Introduction to Integrated marketing communications

first Canadian edition

John Burnett
University of Denver

Sandra Moriarty
University of Colorado-Boulder

E. Stephen Grant
University of New Brunswick

Toronto

Canadian Cataloguing in Publication Data

Burnett, John, 1944–
Introduction to integrated marketing communications

1st Canadian ed.
Includes index.
ISBN 0-13-015668-X

1. Communication in marketing. 2. Advertising campaigns. I. Moriarty, Sandra E. (Sandra Ernst). II. Grant, E. Stephen. III. Title.

HF5415.123.B87 2001 658.8 C00-930896-2

ISBN 0-13-015668-X

Vice President, Editorial Director: Michael Young
Acquisitions Editor: Mike Ryan
Marketing Manager: James Buchanan
Associate Editor: Veronica Tomaiuolo
Production Editor: Marisa D'Andrea
Copy Editor: Dianne Broad
Production Coordinator: Janette Lush
Page Layout: Christine Velakis
Permissions Research: Vicky Oskroba
Art Director: Mary Opper
Interior Design: Sarah Battersby
Cover Design: Sarah Battersby
Cover Image: Malcolm Piers/The Image Bank

1 2 3 4 5 05 04 03 02 01

Printed and bound in USA.

Brief Table of Contents

Table of Contents

Preface

Pick up a magazine, navigate the Web, watch TV, or drive to the shopping mall; marketing messages will bombard you. In today's information-filled world, marketers have to fight to grab and hold consumer attention. To do so, they must use effective *marketing communication*—the process of communicating marketing messages to promote products, services, and ideas. This text introduces students to the marketing communication tools, techniques, and media that practitioners use to promote their products. It also gives special emphasis to *integrated marketing communication* (IMC)—a strategy of coordinating and combining messages for maximum impact. Some text highlights follow.

- *Balanced coverage of all marketing communication tools.* Unlike other texts that devote the bulk of their coverage to advertising, we balance our coverage of the key marketing communication areas throughout the entire text.
- *Integrated international, ethical, and technology coverage.* Rather than treat the international, ethical, and technological aspects of marketing communication as isolated topics, the text demonstrates how these topics relate to many issues with integrated coverage.
- *Current examples from all types and sizes of businesses.* The current examples used in the text discussion, opening vignettes, features, and end-of-chapter materials show students how marketing communication concepts apply to a wide spectrum of business practice.
- *A focus on key marketing communication concepts and applications.* By eliminating excess detail, instructors and students have more opportunity to cover the basics well.
- *An integrated learning system.* Our learning system helps students move progressively from recall to mastering concepts to critical thinking. This system is used in end-of-chapter questions, the test bank, and our Web site to strengthen students' learning experience and skill development.

Balanced, Consistent Coverage

The text emphasizes how the various marketing communication areas work together to create a cohesive message. As a result, it does more than define and explain the various marketing communication areas and their comparative strengths and weaknesses (Chapters 9–13). It also stresses how to best "mix" marketing communication tools in a strategic, integrated plan (Chapters 1–4); how to plan for and use media in all marketing communication areas (Chapters 14 and 15); and how to budget and evaluate programs for all those areas (Chapters 16 and 17). The book closes with a chapter that integrates all parts of the text as it shows students how one business planned, budgeted for, executed, and evaluated a marketing communication campaign that is still ongoing (Chapter 18). The benefit of this complete coverage? Students will learn from start to finish how to plan, execute, and evaluate a marketing communication program and message strategy that is effective and efficient.

International, Ethical, and Technology Coverage

Introduction to Integrated Marketing Communications recognizes the importance of how the global community affects marketing communication practices. The international discussion occurs seamlessly in the text through examples and discussion where it is most relevant, with particular emphasis in Chapters 6 and 7 in Part II (The IMC Context).

The ethical implications of marketing communication are covered in Chapter 7 and are also infused throughout the text in You Decide features. These features highlight ethical concerns and pose questions that force students to wrestle with issues that are rarely black-and-white. Because the aim of these features is to sensitize students to situations that can and do arise in practice, each You Decide feature uses a real-world situation as the teaching tool.

Technology is altering many marketing communication practices. Direct marketing databases, sophisticated media tracking, and the use of the World Wide Web to communicate with consumers are only a few examples. We weave technology coverage throughout the text, features, and end-of-chapter materials. Notably, 16 chapters have Internet projects so that students can learn about the strengths and weaknesses of this medium.

Current Examples From All Types and Sizes of Business

This book demonstrates how companies use IMC. In fact, examples abound, not only in the text discussion but also in opening vignettes, IMC in Action and Profile features, and in end-of-chapter cases. The examples and stories bring the theory to life, showing students the relevance of what they are reading. We make the examples vivid, current, and varied. They range from large multinational companies such as Procter & Gamble and Gillette to smaller, privately-held businesses such as Ch!ckaboom (a retailer that targets clothes-crazy female "tweens" (girls 5 to 13)) and Internet service provider The NET IDEA. We also focus on international companies of all sizes, ranging from Ecover (a small manufacturer of toxic-free detergents) to Bennetton Group SpA.

A Clear, Effective Organization

Time is a precious commodity for instructors and students. Market feedback revealed that instructors want an introductory marketing communication text that 1) covers the basics well and 2) omits unnecessary detail. Careful selection of topics, appropriate depth of coverage, and concise writing helped us meet those two objectives. Instead of the typical 22–25 chapters, *Introduction to Integrated Marketing Communications* offers 18 chapters of manageable length.

Introduction to Integrated Marketing Communications is divided into five parts—Understanding IMC; The IMC Situation; The Tools of IMC: Media of IMC; and IMC Appropriation, Evaluation, and Campaign Planning. We briefly describe each part next.

- **Part I, Understanding IMC:** Chapter 1 explains the concepts of marketing communication and integrated marketing communication. Chapter 2 reviews the marketing mix but not in the traditional way. It focuses on the communication dimensions of the marketing mix and how marketing mix decisions drive the marketing communication strategy. The third chapter describes how companies organize marketing and marketing communication teams—internally through departments and externally with agencies. Chapter 4 presents ways to develop marketing communication strategy and the planning process.
- **Part II, The IMC Situation:** This section focuses on the marketing communication context, including the effects of the internal and external environment on those who communicate and receive marketing messages. Chapter 5 reviews the sociocultural environment and Chapter 6 explores how consumers make decisions. Chapter 7 examines the legal, ethical, and global environment of marketing communication. Chapter 8 looks at the communication process.
- **Part III, The Tools of IMC:** Part III surveys different areas of marketing communication—advertising (Chapter 9), sales promotion (Chapter 10), public relations (Chapter 11), direct marketing (Chapter 12), and personal selling (Chapter 13).
- **Part IV, Media of IMC:** Chapters 14 and 15 deal specifically with media and other message delivery systems, the means used to carry integrated marketing communication messages (such as TV, radio, the Internet, and so on). Unlike other texts, this part describes how practitioners can combine media to create synergy.
- **Part V, IMC Appropriation, Evaluation, and Campaign Planning:** Chapter 16 examines the appropriation and budgeting methods for an entire marketing communication plan. Chapter 17 describes how to measure IMC performance. We close the book with a unique chapter on campaign planning. This chapter shows students how a real company (Chapters Online Inc) planned, implemented, and evaluated its IMC campaign.

Helpful Pedagogy

To reinforce learning and build business skills that students can use on the job, we introduce several features that no other marketing communication text offers. Our comprehensive learning system helps students master material quickly and thoroughly. Some features of that system include *opening vignettes, performance-based learning objectives,* and *chapter summaries that link directly to the learning objectives.* We also include the following features that distinguish us from other texts:

- **Concept Reviews** help students grasp the material as they move through the chapter. This learning device recaps the major points of the previous section so that students can review what they've just read to check for understanding of the major issues.

- **You Decide** and **IMC in Action** features foster critical thinking by posing real-world scenarios and questions that have no right answer. The You Decide features highlight ethical issues. IMC in Action boxes spotlight marketing communication business examples.
- **IMC Concept in Focus** features showcase key or emerging IMC concepts. Examples include such topics as the importance of relationship marketing in business-to-business marketing communication, and zero-based budgeting.
- **Profiles** spotlight young executives from a variety of functional areas and job titles working in different countries. These practitioners describe their jobs, their career paths since college or university, and their views on how to get ahead in marketing communication. The profiles offer a real-world view of the range of careers available in this incredibly diverse industry.
- **End-of-Chapter Exercises** move students through three levels of learning—1) fact, recall, and definition; 2) understanding concepts; and 3) applying concepts to new situations. This three-tiered learning system is also incorporated in the test manual and the Web site so that instructors can better evaluate the level of understanding that students have mastered.
- **Team, Communication, and Internet Projects** challenge students to learn how to learn outside the classroom. Business practice is demanding. Workers must be able to collaborate in small groups, communicate effectively, and master new technology. Suggested projects at the end of every chapter allow students to practice these skills.
- **End-of-chapter Case Studies** foster critical thinking. Students are given actual business scenarios that stress several concepts found in the chapter. End-of-case questions encourage students to spot issues, analyse facts, and solve problems.

CBC Video Vignettes based on segments from the CBC series *Venture* and *Undercurrents* have been specifically designed to complement the text. Each section of the text includes a vignette. This case collection is an excellent tool for bringing students in contact with the world of marketing communication. These programs have extremely high production quality and have been chosen to relate directly to the chapter content.

For a multitude of practice test questions, weblinks to related sites, supplemental text material, and the **Roma's Lite Integrative Case**, visit the *Introduction to Integrated Marketing Communications* **Companion Website** at www.pearsoned.ca/burnett. The Roma's Lite Integrative Case is linked to the text with questions from each chapter that tie directly to a detailed marketing plan. As students move through the book they can work individually or collectively on case study questions that encourage them to apply what they have learned in each chapter. In doing so, they build their own integrated marketing communication campaign plans. This skill-building, integrated case teaches students the how-to of campaign planning—a skill that they can use on the job.

Instructor Resources

The goal of *Introduction to Integrated Marketing Communications* is simple: to make teaching and learning marketing communication successful experiences.

We designed each supplemental resource to work hand-in-glove with the text and to add extra value to instructors and students alike.

Instructor's Resource Manual (IRM)

The *Instructor's Resource Manual* contains course-preparation materials. This handy lecture tool provides a chapter overview, detailed chapter outline, chapter objectives, a summary of all features, and suggested answers to critical thinking questions posed in the chapter. It also includes lecture tips, discussion guidelines, key figures and tables, a chapter summary, answers to all end-of-chapter exercises, a case analysis, and guidelines for integrative case question answers.

Test Bank

The test bank provides a file of question types including multiple choice, true/false, and essay. Many of these questions target issues from chapter features such as You Decide and IMC in Action.

Pearson Education Canada Custom Test: DOS, Windows, or Mac Versions

Based on Engineering Software Associates top-selling, state-of-the-art test-generation software program, *Pearson Education Canada Custom Test* allows complete flexibility. First, you can customize tests to suit your course needs—from simple pop quizzes to multiple versions of a comprehensive exam. With its user-friendly test creation and powerful algorithmic generation, tailor-made tests can be developed quickly, simply, and without error. Whether you work on Macintosh, Windows, or DOS, you can administer your exams traditionally or online, evaluate and track students results, and analyze the success of the exam—all with a click of the mouse or push of a button.

Electronic PowerPoint Slides

We offer over 150 PowerPoint full-color electronic presentation screens that are original, rather than taken from the text. This visual package gives instructors a complete array of helpful presentation aids.

The Bessies

The Television Bureau of Canada recognizes excellence in Canadian television advertising with the annual Bessies awards program. The bureau has made copies of the 1999 and 2000 show reels available to instructors who are using *Introduction to Integrated Marketing Communications, First Canadian Edition*. These tapes feature the best advertisements that have been created for Canadian audiences by companies incorporated in Canada. Please contact your Pearson Education Canada sales representative for details. These videos are subject to availability.

For further information about The Bessies, or to inquire about the Television Bureau of Canada's library of nearly 30 000 commercials, please contact them at 890 Yonge Street, Suite 700, Toronto, Ontario, M4W 3P4, 416-923-8813. You may also visit their web site at www.tvb.ca.

Acknowledgments

A book like this is a major undertaking. It would not have happened without the help of a great many significant others. Special thanks go to Pearson Education Canada and Michael Ryan, Executive Editor, for having faith in this project from the outset. Our sincere thanks also to the editorial team: Sherry Torchinsky, Developmental Editor, for her encouragement during the text's early development; Nicole Mellow, Developmental Editor, for her extremely insightful, creative, and constructive suggestions; Dianne Broad for her professional approach to copyediting; Marisa D'Andrea, Production Editor, for her shepherding of the text through the production process; and Veronica Tomaiuolo, Associate Editor, for overseeing all of the many details of the project in its final stages. Without the hard work and professionalism of this editorial team we would not have made the tight deadlines associated with this project.

This book has been through an extensive review process. The reviewers who have looked at several drafts of the manuscript and made thoughtful and important suggestions deserve special recognition. Most notably, we would like to thank Dr. Jim Dupree for his assistance on the manuscript, the instructors resource manual, and the test bank. Also, University of New Brunswick BBA student Jeff Miller deserves a special thank you for his assistance in the preparation of the PowerPoint slide supplement. We also wish to thank all of the professors and instructors who provided suggestions on how to improve the text. Reviewers who provided thoughtful critique include:

Eli Winston Baker, University of New Brunswick

Michael Guolla, University of Ottawa

Anne Lavack, University of Winnipeg

Barry Mills, College of the North Atlantic

Judy Roy, University of New Brunswick

Harold J. Simpkins, Concordia University

Brock Smith, University of Victoria

Robert G. Wyckham, Simon Fraser University

To my beautiful wife, Kimberly, and my supportive parents, Ernest and Treva. Thank you for your constant understanding and encouragement.

E.S.G.

About the Authors

Dr. John Burnett

John Burnett holds a D.B.A. degree in Marketing from the University of Kentucky. He is a Professor of Marketing at the University of Denver. Dr. Burnett is the author of *Promotion Management*, now in its third edition, and a co-author of *Advertising Principles and Practices*. In addition, he has had numerous articles and research papers published in a wide variety of professional and academic journals.

In addition to his teaching, writing, and research activities, Dr. Burnett is an active marketing and marketing communication consultant for a wide range of industries. He has worked, for instance, as a consultant for AT&T, the Dallas Mart, the AAFES organization, and Scott & White Hospitals. Dr. Burnett has also won several teaching awards and serves as faculty advisor for student chapters of the American Marketing Association.

Dr. Sandra E. Moriarty

Sandra Moriarty holds a B.J. and M.S. in journalism from the University of Missouri and a Ph.D. in instructional communication from Kansas State University. She started her career as a government information officer. Dr. Moriarty has owned her own public relations and advertising agency, worked as a copywriter, done public relations consulting, and directed a university public relations program. She has also taught at Michigan State University and the University of Kansas. Currently, Dr. Moriarty is a professor at the University of Colorado–Boulder where she teaches in the Integrated Marketing Communication graduate program.

In addition to an extensive list of articles in both scholarly and trade journals, Dr. Moriarty has authored or co-authored eight other books, including *Driving Brand Value: Using Integrated Marketing to Manage Profitable Stakeholder Relationships; Creative Advertising; Advertising: Principles and Practices; and The Creative Package.*

Dr. E. Stephen Grant

E. Stephen Grant holds a PhD in Business Administration with a concentration in marketing from the University of Memphis, Fogelman College of Business and Economics. He is Associate Professor of Marketing at the University of New Brunswick. Dr. Grant is a co-author of *Marketing: Canadian Insights and Applications*. In addition, he has had numerous articles and research papers published in academic journals and proceedings of national scholarly conferences. Dr. Grant's research activities have been recognized through an assortment of awards, contracts, grants, and fellowships.

In addition to his writing and research activities, Dr. Grant regularly teaches marketing principles and an assortment of advanced topic courses in marketing at the undergraduate and graduate level. He is also involved in marketing consulting and small business case writing.

Expert Roundtable

In today's information-filled world we all need the help of experts to stay abreast of the continuous state of change. To further aid development and to inject realism, we assembled a highly qualified group of experts to form an **Expert Roundtable.** The Roundtable members represent a broad spectrum of experts from many different organizations. The brief biographies provided here identify their current positions and relevant professional experiences. All Roundtable members contributed to the development of this text.

Graham Barker, President of Phoenix Group. Regarded by many as Saskatchewan's foremost communications professional, Graham offers clients an outstanding wealth of insight and a unique humanistic perspective gained through his 21-year agency career.

A demanding marketing professional, Graham understands the intrinsic importance of strategy, a perspective that has allowed him to create and execute award-winning communications programs that discernibly shift attitudes and, later, behaviour.

His results-oriented approach to communications and marketing is appreciated by a wide range of private- and public-sector clients with local, national, and international business interests. The success of Phoenix Group can most certainly be attributed to Graham's unwavering dedication to communications excellence and his ability to embrace change and innovation.

Michael G. Beairsto, Partner, Fraser Milner/Casgrain Barristers & Solicitors. Michael Beairsto is a partner with the law firm of Fraser Milner/Casgrain, practicing corporate/commercial law with a specialization in information technology and electronic commerce matters. He has a Bachelor of Business Administration from the University of New Brunswick (1985) and an LL.B. from the University of New Brunswick (1987).

Mr. Beairsto is a member of the Computer Law Association, Toronto Computer Lawyers Group, and the Canadian Bar Association of Ontario. He has written numerous papers for and participated in conferences and seminars on the information technology industry. Mr. Beairsto also sits on the board of directors for various technology and Internet-related companies.

Dr. Deirdre Grondin, Professor of Marketing, University of New Brunswick. Dr. Grondin is a professor of marketing in the Faculty of Administration at the University of New Brunswick. She received her PhD from Purdue University, specializing in marketing.

Formerly, Dr. Grondin was Promotion Specialist, then, Head of the Agricultural Marketing Section for the Province of New Brunswick. While in this position, she was responsible for the marketing and promotion of natural products and the management of the department's Marketing Communication Program.

Dr. Grondin's major teaching, consulting, and research interests include Consumer Behaviour, Marketing Communications, and Women in Entrepreneurship and Export. She is the author of a number of government documents and publications on these topics.

Bruce MacLellan, President and Partner, Environics Communications Inc. Bruce MacLellan has been a public relations counselor since 1980. In 1993, he won the Canadian Public Relations Society's Award of Excellence for External Communications. In 1994, he became the founding president and partner of Environics Communications Inc., a position he still holds. In 1995, Environics Communications became the first Canadian-owned PR agency to open an office in the United States. In 1996, he was one of only four PR agency executives selected to *Marketing* magazines Top 100 Marketing Communicators list.

He has a BA and an MA from the University of Toronto. He is a volunteer member of the Public Awareness Committee of the Salvation Army of Canada and is an Ontario board member of The Nature Conservancy of Canada.

Mark W. M. McCauley, Vice President of Marketing, McCain Foods (Canada). As Vice President of Marketing for McCain Foods (Canada), Mark McCauley has overall responsibility for the marketing function.

Originally from Perth-Andover, N.B., and a 1979 graduate of Southern Victoria High School, Mr. McCauley earned a Bachelor of Science degree in biology from Dalhousie University in 1982 and a Master of Business Administration from McGill University in 1984.

He joined the McCain Foods sales force in Montreal in 1984 and was later promoted to sales territory manager. In 1992 Mr. McCauley became an assistant product manager with the marketing department of McCain Foods in Florenceville.

He was promoted to Product Manager in 1993 and to Group Product Manager in 1995. In early 1997 he became Marketing Manager with responsibility for food service products, retail potato products, and vegetables. In June 1998, Mr. McCauley was promoted to his current position, vice president.
Mark and his wife Nancy reside in Florenceville with their children Brendan and Lindsay. Mountain biking, skiing, golf, and hockey are among his favourite leisure pursuits.

Perry Miele, Co-chairman, DraftWorldwide Canada. Perry brings to his clients over 15 years of progressive and senior level experience as a promotion and brand building communications specialist —a position he has earned across a broad range of categories.

After graduating from the University of Western Ontario, Perry began his career with the federal government, rising to the position of Chief of Staff to the Honourable Pat Carney, during the NAFTA negotiations. He joined Gingko in 1987 as a partner and quickly helped the firm to grow to its present size and stature, leading to the merger with DraftWorldwide out of Chicago.

During his career, Perry has launched several new products and lines and extended a number of major brand names. He is well-versed in consumer insight and research methodology, and has a well-developed reputation as both a strategist and creative thinker. Perry has worked in every marketing discipline including advertising, sales promotion, public relations, direct marketing, telemarketing, and new media technologies, such as the Internet. As President of DraftWorldwide International, Perry is responsible for 30 offices in 21 countries around the world.

Perry has worked closely with such clients as American Express, Royal Bank, Foodland, Kodak, Ontario Lottery Corporation, Federal Government, Pitney Bowes, Bayer Canada, Molson, and Kellogg, and has played a key roll in developing national advertising and promotion campaigns for these clients.

Heather Reid, Chairman, Canada Porter Novelli. Heather deeply believes in the importance of public relations within the marketing mix. Indeed, she was one the first people in Canada to recognize the need to integrate these two marketing functions, ensuring clients benefit from truly full-service marketing solutions.

Heather's vision of marketing-based public relations colours every communications service Canada Porter Novelli provides its clients. These dynamic solutions have allowed Heather and her team to provide Canada Porter Novelli clients with fresh approaches to public relations services. Her energy, marketing savvy, industry contacts and business sense are what attract and keep clients, some of whom have stayed with her team for close to 20 years.

As founder and president of Heather Reid & Associates—the forerunner of Canada Porter Novelli (CPN)—and now as chairman of CPN, she brings strong leadership and strategic marketing expertise to agency programs, and provides the objective, creative, and results-oriented thinking that makes CPN one of the top-ranked public relations firms in Canada.

Alison Simpson, Vice President and General Manger of Enterprise Creative Selling. Alison brings 11 years of expertise in advertising, marketing, and sales to Enterprise Creative Selling. The majority of her career has been spent with the top advertising agencies in Canada, where her ability to develop more creative solutions—that drive sales—has set her apart from those around her.

Alison worked at BBDO (Vancouver and Toronto) and MacLaren McCann (Toronto) before taking on the lead position at Enterprise Creative Selling.

Alison's unique philosophy compares great marketing to blood-stained wallpaper: no matter how much wallpaper there is, it's the blood you remember.

In addition to strong business results, Alison's advertising initiatives have also been recognized by numerous national and international awards. Alison's career client roster follows: Tim Hortons, Molson Breweries, Rogers Cable, Campbells, Effem (Mars, M&Ms), Scott Paper Company, Apple Computers, The Toronto Star, Oral-B, EyeMasters, Vtech, Block Drugs, Nestle Canada, Canadian Pacific Hotels & Resorts, BC Tel, Bayer Consumer Care Division, Tourism BC, and McCormick Spices.

The Pearson Education Canada companion Website...

Your Internet companion to the most exciting, state-of-the-art educational tools on the Web!

The Pearson Education Canada Companion Website is easy to navigate and is organized to correspond to the chapters in this textbook. The Companion Website is comprised of four distinct, functional features:

1) **Customized Online Resources**

2) **Online Study Guide**

3) **Reference Material**

4) **Communication**

Explore the four areas in this Companion Website. Students and distance learners will discover resources for indepth study, research and communication, empowering them in their quest for greater knowledge and maximizing their potential for success in the course.

A NEW WAY TO DELIVER EDUCATIONAL CONTENT

1) Customized Online Resources

Our Companion Websites provide instructors and students with a range of options to access, view, and exchange content.

- **Syllabus Builder** provides *instructors* with the option to create online classes and construct an online syllabus linked to specific modules in the Companion Website.
- **Mailing lists** enable *instructors* and *students* to receive customized promotional literature.
- **Preferences** enable *students* to customize the sending of results to various recipients, and also to customize how the material is sent, e.g., as html, text, or as an attachment.
- **Help** includes an evaluation of the user's system and a tune-up area that makes updating browsers and plug-ins easier. This new feature will enhance the user's experience with Companion Websites.

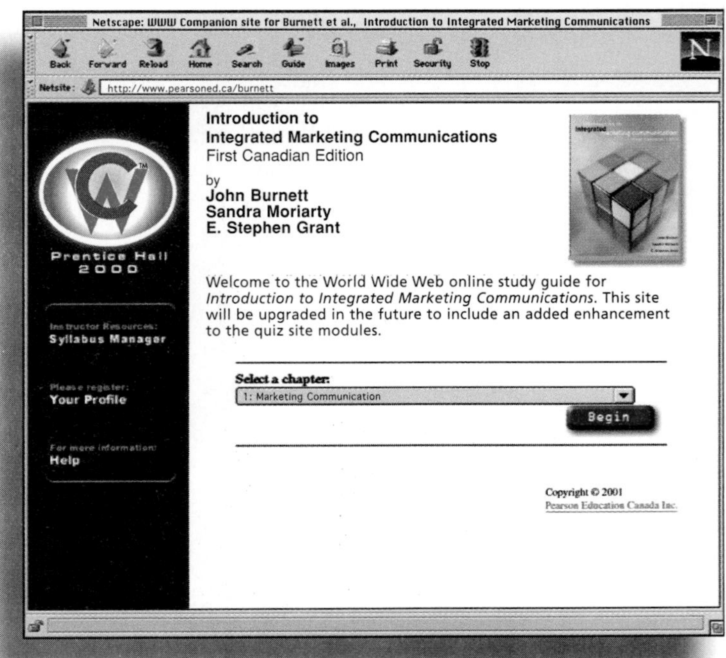

www.pearsoned.ca/burnett

2) Online Study Guide

Interactive Study Guide modules form the core of the student learning experience in the Companion Website. These modules are categorized according to their functionality:

- True-False
- Multiple Choice
- Short Answer
- Internet Questions

The True-False, Multiple Choice, Essay and Internet Questions modules provide students with the ability to send answers to our grader and receive instant feedback on their progress through our Results Reporter. Coaching comments and references back to the textbook ensure that students take advantage of all resources available to enhance their learning experience.

3) Reference Material

Reference material broadens text coverage with up-to-date resources for learning. **Web Destinations** provides a directory of Web sites relevant to the subject matter in each chapter. **NetNews (Internet Newsgroups)** are a fundamental source of information about a discipline, containing a wealth of brief, opinionated postings. **NetSearch** simplifies key term search using Internet search engines.

4) Communication

Companion Websites contain the communication tools necessary to deliver courses in a **Distance Learning** environment. **Message Board** allows users to post messages and check back periodically for responses.

Communication Facilities of Companion Websites provide a key element for distributed learning environments. One type of communication facility currently in use in Companion Websites is:

- **Message Board** – this module takes advantage of browser technology providing the users of each Companion Website with a national newsgroup to post and reply to relevant course topics.

Companion Websites are currently available for:

- Evans: Marketing
- Evans: Marketing Essentials
- Kotler: Principles of Marketing
- Horngren: Cost Accounting
- Horngren: Introduction to Financial Accounting

Note: CW '99 content will vary slightly from site to site depending on discipline requirements.

The Companion Website can be found at:

www.pearsoned.ca/burnett

PEARSON EDUCATION CANADA

26 Prince Andrew Place
Don Mills, Ontario M3C 2T8

To order:
Call: 1-800-567-3800
Fax: 1-800-263-7733

For samples:
Call: 1-800-850-5813
Fax: (416) 447-2819
E-mail: phcinfo.pubcanada@pearsoned.com

1 Marketing Communication

chapter objectives

After completing your work on this chapter, you should be able to

- Explain what marketing communication is and how it is used to promote a product.
- Describe the types of marketing communication messages.
- Define integrated marketing communication (IMC).
- Discuss the benefits of IMC.
- Describe how IMC relates to marketing.

Marketing Communication in Canada: Continuous Change

The marketplace, on a global basis, is experiencing continuous change. The marketing communication field in Canada is no exception. In fact, most marketing experts would tell you that change for the purpose of continuous improvements in communication effectiveness and cost efficiency is especially critical in the Canadian environment. Why? There is no single explanation, but rather a number of factors that help explain why Canadian marketing practitioners are being driven to find smarter communication solutions that are more effective and less costly than solutions used in the past. Some of the factors that help explain this drive for continuous improvement include the following:

- The Ten Percent Rule. Unlike their counterparts in the United States, Canadian marketing practitioners are often marketing to a much smaller domestic market. Although the 10 percent rule does not always apply, it's true that most consumer and industrial markets in Canada are only one-tenth the size of the U.S. domestic market. Unfortunately, market size and the cost of communication tools are not directly proportional; thus it's seldom an option to replicate U.S. communication strategy on a smaller scale.
- Diversity. The Canadian population continues to grow more diverse, thus offering a unique challenge for firms wishing to devote marketing efforts that specifically cater to ethnic groups and other subcultures. And it's not a simple matter of catering to French and English Canadians. Although over four million Canadians can speak both English and French, approximately 20 percent of the Canadian population is composed of people classified as either First Nations People or people from China, Southeast Asia, Africa, and India.
- Technology. Technology, specifically the development of costly information technologies, has had a profound impact on marketing communications in Canada. For example, increased use of electronic commerce has resulted in the need for effective Web-site design and the development of techniques to accurately assess Web page effectiveness. Also, technology has advanced the science of audience measurement, customer segmentation, and analysis, and has enabled marketing specialists to better assess alternative media choices and monitor communication plans. Perhaps the biggest impact of technology is that it has provided more choices for consumers. Gone are the days of the one-newspaper, four-television-channel family.
- A New Corporate Landscape. Driven, in part, by increased global competition, takeovers and mergers in the 1990s have resulted in the restructuring of many businesses. This restructuring

has had a profound impact on the economics of marketing communication in Canada. New giant media conglomerates have gained economic efficiencies and many strategic alliances have formed between communications firms in order to gain efficiencies and economies of scale in media purchasing. These structural changes have made it increasingly difficult for small independents to purchase effective and cost-sensitive communication solutions.

Have Canadian marketers found a way to deliver communication solutions that are more effective and more cost-efficient than the solutions of the past? Most Canadian marketers recognize that there are no quick fixes, but many have discovered that an integrated approach is the blueprint for success in marketing communications. Although many small and resourceful businesses have practised an integrated approach to marketing communications for years, it's one of the most important communication trends of the past decade. What does this really mean? Although we will define and discuss the concept of integrated marketing communications (IMC) in greater detail later in this chapter, in practice IMC means that all communication tools—advertising, sales promotion, public relations, direct marketing, personal selling, point-of-purchase, packaging, sponsorships, and so on—work together to send target audiences a consistent, persuasive message that promotes company goals.

Chapter Overview

Procter & Gamble
www.pg.com

Consumers are skeptical of many marketing efforts, so getting and holding their attention is extremely difficult. Even market leaders such as Procter & Gamble, General Motors, and Microsoft are no longer secure in their market dominance. To ensure that a product will sell successfully, businesses must do more than produce the best product, charge the lowest price, or place the product in the best or largest number of stores.* Companies must market their products with creative, informative, and interesting messages that show how the products meet the needs and wants of consumers. A key factor in marketing a product is effective and cost-efficient communication, as illustrated by the opening vignette.

This text explains the basic concepts of marketing communication. We begin this chapter by examining what marketing is. Next, we define and describe integrated marketing communication and explain the reasons for its use in business. Finally, we conclude with a framework that shows how integrated marketing communication fits into a firm's marketing program.

Marketing Communication

Marketing communication
The process of effectively communicating product information or ideas to target audiences.

Target audience
A group of people who receive marketing messages and have significant potential to respond to the messages.

Marketing communication is the process of effectively communicating product information or ideas to target audiences. No business can operate in every market to satisfy everyone's needs. Instead, a company succeeds when it targets a market of those people most likely to be interested in its marketing program. A **target audience** is a group of people who receives marketing messages and has significant potential to respond to the messages. Even mass-marketers like

*Note that here and throughout the text, "product" refers to a good, a service, or an idea.

"Diner": *Pepsi-Cola via BBDO Worldwide*

This Pepsi-Cola ad targeted an audience of older consumers that enjoy a non-diet soft drink.

Coca-Cola Enterprises and Pepsico target specific audiences to promote their products. For example, the target market for Diet Coke consists of all diet-conscious pop drinkers. Diet Coke, then, targets an audience of those who are most likely to be diet conscious—12- to 24-year-olds of both sexes and women aged 25 to 45.

To communicate a marketing message effectively, companies must realize that everything they do can send a message. For instance, outfitting a car with a CD-player and leather upholstery sends a strong message about the car's quality. The price of a product can also communicate to an audience—a 99-cent pen will probably not be as durable or luxurious as a $50 pen. A company that distributes its product only through discount stores tells the consumer a great deal about the status of its product.

Product, price, and distribution can communicate market information to audiences. These three marketing activities—price, product, and channel of distribution—combined with marketing communication, make up the **marketing mix**. Marketing communication is the element of the marketing mix used to showcase important features of the other three to increase the odds the consumer will buy a product. If marketing communication is based on a comprehensive, well-conceived marketing plan, it will produce a "Big Idea" that is persuasive to the target audience.

Marketing mix
Price, product, and channel of distribution (three marketing activities), combined with marketing communication, make up the marketing mix.

Marketing plan
A document that analyses the current marketing situation, identifies market opportunities and threats, sets objectives, and develops action plans to achieve objectives; the central instrument for directing and coordinating the marketing effort.

Marketing communication and the other three marketing mix elements are the four categories of strategic decision making in a marketing plan. A **marketing plan** is a document that analyses the current marketing situation, identifies market opportunities and threats, sets objectives, and develops action plans to achieve objectives. Each of the marketing mix areas has its own set of objectives and strategies. A pricing objective and strategy, for example, might be to increase sales in a certain geographical market by pricing a product lower than a competitor. Marketing communication presents the overall marketing strategy to target audiences, sending messages about product, price, and distribution to excite interest or make a convincing point. Figure 1.1 shows how the marketing plan and the marketing mix relate.

All marketing communication involves five factors: persuasion, objectives, contact points, stakeholders, and various types of marketing communication activities. We will consider these factors in detail one by one.

PERSUASION

All marketing communication tries to persuade the target audience to change an attitude or behaviour or provides information. For example, Kraft wants consumers to believe that its cheese is the best value compared to all other

Figure 1.1 THE MARKETING PLAN AND THE MARKETING MIX

Hallmark
www.hallmark.com

cheese brands. Hallmark wants purchasers to think of its cards "when you care enough to send the very best." Marketers can persuade in many ways. They can provide information, reasons, and incentives. They can also listen actively to the concerns of people in the market.

Objectives

All marketing communication should be goal directed. Marketing communication objectives are the goals of the communication program. Generally, those objectives are to create brand awareness, deliver information, educate the market, and advance a positive image for the brand or company. The ultimate goal of the marketing communication strategy is to help sell the product to keep the company in business.

Contact Points

Successful marketing requires managing and coordinating marketing messages at every contact point the brand or company has with its target audience. Contact points can range from the store where the customer sees the product, the 800 number or Web site the customer contacts for information, or the living room where the TV airs a commercial. Marketers can plan formal contacts, such as an advertisement; however, many contacts are unplanned. The unplanned contacts can communicate informal messages that audiences infer. For instance, a store's design can send a message that it retails inexpensive products. Or an unhelpful salesperson can send a message that the company doesn't care about customer service. Successful persuasion requires that messages at every contact point work together.

Stakeholders

Stakeholder
Anyone who has a stake in the success of a company or its products.

The target audience includes more than the target market of potential consumers. A **stakeholder** is anyone who has a stake in the success of a company or its products. Stakeholder audiences include all those who might influence the purchase of products and the success of the company, such as employees, retailers and distributors, suppliers, the local community, the media, and government regulators, as well as customers.

Diet Coke's target market consists of diet-conscious consumers. Stakeholder audiences might include Diet Coke retailers and distributors because they can influence how and when the product reaches consumers, financial analysts who influence the company's shareholders, and local communities where Diet Coke distributors are located.

Competitors can even be important stakeholders. In Asia, for example, Cathay Pacific, Singapore International Airlines, Thai Airways International, and the Malaysian Airline Systems introduced a cooperative frequent-flyer program to protect themselves from the large international carriers that fly into their markets and offer such programs.

Toronto Dominion Bank
www.tdbank.ca

Government regulators often can have an important say about the success of a business or industry, even those as dominant as cigarette manufacturers or banks. When the TD Bank announced plans to purchase Canada Trust, it found it needed special messages for both regulators and competitors who feared its monopoly potential.

Marketing Communication Messages

Hundreds of different communication activities can deliver messages both formally through explicit marketing communication programs and informally through the marketing mix and other corporate contact points. As depicted in Figure 1.2, the two key types of messages used to reach marketing communication goals are planned and unplanned messages.

Figure 1.2 Marketing Communication Messages

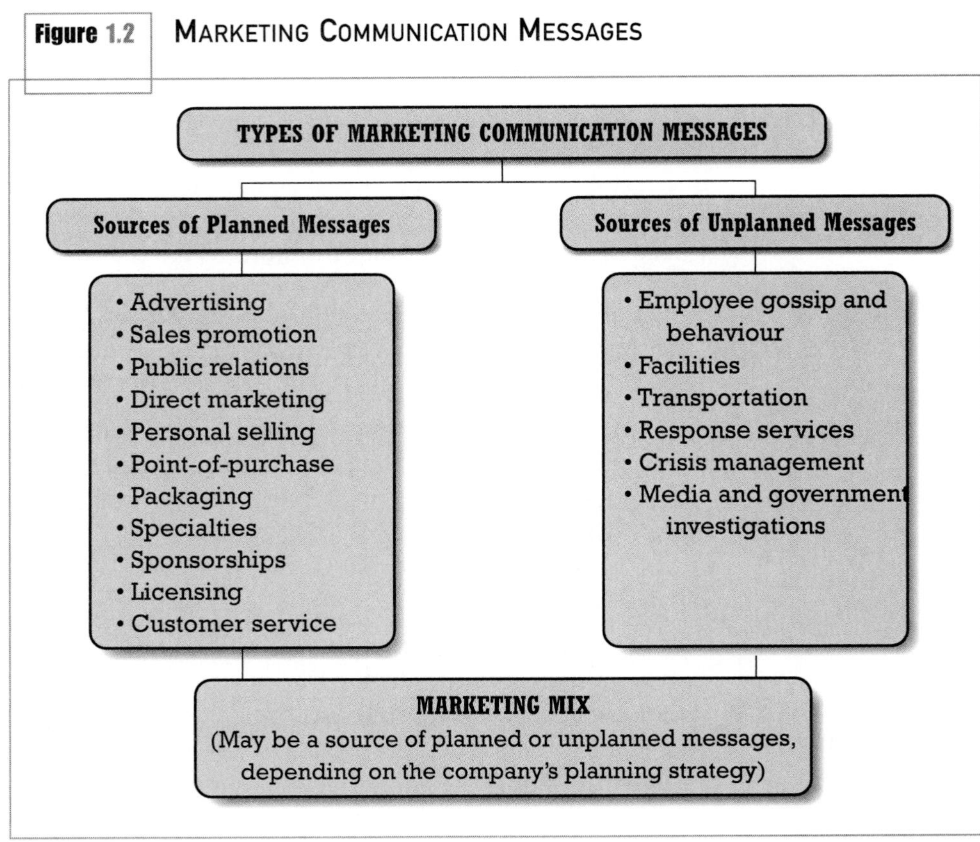

Planned messages
Deliberate messages delivered formally through explicit marketing communication programs.

Planned messages are delivered through the following marketing communication tools:

- *Advertising*—Any paid form of communication by an identified sponsor that promotes products. Although some advertising (such as direct mail) is directed at specific individuals, most advertising messages are tailored to a target group and use media such as radio, television, the Internet, newspapers, and magazines.
- *Sales promotion*—Marketing activities that add to the basic value of the product or service for a limited time and directly stimulate consumer purchasing (for example, coupons and product sampling), the cooperation of distributors, or stimulate the effort of the sales force.
- *Public relations*—A coordinated attempt to create a favourable product image in the mind of the public by supporting certain activities or programs, publishing commercially significant news in a widely circulated medium, or obtaining favourable publicity on radio, television, or stage that is not paid for by the company selling the product.
- *Direct marketing*—An interactive form of marketing that allows the consumer to access information, purchase the product through a variety of media, or both. Examples include direct mail, catalogues, and online catalogue services.
- *Personal selling*—An interpersonal communication with one or more prospective buyers for the sake of making sales. Examples include sales calls to a business by a field representative (field selling), in-store assistance of a salesclerk (retail selling), a representative calling at homes (door-to-door selling), or a sales call made via telephone (telemarketing selling).
- *Point-of-purchase or merchandise materials*—Materials that deliver marketing communication messages at the point of sale that facilitate the consumer's likelihood to purchase. These materials, such as in-store coupons, remind the consumer of the product, deliver a selling message, or inform the consumer of a special reason to buy.
- *Packaging*—A package is both a container for a product and a display for a marketing communication message. Packaging is the last marketing message a consumer sees before making a product purchase decision and thus has an extremely critical role in the persuasion process.
- *Specialties*—Free gifts used as reminder items because they carry the brand or corporate identification.
- *Sponsorships*—A company's financial support of an event or cause in exchange for an affiliation with the organization or event sponsored. Sponsorships can create goodwill and positive associations that companies can feature through other communication tools such as advertising.
- *Licensing*—The practice of selling the right to use a company's character or logo (product symbol) on another company's products. When your university makes it possible for a sweatshirt manufacturer to produce a sweatshirt with your school's logo on it, the university will control such use through a contract that licenses the right to use the logo to the manufacturer.

- *Customer service*—An important part of marketing communication is "aftermarketing," that is, dealing with customers after they have bought the product. Customer service programs are designed to deal with customers' ongoing needs. Other tools that attempt to make the aftermarketing experience positive are warranties and guarantees.

Unplanned messages
Elements associated with a company or brand that are capable of delivering implicit messages to consumers.

Unplanned messages include all the other elements associated with the company or brand that are capable of delivering implicit messages to consumers. For example, dirty delivery trucks or unsafe parking lots, unfriendly receptionists, angry employees, and busy telephones all deliver negative messages that may have more impact than all the planned marketing communication messages. Customer service representatives and other employees may deliver unwanted or unintended messages if they have not been trained to consider the communication impact of their actions and words. Although these unplanned company messages are not always considered the responsibility of the marketing communication team, those in charge should anticipate and eliminate messages inconsistent with the communication strategy and reinforce the consistent ones.

High Hopes for Hemp

The "times are a changing," and so is the law. The weed once strictly prohibited in this country because of confusion with its distant cousin, marijuana, is now legal. The first hemp crops were harvested in southwestern Ontario in the summer of 1998, giving Canada a headstart on U.S. competition. Despite hemp's benign nature, strength, and many potential uses, its cultivation remains illegal in the United States, forcing Americans to import US$100 million worth of hemp per year, mostly from Asia and Eastern Europe.

Geof Kime, founder of Hempline, which last summer grew 200 hectares of hemp in Delaware, Ontario, isn't shy about discussing his company. Kime is regularly quoted in print ads and on television—including a segment on CBC-TV's ***Venture.*** However, to reach this point, Kime spent two years convincing Members of Parliament and senators that you can't smoke hemp but can make a variety of high-quality products out of it.

Hempline has two core products: one is Hemp Chips—equine (horse) bedding. To promote this product, Hempline has sponsored horse shows, and run ads through Maire McKaskell Art & Design of London,

Ontario, in horse magazines. Hempline's other core product is hemp fibre, which is a high-strength, mould-, and mildew-resistant crop. Hempline's entire crop has been bought up by U.S. carpet and upholstery manufacturers.

The real action for Hemp promises to be in the edibles. Jerzy Prytyk, Quebec City-based president of the Canadian Industrial Hemp Council, explains, "We think the fastest-growing hemp market will be in food products, where the infrastructure exists to process hemp grain into many nutritious and edible products."

Despite the promise of attractive markets for hemp based products, marijuana-related misconceptions still haunt those trying to bring the industry into the mainstream and remove the connection to hemp's original proponent—the drug subculture.

Regardless of the image, hemp's legal agricultural status in Canada could give Canada a foothold in the United States, but as noted by Bud Sholts, chair of the North American Industrial Hemp Council in Madison, Wisconsin, Canada's prospects will be vastly improved when the U.S. government sees the light and legalizes it there too: "Our manufacturers aren't really going to gear up for hemp until they know there's a guaranteed supply in North America. So Canadians will really see their markets expand when we can grow here as well, because that's when things will really start to happen.

You Decide

1. What different marketing messages do you think hemp growers send when they acknowledge public confusion with hemp's distant cousin, marijuana? Are those messages helpful or harmful? Explain.
2. To what extent, if any, should Canadian hemp growers attempt to influence the legalization of hemp growing in the United States?

Sources: Phil Novak, "High Hopes for Hemp," (March 8, 1999), 22.

Canadian Industrial Hemp Council
www.cinevision.com/cihc

The marketing mix activities may be either planned or unplanned messages, depending on the circumstances. Marketing mix decisions, such as where the product is sold, how reliable the product is, and whether a fair price is being charged, strongly affect the consumer's level of interest in the product. The marketing mix is in the hands of the marketing manager, so in that sense mix decisions are controlled. Marketing mix decisions are not, however, always considered from the communication viewpoint, and the marketing communication team may not be involved in planning the marketing mix. In cases where the marketing communication team does not help plan the marketing mix and consider its message effects, then that mix is considered an unplanned message. In cases where the marketing communication team does help plan the mix and its message effects, the marketing mix is viewed as a planned message.

As Figure 1.2 shows, planned and unplanned communication messages deliver all the messages consumers and other stakeholders receive. Clearly, both types of communication are crucial. Ideally, they work together and deliver a unified story. Advertising and public relations, for example, inform and persuade consumers so they enter the store equipped with brand awareness, product information, and a positive attitude. Sales promotion provides an extra incentive to buy. Then the product and store attributes—such as packaging, merchandising signs, cleanliness of the store, and friendliness of the sales staff—take over. All work together to influence the consumer's decision to buy the product.

Marketing communication can create positive impressions that enhance the buyer's satisfaction and thus add to the real value of the company's product. For instance, for many consumers buying a pair of Levi's means a lot more than buying just any pair of denim jeans because Levi Strauss & Co. creates a quality image through its advertising and merchandising. But even great marketing communication cannot save a bad product. In fact, the fastest way to kill a poor product is with a good communication program. Such a program will quickly expose the weakness of the product to its target audience, the people who count the most.

concept review

Marketing Communications

A key part of any marketing program is communication.

1. Marketing communication is the process of effectively communicating product information to target audiences.
2. Planned marketing communication message sources include advertising, sales promotion, public relations, direct marketing, personal selling, point-of-purchase/merchandising, packaging, sponsorships, licensing, and aftermarketing customer service.
3. Unplanned marketing communication messages include all the other elements associated with the company or brand that are capable of delivering implicit messages to consumers.
4. The marketing mix may be either a planned or unplanned message source.

IMC: A Blueprint for Success in Marketing Communication

Here's a quiz: Which battery product features a pink rabbit beating a big drum? Almost half of the consumers who answer this question say Duracell. Wrong! The correct answer is Energizer. For all the money spent on the Energizer bunny campaign, many consumers have had a hard time associating the campaign with Energizer, particularly in the early years of the campaign. One of the main reasons for the difficulty is that for many years the pink bunny was strictly an advertising campaign: The bunny wasn't used in sales promotion, packaging, or in-store promotions until much later. Once it became an integrated communication strategy, then the brand association scores began to increase.

What Is IMC?

Integrated marketing communication (IMC) The practice of unifying all marketing communication tools—from advertising to packaging—to send target audiences a consistent, persuasive message that promotes company goals.

One of the most important communication trends of this decade is a shift to **integrated marketing communication (IMC),** which is the practice of unifying all marketing communication tools—from advertising to packaging—to send target audiences a consistent, persuasive message that promotes company goals. According to marketing experts IMC is "a new way of looking at the whole, where once we saw only parts such as advertising, public relations, sales promotion, purchasing, employee communications, and so forth." IMC realigns marketing communication "to look at it the way the consumer sees it—as a flow of information from indistinguishable sources."[1]

An example of a successful IMC strategy is the RCA campaign for its television products. By bringing back the familiar image of RCA's white-and-black dog, teaming it with a new puppy, and juxtaposing them against newer, more advanced products and more lively graphics, RCA was able to appeal to younger consumers yet retain the older users who still remember the original RCA image. Print and television ads, point-of-purchase materials, and packaging all sent the same message—RCA's long-term commitment to the entertainment industry guarantees quality and innovation. The message strategy worked and continues to do so because advertising, sales promotion, point of purchase, and packaging work together to send messages to various age groups.

As discussed earlier in this chapter, the marketing mix of product, price, distribution, and communication sends planned and unplanned messages to target audiences. Marketing communicators use tools to send planned messages and attempt to anticipate and control unplanned messages. In companies that do not use IMC, the marketing communication tools, such as advertising and public relations, are not used together for maximum impact. In companies that do use IMC, marketing communicators coordinate all the tools to create *communication synergy,* which means each tool has more impact working jointly to promote a product than it would working on its own. That is, the whole is greater than the sum of the parts.

To create synergy, marketing communicators must understand how each tool works best and how they work together. Each tool can reach audiences in different ways, some of which complement one another and reinforce each other's efforts. Furthermore, marketing communicators must understand what each activity can do best and what its strengths and weaknesses are. For example, advertising is capable of reaching a mass audience simultaneously and repeatedly. It is also effective at informing customers about new products or new product features and reminding customers about positive past experiences with a product. Public relations is effective at creating highly credible messages. Sales promotion may be most effective at stimulating an immediate response, such as when a company offers an incentive to try a new product.

The important thing to remember is that all these tools have strengths and weaknesses, such that different tools can accomplish different objectives. In an integrated marketing communication program marketing communicators plan how each tool can work with all the others to accomplish marketing communication objectives.

Reasons for IMC

Although some critics say that IMC may be a fad, more and more businesses are using it with success. According to one study, 60 percent of the 100 leading senior-level marketing executives surveyed rated IMC as the most important factor in devising a marketing strategy.[2] Table 1.1 shows the survey results.

What is driving integration? As discussed in the opening vignette, integration is being driven in Canada by a number of factors that are forcing continuous improvements in communication effectiveness and cost efficiency. However, integration is not a trend unique to the Canadian situation. With heightened global competition, technological advances, and more informed consumers, North American businesses demand more efficiency, stronger customer loyalty, an image that can be transmitted globally, and a more powerful impact. In the marketing context, this means that businesses want better

Table 1.1 FACTORS INFLUENCING MARKETING STRATEGIES

Factor	Importance Rank (%)
Integrated marketing communications	60
Consumer lifestyle changes	55
Economic trends	45
Everyday low-pricing strategies	32
New retail formats	29
Integration of consumer and trade promotion	27
Globalization	26

Source: NPO Group. Reprinted with permission from *Advertising Age*, March 22, 1995, 2. Copyright, Crain Communications, Inc. 1993.

results from the marketing communication plan and budget. IMC is a cost-effective practice because it carefully coordinates and communicates each part of the marketing mix. This is especially true for smaller, cost-conscious companies that can't afford to gamble all their marketing communication dollars on a single ad campaign.[3]

Next we discuss the four main reasons for the growth of IMC: greater efficiency, stronger customer loyalty, international marketing, and added impact.

GREATER EFFICIENCY

In the last decade new data-gathering technology, such as scanners and relational databases, have allowed businesses to attract and predict consumer buying behaviour with ever-increasing accuracy. As a result, firms can segment and target their audiences more efficiently using new message-delivering technologies instead of spending huge sums on a mass-marketed advertising campaign. These technologies range from interactive media to digital TV to the Internet.

At the same time, companies are demanding greater efficiency from their marketing communication programs. Integrated marketing communication is "the most cost-effective means for achieving marketing goals because it carefully evaluates each component of the marketing mix."[4] Through strategic, careful planning and management of all messages, companies can expect more impact from the marketing communication program.

STRONGER CUSTOMER LOYALTY

Kodak Canada
www.kodak.ca

Businesses and marketers alike are concerned about the decline of brand loyalty due to the quantity of products available and the growth of sales promotion. Marketing analyst William Weilbacher claims that the explosion of new brands causes consumers to drown in "unfathomable and largely insignificant product differences" and that is making it more difficult, if not impossible, for advertising to create the psychological value embodied in the great brands of the past—such as Kodak, Coca-Cola and Green Giant.[5]

The indiscriminate use of sales promotion conditions even the most loyal customers to wait for special deals and reduced prices. With some products with little perceived difference in quality, customers only buy a product when it is on sale. The overuse of sales promotion makes it difficult for companies to maintain brand loyalty because for some consumers price becomes more important than brand preference.

The interesting change, however, is that marketing communicators are learning to use diverse marketing communication tools, including sales promotion, to help build brand loyalty. A sophisticated brand marketing program may not use as much advertising as in the past, but it is likely to use more public relations, direct marketing, event marketing, and, yes, even sales promotion, to build loyalty.

The concerns about brand loyalty decline are justified. The advance in database technology has identified a very demanding consumer rather than a passive audience, a consumer who wants relevant content, extra incentives, and signs of company commitment to things that matter, such as health and ecology. Most of all, this new consumer wants to be in touch with companies and brands on his or her own time and has very little patience with intrusive communication forms such as advertising.

The North American consumer's skepticism is mirrored in the attitudes of some governments on other continents that so distrust advertising and other forms of marketing communication that they actively discourage their use. Some East Asian and Muslim countries tightly control the content of advertising. Germany has strict laws about selling information about consumers for use in direct marketing. Whether the distrust lies with the consumer or government, intrusive marketing communication faces an increasingly hostile audience.

New technology is opening up new opportunities for two-way communication, communication that involves a dialogue between company and customer and communication that can be initiated by the customer. These types of communication will supplement or substitute for the mass forms of communication used exclusively in the past.

Relationship marketing
A type of marketing that builds long-standing positive relationships with customers and other important stakeholder groups.

To combat the decrease in brand loyalty, many firms are emphasizing **relationship marketing**—a type of marketing that builds long-standing positive relationships with customers and other important stakeholder groups. Relationship marketing identifies "high value" customers and prospects and bonds them to the brand through personal attention.[6] Most executives focus marketing communication on the needs, wants, and desires that are personally relevant to customers. The best way to manage the whole process is through a database that stores critical information about customers and their interactions with the brand or company.

As author Terry Varva explains, "Treat your customers and clients as you would have other marketers treat you."[7] Many companies think of sales transactions as isolated events rather than steps in lifelong relationships with customers. Furthermore, because many businesses haven't accounted for the lifelong value of a customer relationship, companies think that a bad experience just represents the cost of a simple sale. Varva believes that the value of organizations' relationships with their current customers and other important constituencies leads to more intensified customer loyalty. Indeed, research has found that the average dissatisfied customer tells nine to ten people about the experience, while 13 percent of dissatisfied customers spread the news to more than 20 people. The damage may be far greater than a single lost sale.[8]

Ch!ckaboom Understands Relationship Marketing

Canada's clothes-crazy female "tweens" (girls aged 5 to 13) have become the newest retail fashion trend. Who woulda' thought it? Nancy Dennis, that's who.

Nancy Dennis, a former buyer and merchandise manager for Canadian retail giants like Eaton's, The Bay, and Dylex, recognized the potential of this largely untapped market, and in 1997 launched her own store in Toronto called Ch!ckaboom. Having already experienced significant growth, Dennis ultimately wants to expand to other cities.

Clearly, Ch!ckaboom has found a market that's just waiting to be catered to. According to a 1998 YTV Tween Report, this is a unique and sizable market with about $700 million in discretionary income. This is a target market that is "brand-conscious, mall-wise, and extremely savvy." Moreover, girls are twice as likely as boys to spend cash on clothes.

Ch!ckaboom is not alone in the market for tween spending on clothing. Other retailers like La Senza Inc. and Le Chateau see this market as both sizable and important to their future. These retailers understand that it's essential to understand this market. According to Maureen Atkinson, a senior partner and J.C. Williams Group in Toronto, "You absolutely have to talk to them (the tweens) and not to

ch!ckaboom
yorkdale

Many experts believe that relationship marketing represents a major change in the philosophy of marketing and marketing communication.[9] Relationship marketing is relevant to IMC because a relationship program needs more than just mass-media advertising. It needs a totally integrated communication process that manages every type of message and every aspect of a brand or company's communication and moves the communication as close as possible to one-on-one communication. As you read through this text, you will see how this process can be accomplished in a marketing communication program. The IMC in Action feature shows how Ch!ckaboom has grown a business based on a relationship approach.

International Marketing

Another factor driving the need to integrate marketing communication efforts is the continued growth of international or global marketing efforts. Not only do companies have to deal with departments, divisions, and brand management responsibilities, but they also have to manage across regions, countries, continents, and the globe. This scope complicates the objective of delivering a consistent image and message.

The international communication challenges focus on questions of what to standardize and what to localize. In international advertising, for example, the campaign strategy is often globalized—the company uses the same product positioning and target audience in every country—but the individual ads may anybody else. And certainly you can't talk to their parents. But there's a lot about teenagedom that parents really fear, so I think it's making it comfortable for the parent, but still being able to appeal to that kid directly is critical. It's touchy, because how do you make it cool without making it not cool?" It seems Nancy Dennis knows something about making it cool without making it not cool.

Although Dennis understands that it's Mom's or Dad's credit card, she ensures that her store speaks directly to Susie and her friends—and not her parents. According to Dennis, "the best practice in retail is to respect my customer ... she's the queen when she comes in here. Her mom comes along and pays, but this echo boom generation has tremendous influence, and at least my store, Ch!ckaboom, is theirs."

So far Ch!ckaboom has the names of several thousand of those girls in its database. Relationship marketing, says Dennis, is what it's all about. Girls who join the birthday club can expect to receive a card and a gift certificate on their birthdays. They can also attend special Valentine and Halloween parties—and, of course, what would a tween shop be without a shriekingly fantastic Spice Girls Day? Dennis also gives back to the community: $5 from each sale of a Ch!ckaboom T-shirt goes to the Hospital for Sick Children in Toronto.

Keenly aware that competitors also see this sizable market, Dennis is comfortable with her relationship approach to marketing communications. According to Dennis, Ch!ckaboom is different: "We market to the little girl and our events are for her. So I'm completely comfortable that Ch!ckaboom is one of a kind."

Food for Thought

1. Do you think focusing on relationships is always good marketing communication strategy? Explain your answer. If you think it is, then why do you think some companies don't use it?
2. Suppose you were a Ch!ckaboom competitor. What strategies would you suggest to your company's marketing communication director to combat Ch!ckaboom's understanding of its consumers?
3. Now suppose you were hired as an outside consultant to evaluate Ch!ckaboom's marketing communication program. What additional marketing communication tools would you suggest be used to send tweens a consistent, persuasive message that promotes the company's goal to speak directly to its customer?

Sources: Mikala Folb, "Totally Girl," ***Marketing*** (January 4/11, 1999), 10, 12; personal interview with Nancy Dennis, June 1, 1999. Used with permission.

be produced locally to allow for different language, setting, culture, and physical appearance. Finding the best blend of standardization and localization is crucial for effective message communication.

Added Impact

Impact involves grabbing the consumer's attention. In message design knowing what to say at the right time to the right person can be more effective than mass broadcasting a general idea. Furthermore, the same idea repeated from a variety of different sources can intensify its memorability. For instance, Creative Artists Agency's Coca-Cola campaign targeted each of Coke's market segments differently. Even though Coca-Cola is a mass-marketed product, Coke's marketing managers recognized that many different types of people buy Coke—from teenagers to senior citizens—and you don't talk to them all with the same message, an approach often referred to as a "same voice" or "one look" strategy. Although the varied advertisements used different styles and tone of voice, they were unified by a consistent campaign theme, "Always Coca-Cola," the logo, and the Spencerian script brand name. It was a highly successful experiment in creating diverse messages with a consistent core theme. The company claims the experiment has had tremendous impact.

IMC creates more impact than traditional marketing programs because it eliminates message conflict. The more consistent the message, the greater the impact. People who perceive various messages automatically try to integrate

Brooke DeLong

Communication Specialist, The Canadian Association of Insurance and Financial Advisors

As the primary point of contact for the Canadian Association of Insurance and Financial Advisors' (CAIFA) 1500 volunteer leaders, Brooke DeLong often hears first-hand how things are working in the field. With over 18 000 members and 59 chapters across Canada, DeLong must constantly keep on top of members' attitudes and opinions in order to find new and better ways to service their needs.

In her position as Communication Specialist—Chapter Relations and Website, DeLong acts as the liaison between the Association, its board of directors, and the volunteer chapter leaders. Her main responsibilities include communicating to the leaders about what the Association is doing for its members and supporting them in their activities at the local level.

As DeLong is quick to point out, an open mind and a little creativity can go a long way when you're supporting programs in 59 different communities across Canada. "I quickly realized that each chapter has its own unique needs and concerns," she explains. "What works in one area of the country may not work in another. Part of my role is to help chapters identify their strengths and capitalize on them through a variety of public relations and communication activities. Then I try to provide them with the tools they need to carry out these activities, whether it is media relations training or insight on best practices in association management."

While the administration of CAIFA's chapter recognition program allows DeLong to maintain regular, two-way communication with the chapter leaders, the association's Web site, www.caifa.com, is quickly proving to be the most powerful marketing-communications tool in CAIFA's 93-year history.

The site, complete with current industry information for consumers, discussion areas, and communication materials for chapters, provides CAIFA staff and members with a quick and up-to-date two-way communication tool. CAIFA has also integrated and expanded its member-marketing strategies through new developments to its Web site, such as weekly online newsletters and regular member surveys.

DeLong notes that when she began working with CAIFA in 1998, she found herself in a rather unique position, much to her good fortune. "CAIFA was going through a growth spurt when I came on board," she says. "The Association, formerly the Life Underwriters Association of Canada, had recently changed both its name and its overall strategic direction. Marketing-communication strategies were being focused on member retention and increasing member-value.

"I was given the opportunity to explore new ways to communicate with members, while working with leaders to develop stronger chapter programs. On top of that, I was also responsible for building a more strategic and professional Web presence for the Association. It was a lot of work for someone fresh out of university but once the challenge was issued, I quickly got to work. And it's definitely been worth it."

Academic Background

In 1995, DeLong graduated with a Bachelor of Arts degree in Honours History from the University of New Brunswick in Fredericton. That same year, she also served as vice-president of her graduating class. DeLong credits this experience and some rather interesting job opportunities along the way as being instrumental in her decision to begin studies in public relations.

Fluently bilingual in English and French, DeLong had spent the previous six summers working with the Fredericton Tourism Department, giving tours and administering programs for visitors to the city. In 1994, her bilingualism and history background proved invaluable as she travelled to Vimy, France to work as a site interpreter at the Vimy Ridge Memorial Park. For DeLong, a career in public relations ended up being the most natural progression given her past work experience.

During the fall of 1995, she began the Bachelor of Public Relations program at Mount Saint Vincent University (MSVU) in Halifax. DeLong chose to study at MSVU based on its reputation for providing a solid public relations background and also because at the time, MSVU offered the only degree program in public relations in Canada. However, according to DeLong, the most attractive part of this program ended up being the cooperative education option available to students.

When she graduated three years later, DeLong had a well-rounded background in public relations theory and practice, media relations, and news writing. She had also completed three cooperative education placements, working at the Treasury Board Secretariat of Canada in Ottawa, Atlantic Canada Opportunities Agency in Fredericton, and Noranda Inc. in Toronto. She points out that her co-op experience has proven invaluable in helping her make the transition from university to the workplace.

"My co-op terms gave me 'real-life' experience that I simply couldn't learn from a textbook or a lecture," she says. "By the time the third co-op term rolled around, I was more than ready to get a 'real job.' I was anxious to get out there and start trying things for myself."

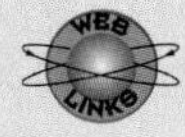

Canadian Association of Insurance and Financial Advisors
www.caifa.com

Soon after finishing her public relations degree, DeLong began work at CAIFA. Even though she's now officially joined the workforce, she continues to attend seminars and other training programs as needed, to keep her skills sharp. She is also an active volunteer with the International Association of Business Communicators (IABC), a professional organization she joined soon after starting her public relations studies. DeLong says that her experience as a volunteer with IABC helps her relate even more to CAIFA's volunteer leaders because, like her, they contribute much of their time and efforts above and beyond their regular work schedules.

Advice

DeLong admits that the two-way communication she enjoys with CAIFA's chapter leaders would not have been possible without taking the time to really learn and understand as much as she could about the leaders and their relationship to the organization. She believes that now, more than ever, the onus is on marketing-communication practitioners to really know their audience, their opinions, their needs, and their expectations.

"In my job, it's been especially important to get to know people as individuals," she says. "I need to know how each one likes to communicate and how to keep them motivated in a competitive and constantly changing industry. People need to be reassured that their needs and concerns are number one and that we haven't forgotten that."

DeLong also points out that every day she learns something new. This has helped her become more successful at her job. "By remaining open to new ideas and suggestions, I've often come up with the best solutions to situations that previously seemed like problems," she says. "There's so much to learn by simply listening to and observing the people around you."

DeLong believes that keeping a pulse on emerging trends and issues in marketing-communication has helped ensure that she is providing members with the most current and relevant information and service possible.

them into some kind of central thought or idea. If the messages are consistent and work together, then the integration leads to more impact than any one message by itself. If they do not work together, then the messages can lead to confusion and irritation. An effective IMC program, then, works with and not against the natural process of perception.

In many companies a lack of coordination creates a consistency problem. The public relations team, for example, may be communicating good citizenship or quality whereas other teams, such as advertising and sales promotion, may be communicating about a new product feature or price reduction. How do all these different messages add up to a coherent image or position for the company or brand?

A fragmented approach does more to destroy a corporate or brand image than it does to reinforce the image, especially when corporate and brand messages conflict. For example, a company that tells shareholders that this will be a banner year and tells employees that there will be no salary increases because of higher production costs could easily lose credibility with both audiences. Integrated marketing communication provides a mechanism for identifying such message conflict, which is important because stakeholder groups often overlap. An employee may also be a shareholder, a community leader may also be a supplier that does business with the company, and so on. This overlap makes it likely that people in an audience group may receive a message intended for another group.

IMC strives to manage or respond to all the messages sent to or by all the various stakeholders. This message management involves tremendous coordination and cooperation within the company across all divisions, not just the traditional marketing communication areas that will be discussed in Chapter 2. As more people accept IMC, however, planning across the company will become easier.

The IMC Model

The model shown in Figure 1.3 depicts the IMC process presented in this text. It incorporates the marketing communication messages from Figure 1.2 and illustrates how they relate to the marketing plan. Marketing communication is determined by the overall marketing plan and its objectives. In a traditional marketing plan, four areas—marketing communication, distribution, price, and product—make up the marketing mix. In the IMC plan, however, message planners recognize that the marketing communication element of the mix is not the only one that can send a message. In fact, the other three elements also communicate messages that can be more important in consumer decision making than the planned marketing communication messages. In our IMC model we show communication as supporting the other three areas. In other words the marketing communication element ties together the other elements of the marketing mix. The second half of the model details the marketing communication plan. That plan, however, takes an IMC approach, which includes planned and unplanned marketing messages.

Figure 1.3 shows a basic model for marketing communication that identifies the critical elements of a dynamic marketing program, one that is both strategically sound and flexible enough to accommodate the demands of a changing marketplace.

Figure 1.3 IMC Model

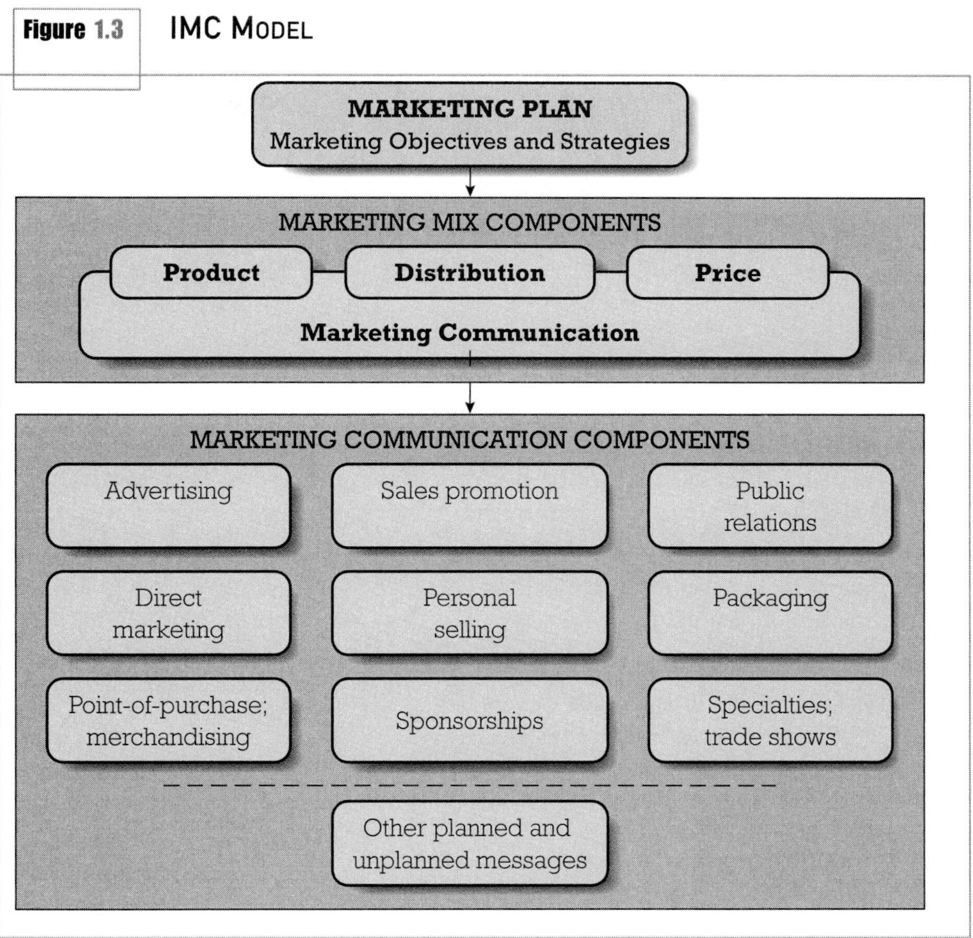

concept review

IMC: A Blueprint for Success in Marketing Communication

1. The IMC goal is to create communication *synergy*, which means that coordinating marketing communication tools creates more impact than the tools would have without such coordination.
2. Integration promises more efficiency, customer loyalty, and impact for the marketing communication program and helps maintain consistency in global marketing programs.

A Closing Thought:

Revolution and Evolution

Marketers know intuitively that communication coordination is a good idea, but the problem continues to be how to do it. IMC is a revolutionary concept in marketing communication in one sense because, as we will see later in the text, it calls for tearing down walls between departments. In another sense it is evolutionary because IMC makes it possible to truly implement marketing objectives that lead to long-term relationships. Why? Those objectives are based on more targeted communication with consumers and other stakeholders. Regardless of how much is revolution and how much is evolution, IMC represents a major change in marketing communication that is gaining momentum both in industry as well as in education.

summary 

1. Explain what marketing communication is and how it is used to promote a product.

   One of the four elements of the marketing mix, marketing communication is the process of effectively communicating product information to target audiences. It uses persuasion to target audiences at all points that audiences might come in contact with the company or brand. The marketing communication plan sets objectives, analyzes unplanned messages, and uses marketing communication tools to communicate the marketing message.

2. Describe the types of messages that are used in marketing communication.

   Two main types of messages communicate with the target market and stakeholder audiences: planned and unplanned. Planned messages are those that marketing communicators intend to send to target audiences via such activities (or tools) as advertising, direct mail, personal selling, sales promotion, and public relations. Unplanned messages are those that audiences infer. Unplanned marketing communication message sources include all elements associated with the company or brand that are capable of delivering implicit messages to consumers, ranging from the courtesy and knowledge of a salesperson to the condition of the company parking lot. In a traditional marketing program, the marketing mix typically sends unplanned messages. In an IMC program, the marketing mix is part of the communication plan, so it is a planned message strategy.

3. Define integrated marketing communication.

   Integrated marketing communication (IMC) is the practice of unifying all marketing communication tools—from advertising to packaging—to send target audiences a consistent, persuasive message that promotes company goals.

4. Discuss the benefits of integrated marketing communication (IMC).

   IMC creates communicate synergy by coordinating all marketing communication activities to send a consistent message that target audiences will perceive and remember. This synergy is more efficient because combined, consistent messages have more impact than independent or inconsistent messages. It creates more customer loyalty by focusing on long-term relationships with customers and other stakeholders. It helps with internationalization because it helps control the consistency of messages being delivered in a variety of countries. Finally, it offers tremendous impact because it eliminates message conflict. As a result, the consistency of the message works with the natural process of perception so that audiences are more likely to remember and appreciate that message.

5. Describe how integrated marketing communication relates to marketing.

   The company's marketing plan and its objectives determine the integrated marketing communication plan's strategies and objectives. The IMC plan recognizes that all marketing mix elements—product, price, distribution, and marketing communication—can communicate messages, though the marketing communication element provides the foundation for such messages.

points to ponder

Review the Facts

1. In your own words, define marketing communication and integrated marketing communication.
2. What is relationship marketing?
3. What is a contact point?
4. What is a stakeholder?

Master the Concepts

5. How do traditional marketing communication and integrated marketing communication differ?
6. Explain the difference between planned and unplanned messages.
7. Why do you think there is a decreasing emphasis on advertising? Explain.
8. How does relationship marketing fit in an integrated marketing communication program?
9. Explain how the demand for efficiency has affected integrated marketing communication.
10. How does internationalization complicate a company's efforts to maintain strategic control over its messages?

Apply Your Knowledge

11. Explain the components of the integrated marketing communication model used in this chapter. Does this model make sense to you? How would you refine it if you were the marketing director for a medium-sized business and the CEO asked you to develop a model of your company's marketing communication?
12. Develop an analysis of all the stakeholders for your university or school. If you were the public relations director for your school, which stakeholders would you consider to be the most important? Explain.

suggested projects

1. If you were to go to work for General Motors Canada, how would you begin to analyse all the places where coordination in message strategies are needed? How does the auto industry, and this company in particular, work in terms of all the various functions, departments, and divisions that are communicating messages?
2. Choose your favourite brand of any product, and collect or research all the different types of marketing communication for that brand that you can find. What tools does the company seem to rely on most? Do the different tools deliver consistent messages? Are there any message conflicts?
3. (Writing Project) Assume your university or school became embroiled in a high-profile scandal in which two high-level administrators were charged with diverting $500 000 earmarked for computer facilities for the business school. Building on your stakeholder analysis in Points to Ponder question 12, craft a brief memo that outlines the contact points key stakeholders might have with the school and how the school could send messages from the contact points to influence stakeholders' perceptions.
4. (Internet and Team Project) Break into small groups of three to six people. Choose a product or service that your group wants to research. Each group member should search the Internet, find two organizations that offer the product or service, and visit the home page of each organization. (Note: You do not need to limit your search to business organizations.) Follow the links in the site and make a list of the audiences the Web site seems to target. Then assess the messages the site tries to communicate to its audiences. Are the messages effective? Consistent? Is there an effort to practise integrated marketing communication (IMC)?

   Meet as a group to discuss your findings, then select the best examples of effective marketing communications. Choose a spokesperson who will present and explain the reasons for your choices in a five-minute oral presentation to the class.

case 1 Promoting CallMall™ & Vista 350*: A High-Tech Service Introduction

Background

It was August. The final technical issues relating to NBTel's Vista 350 telephone system were identified and would be eliminated in the next manufacturing run. Working forward with dates, this meant an early November launch was possible. This was as late as was logically feasible and there was still a fear of getting lost in the Christmas rush. Since NBTel was introducing the Vista 350 and CallMall in North America, the budget for marketing would be liberal, but not excessive.

It was getting down to the wire. Given the November date, this meant that depending on what marketing communication tools were used, decisions would have to be made within two weeks to get production started. Executives at NBTel wondered what would be the lowest cost option to meet the objectives. What marketing communications concepts should be implemented?

Industry, Company, and Product

The New Brunswick Telephone Company, Limited (NBTel) is an acknowledged world leader in telecommunications. It invests in people and technology. Serving more than 300 000 customers in New Brunswick, NBTel's expertise is in developing and delivering local and long distance telephone services, wireless services, advanced network services, and interactive multimedia applications that provide a competitive advantage to businesses and enrich the day-to-day lives of consumers.

Known as an innovator and pace setter in the industry, NBTel has had many "firsts" to its credit. For example, NBTel was the first telephone company in Canada to introduce community calling service, call display, and province-wide Internet access service on both a dial-up and dedicated-access basis. NBTel Mobility's Caller Pays service is also a first in Canada. TalkMailTM, a universal voice-messaging service provided to customers along with their basic local telephone service, and CallMallTM, a joint venture with Northern Telecom (Nortel) that provides customers with access to home-based banking, shopping, and information services, are both world firsts.

The Vista 350 is one of the newest phone sets available with features such as an eight-line, back-lit display screen; message waiting light; speaker phone; caller's log; and a directory of names and numbers. What makes the phone unique is the ADSI-based display that allows connection with a computer server and the downloading of information based on the customer's request.

The two services offered with the set were CallMall and QuickAds:

- CallMall is a customer-initiated connection to a computer that allows the customer to see, read, and hear information, and to complete transactions for banking and catalogue shopping.
- QuickAds allow customers to select categories of interest. Ads are then displayed on the phone based on these categories.

The telephone would be rented monthly and the additional CallMall and QuickAds services would be added at no cost. Other services such as name display and call answer would also be available at a monthly charge.

The Market

The first launch was set for Moncton, New Brunswick, which represents about 50 000 households. The market is about one-third French, with the balance English speaking. It is a smaller town with a mix of service, logistics, and manufacturing industries—a good representation of the rest of Canada, which was the longer-term target for marketing CallMall and Vista 350.

Objectives

There were two objectives:

1) 10+ percent overall penetration of the service before year end, with excellent retention on each install.
2) 80+ percent local awareness of the new services.

Marketing Communication Options

Everything was on the table; however, the marketing communications plan had to be approved and adopted to meet the objectives at the lowest cost. The options included:

- News conference
- Free trials
- Advertising—TV and/or radio
- Billboards

- Direct mail-targeted or mass market, traditional or a "gimmick"
- Multiple locations for distribution channels

To achieve the aggressive penetration targets, a good marketing communication strategy and plan had to be devised and implemented. There were concerns about offering a free trial because all sets returned would have to be refurbished, adding cost to an already expensive set.

The decision was not in the hands of the launch team. What would the strategy and plan of action be?

Case Questions

1. Refer to Figure 1-2. Identify and discuss the advantages and disadvantages of sources of planned marketing communication messages identified by NBTel as communication options.
2. Prepare a list of strategy and action plan ideas for the launch team. Make sure your suggestions are consistent with the objectives, constraints, etc. discussed in the case.

*Trademark of Nortel, NBTel licensed user.

Source: This case was prepared by Mervyn Hann of NBTel as a basis for classroom discussion, and is not meant to illustrate either effective or ineffective management. Used with permission.

CBC VIDEO VIGNETTES

PR Nightmare: The Case of Hemp

As discussed in this chapter's You Decide feature, it has been a struggle for Geof Kime, founder of Hempline, to convince Members of Parliament and senators that you can't smoke hemp but can make a variety of high-quality products out of this high-strength, mould- and mildew-resistant crop. Although hemp now has legal agricultural status in Canada, it seems the struggle for Kime and other industry advocates is far from over.

Once a popular crop, hemp was banned in 1938 because of the mass hysteria at the time concerning the plant's distant cousin, marijuana. It seems, however, the marijuana-related connection remains a significant threat for those, like Kime, who are trying to bring the industry back into the mainstream. Kime refers to the "giggle factor"—that laugh he too often hears when people, some of whom are potential customers, discuss hemp and the products produced from its fibre.

In addition to the "giggle factor," Kime has discovered that it takes time to work around the many bureaucratic hurtles involved in getting a once-banned crop into the mainstream. From Health Canada permits to Canada Customs inspection of seed bags, all of these processes take time. Unfortunately, time is of the essence for farmers who depend on the kindness of Mother Nature throughout the duration of a short growing season. If seed isn't available at planting time, farmers must plant another crop. Therefore, it's conceivable that one or more bureaucratic hurtles just prior to the growing season could drastically reduce the amount of hemp grown in Canada. A lack of hemp supply is a serious impediment to the growth of the Canadian hemp industry. Large manufacturers lack a willingness to gear up for hemp because of a lack of a reliable source of supply. Therefore, it's essential that all barriers to hemp production be overcome. Perhaps a more serious threat to hemp production than the "giggle factor" is the existing ban on the U.S. cultivation of hemp. Advocates like the North American Industrial Hemp Council understand this issue, as do entrepreneurs like Geof Kime.

QUESTIONS

1. If you where a marketing communication specialist hired to advise Geof Kime on what should be done to promote the Canadian hemp industry, what would your advice be?
2. Should the "giggle factor" be addressed by an advertising campaign designed to promote hemp products?
3. Could the "giggle factor" work to the advantage of hemp advocates?

Video Resource: Based on Hemp Madness, © Venture #704 (November 17, 1998).

2

The Marketing Mix and IMC

chapter objectives

After completing your work on this chapter, you should be able to

- Explain the marketing concept and outline how the business plan, marketing plan, and marketing communication strategy inter-relate.
- Identify the product mix elements and explain how they affect the marketing communication program.
- Describe the distribution mix elements and explain how they influence marketing communication.
- List the price mix elements and analyse how they affect marketing communication strategies.

Cows Inc.—A Quality Mix and the World's Coolest Cow Icons

A Prince Edward Island-based company has taken the cow off the farm and into a business enterprise that has rapidly moo-ved forward. Established in 1983, Cows Inc. has expanded from a small ice-cream kiosk in the P.E.I. tourist resort of Cavendish that sold only vanilla ice cream to a multi-store operation across Canada with a multitude of flavours and an extensive merchandise line featuring the cow. This growth record can be attributed to the company's dedication to its mission, a well-planned marketing mix, innovative yet consistent use of the cow icon, and the tremendous loyalty of its stakeholders—customers, employees, and the community.

Aquatic Cow about to explore marine life off Cavendish Beach P.E.I.

According to Bettie MacPherson, the company's general manager, the success of Cows Inc. can be attributed not only to the popularity of the Holstein cow icon, but also to high-quality products and a company philosophy that is both employee- and customer-oriented. Employee Eric Chatigny couldn't agree more. "I had a blast working for Cows. It's fabulous. I'd say that management is more concerned about people—both on the customer and employee side."

The business has been customer-driven from the start. Island entrepreneur Scott Linkletter began by experimenting with an old family ice-cream recipe. In 1985, he asked his friend Marc Gallant to design some humorous T-shirts with cows on them for the staff doing the scooping. Gallant's whimsical cow creations caught the eye of ice-cream customers, and because there were so many requests for them, the shop introduced its own T-shirt line in 1987. More T-shirt designs were added to the initial two and the line expanded to include cow images on crew-neck shirts, reverse fleece shirts, pajamas, and hats. Now the cows are also featured on a wide range of other merchandise including calendars, notepads, pens, cards, refrigerator magnets, pins, and hot chocolate.

Shortly after the T-shirts were introduced, customers began asking for catalogues, so Cows Inc. started a mail-order division in 1991. It wasn't long after this introduction that the company expanded beyond its home province because people pushed to open franchises. The first out-of-province store was located on Vancouver's Robson Street as a franchise. Cows Inc. has since decided not to franchise anymore but has bought back control of the store. Today there are Cows outlets in Halifax, Park City, Utah, Whistler, Banff, and Ottawa, and seven outlets in Prince Edward Island.

Message consistency in an integrated marketing communications program requires that all messages sent by an organization work synergistically to create a coherent image. In this case, the company's image is consistently communicated through its Holstein cow icon. "There's something about the cow that people like," explains Bettie MacPherson. "It's a warm, gentle creature that gives milk and feeds society, and we keep it all fun."

This image is integrated within Cows' entire marketing mix. Its ice cream is not "run-of-the-mill"—it's a wholesome premium product. A single scoop on a waffle cone costs almost $3, which is a little higher than average, but only the best ingredients are whipped together in a special machine that doesn't pump in air. This means that one scoop can weigh three times as much as cheaper ice cream. Moreover, each scoop is weighed to ensure the customer receives 250 millilitres.

Cows Inc.
www.cows.ca

To remain fun, fresh, and appealing to customers, Cows Inc. continuously innovates with the Holstein cow icon. Each year, six new designs are introduced and sold along with six existing ones in four different coloured shirts. Popular designs that have been discontinued are sold as classics through mail order, but only in white. A design may be revived, as happened when the golfing cow was brought back to tie into interest generated when the prestigious Skins golf tournament that was held on the Island in 1998.

Source: Norma Reveler, "Moo-ving Some Merchandise," *Marketing* (April 12, 1999), 21, 24.

Chapter Overview

Need
A state or feeling of deprivation, such as hunger, the need for affection, knowledge, or self-expression.

Many firms, driven by a **need** to better communicate with their customers and other stakeholders, recognize that marketing "is not a specialized activity at all. It encompasses the entire business. It is the whole business seen from the customer's point of view."[1]

Every aspect of the marketing mix—the product, channels of distribution, price, and marketing communication—affects customers' response to a product. And as we discussed in Chapter 1, the product, price, and distribution affect the marketing communication program. In this chapter we review how the marketing communication program fits into the firm's corporate strategy and its overall marketing strategy. Then we explore how the product type, product life cycle, and product mix affect marketing communication. We also consider the distribution of products, both goods and services, and see how different distribution channels influence marketing communication. Finally, we examine how pricing strategies affect marketing communication.

The Marketing Concept

Marketing
The process of planning and executing the conception, pricing, promotion, and distribution of ideas, goods, and services to create exchanges that satisfy individual (customer) and organizational objectives.

Marketing has been defined as "the process of planning and executing the conception, pricing, promotion, and distribution of ideas, goods, and services to create exchanges that satisfy individual (customer) and organizational objectives."[2] The marketing concept is a business philosophy that defines marketing as a process intended to find, satisfy, and retain customers while the business makes a profit.

Central to both of these definitions is the role of the customer and the customer's relationship to the product, whether that product is a good, service, or idea.

Competitive advantage
When consumers believe that a product satisfies their need better than a competitor's product.

The success of a marketing effort, however, depends on whether a firm can convince consumers that the product has a competitive advantage. Consumers believe a product has a **competitive advantage** when they believe the product satisfies their needs better than a competitor's product. A human **need** is a state or feeling of deprivation, such as hunger, the need for affection, knowledge, or self-expression. These needs can be rational or irrational. Harley-Davidson sells a great many motorcycles because of the product's rough-and-tumble image and its power to satisfy an emotional rather than a rational need.

Exchange
The act of obtaining a desired object from someone by offering something of value in return.

When you shop for a particular style of shirt and you find one that you like, you typically purchase it for a sum of money. In marketing, this act of obtaining a desired object from someone by offering something of value in return is called the **exchange**. Moving consumers to make such an exchange requires a great deal of marketing know-how and effort.

The Business and Marketing Plans

Businesses exist to accomplish goals. These goals, known collectively as the company's "mission," define why the company exists. They embody the organization's core beliefs and values.

This UPS ad touts transportation speed as a competitive advantage that its business audience is likely to appreciate.

Business plan
A long-range plan that outlines the objectives and specific actions the organization will take to reach its goals.

Once a business has established its goals, it then creates a **business plan**—a long-range plan that outlines the objectives and specific actions the organization will take to reach its goals. The business plan objectives are usually measurable. A clothing retailer like Zellers might, for example, state that it plans to increase its market share in the toddler clothing market segment by five percent over the next two years. To be effective, the business plan should be consistent with the company's goals.

After the business plan has been developed, those in charge of marketing create a marketing plan. Recall from Chapter 1 that the marketing plan analyses the marketing situation, identifies a target market, states clear and measurable objectives, develops strategies to achieve those objectives, and specifies the activities (through the marketing mix) to implement these strategies. The marketing plan should be compatible with both the company mission and its business plan. The marketing communication plan, in turn, must be compatible with the marketing plan. Figure 2.1 outlines the entire planning process.

Volvo
www.volvo.com

The problem is that the compatibility between the corporate mission, business objectives, marketing objectives, and marketing communication objectives can sometimes break down at the implementation stage if not carefully managed. For example, Volvo AB had a long historical commitment to honesty and consumer concern as part of its mission and its business and marketing plans. Unfortunately, a few years ago Volvo's ad agency was caught rigging a product demonstration where a monster truck drove over several automobiles and only the Volvo 240 survived. Evidence showed that producers at the commercial shooting had cut the roof supports of the other cars and reinforced the Volvo 240. All the parties associated with the commercial denied blame, but in the end

Figure 2.1 THE COMPANY PLANNING PROCESS

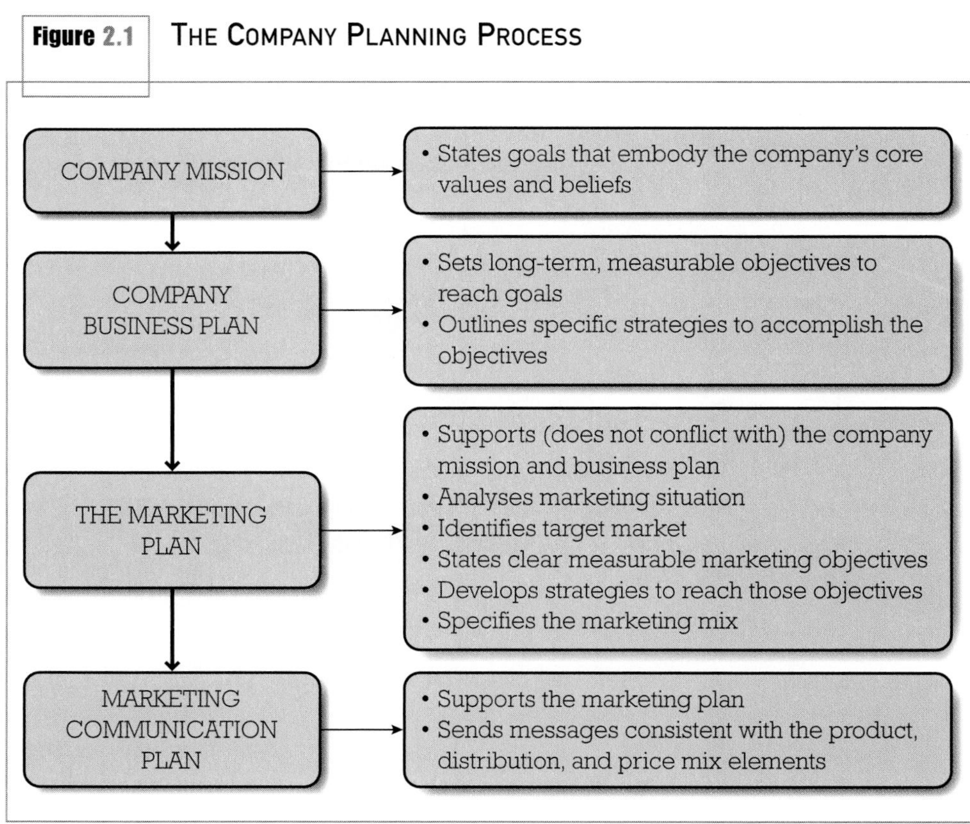

Volvo fired its ad agency of 24 years, Scali, McCabe, Sloves; and Volvo's reputation may never recover completely. The business and marketing plans were not implemented correctly in the advertising.

The Marketing Mix

Generally, a company's marketing mix includes product, distribution, price, and marketing communication (the mix was originally referred to as the 4Ps of product, place, price, promotion). Marketers use the marketing mix as the means to reach marketing goals. Each mix element has many dimensions. In fact, each element has its own mix of strategic decisions—the product mix, distribution mix, and so on.

For instance, we introduced many marketing communication activities (also called marketing communication tools) in Chapter 1, such as direct marketing and sponsorships. Those activities combine to form a marketing communication mix. Likewise, components of the product—product design, features, packaging, maintenance, and warranty—create the product mix. The distribution mix involves where, when, and with whom a company places a product to make it accessible to customers. The price mix establishes the terms of the marketing exchange, which might include the dollar price on the package, a trade-in, a discount, or a rebate. In this chapter we discuss the product, distribution, and price mixes and explain how their planning and management communicate messages that impact the company's marketing communication program.

IMC recognizes that every element in the marketing mix delivers a marketing message. For the best chance of success, all these messages should be integrated so they are consistent, because every facet of the marketing mix communicates. The question is how to manage all the mix decisions so the marketing messages are unified.

Not only are the various components of the marketing mix integrated, they are also message carriers. The design of the product says something about its quality, the price carries a message that establishes the product's value, and the store where the product is displayed says something about convenience and status. Because the marketing mix elements communicate, however, firms must

concept review

The Marketing Concept

Three basic concepts help us understand why marketing communication should be integrated with the other marketing mix elements.

1. Marketing focuses on customer wants and needs. Communication helps customers see how a product will best serve their needs.
2. The marketing plan must be compatible with the company's mission and business plan. In turn, the marketing communication strategies must support, not conflict with, the marketing plan.
3. The marketing mix involves strategic decisions about the product, its pricing, distribution, and its marketing communication. Because all marketing mix elements communicate, marketers should be sure all mix elements deliver a consistent message.

A Do-It-Yourself Mix-Up

The design of the product sends a message about quality, the price carries a message about the product's value, and the store where the product is displayed can signal convenience, accessibility, and quality. Because the marketing mix elements communicate, firms must be careful that the mix doesn't conflict with the overall company, product, or brand communication strategies.

A company that learned how important it is to coordinate marketing communication with its overall communication strategies is Black & Decker, a leader in the do-it-yourself tool market since the 1960s. In the early 1990s Black & Decker began suffering erosion in its professional tool line, caused by fierce competition from Makita, a Japanese manufacturer, and cannibalization from its own consumer brand.

Black & Decker marketed its professional products under the DeWalt brand name, not the Black & Decker brand name. The company had assumed that professionals would not connect Black & Decker products targeted at do-it-yourselfers to its DeWalt products. Instead, professionals saw the ads and products for do-it-yourselfers and found them confusing.

Black & Decker made the decision to relaunch the DeWalt line to professionals in a manner easily distinguishable (beyond just price) from the consumer product line. Products were reassessed, distribution was limited to retail outlets where professionals shop (not Kmart), and a separate pricing strategy was devised in line with its major competitors. Finally, Black & Decker communicated key information about DeWalt products, price, and distribution in print ads in professional magazines, demonstration videos, and through a toll-free number. Recognizing how the marketing mix elements of the DeWalt line were undercut by the consumer product line marketing mix helped Black & Decker increase its sales.

Food For Thought

1. Many big companies are marketing brands that sound home-spun and disguise the name of its parent company. RJR Nabisco, for instance, promotes cigarette brands under the name Moonlight Tobacco Co. Given the Black & Decker experience with its DeWalt line, do you think this is a good idea? Explain your answer.
2. Gillette creates and markets both Waterman and Parker pens. Do you think that these brands are easily distinguishable? What marketing mix strategies do you think Gillette uses effectively or ineffectively to distinguish the two brands?

Sources: Norton Foley, "Back from the Dead," ***Sales & Marketing Management*** (July 1995): 30-1; David W. Stewart, "The Market-Back Approach to the Design of Integrated Communications Programs: A Change in Paradigm and a Focus on Determinants of Success," American Academy of Advertising Special Conference on Integrated Marketing Communication, Norfolk, Va., March 1995.

be careful that the mix doesn't conflict with the overall company or brand communication strategies.

Some marketing experts claim that the idea of IMC cannot be separated from the way a firm defines its business and the customers it elects to serve. Ideally, what requires coordination, then, is not just marketing communication, but the entire communication of a business.[3]

The Product Mix

A good product is at the heart of marketing. (Remember, we use the word *product* in its broadest sense to refer to goods, services, and ideas.) The term *product* refers to the bundle of attributes and features—both tangible and intangible—offered by a firm. It includes the elements supporting the physical product (for example, package, warranty, colours) as well as its emotional components (for example, brand loyalty, status, self-esteem, security, convenience).

To effectively manage the message the product sends, marketing communication managers must become passionately involved with a product as shown in

Products are the heart and soul of marketing. How does this Ginsana ad convey passion for the product?

the accompanying ad. Their involvement should start early and continue throughout the process of product design and delivery. These managers must assess how the types of products they market affect their marketing communication strategies. They must then examine the product's life cycle and plan the strategic components of the product mix.

Product Classifications

Many different types of products exist. There are two main product classifications: the nature of the product (goods, services, or ideas) and the market to which the product is sold and used (consumer or industrial products).

Goods, Services, and Ideas

Goods
Tangible products such as cookies and bicycles.

Services
Intangibles that are represented by activities of people.

Products may be classified as a good, service, or idea. **Goods** are tangible products such as toothpaste, cookies, cars, and bicycles. **Services** are intangibles and are represented by activities of people. Service product examples include insurance, hair salons, health care, banks, entertainment, and education. Both goods and services are intended to satisfy the needs of customers. Ideas can be marketed—such as donating to a good cause, participating in recycling programs, or voting for a particular candidate—and are "sold" through persuasive communication. The objective of marketing ideas is to shape or change opinions.

Goods and services, however, are the focus of most marketing programs. An overlap often occurs between goods and services. Goods are frequently supported by services and vice versa. In automotive marketing, the service, repair, or financing departments are integral parts of the product. Conversely, in a service industry such as restaurants, tangible products (hamburgers, pizzas, and tacos) are served. To classify whether the product is a good or service, look at its dominant characteristics. Tim Hortons may provide donuts, which are tangible, but its primary role is to serve ready-to-eat food quickly, as shown by its drive-in window, its standardized menu, and its staff. Its dominant characteristics show that it is a service. Service products are commonly distinguished from goods products by the four characteristics that are listed in Table 2.1. These four characteristics are referred to as the four I's of services.

Tim Hortons
www.timhortons.com

Of particular relevance to the marketing communication effort is the notion of tangibility. Every product has both tangible and intangible characteristics. A John Deere tractor has obvious tangible features, but it also has intangible

Table 2.1 THE FOUR I'S OF SERVICES

Characteristic	Description
1. Intangibility	Service products cannot be tasted, felt, seen, heard, or smelled. Thus the communication program, especially personal selling and advertising, must describe the benefits derived from the service. Mass advertising can stimulate demand through the use of testimonials and other techniques that show service products' appealing benefits. Example: A hotel chain might highlight symbolic representations of the product such as an easy check-in process or the spectacular view from the room.
2. Inseparability	For many services, the product cannot be created or delivered without the customer's presence. Examples include haircuts and medical care. As a consequence, the marketing communication must convince the consumer that the feeling gained from the service is worth buying it. Example: A sporting event such as a university football game is promoted by focusing on the excitement of the event and the enthusiasm of the spectators.
3. Inconsistency (also referred to as heterogeneity)	For many services, it is virtually impossible to standardize the service product, nor is it easy to predict the quality of the service delivered as it can vary from one time to another and from one service provider to another. That's why training is so important in service industries. Example: McDonald's has trained its staff to comply with standards so that customers have the same experience no matter which McDonald's they visit.
4. Inventory (also referred to as perishability)	Service products, such as seats on a scheduled airline flight, cannot be stored, and the demand level is difficult to forecast. Marketing communication, therefore, attempts to encourage consumers to use it in a more predictable pattern. Example: Airlines offer frequent flyer programs and lower prices if customers are willing to fly at certain times of the day, days of the week, or certain times of the year.

elements, such as the warranty, ease of maintenance, available financing, and brand reputation. A goods product tends to have *more* tangible elements than intangible. This does not mean, however, that the consumer values these tangible elements over the intangible. For example, in Canada some car buyers perceive automobiles made in Germany as offering superior quality and cars made in Japan as offering better gas consumption and higher levels of durability than cars made in North America. Thus, the intangible, symbolic attributes of these foreign-made automobiles may be more important than tangible ones such as four wheels, seats, brakes, and a steering wheel. Figure 2.2 illustrates the interplay between these tangible and intangible product characteristics.

The goods or services classification provides specific implications for the message strategy. In general, the challenge is to make dull tangible features exciting and to make vague, hard-to-visualize intangible features clear and concrete. Consider the packaged cookie. An intangible feature that would need to be made more concrete could be a reputable brand name, such as Christie, that guarantees consistent quality. A marketing message might say, "Mr. Christie, you make good cookies!" The tangible features include the sugar, flour, chocolate, and baking powder used to make the cookie. However, these ingredients are too far removed from the real benefits that interest consumers—such as "tastes like homemade" or "rich double-chocolate flavour." Because taste and quality are the benefits consumers want to learn about, marketers need to focus on this information.

The goods or services classification has other marketing message implications. For instance, many service firms depend heavily on personal selling because of the difficulty the customer often has understanding service products.

Figure 2.2 TANGIBLE AND INTANGIBLE PRODUCT CHARACTERISTICS

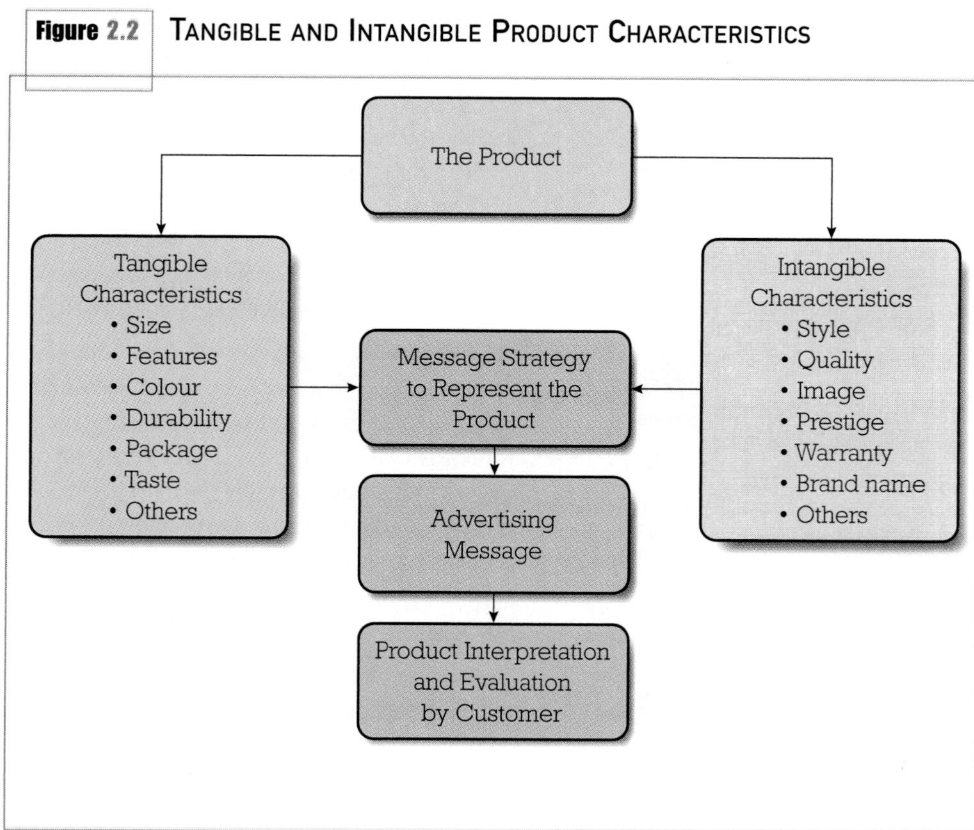

The travel, banking, entertainment, and educational industries all employ many individuals who act as salespersons, explaining the intangible benefits of the service product, answering questions, and prompting action.

In the case of goods products, such as television sets or clothing, the consumer has access to product specifications and can test or try on the product. The salesperson, then, may simply take the order and ring up the sale.

Marketers of service products often rely heavily on public relations. Because service products cannot be readily experienced, consumers tend to trust word of mouth and expert opinions to gauge quality. Restaurants, concert promoters, and the movie industry all rely on critics to give positive reviews. Similarly, banks and investment companies offer free seminars to existing and prospective customers. All of these efforts try to create a positive image for an intangible product.

Consumer and Industrial Products

Consumer products
Products purchased for personal or family consumption with no intention of resale.

Industrial products
Products purchased by an organization or an individual that will be used to make another product, will be distributed to an industrial customer for a profit, or used to meet some other business objective.

Products may also be classified according to who uses them. Products purchased for personal or family consumption with no intention of resale are **consumer products**. Products purchased by an organization or an individual that will be used to make another product, distributed to an industrial customer for a profit, or used to meet some other business objective are called **industrial** or **business-to-business products.**

Goods such as raw materials used in construction and the services of professionals who use these supplies to make or do something, such as building a home or cleaning an office, are industrial products. When a company or an entire industry expresses a viewpoint about something that affects the way it does business, such as the cigarette industry promoting commercial free speech or self-regulation, it is participating in industry idea marketing.

The distinction between consumer and industrial products has marketing communication implications, as shown in Table 2.2. Because the decision to buy industrial products is usually made by professional purchasing agents or committees that place great importance on cost, marketers assume the decision is based mainly on factual information rather than emotional appeals. Thus, the marketing communication effort for industrial products often includes, in order of emphasis: 1) personal selling, 2) sales promotion, especially if presented by salespeople, and 3) trade advertising that uses print media filled with product information and a toll-free telephone number or Internet address that allows customers to request additional information.

Table 2.2 Marketing Communication Emphasis: Consumer versus Industrial Products

Marketing Communication Emphasis	Consumer Products	Industrial Products
Advertising	✓✓✓✓	✓✓
Sales promotion	✓✓✓	✓✓✓
Public relations	✓✓	✓
Personal selling	✓	✓✓✓✓

Generally, marketing communication aimed at consumers uses a more emotional appeal. Often the focus is on mass selling through television and print advertising, sales promotion at the point of purchase, and public relations to provide credibility and remind the consumer about the product's positive image. Personal selling becomes relevant when the consumer product is expensive or technically complex and needs demonstration and explanation. The business service ad from The Marketing Store Worldwide illustrates a trait of industrial product advertising.

Product Life Cycle

The concept of the product life cycle (PLC), is based on a metaphor that treats products as people and assumes products move through predictable stages in their lifetimes.[4] From birth to death, products exist in different stages and different competitive environments. The product life cycle is typically divided into four stages: introduction, growth, maturity, and decline. The length of each

This ad for The Marketing Store Worldwide promotes a member of the firm's senior management team and its brand building services. This ad is targeted to a business market and provides information to help sell the firm's expertise.

The Marketing Store Worldwide launches major Promotion in Canada

Terri Perras
Senior Vice President Promotions & Advertising

The Marketing Store Worldwide, L.P.
20 Duncan St., 2nd Floor, Toronto, Ontario, Canada M5H 3G8
Phone: 416-977-TMSW (8679)
Fax: 416-977-3501

Well established as one of Canada's top promotional marketers, Terri Perras joins the ever expanding senior management team of Canada's only truly integrated one stop brand building shop; **The Marketing Store Worldwide.**

A past recipient of Canada's "Promotional Professional of the Year", Terri comes with a slew of other awards and accolades, as well as over 15 years working within the packaged goods, fast food and entertainment industries. While with YTV Terri gained significant experience in kid's marketing and media leveraging.

Terri is just the latest recruit to the agency's innovative concept of **Total Brand Experience** delivered via strategic based planning.

If you company is in need of the best promotions that Canada has to offer, e-mail **terri.perras@tmsw.com**

The Marketing Store Worldwide 

stage and the entire life cycle vary among products. Furthermore, not all products go through the four stages. Marketing communication for a product depends in part on the stage of the product life cycle because a different communication mix is often needed.

Introductory Stage

In most cases new product stories are built on new ideas, new product features, or a new formulation—some innovation that is worthwhile for the customer. The marketing communication program stimulates *primary* rather than *secondary* demand, particularly if it has no competition. That is, it emphasizes the type of product rather than the brand. The problem with new product launches is that often the bugs aren't worked out and the company must be prepared to handle customer complaints.

A company often launches a new product with a high price to recover as much cost per unit as possible, and therefore it must support the high price with extensive marketing communication. It may take an enormous amount of mass advertising and personal selling to convince the market of the product's merits at the premium price level. A high level of sales promotion serves to accelerate the rate of market penetration because sales promotion is particularly good at stimulating trial. For example, when Gillette introduced its Sensor shaving system in North America, it spent a spectacular $245 million on an integrated marketing communication campaign that included mass-media advertising, coupons, point-of-sale displays, product sampling, and public relations that stressed the new technology of the razor. The product grabbed more than three percent of the market within three months of introduction—making it one of the most successful new product launches in history.

Growth Stage

By the time the good or service has reached the beginning of the growth stage, its market acceptance has been assured. Previous purchasers continue their purchasing, and new buyers enter in even larger numbers as word gets out. The success of a new product attracts competition. However, these firms require time to introduce their own versions of the product, so there is a short time during which the new product owns the market and can establish its dominance. As technology makes new product innovation easier, the window of time decreases. To stay ahead of the pack, firms may add new product features and refinement to their products quickly to address the needs of the market.

During the growth stage, companies maintain their marketing communication expenditures at the same or slightly higher level to meet competition and to continue educating the market. The aim of advertising shifts from building product awareness to creating brand loyalty and securing repeat purchases. Finally, as more competitors enter the market, the role of personal selling changes. Now the salesperson must deal with distributors more aggressively. Shelf space is at a premium, and a variety of trade deals is common. As the ultimate consumer is inundated with choices, sales promotion tools such as discounts, coupons, and rebates may become more important in the consumer decision process.

Maturity Stage

In the maturity stage of the PLC, sales increases may continue although the rate of the increase is slowing down and profits may start to decline. Competitive effort is spent on generating small changes in market share. Marginal producers drop out of the market as price competition becomes increasingly severe. Coca-Cola and Pepsi products are in this stage in most countries. The products are still selling well, but both companies must fight harder to retain market share. Keep in mind, increasing market share by one percentage point for Coke in the U.S. market is equivalent to almost $1.4 billion.(Coke and Pepsi are both entering new markets as they continue to expand globally. In those markets, they find themselves back in the new product stage.) It is also during this stage that manufacturers fight constantly to retain distributors and shelf space, and even more of the budget is allocated to trade deals and consumer sales promotion.

Over time it becomes more difficult to identify important product features that can be effectively featured in marketing communication. Essentially, all the competitors have the necessary technology to match one another, thereby creating commodity products that are substitutable in the mind of the consumer. The only point of difference, then, becomes the imagery communicated by marketing communication. B.C.'s Columbia Brewing Company has, for example, successfully differentiated its Kokanee Beer by promoting it as the beer that fits the image of a 20-year-old's lifestyle. This approach has helped to build market share in the young male-dominated market.[5]

Decline Stage

A product enters the decline stage when consumer demand decreases, such as the market for eight-track tapes or record albums. This stage highlights why firms should continue to develop new products. It is better to lose sales of an older product to one's own new product than lose sales to competitors. As the market declines, the marketing communication budget and selling efforts decrease. The decline stage does not affect all products. Some long-time products, such as Ivory soap and Campbell's soup, for example, have never entered the decline stage.

Campbell's
www.campbellsoups.com

One of the most common reasons for decline is a market change. An example is the Cray computer, a huge computer system prized by large users such as weapons engineers, rocket scientists, and government purchasing agencies.[6] In the 1990s, the arrival of cheap and powerful microprocessor chips transformed the computing world and dramatically decreased demand for big systems like Cray. The Cray supercomputers became obsolete, and Cray was unable to keep pace with these market changes.

In summary, the product life cycle is a very useful planning tool for marketing communication. Although it tends to be product-specific, Figure 2.3 shows the general communication strategies that should be emphasized as we move from introduction to decline.

Strategies for Product Mix Communication

For every product, regardless of where it is in its life cycle, marketers must make certain strategic decisions. The key product mix decision-making areas include research and design, product features, packaging, branding, and support services. In many organizations, these decisions are made by the product manager who uses extensive research to carefully assess the relative importance of these

Figure 2.3 MARKETING COMMUNICATION EMPHASIS OVER A PRODUCT'S LIFE CYCLE

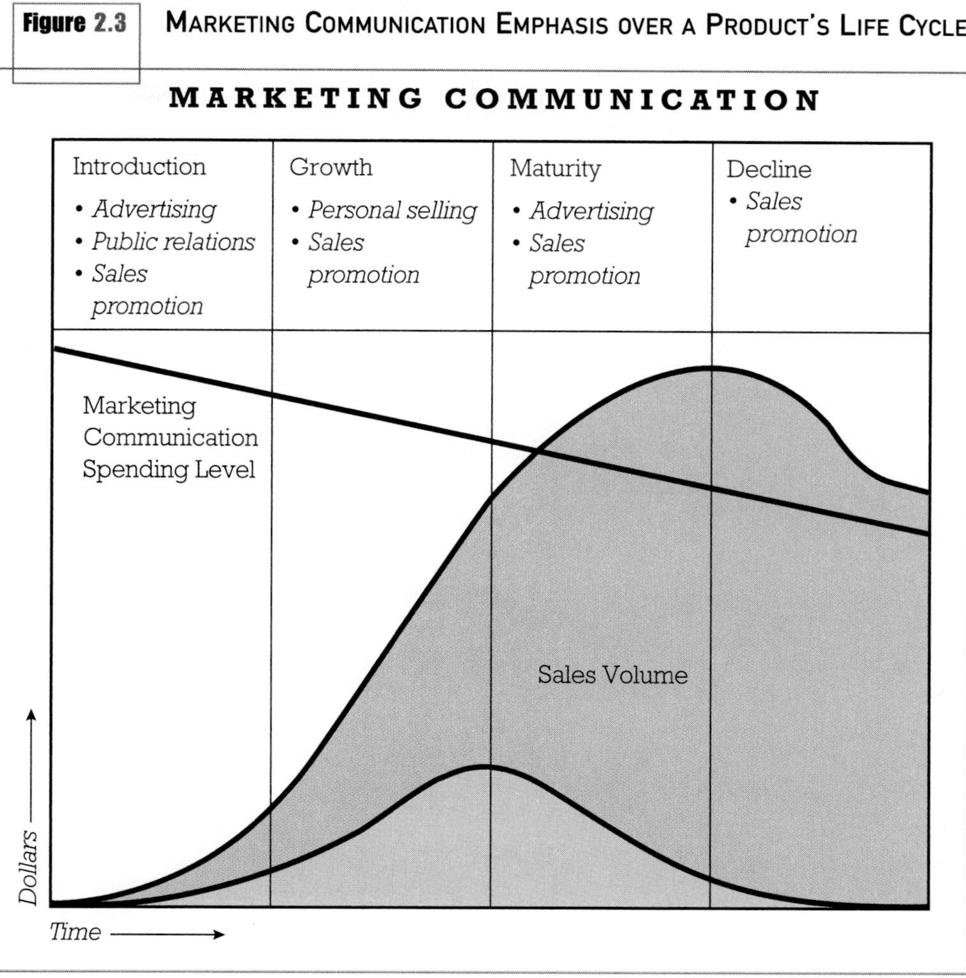

Hospital for Sick Children
www.sickkids.on.ca

product-related elements in the minds of the customer or potential customer. For computer customers, the key elements are features and compatibility. For Toronto's Hospital for Sick Children, it is reputation and availability of skilled physicians. For Armani, the brand name may take precedence over features.

PRODUCT DESIGN

The opening story about Cows Inc.'s wholesome premium ice cream underscores the importance of product development and how the product can drive a marketing communication program. In a marketing-driven organization, research and development (R&D) must work closely with marketing to determine consumer needs and product features that will be most useful to potential customers. Engineers and marketing researchers should partner with strategists. In well-integrated companies, these groups work closely together, often in teams.

Microsoft is an example of a company that is market driven. As discussed in the Profile feature that follows, the Encarta product design story involved much more than a simple conversion of an encyclopedia to an electronic format. Product designer Bill Flora had to design the product so that users could navigate their way through complex electronic files. He also knew that the Encarta product instructions had to be consumer-friendly.

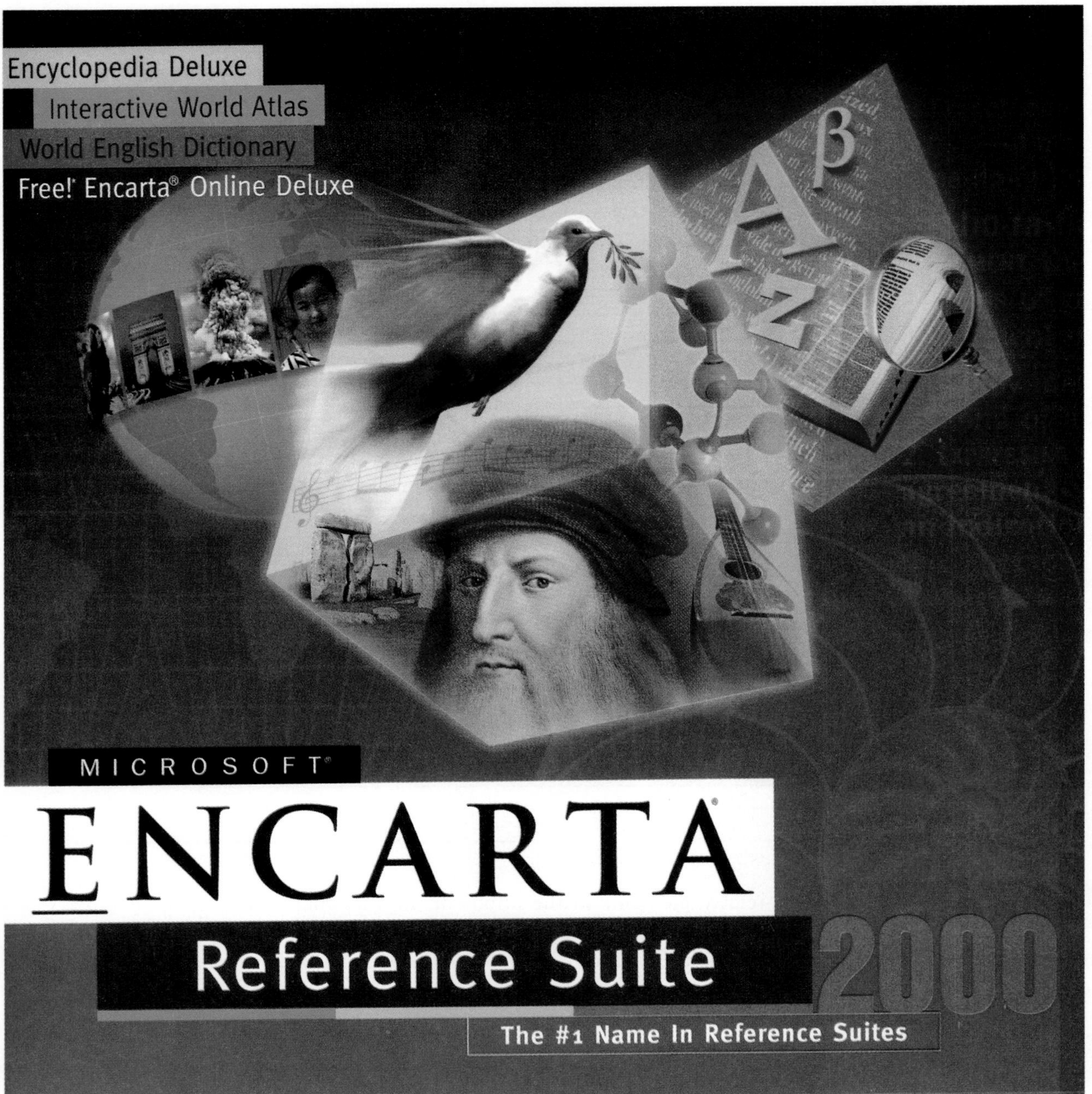

Microsoft's electronic encyclopedia, Encarta, was an interesting design challenge for computer graphics whiz Bill Flora, who had to develop an easy-to-use navigation system that would let novice computer users move easily through complex files of information.

Product Features

Product features for goods include form, colour, size, weight, texture, and materials. For service products, the features include expertise, physical surroundings, and people. Features create unique qualities, benefits, and appeals that can be used in marketing communication. For example, a new car offers many features—some critical to consumers and some trivial, some better than competitors' and some not. All automobile manufacturers offer safety features such as seat belts, reliable tires, bumpers, and safety windshields.

Marketing communication managers analyse what product features will say to an audience. A car that has anti-lock brakes, for example, communicates safety and top quality. Next, the manager must decide how to communicate the features to the target audience and how to do that with an integrated, consistent message. Armstrong Floors, for instance, sends the same message to both consumers and industrial users—durability and variety at a fair price. Its sales promotion effort includes sample sheets, videos demonstrating the various floors, and an iron-clad guarantee. Walk into a store selling Armstrong Floor products and you will find a salesperson thoroughly trained and responsive to customer needs.

The complexity of the product also suggests specific communication strategies. When products are complex, companies may rely on personal selling and other sales promotion tools that inform such as printed brochures, demonstrations, and point-of-purchase displays. Salespeople and product demonstrations allow consumers to experience the product and ask questions. To get across simple ideas or to make consumers aware of a product that does not have complex features, firms usually use image advertising—advertising that focuses on one or two general ideas about the brand.

Packaging

Traditionally viewed as the container that holds the product, packaging is primarily a concern for a goods product, although a service product can also be "packaged" in the way it is presented to the customer. For example, Avon's customer contacts are well packaged—the phone call appointment, the door hangers left when potential customers are not at home, and the leave-behind product catalogue. When we speak of packaging, we are primarily referring to goods and the physical containers that not only protect the products but also deliver an important selling message at the point of purchase. Packaging is so crucial in some product categories—toothpaste, detergents, food products—that the phrase "package goods" is often used to refer to these products.

Packaging serves three purposes: functional, informational, and persuasive. The functional features of packaging include convenience, safety, and preassortment—that is, placing the product in an individual or a grouped unit, such as a four-pack of Snapple. Easy-open spouts, safety lids, recyclable packaging, and oven-proof paperboard are all examples of package functions that move beyond protecting the product to a marketable product feature. Information can be conveyed through a listing of product ingredients, special instructions, price, and so forth. A package can persuade if the design incorporates a special offer, contest announcement, or perhaps a testimonial.

Conversely, packaging—particularly wasteful over-packaging with multiple wrapping—may provide environmentally concerned consumers with a reason to avoid buying the product. The "long-boxes" that packaged some CDs generated consumer resistance because they were wasteful.

Brand
The name, design, symbol, or any other feature that identifies the good, service, institution, or idea sold by a marketer.

Brand name
That part of a brand that can be spoken, such as words, letters, or numbers.

Brand mark, or logo
The part of the brand that cannot be spoken, such as a symbol, picture, design, colour combination, or distinctive lettering.

Branding

A **brand** is the name, design, symbol, or any other feature that identifies the good, service, institution, or idea sold by a marketer. The **brand name** is that part of a brand that can be spoken, such as words, letters, or numbers. The **brand mark,** also known as the logo, is that part of the brand that cannot be spoken. It can be a symbol (Nike's swoosh), picture (Green Giant's jolly green giant), colour combination (IBM's use of blue), or distinctive lettering (the distinctive

Bill Flora

Creative Director—Microsoft's Encarta

As creative director, Bill Flora is lead designer for Microsoft's Encarta, an electronic encyclopedia. He is involved in both art direction and product design. His goals are to invent new ways for people to navigate through complex sets of information, make an attractive and visually fascinating product, and develop a useful program for people who have only minimal computer experience.

Bill's job responsibilities include the following:

- Directing the art content of the encyclopedia
- Managing a team of up to five other interactive designers
- Understanding the customer, the market, and the technology
- Designing the functional elements of the product—such as the product's organization
- Designing the interface —that is, developing the look and feel of the product
- Proposing and prototyping design solutions to communication problems
- Applying new styles of information presentation and learning adapted from such activities as interpretive museum exhibits, film documentaries, and new data visualization techniques

An interesting aspect of Flora's work is that the product is redesigned every year to keep up with content changes. For instance, the Encarta 95 edition made major changes to the product's user interface for several reasons. "We wanted to improve it, make it easier to use, less intimidating, and more integrated." The second and more important reason is that "we wanted a new visual appeal—more approachable, more fun, and in our case more sophisticated." Flora notes, "Our main goal was to create an 'experience,' and to make that experience engaging."

The success of the Encarta program led to coverage of Flora's work in a number of trade and general interest magazines. His string of awards for Encarta include the Industrial Design Society of America (IDSA) Design Excellence Silver Award, an Honorable Mention for Encarta 95 in *ID* Magazine, and Communication Arts' Interactive Multimedia Award.

Academic Background

Flora graduated from the University of Colorado with a B.S. in Business in 1987. During that time he worked as advertising director for the Campus Press, the School of Journalism's campus newspaper. Flora feels his best school experience, aside from his degree program, was working on the campus newspaper. He values the sales,

Trademark
A brand name or brand mark that is legally protected through a registration process.

Branding strategy
The process of developing and selecting brand names, brand marks, and the supporting marketing campaign.

Spencerian script used to write the Coca-Cola brand name). When a brand name or brand mark is legally protected through registration with the Canadian Intellectual Property Office (CIPO), a special operating agency associated with Industry Canada, it becomes a **trademark**. The process of developing and selecting brand names, brand marks, and the supporting marketing campaign is called a **branding strategy**.

The power of a brand name recently has been demonstrated by a number of companies. Eastman Kodak, for example, used its name and package design to enter the battery business, even though it does not manufacture the batteries it sells. Kodak buys the batteries from suppliers and then gives them the company's familiar yellow "trade dress" found on most of its film products. By the end of the first year, the battery line had won 5 to 10 percent of the $7 billion worldwide market.

organizational, and people skills that he acquired during that job. He feels that sales experience is especially handy now because he must sell his ideas and build consensus.

For a year after graduation, he lived and worked with artists and designers in Cologne, Germany, then returned and attended the Art Center College of Design in Pasadena, California, where he got a B.F.A. in the Graphic Design and Packaging program and graduated with honours in 1992.

Career Track

After graduation from the Design Center in 1992, he was offered a position with Microsoft in Redmond, Washington, in its Visual Interface Design Group. He has been at Microsoft since then and has advanced to the position of Microsoft Encarta lead designer.

Typical Day

Flora says a typical day begins with reading e-mail, checking voice mail, and solving any immediate problems. He meets with his designers and reviews their work. Then he turns to his own work. A lot of his time is taken up with meetings with editors, programmers, and program managers to define and refine tasks and get design feedback. He spends a lot of time trying to keep current with other design work outside Microsoft, and he meets as often as possible with other Microsoft designers to share work and ideas.

Day by day, he moves through the annual Encarta product development process:

- Studying the current version and user feedback
- Integrating the feedback and new research data into design refinement proposals
- Initiating new feature ideas
- Prototyping new features; getting feedback on them
- Prioritizing features and changes to be developed
- Communicating and specifying new features to programmers
- Reviewing programmers' final versions and suggesting refinements
- Producing and shipping the product

Microsoft
www.microsoft.com

concept review

The Product Mix

Product refers to a bundle of attributes, either tangible or intangible, offered by the company. The following elements of the product mix must be integrated with the marketing communication strategies:

1. Product classification—industrial versus consumer products, and goods products versus service products.
2. Life cycle of the product—its introductory, growth, maturity, and decline stages.
3. Strategic components of the product mix—product design, product features, packaging, and branding.

Coca-Cola is one of the most powerful brands in the world. The 750 million daily points of contact with its package provide the experiences that build brand loyalty.

The Distribution Mix

Channel of distribution
All the institutions, processes, and relationships that help the product from the manufacturer to the ultimate buyer, either industrial or consumer.

Resellers
Wholesalers, brokers, and retailers.

All products, whether goods or services, have a channel of distribution through which the product is delivered to customers. A **channel of distribution** includes all the institutions, processes, and relationships that help the product from the manufacturer to the ultimate buyer, either industrial or consumer. For example, if a manufacturer uses direct mail to distribute products, then the distribution strategy revolves around the design of a system for taking orders and delivering the product to the consumer, for receiving payment, and for handling returns. In contrast, the distribution strategy of a manufacturer of machine parts focuses on identifying wholesalers or brokers who will locate retail outlets and retailers who will sell the product to customers and make sure it is delivered and serviced. Wholesalers, brokers, and retailers are collectively called **resellers** (also referred to as intermediaries).

Distribution and Communication Strategy

A marketer must constantly consider how its channel of distribution conveys a message. For example, the image of a possible retail outlet can negatively or positively impact on a brand image. The store's image depends on the consumer's attitude toward the retailer's communication strategy, its services, convenience, layout, exterior and interior appearance, location, personnel, and product mix. The strategy is to match the image of the store to the image of the marketer's product. Therefore, Rolex would not expect Zellers to implement its upscale marketing communication strategy. To ensure marketing mix consistency, Birks Jewellers would be a better channel for distributing Rolex watches.

The communication and distribution elements of the marketing mix are becoming increasingly indistinguishable.[7] In some cases, as in direct response marketing, the distribution channel and the communication activity are one and the same. A catalogue such as L.L. Bean, for example, is both the primary mechanism for purchasing the product and the main communication vehicle, listing products along with descriptions, prices, and so forth.

L.L. Bean
www.llbean.com

Wholesalers and Retailers

Wholesaler
A distribution channel member who receives products from a manufacturer or other wholesaler and distributes them to a retailer or another wholesaler.

A **wholesaler** is a channel member who receives products from a manufacturer or other wholesaler and distributes them to a retailer or another wholesaler. Wholesalers tend to act as "intermediaries" and typically don't deal with ultimate users. If we consider the marketing communication mix, the greatest strength of wholesalers is personal selling. As much as 80 to 90 percent of their

Sometimes it feels great to yell the
f-word
"FREE"
Free stock quotes
Free online portfolio
Free mutual fund look-up
Quicken .ca
www.quicken.ca
Canada's personal finance and investment Web site
ROGERS

This magazine ad for Quicken's personal finance and investment Web site effectively communicates price information using humorous appeal and it provides the produces Web site address.

marketing communication budget goes to this activity. Wholesalers often use other communication techniques such as direct mail, trade publication ads, product catalogues, and trade shows (a meeting of people in the industry where businesses set up booths to demonstrate or distribute information about products). However, these are usually intended to support the activities of the sales force. Trade shows, for example, are a primary source for sales leads.

Retailers
A channel member who receives products from wholesalers and then sells them to ultimate users.

Retailers are those who receive products from wholesalers, or possibly from manufacturers, and then sell that product to ultimate users. Without retailers many manufacturers would not have profitable access to customers. The marketing communication activities of retailers are broader than those of wholesalers. At one end of the continuum is a company such as Sears, which has the capacity to match the communication efforts of the largest manufacturer. At the other end is an individual operating a shoe-repair shop, whose entire marketing communication strategy is providing good customer service and placing a small ad in the Yellow Pages.

Retail communications often focus on price and availability. This postcard for Ch!ckaboom creatively blends product, price, and availability information.

Regardless of size, every retailer should consider some questions when designing its communication strategy. First, what types of products are carried by the retailer? If the products are indistinguishable and price is the major selling attribute, price should be featured prominently in advertising and, perhaps, store coupons should be made available. Second, what market does the retailer target? For example, if the target market is concerned with quality at any price, such as Rolex watches, then retailers use image advertising, personal selling, and elaborate point-of-purchase displays. Conversely, a price-conscious target market would prompt communication strategies that emphasize price and sales promotions (sales prices, rebates, coupons). Third, is the manufacturer willing to supplement the retailer's advertising, either financially or through technical expertise (a practice known as **cooperative advertising**)? If so, the advertising program may be more extensive and sophisticated than that supported by a retailer that lacks such cooperation.

Cooperative advertising
An advertising program in which a manufacturer supplements a retailer's advertising, either financially or through technical expertise.

Service Providers

Service product marketers also use a channel of distribution for the product. A hospital, for example, moves the consumer (patient) through a channel that may include an admissions stage, an assessment stage, an action stage (the treatment), a recovery stage, and a follow-up stage. Each stage requires different

Quebec's Legal Profession Discovers Marketing

Quebec law firms are discovering that well-targeted marketing can help them argue their case with new clients. Until recently, Quebec law firms were only allowed to promote themselves through business cards and a listing in the Yellow Pages. Since the Quebec Bar Association significantly loosened those restrictions, lawyers can now use everything from billboards to business cards to advertise their services.

The new situation in Quebec is similar to current regulations in other provinces, where lawyers can use media to promote their services as long as they don't use testimonials from clients, refer to themselves as experts in a particular field of law, or claim superiority over other members of the bar.

Although opinions on the use and effectiveness of marketing communications vary within the legal profession, a growing number of law firms have discovered that the "more is better" approach to advertising doesn't necessarily bring in significant numbers of new clients. As a case in point, the Quebec law firm of Langlois Gaudreau recently restructured its approach to marketing communications. The new approach involved a coordinated marketing strategy and development of a series of seven print ads featuring various partners each wearing a different hat. According to Michel Farrah, the firm's general manager, his firm wanted to put a face to its partners and lawyers.

To evaluate its marketing strategy, Langlois Gaudreau hired Impact Research of Montreal to interview 100 clients and potential clients about whether they saw the print campaign, what they thought of it, and whether it motivated them to call the firm. "We're persuaded that some of our clients came to us after seeing the campaign," Farrah says. The firm plans to add three new print ads, focus more on media relations, and train lawyers on how to best approach potential clients. It's also considering doing an English-language campaign.

Aware of increasing use of communications and marketing in the legal profession, the Quebec Bar Association published a handbook entitled ***Mieux*** *comprendre la communication* (Understanding Communication Better). Co-author Louis Delage, who works for Optimum Public Relations in Quebec City, says the law firms have generally jumped on the advertising and marketing bandwagon without clearly defining how their product differs from that of the competition and without defining ways to measure results. "They didn't look at the marketing mix," he says. "They saw communications as a way to get new clients rather than first looking at their products."

Quebec Bar Association
www.barreau.qc.ca

You Decide

1. Should Canadian lawyers be allowed to use client testimonials in their advertisements? Why or why not? Explain your answer.
2. If all marketing communications restrictions were removed, what would the implications be for the legal profession and its clients?
3. If you were a marketing communications manager for a large law firm and you were asked to focus on growing new client business, what would you do to attract clients?

Sources: Hanna Katz, "Legal Matters," *Marketing* (March 22, 1999): 12-13.

expertise and communication objectives. Hospitals also use other service and goods marketers to support their efforts, such as ambulance services, pharmacies, and in-home nursing services.

Aspects of marketing communication are a topical issue in Canada for professional service providers such as members of the legal profession, as the accompanying You Decide feature explains.

concept review

The Distribution Mix

The channel of distribution is the marketing mechanism used to present, deliver, and service the product for customers. The channel of distribution for goods and services affects the product's marketing communication efforts.

1. A goods product is distributed by wholesalers, retailers, or both. Each distributor uses different marketing communication activities. Wholesalers typically rely on personal selling and sales promotion, whereas retailers usually rely on advertising and sales promotion.
2. Service product marketers rely on intangible channels and communication efforts to create tangible benefits for each channel element.

The Price Mix

Price
The value assigned to the product by the seller and the buyer.

Superficially, price is easy to define. **Price** is the value assigned to the product by the seller and the buyer. However, a price has different meanings for sellers and buyers. For the seller, it is a series of cost components and an expected profit margin. Most companies cannot operate successfully unless their price guarantees a specific profit. For the buyer, it is a calculation of the historical price of the product, the competitive price (or the price for comparable products), the expected price, risk, and the perceived need for the product. That is, a business like Procter & Gamble ensures that the price charged for its laundry detergent covers the cost of research and development, materials, marketing, and other costs, and generates a profit. Consumers purchasing detergent, however, don't care about the company's costs and profit margins. Instead they look at how the current price compares to last week's, what other stores are charging for the same product, and what other brands of laundry detergent cost.

Marketing communication must present price from the consumers' perspective, and all the elements of the price message must be consistent. To illustrate, an ad for a $105 000 BMW would be remiss to use poor photography or improper grammar. The ad should focus on the value of the car (such as, "The safest, most luxurious ride ever") and anticipate reaction to a high price.

Pricing Strategies

Firms use pricing strategies for three reasons: to stay competitive, to shape consumer attitudes, and to create brand differentiation. First, a firm remains competitive when it offers comparable satisfaction at lower prices. When marketers decide to use price as a competitive weapon, they should show how their price matches or beats competitors' prices. Price can also be used to counter a competitive move. For example, when The Walt Disney Company announced that it planned to enter the cruise industry with 2400-passenger "mega-ships," the four biggest lines—Carnival, Royal Caribbean, Princess Cruises, and Norwegian Cruise Line—all announced price discounts to encourage early bookings on their ships.

Walt Disney Company
www.disney.com

Second, the price helps shape attitudes toward a product. For marketing communication to be effective, the message sent by both the price and the communication must be consistent. For example, a luxury item must have a high enough price to signal high quality. Running a sale or offering a rebate on Armani suits undercuts the elite image of paying top dollar for a status product.

Third, a high price is often accompanied by heavy advertising that creates brand differentiation. In the case of high-priced products, brand differentiation justifies the price. Intelligent marketers create brand differentiation only if they know how consumers perceive the brand, the price being charged, the prices charged by the competition, and how consumers feel about price reductions and increases.

Price Communication

Information about pricing is probably the most important message that can be transmitted to consumers. The price information on the package, signage, point-of-purchase materials, coupons, and advertising all deliver price messages. Advertising that touts price as the dominant marketing mix element is referred to as **price copy advertising**. Supermarket retailers often use this type of advertising because their customers usually view price information as the most important factor in their product choice.

Price copy advertising
Advertising that touts price as the dominant marketing mix element.

Pricing information is often a key factor in motivating consumers to act. Price discounts, rebates, and coupons are all price adjustments intended to spur purchase. Industrial buyers are also responsive to price changes. In fact, negotiating for a lower price, rebates, and other price deals are quite normal in many industries. For both consumers and industrial buyers, **price bundling**—the practice of selling multiple units of a product or combination of complementary products for a lower total price than if sold separately—is also common.

Price bundling
The practice of selling multiple units of a product or combination of complementary products for a lower total price than if sold separately.

concept review

The Price Mix

1. The price is the total value assigned to the product by the seller and the buyer. Firms use a pricing strategy for the following reasons:
   - To stay competitive
   - To shape customer attitudes
   - To differentiate the brand
2. Firms communicate prices through packaging, coupons, signage, price copy advertising, price concessions, and price bundling.

A Closing Thought:

You Cannot *NOT* Communicate

The purpose of any product or service is to meet the needs and wants of target markets. This purpose cannot be satisfied, however, without a product that benefits consumers, a distribution program that delivers a product that is accessible to customers, a pricing strategy that clearly determines the worth of the value of the product to customers, and a communication program that tells customers how the product meets their needs and wants. Thus, the linkage between the product, the distribution, the price, and marketing communication is critical.

Why is this link so critical? Every marketing mix element communicates. Furthermore, in any marketing situation, you cannot not communicate. The notion of a mix of marketing tools and programs challenges any planner to make the product, price, and distribution decisions work together strategically to communicate the same message. It is an extremely important—and difficult—management task.

summary

1. Explain the marketing concept and outline how the business plan, marketing plan, and marketing communication strategy inter-relate.

   Marketing focuses on satisfying customer wants and needs. The goals in the company's mission and business plan determine the marketing plan objectives and strategies, and the marketing plan must be compatible with both. In turn, the marketing communication plan must support, not conflict with, the marketing plan. The marketing plan outlines the marketing mix of product, distribution, pricing, and marketing communication.

2. Identify the product mix elements and explain how they affect the product's marketing communication program.

   The term product refers to a bundle of attributes, either tangible or intangible, of a good, service, or idea offered by a company. The product mix consists of three main elements. The first element is product classification. Is it a good or a service, and is it a consumer or industrial product? The second element is the life cycle of the product. Is it in the introductory, growth, maturity, or decline stage? The third element is the group of strategic product mix components—research and development, product features, packaging, and branding. Each of these elements must be integrated with the marketing communication strategies because all marketing mix elements communicate. Marketers should be sure all mix elements deliver a consistent message.

3. Explain the distribution mix elements and how they influence marketing communication.

   Marketing communication planners must understand the informational needs and communication capabilities of the channels of distribution. For goods products there are two primary types of resellers: wholesalers and retailers. Wholesalers communicate the benefits of the manufacturer's product to retailers primarily through personal selling and sales promotion. Retailers communicate product features and store services through mass advertising and sales promotion, especially point-of-purchase displays and price discounts. Service providers are also retailers and rely on other intermediaries to help them provide their services.

4. List the price mix elements and analyse how they affect marketing communication strategies.

   Price, a crucial factor in the marketing mix, helps consumers estimate the value of the product. The three purposes of price are to stay competitive, shape consumer attitudes, and differentiate the brand. Pricing is communicated through such elements as the package, store signage, point-of-purchase materials, coupons, and advertising. A price that is too high given the product quality or the distribution channel sends a conflicting message that will confuse consumers. Conversely, a price that is too low given the other mix elements will also send a conflicting message.

points to ponder

Review the Facts

1. What is the marketing concept?
2. How does the notion of exchange help explain a marketing focus?
3. What are the four stages in the product life cycle? Give an example of a product in each of the stages.
4. Define a product.
5. Explain branding and what it contributes to the marketing strategy of a product.
6. What is price bundling? Identify three examples.

Master the Concepts

7. Describe how the marketing concept relates to integrated marketing communication.
8. Discuss why the company's mission and business plan, the marketing strategy, and the marketing communication strategies should all be in harmony. How can a firm ensure that such coordination happens?
9. The marketing of services is receiving more attention since consumer spending on services has risen. How does the promotion of services differ from the promotion of goods products?
10. Describe how marketing communication for industrial products differs from that of consumer products.
11. Outline the role of advertising and personal selling in the various stages of a product life cycle.
12. Discuss a situation in which pricing would be easy to promote and one in which it would be difficult.

Apply Your Knowledge

13. You are the marketing director for Coca-Cola in India. The company has only recently received government approval to begin selling the product in this very large market. How would your communication strategy differ from that of your colleagues in various European countries where the product has been selling for years?
14. As competition moves into the household and automotive goods market, Canadian Tire is already feeling the pressure, particularly on price. How can the company improve its marketing mix and marketing communication strategies to stay competitive? How does an innovative company like this stay ahead of the market?

suggested projects

1. (Writing Project) Select two products in your supermarket that are at opposite ends of the product life cycle. Collect marketing communication material supporting each product. In a brief memo, compare and contrast the information about the marketing mix found in these promotions. How does the information differ? How is it the same? How does the marketing communication information you found compare with the product life cycle discussion in the chapter?
2. (Oral Communication) Interview the managers of three types of retail stores. Determine what types of marketing communication they use and ask them to assess the relative success of each type. How do their assessments compare with the discussion of retailers' marketing communication strategies in this chapter? If you were introducing a new product that would be distributed through these stores, what type of marketing communication program would you recommend to get the most retailer support?
3. (Internet Project) Visit the Body Shop Canada home page on the World Wide Web (www.thebodyshop.ca). Find the company mission statement. Now research some of the company's products, pricing, distribution, and marketing communication strategies. Do they seem consistent with the company's mission statement?

Recruiting Volunteer Business Executives For Corporate Fundraising

How does an unknown performing arts centre, perceived to be an amateur community theatre, attract corporate support in a cost-effective manner? Just ask Bill Murray.

Bill Murray was the Audience and Business Development Officer for a newly opened, non-profit performing arts centre located in a major suburb of Vancouver. Bill's primary objectives were to increase the Centre's corporate profile in the surrounding business community and to recruit business executives who would volunteer their time for corporate fundraising.

The performing arts centre had been open for two years and most of the events presented were local amateur productions of theatre, dance, and music. Other events booked in to the Centre were non-performance related, such as seminars, workshops, and conferences.

Unfortunately, there were not enough local performing and non-performing events to generate the rental and ticket sale revenues required by the Centre to break even. As well, the Centre had an image of being a "community theatre" as opposed to a "professional-regional" performing arts centre.

To address the issues of revenue shortfalls and poor quality image, the board of directors decided to put on its own professional theatre and children's music series. The theatre series consisted of five professional theatrical productions per year. Three of the productions were produced in house by the Centre, and two touring productions were purchased by the Centre. Each production ran for 14 days. The children's series consisted of five children's entertainers who performed two shows per day over a three-day period. Both the theatre and the children's music series were sold as annual season subscriptions or as single tickets.

To ensure that the Centre could afford to present those potentially riskier but more profitable professional programs, the board of directors needed to attract corporate support from the local business community.

Bill's Solution

An integrated and direct marketing communications strategy was developed and employed over a 12-month period. The four-step strategy was as follows:

1. Introduce the Centre and its key personnel to the local business community. The Centre joined the suburb's 525-member Chamber of Commerce. Along with Bill, the Centre's general manager and the board's president made the presentation to the Chamber members at one of its business luncheons.
2. Invite the business community to the Centre's professional theatre productions. All 525 business executives who were members of the Chamber were invited to opening-night performances of the Centre's

first two theatrical productions. The invitations were designed so that attendees had to fill out information about themselves and their company, and then provide it to box-office officials upon arrival. Box-office staff then issued a pair of tickets for the best house seats, two free refreshment tickets, and a special reception name tag allowing them to attend a backstage cast reception.

3. Recruit business executive attendees to become involved in the volunteer corporate fundraising campaign. Bill recruited a campaign chair from the invited attendees. Then, on behalf of the campaign chair, Bill sent a letter to all attendees asked them to attend a corporate fundraising campaign meeting. At the campaign meeting, those who attended were officially recruited to be on the Centre's corporate fundraising team. Team members received a volunteer appreciation gift, a bronze key chain in the shape of the Centre's ticket stub.
4. Implement the corporate fundraising campaign. Fundraising team members were each asked to identify 10 companies as potential corporate supporters. The Centre, on the volunteer's behalf, mailed these 10 identified company executives information on the corporate campaign and the Centre's operations. The volunteers then followed up with a personal phone call and/or visit to encourage their 10 identified companies to financially support the Centre.

Results

The following results were associated with Bill's corporate fundraising campaign:

- Of the 525 invitations sent out, 64 business executives accepted and attended the theatrical production (a response rate of 12 percent).
- Of the 64 business executives, 20 were recruited to be volunteers for the corporate fundraising campaign (a response rate of 31 percent).
- Of the 200 companies identified and approached by the 20-member fundraising team, 110 companies (a response rate of 55 percent) gave an average financial donation of $105, for a total of $11 500.
- Of the 20 volunteers, 15 purchased corporate theatre subscriptions for the next theatre season, which amounted to $3600 in revenue (a response rate of 75 percent).
- The campaign also identified six companies interested in sponsoring Centre events the following season. Five of these companies became sponsors and contributed a total of $30 000.

Bill was very pleased with the results of his fundraising strategy. He estimated the direct costs associated with this strategy (mailings, stationery, etc.) to be $1500. More important, perhaps, than the revenues associated with the strategy to date, Bill believed a number of marketing relationships had been formed that would serve to ensure the continued success of the Centre for many years to come.

Case Questions:

1. What elements of the marketing mix were used as a means to reach the Centre's fundraising objective?
2. Critically assess the strengths and weaknesses of Bill's solution. Identify the marketing communications components (refer back to Chapter 1, Figure 1.3) not incorporated in Bill's solution that you believe could enhance the effectiveness of the campaign.
3. Review the response rates reported above for the first four results items. Why did the response rates increase?

Source: Prepared by Lloyd Salomone, President of Precision Target Marketing Ltd., Fredericton, N.B. Used with permission. Names and locations have been disguised. This case serves as a basis for discussion rather than an illustration of either effective or ineffective handling of an administrative situation.

Organizing for Integrated Marketing Communication

chapter objectives

After completing your work on this chapter, you should be able to

- Explain how the organization of a business affects marketing communication.
- Distinguish between integrated marketing and integrated marketing communication.
- Discuss the development of integrated marketing and why some firms have trouble implementing it.
- Describe the typical organizational elements in a marketing communication program.
- Outline the characteristics of an IMC organization.

Kraft Gets Its Act Together

In the 1980s, Philip Morris Incorporated, parent company of Kraft, bought General Foods Corporation to create a food giant, Kraft General Foods, Inc.. Philip Morris formed Kraft General Foods thinking the newly combined food conglomerate would have more marketing synergy and savings than either company had separately. Combined, the companies should have had stronger purchasing power and been able to cut costs through staff reductions. But because Kraft and General Foods maintained headquarters in different regions, and the two had vastly different corporate cultures, Philip Morris was unable to take advantage of potential synergies. One marketing executive explained that each division "had its own structures and priorities: it was very difficult to make things happen."

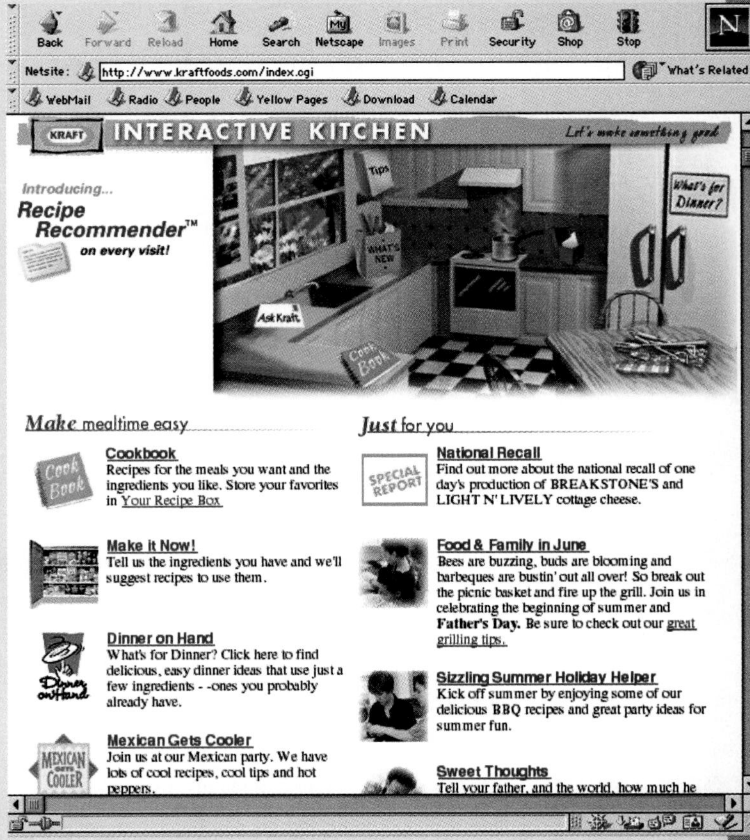

However, under the leadership of a new CEO, the synergy at Kraft General Foods began to sizzle. In a symbolic move, the CEO decided to drop General Foods from the company name, calling the company Kraft Foods. Then the CEO took a major step to unify both Kraft's operation and its corporate culture by combining the Kraft and General Foods salesforces. The salesforce integration eliminated internal competition and reduced duplicative sales activity. The 3500 sales representatives now work in integrated sales teams that are responsible for entire product portfolios—which include such brands as Jell-O, Louis Rich lunch meat, Maxwell House, Post and Nabisco cereals, Tombstone Pizza, Kool-Aid and Crystal Light, Entenmann's, Kraft products, and Oscar Mayer.

The company's next major step was to consolidate the marketing communication programs so that the marketing messages for all Kraft Food products are consistent. Those messages range from sales promotion coupons to the Kraft Interactive Kitchen Web site, an Internet food site that offers product information, recipes with Kraft products, and shopping tips. The result of the consolidation has been greater impact, lower marketing costs, and more efficiency.

The lessons for Philip Morris? A company's organization can affect its success. And the way a company is organized can have tremendous implications for its marketing communication program.

Kraft Foods
www.kraftfoods.com

Sources: Glenn Collins, "Make Room in the Kitchen for Yet Another Appliance," *New York Times*, 16 September 1996, C6; Kate Fitzgerald, "Kraft Goes 'Universal' as Others Refigure Couponing," *Advertising Age*, June 24, 1996, 9; Julie Liesse, "Kraft Retires General in Reorganization," *Advertising Age*, January 9, 1995, 4.

Chapter Overview

This chapter explores the role of marketing communication within a company. We begin with a big picture discussion of integrated marketing before exploring the role of IMC in a company. Then we investigate how firms organize the marketing communication staff, particularly for an IMC program. Next we explore various marketing communication tools and how they fit or do not fit in a marketing program, as illustrated by companies such as Kraft Foods. Finally, we examine how firms may choose different approaches to implement an integrated marketing communication program.

Importance of the Organization's Structure

The success of any business strategy often depends on whether the company has the appropriate structure to support its activities. This is no less true for marketing communication strategies, which can require a large cadre of experts and support staff to implement the communication objectives. Every business must determine whether the existing organizational structure is adequate to reach objectives or whether reorganization is necessary.

To create effective marketing communication, firms must understand how to organize their marketing communication teams and decide whether to make any other changes in the firms' structure. The dynamics of moving to integrated marketing communication, for instance, often requires changes in the organization of the business. Some firms may choose to integrate all marketing and management activities from the CEO level to managers to employees. This is a rare organization. Other businesses may integrate their functional areas, such as marketing, finance, and human resources. The most effective way to integrate marketing communication is to start by integrating the entire marketing function.

Integrated Marketing and IMC

Integrated marketing communication works best when all the marketing mix elements, and other operating divisions within the company, work together

Integrated marketing
The process of understanding the needs of the customer (and other stakeholders), orienting the firm's manufacturing and sales processes to meet these needs, and applying integrated thinking to all marketing and management decisions.

under a common philosophy of customer-focused marketing. **Integrated marketing** is a process of understanding the needs of the customer (and other stakeholders), orienting the firm's manufacturing and sales processes to meet those needs, and applying integrated thinking to all marketing and management decisions. At the corporate level, all managers share a corporate vision as well as an organizational structure that makes it possible for departments and divisions to share information and participate in joint planning.

That approach represents the direction in which many companies, including Kraft and Disney, are moving. To be truly integrated, every decision at each level should support decisions made at all the other levels. To illustrate, let's say that the corporate goal is to maximize profit. A marketing plan objective to increase sales by marketing new products matches that goal. A marketing communication strategy to promote the new products supports the business and marketing objectives. If all objectives support all others, then integration is much easier to manage.

From a communication perspective, integrated marketing focuses on coordinating all marketing activities to reach the marketing objectives and control or influence the messages they send. In Chapters 1 and 2, we investigated how all marketing activities—from the appearance of the store to the price, design, or packaging of the product to the advertising—could send messages to target audiences. Planning and integrating all those activities, then, means the marketing communication messages have more impact and efficiency and lower cost than those sent through a traditional marketing communication program.

Integrated marketing tries to coordinate all company-based marketing messages—those sent by the marketing mix, the unplanned messages (such as a dirty parking lot), and planned messages sent through marketing communication. In contrast, integrated marketing communication refers only to the strategic coordination of the planned marketing communication areas identified in Chapter 1 such as advertising, sales promotion, public relations, direct marketing, packaging, telemarketing, event marketing, and so on. IMC is the focus of this text, but it is useful to understand the bigger picture of integration at the corporate and marketing levels. Although integrated marketing is still more an ideal than a practice, companies such as Disney suggest it is catching on successfully.

Evolution of Integration

Although the concept of integration is nothing new, growing specialization in all business areas, including marketing and its various specialties, leads to internal competition for resources and much more isolation between departments. Admittedly, specialization is important—there will always be a need for experts in the various marketing communication areas. However, specialization becomes dysfunctional when it leads to what management experts call "silos." Communication experts Michael Hammer and James Champy note, "Companies today consist of functional silos, or stovepipes, vertical structures built on narrow pieces of processes."[1] One study found that the main problem with implementing integration was "turf battles" as specialists in their functional silos tried to protect their budgets and activities from encroachment by other marketing communication professionals.[2] Breaking down the walls between departments is a serious challenge in any marketing program. Integrated marketing (IM) and integrated marketing communication (IMC) are both attempts to do just that.

Small companies, particularly new companies, have found that they have a real advantage in gearing up for integration because they are usually not as bound by tradition or inertia. Oticon Holding A/S is a Danish hearing aid company that has turned its performance around and become a company on the fast track in a flat market by abolishing the traditional organization.[3] The work is organized around projects, not functions or departments. Everyone has a small office or "workstation" on wheels that they can move to create work teams so that cross-functional planning is much easier. Oticon's R&D leader explains that this approach also avoids turf battles and jealousies because employees learn to respect what other people do. "It's hard to maintain 'enemy pictures' in this company—they're not 'those bloody fools in marketing.' " Instead, marketers are part of the team.

Institute of Canadian Advertising
www.ica-ad.com

Cossette Communication Group
www.cossette.com

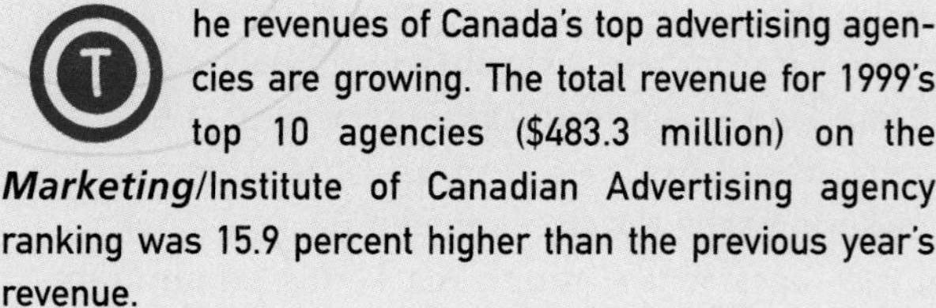

Growing the Cossette Communication Group

The revenues of Canada's top advertising agencies are growing. The total revenue for 1999's top 10 agencies ($483.3 million) on the *Marketing*/Institute of Canadian Advertising agency ranking was 15.9 percent higher than the previous year's revenue.

Despite massive growth at Wolf, the expansion activities causing the most buzz in the industry are those of Cossette Communication Group, Canada's largest advertising agency. Already a giant, Cossette's gross revenues of $82.4 million for its year ending September 30, 1998 are the highest recorded for a Canadian ad agency since *Marketing* magazine began ranking agencies by gross revenues in 1990.

Much of the buzz concerning Cossette's expansion has been based on its decision to go public as its means to raise money for expansion. Although not the first Canadian agency to go public, this approach to agency growth has not been widely practised in Canada. In fact, observers cautioned Cossette's approach and warned against walking the path of Cockfield Brown, at one time Canada's largest ad shop, and the country's only public advertising agency when it went under in 1983. As was demonstrated in the case of Cockfield Brown, a major concern of going public is vulnerability to a hostile takeover.

Why did Cossette go public? Jean Royer, vice-president and financial officer, explains: "The principal shareholders of Cossette have decided, given the context of the industry and consolidation, they want to grow externally, so they needed external capital." In Canada, that growth could be regional or in the businesses Cossette operates in, including advertising, promotions, public relations, graphic design, branding, and research.

South of the border, Cossette's public relations arm Optimum, which has an office in Washington, D.C., is its only presence. However, Cossette president and CEO Claude Lessard said in a speech to the Board of Trade in Metropolitan Montreal that he hopes to have 25 percent of Cossette's annual billings coming from the United States within five year.

Although too early to assess the success of Cossette's expansion plans, its initial public offering (IPO) was well received by institutional investors. Priced at $12.25 a share, the company initially issued 3 158 452 shares and expected to raise a total of $38.7 million. But before the IPO closed, Cossette issued an additional 473 767 shares, raising a total of $44.5 million. On its first day of trading, the stock (KOS) closed at $14 on the Toronto Stock Exchange. This success has others in the advertising-services community considering IPOs of their own.

Food for Thought

1. How could further expansion of Cossette Communication Group facilitate its ability to practise integrated marketing communications? Explain.
2. How might planned expansion south to the Canadian border benefit Cossette's: a) internal operations; b) Canadian-based clients; and c) U.S.-based clients?

Sources: Lesley Daw, "Cossette Builds War Chest with IPO," *Marketing*, (June 28, 1999), 2; Lesley Daw, "Canada's Top Agencies," *Marketing* (June 28, 1999), 11; Editorial, "Cossette's Year," *Marketing* (June 28, 1999), 46. Used with permission.

A manager's background and expertise may pose a problem if they chain the manager to a limited viewpoint. The lack of understanding and appreciation for the strengths and weaknesses of all the communication areas may make it difficult for a manager to make effective strategic decisions. The management of an integrated communication program requires the skills of a generalist rather than a specialist, and the ability to adapt to and feel comfortable with changes.

Another problem for agencies trying to offer integrated marketing communication services is the difficulty of organizing for integrated planning. Many advertising agencies and other marketing communication organizations, such as those in public relations and direct marketing, acquired related firms to position themselves as integration experts. However, no matter how many services an organization can offer, if its IMC program is not planned cohesively and the strategies implemented according to the plan, the program will probably not be integrated.

A successful IMC agency meets the needs of its customers and plans and implements marketing communication programs in a unified manner. Seiko Time Corp. vice president for advertising, Cheri McKenzie, praises the Martin Agency of Atlanta as an example of an agency trying to become an integrated marketing communication firm. McKenzie observes that: "They look at what is the right marketing communication solution for our needs. . . . They not only develop our ad campaigns, but they do all our marketing communications work—direct marketing, promotional programs, sponsorships; they act as creative consultants in trade show booth design and design our displays. And Martin Public Relations is our PR agency. They are part of virtually every facet of our business."

Corporations may also initiate IMC. NEC Corp. recently announced a sweeping plan to coordinate advertising, logo, and product design, packaging, and point-of-purchase materials. Lever-Pond also recently implemented an IMC campaign in the Canadian market for its Sunlight laundry detergent. The Consider This feature in Chapter 9 details the Sunlight IMC campaign.

Although the acceptance of IMC has come a long way during the past decade, serious problems serve as major deterrents for many companies, which we explore next.

Difficulties in Integration

Integration, whether at the marketing level or the marketing communication level, faces certain problems that make implementation difficult. Three basic problems that haunt integration include information sharing, leadership and infringement issues, and integrity.

Information Sharing

Communication across divisions is a problem in any organization and a serious obstacle for companies trying to implement integration.[4] Some even argue that organizational integration only exists to the extent that there is a continuous exchange of information between the units.

In a company with a strong information culture, an increased communication flow promotes information exchange as shown in the Xerox ad. Organizations with greater levels of communication also have fewer problems with the "not-invented-here syndrome." This refers to the tendency of a department or division to ignore communication that was initiated somewhere else in the organization.

An example of the importance of information sharing in new organizational structures is the story of VeriFone Inc., an international company that provides the hardware and, increasingly, the software through which retailers "swipe" credit cards to receive authorization from a credit card company.[5] The company has no corporate headquarters, although it's officially registered in Delaware. It generates more than one-third of its revenues and stations more than one-half of its workers outside the United States. As a global company, its workday is 24 hours long, and business management is moved from one office to another around the globe as it follows the sun. A customer problem that can't be solved by the close of day in one time zone, for instance, is sent to an earlier time zone so that the problem can be worked on nonstop. The only way such a company can operate is through extensive use of e-mail and information systems. Everyone in the company, including the one-third of the workforce that is travelling at any moment, are all in touch with each other, senior management, and the company's information system.

This example points to the need for companies to identify types of information and policies about sharing certain information to aid integration. The more this is done, the more likely integration will be successful.

The notion that flow of information is critical to efficient operation of an organization is captured in this ad by Xerox.

Leadership and Infringement

Any time an organizational structure changes, there are questions about who will be in charge, who will lose power, and who will lose resources. The problem is how to structure an organizational environment in which all the people, with their various interests and skills, will be most productive. However, the attitude problem—one function is better than the other, or one function should lead and the others should follow—continues to be a hindrance in implementing integration. The Lotus SmartSuite ad illustrates the way many organizations are organized into boxes and silos.

Two areas where a negative attitude can be a problem is in integrating marketing communication budgets and public relations. Many turf wars exist over who gets what. That is, many managers evaluate their success and power in terms of budget size. Integrating communication functions brings up a host of budget-related questions. How is the budget divided? How do you charge for services provided? Who is charged for unexpected expenses? IMC scholar Tom Duncan proposes *zero-based communication planning* as a possible solution. With this type of planning, the marketing communication budgets are built annually on the basis of what needs to be done and which activities will make the strongest contributions to achieve that year's marketing communication objectives. Rather than using last year's plan as a starting point for this year's, zero-based planning means starting with a blank sheet. This year's plan may be entirely different from last year's or next year's.[6]

The walls between departments are caused not only by specialization but also by inadequate communication systems that don't permit people to talk to one another. This ad by Lotus Development Corp. describes how electronic communication can break down these walls.

Infringement issues also arise in an IMC program, particularly with public relations. Some public relations practitioners believe that marketing communicators are focused exclusively on customers and selling and don't understand the wider range of stakeholders that public relations must address. Additionally, these PR managers view IMC as an attempt to encroach further into their territory on the part of advertising agencies.[7] Fortunately, many public relations practitioners understand that the driving purpose behind IMC is to better integrate all communication messages and reach a much broader set of stakeholders, regardless of whether the messages have a PR or advertising focus.

Integrity Problems

Ethical behaviour is critical to the success of any marketing program because actions speak louder than words. That is, any lapses in a company's ethical behaviour overshadow messages in advertising or public relations and therefore directly affect the company's reputation. People working in marketing and marketing communication are aware of how difficult it is to manage their people and programs so that ethical problems are minimized. Integration introduces many strangers into the people mix so that controlling for such miscues appears next to impossible. It also means that errors in judgment that occur in one part of the integrated organization are attributed to everyone. Delays or dishonesty in one IMC component such as a news release can risk damaging an organization's image.

concept review

Importance of the Organizational Structure

The structure of a company has a strong effect on its marketing communication program.

1. **Integrated marketing is the process of coordinating the entire marketing function, such as all marketing mix elements and all unplanned and planned marketing messages.**
2. **The evolution of integration has been slow and difficult due to the business trend of increased specialization and the creation of organizational silos. Integration requires that businesses break down these silos.**
3. **The difficulties associated with integration include problems with information sharing, leadership and infringement, and integrity.**

Marketing Communication and the Organization

Before we look at the organizational requirements for implementing an integrated communication strategy, it is helpful to discuss the general organizational structure and terminology that marketing communication managers may encounter.

Managers control the marketing strategy that helps achieve the company's objectives. They manage all decisions about the marketing mix and allocate

Vice president of marketing, or director of marketing
The top executive in charge of the marketing effort.

Marketing services
A department of people that specialize in managing various marketing communication tools, such as advertising and sales promotion.

Brand manager
The business leader for a brand who has ultimate responsibility for coordinating sales, product development , budget, profits, and marketing communications.

budgets to the various marketing teams. The top executive in charge of the marketing effort may have the title of **vice president of marketing** or **director of marketing**. The marketing director may also oversee a department of people, called **marketing services**, that specializes in managing various marketing communication tools, such as advertising and sales promotion. An external or outside agency that aids a firm's marketing communication efforts may refer to the company's marketing team as "the client" or "the account."

A multiple-brand, consumer-products company may divide marketing responsibility by brand—that is, each brand is the responsibility of a brand or product manager. The **brand manager** is the business leader for that brand and has ultimate responsibility for coordinating sales, product development, budget, profits, and marketing communications. For example, the brand manager of Cheer laundry detergent (a brand of Procter & Gamble) must coordinate product distribution, sales territory allocation, mass advertising, coupon programs, public relations activities, and packaging changes, to name but a few assigned activities. As marketing services expertise has developed in larger companies, brand leaders often manage a cross-functional team consisting of research and development, manufacturing, human resources, financial planning, marketing, distribution, international operations, and so forth.

In cutting-edge companies, particularly business-to-business, that team is customer focused rather than brand focused. A customer-focused organization ensures that all team members are doing what they need to do to satisfy the needs and wants of the customer. In other words, a company may be organized by customer group and by how they use the company's products, rather than by brand.

Organizing Marketing Communication Activities

Departments
The marketing functions are divided up into departments to achieve internal control and to organize marketing communication activities.

External agency
Communication expert that provides a service to a company for a contractual fee.

Marketing communication manager
The person responsible for planning and implementing marketing communication.

Marketing communication activities can be organized in a variety of ways. A company may control all the activities internally through **departments** (the advertising department, the sales department, the public relations department, and so on) or through in-house agencies. An in-house agency is staffed by corporate employees who are responsible for creating an advertising campaign, special event, or other communication activity. An **external agency**, such as an advertising or public relations agency, is an organization that helps the client company with marketing communication activities, usually because the company feels the agency has greater expertise or can perform the activity more efficiently. Some companies use a combination of both internal departments and in-house agency work for some activities and use external agencies for major activities that demand more expertise or personnel than is available internally.

Although the terms **marketing communication manager** or **marketing communicator** are used throughout this text, in many companies the person with the title of director of marketing or director of advertising is the one person responsible for planning and implementing marketing communication. In a small organization, the owner or manager may perform all of these tasks or might have one person or a small staff that manages all the marketing communication activities.

Individuals who are in charge of marketing communication have a variety of responsibilities, some of which they accomplish themselves and some of which they may delegate to external agencies or freelancers. These duties are outlined in Table 3.1 on the next page.

Table 3.1 MARKETING COMMUNICATION MANAGER'S RESPONSIBILITIES

- Decide what products, institutions, or ideas to promote
- Develop the marketing communication plan, including how to use the marketing communication tools
- Identify target audiences, basic message strategies, and message objectives
- Allocate the budget for the various marketing communication tools
- Decide whether to conduct the marketing work internally or hire specialists externally
- Give directions to internal staff, external agencies, and freelancers as needed
- Review, approve, and help develop programs created by internal staff, external agencies, and freelancers
- Pay the bills
- Evaluate all work to make sure it is integrated, consistent, and accomplishes communication objectives

The larger the company, the more likely each of these activities will be managed by different specialists. The more specialized the team, the more likely problems with turf battles and lack of communication between team members will arise.

To understand how companies coordinate their marketing communication teams, let's look at three types of staffing arrangements in more detail: internal departments and in-house agencies, external agencies, and freelancers.

INTERNAL DEPARTMENTS AND IN-HOUSE AGENCIES

Often a specialist working for the company manages a part of a firm's marketing communication strategy, such as an advertising manager, sales promotion manager, or special events coordinator. These experts produce, support, and supervise work in their areas of expertise. The advertising manager, for example, is usually responsible for approving advertising ideas before those ideas undergo preliminary testing with consumers. The advertising manager may also hire an outside ad agency who will create the ads, allocate the budget, pay the bills, and determine whether objectives have been reached.

Typically, the larger the marketing communication budget, the larger the marketing communication staff, and the more likely it is that the business will seek outside expertise to ensure the highest possible quality of work. Size of program, however, generally varies with the type of marketing program. Business-to-business marketers, for instance, usually have much smaller marketing staffs than package goods manufacturers, because they rely more on personal sales.

In-house agency
A group of internal marketing communication specialists that operates as its own profit centre and handles all the marketing communication work for its primary client—the company to which it is affiliated.

An **in-house agency** is a group of internal marketing communication specialists that operates as its own profit centre and handles all the marketing communication work for its primary client—the company to which it is affiliated. In-house agencies may also handle outside work, particularly for suppliers, vendors, and distributors who work with the company. Many retailers have in-

The Bay
www.thebay.com

house agencies (such as Pier 1 and The Bay) that specialize in retail advertising. Retailers tend to operate with small profit margins and find they can save money by doing their own advertising. Also, retailers must develop and place their ads under extremely tight deadlines. There is seldom time to work with an outside advertising consultant. Finally, retailers often receive advertising materials either free or at a reduced cost from manufacturers and trade associations, such as free creative and production assistance.

Table 3.2 summarizes the pros and cons of using an in-house agency.

External Agencies

A business may choose to use outside professional services for the marketing communication programs ranging from advertising and public relations to package design to special events and direct marketing. Companies use external agencies (communication experts that provide services for a contractual fee) that have more expertise in marketing communication tools than an internal department or in-house agency can provide. Some companies partner with such agencies for a very long time, establishing a familiarity and level of trust comparable to a good marriage. Other client-agency relationships are short term, requiring that the agency perform a very specific task. Agencies that specialize in organizing sporting event promotions, for instance, may only work with a client for a few weeks or months.

Table 3.2 The Pros and Cons of an In-house Agency

Pros	Cons
Savings	
Saves money because the in-house agency isn't trying to make a profit off its client	Size of external agency may result in bigger savings due to economies of scale
Technical Specialization	
In-house agencies allow individuals to become technical experts on the product(s) being promoted	Creative individuals with varied experiences may provide fresh insight and approaches to communicating about a technical product
Priority Service	
The in-house agency works only for the client and gives priority to the client's needs	Total commitment to one task may mean other tasks, with greater importance, are not considered
Minimum Staffing	
In-house agencies use minimum staffing, employing freelancers when available	Freelancers may not be available when needed, or the quality of those appropriate may be inadequate

Freelancer
Self-employed specialist who is hired by a company to work on a specific project, but is not on the company's payroll.

Freelancers

Self-employed specialists are called **freelancers**. Marketing communication freelancers include copywriters, art directors, computer graphic experts, photographers, cartoonists and other illustrators, Web-page designers, broadcast producers, casting directors, commercial directors, and researchers.

Typically, freelancers work alone, although they may be a part of a network of other freelancers with whom they partner as the job demands. A copywriter and art director, for example, may team up on an advertising assignment for either the advertiser or an advertising agency that handles the account. From a company's standpoint, freelancers are used when it needs highly specialized people who are not on the company's payroll. They are also used to help with an overload of work that can't be handled by the regular staff or if schedules can't be met.

concept review

Marketing Communication and the Organization

Several organizational features and terms help us understand marketing communication.

1. Typically, the manager responsible for marketing communication is titled vice president of marketing or director of marketing, although in a multiple-brand company, a brand manager may be in charge.
2. Marketing communication may be controlled through departments or through in-house agencies. External agencies may also have primary responsibility for marketing communication. There are specific reasons why one form of control should be used instead of another.
3. Self-employed specialists, called freelancers, often are used to assist with the marketing communication effort.

Organizing to Use Marketing Communication Activities

The next section will briefly review how key marketing communication functional areas organize their activities. We examine the organization of the following areas: advertising, sales promotion, public relations agencies, direct marketing companies, sales departments, event organizers, and packaging and design firms.

Advertising Departments and Agencies

Advertising is a big business in terms of both dollars and complexity. At one extreme, a single individual may create, approve, and place ads in the media. At the other extreme, a business may retain a full-service advertising agency to create advertising and make the media buys. Full service means the agency provides creative services, media planning and buying, market research, and all other planning services.

Account managers, or account executives
Advertising agency employees who work as liaisons and work out strategies and details of the assignment with the clients' marketing communication managers.

Researcher, and account planner
A person who conducts consumer research on a particular segment of the population with a specific product or brand in mind.

Creative staff
The copywriters, art directors, and broadcast producers who design and produce the advertising for media.

Media planners
The people who make decisions and implement the media mix that best fits the client's marketing strategy.

Media buyers
People who negotiate the deals for media time and space.

Traffic managers
Those who schedule and track an ad as it is produced and hire production specialists.

Advertising Agencies

The most important reason for using an external advertising agency is to have access to the talented people employed there. A full-service agency is staffed to provide highly specialized services that clients can rarely afford to provide for themselves, such as research statisticians and people who negotiate with networks. Only large agencies with many accounts can afford to employ such specialists full time.

Most advertising agencies have five main departments: account management, creative services, media buyers and planners, research, and traffic. **Account managers**, also called **account executives**, are liaisons to the client's marketing communication manager. They work out the strategy and the details of the assignment with the client and bring that information back to the agency staff. **Researchers and account planners** conduct consumer research and analyse consumer trends and buyer decisions. The **creative staff**—the copywriters, art directors, and broadcast producers—design and produce the advertising for media. The media department consists of **media planners**, people who decide what media mix best fits the client's marketing strategy, and **media buyers**, people who actually negotiate the deals for media time and space. **Traffic managers** are those who schedule and track an ad as it is produced and hire production specialists, such as freelance artists and photo retouchers.

There are also the usual business functions. Human resource managers handle training, staffing, and other personnel issues. The finance and accounting staff monitors budgeting, cash flow, and other monetary activities.

Creative Boutiques

Creative boutiques are small agencies that concentrate entirely on preparing the creative elements for a client. They are generally a small group of individuals—both copywriters and art directors—and are frequently organized as a partnership. Creative boutiques are often hired by companies that do a lot of marketing communication management in-house and only need outside specialists to help develop and execute creative ideas.

Media Buying Agencies

Media buying agencies have emerged as a result of large agencies attempting to make all their departments separate profit centres and because many clients feel they save money and get better results when media is handled separately. Take OMD Canada as an example. It is an independent subsidiary of Omnicom Canada that buys all the media for the client Chrysler Canada. OMD Canada handles the media buying for all the agencies that work for Omnicom, thus creating synergy and cash savings.[8]

Chrysler Canada
www.chryslercorp.com

Media Suppliers

Media suppliers—the broadcasting stations, cable networks, newspapers, magazines, and so on—play a major role in the advertising industry. Each media supplier has its own sales staff to call on agencies and advertisers to persuade them to spend more money with that particular media provider. To encourage business, media suppliers often offer ad writing, design, and production help to advertisers. Media suppliers, then, often hire a professional advertising staff that specializes in producing ads for that medium.

Consumer sales promotion specialists
Those whose role is to understand how and when to use price deals such as sales, coupons, samples, contests and sweepstakes, refunds and rebates, loyalty programs, and premiums or gifts that encourage purchase.

Trade promotion specialists
Experts who know how and when to use in-store merchandising materials, dealer and salesperson contests and sweepstakes, and trade shows and exhibits.

Trade deals
Allowances, discounts, goods, or cash given to a retailer in return for handling a special promotion.

Sales promotion managers
People who set objectives and budgets and evaluate the success of promotions.

Sales Promotion Organizations

Because of the complexity of sales promotion, many people may be part of a sales promotion organization. In a sales promotion department or agency, **consumer sales promotion specialists** are those whose role is to understand how and when to use price deals such as sales, coupons, samples, contests and sweepstakes, refunds and rebates, loyalty programs, and premiums or gifts that encourage purchase. **Trade promotion specialists** are specialists who know how and when to use point-of-purchase displays and other in-store merchandising materials, dealer and salesperson contests and sweepstakes, and trade shows and exhibits. They also specialize in negotiating trade incentives such **as trade deals**, which are allowances, discounts, goods, or cash given to a retailer in return for handling a special promotion.

Sales promotion managers are people who set objectives and budgets and evaluate the success of promotions. Outside specialists are usually hired to handle the specific details of programs such as sampling, product demonstrations, rebates, contests and sweepstakes, and coupon distributions. Each of these promotional activities may require special expertise. A manufacturer's coupon promotion, for example, needs a procedure for distribution—advertising, mail, inserts in newspapers and magazines, and so forth—arrangements with stores for honouring the coupons, plus a coupon redemption procedure. Specialists are involved at each step in the process and most are hired from outside the client company.

Urban Lites, a Canadian outdoor advertising supplier, demonstrates its passion for advertising in this colourful, eye-catching advertisement.

Public Relations Departments and Agencies

Unlike advertising where most professionals work for an advertising agency, most public relations professionals work for the client, though public relations agencies exist and handle big assignments for major companies. Internally, a public relations department may counsel management about public opinion, crisis management, or employee relations. It may also prepare information and publicity materials about the company for an external audience. Almost every organization, firm, or non-profit company, if it is any size at all, will have a public relations professional on staff to deal with company news, prepare brochures about the company or brand, and produce newsletters to keep all the company's key stakeholders informed. Companies that have their own public relations staff may also consult with public relations agencies about special problems or projects.

Public relations specialists may manage such areas as *corporate public relations, crisis management, media relations, internal employee communication, financial relations* (communicating with the financial community), *public affairs* (working with government and the local community), and *marketing public relations* (MPR), which focuses specifically on publicity and other public relations activities for products. Specialists for these areas may be on a company's staff or they may be hired by outside general public relations agencies or agencies that specialize in areas such as financial relations.

Public relations, particularly MPR, plays a key role in an integrated communication program, so public relations professionals should be consulted and involved in IMC planning. These professionals often understand the importance of stakeholders and relationships more fully than other marketing professionals and thus contribute a great deal to a total communication program.

Direct Marketing Companies

More and more businesses have moved to direct forms of communication with their customers. As a result of advances in computer technology and electronic communication systems, direct marketing can occur through mail, video, telephone, and computers. In any of those media, a business can send a marketing message, sell, and deliver its products directly to the buyer without an intermediary reseller or retailer. In this respect direct marketing is more than just a marketing communication tool because it combines channels of communication with channels of distribution. However, it relies on other marketing communication tools such as advertising and direct mail, so it is usually discussed as a marketing communication activity.

Direct marketing specialists have copywriting, graphic design, and research skills that enable them to design a compelling offer powerful enough to move people to immediate action. These specialists manage mail order and broadcast offers through advertising and infomercials (longer advertisements that tell a more in-depth product story). They may also manage telemarketing, e-mail, and Internet offers. Finally, direct marketing experts also understand how to manage a system for fulfillment of an order.

Databases
Files of information that include names, addresses, telephone numbers, e-mail addresses, and demographic and buying-behaviour data.

Another type of direct marketing expert is one who can create and manage a sophisticated database. **Databases** are files of information that include names, addresses, telephone numbers, e-mail addresses, and demographic and buying behaviour data. These files make it possible for a marketer to engage in a dialogue with those people thought most likely to be in the market for a certain product.

Historically, direct marketing was the first area of marketing communication to adopt the integrated philosophy. In fact, we could refer to this activity as integrated direct marketing because it uses other marketing communication tools to deliver its messages. Instead of treating each medium separately, integrated direct marketing seeks to achieve precise, synchronized use of the right medium at the right time with a measurable return on dollars spent.

An advertisement, for example, may be used to tell consumers how to obtain a company's catalogue and to provide either an order coupon or a toll-free telephone number. Once the customer receives a catalogue, that mailing may also contain a toll-free number that puts the consumer in direct contact with a salesperson who can answer questions or take an order. A phone call that follows a mailing or telephone inquiry is an effective step to increase response rates dramatically. Our example only integrates five forms of contact—an advertisement, a coupon sales promotion, a catalogue, personal selling, and telemarketing—but shows how various forms of marketing communication can be combined for more effective direct marketing.

Sales Departments

Historically, many companies manage the sales and marketing departments separately. Even though personal sales is an extremely important part of a company's total communication package, rivalries often exist between marketing and sales. Sales representatives are separated from marketing and promotion staff not only by organizational charts but also by different viewpoints.

On the organizational chart, sales and marketing may report to top management through entirely different people. In such a situation, the only way that personal selling will be integrated with other aspects of marketing communication is through the concerted efforts of top management. The differing viewpoints often stem from the direct client contact that sales representatives have. An overstatement or inaccuracy in a marketing communication message (an ad promises delivery of products by December 1, but they don't arrive until December 21) or failure to support a sales effort puts the sales and marketing teams at odds. Why? Salespeople take the heat from clients for what clients perceive to be a marketing mistake.

Obviously the two functions complement each other and should work closely together. For example, salespeople work on the front line so they can find out what customers need and want in a more personal way than marketing research can. This information should be shared with the marketing people. The marketing people, in return, provide the information and sales materials (product literature, consumer research data, brand profile information) used by the sales representatives. If the materials don't work, then salespeople need to inform marketing. For the most effective marketing and selling, both groups need to share information continually at the planning and implementation stages.

Integrating personal selling with the rest of the marketing communication program is difficult for a number of reasons, including the separation between sales and marketing. The task and the problems of personal selling primarily involve interpersonal relations and communication between salespeople and their customers, salespeople and their supervisors, and salespeople and other departments in the organization.

Because salespeople have the most direct and personal contact with customers, they must understand and buy into the company's communication objectives, or the company runs the risk of an ineffective marketing communication program. This understanding and belief is especially critical in industrial selling, where sales is the key method of marketing. A roundtable of high-level business executives concluded that marketing and sales must be more integrated or companies would "pay the price in the 21st century."

Event Organizers

Event marketing involves both consumer and trade participation. Trade members help produce and promote events, and consumers attend the events as do some trade members. In fact, many companies use event sponsorships as a way to develop reward systems for their employees who are invited to attend free if they reach certain goals, such as sales goals or customer contacts.

Events are often planned as part of some other program, such as a sales promotion or a public relations campaign. For that reason special events and event marketing overlap with other areas. For example, a special event such as an open house almost certainly will be handled by public relations. In contrast, a company-sponsored competition, such as Molson Breweries' sponsorship of the Molson Indy auto racing, might be handled by either the marketing or sales promotion department.

Molson Breweries
www.molson.com

Regardless of who is in charge, the problem is the same—details, details, details. Event management companies that have developed systems for running complex activities are often hired to plan and manage the event. The event companies, in turn, may hire agencies or freelancers to handle the event advertising and other services such as security, catering, and publicity. The tasks of finding locations, negotiating with other sponsors, producing and receiving registration materials, arranging for equipment needed at the event, handling crowd control, and arranging for prizes can be handled internally though many are farmed out.

Packaging and Design Firms

Logo
The imprint that is used for immediate identification of a business.

Major companies rarely maintain their own designers, though they often use design firms. The most important corporate design element is the company's **logo**, which is the imprint that is used for immediate identification. Many thousands of dollars are spent creating and revising logos. In addition to logo design, corporate stationery and signage are also the focus of designers who try to make a company's appearance dovetail with its mission and corporate culture. Even delivery trucks and physical spaces like lobbies are part of the total corporate design package. Usually a company will turn to external agencies that specialize in corporate design and logo design for these kinds of projects.

Another important graphic design area is the product's package. We mentioned in Chapter 2 that packaging can serve two functions: 1) containing and protecting the product and 2) communicating a marketing message to consumers at the point of purchase. Most companies prefer to use packaging design firms instead of keeping packaging specialists on staff. External design consultants keep busy creating, refining, and redesigning product packages for many different clients because packages are constantly changing.

The package for Simply Accounting software that is shown in the lower right corner of this ad does more than protect the product. It communicates at the point of purchase the software's performance features, its user friendliness and it offers a rebate for existing users.

concept review

Organizing to Use Marketing Communication Activities

There are a number of ways to organize marketing communication tools.

1. Advertising agencies that are full-service include account managers, researchers and account planners, creative staff, media planners and buyers, and traffic managers.
2. Sales promotion people plan and implement programs for consumer and trade audiences.
3. Public relations is usually organized as a department within a business, though outside agencies exist. The PR staff can counsel management or communicate about company issues to an external audience, such as the government or financial stakeholders.
4. Direct marketing uses a variety of methods to deliver messages and fulfil orders, a fact that makes it one of the first marketing communication areas to adopt an integrated organizational strategy.
5. Personal sales is often managed by departments separate from marketing, which is one reason why it is hard to integrate the efforts of the two.
6. Events are handled both by marketing and public relations staffs, as well as by people and companies who specialize in handling all the details involved in producing events.
7. Packaging and design staffs are concerned with the physical presentation of the brand, the product, and the company.

The IMC Organization

Let's look now at the organizational dimensions of a business that uses IMC.

Integrating marketing communication usually begins with a system-wide restructuring of marketing communication activities. This restructuring is based on the observation that most internal activities (employee relations and customer service, for example) are not usually considered part of the marketing communication mix. Author Dan Logan has proposed that IMC is a process of understanding the targeted customer and applying IMC to all marketing functions.[9] In other words, integration requires participation by all parts of the company that affect the customer. At this level, integration must reflect a shared corporate vision as well as an organizational structure that makes it possible for all departments and divisions to share information and strategies.

Increasingly, as illustrated by this chapter's IMC in Action, Canadian advertising agencies and marketers are attempting to apply IMC in a global context. Organizing for IMC with international management and global dispersion of marketing communication requires a system of active promotional management that strategically coordinates global communications. IMC scholars Andreas F. Grein and Stephen J. Gould called for agencies and marketers to work towards the application of a concept called Globally Integrated Marketing Communications (GIMC).[10] The accompanying IMC Concept in Focus discusses this emerging IMC concept.

IMC Concept in Focus

Global IMC (GIMC)

Recent marketplace developments involving the increasing international management and dispersion of marketing communication suggest that the impact of globalization on integrated marketing communications should be examined. Toward that end, IMC scholars Andreas F. Grein and Stephen J. Gould proposed the concept of Globally Integrated Marketing Communications (GIMC) and indicated that it applied to both global advertising agencies and multinational marketers.

The GIMC concept exceeds IMC by adding the international dimension, across country offices, to that of the marketing communication disciplines (i.e., PR, sales promotion, advertising, etc.). Grein and Gould define Globally Integrated Marketing Communications (GIMC) as "... a system of active promotional management which strategically coordinates global communications in all of its component parts both horizontally in terms of countries and organizations and vertically in terms of promotion disciplines." Application of this concept entails making strategic communication decisions through the integrated tracking, comparison, and coordination of marketing communications across all relevant global markets, units, or offices to maximize both organizational learning and the efficient allocation of resources.

In contrast to the widely heralded dichotomy of standardized versus customized communications (to be discussed in Chapter 5), GIMC instead argues for global managerial coordination, no matter which of the two is applied.

Source: Stephen J. Gould, Dawn B. Lerman, and Andreas F. Grein, "Agency Perceptions and Practices on Global IMC," *Journal of Advertising Research*, January/February 1999, pp. 7-20; Andreas F. Grein and Stephen J. Gould, "Globally Integrated Marketing Communications," *Journal of Marketing Communications*, 2 (3), 1996, pp. 141-58.

Top-down management
Management approach where top-level executives control various marketing communications programs and manage their integration.

Bottom-up approach
The communication-management approach where managers are in close daily contact with customers and other stakeholders and where cross-functional teams cooperate across departmental boundaries.

Cross-functional management
The process by which teams oversee "horizontal functions," such as PR, sales promotion, packaging, and so forth.

General contractor
An agency that, for a fee, develops an overall strategy and retains outside specialist agencies needed to carry out the plan.

IMC firms have experimented with two ways to organize for IMC—top-down management and cross-functional teams. Some experts proposed that a "communication czar," who has the power and authority to control various marketing communication programs, manage the integration. This approach is referred to as **top-down management**. Although this is one way to organize for a tightly controlled program, researchers have focused on approaches that involve various stakeholders in partnerships or teams, an organizational approach referred to as a **bottom-up approach**.[11] Research has found that the most effective communication management took place in companies using a bottom-up approach where managers were in close contact daily with customers and other stakeholders and where cross-functional teams were used to coordinate across functions or boundaries. **Cross-functional management**, also referred to as boundary spanning, is a process by which teams oversee "horizontal functions," such as PR, sales promotion, packaging, and so forth. In employing IMC, for example, maintaining brand image, corporate reputation, and product quality could be cross-functional objectives.

A problem with using an outside agency to manage an IMC program is that most agencies don't have expertise in all the areas of marketing communication tools that must be integrated. One solution to the specialization problem is to adopt a **general contractor** approach, a solution pioneered by the Interpublic Group. For a fee, an Interpublic agency will develop an overall strategy and retain outside specialist agencies needed to carry out the plan.[12]

Strategic alliances
Agreements between firms of different marketing specialties to complement each others' services and provide referrals.

Smaller agencies without the resources of giant conglomerates like Interpublic can compete for IMC business through strategic alliances. **Strategic alliances** are agreements between firms of different marketing specialties to complement each others' services and provide referrals.

concept review

THE IMC ORGANIZATION

An IMC organization often requires system-wide restructuring through the following three tactics:

- information sharing
- cross-functional management
- organizational alliances

A CLOSING THOUGHT:

PUTTING THE PRESS ON BAD PRESS

Errant departments and divisions can create marketing communication problems. Public relations personnel are particularly concerned about the damage that advertising and promotional planning errors can cause. Sales promotion, for example, can sometimes set up poorly planned programs that harm the company's image. To illustrate, Kraft's sales promotion division held a sweepstakes contest in which a printing error on the entry forms led to many thousands of winners. The company had to endure bad press plus a substantial cost to buy out unhappy winners.

This incident reflects sloppy planning, but it also reflects a lack of coordination from one marketing unit to another. Public relations professionals are skilled at identifying potential crisis situations and should be involved in all these planning sessions to help avoid unwanted negative repercussions. In many companies lawyers have taken over this role, but even though they are very much concerned about legal liability, they seldom concern themselves with the negative communication impact of poorly designed marketing communication programs.

summary

1. Explain how the organization of a business affects marketing communication.

   The structure of an organization can have tremendous implications for marketing communication because the dynamics of moving to integrated marketing communication often require changes in the organization of the business. The most effective way to integrate marketing communication is to start by integrating the entire marketing area and all the communication functions in cross-functional teams.

2. Distinguish between integrated marketing and integrated marketing communication.

   Integrated marketing means that all managers share a corporate vision and an organizational structure that make it possible for departments and divisions to exchange information and participate in joint planning. Integrated marketing tries to coordinate all messages sent by a company or brand. In contrast, integrated marketing communication refers only to the strategic coordination of the planned marketing communication areas such as advertising, sales promotion, public relations, direct marketing, packaging, telemarketing, event marketing, and so on.

3. Discuss the development of integrated marketing and why some firms have trouble implementing it.

   As businesses rely on more specialists, organizational structures must encourage coordination. Problems that make implementation difficult include turf battles and fear of encroachment.

4. Describe the typical organizational elements in a marketing communication program.

   The organizational components that are part of most marketing communication typically include internal departments, in-house agencies, external agencies, and freelancers. Each marketing communicaton activity, such as public relations and sales promotion, requires people with different skills who can plan, implement, and evaluate their communication.

5. Outline the characteristics of an IMC organization.

   Generally, organizations that have integrated communication programs either use a top-down approach with a communication coordinator to oversee the efforts or a bottom-up approach that involves people in cross-functional planning and monitoring teams. The bottom-up approach is more common. IMC agencies tend to operate as "general contractors," working directly with the client and hiring specialist agencies to work as part of the marketing communication team under the direction of the IMC agency.

points to ponder

Review the Facts

1. Identify the different levels in a company where coordinated planning needs to occur.
2. Who typically manages the various marketing activities in a company's marketing program? What are their job titles and what do they do?
3. What is infringement, and why does it create a problem for organizations trying to move into IMC?

Master the Concepts

4. How does cross-functional management differ from top-down and bottom-up management approaches? Do you think one management approach is more effective than the other? Explain.
5. Explain the different models discussed here for managing external agencies.
6. What are the primary problems encountered in reorganizing a marketing communication program? Can you think of any other problems that might arise? Explain.

Apply Your Knowledge

7. Find an organizational chart, either in a textbook or from a company that you have connections with, and analyse whether it looks like the company is using a top-down or bottom-up approach to organization.

8. Find a company that uses cross-functional management teams and interview people who have worked in that environment. Find out what those people think about planning and decision making in this type of organization. Do they view the cross-functional approach as more or less effective than a traditional organization?

9. Interview a person who works in sales. How does the sales department work with the company's marketing department? Are the relationships good or are there problems in the coordination of these two functions?

suggested projects 

1. (Writing Project) Interview a senior marketing manager in a company to discuss who is involved in marketing and what they do. Be sure to find out what really happens, not what's supposed to happen according to the business organizational chart. Based on your interview, draw a map of the organization showing where marketing and marketing communication fit in the company structure. Also, write a brief memo that explains who is responsible for marketing communication and what that person does.
2. (Oral Communication) Interview a senior manager in some type of marketing communication agency and determine if the agency is involved in any cross-functional activities. If so, what are those activities? Also, what type of organizational model does the agency represent? Prepare a brief (five-minute) oral presentation of your findings for the class.
3. (Internet Project) Visit the sites of at least two marketing communication companies. Search the sites to see whether the company is organized for or engaged in integrated marketing communication.

case 3 WORLDWIDE NETWORKING: THE STRATEGIC MERGER OPTION

Every year, several Canadian-owned marketing agencies are sold to multinational networks. Consistent with this trend, Canadian-owned Gingko Group joined DraftWorldwide, one of the largest networks in the world, in January 1999. Why? According to Perry Miele, Gingko's co-chairman, this is a question he's been asked frequently and it's a question Gingko struggled with over the past few years as it tried to balance its desire to grow, while maintaining independence.

As explained by Miele, "Our situation was similar to that of many medium-sized Canadian agencies with four to five years of solid double-digit growth; agencies generating $6 million to $10 million in revenue, employing 40 to 70 people, and maintaining a strong mix of blue-chip clients." For a company of this size to be considered a large Canadian agency, revenues would have to double. In the case of Gingko, Perry Miele explains that "this would have required a large investment in all the core competencies of an integrated marketing communications agency, including creative, production and account servicing, as well as growing our direct response and promotion capabilities."

Another option, the one deemed more practical by Gingko, was to join a worldwide network. Through a strategic merger with a worldwide network Gingko gained the ability to take on the challenges of larger marketing assignments and benefits from the network's deep resources to help deliver results.

The challenging task for Gingko was to choose the right partner. According to Miele, "We knew that finding the interested buyers would not be difficult, but identifying a multinational agency that was committed to integrated marketing and that fit our criteria would be." Gingko had three criteria: a similar culture, a parallel vision for future direction, and a commitment to building resources necessary to continue growing.

For Gingko, culture fit was a "must" and a significant challenge because Gingko had a very different culture than most multinational agencies. First, it had always been committed to strategically driven integrated programs. As well, Gingko had maintained an entrepreneurial spirit and a horizontal organizational structure free from bureaucracy that stifles out-of-the-box thinking.

As one of the major networks owned by Interpublic Group of New York, DraftWorldwide had a culture distinct from other agency networks. According to Miele, it "was clear during our first meetings with Howard Draft, chairman and CEO, and Jordan Rednor, president and COO, that they shared our entrepreneurial spirit. They too considered their number-one objective to be 'consumer-centric' marketing driven with a strong belief in a quantitative approach to building successful campaigns for clients."

Also appealing to Miele was Draft's strong belief that success of an agency should be based on maintaining its autonomy, while supporting and integrating with worldwide resources, such as database technology, services, research and lifestyle marketing, it had a similar culture and would allow the Gingko Group to continue operating independently. According to Miele, "This has been a successful partnership for the agency, our employees, and our clients."

Case Questions

1. How could Gingko's alliance with a worldwide network benefit its Canadian clients?
2. Explain what you believe Perry Miele means when he refers to: a) a marketing objective as being "consumer-centric" driven, and b) a strong belief in a quantitative approach to building successful campaigns?
3. Why do you believe a large number of Canadian-owned marketing agencies are being sold to multinational networks?

Source: Perry Miele, "A Perfect Match," ***Marketing*** (June 28, 1999), 24. Used with permission.

4

Marketing Communication Strategy and Planning

chapter objectives

After completing your work on this chapter, you should be able to

- Describe the critical decisions determined through strategic planning.
- Explain the elements of the marketing plan.
- Analyse the hierarchy of effects models and relate them to marketing communication planning.
- Describe the marketing communication plan and the marketing communication planning process.
- Evaluate the strategic implications of IMC planning.

Healthy Choice Based on a Healthy Strategy

Research, planning, and implementation—a healthy strategy for a healthy company. In the 13 years since its inception, Healthy Choice has expanded its product line from 14 to more than 264 products, and has 90 percent consumer awareness. Its Web site (www.healthychoice.com) has thousands of page views a week from consumers who want information or free product coupons. In one year alone, Healthy Choice introduced Healthy Choice Microwave Popcorn, Healthy Choice Bread, Hearty Handfuls (six hot pocket sandwiches), Healthy Choice Special Creations (10 ice-cream flavours), and many more products.

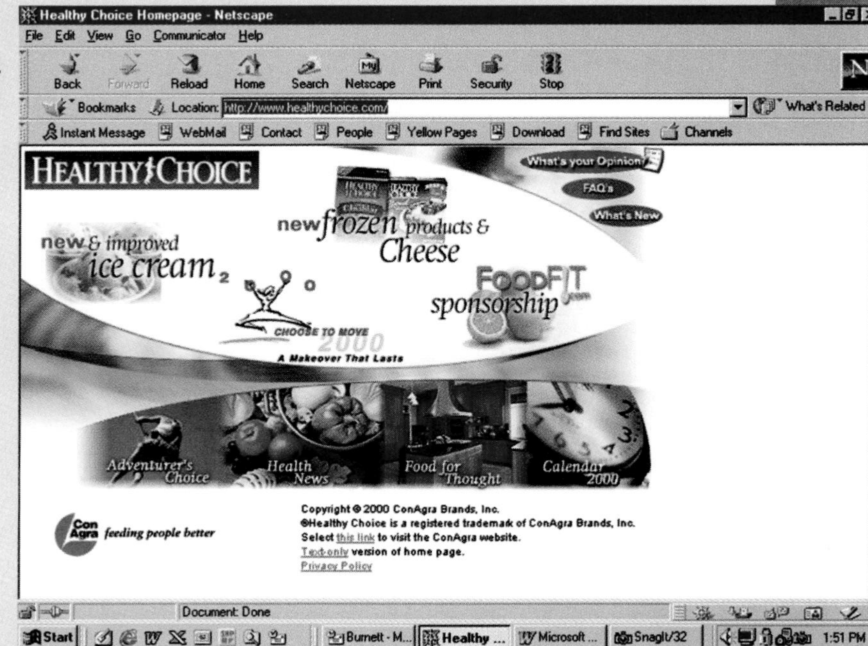

How did the Healthy Choice low-calorie, sodium-controlled frozen-food line become so prominent?

In 1985, Mike Harper, ConAgra's CEO, suffered a heart attack. During his recovery, it became his personal crusade to help consumers enjoy the foods they love, but without the fat, calories, and cholesterol that can have a negative impact on health. As a direct result, ConAgra introduced its first line of Healthy Choice products three years later.

Healthy Choice was developed to draw a health-conscious market of people who had few good-tasting choices in the frozen-food market. Research conducted in the mid-1980s showed a clear opportunity for a new growth segment. According to the research, 20 percent of North Americans were restricted dieters, and a surprising 30 percent were so-called health-conscious eaters.

Research also showed that Healthy Choice had to taste good to succeed. The product needed to deliver on taste to make it mainstream. Extensive test-marketing of the entire line in 18 test markets and careful strategic positioning ensured the product would be perceived as food that tastes good as well as food that lowers the risk of heart attacks.

A public relations campaign set the stage for Healthy Choice's rapid national rollout. Healthy Choice was exhibited at health conventions and the company sent mailings to dietitians informing them of the new products' benefits. The PR agency staged a national press conference, where Mike Harper discussed his heart attack and how his wife was able to make his sodium-controlled diet interesting. By the time it achieved national distribution, word of mouth was rampant. The PR campaign was backed with carefully targeted advertising.

Although plagued by tight freezer space, food stores either enlarged their frozen sections or dropped poor sellers to add the new line. ConAgra's suggested price points were accepted by the trade and successful with consumers.

ConAgra hoped to get five to seven percent of the frozen-dinner segment during the first year. Within seven months of its introduction, the green-boxed 14-item line grabbed a 25 percent share. The people at Healthy Choice sum up the reason for this initial success as follows: "Every detail was thoroughly planned. We were on strategy at all times. Our packaging, advertising, and communication defined us as a unique new product, and the retail community was very aware how health conscious the consumer has become."

Healthy Choice
www.healthychoice.com

Sources: Pamela Ellis-Simons, "One from the Heart," ***Marketing and Media Decisions—3*** (March 1990): 32–6; "ConAgra Products Named the Best of 1995," PRNewswire, May 2, 1996; "What's on the Menu at the Healthy Choice Web Site," PRNewswire, December 21, 1995.

Chapter Overview

The Healthy Choice example demonstrates that a good idea, supported with effective planning and strategic implementation, greatly increases the chances of success. In this chapter we will discuss strategic planning in a marketing program as well as strategic planning for marketing communication. Then we will review the nine steps in marketing communication planning and the specific dimensions of IMC planning that distinguish it from other types of marketing communication planning.

Strategic Planning

Marketing communication managers know that marketing communication is just one piece of the larger business plan. Careful business planning is a crucial survival tool, and the quality of the marketing communication plan can be no better than the quality of the business plan and the strategic planning that guides it. **Strategic planning** is the process of developing and maintaining a viable fit between the organization's objectives, its resources, and its changing market opportunities. The purpose of this process is to produce satisfactory profits and growth, given the company's mission.

Strategic planning
The process of developing and maintaining a viable fit between the organization's objectives, its resources, and its changing market opportunities.

In general, strategic planning guides three critical types of decisions: It identifies *objectives* (a statement of what the plan is intended to accomplish), decides on *strategies* (an outline of how to accomplish objectives), and implements the *tactics* (the short-term decisions about specific, tangible tasks that ensure that strategies are realized).

To illustrate, consider the Healthy Choice objective to establish and then increase its market share in the specialty food market. To achieve that objective, its strategic plan was to introduce five new types of low-fat cookies in a joint venture with Nabisco Brands, Inc. The tactics included decisions to price the cookies at $2.49 per package, start with five flavours, introduce the product in the northeast region of the United States, maintain the familiar green packaging, develop several TV commercials to announce the cookies, distribute coupon inserts in Sunday newspapers, and develop special point-of-sale material.

Marketing Research

Marketing intelligence
Information from internal or external sources that is useful in developing the marketing strategy.

Secondary information
Information that already exists.

Primary information
Information collected for the first time.

Marketing research is essential for informed strategic decisions. Planning is based on information; information is collected through formal research and informal scanning of the environment. **Marketing intelligence** is information from internal or external sources that is useful in developing the marketing strategy.

A systematic research process is used to collect **secondary information** (information that already exists, such as census data) and **primary information** (information collected for the first time) about the market environment, the consumer, and how the consumer responds to elements of the marketing mix. Determining the positive and negative opinions and attitudes of consumers is crucial. For instance, Biofoam, a company that produces an all-natural

Biofoam learned that consumers were concerned about polystyrene packing material and developed an ecologically safe alternative. Such responsiveness can only happen if the company has a research program in place to capture consumer comments, attitudes, and behaviours.

biodegradable packing material, used research to learn about consumer attitudes, though its research took an unexpected turn. The founders were researching new snack foods when they stumbled on this "puffed," ecologically safe packing material that competes with foam peanuts made of polystyrene. The packing material is even edible!

THE MARKETING PLAN

The marketing plan must be consistent with and support the company's overall business plan and mission. Recall from Chapter 2 that the business mission states the company's overall core goals, as well as the type and scope of its business. The business plan, which guides the marketing plan, is based on an in-depth understanding of the firm's market environment—the industry, the economy, and society—with special focus on competitors and customers. The business plan deals primarily with projecting sales and profits and indicates alternative actions if projected sales are less than actual sales.

At some point in the strategic planning process, the company's director of marketing meets with the chief executive officer to offer input about what business goals are relevant to the marketing team. Such goals as increasing sales or market share or moving into a new market require marketing involvement.

Once it is determined that marketing is crucial to reach certain corporate goals, the marketing director's next task is designing a marketing plan. The **marketing plan** is the central instrument for directing and coordinating the marketing effort. It consists of a situation analysis that summarizes research into the marketing environment, basic decisions on marketing objectives, the marketing mix strategy and implementation tactics, and the total marketing expenditures and marketing allocations. As shown in Figure 4.1, the seven steps in the marketing planning process parallel the stages used to develop the overall business plan.

The actual presentation format of a marketing plan may not exactly follow the steps shown in Figure 4.1, but for a marketing plan to be considered comprehensive, it should include:

- A **situation analysis**: an assessment of the environmental conditions and an interpretation of the findings to identify strengths, weaknesses, opportunities, and threats. One technique for this analysis is called *SWOT analysis*.
- Marketing objectives: examining explicit and implicit objectives.
- Market strategy: whether to approach the market as **heterogeneous** (as a market composed of separate, smaller groups known as segments) or **homogeneous** (as a single, large unit).
- Target market selection: determining market segments.
- Competitive strategies, such as **product positioning,** which involves determining how the company can best market its product based on the customer's view of the product compared to the competition; and **branding strategy,** which is the process of developing and selecting brand names, trademarks, and the supporting marketing campaign.
- Implementation tactics: how the marketing mix comes together.
- Evaluation: before and after marketing plan implementation.

Marketing plan
A document that analyses the current marketing situation, identifies market opportunities and threats, sets objectives, and develops action plans to achieve objectives: the central instrument for directing and coordinating the marketing effort.

Situation analysis
A section of the marketing plan that identifies and appraises all environmental factors that affect the marketing program.

Heterogeneous
The type of market composed of separate, smaller groups known as segments.

Homogeneous
The type of market that marketers treat as a single, large unit.

Product positioning
Determining how the company can best market its product based on the customer's view of the product compared to the competition.

Branding strategy
The process of developing and selecting brand names, trademarks, and the supporting marketing campaign.

Figure 4.1 STEPS IN THE MARKETING PLANNING PROCESS

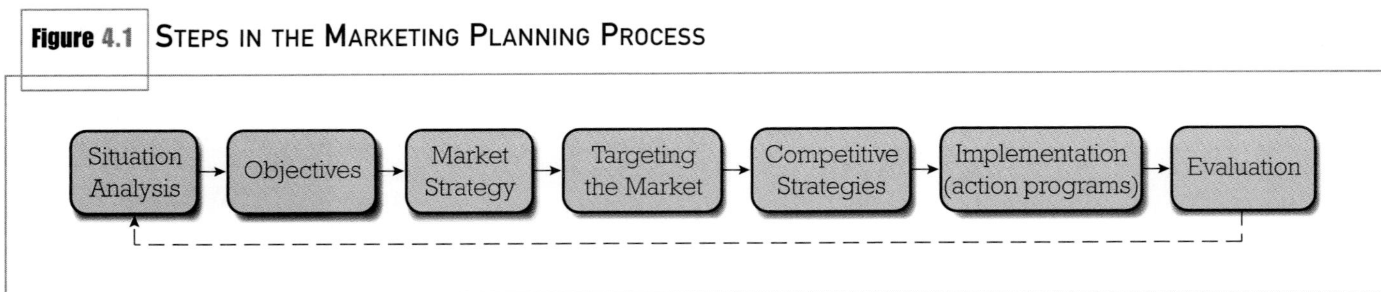

More information about marketing plans may be found at this textbook's Web site at http://www.pearsoned.ca/burnett.

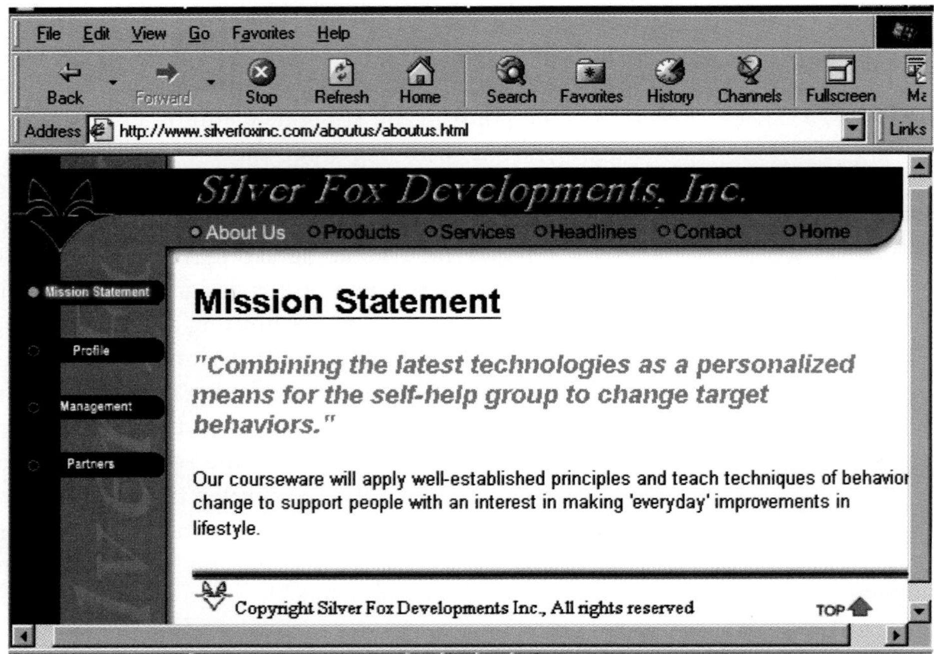

This web page for Silver Fox Developments Inc. of Miramichi, New Brunswick, outlines the company's mission.

concept review

STRATEGIC PLANNING AND MARKETING RESEARCH

1. To be successful, every business must engage in strategic planning, which is the process of developing and maintaining a viable fit between the organization's objectives, its resources, and its changing market opportunities.
2. Strategic planning forces decision makers to determine objectives, strategies, and tactics.
3. Marketing research is essential to strategic planning. Market researchers collect market intelligence—information that is useful in developing the marketing strategy.
4. The marketing plan is the central instrument for directing and coordinating the marketing effort.

Positioning "Buy" the Book

Michael Treacy and Fred Wiersema, consultants for an international consulting firm called CSC, developed an aggressive scheme to position their book, ***Discipline of Market Leaders,*** on the ***New York Times*** best-seller list. The thesis of the book urged companies to dominate their markets by narrowing their focus and disciplining themselves to do well at what they do best. Clearly, the authors took their thesis to heart, and may have taken it too far.

An investigation by ***Business Week*** found that Treacy and Wiersema used an "over-energetic marketing scheme" to inflate the sales of their book. First, they researched how to ensure best-seller status on the ***New York Times*** book list. They contacted a number of prominent booksellers to gather ideas on marketing the book and found, according to ***Business Week***, that to become a best-seller, massive book purchases had to be spread nationwide among certain bookstores. The purchases had to be carefully spaced so as not to alert the ***Times***' computers, and the purchases could not be traceable to the authors.

Next, they spent an estimated $350 000 on bogus purchases from bookstores to inflate book sales. CSC, clients, and friends bought 40 000 copies of the book in quantities of 25 to 1000 from bookstores all over the country. Dozens of bookstores unwittingly filled orders for multiple copies that were sent directly from the publisher to various corporate addresses in San Francisco, none of which were traceable to the authors or CSC. To what end? Aside from the royalties from actual book sales, the authors knew that having a ***New York Times*** best-seller would open up new, lucrative consulting contracts and speaking engagements.

No one knows if any laws were broken, but there are some real questions about the ethics of phony sales to manipulate the lists. The idea of planning purchases to distort the actual demand for a book outrages many people in publishing who see buying their way onto a best-seller list as misleading to buyers and sellers. Treacy and Wiersema admit that they aggressively and energetically marketed the book." Did we cross the line?" asks Treacy. "No way we did anything unethical."

You Decide

1. Do you think their marketing strategy was ethical? Explain.
2. What position do you think they may have achieved as a result of the publicity?

Sources: Willy Stern, "Did Dirty Tricks Create a Best-Seller?" ***Business Week***, August 7, 1995, 22û5; Willy Stern, "The Unmasking of a Best-Seller: Chapter 2," ***Business Week***, August 13, 1995, 41.

concept review

The Marketing Plan

The marketing plan is similar to the business plan although it contains important decisions about the target market and budget. The key sections are

1. Situation analysis: an assessment of the environmental conditions and an interpretation of the findings to identify strengths, weaknesses, opportunities, and threats.
2. Marketing objectives: examining explicit and implicit objectives.
3. Market strategy: whether to approach the market as heterogeneous or homogeneous.
4. Target market selection: determining market segments.
5. Competitive strategies, such as:
   - Positioning the product
   - Branding
6. Implementation tactics: how the marketing mix comes together.
7. Evaluation: before and after marketing plan implementation.

Hierarchy of Effects Models

Before discussing the specific steps in marketing communication planning, we first consider the hierarchy of effects models, which provide a general framework for analysing the impact of communication. Although we discuss communication processes and theories in more detail in Chapter 8, we present these models here because they are relevant to marketing communication planning.

Communication models are useful in planning message strategies. These models, referred to as hierarchy of effects, assume that consumers move through a step-by-step process as they receive marketing information and move toward a decision. An advertisement, for example, is considered effective when it helps move the consumer a step further in the buying decision process. We examine three hierarchy of effects models: the traditional AIDA model, the think-feel-do model, and the domains model.

AIDA model
Describes the effect of marketing as beginning with awareness, then moving to interest, then to desire, and finally to action.

Think-feel-do model
Presumes that we approach a purchase using the following sequence of responses: We think about the cue, then we form an attitude or opinion about it, and finally we take action and respond to it.

Hierarchy of effects models help analyse message impact and provide a structure for setting communication objectives. One classic approach, the **AIDA model**, describes the effect of marketing as beginning with awareness, then moving to interest, then desire, and finally action.[1] A variation of AIDA is the DAGMAR model (Defining Advertising Goals for Measured Advertising Results), which begins with awareness, moves to comprehension, then conviction, and ends with action.[2] In both models the initial effects are easier to create than the ones at the end of the process. The use of cute puppies, kittens, and babies are surefire methods for gaining attention, but getting customers to take action is another story.

The **think-feel-do model** of message effects[3] presumes that we approach a purchase situation using the following sequence of responses: we (think) about the cue, then we form an attitude or opinion about it (feel), and finally we take

Figure 4.2 THE THINK-FEEL-DO MODEL

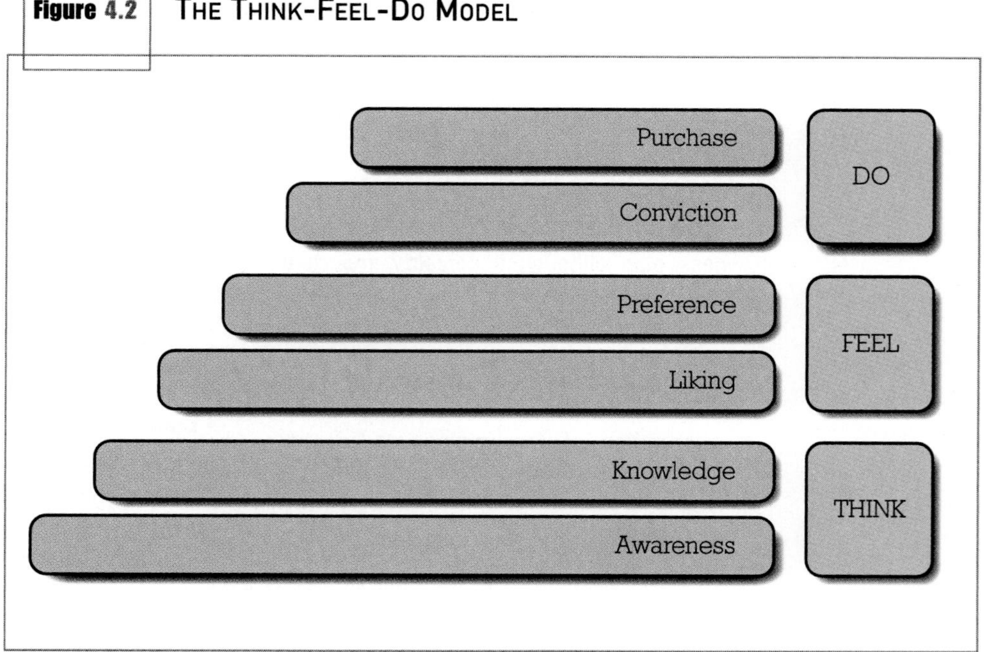

action and respond to it (do). As illustrated in Figure 4.2, the think-feel-do model parallels the AIDA model. The think-feel-do model is also called the high-involvement model because it depicts the responses typically found with consumers who actively participate in the process of gathering information. These consumers are "active" thinkers considering high-priced, high-risk, or complex product categories where there is a need for information. Advertising for these types of products usually provides many product details and is very informative.

The Foote, Cone, and Belding ad agency's (FCB) model[4] is an adaptation of the basic think-feel-do model except that it accommodates both high and low involvement. It creates a matrix with four types of responses, product categories, and situations that are characterized by different orderings of "think-feel-do," as shown in Figure 4.3. For instance, when there is little interest in the product—such as an impulse buy—or a minimal difference between products, the FCB model shows that consumers try a product and then form an opinion—that is, consumers "do-feel-think."

Domains model
The idea that changing perceptions, providing education, and persuading consumers are the primary objectives for marketing communication.

Communication objectives can also be built on domains of effect. The **domains model** in Table 4.1 is based on the idea that changing perceptions, providing education, and persuading consumers are the primary objectives for marketing communication.[5] The model recognizes that marketing communication affects many different areas of the heart and mind simultaneously rather than sequentially. Marketing communication planners, then, must select the factors that are most important to consumers and focus on that part of the message. Table 4.1 explains what kinds of effects are measured in the areas of perception, education, and persuasion.

Figure 4.3 THE FOOTE, CONE, AND BELDING MODEL

	Thinking	**Feeling**
High Involvement	1. Informative (thinking) *Model:* think-feel-do *Products:* car, house *Creative:* demonstration, specific details	2. Affective (feeling) *Model:* feel-think-do *Products:* jewelry, cosmetics *Creative:* execution impact
Low Involvement	3. Habit formation (doing) *Model:* do-think-feel *Products:* liquor, household items *Creative:* reminder	4. Self-satisfaction (reacting) *Model:* do-feel-think *Products:* cigarettes, liquor, candy, gum *Creative:* attention

Table 4.1 THE DOMAINS MODEL MEASURES EFFECTS IN PERCEPTION, EDUCATION, AND PERSUASION

Perception	Education	Persuasion
ATTENTION • PRODUCT, BRAND, AD AWARENESS INTEREST • HOW MUCH CONCERN, EXCITEMENT GENERATED MEMORY • RECOGNITION OF AD, IMAGE, SLOGAN, LOGO, COPY POINTS, POSITION • RECOGNITION OF BRAND, PRODUCT • RECALL OF AD, IMAGE, SLOGAN, LOGO, COPY POINTS, POSITION • RECALL OF BRAND	LEARNING • THE AMOUNT THE CLAIM, FEATURES, AND SELLING PREMISE REGISTERS • THE AMOUNT OF PRODUCT ASSOCIATION WITH LOGO, SLOGAN, THEME, KEY VISUAL, JINGLE, LIFESTYLE, IMAGE, MOOD • WHETHER PRODUCT POSITION OR REPOSITION AND SELLING PREMISE ARE UNDERSTOOD • WHETHER FEATURES, CLAIMS ARE DIFFERENTIATED	EMOTION • RESPONSE TO APPEAL ATTITUDES • POSITIVE OR NEGATIVE DISPOSITION TO PRODUCT • POSITIVE OR NEGATIVE EVALUATION OF FEATURES, CLAIMS, VIEWS • BRAND PREFERENCE ARGUMENT • ACCEPTABILITY OF CLAIM • PERSUASIVENESS OF REASON, PROMISE • WHETHER FALSE IMPRESSION HAS BEEN CORRECTED • WHETHER CONSUMERS CHALLENGE POSITION, CLAIM, VIEWPOINT • WHETHER COUNTER FACTS EXIST BEHAVIOUR • TRAFFIC INCREASES • STIMULATION OF INQUIRIES, TRIAL, PURCHASES, REPURCHASES

concept review

HIERARCHY OF EFFECTS MODEL

Before examining the steps in the communication plan, marketing communicators should consider the hierarchy of effects model to determine the potential effects of their communication plan on their audience. The main versions of the hierarchy of effects model include:

1. The AIDA model
2. The think-feel-do and FCB models
3. The domains model

THE MARKETING COMMUNICATION PLAN

The marketing communication plan evolves from the marketing plan. In the marketing communication plan, however, the objectives are to make the most effective use of all marketing communication functions—advertising, public relations, sales promotion, direct marketing, personal selling, and packaging—and to control the communication impact of the other marketing mix elements.

Each function will have its own section in the marketing communication plan. That section explains how the functional area plans to accomplish marketing and communication objectives and details its implementation activities. The overall marketing communication plan identifies the most efficient and effective combination of activities, media, and messages. Let's consider how that plan is built by examining the nine steps in the marketing communication planning process.

The Marketing Communication Planning Process

A nine-step planning process guides the development of a marketing communication plan. These steps, similar to the business and marketing planning steps, can also be used to create a plan for a specific communication function, such as sales promotion or advertising.

Step 1: Determine a Problem or Opportunity

An analysis of problems and opportunities is derived from a comprehensive situation analysis, discussed earlier. Marketers rely on research, past experience, and a competitive analysis to identify problems and opportunities relevant to the communication plan. The SWOT analysis of the marketing plan may also be reapplied at this stage. Here, of course, the concern is for problems and opportunities that affect marketing messages. Marketing communication can only solve message-related problems such as image, attitude, perception, and knowledge or information. It cannot solve problems related to product price or availability, but it can refocus consumer perceptions and identify problematic messages sent by the marketing mix or other areas that undermine the marketing communication strategy.

Say, for instance, that the marketing plan identifies the product's high price or limited distribution as a weakness. The marketing communication plan may focus on both quality and value to justify price, and exclusivity to justify limited distribution. In an IMC program, a cross-functional team would have worked on the price and distribution decisions together at the marketing planning stage and hammered out the communication implications.

Step 2: Determine the Objectives

The statement of marketing communication objectives evolves directly from the marketing objectives and the problems and opportunity analysis. For example, take Kodak's launch of its disposable camera. Kodak's marketing objective was to gain 50 percent market share for the "novice" photographer segment. However, the price of the product ($8.95–$15.95) created a serious problem in the minds of consumers. The marketing communication objectives therefore emphasized the use of mass media to reach a broad range of consumers, a focus on convenience and picture quality, and an attempt to diminish the high price through product sampling and coupons.

Communication objectives can be planned using the hierarchy of effects models as a basis for identifying how the plan will affect consumers. Marketing communication objectives generally fall into five categories: 1) creating awareness, 2) creating understanding, 3) creating changes in attitudes and perceptions, 4) creating changes in behaviour, and 5) reinforcing previous decisions and attitudes. Certain marketing communication tools are better than others in achieving a given objective, which is an important factor in developing the marketing communication mix in step 4.

Marketing communication objectives should be: 1) specific, 2) measurable, 3) linked to a time frame, and, 4) focused on a target segment.

Advertising that works must make clear its target audience and what the benefits are to that audience. In this ad, the Waterman line of pens is targeted to a relatively upscale audience, as shown by the clothing the models wear. The message, however, relates different pen designs to different family members, who are representative of different target audience segments.

STEP 3: SELECT THE TARGET AUDIENCE

A message delivered to the wrong audience is doomed to fail. In marketing plans, *target markets* are identified as groups of people who are in the market for a product or service; in marketing communication plans, *target audiences* are identified for special communication efforts. There is a subtle difference. For example, the target market for children's toys is primarily children. In contrast, the target audiences might include parents, grandparents, various government agencies concerned with the product safety of children's toys, and consumer activist groups, as well as children. In this case the target audience is much greater than the target market.

The opposite is also possible. The target market for long-distance telephone service for small businesses is all businesses that spend $200 to $1400 a month for long distance. Yet MCI may design a "win-back" (former customers) sales promotion campaign targeted only at Sprint customers.

Sprint Canada
www.sprint.ca

To properly identify the appropriate target audiences, marketing communication managers need detailed information about the product and the market, who produces and sells the product, who uses the product and how it is used, who influences purchase decisions, and the perceptions of consumers.

Targeting is particularly complex in an integrated marketing communication program. In IMC planning, a set of stakeholder audiences may be targeted because they all need to know about or be involved in a company's new product or promotion, such as sales staff, resellers, employees, and the financial community for publicly held companies. Because the audience may be much larger than customers, IMC planning is often more complicated than traditional marketing communication planning that targets only the consumer audience.

The launch of a new product, for example, demands a complex list of target audiences other than consumers and messages that need to be directed to those audiences. Overall the marketer must provide a central message about the value that this new product offers. Shareholders may want to know about the research and development costs and how the new product will affect shareholder returns. The local community will be interested in whether the new product means more jobs and plant expansion. Employees must be notified because some will help with production, so their support will aid quality. Furthermore, they are often sources of information for family and friends. The media—local, national, trade, and financial—will be interested in news aspects of the product development that affect the community. Suppliers and vendors will want to know what opportunities they will have for providing new resources and services to the company. Retailers will need to be informed and motivated to provide space in their stores for the new product.

Step 4: Select the Marketing Communication Mix

One of the most important functions of the marketing communication plan is to determine the marketing communication mix. A recent survey identified the most common marketing communication mix activities used in consumer marketing. The survey respondents spent an average of 2.25 percent of sales revenue on marketing communication and 1.65 percent on personal sales. This pattern contrasts with business-to-business marketing, which spends most of its marketing budget on personal sales.

Marketing communication mix
The activities (or tools) used to achieve the marketing communication objectives.

The activities (or tools) used to achieve the marketing communication objectives make up the **marketing communication mix**. After the target market and audience are selected, the marketer customizes and refines the marketing communication mix to fit the target audience as precisely as possible. The mix will be different for different segments and problem situations. Industry and consumer audiences, for instance, demand entirely different messages. Table 4.2 (on page 92) identifies some general strengths and weaknesses of the most important marketing communication tools.

In IMC planning, the strengths of the various tools are matched against the problems and opportunities to decide which ones are best able to meet the marketing communication objectives. Despite the advantages and disadvantages associated with each tool, several tools may be able to accomplish the same objective. The flexibility of being able to choose among tools is important because it allows managers to match the objective and message needs with budgets.

The "Best" message—no matter what the language—reminds consumers of Gillette's image and quality, as it does in this product display in Shanghai.

Table 4.2 MARKETING COMMUNICATION TOOLS—STRENGTHS AND WEAKNESSES

Tool	Strengths	Weaknesses
Advertising	Creates awareness of a product and informs large mass audiences about a product, service, or idea	Is intrusive, operates in a very cluttered environment, and is expensive
Sales Promotion	Not only does this tool stimulate immediate response by adding incentives and creating tangible extra values, it also creates excitement, increases repeat behaviours, motivates industry support	Can add to communication clutter, creates expectations of lower prices, and may undercut brand image and long-term loyalty
Public Relations	Can create goodwill; can place messages in the media that benefit from the media's credibility and focus on newsworthy information; monitors attitudes to assess a company or brand image; understands and communicates with many stakeholder audiences	Effectiveness is hard to measure; does not usually trigger sales directly
Direct Marketing	Can be highly targeted; excellent for reaching small or niche audiences; economical with small audiences; and can create one-on-one communication because it can be personalized, offers a means for customer feedback and self-selection	Effectiveness often depends on accurate database; often disregarded due to clutter; expensive if large audience
Personal Selling	In business-to-business products, it is the most personalized tool and delivers the most informative and persuasive messages	The most expensive form of marketing communication; can be irritating if the customer does not appreciate the sales call
Event Sponsorship	Can be highly targeted and self-selecting; creates the highest level of participation and involvement; if philanthropic, it also contributes to the corporate good citizen image; and creates news opportunities	Rarely reaches a large audience; does not allow marketers to repeat their messages often; has a high cost given the number of impressions created
Packaging	Makes a strong visual statement about a product; a low-cost reminder message; highly targeted because it is the last message seen before a purchase decision is made	May cause environmental problems; must stand out in a cluttered environment; reaches a small audience
Cause Marketing	Creates positive feelings about the company by associating the business or brand with a philanthropic gesture	If cause does not concern a large audience, or if too many sponsors support it, the effort may get lost; may be seen as self-serving

STEP 5: SELECT THE MESSAGE STRATEGY

Determining exactly what to say to the targeted audience groups is a difficult and important process. Message strategies depend on the nature and extent of the opportunity, as well as strengths, weaknesses, and threats identified in the situation analysis. For example, it is always more effective to promote a product that satisfies a consumer trend. ConAgra, for instance, has followed the health-oriented trend.

Concept in Focus

Zero-Based Planning

In integrated marketing communication planning, there is one important thing to remember: The plans for the functional areas should start with a "zero base." Many firms build plans based on last year's plan because it is simple to do so. Starting with a zero base means that the firm starts from scratch. The plan depends solely on this year's situational analysis, objectives, strategies, marketing communication mix, and budget. Although starting with a zero base requires more time and effort than revising last year's plan, the zero-base method ensures that the firm will use the best tools to solve a problem or seize an opportunity.

Zero-based budgeting, discussed in Chapter 3, is often part of zero-based planning. Starting with a clean balance sheet and building the budget based on the marketing communication tools that will most effectively implement the plan's strategies is the best approach for a constantly changing marketplace.

Source: Tom Duncan, "A Macro Model of Integrated Marketing Communication," American Academy of Advertising Annual Conference, Norfolk, Va., March 1995, 118.

Although different target audiences have different message needs, messages must be consistent with the company, brand, or product's overall message. This message or central theme focuses the marketing effort and provides consistency.

Step 6: Select the Message Delivery Systems or Media

The media planner is the person who identifies how to reach the target audiences at their most important contact points. The development of the media strategy works hand-in-hand with the development of the message strategy and the budget analysis. A planner cannot create a strategy for a television commercial, for instance, if there is no budget for TV advertising. If direct marketing is used, what media will carry the messages—TV or print advertisement, or materials mailed directly to the home or office, or over the Internet? The message strategy differs for each medium, so writers and media planners must coordinate their actions.

To plan the media delivery system, media planning tools (discussed in Chapter 15) include a disciplined analysis of the media options and a rating system that makes it obvious to others how and why various media vehicles were selected. A pie chart is used to show how the media budget is split up, and a balance sheet is used to show what the various elements cost and how they add up. Typically, a flow chart is used to demonstrate the scheduling strategy.

Step 7: Determine a Budget

One key factor that determines which and to what extent each tool will be used in the marketing communication mix is the budget. Ideally, the budget should not enter the planning process until after the major strategic decisions have been made. For this reason, we list budget determination seventh in the planning process. In reality, however, the budget is often a given as it is allocated in the marketing plan, so that a marketing communication manager would be told that the marketing communication budget is $3 million next year, and the plans are made accordingly. This process of arriving at a budget figure is described in more detail in Chapter 16.

Once the overall marketing communication budget is set, a percentage of it is assigned to each tool. For example, the initial promotional mix for Ralston Purina Puppy Chow might look something like this: 40 percent advertising, 30 percent sales promotion, 25 percent personal selling, and 5 percent public relations. Each category would then be broken down into smaller, more specific budget allocations. The advertising component, for example, might be allocated as follows: 30 percent network television, 25 percent magazines, 15 percent newspapers, 10 percent radio, 5 percent outdoor. Another 10 percent might be used for direct mail advertising and 5 percent for specialty items.

An important step after the budgeting stage is to estimate the dollar amounts to be spent on each planned marketing communication activity. How much does advertising during each network television program cost? What does it cost to produce and distribute 500 000 product samples or to produce a sweepstakes campaign? How much does a mailing list cost? To answer this lengthy list of questions, marketing communicators must consult people inside and outside of the organization who can estimate such costs with accuracy. The final budget estimate is often much greater than the amount the company planned to spend. That difference usually spurs plan revisions to cut back activities, adjust the budget, or both.

Step 8: Implement the Strategy

The success of any marketing communication strategy is largely a function of how well it is implemented. Implementation involves three separate stages. First, the marketing communication manager must make specific decisions about all the elements of the plan, including types of media, dates, times, sizes, talent, photographers and artists, and production schedules. Next, the manager must ensure that all these decisions can be implemented and that people are assigned to each task. Finally, the manager must monitor the activities to make sure all decisions were implemented correctly.

A successful implementation coordinates the efforts of all the specialists involved. The advertising program consists of a series of related, well-timed, and carefully placed ads. The sales materials must be planned and produced so they are available when the ads are shown or published. The salespeople also have to be fully informed about the advertising part of the program—the theme, media used, schedule of ad appearances, and so on. The salespeople then inform resellers and retailers about this marketing communication program and convince them to incorporate the merchandising materials, point-of-sale displays, signage, and sales promotions into their marketing efforts. Personnel responsible for physical distribution activities should ensure that adequate stocks of the product are available in all outlets before the start of the program. People working in public relations should also be alerted to new product stories, product demonstrations, new product applications, special events, and so forth.

Marketing communicators should provide enough lead time in all of these areas so the materials and activities are all available on schedule and do not conflict. Conflicting activities overload the trade and the sales staff, who may have to push two different campaign efforts at the same time. Timing and scheduling considerations affect all stakeholders. Usually employees need to know about new programs first, then investors, later the community and the media, and then consumers. If the new program or product design involves government regulators, the company might need to consult the regulators first.

Step 9: Evaluate the Results

After the implementation step, the marketing communication manager must determine if the promotional effort met the stated objectives. External agencies often perform this evaluation because they have greater expertise with marketing communication measurement techniques.

Three tasks must be completed to measure the results of a marketing communication program. First, marketing communication managers must develop standards for effectiveness so that the planners, those who implement the plan, and evaluators understand exactly what the promotion reasonably should have accomplished. The standards should be as specific and measurable as possible. Second, the marketing communication managers must monitor actual promotional performance against the objectives, often through consumer surveys. Third, the manager must compare performance measures against the standards to determine if the performance was effective and efficient.

Once the firm evaluates a marketing communication strategy, the planner is then able to identify deficiencies and prescribe any needed corrective action. Also, the planner can use insights gained from the evaluation as guides for the next planning effort.

concept review

The Marketing Communication Plan

The marketing communication plan provides the framework for the communication effort. The nine steps in the marketing communication planning process include:

1. Determine problems or opportunities
2. Determine the objectives
3. Select the target audience
4. Select the marketing communication mix
5. Select the message strategy
6. Select the message delivery systems or media
7. Determine a budget
8. Implement the strategy
9. Evaluate the results

Strategic IMC Decisions

The goal of IMC is to coordinate all long- and short-term marketing communication efforts. In addition, effective integrated communication programs must consider all messages stakeholders receive each time stakeholders come in contact with a company. The following section identifies the dimensions of IMC that have the strongest effect on planning.

Coordinated Planning

People Magazine
www.people.aol.com

The leaders of each marketing communication area, such as the advertising and sales directors, should plan the marketing communication program together. Coordinated planning efforts should lead to consistent marketing communication efforts. A recent advertisement for NBC's "Dateline" and *People* showed how coordinated marketing efforts can be effective. The ad featured the show and the magazine and reminded consumers that the two team up to "tell some of America's most compelling stories." In contrast, suppose a hospital's marketing plan calls for cost containment, but its medical education seminars stress the use of costly new procedures. What are the hospital's clients, the health maintenance and managed care programs, to make of such conflicting messages? Coordinated planning can reduce this conflict. A seminar could focus on how to use new technology to keep costs down, for instance, but that kind of planning can only occur if the seminar director participates in the marketing communication planning discussions. Such coordination is often difficult to manage in large organizations like hospitals.

Managed Contact Points

As mentioned briefly in Chapter 1, there are a variety of message opportunities, or *contact points,* through which people receive important messages about a brand or company. A coordinated communication program will either control or influence as many of these communication opportunities as possible.

For any product or service, a marketing communication manager can draw up a long list of ways in which people come in contact with the brand or company. The common contact points may include those made through formal marketing communication, such as advertising, articles in the press, sales promotion activities, and in-store merchandising. But informal contact points deliver messages that may speak louder than the formal marketing communication messages. For example, if you manage a hand-lotion brand, then consumers will probably see the product in advertisements and on store shelves. However, the product may also be seen in restrooms, doctor's offices, and in friends' houses. These other locations serve as an informal testimony for the product.

The point is that every contact sends a message—the delivery truck and its driver, the company's plant, the receptionist who answers the phone, and the person who demonstrates the product in the store. Any good IMC plan should include an analysis of all possible contact points and evaluate their importance and impact.

Varied Stakeholder Messages

In a sophisticated integrated communication program, you don't just say the same thing to everyone to maximize consistency. Instead, you tailor the message to each market segment you target while staying consistent with the central themes of the marketing communication program. This is the heart of **strategic consistency.**

Strategic consistency
Tailoring the message to each targeted market segment while remaining consistent with the central themes of the marketing communication program.

After analysing all contact points, IMC planners should evaluate what kind of communication the various stakeholder audiences need to participate in and prioritize the importance of each audience to the company, brand, or product. Specifying and prioritizing the range of possible target audiences help planners decide which communication specialists should address each target market and with what type of message and with how much effort. This process ensures that each stakeholder group is reached in the most effective and efficient manner and that opportunities are created for stakeholders to initiate contact with the company.

It is important for IMC planners to understand that what customers and other stakeholders need is not necessarily one-way communication directed at them by the company. The new era of electronic communication recognizes that two-way communication can be more effective than one-way because it deals with real feedback. As marketing scholar David Stewart explains, "There remains a persistent belief that marketing communication has a powerful influence on consumers. However, what was once a captive audience is increasingly free and increasingly in control of the information flow." He suggests that IMC planners recognize that "consumers will be addressable only to the extent that they choose to be. Marketers may manage and coordinate, but they cannot make consumers attend to, process, or integrate communications."[6]

concept review

Strategic IMC Decisions

Employing an IMC approach toward marketing communication planning requires certain adjustments in the planning process.

1. Strategies must be carefully coordinated.
2. All contact points must be managed.
3. Strategic consistency means that careful consideration must be given to the needs of stakeholders.

A Closing Thought:

Every Company Is a Communicator

Many years ago someone coined the phrase, "Nothing happens until somebody sells something." This statement signifies how crucial marketing communication activities are to business today. Marketing requires more than developing a good product, pricing it fairly, and making it readily available. These facets of marketing are insufficient to generate enough sales and profits for the firm to survive. Without marketing communication, potential buyers would never become aware of, or be persuaded by, the merits of the product. Why? Competition is so fierce and the marketplace so dynamic that the company must develop a comprehensive and effective program of communication. Every company must communicate. The only choice companies have is to decide how well they will communicate.

summary 

1. Describe the critical decisions determined through strategic planning.

   The three most important decisions that are determined by strategic planning include setting objectives, identifying strategies, and developing implementation tactics.

2. Explain the elements of the marketing plan.

   Similar to a business plan, a marketing plan includes a situation analysis, objectives, market strategies, the target market, competitive strategies, implementation, and evaluation.

3. Analyse the hierarchy of effects models and relate them to marketing communication planning.

   Hierarchy of effects models identify the effects of communication. Marketing communicators use these models to assess how communication efforts may affect their audiences and to help define communication goals. The AIDA model describes the effect of marketing communication as a four-step sequence (awareness, interest, desire, and action). The think-feel-do model assumes a three-step sequence of communication responses: We (think) about the cue, then we form an attitude or opinion about it (feel), and finally we take action and respond to it (do). The Domains Model assumes we respond simultaneously in many ways to communication and identifies three categories of effects: perception, education, and persuasion.

4. Describe the marketing communication plan and the marketing communication planning process.

   The marketing communication plan focuses on producing an effective IMC strategy using elements such as advertising, sales promotion, public relations, personal selling, direct marketing, and packaging. The marketing communication planning process consists of nine critical steps:

   1) determining a problem or opportunity, 2) determining the objectives, 3) selecting the audience, 4) selecting the marketing communication mix, 5) selecting the message strategy, 6) selecting the delivery systems or media, 7) determining the budget, 8) implementing the strategy, and 9) evaluating the results and taking corrective action.

5. Evaluate the strategic implications of IMC planning.

   In an integrated marketing communication plan, the strategies must also consider coordinated planning, strategic consistency even with messages that are designed to speak to the individual needs of stakeholders, and the various contact points at which messages about a company or brand are delivered.

points to ponder

Review the Facts

1. In your own words, describe strategic planning.
2. What is a market intelligence?

Master the Concepts

3. Explain why strategic planning must begin with a business mission.
4. Compare the elements of a marketing plan and a marketing communication plan. How are they similar and how are they different? Why are there differences?

Apply Your Knowledge

5. Your company markets microwaveable dinners. Your research suggests that 40 percent of your customers use coupons. What additional information would you need from your research division to determine whether this percentage is a potentially profitable market?
6. Assume that you own a small manufacturing business that produces men's knit shirts. For your business, develop the following: a set of at least three marketing communication objectives and a strategy for each one. Use one of the hierarchy of effects models to structure your objectives.
7. Cite examples of how either advertising or some other form of marketing communication led you to purchase a product. What need did it satisfy? Could any other form of marketing communication also lead you to the purchase of this product?

suggested projects

1. (Oral Communication) Contact two local businesses and determine through at least one interview what kind of planning they use at the corporate or business level, the marketing level, and the marketing communication level. Is the plan for each level formal (written) or informal (most of the information is in someone's head)? How does the interviewee feel about the usefulness and the success of planning? Prepare a five-minute class report on your interviews.
2. (Writing Project) Identify two ads that appeal to unique target audiences and explain what audience segment(s) you think have been targeted and why you think they are successful in targeting those segments. Now rewrite the two ads to demonstrate how the product might be aimed at a different target audience. Explain your new targeting strategy.
3. (Writing Project) Assume that the top management of General Electronics has hired you to determine if a promotional opportunity exists for a new technology that lets consumers record their own compact discs. Where would you begin your investigation? What marketing factors would be most important in developing a strategic marketing communication plan for this product? Outline the key decisions you would need to make in the marketing communication plan to launch such a product.
4. (Internet Project) As this chapter explains, planning requires research. The Internet can be an excellent research tool. Suppose that you decide to conduct some Internet research to assist you with the launch plans described in Project 3. Explore at least two different search engines to find out more about MP3 technology. Some free search engines that you might want to visit include the following:

Alta Vista	altavista.com
Excite	www.excite.com
HotBot	www.hotbot.com
Lycos	www.lycos.com
WebCrawler	webcrawler.com
Yahoo	www.yahoo.ca
	For each engine, try a search for MP3.

Review the list of sources from each search and explore the sources you feel are most relevant. Which search engine provided you the best information? Why? In a brief memo, explain your conclusions.

case 4 Cleaning Helps Ecover Clean Up

Doing the laundry, washing dishes, cleaning the windows—these mundane activities are a $28 billion industry in North America alone—and one of the worst sources of environmental damage. Enter Ecover, a small company from Belgium that is challenging big package goods manufacturers such as Procter & Gamble and Lever Bros. Co. Ecover makes all kinds of cleaning supplies, everything from laundry powder and dishwashing liquid to shampoos and car wax. The difference is that its products use only natural soaps and renewable raw materials such as vegetable extracts, sugar derivatives, and natural oils.

Ecover's sales are around $40 million a year and increasing dramatically, but its impact far exceeds its size because it is helping to shape the debate worldwide on the future of one of the world's dirtiest industries. Its ecologically sound factory has become a biodegradable tourist attraction drawing activists from all over the world. A huge grass roof keeps the factory cool in summer and warm in winter. The water-treatment system operates on wind and solar energy.

The company is not relying on its "green" image to find a position in the market. The fact is there isn't a mass consumer revolt against cleaning products even though one-third of all household pollution comes from cleaning products. It is competing head-to-head with industry giants in terms of pricing and other product features. However, it beats the industry on cleanliness. Not only does its soap clean as well as Tide, but it is also 6000 times less toxic. And Ecover products are more healthy.

The company's strategy has been to roll out its products in European countries whose consumers are environmentally aware and health conscious, such as the Netherlands and Switzerland. It even developed a specially formulated detergent for Amsterdam that is designed to work with the city's water. The product has the city's coat of arms on the package. It now sells products in 34 countries and in 15 000 retail outlets. It is also targeting the business market, primarily office buildings and hotels, which Ecover identifies as "industrial society's great silent polluters." It has limited distribution in the United States and sells through a few environmentally concerned retailers, such as Ecowash in New York City.

Ecover is also a pioneer in marketing communication. In Antwerp the company bought numerous billboards that carried ads for competitors. Then it sponsored a contest for artists to recycle the boards—tear them apart, reassemble them, and create billboards for Ecover. The recycled billboards were colourful, cheerful, provocative, and artistic. Then the company organized walking tours and asked people to look at the billboards as if they were an art exhibit.

Not only is the company reinventing the cleaning business, it's also reinventing marketing communication.

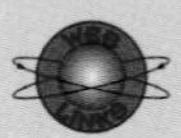

Ecover
www.ecover.com

Case Questions

1. Develop an outline of what you think Ecover's marketing plan would look like. Start with what you think Ecover's mission statement would say.
2. You are director of marketing for Ecover and your senior management is considering making a major entrance into the Canadian market. What would the marketing research need to include to help you decide if the time is right for this move?
3. Ecover's billboards have been a marvellous marketing communication opportunity. If you were in charge of planning the company's marketing communication, what would you recommend for the next innovative marketing communication effort?

Sources: "Save the Planet: Getting Clean, Staying Green," *Glamour* (October 19, 1996): Internet (www.ecomat.com/Glamour_mag.html); "Gunter Pauli Cleans Up," *Fast Company* (November 1993): Internet (www.fastcompany.com).

5 The Sociocultural Environment

chapter objectives

After completing your work on this chapter, you should be able to

- Describe how culture and subculture affect marketing communication.
- List and explain demographic factors that influence marketing communication.
- Discuss the role that social class plays in a culture.
- Summarize how social groups can influence and are influenced by marketing communication.

Burger King Commits to Multicultural Marketing

For George Michel, it's almost personal. As a person with a mixed-Palestinian heritage who was born in Jerusalem and lived there for 17 years, he recognizes that most brands fail to cater to the Canadian multicultural community. But as president of Toronto-based Burger King Restaurants of Canada (hereafter referred to as BK), a chain of fast-food restaurants with almost 300 outlets, he also sees an opportunity for change.

When he and Chuck McAulay, BK's director of marketing, decided the chain would get into ethnic marketing, they zeroed in on the largest ethnic group in Canada—the Chinese—through an ad campaign and several other strategically coordinated moves. In doing so, BK was one of the first fast-food chains in Canada to try such marketing. Michel and McAulay say the campaign was a success and are looking at ways to deepen BK's commitment to multicultural marketing.

To connect with the Italian community, McAulay came up with the idea for an Italian-language ad to air on television sports channel TNN when Italy was playing in the World Cup Soccer finals. Their strategy worked and based on that ad, and the success of the U.S. chain's efforts, BK approached ethnic marketing agency EthnoWorks Inc. in Toronto to create its campaign targeting the Toronto Chinese community.

BK believed it was necessary to create a new campaign, rather than just dubbing over an existing one. "You can't (just dub)," explains Michel. "It's like you can't take Parisian French and put it into Quebec. You need to go by the dialect people speak and, more importantly, the meaning of certain words."

BK chose to use Cantonese in its "Now we're speaking the same language" campaign because it was the most common dialect used in the Canadian Chinese community. BK and EthnoWorks also decided to use two local celebrities—Anson Wong and Hannah Hsu, on-air hosts on Toronto's CHIN radio—to appear in the three print ads in publications such as the ***Sing Tao*** weekly Chinese newspaper (Toronto circulation) and one television spot.

Culturally, everything must have dead-on accuracy to be effective, says David Bray, senior vice-president and creative director at EthnoWorks. "Cantonese is quite a complex language, especially when you get into singing it," he explains. "When you're working with tones, you've got to be sure that it's done correctly. And colloquialisms have to be appropriate." Bray adds: "Everything has to be right, from making sure there's the right colours, the right numbers, the right everything." While it doesn't relate to BK spots, he uses the examples of white flowers, which are symbols of death. So if a wedding shot is called for, white flowers certainly aren't.

But BK's multicultural targeting effort went beyond simply an ad campaign. It was also looking at strategic locations in the Toronto and Vancouver areas. "When we're looking at locations, especially in urban markets, we're looking at the mix in the area's population and their ethnic backgrounds so we can understand how we can communicate with them through local newspapers and through the kinds of products we might serve," says Michel. The chain also ensures that staff are in place who speak the language.

"I think as we evolve our business in Canada, we need to be extremely careful of the cultural diversity in the Canadian marketplace, especially in cities like Montreal, Toronto, and Vancouver, where there's a high mix of people with ethnic backgrounds sticking to their culture," says Michel. "You've just got to be careful of where you're doing it and how you're doing it."

Burger King Corporation
www.burgerking.com

Source: Astrid Van Den Broek, "Speaking the Same Language: Burger King Cooks Up a Multicultural Menu," ***Marketing***, June 21, 1999, p. 13.

Chapter Overview

Sociocultural environment
Consists of four factors: culture and subculture, demographics, social class, and groups that influence.

External influences affect consumer decision making. One external element is the marketing mix, discussed in Chapter 2. Another powerful element is the sociocultural environment. The **sociocultural environment** reflects those factors outside the individual—the person's world. As shown in Figure 5.1, the sociocultural environment consists of four main factors: culture and subculture, demographics, social class, and groups that influence. In this chapter we explore these four factors and how each affects the marketing communication program.

The sociocultural environment is dynamic. As consumers' culture, demographics, social class, and family values change, their reactions to products and marketing communication programs change also. Burger King Restaurants of Canada understood this and decided to deepen its commitment to multicultural marketing. Marketing communication managers must constantly track sociocultural changes to understand how consumers make decisions. We begin our discussion with the broadest factors—cultures and subcultures.

Figure 5.1 COMPONENTS OF THE SOCIOCULTURAL ENVIRONMENT

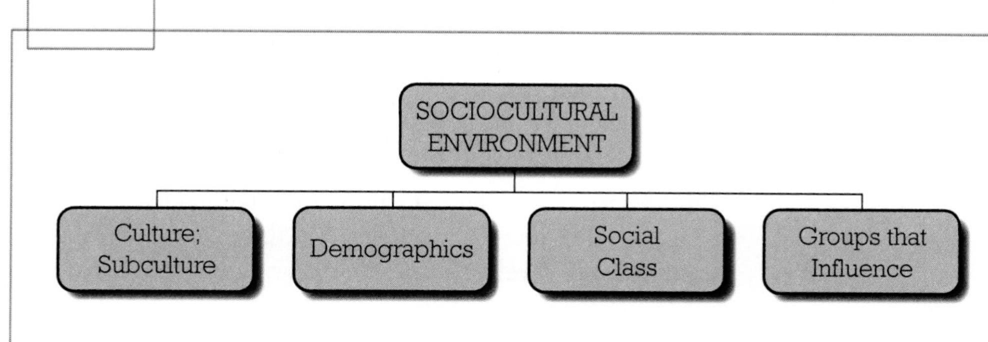

Cultures and Subcultures

Culture
The sum of learned beliefs, values, and customs that regulate the behaviour of members of a particular society.

Belief
An opinion that reflects a person's particular knowledge and assessment of something.

Values
General statements that guide behaviour and influence beliefs and attitudes.

Customs
Overt modes of behaviour that constitute culturally approved ways of behaving in specific situations.

All of us are part of a cultural fabric that affects our behaviour, including our behaviour as consumers. **Culture** is the sum of learned beliefs, values, and customs that regulate the behaviour of members of a particular society. Through our culture, we are taught how to adjust to the environmental, biological, psychological, and historical parts of our environment.

Beliefs and values are guides for behaviour, and customs are acceptable ways of behaving. A **belief** is an opinion that reflects a person's particular knowledge and assessment of something (that is, "I believe that. . . ."). **Values** are general statements that guide behaviour and influence beliefs and attitudes ("Honesty is the best policy"). A value system helps people choose between alternatives in everyday life.[1] **Customs** are overt modes of behaviour that constitute culturally approved ways of behaving in specific situations. Customs vary among countries, regions, and even families. In Arab societies, for instance, usury (payment of interest) is prohibited, so special Islamic banks exist that provide three types of accounts: nonprofit accounts, profit-sharing deposit accounts, and social services funds. A Canadian custom is to eat turkey on Thanksgiving Day; however, the exact Thanksgiving Day menu may depend on family customs.

Cultural Values and Psychographics

Core values
Dominant cultural values.

Psychographics
A tool that determines how people spend their time and resources (activities), what they consider important (interests and values), and what they think of themselves and the world around them (opinions).

Cultural values influence consumer behaviour. Because it is more time- and cost-effective to gather information about cultural values instead of personal values, marketers are forced to concentrate on dominant cultural values.[2] Dominant cultural values are referred to as **core values**; they tend to affect and reflect the core character of a particular society. For example, if a culture does not value efficiency but does value a sense of belonging and neighbourliness, few people in the culture will want to use automatic teller machines.[3]

Marketers track trends in cultural values and target their efforts to address core values. A grouping technique that is particularly useful for tracking trends in cultural values is psychographics (or lifestyle analysis). We can define **psychographics** as a tool that determines how people spend their time and resources (activities), what they consider important (interests and values), and what they think of themselves and the world around them (opinions).[4] Psychographics has become a popular tool with marketers as measurement techniques have become more accurate and the consumer categories that result from the process are easily applied in marketing strategy decisions. As a result, marketers are using psychographic research to target their products and communications to various lifestyle segments.

Stanford Research Institute
www.sri.com

Among private research firms that monitor cultural values and look for psychographic or lifestyle segments, Stanford Research Institute (SRI) provides the most well-known and widely used segmentation system in North America known as VALS (Values and Lifestyles).

SRI's latest product, VALS 2, divides people into three basic categories: those who are principle-oriented, status-oriented, and action-oriented. Then it estimates the resources consumers can draw upon, such as education, income, health, energy level, self-confidence, and degree of consumerism. The result is eight subcategories. Figure 5.2 shows how the VALS 2 categories and resources interact.[5]

Figure 5.2 A METHOD FOR CLASSIFYING CONSUMER VALUES

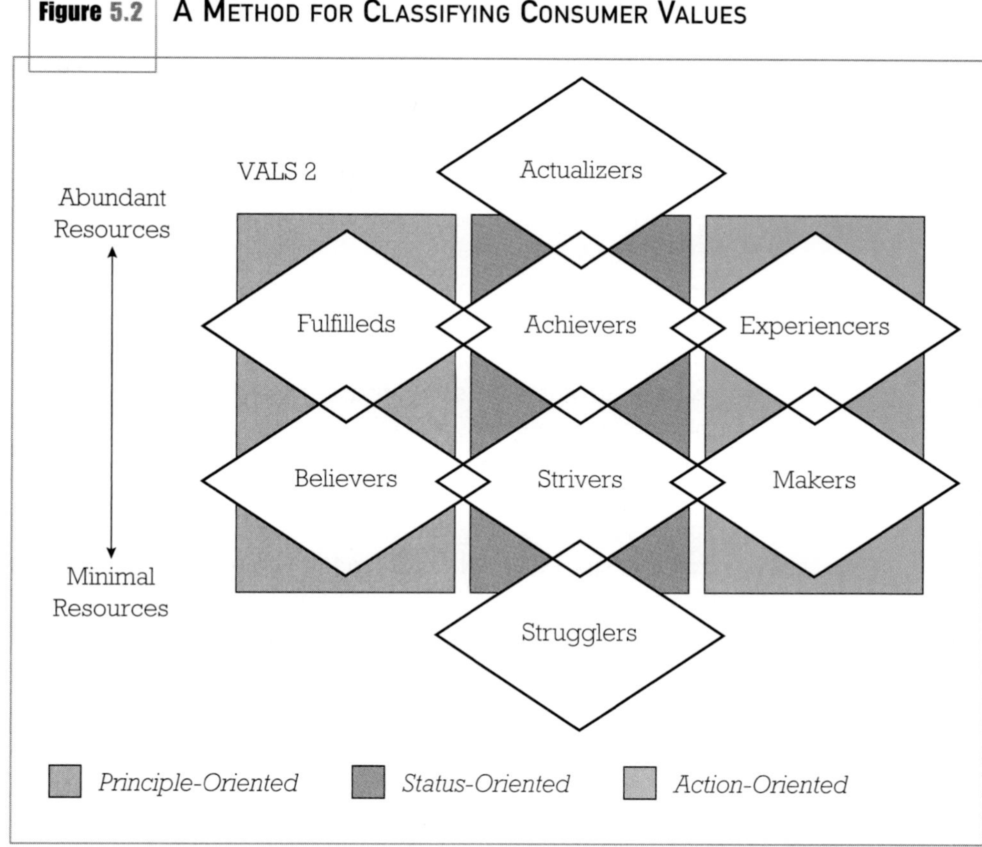

Note in Figure 5.2 that the three main categories and subcategories are arranged in a rectangle. They are stacked vertically by amount of resources (minimal to abundant) and horizontally by principle-oriented, status-oriented, and action-oriented. We see from Figure 5.2 that principle-oriented consumers are guided by their views of how the world is or should be; status-oriented consumers, by the action and opinions of others; and action-oriented consumers, by a desire for social or physical activity, variety, and risk taking.

The two principle-oriented segments, for instance, are fulfilleds and believers. Fulfilled consumers are mature, responsible, well-educated professionals. Their leisure activities centre on their homes, but they are well informed about what goes on in the world, and they are open to new ideas and social change. They have high incomes, but they are practical, value-oriented consumers. Believers have more modest incomes. They are typically conservative and predictable consumers who favour established brands. Their lives are centred on family, religion, community, and the nation. Do you know anyone who would be in either of these VALS groups?

An annual subscription to VALS provides businesses with a range of products and services. Businesses that do market research can include VALS questions in their own questionnaires. SRI will analyse the results, and businesses can then tabulate the rest of their market research according to VALS classifications.

The VALS 2 system is used by various companies, including Mercedes-Benz, Chevron Corporation, Eastman Kodak, and Ketchum Communications. Chevron, for example, uses the VALS 2 classifications to categorize all its consumers into types that are then combined with information about the size of the market and geographic distribution. Chevron uses the results to target its sales promotions.

SRI provides online access to VALS. Check it out at future.sri.com/vals/survey.shtml. Although the segmentation scheme has been developed for the U.S. population, the values, activities, and lifestyle questions are also relevant to Canadians. It takes about 10 minutes to log on, answer the questions and determine which VALS 2 segment best describes your values and lifestyle.

In Canada there are many large-scale consumer survey studies that marketing communication specialists purchase. Some of these studies provide similar lifestyle insights to the VALS 2 segmentation system. Many of the firms that conduct these studies are operated by advertising agencies to enable them to remain current with sociocultural trends in order to effectively develop communications on behalf of their clients. For example, the WPP Group's Goldfarb Consultants of Toronto offers a Canadian population-based product similar to VALS 2 known as the Goldfarb Psychographics Segments. Like VALS 2, this product provides insight into key factors in developing marketing communication messages that will reach and motivate a particular target audience.[6] Details of this and other Goldfarb Consultants' products are available on the firm's Web site (www.goldfarbconsultants.com).

Goldfarb Consultants
www.goldfarbconsultants.com

Angus Reid Group
www.angusreid.com

Environics Research Group
www.environics.net

Other research firms that track lifestyle and other consumer trends in Canada include the Angus Reid Group, BBM Bureau of Measurement, and Environics Research Group Ltd. Check out their respective Web sites to see the

IMC Concept in Focus

Syncographics

One of the newest lifestyle extensions is known as syncographics. This is the short-term period when something is either about to happen, has recently happened, or is happening in people's lives. This period, generally identified as a lifestyle change—graduating university, getting married, having a baby, buying a home, retiring—qualifies consumers as prime targets for specific products and services.

Syncographics identifies people going through demographic changes. The segment has movement; it's not static like others. It allows marketing communicators to hone in on a key niche market and avoid wasting money on mass markets. For example, a woman getting divorced generally wants to take back her name. She wants a charge card with her own name, so credit cards are a natural for this market. People who have been widowed or divorced recently also become more interested in financial services.

Reaching customers experiencing lifestyle changes may cost a little more per contact, but the results typically are much greater. For example, businesses that offer baby products can target a pregnant woman before she gives birth. When she visits her obstetrician early in the pregnancy, she often will receive a gift pack filled with samples of diapers and formula. Many businesses place a product sample or coupon in the pack. Still others buy the names of the women who complete an information card distributed in the pack. The information card asks such questions as, "What is your name?", "Is this your first baby?", "When are you expecting?", and "What is your telephone number?" Generally the response rate of pregnant women who fill out the card is high, 20 to 35 percent.

By targeting markets in motion, businesses can zero in on the proper target and spend communication dollars more wisely.

Sources: Tracy Finley, "Targeting 'Consumers in Motion,'" ***Marketing News***, August 28, 1995, 7; Paul Mergenhagen, "Seizing the Day," ***American Demographics*** (July 1995): 22–3.

latest studies available for purchase from these firms (www.angusreid.com, www.bbm.ca, www.environics.net).

As indicated in the IMC Concept in Focus Feature, people in transition face an interesting lifestyle challenge that is of interest to marketing communicators.

Core values are slow and difficult to change. Consequently, marketing communication strategies must accurately portray and reflect these values.

Secondary values
Impermanent values that can sometimes be influenced by marketing communication.

Secondary values also exist in any culture. Secondary values are less permanent values that can sometimes be influenced by marketing communication. In addition, secondary values are often shared by some people but not others. These values serve as the basis for subcultures.

SUBCULTURES

Subculture
A group of people who share a set of secondary values.

A natural evolution that occurs in any culture is the emergence of subcultures. Core values are held by virtually an entire culture, whereas secondary values are not. A **subculture** is a group of people who share a set of secondary values. Examples include Gen-Xers and environmentally concerned people. Many factors can place an individual in one or several subcultures. Five of the most important factors that create subcultures follow:[7]

- *Material culture*. People with similar income may create a subculture. The poor, the affluent, and the white-collar middle class are examples of material subcultures.
- *Social institutions*. Those who participate in a social institution may form a subculture. Examples include participation in marriage, parenthood, a retirement community, the armed forces, and so on.
- *Belief systems*. People with shared beliefs may create a subculture, such as shared beliefs in religion or politics. For example, traditional Amish do not use several types of products, including electricity and automobiles.
- *Aesthetics*. Artistic people often form a subculture of their own associated with their common interests—including art, music, dance, drama, and folklore.
- *Language*. People with similar dialects, accents, and vocabulary can form a subculture. Canada's rich ethnic diversity provides many subcultures with unique language characteristics. Even within the large French- and English-speaking population there are subcultures identifiable by their unique dialects, such as the Acadian French of New Brunswick and Nova Scotia, and the French Quebecois in Quebec.

To illustrate, let's examine a subculture that has received a great deal of attention during the last decade—the gay and lesbian community. For many marketers the gay and lesbian market represents an untapped gold mine. Because many gays are highly educated and often have no dependants, they have high levels of disposable income. Geographic concentration and a strong word-of-mouth network make them easy to reach.[8]

Currently, limited research exists to provide insights about product or media usage in the homosexual community. However, Simmons Market Research Bureau has linked readership of gay publications with purchase behaviour. Readers of gay magazines and newspapers are more likely to buy many discretionary items, from sparkling water to consumer electronics and health club memberships. This upscale profile indicates a level of affluence borne out by

To effectively communicate marketing messages to Quebec consumers, the full extent of the cultural differences relative to English Canada should not be underestimated.

linking readership with demographic characteristics. The drawback to measuring consumer behaviour through gay publications, however, is that lesbian women don't tend to read them.[9]

More firms are targeting this growing subculture with separate marketing communication efforts, such as *OUT* magazine, or sponsorship of gay events like the annual Gay Games in Vancouver, British Columbia.

The French Quebec market is a Canadian subculture that marketing communicators need to understand. To reach and effectively transfer marketing messages to Quebec consumers, the full extent of this group's cultural differences relative to English Canada should not be underestimated. Large companies, such as Pepsi, that have taken the time to research and design specific Quebec communication campaigns have had market success. Pepsi's long-running campaign featuring comedian Claude Meuniere helped make Quebec one of the few geographic markets where Pepsi has outperformed Coke. The implication of Quebec's unique culture is clear—to be understood by Quebecers, you must speak to them as a Quebecer.

Association of Quebec Advertising Agencies

www.aapq.qc.ca

To educate marketing communicators, the Association of Quebec Advertising Agencies has produced videos and print materials that describe many of the things that make Quebec a unique market. Select extracts from the Association's Web site that explain media habits are provided in Table 5.1. Check out this Web site for more information about the Association of Quebec Advertising Agencies.

Table 5.1 QUEBEC AS A UNIQUE MARKET: MEDIA HABITS

Medium	Description
TELEVISION	QUEBECERS WATCH MORE TELEVISION THAN OTHER CANADIANS: AN AVERAGE OF 26 HOURS 44 MINUTES A WEEK COMPARED TO 22 HOURS AND 54 MINUTES.
RADIO	QUEBECERS LISTEN TO THE RADIO MORE THAN OTHER CANADIANS: 24 HOURS A WEEK COMPARED TO 21 HOURS 58 MINUTES.
MAGAZINES	QUEBECERS READ FAR MORE FRENCH MAGAZINES PRODUCED IN QUEBEC THAN THOSE IN THE REST OF CANADA, THE UNITED STATES, OR EUROPE.
DAILY NEWSPAPERS	QUEBECERS READ FRENCH DAILIES MORE THAN ANY OTHER: 10 OF THE 13 DAILIES PRODUCED IN QUEBEC ARE FRENCH AND THESE ACCOUNT FOR 85 PERCENT OF READERSHIP OF ALL QUEBEC DAILIES.

Source: Statistics compiled by the Association of Quebec Advertising Agencies. Used with permission.

OUT magazine is among the brand-name publications that target the lesbian and gay community in print and online.

Understanding Other Cultures Around the World

Adjusting to cultural differences is perhaps the most difficult task facing marketing communicators who operate in other countries. Before entering a foreign market, a company must decide to what extent it is willing to customize its marketing effort to accommodate each foreign market. Naturally, the more the company standardizes its effort, the less trouble it incurs and the greater the assumed profitability. But is some customization inevitable?

Theodore Levitt, a Harvard professor, has argued against customization. In *The Globalization of Markets,* he suggested that world markets are being driven "toward a converging commonality" in which people everywhere are motivated by two common needs: high quality and reasonable price. Therefore, the "global corporation sells the same thing in the same way everywhere."[10]

Critics argue that Levitt's assumptions are unrealistic. Products and strategies must be adapted to the cultural needs of each country. Philip Kotler, a professor of marketing at Northwestern University, champions the tried-and-true method of selling: tailoring to the local culture. Each national market is different, hence products and promotional strategies must be designed to fit the local culture. He cites several examples to support his position, including M&M/Mars' attempt to enter the European market by creating versions of its candy bars with a better grade of chocolate to compete with Swiss Nestle and Cadbury Schweppes.[11]

Table 5.2 A Sampling of Cultural Variations

Country-Region	Body Motions	Greetings	Colours	Numbers	Shape, Sizes, Symbols
Japan	Pointing to one's own chest with a forefinger indicates one wants a bath. Pointing a fore-finger to the nose indicates "me."	Bowing is the traditional form of greeting.	Positive colours are in muted shades. Combinations of black, dark gray, and white have negative overtones.	Positive numbers are 1, 3, 5, 8. Negative numbers are 4, 9.	Pine, bamboo, or plum patterns are positive. Cultural shapes such as Buddha-shaped jars should be avoided.
India	Kissing is considered offensive and not seen on television, in movies, or in public places.	The palms of the hands are placed together and the head is nodded for greeting. It is considered rude to touch a woman or to shake hands.	Positive colours are bold colours such as green, red, yellow, or orange. Negative colours are black and white if they appear in relation to weddings.	To create brand awareness, numbers are often used as a brand name.	Animals such as parrots, elephants, tigers, or cheetahs are often used as brand names or on packaging. Sexually explicit symbols are avoided.
Europe	Raising only the index finger signifies a person wants two items.	It is acceptable to send flowers in thanks for a dinner invitation, but not	Generally, white and blue are considered positive.	The number 3 or 7 is usually positive.	Circles are symbols of perfection.

Are there global markets? The answer is yes. Many countries have market segments with similar demands for the same product. Timex, for example, has sold standard products in similar fashion worldwide for decades. Does the world represent a global market? Hardly. There will always be obstacles to standardization, including cultural, political, economic, technological, and other environmental factors. McDonald's restaurants in Hawaii and Japan offer sushi; those in Germany serve beer. In India, a culture that holds the cow sacred, McDonald's offers beef-less patties and calls its Big Mac the Maharaja Mac.[12]

Whether a company assumes a standardized or a customized posture toward foreign markets has a direct bearing on the marketing communication effort. Standardization means taking the existing marketing communication strategy, ensuring that everything is translated properly, and otherwise using it unchanged in a foreign country. Customization has far greater implications and makes marketing communication very complex. Extensive research is conducted on a country-by-country basis. Separate agencies may be hired for each market, and separate strategies are developed, as shown in Table 5.2.

What may be more likely to happen is a modularized approach to international marketing communication. A company may select some features as standard for all its communications and localize some others. Campbell Soup Co., for instance, maintains its well-known package and logo on all its ads, but customizes copy and visuals for each country.

Country-Region	Body Motions	Greetings	Colours	Numbers	Shape, Sizes, Symbols
Europe continued	When counting on the fingers, "one" is often indicated by thumb, "two" by thumb and forefinger.	roses (associated with sweethearts) or chrysanthemums (associated with funerals).	Black often has negative overtones.	13 is a negative number.	Hearts are considered favourably at Christmas.
Latin America	General arm gestures are used for emphasis.	The traditional form of greeting is a hearty embrace followed by a friendly slap on the back.	Popular colours are generally bright or bold yellow, red, blue, or green.	Generally, 7 is a positive number. Negative numbers are 13, 14.	Religious symbols should be respected. Avoid national symbols such as flag colours.
Middle East	The raised eyebrow facial expression indicates "yes."	The word "no" must be mentioned three times before it is accepted.	Positive colours are brown, black, dark blues, and reds. Pink, violets, and yellows are not favoured.	Positive numbers are 3, 7, 5, 9, whereas 13, 15 are negative.	Round or square shapes are acceptable. Symbols of six-pointed star, raised thumb, or Koranic sayings are avoided.

Sources: Philip R. Harris and Robert T. Moran, *Managing Cultural Differences*, 3rd ed. (Houston Gulf Publishing Co., 1991), 345–50; James C. Simmons, "A Matter of Interpretation," *American Way* (April 1983):106–11; and "Adapting Export Packaging to Cultural Differences," *Business America*, December 3, 1979, 3–7.

Culture, Subculture, and IMC

Understanding the culture and subculture in which you are marketing has important implications for integrating marketing communication. Most notably, all communication must be accurate and consistent within the particular culture or subculture. To communicate a message on a birth-control device in France, you must consider the values and attitudes the French hold toward such technology. However, the communication might be adjusted in Switzerland, where French, Italian, German, and Swiss subcultures exist. Cultures and subcultures represent the starting point for research that serves as the foundation for IMC.

This Bijan ad illustrates how gender-role identities are culturally bound by contrasting the expectations of how women should appear in two different countries.

concept review

Cultures and Subcultures

1. A culture is the sum of learned beliefs, values, and customs that regulate the behaviour of members of a particular society.
2. Values are thought to shape behaviour, but no researchers can identify and agree about a set of core values in the North American culture. Searches for general core values have been conducted by research firms such as SRI International (VALS 2) and Goldfarb Consultants (the Goldfarb Segments). The values segments identified by these firms are known as psychographic (of values and lifestyle) segments.
3. Subcultures are based on secondary values. Five factors influence the formation of subcultures:
   - Material culture
   - Social institutions
   - Belief systems
   - Aesthetics
   - Language
4. Marketing in foreign subcultures typically requires major adjustments.

Demographic Changes

Demographics
The observable characteristics of individuals living in the culture.

Whereas beliefs, values, and customs describe the characteristics of a culture and subculture, **demographics** describe the observable characteristics of individuals living in the culture. Demographics include our physical traits, such as gender, race, age, and height; our economic traits, such as income, savings, and net worth; our occupation-related traits, including education; our location-related traits; and our family-related traits, such as marital status and number and age of children. Demographic trait compositions are constantly changing.

University of Toronto
www.utoronto.ca

According to David Foot, a University of Toronto professor and author of *Boom, Bust & Echo: How to Profit from the Coming Demographic Shift*, demographics explain about two-thirds of everything. For example, how do you explain a 38 percent increase in the popularity of golf over the last 25 years? This is explained by golf's popularity among aging baby-boomers who are entering a stage of life that enables them to spend more time on the golf course.[13]

There is no average family, no ordinary worker, no everyday wage, and no traditional middle class. Still, marketing communicators must understand consumers intimately. Often, the best they can do is take a demographic snapshot and try to understand what is happening in our cultures. Next, we examine six demographic trends and how they affect marketing communicators.

1. *Aging population.* The single most notable demographic trend in Canada is the aging population. Sometimes referred to as the mature or greying market, the over-50 age segment is expected to exceed nine million (or 28.6 percent of the population) by 2001 and may exceed 13.7 million (or 37 percent of the population) by the year 2016.[14] Because age affects needs, values, and ultimately purchase behaviour, marketing communicators should plan for a great number of middle-aged households with accumulated wealth (real property, financial securities, pension assets), and consumers who are experienced and have a better understanding of price and value. These consumers will have an interest in high-quality household goods, travel and leisure services, and in-home health care services.

2. *Relatively slow population growth.* The population of Canada is expected to exceed 31 million by 2001 and may reach 37 million by the year 2016.[15] Although this growth projection indicates some Canadian businesses will face growing domestic markets, opportunities should be explored in developing countries where it is believed much of the growth in the world population will take place. As discussed earlier, adjusting to cultural differences is perhaps the most difficult task facing marketing communicators. Moreover, marketing communicators need to understand that population size and growth rate do not tell the whole story. Economic and other marketing environment factors shape consumers' consumption behaviour.

3. *Continued increase in education and service sector employment.* The Canadian population is becoming better educated. More and more people have attended some college or university. This trend corresponds with a workforce that is becoming more white collar. Virtually all job growth during the next 10 years will take place among service providers, especially in health care and social services.

   This trend suggests a continued growth in demand for quality products, computers, books, and travel. For marketing communicators, this trend means more knowledgeable and sophisticated consumers who expect more information about product attributes and benefits before making a purchase.

4. *Increasing ethnic diversity*. Although many observers characterize Canadians as being of either French or English descent, the population of Canada is composed of mixed races as the result of changing patterns of immigration that have had a significant impact on population growth. In past decades most immigrants came from Europe. Today, immigrants from Asia, the Americas (including the Caribbean and Bermuda), Africa, and the Middle East outnumber those arriving from Europe, and many ethnic markets in Canada are growing.[16] Much of the ethnic population can be found in major metropolitan areas such as Toronto, Vancouver, Montreal, and Calgary. This concentration of ethnic segments helps marketing communicators efficiently reach ethnic market segments.

As is indicated in this chapter's IMC in Action feature, those who are not from the ethnic group must understand how to communicate with the group or risk inept communication.

Multicultural Creative

When marketers decide to venture into multicultural marketing, whether the target sector be Asian, French or Hispanic, they have an opportunity to reach a very focused group with a distinctive culture. It makes sense to create a targeted message to take full advantage of this unique audience.

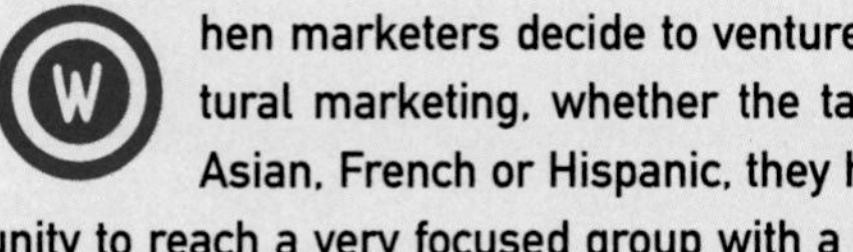

Unlike the case of Burger King as described in this chapter's opening *Consider This* feature, agency clients often do not see ethnic advertising as segmentation marketing; they see it as marketing with a language issue. The key to ethnic marketing is to gain an in-depth understanding of the target group's culture. Only then can truly meaningful messages be conveyed. Like segmentation marketing, media alternatives must be examined and messages must be tailor-made so as to "single to the hearts" and "push the hot buttons" of the target audience. In short, to do it well, you need to be committed to the development of original creative communications for the targeted sector.

The key to this commitment is knowing the contribution it could make to your market share. Research and analysis are needed to assess your product's market share potential. It's an investment of both effort and money. But if your study shows that an ethnic group can deliver a substantial new market, it's often worth doing it right. An ethnic market can be less competitive than the mainstream scene, and the cost to gain a market share can be reasonable. Moreover, ethnic consumers can be loyal brand followers.

Brand erosion is a real and logical concern. Agency clients often say they do not want conflicting brand messages out there. According to Ken Koo, president of Koo Creative Group in Vancouver, two questions from agency clients keep emerging: 1) What if the ethnic group is exposed to the mainstream campaign as well?, and 2) Aren't we sending confusing messages if the ethnic campaign is original? To answer, Koo argues that "... to run an additional segmented campaign with original creative specifically made ... will show how committed the client is to earning their business, as well as demonstrating the relevance to their (the targeted audiences) way of life. If anything, it (the original creative for the ethnic segment) may enhance the main branding campaign." Koo adds that it's also "... possible to develop creative concepts that cross cultural barriers without losing much of their effectiveness. That means bringing in an ethnic marketing agency to partner with the mainstream agency and ensure the concept has equal potential for both markets."

In Koo's opinion, "if an ethnic group's market is meaningful enough for your business to target it separately, then you might as well tailor-make your message to maximize your investment."

Food for Thought

1. This feature suggests marketing communicators should adjust to communicate with different ethnic groups in Canada. Do you agree with the opinions and arguments presented in this feature? Explain.
2. Locate a print ad that targets one or more ethnic segments and assess how it is unique.

Source: Adapted from: Ken Koo, "Cross-culture Creative," ***Marketing***, June 21, 1999, p. 23. Ken Koo is president of Koo Creative Group in Vancouver.

5. *The demise of the traditional family.* What is a traditional family? Married couples are a bare majority of Canadian households and couples with no children under 18 now comprise almost half of all families. Also, non-family and single-parent households is the fastest-growing category of Canadians households.[17] Although married couples dominate the affluent market, there has been a long-term trend of high growth in non-traditional types of households and a lack of growth among married couples. This trend can only mean further segmentation of an already segmented marketplace.
6. *Geographic mobility of the population.* There has been a long-term trend of movement from rural to urban areas. Because urban dwellers have been moving from the city to the suburbs, this movement has formed what Statistics Canada calls Census Metropolitan Areas (CMAs). Approximately 40 percent of Canada's population lives in the top five CMAs. Canada's top 20 CMA Markets are listed in Table 5.3 along with projected retail sales for each area for 2004.

Despite Canada's large geographic mass and regional dispersion of the population, these trends indicate potential marketing opportunities that are concentrated in relatively few urban areas. These large geographic labour market areas are allowing marketing communicators to efficiently reach large segments of the population.

Table 5.3 THE TOP 20 CMA MARKETS IN CANADA*

Rank	City	Population (000)	Total Retail Sales (mil $)	Per Capita Retail Sales
1	Toronto	5 306	48 443	9 100
2	Montreal	3 607	38 072	10 600
3	Vancouver	2 123	21 128	10 000
4	Ottawa-Hull	1 168	9 660	9 600
5	Calgary	1 004	9 660	9 600
6	Edmonton	937	10 262	11 000
7	Québec	711	7 911	11 100
8	Hamilton	710	6 943	9 800
9	Winnipeg	708	7 282	10 300
10	London	446	4 633	10 400
11	Kitchener	422	4 333	10 300
12	St. Catharines/Niagara	410	4 204	10 500
13	Halifax	368	3 770	10 200
14	Victoria	334	3 581	10 700
15	Windsor	320	2 991	9 300
16	Oshawa	308	2 982	9 700
17	Saskatoon	242	2 466	10 200
18	Regina	210	2 122	10 100
19	St. John's	188	1 981	10 500
20	Chicoutimi-Jonquiére	169	2 071	12 300

*All numbers are projected for the year 2004.

Source: 1999 FB Markets—Canadian Demographics, *Financial Post*. Used with permission.

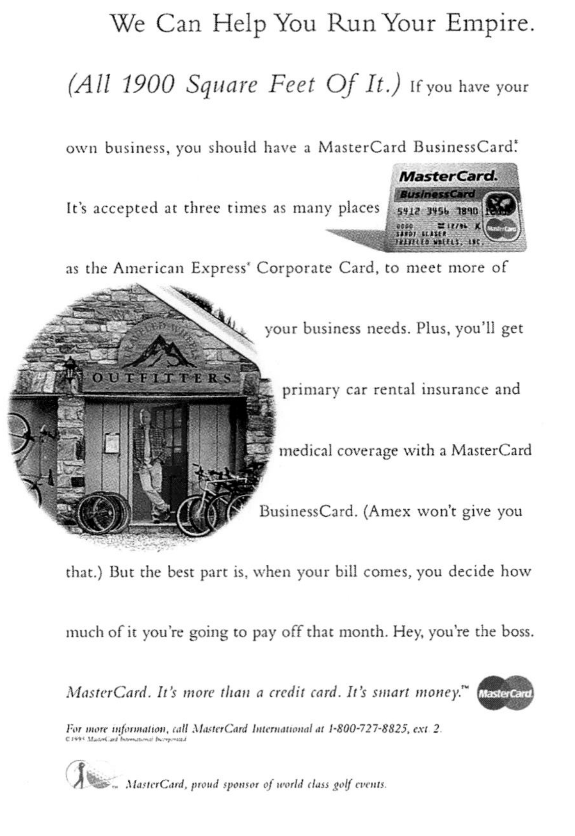

This ad targets the small-business owner. Do you think it does a good job highlighting issues that might concern its target market?

Demographic Groupings

In addition to understanding general demographic trends, marketing communicators must also recognize demographic groupings that may turn out to be market segments because of their enormous size, similar socioeconomic characteristics, or shared values. Michael Adams, president of Environics Research Group Ltd., in his book *Sex in the Snow* divided the Canadian population into three demographic groups that have become dominant market segments: Elders, Boomers, and Gen-Xers. According to Adams, 12 value-based "tribes" exist within these broader demographic groups. Their relative size, motives, values, and exemplars are illustrated in Table 5.4.

Given the diversity of each demographic grouping, what are the possibilities that an integrated marketing communications strategy can be targeted at one group? The key is in understanding the sub-segments (or "tribes") within each grouping. Since Adams' classification describes motivators, values, and exemplars of each group, it serves as a very useful tool for marketing communicators. For example, several of the Gen-Xers' tribes have a common motivator, experience-seeking, that alone or in conjunction with other shared characteristics could serve as a point of distinction. Their experience-seeking motive and desire to have fun or live dangerously suggests that creative communication content depicting these features would prove effective. Ultimately, marketing communications managers would be wise not to make assumptions about large demographic groups and should conduct primary research on their specific target audience.

Table 5.4 A GUIDE TO THE GENERATIONS OF CANADA

Groups	% Pop & Size	Motivators	Values	Exemplar
The Elders:				
Rational Traditionalists	15% 3.5 M	Financial independence, stability, and security.	Value safety, reason, tradition, and authority. Religious.	Winston Churchill
Extroverted Traditionalists	7% 1.7M	Traditional communities and institutions. Social Status.	Value tradition, duty, family, and institutions. Religious.	Jean Chrétien
Cosmopolitan Modernists	6% 1.4M	Traditional institutions. Nomadic, experience seeking.	Education, affluence, innovation, progress, self-confidence, world-perspective.	Pierre Trudeau
The Boomers:				
Disengaged Darwinists	18% 4.3M	Financial independence, stability, and security.	Self-preservation, nostalgia for the past.	Mike Harris
Autonomous Rebels	10% 2.4M	Personal autonomy, self-fulfilment, and new experiences.	Egalitarian, abhor corruption, personal fulfilment, education. Suspicion of authority and big government.	John Lennon
Anxious Communitarians	9% 2.1M	Traditional communities, big government, and social status.	Family, community, generosity, duty. Needs self-respect. Fearful.	Martha Stewart
The Gen-Xers:				
Aimless Dependents	8% 1.9M	Financial independence, stability, security. Fearful.	Desire for independence. Disengagement.	Courtney Love
Thrill-Seeking Materialists	7% 1.7M	Traditional communities, social status, experience-seeking.	Money, material possessions, recognition, living dangerously.	Calvin Klein
Autonomous Postmaterialists	6% 1.4M	Personal autonomy and self-fulfilment.	Freedom, human rights, egalitarian, quality of life.	Bart Simpson
Social Hedonists	4% .9M	Experience seeking, new communities.	Esthetics, hedonism, sexual freedom, instant gratification.	Janet Jackson
New Aquarians	4% .9M	Experience seeking, new communities.	Ecologism, hedonism.	Tori Amos

Source: Philip Kotler, Gary Armstrong, and Peggy H. Cunningham, *Principles of Marketing*, 4th Canadian Edition (Scarborough, ON: Prentice-Hall of Canada Inc., 1999), p. 168 as adapted from information in: Michael Adams, "The Demise of Demography," *The Globe and Mail,* January 8, 1997, D5; Ann Walmsley, "Canadians Specific," *Report on Business*, March 1997, pp. 15-16

SOCIAL CLASS

Social class
A position on a social scale based on criteria such as occupation, education, and income.

Social class refers to position on a social scale based on criteria such as occupation, education, and income. These characteristics define the prestige or power of the individual and, therefore, his or her social position. Members of the same social class may never meet or communicate, but they are likely to share certain values, attitudes, and behaviour because of similar socioeconomic characteristics.

This AOL Canada ad seems to target Gen-Xers. Do you think this ad is effective?

Unlike the rigid social caste system found in India, the social class system in Canada is an open system because people can move from one class to another.

Lower class
The traditional view of the working class.

Middle class
The social class falling between the upper class and the working class. People in business and the professions.

Upper class
The wealthiest social class.

Although there are a number of techniques available to place an individual in a particular social class, these results are uncertain. For the marketing communication manager, the traditional **lower, middle,** and **upper class** is sufficient for planning purposes. The assumption that can be made is that to some degree, people within these three social classes develop and assume different patterns of behaviour.

For example, time patterns differ sharply by social class. People in the upper social class perform most daily activities an hour or so later than people in the lower social class. The use of language and symbols also differs. Middle-income people use more subtle and complex forms of expression than lower-income people. Simile and analogy are considered more meaningful to middle-class people than to lower-class people.

This ad targets a reference group. Can you identify the type of reference group it targets?

Perceived risk also separates the social classes. In general, the lower-class segment sees the world as risky and perhaps dangerous. People without much income may not feel adequate to cope with loss or adversity, they are risk averse, and they value personal security. Upper-class people feel risk implies both danger and opportunity; the degree of negative risk is proportional to the rate of positive return.[18]

In cases where social classes differ in at least some purchasing attitudes and behaviour, marketers often use social class variations to design communication strategies. For example, banks that market to different social classes should develop marketing communication strategies that match the spending, saving, and investment strategies for each class. Generally, upper-class individuals save more money than people in the lower class. They are concerned about quick and easy access to funds and the rate of return they will receive from investments. Lower-class consumers often save only to accumulate money for a specific purchase, so they may not be concerned about the rate of return they receive. Credit is used more by upper-class consumers, but for different reasons than people in

Fairchild Television recognizes that advertisers need to cultivate a diverse customer base.

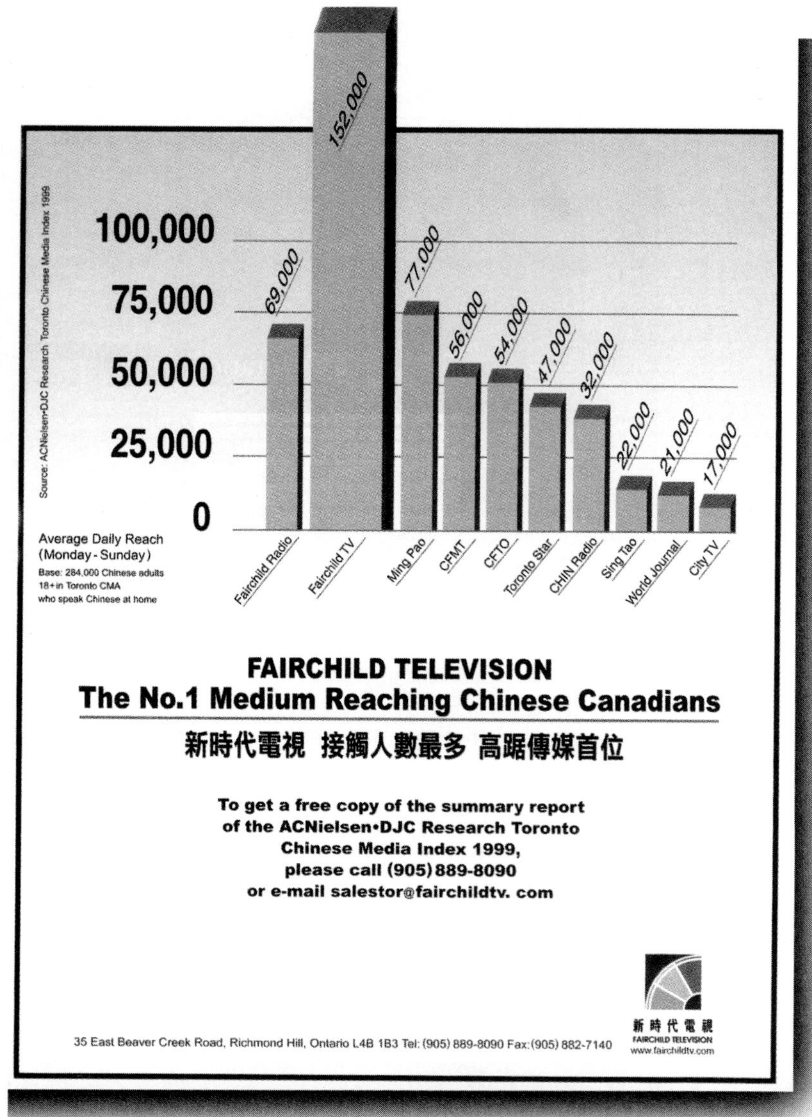

the lower class. Upper-class consumers use credit cards for convenience, whereas lower-class consumers use cards as a type of financial loan.[19]

A final example, and one of particular interest to communication managers, is the differences in media habits. Lower-class consumers tend to depend more on broadcasting for news and sports, and they are devoted to television for entertainment. The late-night television audience is largely upper class. These viewers also watch public affairs programs and public broadcasting, prefer FM to AM radio, read the daily morning newspaper, and prefer magazines targeted at their class.[20]

Groups that Influence

Group
Two or more people who interact to accomplish individual or mutual goals.

A **group** may be defined as two or more people who interact to accomplish either individual or mutual goals. For marketing communication managers, two types of groups strongly influence others' buying behaviour, so they have special relevance: reference groups and families. We examine these two groups in the following sections.

concept review

Demographic Changes, Groupings, and Social Class

1. Demographic changes can strongly influence marketing communication because they often lead to behavioural changes.
2. Demographic groupings based on factors such as size, socioeconomics, age, and values are meaningful to marketing communicators because these groupings often become market segments.
3. Social class is the position an individual has on the social scale, based on objective indicators such as occupation, education, and income, or subjective assessment. When social class differences influence buying behaviour, marketing communicators should devise strategies that match the patterns of the target class.

Reference group
Any person or group that serves as a point of comparison (or reference) for an individual in the formation of general or specific values, attitudes, or behaviour.

Contractual reference group
A group in which a person holds membership or with which he or she has regular face-to-face contact; this person approves of the group's values, attitudes, and standards.

Aspirational reference group
A group in which a person does not hold membership or with which he or she does not have face-to-face contact, but to which this person wants to belong.

Disclaimant group
A group in which a person holds membership or with which he or she has face-to-face contact, but this person disapproves of the group's values, attitudes, and behaviour.

Avoidance group
A group in which a person does not hold membership or with which he or she does not have face-to-face contact, and whose values, attitudes, and behaviour he or she disapproves of.

Norms
Expectations about what behaviour is appropriate.

Role
A prescribed way of behaving based on the position of the group member in a specific situation.

Conformity
Obedience to group norms and rules.

Reference Groups and Their Effects

A **reference group** is defined as any person or group that serves as a point of comparison (or reference) for an individual in the formation of general or specific values, attitudes, or behaviour.[21] Although reference groups are normally very specific, for practical reasons marketers classify reference groups into four types: contractual, aspirational, disclaimant, and avoidance. A **contractual reference group** is a group in which a person holds membership or has regular face-to-face contact with, and that person approves of the group's values, attitudes, and standards (for example, family, friends, neighbours, coworkers). Family and friends serve as the reference group highlighted in many marketing ommunication messages.

An **aspirational reference group** is one in which a person does not hold membership or have face-to-face contact with, but of which he or she wants to be a member. This type of group often positively influences the person's attitudes or behaviour. Most university students study and attend class because they aspire to be members of the employed reference group. A **disclaimant group** is one in which a person holds membership and does have face-to-face contact with, but he or she disapproves of the group's values, attitudes, and behaviour. For instance, the "Don't drive drunk" campaign encourages teenagers to disassociate themselves from other teenagers who drink. Finally, an **avoidance group** is one in which a person does not hold membership or have face-to-face contact with, and whose values, attitudes, and behaviour he or she disapproves of. For example, many students avoid contact with students who have flunked out.

Although we may belong to many groups, in a particular situation we generally use only one group as a point of reference. For a university student, other students tend to be the primary reference group. Reference groups have wide-ranging influence on individuals and thus on their behaviour as consumers.

Reference groups influence one another through norms, roles, and conformity. Every group has **norms**, which are expectations about what behaviour is appropriate. A **role** is a prescribed way of behaving based on the position of the group member in a specific situation. **Conformity** is obedience to these group norms and rules.

Group Communications Through Opinion Leaders

The reference group influences the communication process. Although information is ultimately processed by an individual, in many cases one or more members of a group filter, interpret, or provide information for the group. Whether people are selecting a restaurant, a lawyer, an automobile, or a brand of cake mix, they seek the advice of knowledgeable friends or acquaintances who can provide information, give advice, or actually make the decision. The individual who provides this service is called an *opinion leader*.

For several years, identifying and influencing the opinion leader have been major objectives of marketing communicators. These tasks have been complicated by the fact that opinion leaders are product specific and tend to be similar, both demographically and in personality, to those they influence. For example, both the opinion leader who shares information about stock investments and the interested investor tend to share many characteristics. However, opinion leaders view or listen to mass media, particularly media that concentrate on their area of leadership. This involvement provides a partial solution to the identification problem. It is logical to assume that people who subscribe to one or more publications on sailing are opinion leaders on sailing. These clues—involvement with sailing, their knowledge, and their subscriptions to sailing publications—signal that they may influence others in this area.

Martha Stewart
www.marthastewart.com

Some product categories have professional opinion leaders who are easy to identify. Examples include auto mechanics, beauticians, stockbrokers, and lawn and garden experts. Martha Stewart is an opinion leader in the culinary field. Perhaps the most prominent opinion leaders as a group are physicians. Not only do they suggest medications and recommend other physicians, but they also may prescribe exercise equipment, wheelchair brands, diets, or vacation sites. Consequently, marketers of medical supplies have long directed their marketing communication to the opinion leader physician rather than the patient, the ultimate user of the product.

Product usage tests, tests of advertising campaigns, and media preference studies are usually conducted on samples of individuals who are most likely to be opinion leaders. It is important that these people not only approve of the marketing mix but feel strongly enough about it to tell others. (The You Decide feature deals with many of the aspects of societal norms and group influences.)

For the marketing communicator, knowledge of reference groups serves several useful purposes. For example, you wouldn't want to use couponing if your target audience viewed coupon clippers as an avoidance group. Likewise, you wouldn't advertise in the *National Enquirer* if your target audience disliked those who read that newspaper. Finally, you would design messages using reference groups that the audience relates to in a positive manner. In this context a reference group is called a source, a topic discussed in more detail in Chapter 8.

The Family

The family remains one of the most influential elements in the macroenvironment. Our values, attitudes, and perceptions of life and the world are all formed by our families. The family is a key agent of socialization, the process by which people acquire the skills, knowledge, and attitudes necessary to function in society.

Clearly, purchasing and consumption patterns are behaviours, reflecting attitudes and skills strongly influenced by the family unit. These patterns depend in part on the type of family involved, the stage of the family's life cycle, and the method of decision making used by the family. We explore these factors next.

The Problems of Being Ethical

Business ethics catchphrases typically include no use of animals in product testing, domestic partners' benefits, concern for the rain forest, refusal to do business in China, and so forth. Express full-fledged support of a politically correct agenda and the public cheers.

Many applauded the mission of Anita Roddick's Body Shop: natural cosmetics and "Products for People Tested by People." Readers objected, however, when Jon Entine published articles in ***Business Ethics*** that exposed the Body Shop's false advertising claims, unfair treatment of franchises, and other ethical slips. Gordon Roddick, Anita's husband, objected, too. His response, however, confirmed some key points—the Body Shop used synthetics to colour, perfume, and preserve its products.

Ben & Jerry's Homemade Inc. is often cited as a model of social responsibility. Its ice cream contains all-natural ingredients; its founders donate profits to charity. But the company's self-audit, eventually released to shareholders and the public, showed that the Cherry Garcia flavour contained sulphur dioxide preservatives, and some flavours contained margarine, not butter. Further, due to lacklustre financial performance and stiff competition, charitable contributions were decreased.

An ethical business does more than tout its ethics agenda. Once the agenda is set, then, we shouldn't stop asking questions about basic ethical issues. Which is more important—no animal testing or the fair and honest treatment of franchises? Commitment to the rain forests or truth in labelling? Charitable contributions or fairness to shareholders?

Should a business ethics agenda set ethical standards? No one checks to see that firms with commendable social agendas aren't just using them as marketing ploys designed to maximize returns. Stating certain social goals is not the equivalent of acting ethically in business. Though we may want to believe that commitment to social issues is a good measure of ethical conduct, it is not an absolute determinant of fairness and honesty.

You Decide

1. Do you feel that these companies were misleading to position themselves as socially responsible?
2. How should these companies respond to consumers about the conflicts between their images and their actions?
3. Now assume you are a stockholder of these companies. Do your views of their actions change?

Source: Adapted from Marianne M. Jennings, "Confessions of a Business Ethicist," *Wall Street Journal*, 25 September 1995, A14; Marianne M. Jennings, "What's Going On," originally aired on National Public Radio, All Things Considered, 18 March 1996. Internet: www.swcollege.com/bef/jennings/br_whats_going_3.18.96.

The Body Shop
www.bodyshop.com

Nuclear family
Two adults of the opposite sex, living with their own or adopted children.

The Canadian Family

Approximately 50 percent of Canadians marry and spend the majority of their adult lives as members of a **nuclear family**, which consists of two adults of the opposite sex, living in a socially approved sexual relationship, and their own or adopted children. A nuclear family may be the family of orientation, which is the family a person is born or adopted into, or the family of procreation, which is the family formed by marriage. The family of orientation is the source of many of our attitudes and values. Although we carry many of these values and attitudes into the family of procreation, lifestyle and purchasing patterns usually shift drastically after marriage. The *extended family* is the nuclear family plus all other close relations—grandparents, aunts, uncles, and cousins. Since World War II, the extended family has become less important to Canadians but remains influential in some subcultures.

Within traditional nuclear families in Canada, one important change has occurred: We have become a nation of small families. Lower birth rates mean fewer children per family. Consequently, most Canadians are not likely to

As the middle-age group of consumers grows, discretionary spending on luxury automobiles is likely to increase. This Jaguar ad is aimed at people who want an exceptional automobile.

identify with a portrayal of a large family interacting in a television ad. In fact, the ad might create a negative response. However, for single mothers with even a few children, providing a good education can be difficult. The Toyota ad on the next page addresses this issue.

Divorce is a significant phenomenon that impacts many Canadian families. Approximately 50 percent of all first marriages in Canada end in divorce although most first marriage divorces are followed by remarriage. The result of these remarriages is often an aggregate, or blended, family, in which two previously separate families are merged into one family unit.

Of course, divorce may also create a household made of just one person or a household headed by a single parent. Single-parent households represent about 15 percent of all family units in Canada. The sheer size of this family category has definite marketing implications. For example, convenience items, day-care centres, and appliances safe enough for young children to use without supervision have all become important to the single-parent family. When and what type of media should be used to deliver the marketing communication message must be adjusted to reach this type of family. Most single parents do not have time to read newspapers and magazines regularly. Nor do single parents watch television until late at night after the children go to bed and the kitchen is cleaned. A message delivered through late-night television or direct mail, then, is more likely to be seen or read.

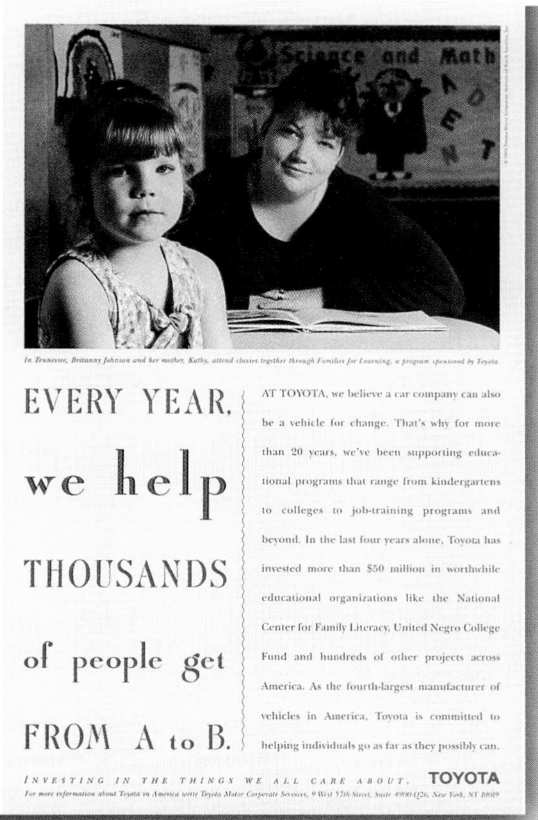

This ad by Toyota targets an ongoing concern for Canadian families. Do you think the ad is effective?

Family Decision Making

For more than 40 years, marketers have been studying how families make their purchasing decisions. How many members are involved in each decision? How are they involved? How does their influence work on the outcome? And what is the best way to reach each of them?

Table 5.5 shows some consumer roles played by members of a typical family. Decisions about purchases depend in part on which family member takes on which role. Studies of husband-wife decision making usually classify the decisions as being husband-dominated, wife-dominated, joint, or autonomous. These influences are quite fluid and depend on the specific product features under consideration. Consequently, marketing communicators must ensure that they are portraying the husband and wife correctly in various decision-making scenarios.

Children play an important role in family decision making. Researchers in one study observed the interaction between parents and children during the purchase of breakfast foods. In 516 episodes the two most frequent scenarios were (1) the child demands a particular brand of cereal and the parent yields (30 percent), and (2) the parent invites the child to select a brand, the child does so, and the parent agrees with the selection (19 percent). Regardless of whether the parent or the child initiates the selection, the child seems to direct the brand selection for breakfast food. Recognizing the influence of children, many firms target young children in their promotions. Cereals are often positioned as after-school snacks and include toys and games as part of the package or offer a prize or premium.

Table 5.5 CONSUMER ROLES WITHIN A FAMILY

Role	Description
Stimulator	First mentions the product or service
Filter	Regulates the flow of information about consumer goods
Influencer	Helps shape other people's evaluation of goods or services
Decider	Makes the decision to buy or consume the product
Preparer	Converts the goods to a form that can be consumed
Consumer	Uses or consumes the product
Monitor	Regulates consumption by other family members
Maintainer	Services or repairs goods
Disposer	Discards goods that are no longer wanted or needed

Source: Robert B. Settle and Pamela L. Alreck, ***Why They Buy: American Consumers Inside and Out***. Copyright 1986 by John Wiley & Sons. Reprinted by permission of John Wiley & Sons, Inc.

THE FAMILY LIFE CYCLE

According to *the family life cycle theory* a family's needs and wants change as it moves through a series of distinct stages. A number of classification systems are available to define stages of the family life cycle. All such systems use age, assumed income, marital status, and the presence of children as the variables that define a family's life cycle stage. According to this theory, financial burden and the presence of children dramatically impact purchase decisions. To illustrate, the purchase priorities of single parents with preschool children will be very different from those of middle-aged married couples with no dependent children.

For marketing communication managers, changes in the family life cycle offer opportunities to match strategies with particular life stages. A company such as Eastman Kodak uses diverse ads in different media to match the stage of the family life cycle. On the one hand, the "young, unmarried, childless" individual has little money for photography and associates picture taking with pleasurable events such as vacations. With this in mind, the Kodak ads in such magazines as *Seventeen* and *Rolling Stone* emphasize the low cost of Kodak cameras and show young people preserving enjoyable times. The "married with preschool children" group, on the other hand, is very involved in picture taking. Network television, direct mail, and print ads in magazines such as *Parents* portray the joy of saving the moments of childhood through photographs.

This London Life ad targets older consumers who are interested in financial services that will protect their assets in later years.

concept review

Groups that Influence

Two main types of groups influence the consumer: reference groups and the family.

1. The reference group serves as a point of comparison for an individual in the formation of general or specific values.
2. The family forms many of our values, attitudes, and perceptions of life and the world.

summary

1. Describe how culture and subculture affect marketing communication.

   Marketing communication strategists who plan to operate in the dynamic marketing environment of the twenty-first century must continuously monitor and evaluate the sociocultural environment. Culture, the broadest element of the sociocultural environment, consists of three components. The first, beliefs, reflects our knowledge and assessment of something. The second component, values, is divided into core values and secondary values. Core values predominate within a culture, whereas secondary values predominate at the subculture or personal level. Both types help us make choices in everyday life. The final component is customs, overt modes of behaviour prescribed in a culture.

2. List and explain demographic factors that influence marketing communication.

   Demographic characteristics are elements we can observe about the individual. Six general demographic trends that influence marketing communication in Canada are the following: aging population, relatively slow population growth, continued increase in education and white-collar employment, increasing ethnic diversity, decline of the traditional family, and geographic mobility of the population. In addition, three age-related demographic segments (elders, boomers, and Gen-Xers) have communication implications because each responds uniquely to communication.

3. Discuss the role that social class plays in a culture.

   Demographic traits are often related to another key element of the sociocultural environment: social class. People in different social classes tend to follow different lifestyles, but the relevance of social class to promotion strategies depends on the product involved.

4. Summarize how social groups can influence and are influenced by marketing communication.

   The family and other reference groups shape values, attitudes, and behaviour. People tend to conform to the norms and roles established by their reference groups, and they often turn to opinion leaders within these groups for guidance. The most important reference group remains the family, which is the key agent of socialization. Consumer purchases are influenced by the type of household people live in, by their current stage in the family life cycle, and by their methods of family decision making. Changes in families and households, such as recent increases in the numbers of single-person and single-parent households, offer dramatic challenges and opportunities for marketing communication managers.

points to ponder

Review the Facts

1. Define the sociocultural environment.
2. What are core values? Secondary values?
3. What is a subculture?
4. What are norms? Roles? Conformity?

Master the Concepts

5. What factors can be used to distinguish one subculture from others? What does a culture have in common with its subcultures?
6. Outline the major demographic trends in Canada.

Apply Your Knowledge

7. Boomers were presented as one of the most important demographic groups. Identify three specific marketing communication strategies that would be appropriate for reaching (1) the older baby boomers and (2) the youngest baby boomers.
8. Describe a marketing communication strategy for a compact disc player that would be appropriate for Gen-Xers.
9. Gold Star is a company that manufactures dual-track video players. It would like to design a marketing communication strategy targeted at the Canadian family. What are the key considerations Gold Star should identify before targeting this group? Is there a typical Canadian family?

suggested projects

1. (Writing Project) Trace the baby-boom generation through the year 2020. Graphically show the kinds of goods and services baby boomers will need as they move toward that date. Write a brief memo (1 to 2 pages) analysing how you arrived at the conclusions shown on your graph.
2. Review the purchase decision-making process your family has followed during the last year. Are purchasing decisions made exclusively by one member of your family? Jointly?
3. (Internet Project) As discussed in this chapter, the Stanford Research Institute's (SRI) Values and Lifestyles Program 2 (VALS2) can help marketers understand consumer psychographics and increase marketing communication effectiveness. Log on to SRI's Web site (future.sri.com) and follow the site's links to the VALS2 page. What kind of companies have used VALS2 and for what purpose?

   Now determine your own psychographic profile by navigating to the on-screen survey and entering your responses. What is your primary type in the VALS 2 framework?

The Poor as a Market Segment

People tend to think of others as being like themselves. When you hear the phrase "young adults," you probably think of other students, not of 20-year-olds living in poverty with no job, income, or prospects. This tendency holds true in corporate boardrooms and in advertising agencies, and, because top executives and marketers are generally better off than the average person, many marketing campaigns are pitched at richer customers. As Harvard Business School professor John Quelch puts it, "The marketing community has no aspirations to address the needs of a demographic group of which it is not a member."

S. C. Johnson & Son, Inc., manufacturer of Raid, is an exception to this rule. It all began in 1992 when Lisa Peters, account supervisor at BR & R Communication was faced with the unenviable task of finding new market opportunities for the 40-year-old Raid brand. With the migration of the North American population toward urban housing, improvements in insulation, and the popularity of commercial exterminators, the market for home pest-exterminator products such as Raid had declined steadily.

After several months of research, Lisa determined that there was one market segment that still had a need for products such as Raid. Her research found that in the United States, 78 to 98 percent of inner-city urban homes and apartments are infested with cockroaches. Market testing indicated that the current Raid formulation was not effective in dealing with these super bugs.

The lab went to work and produced a new-and-improved version of Raid they named Raid Max. Next, the product was test-marketed in several Chicago housing developments—samples were distributed to 1500 families. After 30 days, test families were queried about both the effectiveness of the product and its affordability. The product would prove profitable if a 650-mL aerosol can could be sold for at least $1.75. Lisa's research indicated that this low-income consumer group could and would pay this amount. The product was launched in the spring of 1993.

The following year the company added a health spin. It seems that in addition to being unsightly, the little devils are the leading cause of asthma and allergies in many urban cities. Johnson hired medical specialists to test people for cockroach allergies and recruited two minority entomologists to answer questions about cockroach asthma and allergies and tell consumers how to control the bugs. At the same time, the company rolled out its Raid Max Roach Bait Plus Egg Stoppers, which uses a special ingredient that the company claims "renders cockroaches sterile."

The company also developed a series of educational brochures. The copy was kept simple and there were a lot of graphics. The company tapped into community leaders to help make the pitch. "We want to be invited in," Peters said. "We don't want to just appear on a billboard . . . . when consumers go into the store, they remember that the company cared enough to come into the neighbourhoods and provided them with something they can use to make a difference."

Case Questions

1. Which sociocultural factors proved most important in the success of Raid Max?
2. How would you evaluate the approach Johnson used in marketing to this consumer group?
3. If you were the marketing communications director with this information, what consistent theme or themes would you use to promote Raid Plus Egg Stoppers? Name three types of marketing communication you would use and explain your choices.

Sources: Jan Larsen, "Fact, Fiction and Homeless," ***American Demographics***, August 1996, pp. 14–15; Paula Mergenhagen, "What Can Minimum Wage Buy?," ***American Demographics***, January 1996, pp. 32–36; Donald L. Bartlett and James B. Steele, "American Dream Turns Into Nightmare For Many," ***The Denver Post***, Sunday September 1996, 31A–32A.

S.C. Johnson & Son, Inc.
www.scjohnsonwax.com

6

Decision Making in the New Marketplace

chapter objectives

After completing your work on this chapter, you should be able to

- Describe how the psychological factors of motivation, learning, and attitudes affect consumer decision making.
- Explain how consumers make complex and simple decisions and how marketing communication can influence this process.
- Contrast organizational and consumer buying behaviour.

Financial Service Clients and Their Needs

The financial services sector in North America is undergoing a significant degree of change. Perhaps the most notable change is what analysts have dubbed the "melting pot of financial services." What does this mean? This expression is used to describe the unprecedented number of mergers, acquisitions, and regulatory changes that have resulted in a notable decrease in the number of financial service providers, and an increase in the number of services offered by the remaining firms.

It has been argued by some that this is good news for consumers because of the evolution towards convenient one-stop shopping. For instance, major Canadian banks now offer a limited line of insurance products, and some insurance and investment firms offer mortgage financing. Only time will tell whether these changes will really benefit consumers in the long term. However, analysts generally agree that these changes are driven, in part, by pressure on this sector to provide the level of value demanded by today's consumers. Unfortunately, individual clients' needs vary greatly.

How do you attract prospective clients and retain their business over the long haul? Ask financial service professionals, and you're likely to hear one phrase continually repeated: needs-based selling. It means identifying an individual's needs and recommending an appropriate plan to help satisfy those needs. This approach enables marketers with numerous products to modify their sales strategies to accommodate the demands of most clients.

Blair D. Hayden, a manager with London Life, uses this approach and he ensures his salespeople use it religiously. According to Hayden, "There's no better way to build long-term relationships with clients." To retain clients, you need to know your products, but of equal importance is the ability to be authentic and human, not mechanical and sales-oriented. Focusing on a client's needs instead of trying to sell a particular product is the best way to accomplish this goal."

James Pinnock agrees. Pinnock is managing director of Stanley Mutual Insurance. Stanley Mutual is a small but progressive insurance mutual that is successful in the face of increasing competition. He manages his sales force so that clients and prospects feel as if they have a strong relationship with both their agent and Stanley Mutual. "My agents need to analyse each client's insurance needs," he says. "Then, using Stanley Mutual's product line or by working with our professionals to develop a product, the agent recommends what is appropriate for that client." Pinnock admits that having agents building business through needs-based selling is more time-consuming than selling standardized product over the Internet, but he says it's worth it. "People develop a level of trust and they come to realize that we're here for them when they have an insurance claim and have questions regarding their policy or coverage needs."

While there are as many ways to practise needs-based selling as there are investment professionals, the bottom line on this strategy is that it's well received by most individuals. And understandably so. Most people respond favourably to those who want to help.

Source: Quotations extracted from Blair Hayden's presentation to sales force management students at the University of New Brunswick (February 1999), and a personal interview with James Pinnock (June 1998). Used with permission.

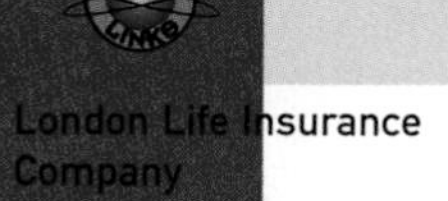

London Life Insurance Company
www.londonlife.com

Chapter Overview

In Chapter 1 we stressed that to succeed in today's business environment marketers must focus on customers' needs and serve those needs well. Whether the term for this approach is relationship marketing or needs-based selling, the outcome should be the same—a mutual commitment and trust between the marketer and the customer.

Chapter 5 described sociocultural factors—such as culture, social class, and reference groups—that marketing communicators must understand to influence buyer behaviour. But marketing communicators must also understand the psychological factors that influence consumer decisions. These factors include motives, attitudes, and personalities.

In this chapter we investigate psychological traits that affect purchasing decisions, the types and process of consumer decision making, and purchase and postpurchase consumer behaviour. Most importantly, we see how the psychology of consumer behaviour affects marketing communication programs. We also examine how organizations, and the people in them, make decisions and how the psychology of those decisions affects marketing communication programs.

The difficulties in understanding buyer behaviour are daunting. People themselves often do not understand why they buy some products rather than others. Countless variations in consumer behaviour occur simply because each person is an individual with a unique personality. Predicting consumer behaviour becomes even more difficult for companies that are trying to influence the consumer decisions of people from many different cultures. Despite difficulties, businesses must search for common threads so that they can appeal to many people with one marketing communication program.

We start with a model of consumer decision making, as shown in Figure 6.1. Our focus is on answering this question: What does the marketing

Figure 6.1 EXTERNAL INFLUENCES AND INTERNAL FACTORS AND PROCESSES

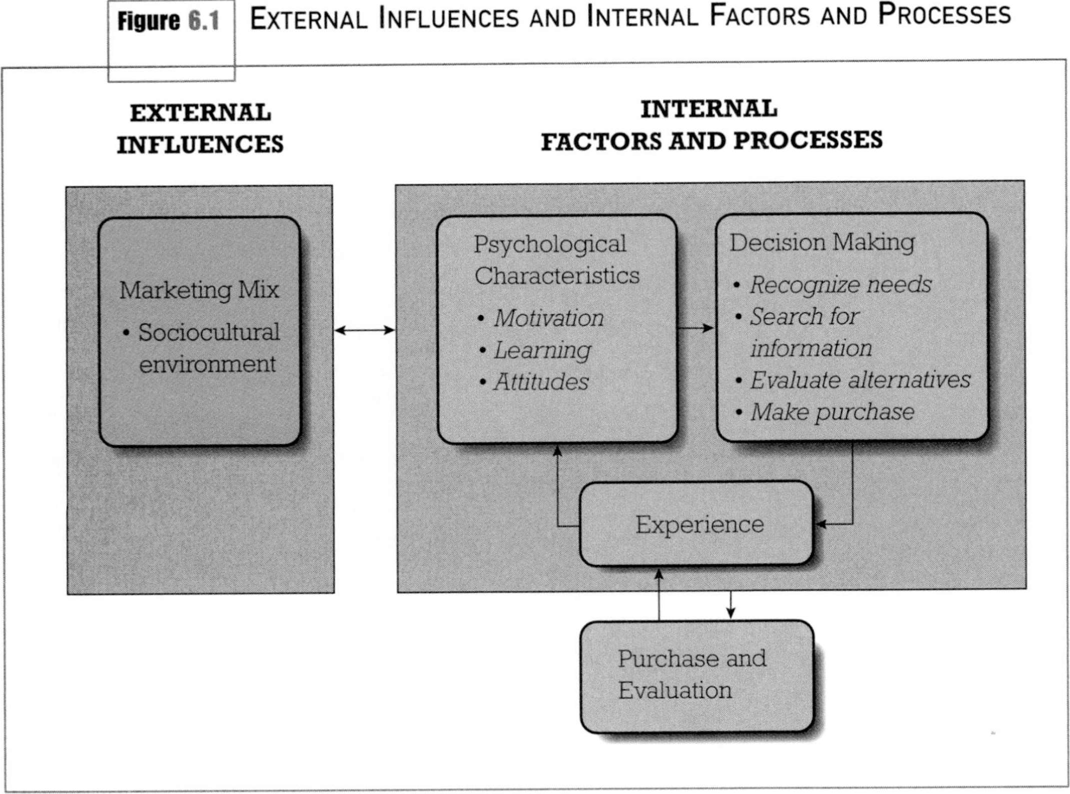

communication strategist need to know about human behaviour to create effective messages? We first examine the psychological characteristics of motivation, learning, and attitudes shown in Figure 6.1.

THE PSYCHOLOGICAL BACKGROUND

Although we focus on individual consumers throughout this chapter, all the members of the stakeholder audiences—employees, community members, suppliers, resellers, and so forth—are people who exhibit and are influenced by psychological factors. The buying behaviour we explore here applies to all types of audience members, though integrated marketing communication managers may have to adapt their communication strategy to each audience group. For instance, motivating an employee to work harder to prepare more pizza may require a different set of cues (such as financial incentives or more responsibility) than motivating a consumer to purchase pizza, or a cheese supplier to deliver its product to the pizza maker on time.

Regardless of which stakeholder audience group we choose to communicate with, a basic understanding of what makes that person tick is essential. Suppose you were trying to sell lights to a buyer in an industrial plant who wanted powerful outdoor security lights. Trying to sell that buyer decorative lamps would probably get you nowhere. If sellers do not appeal to the right motive, they will likely lose the sale. Similarly, a business that does not accommodate its customers' beliefs, interests, attitudes, self-images, or other psychological characteristics risks losing customers. A business should learn about its customers—why customers do or do not buy their products, where and how they make purchases, and when. Gathering such information may reveal marketing communication opportunities. Next, we introduce three key aspects of consumer behaviour psychology: motivation, learning, and attitudes.

MOTIVATION

Motive
An inner drive or pressure to act in order to eliminate tension, to satisfy a need or want, to solve a problem, or to restore a sense of equilibrium.

A **motive** is an inner drive or pressure to act in order to eliminate tension, to satisfy a need or want, to solve a problem, or to restore a sense of equilibrium. A need or desire must be aroused to serve as a motive. The sources of arousal may be internal (biological or psychological) or environmental. Hunger, for example, may be stimulated by a lack of food, by thoughts about food, or by a food commercial that shows a remarkable picture of your favourite meal.

Marketing communication managers need to understand what motives stimulate consumer behaviour and how these motives and behaviours are influenced by specific situations. Identifying motives is the first step in this task. Because each individual's personal development is unique, so are each person's motives.[1] For example, if you buy a particular brand of soft drink on a hot summer day, that decision may reflect both your need to satisfy thirst and your need for self-expression. Although marketers cannot control your thirst, they can influence your choice of a soft drink.

Ford Motor Company of Canada
www.ford.ca

The number of possible motives for consumer behaviour is vast. Many have attempted to classify these motives, but no one classification is complete or universally accepted. Probably the classification most closely associated with marketing communication divides motives into rational and emotional motives.

Rational motives
Are supported by a reasoning process that consumers perceive as being acceptable to their peers.

Rational motives are supported by a reasoning process that consumers perceive as being rational (that is, acceptable) to their peers. For example, an investor may decide to invest in Ford Motors stock because her father always bought Fords. Whether this reasoning is sound is irrelevant. What matters is that the individual believes the motivation is rational. Rational motives commonly include criteria such as convenience, price, risk, performance, endurance, delivery time, and reliability.

Emotional motives
Are characterized by feelings that may emerge without careful thought or consideration of social consequences.

Latent motives
Emotional motives that lie below consciousness.

Manifest motives
Motives that people are conscious of but are often unwilling to acknowledge.

Emotional motives are characterized by feelings that may emerge without careful thought or consideration of social consequences.[2] People are often unwilling to admit emotional motives openly. Sometimes these motives—known as **latent motives**—lie below consciousness. It would probably be unwise to emphasize these motives in marketing messages because consumers might not recognize that they are relevant. Motives that people are conscious of but are often unwilling to acknowledge are **manifest motives**. Being afraid of snakes might be an example. A great many emotional motives exist, but generally those most important in marketing include status, prestige, conformity, sex, loneliness, self-esteem, and the desire to be different.

Motives, both rational and emotional, may be stimulated through the use of marketing communication tools that provide product information, extra incentives, entertainment, and so forth. Motorola, for instance, uses a special year-long team event to motivate its employees. The event is motivating because it addresses employees' need to increase self-esteem, improve status, and gain financial reward. The event is called the Total Customer Satisfaction Team Competition. The winning teams, selected by Motorola's top managers, are judged both by how they achieved superior customer service and how that service resulted in bottom-line benefits.[3]

Learning
A process of taking in information, processing it along with existing information, and producing new knowledge.

Cue
Persuades the direction the individual will follow to satisfy the goal of the ad.

Learning

Learning starts with motivation. Needs and goals stimulate motivation, which in turn, spurs learning. **Learning** is a process of taking in information, processing it along with existing information, and producing new knowledge. Suppose a customer is motivated to begin an exercise program because he or she is gaining weight and feeling lethargic. A **cue**—in this case an ad for a new health club—persuades the direction the individual will follow to satisfy the goal of losing weight. The message in the health club ad, however, will only serve as a cue if it is consistent with the person's expectations. If he or she has already tried to lose weight at other health clubs, the ad will not create a response. Can you spot the message designed to serve as a cue in the ad for Cantel AT&T™'s national Digital PCs network?

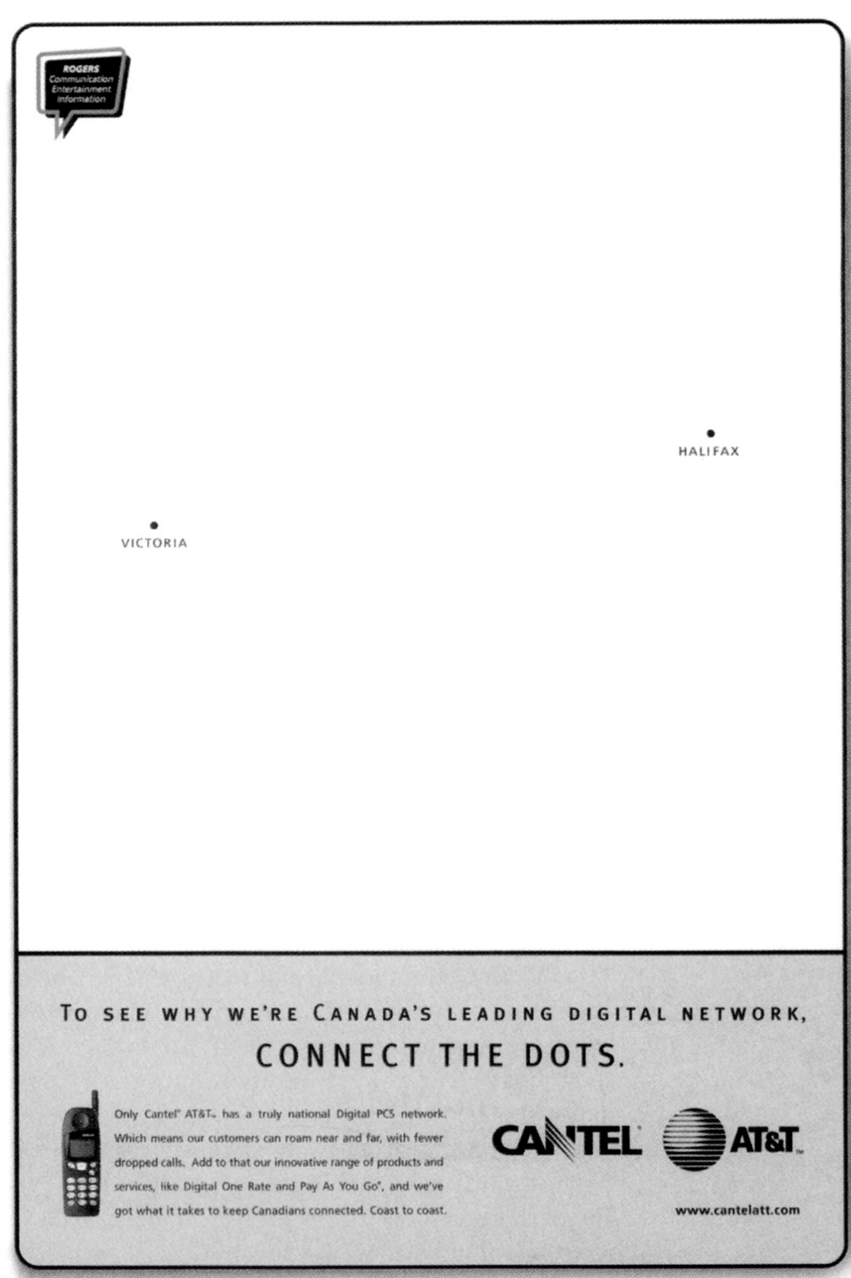

Can you spot the message in this ad for Cantel AT&T™ that is designed to serve as a cue?

The Spike Lee ad for milk is designed to create a conditioned response—those consumers who like Spike should now feel positively about milk.

Response
How an individual reacts to a cue.

Positive reinforcement
A positive response to a cue.

Negative reinforcement
A negative response to a cue.

Classical conditioning
A response learned as a result of the pairing of two stimuli.

Conditioned response
That which has been learned as a result of the pairing of stimuli.

Instrumental conditioning
A response learned or strengthened because it has been associated with certain consequences.

Reinforced
The resulting condition of a behaviour when a consumer has a positive or negative response to a product.

How an individual reacts to a cue constitutes his or her **response**. Learning can take place even if the response is not overt. A positive response to a cue is called **positive reinforcement**; in the future the same cue is again likely to produce a similar reaction. If a past response to a cue produced an unpleasant experience, then **negative reinforcement** has taken place.

Psychologists distinguish two basic types of behavioural learning: classical conditioning and instrumental conditioning. In **classical conditioning** a response is learned as a result of the pairing of two stimuli. Assume that Spike Lee elicits positive feelings in members of an audience. If they repeatedly see him and milk together in a commercial, then eventually the sight of milk alone will elicit those positive feelings. In the language of classical conditioning, Spike Lee and milk are stimuli that have been paired. The positive reaction to milk is a **conditioned response** that has been learned as a result of the pairing of the stimuli.

In **instrumental conditioning** a response is learned or strengthened because it has been associated with certain consequences. If buying milk brings the reward of a good-tasting, healthy drink, then the act of buying milk is **reinforced** and is more likely to occur in the future.

Attitudes

Attitude
An enduring disposition, favourable or unfavourable, toward an idea, a person, a thing, or a situation.

Motivation and learning both play a part in forming the third component of the psychological background for consumer behaviour: attitudes. An **attitude** is an enduring disposition, favourable or unfavourable, toward an idea, a person, a thing, or a situation. Thus, attitudes toward brands are tendencies to evaluate brands in a consistently favourable or unfavourable way. Each attitude has three components: cognitive, affective, or behavioural. All three components must be consistent for enduring attitudes to result.

Cognitive component
Includes beliefs and knowledge about the object of the attitude.

The **cognitive component** includes beliefs and knowledge about the object of the attitude. For example, you might believe that Shell Oil is a major petroleum manufacturer, an aggressive marketer, and is socially responsible. Each of these beliefs reflects knowledge about an attribute of the company. The sum of your beliefs about Shell Oil represents the cognitive component of an attitude toward the company.

Affective component
Feelings expressed toward the object advertised.

If you say "I hate Shell Oil" or "I feel like the gasoline from Shell Oil is better than any other," you are expressing the **affective aspect** of an attitude. Feelings about the object make up the affective component of an attitude.

Behavioural component
Actions taken toward the object of an attitude.

Actions taken toward the object of an attitude constitute the **behavioural component** of an attitude. Buying a product, recommending a company to friends, or requesting information are examples of behavioural components. Behaviour is usually directed toward an entire object and is therefore not likely to be attribute specific.

A great deal of marketing strategy is based on the idea that the cognitive, affective, and behavioural components of an attitude tend to be consistent. Thus, if a company like Intel can change the cognitive component of people's attitudes—that is, change people's beliefs about the firm—their feelings and actions about the company may also change.[4] However, this assumption is more true in certain decision settings than others.[5]

The situation, or consumer attitudes toward the situation, play an important role in how well attitudes predict behaviour. For example, suppose a consumer loves thick-crust pizza but does not like the fact that the pizza restaurant serving the product allows smoking. Regardless of his or her positive feelings about the product, the situation precludes the possibility that a purchase will be made.

Air Canada
www.aircanada.ca

The Multiattribute Attitude Model

In general, the simple linkage between beliefs, feelings, and behaviour has not held up. Instead, attitude research has shown that these three elements are not equivalent. Rather, some components are far more important than others in forming attitudes. For instance, the fact that Air Canada experienced extended flight delays during an ice storm in 1998 is an event that consumers may focus on rather than Air Canada's safety record or advertising.

Multiattribute attitude model
Helpful with message strategy, it systematically predicts individuals' attitudes toward an object by examining their reactions to specific object attributes.

Each element contains a set of attributes relevant to the object considered. Marketing communication managers who know which attitude is most salient can design their message strategy with that attribute in mind. The **multiattribute attitude model** is quite helpful with message strategy in that it systematically predicts individuals' attitudes toward an object by examining their reactions to specific object attributes.[6]

According to the multiattribute attitude model, a person's overall attitude toward a brand can be measured by determining (1) the consumer's evaluation of individual brand or product attributes, (2) the consumer's ideal for those attributes, and (3) the importance the consumer assigns to those attributes. The difference between the evaluation of each attribute and the customer's ideal, weighted by the importance of that attribute, determines the strength of the attitude. This definition may be formulated in the following way:

$$A_b = \sum_{l=i}^{n} W_i[I_i - X_{ib}]$$

in which:

$A_{(b)}$	=	the consumer's attitude toward a particular object
$W_{(i)}$	=	the importance the consumer attaches to attribute i
$I(i)$	=	the consumer's ideal performance on attribute i
$X_{(ib)}$	=	the consumer's belief about object b's performance on attribute i
n	=	number of attributes considered

As an example, suppose that a consumer perceives Crest toothpaste to have the following levels of performance on four attributes:

	1	2	3	4	5	6	7	
Low price		1			X			High price
Good taste			1	X				Poor taste
High cavity prevention	1	X						Low cavity prevention
Good breath freshener		1				X		Poor breath freshener

In this example, as shown by the Xs, the consumer believes that Crest has a fairly high price, has a fair taste, has better-than-average cavity prevention, and is a poor breath freshener. The consumer's ideal toothpaste, as shown by the Is, would be low priced, taste good, prevent cavities, and be a good breath freshener. For each attribute, the consumer assigns an importance weight.

Attribute	Importance
Price	10
Taste	20
Cavity prevention	50
Breath freshening	20
Total	100 points

The list shows that cavity prevention is the most important attribute, followed by flavour, breath freshening, and price. Now let's examine each attribute. By taking the difference between the ideal score and the actual score times its weight, we see that the consumer's attitude score toward Crest toothpaste is as follows:

$$
\begin{aligned}
A(\text{Crest}) &= (10)(2 - 5) + (20)(3 - 4) + (50)(1 - 3) + (20)(2 - 6) \\
&= 10(3) + 20(1) + 50(2) + 20(4) \\
&= 30 + 20 + 100 + 80 \\
&= 230
\end{aligned}
$$

Determining whether this attitude score of 230 is good or bad can only be ascertained by computing an attitude index with 0 as the strongest favourable attitude (that is, perceived performance and ideal scores are identical) and the other end of the index reflecting the maximum possible difference between desired and perceived beliefs.

In this example the maximum possible difference is 530. Therefore, an attitude score of 230 suggests a somewhat favourable attitude toward Crest, as it is on the favourable half of the index. A comparison of this attitude score with the scores for competing brands shows how consumers perceive Crest relative to other brands. This comparison might show Crest in a more favourable or less favourable light when compared with competitors.

Crest
www.crestsmiles.com

INFLUENCING ATTITUDES

How easily can attitudes be changed? The answer depends to an extent on two characteristics of the attitude: its centrality and its intensity. **Centrality** depends on the degree to which an attitude is tied to values. Note that although personal values influence attitudes, the two are distinct. Values are not tied to a specific situation or object; they are standards that guide behaviour and influence beliefs and attitudes. People have a large number of beliefs, a smaller number of attitudes, and even fewer values. The stronger the relationship between an attitude and a person's values, the greater the centrality of the attitude.

Centrality
A measure that depends on the degree to which an attitude is tied to values.

For example, for a person who places a high value on thriftiness, social responsibility, and ecology, a favourable attitude toward recyclable containers is likely to have high centrality. If the centrality of an attitude is high, then changing it would create inconsistency between the attitude and a person's values. Not surprisingly, research suggests that the more central an attitude is, the more difficult it is to change.[7]

Intensity depends on the affective component of an attitude. The strength of feeling toward the object of an attitude constitutes the intensity of the attitude. Intense attitudes are difficult to change. Consequently, most marketing efforts are directed at creating minor changes in attitudes—from negative to neutral, from neutral to positive, or from positive to more positive. A person who holds an intensely negative attitude toward a product or idea might best be dropped as a target audience member.

Intensity
A measure of the strength of feeling toward the object of an attitude.

Change in consumers' attitudes is most likely to occur when people are open-minded in their beliefs or when an existing attitude is weak, such as an attitude based on poor information. However, if people have strong brand loyalty, changing their attitudes will be difficult. A marketing communication manager must use highly persuasive communication to change one or more of the three attitude components. For instance, the use of coupons, free samples, or cents-off sales might induce open-minded buyers to change their behavioural

Lack of Continuity Down Under

Australia has been slow to accept programs that offer points as a bonus for customer loyalty. The recent spate of loyalty program activity may prove that its slow start was a costly gamble.

To compete with international carriers, after a merger of Qantas with Australian Airlines, the "new" Qantas launched Australia's first frequent-flyer program. The only other national competitor, Ansett, followed simultaneously. The Qantas program now holds 2.5 million members. According to published industry estimates, the Qantas program has the highest penetration per head of population of any airline loyalty program in the world.

The Qantas co-branded credit card, the Qantas Telstra Visa card, has been rated by Visa as the most successful co-brand ever launched in the world. Members accumulate points mainly through flying with Qantas or its 15 Frequent Flyer airline partners. Points are awarded according to the class of travel and kilometers flown. Points may also be accumulated through qualified transactions with more than 4000 hotels around the world and with selected car rental companies. Points earned in the credit card loyalty programs of American Express and Qantas Telstra Visa and selected programs of a number of banks may be converted to Qantas Frequent Flyer points. Co-branding and partnering with other loyalty programs helped Qantas move ahead in the loyalty program battle.

But the battle continues. Both Qantas and its competitor, Ansett, have opened Web sites that outline their frequent flyer programs and partners. Both companies offer enticing programs. For instance, Qantas has partnered with carriers including British Airways, American Airlines, Cathay Pacific, Aer Lingus, and SAS. Frequent-flyer points count toward increasing privileges and membership status to Blue, Silver, or Gold. With each status upgrade, members earn greater travel privileges, such as priority baggage handling, extra baggage allowance, priority check-in service, and membership in The Qantas Club. Ansett's programs are similarly enticing.

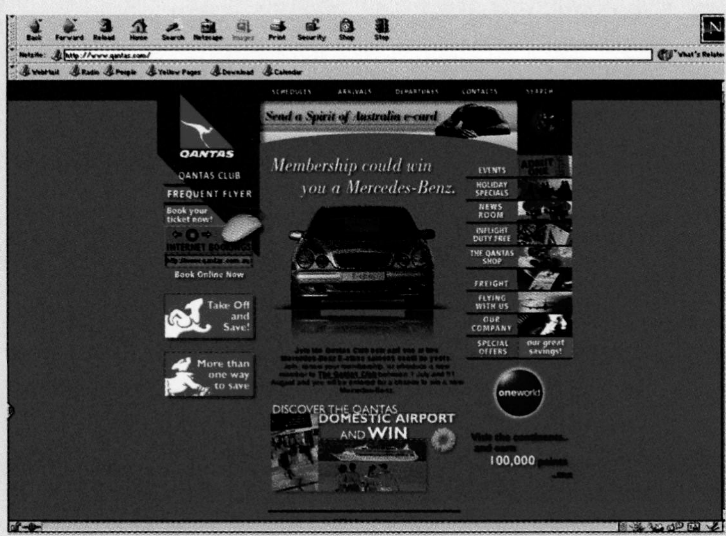

Food for Thought

1. Which component(s) or attitudes are changed through this communication strategy?
2. What happens to attitude changes when all competitors offer the same or similar incentives?
3. Imagine you are the marketing communication director for Qantas. Taking the cost of frequent-flyer miles redemption into consideration, what steps, if any, would you take to improve the frequent-flyer program?

Sources: "Frequent Flyer Membership Programs," Qantas Airlines home page (September 1996): Internet (www.qantas.com); "Ansett Frequent Flyer Travel Services and Membership Levels," Ansett Airlines home page (September 1996): Internet (www.ansett.com.au); Mike DaSilva, "Customer (Dis) Loyalty in Australia," Promo (December 1994): 53.

component—they may try a new brand. The IMC in Action feature shows how the Australian Airline Qantas attempted to change attitudes through new information and by offering incentives.

Regardless of the efforts to change attitudes, the burning question remains whether this is worth it given the uncertainty of attitudes that predict behaviour. The results of a survey conducted by Roper College Track show how attitudes translate into behaviour. The survey asked university students questions regarding their attitudes about food and meals, and what foods they purchased. Essentially, the attitudes of the students indicate that they are willing to trade quality for convenience and speed. Quick and easy meals are most attractive to students, so the microwave is an appliance that plays a major role in students' lives. Cereal is a staple. Far and away the most popular food is pizza, followed by hamburgers. Other highly regarded items are subs, chicken wings, fried mozzarella sticks, onion rings, french fries, Oreos and Chips Ahoy!, Cool Ranch Doritos, Twinkies, Mountain Dew, and Jolt![8] Any of this ring a bell?

Nabisco World
www.oreo.com

The You Decide feature that accompanies this chapter details a product category that consumers have changed their attitudes about—credit cards.

In this section we discussed the psychological background of consumer decision making. In the following sections we explore the types of decisions consumers make and how they make them.

The Curse of Plastic

After a fling with frugality in the early 1990s, consumers are back in love with their credit cards—and not just because the economy has improved. Credit-card marketers keep offering consumers more reasons to whip out plastic. They're coaxing businesses—from supermarket chains to the family dentist—to accept the cards. And by offering airline miles or rebates, they're providing consumers more incentives to use credit cards in place of cash or cheques.

Consumers love rebate products. Credit cards that offer rebates, such as the Bank of Montreal AIR MILES MasterCard, are known in the business as "co-branded" or "affinity" cards. MasterCard now has 49 million co-branded cards outstanding. More people are shopping with more plastic: Anderson Consulting says the average spender held seven cards in 1989. Today, that purse or wallet carries 11.

All the new incentives to use plastic are likely to boost consumer spending, but it's too soon to gauge the exact effect. Of course, new opportunities to charge also mean new opportunities to sink into debt. But card issuers insist that consumers are getting better at managing debt, and indeed delinquent rates are at low levels. Also, they say, a big chunk of charges gets paid the same month. A study done for Visa, for example, shows that 72 percent of grocery charges are paid by the month's end.

But critics note that most consumers don't use separate cards for food or luxury items. When the economy gets worse, they say, it will be tempting to roll over charges for essentials month after month.

Take, for example, the case of Anne Marie Moss, a 26-year-old who is in her final year of a graduate journalism program. Currently, she owes $1600 on her cards and doesn't want to push that amount any higher. "Right now I am just doing the minimum payments," says Moss. "It's just debt paying debt, which is kind of frustrating." Moss turned to plastic last summer for living expenses while serving an unpaid internship at a magazine. Plastic can be a blessing to a grad student—it can be a source of emergency loans and is convenient—but it can also be a curse.

You Decide

1. Do credit-card companies take advantage of our general weakness to spend money we don't have?
2. Is it possible to change the attitudes of consumers who use credit cards irresponsibly? If yes, can you think of any marketing communication strategies you might use to do so? Explain.
3. If you were the marketing communication director for a financial institution and you were asked to target the 17- to-25-year-old consumer market, what would you do to motivate this market to sign up for a credit card with your company?

Sources: Margret Mannix, "Unpaid Debt Can Be a Distraction—and Worse," U.S. News Online (April 30, 1996): Internet (www.usnews.com/Usnews/fair/gbcredit); Russell Mitchell, "Sorry, We Don't Take Cash," Business Week, December 12, 1994, 42.

concept review

The Psychological Background

Three components make up a person's psychological background.

- Motive. The inner drive to take action to eliminate tension, to satisfy a need or problem, or to restore a sense of equilibrium.
- Learning. A process of taking in information, processing it with existing information, and producing new knowledge. Cognitive learning involves thought and conscious awareness. Behavioural learning does not require awareness or conscious effort. It depends on an association between events.
- Attitude. An enduring disposition, favourable or unfavourable, toward an object—an idea, a person, a thing, or a situation.

This ad for office furniture targets consumers who are looking for home office solutions.

Consumer Decision-Making Processes

Complex decision making
A search for information and an evaluation of alternatives leading to a decision.

Simple decision making
A minimal information search and evaluation of alternatives leading to a decision.

So far we have investigated the psychological characteristics that influence consumer decisions. Our next question is, how does the consumer make decisions? What steps are involved in consumer decision making?

The answer depends on whether the consumer engages in simple or complex decision making. Figure 6.2 shows the differences between these two processes. Notice in the figure that **complex decision making** requires a search for information and an evaluation of alternatives, whereas simple decision making does not. In **simple decision making** some information search and alternative evaluation may occur, but these activities are minimized. Note further that evaluation after the purchase always occurs with complex decision making. In simple decision making it may or may not occur.

Figure 6.2 The Process of Complex and Simple Decision Making

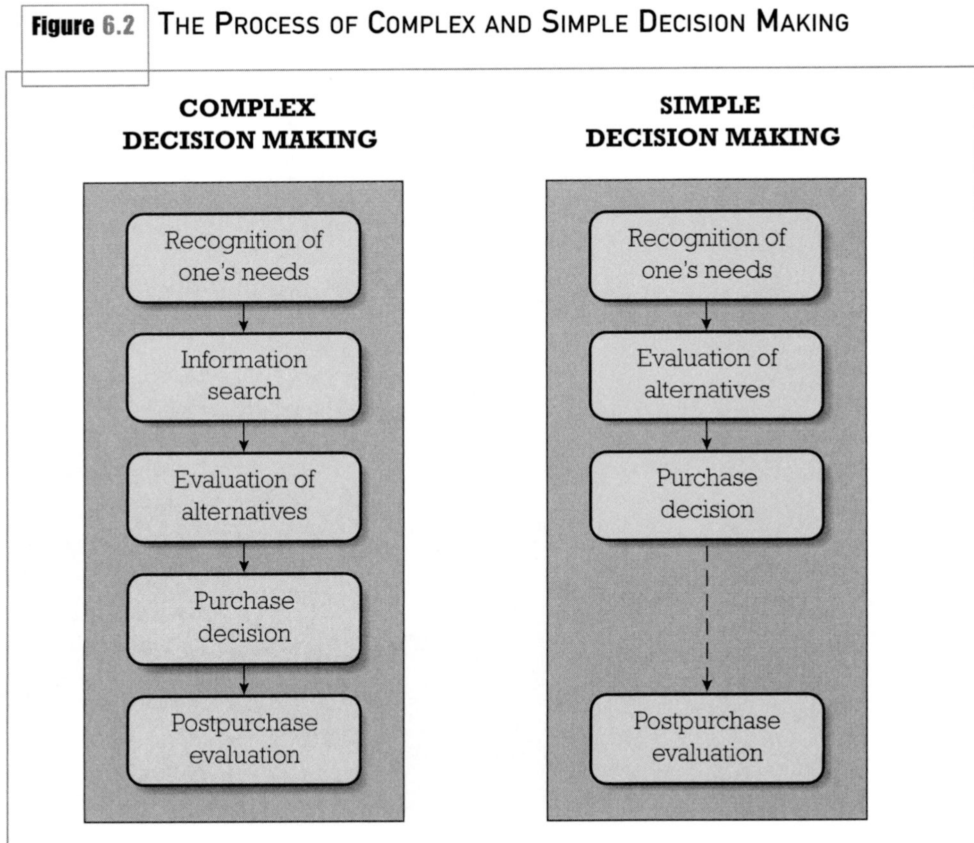

Which type of decision making occurs depends on (1) whether the decision is novel or routine and (2) the extent of the consumer's involvement with the decision.

High-involvement decisions
Those decisions that are important to the consumer.

High-involvement decisions are those that are important to the consumer. Such decisions are closely tied to the consumer's ego and self-image. They also involve some risk to the consumer—financial risk (high-priced items), social risk (products important to the peer group), or psychological risk (the wrong decision might cause the consumer some concern and anxiety). In making these decisions it is worth the consumer's time and energy to consider product alternatives carefully. A complex process of decision making is therefore more likely for high-involvement purchases, such as a new computer or new car.

Low-involvement decisions
Those that are not important to the consumer.

Low-involvement decisions are those that are not important to the consumer, such as buying a pizza or pack of gum. Financial, social, and psychological risks are not nearly as great. In such cases it may not be worth the time and effort to search for information about brands or to consider a wide range of alternatives. Consumers who make a low-involvement purchase, then, generally use a simple decision-making process.[9]

When a consumer has bought a product many times in the past, the decision making is likely to be simple, regardless of whether it is a high- or a low-involvement decision. Suppose after much care and involvement a consumer decided to bank at Scotiabank, was satisfied with the choice, and continued to bank there. The customer's careful consideration of this service product has produced *brand loyalty*, which is the result of involvement with the product decision. Once a consumer is brand loyal, a simple decision-making process is all that is required for subsequent purchases. The consumer now buys the product through **habit,** which means making a decision without the use of additional information or the evaluation of alternative choices. This is a simple but high-involvement decision.

Habit
The act of a consumer making a decision without the use of additional information or the evaluation of alternative choices.

Habitual buying may also reflect low-involvement, simple decision making. If a consumer is not highly involved in the initial decision to buy a product and makes no commitment to the product but simply responds to the positive reinforcement it provides, the person may develop a type of brand loyalty called **inertia.** The consumer thus buys the product passively. An example would be buying the newspaper every morning.

Inertia
The condition when a consumer is not highly involved in the initial decision to buy a product and makes no commitment to the product but simply responds to the positive reinforcement it provides.

Even when a consumer buys a brand for the first time, if it is an inexpensive, unexciting product that is purchased regularly, such as ballpoint pens, the consumer is likely to exert very little thought or effort in choosing the product. This type of process is a simple, low-involvement decision. Now consider the case of a consumer deciding whether to buy for the first time an expensive, personal, or emotion-laden product such as a car or medical care. It is fairly safe to assume that the consumer will expend a great deal of effort on the process. This process is a complex, high-involvement decision.

In the rest of this chapter, we examine a complex decision process to buy a new product and explore each of the steps outlined in Figure 6.2. We turn next to a consideration of how consumers recognize needs.

Recognizing Needs and Problems

Every day people face a myriad of consumption problems. Some are routine, such as filling the car with gasoline or buying milk. Other problems occur infrequently, such as searching for a good life insurance policy or a new mountain bike. Whether the problem is routine or infrequent, the process of solving the problem starts when an unsatisfied need creates tension and thus motivation. As discussed earlier, recognizing that a need exists can be prompted by an ad, attractive packaging, or a cause marketing appeal. Whether people recognize a need exists, however, often depends on the information received and how it is perceived. Your roommate's claims that "We're running out of bread!" for three days doesn't become a felt need until you want to make a sandwich and only the heels remain.

Kim Race

Senior Consultant, Environics Communications Inc.

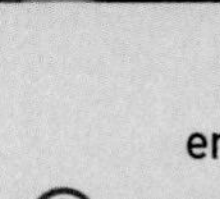

Kim Race is a senior consultant at Environics Communications Inc., a full-service public relations and public affairs agency that specializes in areas of technology, e-commerce, financial services, health care, consumer products, and entertainment.

In her role as senior consultant, Race is responsible for managing and implementing interesting and creative marketing communication programs, often with a media relations focus. Since joining Environics in 1995, she has enjoyed the variety of working with clients in many different industries from international banking and mutual funds to consumer electronics to visual effects for the film and television industry.

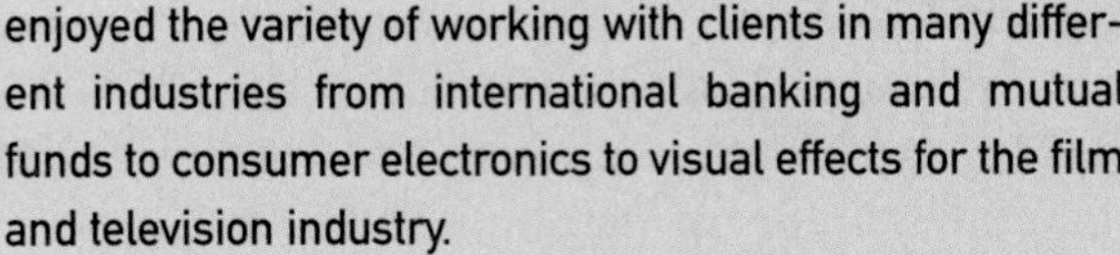

Along with a varied client list, her work at the agency is anything but routine. In her role as a senior consultant, Race has been responsible for developing and writing annual reports, newsletters, speeches and media materials, working with advertising, design and video/photography suppliers, coordinating splashy consumer and media events, representing clients in trade shows, pitching new clients, securing celebrity appearances, and engaging investor relations activities, including on-site management of investor road shows in Montreal and New York City.

Academic Background

Race received a B.A. in Political Science from the University of Western Ontario in 1991. Following her undergraduate degree, she completed the Canadian Securities Course. In 1992, she gained acceptance to the University of Stirling (Scotland) Public Relations graduate degree program and earned her Masters of Science in Public Relations in 1994. Her master's project was a study of "branding," and the role public relations plays in building the brand name of television networks.

Career History/Track

Prior to acceptance in the graduate program at Stirling University, Race's first job was as a sales representative for a transit advertising company. Following her year in Scotland, Race returned to Toronto and was shortly hired into an entry-level position at a small advertising/public relations agency specializing in the high technology industry. Race quickly moved into a consultant position with the agency, working on some key high-technology accounts. In this position, she was responsible for helping to get her Canadian clients' "mindshare" across the border, and soon had several occasions to represent her clients at leading tradeshows such as COMDEX and Networld+Interop in Las Vegas.

Advice

"PR agencies are looking for more than just good communicators. Today they expect consultants to bring additional expertise. Demonstrating a genuine interest in and knowledge of a particular area of an agency's business—for instance, investor relations, healthcare, entertainment or technology—will help set you apart from other job seekers. If you don't have a target interest, think about where you see yourself and cultivate knowledge in that field by reading trade literature or joining relevant associations outside of the communications area."

Even if people recognize a need exists, whether they act to resolve the problem depends on two factors: (1) the magnitude of the discrepancy between what they have and what they need and (2) the importance of the problem. A young mother with two kids under age five must decide whether the need to protect her children by purchasing two new car seats is worth the hassle of going to the mall. She may decide that the car seats she has are good enough.

Every person has his or her own personal hierarchy of needs. For some people, having a cup of coffee first thing every morning is a need with a high priority. This hierarchy varies from person to person, across time, and situations. For buying to occur, people must be motivated both to acknowledge the need and to do something about it. Furthermore, consumers must define the problem so that they can act to solve the problem.

In many cases problem recognition and problem definition occur simultaneously, as happens when a person runs out of toothpaste. But consider a more complicated problem that is involved with status and image—how we want others to see us. Consumers may know that they are not satisfied with their appearance, but because they may not be able to define the problem more precisely, they might not do anything about the situation. Consumers do not usually begin to solve a problem until it is adequately defined. As we discuss in the following section, marketing communication may help consumers both to recognize a need and to define it in a way that makes a particular purchase likely.

Marketing communication managers become involved in the need-recognition stage in two ways. First, if they know what problems consumers are facing, they may help develop a marketing mix to solve those problems. To measure problem recognition, marketers use market research techniques, including surveys, focus groups, observations, and consumer feedback. Marketing communication managers can use this research to select the best communication tools and messages that address how the product solves a consumer problem.

Second, marketers themselves may activate problem recognition. The cooperative ad for Vanilla Fields and Sears, for example, points out a problem that most of us would like to solve at holiday time.

Marketers can also help define the need or problem. If consumers need a new coat, do they define the problem as a need for inexpensive covering, for a way to stay warm on the coldest days, for a garment that will last several years, for a warm covering that will not attract strange looks from peers, or for an article of clothing that will express a personal sense of style? A salesperson or an ad may shape the answers.

Marketing communication managers can influence need definition greatly in part because people usually experience several motives at a time and usually act based on a mixture of rational and emotional motives. That is, when buying a new jacket, the consumer is probably influenced by rational motives such as price and endurance as well as by emotional motives such as a desire for prestige or to look better. Commercials, point-of-purchase displays, and sales presentations often appeal to both types of motives. In fact, when a product inherently appeals to one type of motive, marketing communication managers may find it effective to stress another type of motive. For example, because automobiles and clothing inherently appeal to emotional motives such as self-esteem, it is wise to include appeals to rational motives when promoting these products. This rational appeal allows the consumers to believe that they purchased a product for sound, logical reasons instead of emotional responses. But because the inherent appeal of a lawn mower is probably rational, effective marketing communication is likely to include appeals to emotional motives.

Sometimes needs evolve over time as the culture changes. For example, many homeowners today feel they need protection or security because of a rising fear of crime. Numerous new products and as many new marketing communication strategies have emerged to fill this need. Among the hottest new home security

This ad stimulates our "need" to find the perfect gift and shows how we can do so simply.

products are hand-held personal alarms; video cameras for homeowner surveillance of entry areas; and integrated security, temperature control, and entertainment systems. One of the hottest items is the Electronic Watchdog that growls, barks, and snarls like a real German shepherd when intruders approach.

Information Search and Processing

Problem recognition creates a state of tension that causes the consumer to search for information that will help in decision making. The information search is the second step in complex decision making and involves mental and physical activity. The search takes time, energy, and money and can often require giving up more desirable activities.[10] The benefits of the information search, however, often outweigh the costs. Undergoing a thorough information search may ultimately mean saving money, receiving better quality, or reducing risk.

The consumer becomes involved in two types of information search: internal and external. In an internal search, the consumer attempts to resolve problems by recalling previously stored information. For example, people who suffer from allergies can easily recall what they did last year for relief. When problems cannot be resolved through an internal search, people search externally for additional information. The external sources may include family, friends, professionals, government or corporate publications, ads, sales personnel, or displays.

The sources that a person uses may depend on the importance of the decision, past experience, confidence in particular sources, and psychological makeup. Some consumers find it too troublesome to search for information and are willing to rely on the information provided by a salesperson for a minor purchase. But when these same people buy a new car, they may go through an elaborate search that includes writing for information, comparing government reports, driving from dealership to dealership, and talking with knowledgeable people.

When the search occurs, what do people do with the information? How do they spot, understand, and recall information? Marketing communication managers must understand this process so they can affect buyer behaviour.

Steps in Information Processing

Assessing how a person processes information is not an easy task. Observing the process can help with the assessment, but because we can't see people's thoughts we have to draw some conclusions. Many theories try to explain the process. Figure 6.3 shows an outline of the information-processing sequence. It includes five steps.

Exposure

Exposure
The point at which information processing starts, usually with some source of stimulation such as watching television, going to the supermarket, or driving past a particular billboard.

Information processing starts with consumer **exposure** to some source of stimulation such as watching television, going to the supermarket, or driving past a particular billboard. To start the process, marketing communication managers must attract consumers to the stimulus or put it squarely in the path of people in the target market. For instance, messages that contain celebrity endorsements or coupons to attract consumers should appear in a media mix that consumers will be exposed to.

Attention

Attention
When the consumer must devote mental resources to stimuli in order to process them.

Exposure alone does little unless people pay attention to the stimulus. At any moment, people are bombarded by all sorts of stimuli, but they have a limited capacity to process this input. They must devote mental resources to stimuli in order to process them; in other words, they must pay **attention**. Without attention, no further information processing occurs, and the message is lost. Attention is selective. We have neither the cognitive capability nor the interest to pay attention to all the messages to which we are exposed.

Some stimuli are more attention-getting than others. For example, bright colours and movement both attract attention. Contrast (that is, size of the

Figure 6.3 The Five Steps in Information Processing

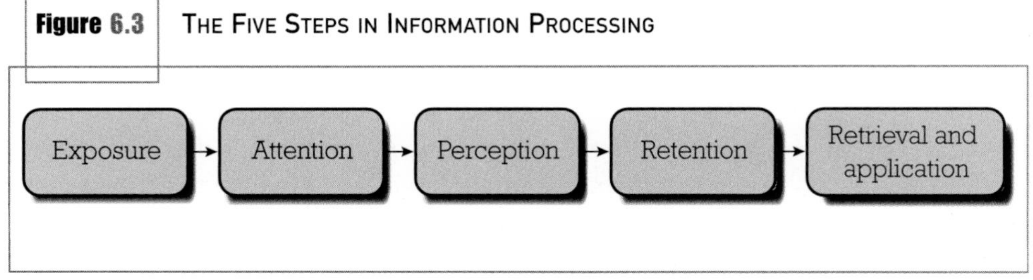

stimulus relative to its background) and intensity (for example, loudness and brightness) also prompt attention.[11] Personal attributes also influence which stimuli will attract attention. People are likely to pay attention to a message when it provides information that is relevant to problems that evoke high involvement and that they are motivated to resolve.[12] People also tend to pay attention to messages that are perceived to be consistent with their attitudes and ignore those perceived as inconsistent.[13]

Several attention-enhancing advertising methods have been identified. For example, ads that are positioned first in a series of ads are more likely to gain attention, as are humorous ads and those that use a sexual appeal.[14] A print ad in a newspaper is more likely to receive attention if it is placed in the centre of the reader's optical field. Buying a full-page ad eliminates this positioning problem.

Employing an IMC approach provides a wide variety of tools to create attention. Effective packaging, point-of-purchase materials, special events, free samples, and annual reports can grab the attention of the target audience. Seeing a McDonald's ad on TV, receiving a coupon in the mail, and listening to a story on the radio about how McDonald's donated food to a local fund-raiser all combine to increase the likelihood that you will visit a McDonald's soon.

Perception

Perception

The assignment of meaning to stimuli received through the senses.

Step three in the information-processing sequence is perception. It involves classifying incoming signals into meaningful categories, forming patterns, and assigning names or images to them. **Perception** is the assignment of meaning to stimuli received through the senses.

Perceptions are shaped by (1) the physical characteristics of the stimuli, (2) the context, and (3) the individual perceiving the stimuli. The senses transmit signals about the shape, colour, sound, and feel of stimuli, but each individual perceives those stimuli within a particular context shaped by the person's own frame of reference. Thus, a person's past learning, attitudes, personality, self-image, and current motivations and emotions shape perception. Some stimuli are perceived totally, some partially, some accurately, some inaccurately. The perceptual process results in a highly personalized mental representation of sensory stimuli.

The actual process of human perception has been well researched. In general, perception is thought to be a three-stage process: selection, organization, and interpretation of stimuli. Although we are not always conscious of it, we select the stimuli we will perceive, depending on our previous experience with the stimuli and our motives. The more experience or familiarity we have with a setting or situation, the more selective we are. A student enters a classroom with a set of expectations about what he or she will see, hear, and smell on entering the room. Given everything is as expected, the student will perceive only those things selected as relevant (for example, an available seat near the door). If expectations can be changed dramatically, it is possible to influence the selection process. This is called creating *contrast*, which is what Infiniti did when the company produced a television ad that did not show the car. Motivation, as discussed earlier, is a somewhat similar phenomenon.

People tend to perceive things they need or want. The stronger the need, the greater the motivation to perceive stimuli that will satisfy their need or want and to ignore stimuli that will not. We tend to organize stimuli into groups and perceive them as unified wholes. This tendency to organize and integrate stimuli into a group greatly simplifies our lives.

This full-page ad uses many attention-getting techniques: the image is bold, the colours are bright, and the model offers a quirky blend of humour and sex appeal. Do you think the ad grabs attention?

Evidence indicates that we automatically group stimuli in a manner that forms a unified picture or impression. We tend to group stimuli to facilitate memory and recall. Telephone numbers and addresses are everyday examples of how we group. Soft drink companies are famous in their attempts to group their products with a positive experience.

We all like to know how an unfinished story, movie, or even joke turns out. This desire reflects our need for closure, organizing perceptions so that they paint a complete picture. Even when a message is incomplete, we tend to consciously or subconsciously complete it. Coke told consumers it was "IT," hoping people would interpret "IT" in a positive way. Pepsi used "Uh-huh" in a similar way.

Finally, an individual interprets stimuli according to a set of prescribed criteria. Although this interpretation can be affected by many factors, there are a few general factors that appear to always operate. Clarity of the stimuli is critical. Stimuli that are ambiguous or fuzzy run the risk of being misperceived. A person's past experience also influences interpretation. Prejudice, either racial or some other type, is simply taking certain stimuli and generalizing from experience, whether accurate or inaccurate. Our motives and interests also influence interpretation. We tend to interpret clearly when we are interested in the topic.

Comprehension is part of the perceptual process, but it goes beyond labelling and identification to produce a more thorough evaluation of the perceived stimuli. Our first exposure to a red bicycle simply provides the perceptual reaction: "This is a red bike." A split second later we add to that assessment through comprehension: "Red bikes are best" or "Red bikes are ugly." In general, people comprehend messages in a way that makes them consistent with pre-existing attitudes and opinions. People who believe that automobiles made in the North America are best, for instance, tend to discount or distort perceptions that challenge this view.

Without the consumer's ability to perceive, integrated marketing communication would not succeed. That is, if consumers were unable to group a variety of cues in some sort of meaningful manner, they could not see how a number of communication techniques blend into a comprehensive message. For example, if you work part-time at a McDonald's restaurant, you are receiving messages as an employee, as a consumer, and as an employee receiving feedback from customers. Perception allows you to understand all these messages, group them, and comprehend them.

RETENTION

Retention
The storage of information for later reference.

Storage of information for later reference, or **retention**, is the fourth step of the information-processing sequence. Actually, the role of memory in the sequence is twofold. First, memory holds information while it is being processed throughout the sequence. For example, for a stimulus to be perceived at all, it must first be held for an extremely brief time in what psychologists call *sensory memory*. Next, memory stores the information for future, long-term use.

Memory itself is a process involving several stages. First is *encoding*: Before a person can remember anything, information must be put into a form the memory system can use. If a person reads a paragraph, for example, she might encode the general meaning of the passage, the image of the printed words, or the sound of the words. Once encoded, information can be stored in memory.

Information can be encoded and stored automatically, without conscious effort, but rehearsal, the mental repetition of material, is often necessary to ensure that these processes occur. Rote repetition is sometimes sufficient, but it is not as effective as elaborative rehearsal, which involves thinking about the information and relating it to other, already stored information. A person might remember a name if he simply repeats it, but he is more likely to remember it if he also thinks about the name and associates it with something else. Prudential Insurance has used the Rock of Gibraltar as a means of creating an association.

Prudential
www.prudential.com

Whenever possible, marketing messages are couched in a way that encourages elaborate rehearsal. Many Kodak ads, for instance, are intended to trigger a stream of pleasant thoughts about milestones in one's life.

Retrieval and Application

Retrieval
The process by which information is recovered from the memory storehouse.

The process by which information is recovered from the memory storehouse is called **retrieval**. Combined with *application* (how we are going to use this information), retrieval represents the final stage in information processing. If consumers can retrieve relevant information about a product, brand, or store, they will apply it to solve a problem or meet a need.

Research findings suggest that the most effective way for marketing communication managers to aid product information retrieval is to provide information about the product's benefits and attributes and then show a strong connection between them. The cereal industry uses this association when it presents the key attribute of high fibre as a means of preventing cancer, a clear benefit. Auto companies that include air bags as standard safety equipment provide a similar connection between the attribute and the benefit—in this case, prevention of serious injury in a car crash.

Identifying and Evaluating Alternatives

Once a need is recognized and defined and the information search is completed, alternatives are identified and evaluated. How people search for alternatives depends in part on such factors as the following:

1. the cost in time and money
2. how much information they already have
3. the perceived risk associated with a wrong decision
4. their predispositions about making choices

Because some people find the process of looking at alternatives to be difficult and disturbing, they tend to keep the number of alternatives to a minimum, even if they do not have enough information to determine that they are looking at their best option. Other people feel compelled to collect a long list of alternatives, a tendency that can slow down decision making.

Once people know their alternatives, how do they evaluate and choose among them? In particular, how do people choose among brands of a product?

Roper Starch Worldwide
www.roper.com

To illustrate this decision for one market segment and one product category, let's revisit the Gen-Xers and how they buy home furnishings. A recent young adult study from consumer researcher Roper Starch Worldwide found 20 percent of those aged 18 to 29 plan to buy furniture in the next year. Many in that age group have jobs that aren't careers because of the difficulty of finding a first career-track job. As a result, their leisure time is more of an expression of themselves than work is, and they want their homes to be as nice as possible. Style and value are the two most important decision criteria. There is also a need to show that their products fit into their lives.[15]

Purchase and Postpurchase Behaviour

After searching and evaluating, at some point consumers must decide whether they are going to buy. Anything marketers can do to simplify the decision making will be attractive to buyers because most people find it hard to make a decision. Perhaps marketers can suggest in their advertising the best size of a product for a particular use or the right wine or drink with a particular food. Sometimes several decision situations can be combined and marketed as one package. For example, travel agents often package travel tours, combining airfare, ground transportation, and hotels.

To do a better marketing job at this stage of the buying process, a seller needs answers to many questions about consumers' shopping behaviour. For instance, how much effort is the consumer willing to spend in shopping for the product? What factors influence where a consumer will shop? Do stores each have an image? If so, is the image important to a shopper when selecting a store? What are the differentiating characteristics, if any, of impulse buyers?

Marketing communication managers can play a key role at the purchase stage. Providing basic product, price, and location information through advertising, personal selling, and public relations is an obvious starting point. Sales promotion, in particular, is critical at this stage. Product sampling, coupons, rebates, and premiums are a few of the sales promotion devices used to encourage the customer to purchase. Communication elements at the point of sale may also be important. Packaging, signage, store appearance, merchandise techniques, and attitude of the sales and management personnel are relevant in closing a sale.

For instance, E-Lab, a small market research and design firm, discovered why Hallmark's Showcase stores weren't generating higher sales. Researchers videotaped customers in the stores to record their behaviour. The footage revealed a recurring set of images—shoppers would move slowly through the aisles, appear discouraged, and leave with only a greeting card. The conclusion? Store layout was confusing, signage was unclear, and high-turnover products were hard to find. Based on the research, Hallmark redesigned its stores, signage, and merchandising displays to make them easier and more fun to navigate.[16]

Integrating all these marketing communication tools so they coincide with the decision criteria of the individual can make all the difference. For many purchase decisions, the salesperson is the key. This is particularly true for industrial products and retail sales. In recent years direct marketers have played a prominent role in reshaping the purchasing process of millions of consumers. Because of time constraints and the risks alleviated through warranties and guarantees, purchasing through direct marketing is now an alternative for virtually all consumers. These benefits are highlighted in marketing messages produced by direct marketers.

These coupons for Melitta Canada coffee products are distributed as tear-outs in magazine ads. These coupons draw attention to the ad and encourage the consumer to purchase.

A consumer's feelings and evaluations after the sale are also significant to a marketer because they can influence repeat sales and what the consumer tells others about the product or brand. Keeping the customer satisfied is what marketing is all about.

Cognitive dissonance
Postpurchase anxiety after all but routine and inexpensive purchases.

Consumers typically experience some postpurchase anxiety after all but routine and inexpensive purchases. This anxiety reflects a phenomenon called **cognitive dissonance**. According to this theory, people strive for consistency among their cognitions (knowledge, attitudes, beliefs, values). When inconsistencies arise, dissonance is created, which people try to eliminate. In some cases the consumer makes the decision already aware of the dissonant elements. In other instances dissonance is aroused by disturbing information received after the purchase.

To avoid or eliminate dissonance, consumers may avoid negative information. They may change their behaviour, their opinions, or their attitudes. They may seek information or opinions that support their purchase. Sometimes the consumer's attempt to reduce dissonance can produce dire consequences for the marketer. For example, in the process of convincing oneself that the purchase of a new GE microwave oven was a good decision, the consumer seeks additional information from friends. Unfortunately, the consumer's best friend says she had a terrible experience with her GE microwave oven.

Xerox Canada
www.xerox.ca

The marketer may take specific steps to reduce postpurchase dissonance. Advertising that stresses the many positive attributes or confirms the popularity of the product can be helpful. Providing personalized reinforcement has proven effective with big-ticket items such as automobiles and major appliances. Salespeople in these areas may send cards or publicity materials or may even make personal calls to reassure customers about their purchase. One company that has done an excellent job of checking on customer dissonance is Xerox Corp. Xerox uses phone surveys and goes after decision makers exclusively, conducting about 10 000 surveys per month. It has also gone beyond measuring customer satisfaction to gauging customer loyalty.[17]

concept review

Consumer Decision-Making Processes

Consumers go through a specific decision-making process to resolve needs. These decisions can be complex or simple. The following steps outline the complex decision-making process.

1. Recognizing needs and problems: Consumers must be motivated both to acknowledge and resolve a need in order for the buying process to proceed.
2. Information search and processing that includes the following stages:
   - Exposure
   - Attention
   - Perception
   - Retention
   - Retrieval and application
3. Identifying and evaluating alternatives
4. Purchase and postpurchase behaviour

ORGANIZATIONAL MARKET BEHAVIOUR

Those who supply goods and services to consumer markets are themselves in need of goods and services to run their businesses. These organizations—producers, resellers, and governments—make up vast organizational markets that buy a large variety of products, including equipment, raw material, labour, and other services. Some organizations sell exclusively to other organizations and never come in contact with consumer buyers. A common term used to describe these types of exchanges is **business-to-business marketing.**

Business-to-business marketing
Organizations selling exclusively to other organizations and never coming in contact with consumer buyers.

Despite the importance of organizational markets, far less research has been conducted on factors that influence their behaviour than on factors that influence consumers. However, we can identify characteristics that distinguish organizational buying from consumer buying and typical steps in the organizational buying process.

CHARACTERISTICS OF ORGANIZATIONAL BUYING

Many elements of the sociocultural environment discussed in the previous chapter influence both organizational and consumer buying, but additional forces arise only in the organizational setting. In particular, each organization has its own business philosophy that guides its actions in resolving conflicts, handling uncertainty and risk, searching for solutions, and adapting to change.

Five characteristics mark the organizational buying process:[18]

1. In organizations many individuals are involved in making buying decisions.
2. The organizational buyer is motivated by both rational and emotional factors in choosing products and services. Although the use of rational and quantitative criteria dominate in most organizational decisions, the decision makers are people, subject to many of the same emotional criteria used in personal purchases.
3. Organizational buying decisions frequently involve a range of complex technical dimensions. A purchasing agent for Volvo AB, for example, must consider a number of technical factors before ordering a radio to go into the 740 SL model. The electronic system, the acoustics of the interior, and the shape of the dashboard are a few of these considerations.
4. The organizational decision process frequently spans a considerable time, creating a significant lag between the marketing communicators' initial contact with the customer and the purchasing decision. Because many new factors can enter the picture during this lag time, the marketer's ability to monitor and adjust to these changes is critical.
5. Organizations cannot be grouped into precise categories. Each organization has a characteristic way of functioning and a personality.

The first item in this list of characteristics has important implications. Unlike the consumer buying process, groups making organizational buying decisions must generally follow enforced decision-making rules. The group dynamic greatly complicates the task of understanding the buying process. For example, to predict the buying behaviour of an organization with certainty, we need to know who will take part in the buying process, what criteria each member uses in evaluating prospective suppliers, and what influence each member has. We should also understand something not only about the psychology of the individuals involved but also how they work as a group.

Who makes the decision to buy depends in part on the situation. Three main types of buying situations exist: the straight rebuy, the modified rebuy, and the new task. The straight rebuy is the simplest situation: The company reorders a good or service without any modifications. The transaction tends to be routine and may be handled totally by a purchasing agent. With the modified rebuy, the buyer is seeking to modify product specifications, prices, and so on. The purchaser is interested in negotiation, and several participants may participate in the buying decision. A company faces a new task when it considers buying a product for the first time. The number of participants and the amount of information sought tend to increase with the cost and risks associated with the transaction. This situation represents the best opportunity for the marketer because the customer is open to new information and alternatives.

Purchasing Objectives

As you can see in the ENN (Elevator News Network) advertisement, purchasing objectives in the business market for the most part centre on rational, pragmatic considerations such as price, service, quality, and assurance of supply. The ENN ad assures business purchasers that the company offers an expertise reaching the business and audience when they're at work, an affirmation it backs up with discussion of the approach it employs.

This business-to-business ad makes a rational appeal.

1. *Price*. Buyers in the business arena are more concerned than ordinary consumers with the cost of owning and using a product. Most notably, the large volume of a particular product purchased, or the high per-unit cost, means that businesses spend thousands or millions of dollars with each purchase decision. In evaluating price, therefore, businesses consider a variety of factors that generate or minimize costs, such as: What amount of scrap or waste will result from the use of the material? What will the cost of processing the material be? How much power will the machine consume?
2. *Services*. Business buyers require multiple services, such as technical assistance, availability of spare parts, repair capability, and training information. Thus, the technical contributions of suppliers are highly valued wherever equipment, materials, or parts are in use.
3. *Quality*. Organizational customers search for quality levels consistent with specifications. They are reluctant to pay for extra quality or to compromise specifications for a reduced price. The crucial factor is uniformity or consistency in product quality that will guarantee uniformity in end products, reduce the need for costly inspections and testing of incoming shipments, and ensure a smooth blending with the production process.
4. *Assurance of supply*. Interruptions in the flow of parts and materials can shut down the production process, resulting in costly delays and lost sales. To guard against interruptions in supply, business firms rely on a supplier's established reputation for delivery.

The organizational buying process has eight stages, or key phases, as illustrated in Figure 6.4.[19] Although these stages parallel those of the consumer buying process, some key differences have a direct bearing on the marketing communication strategy. The complete process only occurs in the case of a new task. Even in this situation, however, the process is far more formal for the industri-

Figure 6.4 ORGANIZATIONAL MARKET BEHAVIOUR

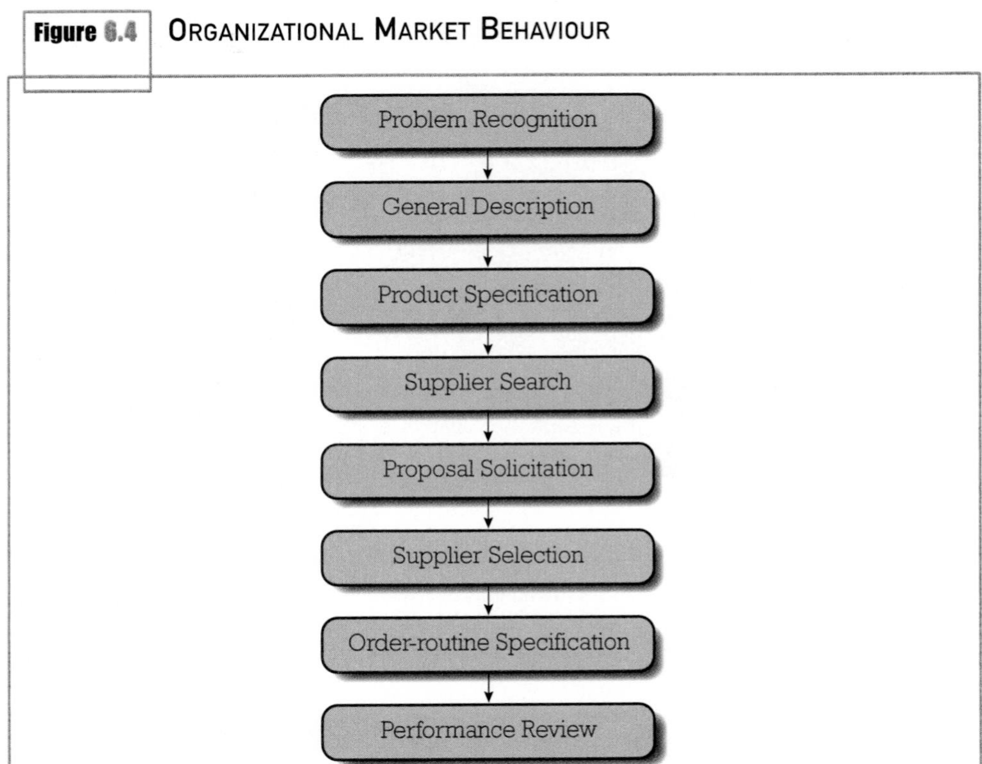

al buying process than for the consumer buying process. Most of the information an industrial buyer receives is delivered through direct contacts such as sales representatives or information packets. It is unlikely that an industrial buyer would use the information provided through a trade as the sole basis for making a decision.

For more information on the organizational buying process, refer to this textbook's Web site at http://www.pearsoned.ca/burnett.

concept review

Organizational Market Behaviour

1. Five characteristics of organizational buying are
   - Multiple-decision making
   - Rational and emotional decision factors
   - Complexity
   - Lengthy time frame
   - Diverse classification of organization types
2. Purchasing objectives in the business market for the most part centre on rational, pragmatic consideration such as
   - Price
   - Services
   - Quality
   - Assurance of supply

A Closing Thought:

Build or Break Customer Loyalty?

If specific behaviours do not always follow attitudes, or if social trends do not always parallel business trends, why do marketing communicators think it still is important to understand consumers?

The reason is simple. The savvy marketing communicator knows that having solid trend information at one's disposal, even with its limitations, is a much more desirable alternative to having no information. Even worse, however, is having "information" that is largely or even partly wrong.

Almost all facets of marketing—including marketing communication, product, packaging, and price—are a form of communicating to a target consumer. The better marketing communicators know their targets, the more effectively they can communicate with them. Information about consumers provides marketing communicators with a much more detailed and thorough understanding of the target market than unaided judgment could provide. And that knowledge can greatly increase the chances for campaigns that speak directly to what is on consumers' minds. This approach to the consumer is the heart of relationship marketing.

Because customers have more options and information, firms must strive to meet customers' needs and wants better than competing firms. To create customer loyalty, businesses must build strong relationships not only with their customers, but also with each group that helps the firm serve its customers—suppliers, distributors, resellers, and members of the financial and local communities.

What firms do for their current or potential customers with each and every contact helps build or break customer loyalty. In sum, relationship marketing is customer-focused: It aims to build long-term relationships with each customer.

summary

1. Describe how the psychological factors of motivation, learning, and attitudes affect consumer decision making.

   Consumer decision making is influenced by motivation, learning, and attitudes. A motive is an inner drive or pressure to act to eliminate tension, to satisfy a need or want, to solve a problem, or to restore a sense of equilibrium. Learning is a process of taking in information, processing it along with existing information, and producing new knowledge. An attitude is an enduring favourable or unfavourable disposition toward some object. Motivation spurs learning, and both these factors shape attitudes. Understanding these psychological factors can help marketing communicators stimulate consumer motivation and learning and shape attitudes so that consumers are more likely to buy.

2. Explain how consumers make complex and simple decisions and how marketing communication can influence this process.

   The two main types of decision making are complex or simple decisions. Novelty of the purchase and consumer involvement influence whether the decision-making process is simple or complex. Complex decision making involves five steps: need recognition, information search, evaluation of alternatives, purchase, and postpurchase behaviour. Simple decision making does not require information search or evaluation. This process is based on habit.

   The three psychological factors of motivation, learning, and attitudes influence the various stages of complex decision making. The process begins with need recognition, then moves to information search and processing (internal motivation is necessary for this step), continues with identifying and evaluating alternatives, and concludes with purchase and postpurchase behaviour. Marketing communicators that understand the complex decision process can motivate buyers to learn about and identify their products as the best purchase choice. They can also influence some postpurchase behaviour through planned follow-up and relationship building.

3. Contrast organizational and consumer buying behaviour.

   Organizational buying behaviour differs from consumer decision making in five key ways. First, groups, not individuals, make decisions according to enforced decision-making rules. Second, although the organizational buyer is motivated by both rational and emotional factors in choosing products and services, organizational buying behaviour tends to be less emotional and relies on information. Third, organizational buying decisions often involve complex technical dimensions. Fourth, the organizational decision process often takes a long time, creating a significant gap between the marketing communicators' initial contact with the customer and the purchasing decision. Finally, organizations differ in how they function and their personality.

points to ponder

Review the Facts

1. What is an attitude?
2. List the three elements of the learning process.

Master the Concepts

3. How can marketing communicators influence a person's motivation to take action? How can they facilitate learning?
4. Discuss the components of an attitude. What are the implications for marketing communication?
5. Discuss several reasons why marketers continue to have a hard time understanding, predicting, and explaining consumer behaviour.
6. Present a diagram of the consumer decision process. What is the role of marketing communication in each stage of this process? Consider which marketing communication activities might be most effective for each stage.
7. Distinguish between high-involvement and low-involvement decision making.
8. What are the differences between the consumer decision-making process and the organizational decision-making process?

APPLY YOUR KNOWLEDGE

9. Based on your understanding of consumer motives, develop some general guidelines or directives for practising marketing communication.
10. Use the multiattribute perspective to measure your attitude toward two different brands of jeans.
11. Assume you are training a salesperson to sell industrial products. Although this salesperson has a strong track record, she has been selling consumer products. What would you emphasize during training?

suggested projects 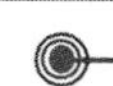

1. Locate an individual who has purchased a new automobile during the last year. Using the five-step decision-making process, ask this person to indicate how he or she accomplished each step.
2. (Writing Project) Contact 10 students. Ask them to list the three primary motives they considered when selecting which university to attend. Ask them whether they would still use these same motives. Have them indicate any new ones. Write a short paper (two to three pages) in which you summarize your findings and address how understanding motives can help marketing communicators understand the decision-making process.
3. (Internet Project) Find the Internet home page for a favourite product, brand, or company. Analyse the Web site to see if its contents attempt to assist consumer decision making. Write a brief (one- or two-page) memo to support your findings. Be as specific as possible. For instance, if you believe the site attempts to reduce cognitive dissonance, describe the approach used and assess the effectiveness of the approach.

So Long to the Van?

Gerri Gayner traded in her new Plymouth Voyager minivan—at a loss—to reclaim her individuality. A single mother of three, she didn't want to be typecast as a cargo-hauling "mommy." "It's not what I am," says Gayner, an entrepreneur who now drives nothing but convertibles. However, Gayner is planning to marry a man with three children of his own. The engagement entailed "a minivan talk," she says. Well, maybe it wasn't much of a discussion. "I said I would never drive one of those things as long as I live," she recalls. Today, her fiancé is shopping for a Chevrolet Suburban, the biggest sport-utility vehicle on the market. It seats nine, about two more than your average minivan.

What's going on? North Americans' love affair with the automobile has crashed into life's practical demands and the evil angst of aging. To some people in their 30s and 40s who feel powerless against the tide of dirty diapers, day-care expenses, and kiddie soccer games, the minivan is starting to look like a good place to draw the line. Students of automotive culture say this rejection of the conventional is predictable behaviour. In fact, some believe historians will look back on the minivan as an aberration, a vehicle whose popularity was almost entirely dependent not on its image but on its practicality. "That has not been the major motivating force of this industry," says Michael Marsden, an expert in the role of the automobile in popular culture. "The mainstay has been excitement, fun, liberation, movement—the feeling that destiny is in your own hands and that you are on the open road."

There are more than six million minivans on North American roads today, and manufacturers expect sales to remain strong. Minivans have become icons of modern suburbia, filling school parking lots across North America. They are invading Europe, and China wants them to help cart around its 1.3 billion people. But just the same, manufacturers know something is going on image-wise: It shows up in focus groups conducted by market researchers. One research consulting firm asked what minivans represent. The answer from one suburbanite: "Family, family, family. Kids, kids, kids. No fun, no fun, no fun."

Manufacturers know that customers may grasp for alternatives like pricey Volvo station wagons or rugged Jeep Cherokees to escape the stigma, but parents, after all, will always need something to haul kids, pets, and sports equipment. It's just that people can be so cruel. When Jane Osgood announced she was expecting twins, she waited for her phone to ring with warm, congratulatory calls. Instead, her pals needled her about the minivan that seemed inevitably to be in her future. "This is it, you're going to have to get a minivan!" her friends gloated, observing that she would soon have a total of three children and a dog. "They were laughing at me," she says.

Case Questions

1. How are learning, attitudes, and perception affecting the purchase of minivans?
2. Identify places where marketing communication could improve minivan buyer behaviour.

Sources: Robyn Meredith, "For Mini-Vans, a Mid-Life Crisis at Age of 14," ***New York Times***, 12 May 1997, A1, C4. Keith Bradsher, "G.M. Sales Decline, but Chrysler's Surge," ***New York Times***, 2 August 1996, C4; Oscar Suris, "It's Useful, Practical, and No One Can Make Me Drive It," ***Wall Street Journal***, 26 February 1995, A-1.

7

The Legal, Ethical, and Global Environment

chapter objectives

After completing your work on this chapter, you should be able to

- Identify the government bodies that control the efforts of marketing communicators.
- Identify the major legal issues that affect marketing communication.
- Analyse the social responsibility issues that affect marketing communication.
- Discuss the role of self-regulation in marketing communication.
- Outline the key global factors that affect marketing communication.

The Tobacco Industry's Communications Challenge

To say cigarette marketers have an ethical dilemma on their hands would be an understatement. Their industry code says they must aim their sales pitch at adults—but market research shows that nearly all smokers start smoking, and become loyal to a specific brand, before adulthood. Research also shows that the percentage of teenaged smokers surged in the 1990s. Yet the cigarette companies insist that their marketing efforts do not intentionally target teenagers. The $7 billion they spend every year on marketing communications, they say, is intended to promote their brands among adults who already smoke.

Adding to tobacco marketers' public relations worries are the growing number of lawsuits that are being made public across North America. For example, the Canadian government recently filed a $1-billion lawsuit in U.S. Federal Court against tobacco companies. The lawsuit alleges that the R.J. Reynolds companies set up a scheme to smuggle cheap cigarettes into the Canadian market. According to Canadian officials, this scheme undermined the government's 1991 increase in taxes and duties on tobacco that was intended to help deter young people from becoming addicted to cigarettes. Due to this smuggling activity, the government was forced to reduce its taxes and duties on tobacco in 1994. According to Health Minister Allan Rock, "The link between low prices and youth smoking is clear . . . since taxes were lowered five years ago, the rate of smoking among 15- to 19-year-olds climbed from 21 to 31 percent."

Undaunted by the industry's PR worries, Imperial Tobacco recently promoted a contest that riled anti-smokers. According to the contest's rules, all Canadians over age 19 were welcome to enter, as long as they were smokers. Contest winners received a trip to a Whistler, B.C. ski resort to hear Big Sugar and The Tea Party perform as part of Imperial's annual du Maurier concert series. To promote the contest, the company ran a print and radio campaign in 10 cities across the country. The ads, which explicitly stated "you must be 19 or older to enter," directed people to a toll-free line where they obtained information on the "exclusive weekend" offer.

What's wrong with Imperial's contest? Alwyn Robertson, executive director at Toronto-based Council for a Tobacco-Free Ontario, explains, "It's absolutely dreadful that they're trying to reward extremely destructive health behaviours." Robertson is not the only one to express concern about this contest. Several other anti-smoking groups, such as the Canadian Cancer Society, have issued complaints to Health Canada, arguing the contest exploits the transitional period in government restrictions on tobacco-related sponsorships.

"We're not in the business to persuade people to smoke," says Paul Forgues, manager of community relations for Imperial Tobacco. According to Forgues, the contest is simply meant to generate brand loyalty among existing smokers.

Regardless of how you feel about the ethics of tobacco marketing, it's fair to say that cigarette marketers face a public relations challenge. Only time will tell what the future holds for the tobacco industry.

Council for a Tabacco-Free Ontario

www.opc.on.ca

Canadian Cancer Solciety

www.cancer.ca

Health Canada

www.hc-sc.gc.ca

Sources: Shawna Cohen, "Imperial's Promo Riles Anti-smokers," *Marketing*, February 28, 2000, p. 2; Sandra Cordon, "Ottawa Takes on Tobacco Giant in $1-billion Lawsuit," *The Canadian Press*, extracted from www.canoe.ca, December 22, 1999; "Canada Files Tobacco Lawsuit," extracted from www.canoe.ca, December 21, 1999.

Chapter Overview

Marketing communicators in the tobacco industry face a paradox. On the one hand, they must convince their clients that the communication strategies they propose achieve objectives, including turning nonsmokers into smokers. On the other hand, they must convince the government and the general public that these same strategies don't affect an underage audience of potential smokers. They must also grapple with the issue of whether it is socially responsible to market a product around the world that is physically harmful.

Marketing communication strategists must work within a tremendously complex legal, ethical, and global environment. The intent of this chapter is threefold:

(1) to provide an overview of legal issues that affect marketing communication,

(2) to examine self-regulation in the marketing communication industry, and

(3) to consider ethical and global issues that affect marketing communication.

Marketing Communication and Government Regulation

Since the 1960s, consumer protection initiatives have been active at the federal, provincial, and local levels. With unprecedented changes in marketing communications practice as the result of developments such as e-commerce and business consolidations, it is unlikely that interest in consumer protection will disappear. One outcome of the consumer protection initiatives has been a proliferation in regulations at all levels of government.

Governments develop public policy—laws and regulations—to guide, control, and in some cases resist marketing communications. Public policy often limits communication activities for the good of consumers and society as a whole. The laws and regulations of the various levels of government often overlap, are subject to interpretation, and are constantly changing. What was prohibited last year may be allowed this year, or could be allowed under a specific set of circumstances.

Two key regulatory bodies "directly" affect marketing communication practice in Canada. First, we turn to Industry Canada, the federal department with the greatest direct impact on marketing communications. Then we discuss the Canadian Radio-television and Telecommunications Commission (CRTC). Finally, we briefly look at other groups that shape the marketing communication environment.

Industry Canada
www.ic.gc.ca

Industry Canada

Industry Canada is the federal department responsible for administrating most federal legislation that regulates business. A partial list of federal laws are listed in Table 7.1. Specific responsibilities of Industry Canada include the following:

1. Working with Canadians throughout the economy and in all parts of the country to improve conditions for investment, improve innovation performance, and increase Canada's share of local trade.
2. Working to build a fair, efficient, and competitive marketplace.
3. Developing and administering programs aimed at developing industry and technology capability, fostering scientific research, setting telecommunications policy, and promoting tourism and small business development.
4. Setting rules and services that support the effective operation of the marketplace.[1]

For more information about Industry Canada, its mission, programs, acts and regulations, check out its Web site.

The key piece of federal legislation is the Competition Act, which was passed in 1985. This act is administered by the Competition Bureau, which is a branch of Industry Canada. The purpose of this act is to ensure a healthy and fair

Table 7.1 A Partial Listing of Federal Laws Designed to Protect Business and Consumers that Affect Marketing Communication

Consumer Legislation:
- Consumer Packaging and Labelling Act

Telecommunications Legislation:
- Radiocommunications Act
- Telecommunications Act

Marketplace and Trade Regulation:
- Competition Act
- Lobbyists Registration Act
- Winding-up and Restructuring Act

Canadian Intellectual Property Legislation:
- Copyright Act
- Industrial Design Act
- Patent Act
- Trademarks Act

competitive marketplace. Current areas of regulation covered in the Competition Act that impact marketing communications include pricing, misleading advertising, promotional contests, tied selling, bait-and-switch selling, and pyramid selling schemes.

Canadian Radio-television and Telecommunications Commission (CRTC)

Canadian broadcasting has been an area of study and regulation for more than a century. Early communications regulation can be traced to the first Telegraph Act that was passed in 1852. In 1928, the Government of Canada created the first Royal Commission on Broadcasting. To this day, the federal government has sought to develop policies to keep pace with changing technology. This has been the federal government's primary goal since the early days of radio and television, to our current information highway era.

Canadian Radio-televison and Telecommunications Commission

www.crtc.gc.ca

Today, the Canadian Radio-television and Telecommunications Commission (CRTC) is the regulatory agency that regulates Canadian broadcasting and telecommunications industries. With routes traceable to a number of reports commissioned by the federal government, the Canadian Radio-television Commission was created in 1968. As a reflection of changes in communications technology, the regulatory agency became the Canadian Radio-television and Telecommunications Commission in 1976.

The CRTC is governed by the Broadcasting Act and Telecommunications Act. The primary objective of the Broadcasting Act is to ensure that all Canadians have access to a wide variety of high-quality Canadian programming. Similarly, the main objective of the Telecommunications Act is to ensure that Canadians have access to reliable telephone and other telecommunications services at affordable prices. Together, these legislative acts mandate the CRTC to ensure that Canadians have access to reasonably priced, high-quality, varied, and innovative communications services that are competitive both nationally and internationally. Moreover, the mandate is to ensure a Canadian broadcasting system that reflects Canadian creativity and talent, our linguistic duality, our multicultural diversity, our social values, and the special place of aboriginal people within our society.[2]

Other Regulatory Bodies

Many additional regulatory bodies also have an impact on marketing communication practice. For example, the Canadian Transport Commission (CTC) regulates airline and rail travel routes and fares, thus having an effect on the communication of pricing policies and product offerings in the transportation sector. Moreover, the state of Canadian law cannot be ascertained by reference to the federal bodies and legislation. Most provincial governments have passed Consumer Protection Acts, referred to as Trade Practices Acts in British Columbia and Ontario, that have direct impact on marketing communication practices.[3]

At the federal and provincial level there are marketing boards and other trade associations that, to varying degrees, impact marketing practice via control of advertising, production quality and quantities, distribution networks, and the pricing of products. Often, marketing boards and trade associations embark upon national communications plans that would be cost prohibitive to individual producers. These national campaigns are most common with agricultural products where the communications objective is to represent the interests of producers.

Canadian Egg Marketing Agency
www.canadaegg.ca

Dairy Farmers of Canada
www.dairybureau.org

The Canadian Egg Marketing Agency and Dairy Farmers of Canada are two organizations with well-recognized national communications campaigns. For example, the main objective of the Dairy Farmers of Canada (DFC) is to promote the interests of Canada's milk producers. The policy and government relations department of this organization coordinates the actions of provincial dairy producer organizations on issues affecting the Canadian dairy industry. Its international trade department monitors trade-related issues, such as negotiations with the World Trade Organization (WTO). Its marketing department is responsible for the promotion and marketing of products such as cheese, butter, and ice cream, and the evaluation of these communications programs is conducted by its Economics and Market Research Department. DFC's nutrition department ensures that effective nutrition communications are directed to health officials and consumers.[4]

The www.myrecipes.org campaign is among the many well-recognized promotional efforts of the Dairy Farmers of Canada.

Marketing Communication and the Law

The federal laws and regulatory bodies discussed so far have a direct impact on marketing communication. Next we will examine how five areas of marketing communication are affected by their legal environments: advertising, sales promotion, public relations, direct marketing, and personal selling.

Competition Bureau
www.strategies.ic.gc.ca

Advertising and the Legal Environment

As noted earlier, the Competition Bureau is the branch of Industry Canada that serves as the primary governing body for the advertising industry via administration of the Competition Act. With respect to advertising, the main focus of the Competition Act is to identify and eliminate ads that are determined to be either false or misleading to consumers. In this section we will begin with a discussion of the act's coverage of misleading advertising. This will be followed with discussion of the use of tests and testimonials in advertising. Finally, we will define and discuss bait and switch advertising. Although the Competition Act does cover a number of additional issues and marketing practices, we limit our discussion to the practices most likely to be of day-to-day concern to marketing communicators.

MISLEADING ADVERTISING

A demonstration of a product or product performance must not mislead viewers. There are instances, in the case of food products for example, when additives or substitutes can be used legally because hot lights, film quality, and other aspects of the filming process do not provide an accurate portrayal of the product. The issue is whether the demonstration shows the product in a normal way in a normal setting without falsely upgrading the consumer's perception of the product. Dropping a truck six metres to show its strength but using special reinforcement of the frame would be an example of a misleading demonstration. Demonstrations are usually evaluated by the Competition Bureau on a case-by-case basis.

An ad that is considered misleading has one or more of the following characteristics: (1) representations as to performance, efficacy, or length of life of a product where such statements are not supported by adequate and proper tests; (2) warranties or guarantees are made where there is no reasonable prospect that the warrantors can make the undertaking, or where the terms of the undertaking are themselves, materially misleading; and (3) representations as to the price at which a product or a like product has been, is or will be ordinarily sold. (For example, "Regularly $14.95, now $7.95," where the price was never above $10.00.)[5]

For a misleading advertising conviction to occur under the Competition Act, the following four requirements must be met:

1. the representation must be made to the public;
2. the representation must be misleading;
3. the representation must be misleading in a material respect; and
4. the representation must be made for the purpose of directly or indirectly promoting the supply or use of a product or a business interest.[6]

What does it really mean for a representation to be material and misleading? According to Canadian legal experts C.J. Michael Flavell and Christopher J. Kent, these are interrelated concepts. Briefly stated, Canadian law " . . . requires that the representations be such as to induce a person into a course of conduct that he or she believes is advantageous. For example, if the misleading aspect of a representation is shown to be determinative of a person's decision to purchase a product, the materiality criterion will be met." With respect to whether a representation is misleading, "courts and the Bureau [the Competition Bureau] are guided by the general impression of the representation, as well as its literal meaning. Several factors are considered in assessing the general impression of representation." These factors include the following:

- the nature and understanding of the person to whom the representation was made;

Eric Swetsky PROFILE

Solicitor and Barrister, Trademark Agent

Toronto, Ontario

Eric Swetsky is a well-known lawyer in Toronto who practises exclusively in the advertising and intellectual property law field, areas such as misleading advertising, the legal structuring of innovative marketing campaigns, copyright law, trade-mark law, merchandising and licensing law, and celebrity endorsement law.

Swetsky publishes a bimonthly "advertising law" newsletter, writes a monthly legal column in ***Marketing*** magazine, and speaks to many groups on advertising law. He is listed in the independent ***LEXPERT*** directory of legal experts as an expert in the advertising and marketing law field. He is one of 12 lawyers from across Canada who sit on the Canadian Bar Association's Trade Marks Committee.

LEXPERT
www.lexpert.ca

Education

Swetsky holds two law degrees, one from the University of Warwick in England, the other from the University of Windsor in Ontario. He obtained an MBA from Queen's University in Kingston, Ontario and has a Bachelor of Commerce degree from Dalhousie University in Halifax, Nova Scotia.

Typical Day

The more interesting advertisements and promotions are often those that are cutting edge and the role of the advertising lawyer is to assist in ensuring that they do not cross the legal line. Each client request is different, so that there is no such thing as a typical day. There is no legal textbook available to assist the advertising lawyer, which is what is particularly enjoyable about practising this area of the law—it's different all the time, and one must stretch him- or herself to come up with innovative solutions to novel legal situations.

Advice

Do what you enjoy doing. If you have a dream, pursue it. Nothing worthwhile comes easy, and if it is worthwhile, you're going to have to work hard to achieve it.

Don't assume that your first career choice must be your ultimate career. The world often does unfold as it should, and you may find that today you are completely unaware of the twists in your career path and that you would never have been able to achieve your ultimate career without those intermediate twists along the way.

- the nature of the medium through which the representation was made; and
- the use of qualifiers such as "usually" and "up to."

The use of such disclaimers are legitimate tools for marketing communicators attempting to limit their liability, provided such disclaimers are displayed or communicated with prominence.[7]

Tests and Testimonials

Before an advertising claim can be made about product performance, the advertiser must have a reasonable basis for making the claim. If the advertiser cannot show that it had proof to support the claim before it developed the ad, the ad is illegal even if the claim is true and the product performs as advertised.

Endorsement or testimonial
Any advertising message that consumers perceive as reflecting the opinions beliefs, or expressions of an individual, group, or institution.

An **endorsement** or **testimonial** is any advertising message that consumers perceive as reflecting the opinions, beliefs, or expressions of an individual, group, or institution. If, however, one can reasonably ascertain that a message does not reflect the announcer's opinion, the message is not an endorsement. Although any one individual can endorse a product or service, some advertisers use the services of motion-picture celebrities, television stars, or sports personalities as endorsers. For example, Wayne Gretzky has served as an endorser of Tylenol in television advertisements in which he claims to use this product to help manage his pain caused by arthritis.

Because consumers rely on expert endorsements to make purchase decisions, it is important that the endorser use the product and be qualified to make expert judgment. When an expert endorses a product, the endorser must use his or her expertise to evaluate the product and must examine it as extensively as would another person with similar credentials. If endorsers compare competing brands, they must also evaluate the selected brands. If an organization makes an endorsement, the organization must use evaluative procedures that will ensure that the endorsement fairly reflects the collective judgment of the organization.

Comparison advertising
The comparison of two or more specifically named or recognizably presented brands of the same generic product or service class in terms of one or more specific product or service attributes.

In narrow terms, **comparison advertising** is the comparison of two or more specifically named or recognizably presented brands of the same generic product or service class in terms of one or more specific product or service attributes.

Although the effect of comparison ads on market share, advertiser image, and competitor image is still uncertain, comparison ads may provide consumers with biased information on the relative importance of two or more brands, and

A company will often compare its product or service directly to that of its competitors. This Cantel "Yak Attack" ad compares itself to Bell Mobility's "Yak" campaign.

disparage brands either by implication or by direct criticism. Suppose that Tagamet HB created a comparison ad with Mylanta. It would be misleading if the information shown was inaccurate or Tagamet only selected decision criteria that favoured the sponsor.

Bait and Switch

Bait advertising
An alluring but insincere offer to sell a product or service that the advertiser does not really intend or want to sell.

Bait advertising is an alluring but insincere offer to sell a product or service that the advertiser does not really intend or want to sell. Bait-and-switch ads that are impermissible are those that do not represent a bona-fide offer to sell the advertised product or those that misrepresent the actual price, quality, or saleability of the product.[8]

The Competition Act specifies defences to allegations of bait-and-switch selling. For example, if the advertiser is unable to supply product, but demonstrates reasonable steps were taken to obtain it; where the advertiser obtained a reasonable quantity of the product, but was unable to meet the demand because the demand surpassed the advertiser's reasonable expectation; or where the advertiser provides rain checks to supply non-available items within a reasonable time and honours the rain checks.[9]

Every country has its own definition of a reasonable claim. For example, recently the Chinese government banned the unstoppable Energizer battery

Defining Copycat Ads: A Legal Perspective

A 1998 decision of the U.S. District Court (S.D. Georgia) nicely reviews some of the legal principles involved with the issue of copycat advertising. However, since additional laws apply in Canada, one must not jump to the conclusion that by merely changing an ad's copy, for example, that the advertiser will be out of the legal woods here.

The U.S. case involves the movie ***Midnight in the Garden of Good and Evil,*** based on the John Berendt book of the same title. Those who have seen the book will recall Jack Leigh's jacket photograph of the sculpture in Savannah's Bonaventure Cemetery, referred to locally as "the Bird Girl." Sculpted by Sylvia Shaw Judson in 1938, it was placed at that time in the burial plot of the Lucy Trosdal family.

In 1997, when Warner Bros. was in the midst of filming, Leigh asked if they would be using his photograph in connection with the film's publicity. Warner Bros. declined the invitation. Warner Bros. received permission from the Judson estate to make a replica of the sculpture. They encountered problems in obtaining permission from the Trosdal family to place the replica in their plot, and therefore placed it elsewhere in the cemetery. When all was said and done, the Warner Bros. photograph of their Bird Girl evoked a resemblance to Leigh's photograph, and both had the same eerie look and feel. Leigh sued for copyright infringement.

Since no copyright exists in an idea, the use of the same subject matter in two works does not in and of itself result in an infringement of copyright. Two people can therefore photograph the same subject. The protection granted to a photographer is in the posing of the subject, lighting, timing, and shading that evokes a desired expression, the selection and arrangement of costumes, the angles photographed from, and other such variants.

Based on these legal principles, the court first decided that Leigh was not entitled to copyright protection of his choice of subject matter, namely the Bird Girl in Bonaventure Cemetery. The court also said that since the sculpture had been in the same position for some 50 years, Leigh could not claim originality in the background of his photograph. Nor could Leigh claim protection for the pose or expression of the statue, since he did not select these or alter the statue's physical appearance in any way.

The court also decided that Leigh could not claim that the eerie or spiritual mood of the photograph was capable of protection, saying: "Statues in cemeteries are often photographed in a manner evoking an eerie or spiritual mood and thus these moods can be said to flow naturally from the subject . . ."

Leigh argued that the statue represented the final judgment on the book's main character. To this, the court said: "The idea of a forlorn cemetery statue representing final judgement cannot be protected by copyright. (Leigh's) original expression of that idea, that being the elements of his photograph over which he exerted original creative control, can be protected. It is these elements that must be compared . . . and not the ideas that they convey."

The court then looked at the copyrightable elements in Leigh's photograph (lighting, shading, timing, angle, background scenes, etc.) and noted that the Warner Bros. photograph was set farther back, and was slightly off-centre. More headstones, and different headstones, were visible, background trees were much larger, light streams were different, and the Warner Bros. photograph had a different tint.

What was the court's conclusion? The court decided the case this way: "(Leigh) may be correct in asserting that if it were not for his idea, the Bird Girl would not be associated with (the film). Nevertheless, copyright law does not protect his idea . . . Warner Bros.' expressions of that idea are original and different from (Leigh's). The only similarity between the images . . . are of the sculpture in the cemetery. This aspect of the images, however, is not copyrightable."

You Decide

1. Despite the court's ruling in this case, do you believe Warner Bros. has a moral obligation to acknowledge Leigh's original work? Explain.
2. If you were the marketing communications director at Warner Bros., would you be concerned about press coverage of Jack Leigh's legal action. If so, what action would be appropriate?

Source: Eric Swetsky, "Copyright in the Garden of Good and Evil," *Marketing* (June 28, 1999), 38. Used with permission. Eric Swetsky is a Toronto lawyer who practises advertising, marketing, and promotion law. His Web site is at http//:advertisinglawyer.wld.com.

bunny because the bunny endurance contest broke new rules that ban superlative claims and comparative advertising. Likewise, Budweiser had to cease using its slogan "King of Beers" or provide statistics proving its claim.

Sales Promotion and the Legal Environment

Most of the laws related to sales promotions deal with incentives offered to consumers. Accordingly, legislation controls procedures that relate to contests, lotteries, and sweepstakes. In addition, there is general sale of good legislation and consumer product warranty legislation that should be of interest to the growing number of marketers using warranties as a promotion tool to stimulate purchase by reducing consumers' risk.

Contest
A promotion that requires some act of skill that requires a judge to make a relative comparison.

Lottery
A payment or other legal consideration in exchange for a chance to win a prize.

Sweepstakes
Games of chance that are lawful only if there is no charge or obligation of any kind for participation.

A **contest** is a competition involving some act of skill that requires a judge to make a relative comparison. A **lottery** involves a payment or other legal consideration in exchange for a chance to win a prize. All three elements—chance, consideration, and prize—must be present, or the promotion is not a lottery. **Sweepstakes** are games of chance based on a random draw of eligible entries and that are lawful only if run by government, licensed, or there is no charge or obligation of any kind for participants. The requirements for promotional contests such as stating the chance of winning, distribution of prizes, and the selection of participants are specifically addressed in the Competition Act.

The Competition Act addresses promotional contests by specifying procedural protections aimed at protecting the contestant. According to the act, when conducting any contest, lottery, game of chance or skill, or mixed chance and skill, there must be: (1) adequate and fair disclosure of the number and approximate value of the prizes; (2) distribution of the prizes such that delivery is not unduly delayed; and (3) selection of participants or distribution of prizes on the basis of skill or on a random basis in any area to which prizes have been allocated.

With respect to warranties, express warranties—those stated in spoken or written words—should be designated as either full or limited. A full warranty should include a statement of the time period during which it will remain operative. A limited warranty must set forth clearly what limitations are included. Moreover, courts now recognize implied warranties—a warranty not actually stated in written words, but intended.

Public Relations and the Legal Environment

Marketing communication managers must also be aware of the laws that affect public relations. We discuss five areas of law: defamation, privacy, copyright, trade-mark, and contract negotiations.

Defamation

Defamation
Any untruthful communication to at least one person (other than the person or entity defamed) that tends to damage a reputation.

Slander
Oral defamation.

Libel
Written defamation.

Defamation is any untruthful communication to at least one other person (other than the person or entity defamed) that tends to damage the reputation of the person or entity defamed. The untruthful communication must clearly identify the defamed party, though not necessarily by name. If the party can be recognized from a description such as "the bald-headed, bearded guy who always sits in the corner of the lunchroom," that identification would be sufficient.

Usually defamation is divided into slander and libel; **slander** is classified as oral defamation and **libel** is classified as written defamation. However, some cases seem to combine both libel and slander. Take, for instance, a television or radio commentator who makes a defamatory remark while reading from a written script. The commentator in such a case is often charged or sued for libel because when the remarks were communicated to an audience they were spoken.

With the emergence of interactive technology, the issue of defamation has become even more confusing. Computer experts are now able to modify a company's Web site and replace the pictures to produce derogatory results. The government has yet to enact laws making it clear who is responsible for monitoring this technology, and the Canadian courts have not yet provided a decision on defamation for cyberspace.

There are two ways public relations practitioners may be involved in libel actions. One of the practitioners' clients might be libelled, or, more likely, the practitioner could be accused of libel through a news release, speech, or other communication.

Privacy

Appropriation
The maximum amount of dollars that management allocates to a specific purpose. Also, the use of private pictures without permission.

The rights of privacy do not apply to a public interest news story about a public figure or to information that is a matter of public record. The right of privacy applies only to people, not to organizations, and it takes four forms: (1) intrusion into solitude; (2) portraying someone in a false light (making the person appear to be someone he or she isn't); (3) public disclosure of private information; and (4) appropriation. **Appropriation,** using private pictures without permission, is the violation that causes most public relations problems. Model and photo releases (forms that give the company permission to use the model or photo in advertising) should be obtained to avoid any PR fiascos. For instance, in 1996 an Amazon chief sued Body Shop International because he alleged the company featured his photo in a publicity poster without his permission.[10] As will be discussed in Chapter 11 in more detail, the suit damaged the Body Shop's image of a company concerned with the environment and all the world's citizens.

Canadian Intellectual Property Office
www.strategies.ic.gc.ca

Copyright

PR experts often use written, artistic, or photographic materials as part of their message strategy. In such cases they must be careful to comply with copyright laws when using others' work. In Canada, copyrights are governed by the Copyright Act which is administered by the Copyright Office, which is part of a larger organization called the Canadian Intellectual Property Office (CIPO).

Under copyright law, users of another person's creative works must understand the fair-dealing exception to the copyright law. It is the primary defence against copyright infringement. The fair-dealing exception allows the use of a part or parts of the work in criticism, research, or private study without seeking permission from the copyright holder. The distinction between "**fair dealing**" and infringement can be a very thin line. What amount of material is allowable is relative, and each case is decided on its own merits. Because so much public relations work is farmed out, public relations freelancers should realize that they may not own the work they produce, since ownership depends on the details of their employment contract.

Fair dealing
An exception to the copyright law that allows the use of a part or parts of a work in criticism, research, or private study without seeking permission from the copyright holder.

Unlike trademarks and patents, a creator of a work for which copyright applies does not have to register the copyright. This protection extends to most foreign countries because international treaties governing copyright have been established. However, in the event of a dispute, registration will establish a presumption of ownership.

Trademark
A brand name or brand mark that is legally protected through registration under the Trademarks Act.

Trademark

Much like the use of copyright material, PR experts often use distinctive logos or symbols such as brand names that are trademarks. A **trademark** is a brand name or brand mark that is legally protected through registration under the Trademarks Act with the Trademarks Office, which is part of a larger agency called the Canadian Intellectual Property Office (CIPO).

Unlike copyright protection, which extends to most foreign countries, if you are selling goods or services in other countries, the CIPO advises that you should consider registration in each of those countries.

Contract Negotiations

Ordinarily, contracts are drafted with the help of a lawyer, but certain business transactions become so familiar that the users forget they are dealing with actual contracts. When a PR practitioner gives a printer a brochure to print, both parties are entering into a contract. Contract negotiations may be equally informal with many other public relations suppliers—photographers, artists, freelance writers, models, typographers, and film producers.

Typically, standard form contracts are used for such transactions. The forms should include these five elements: (1) names of all parties; (2) consideration specified (something of value exchanged); (3) an explanation of the extent of the use of the work (for instance, a photo is to be used in one brochure only); (4) duration of the arrangement; and (5) an indication of any other important factors. Still, these forms should be reviewed periodically, and legal experts should be employed whenever feasible.

Direct Marketing and the Legal Environment

The use of direct-marketing techniques such as telemarketing, direct mail, and use of the Internet as a medium of communication is growing rapidly. The laws and regulations that apply to other forms of marketing communication typically apply to direct marketing. The use of a direct- response technique via the telephone, mail, or Internet does not exempt the marketer from a specific law or regulation.

Of specific interest to direct sellers—sellers who sell at a location other than their permanent place of business, such as door-to-door—all provinces have legislation requiring a registration or licence of direct sellers. To protect consumers, registration will be denied if there are reasonable grounds to believe that business will not be conducted with integrity and honesty. Moreover, a direct sellers' registration or licence can be revoked if the seller does not comply with the provisions of the various acts. Failure to comply with registration requirements is a criminal offence.[11]

Additional consumer protection is afforded to buyers by giving them a cooling-off period—an unconditional right to cancel a contract within a specified period. The intention of a cooling-off provision is to protect consumers who may have been pressured into the purchase of a product that they did not need or want. This type of legislation comes within provincial jurisdiction, thus the actual length of the cooling-off period varies province to province from two to ten days.[12]

The Internet looms as an important and complex direct-marketing medium. The debate over how it should be governed rages as this text goes to print. No one knows exactly the extent to which the Internet will be self-governed or controlled. A recent development is the release of a set of principles for the protection of consumers shopping on-line. The principles are contained in a document, *Principles for Consumer Protection in Electronic Commerce—A Canadian Framework*, that was developed by a working group of Canadian business and consumer organizations, Industry Canada, and the consumer ministries of Alberta, Ontario, and Quebec. According to Nathalie St. Pierre, executive director of Action réseau consommateur (ARC), "the principles set a benchmark for consumer protection on the Internet and will help consumers identify those web sites where they can expect to be dealt with fairly."[13]

Internet expert Martin Cohen comments on one legal Internet issue as it relates to sweepstakes. Consider a standard sweepstakes rule: "enter as often as you like, but each entry must be mailed separately." While it limits entries in a traditional program, if the promotion is offered both on the Internet and via traditional media, the advantage shifts to the electronic entrant. E-mail allows the computer user to forward entries as fast as the fingers can complete the entry form and click "send." To control this, "the rules should include statements limiting the number of e-mail entries, as well as reserving the right to disqualify all entries which violate the limitation."[14]

Personal Selling and the Legal Environment

Historically, personal selling has not been considered an integral part of marketing communication. With the acceptance of an integrated approach to marketing communication, that view has changed. Clearly, the salesperson is often closest to the customer and is the organization's primary communicator. Consequently, the marketing communication manager must be familiar with the laws that impact the salesperson and the sales manager.

Bid-rigging
The act whereby persons, invited to tender for a contract, together and secretly set in advance the terms and conditions under which they will bid.

Price fixing
The illegal act of setting prices in concert with competitors.

Tying arrangement
When a seller forces a buyer to purchase one product to obtain the right to purchase another.

Undoubtedly, laws regarding bid-rigging are particularly significant in industrial and government selling. **Bid-rigging** is the act whereby persons, invited to tender for a contract, together and secretly set in advance the terms and conditions under which they will bid. There are several variations of this practice. The conspirators may agree on the prices to be submitted or arrange that, in consideration for future favours, one or the other of them will not tender for a particular contract offer.[15]

Price fixing is the act of setting prices in concert with competitors. Price fixing occurs most often in concentrated industries where several major competitors exist, for example, steel manufacturing. Often, the price fixers are sales managers. For price fixing to be deemed illegal under Canadian law, it must be demonstrated that the pricing arrangement would likely lessen or prevent competition unduly.

Finally, salespeople are not allowed to engage in tying arrangements. In a **tying arrangement** a seller forces a buyer to purchase one product (the tied product) to obtain the right to purchase another. Under Canadian law, two variations of this practice are also covered: 1) where the supplier will provide the wanted product only on the condition that it is not used in combination with other products not designated by the supplier; and 2) where the supplier does not set an absolute requirement, but seeks to attain the same end by offering to supply the wanted product (the tying product) on more favourable terms and conditions if the buyer agrees also to take tied product or only use tied products in combination with the tying product.[16]

concept review

Marketing Communication and the Law

1. Industry Canada evaluates advertisements that have the capacity to deceive. Deceptive ads may have one or more of the following problems: a misleading claim or demonstration, a false endorsement or testimonial, an unfair comparison, or the use of bait advertising.
2. Sales promotion devices such as contests, lotteries, and sweepstakes each have distinct legal constraints.
3. Legal issues that affect public relations include defamation, privacy, copyright protection, trade-marking, and contract negotiation.
4. Direct-marketing techniques such as direct mail, telemarketing, and the Internet all have important legal limitations.
5. The salesperson and sales managers are affected by three main Competition Act legal issues: bid-rigging, price fixing, and illegal tying arrangements.

MARKETING COMMUNICATION'S RESPONSIBILITY TO SOCIETY

Societal Issues
When the marketing communication activities of a business appear to violate widely held values and, as a result, part of society wants to change the offending actions.

In Chapter 5 we discussed the role of values in cultures and subcultures. Values are guidelines for making judgments, which include honesty, hard work, and love of family. When the marketing communication activities of a business appear to violate widely held values, the actions become **societal issues**. That is, part of society wants to change the offending actions. Even though such activities are not always illegal, the organization that ignores the underlying societal issues risks losing goodwill or business.

Marketing communication managers must be aware of societal issues and be prepared to adapt their strategy (often without advanced notice). These issues differ from one culture to another and from one subculture to another. For instance, a message that goes unnoticed in a large city may become an issue in a small town.

Because marketing communication activities are highly visible, widely varied, and difficult to screen, the general public tends to distrust marketing communications, especially advertising. For instance, a recent survey asked both consumers and advertising executives about their attitudes toward advertising. The findings showed that ad executives are fed up with bad ads produced by their trade—and, importantly, that they're becoming more and more concerned about advertising clutter. "The quality of advertising is really lousy. [Marketing people] feel the bad stuff compromises their work," notes Allison Cohen, president of People Talk, a marketing consulting group in New York.

A large number of consumers in the poll said they "don't care one way or the other" about several types of advertising. Many research experts believe such ambivalence could doom the ad industry. "People care less because there is too much advertising—they're just getting overwhelmed," People Talk's Cohen notes. "They are subject to so much that they tune it out." Perhaps most surprising was the fact that 42.5 percent of the people who work in advertising could not recall an ad seen during the past 24 hours. Only 17 percent of all consumers were able to recall a specific brand name.[17]

It is doubtful that negative attitudes toward advertising will ever disappear, so it is worthwhile to be aware of the social issues facing advertisers. Each of these issues is complex and each involves balancing the public welfare against the right to free speech and freedom of choice. The collective marketing communications industry, including advertising agencies, advertisers, and the media, has an important stake in how the public and legislators view these social issues.

Consequently, the advertising industry has taken a proactive strategy in defending its image and informing the public about the virtues of the industry. The ad for the advertising industry illustrates the approach being used to enhance their image.

ISSUES OF SOCIAL RESPONSIBILITY

In the following sections we briefly explore six societal issues that affect marketing communicators: manipulation and subliminal messaging, the right to privacy, puffery, offensive products and appeals, stereotyping, and advertising to children.

This Advertising Standards Canada (ASC) ad indicates that the Canadian advertising industry listens to the public's concerns about advertising.

Everyone Has Something To Say About Advertising.

And We Listen.

That's what we're here for. So what do you do if an ad causes you concern? Simple. Let us know. We're Advertising Standards Canada, the industry's self-regulatory body. We administer the Canadian Code of Advertising Standards; a code developed by and for the advertising industry. It sets the standards for responsible advertising in Canada. For more information, call our toll-free line. If you have a concern about an ad, write to us. We guarantee a prompt response.

ADVERTISING STANDARDS CANADA

You respond to advertising. We respond to you.

350 Bloor Street East, Suite 402, Toronto, Ontario, M4W 1H5 • 1-877-656-8646 • www.adstandards.com

Manipulation and Subliminal Messaging

Critics claim that marketing communication manipulates people so that they purchase products and services that they neither need or want. This criticism raises an extremely difficult issue. On the one hand, there are gullible people who believe everything they hear or read. And some people buy everything they see, regardless of whether they can afford it. Other people—including children, the senile, or the poorly educated—may not have the intellectual or physical capabilities to judge good from bad or real from unreal. The extent to which marketing communication influences these people is impossible to determine. On the other hand, no amount of marketing communication will make most people do something they do not want to do. Even a smooth-talking, aggressive salesperson cannot make the customer sign on the dotted line. Freedom of choice is a right that marketing communication cannot negate.

Subliminal message
A message that is sent in such a way that the receiver is not consciously aware of receiving it.

This same freedom does not exist, however, in the case of subliminal techniques. A **subliminal message** is one that is sent in such a way that the receiver is not consciously aware of receiving it. This usually means that the symbols are too faint or too brief to be clearly recognized. In essence it is a type of brainwashing and is morally wrong.

So, the critical question is whether advertisers engage in subliminal messaging. There is no evidence that they do, or should. First, the risk of engaging in such an underhanded activity is too great compared with possible benefits. Second, the potential benefits are uncertain as well. No evidence supports the claim that symbols subliminally perceived by one person are perceived in the same way by another person. Third, marketing communicators cannot predict how, where, and in what context the audience will receive the subliminal message. Because of these factors, the effect of any subliminal message strategy would be, at best, limited and inconsistent—especially when compared with the risk communicators would face if consumers learned the business used such techniques.

Privacy

One basic human right is privacy—the right to be left alone. Critics argue that marketing communication violates our personal privacy. Ads seem to confront us everywhere—on parking meters, grocery store shopping carts, movie screens, rented videocassettes, and television monitors at airports. Ads are sent to fax machines, and few nights go by without a household's receiving at least one telemarketer's sales call, usually during dinner. The criticism of privacy violation appears valid. Marketing communication strategists must find less offensive ways of reaching consumers than bombarding them wherever they go. Doing a better job of identifying consumers who are truly interested in the product is part of the solution. Providing a mechanism for consumers to initiate the communication process—by calling a toll-free number, for example—is also helpful.

Puffery

Puffery
Advertising or other sales representations that praise the product or service with subjective opinions, superlatives, or exaggerations, vaguely and generally, without substantiation.

Consumers do not like to be lied to. But do they mind puffery? **Puffery** is advertising or other sales representations that praise the product or service with subjective opinions, superlatives, or exaggerations, vaguely and generally, stating no specific facts.[18] Statements such as "Nestlé makes the very best chocolate" and "When you say Budweiser, you've said it all" are mild forms of puffery.

Regulators who deal with misleading messages have no jurisdiction over those that exaggerate. Critics argue that promotional messages should contain useful information, but not puffery. Defenders suggest that reasonable people know that puffery merely shows enthusiasm for a product and that consumers understand this persuasive type of selling. Clearly, puffery can be risky because overexaggerating can dissuade an audience. Defining puffery and determining whether to encourage, tolerate, or avoid it require the marketing communication manager to make a careful evaluation.

Offensive Products and Appeals

We have come a long way since the 1950s, when an advertising executive coined the term B.O. (body odour) for use in a print ad for a deodorant because consumers would be offended by the word sweat. Nevertheless, consumers may still be offended or irritated by certain types of appeals and by promotions for certain products. Feminine hygiene products, hemorrhoid cures, condoms, and jock itch treatments are a few products whose advertisements offend some people. Sexual appeals and fear appeals may also offend.

Marketing communication managers who use controversial appeals and promote controversial products argue that their messages are appropriate for the target audience. But managers must be sensitive to the fact that people outside the target audience may also receive the messages. When people feel that

Many consumers have negative perceptions about advertising, some of which are effectively challenged in this eye-catching ad.

marketing communicators have gone too far, they are likely to pressure marketers to change their messages and resellers to stop carrying the products.

This problem of being sensitive to other people's tastes becomes even more complicated when communicating in other cultures. In South Korea, for example, marketing communicators are not allowed to advertise products such as beer, liquor, and cigarettes. Keeping pet animals used to be regarded as a luxury in Korea, and the government opposed advertising pet-related products on the grounds that it was inappropriate to advertise such products while some families had difficulty feeding their children.

Stereotyping

Stereotyping
Ignoring the differences among individuals and presenting the group in an unvarying pattern.

The portrayal of people, not products, has also become a social issue. Marketing communications are accused of being discriminatory by presenting stereotypes in their promotions. **Stereotyping** ignores differences among individuals and presents a group in an unvarying pattern. Stereotypes of women are one prominent target of criticism. Recent studies have shown that females are more scantily dressed than their male counterparts in the same ad. Ads often depict women as sexualized bodies, with their status based on how they look.[19] The two most prominent images of women presented in ad campaigns, those of the "innocent virgin" and of the "dark lady," pit innocence and romance against knowledge and sexuality. Although there is still concern about sexual stereotyping, more marketing communicators are recognizing the diversity of women's roles.

Racial and ethnic groups also complain of stereotyping in marketing communication. Minorities may be the basis of a joke or, alternatively, consigned to the background. Other critics complain that minorities are under-represented in advertisements. Communication that perpetuates stereotypes can offend society at large and promote biases.

Another group frequently stereotyped is senior citizens. Critics often object to the use of older people in roles that portray them as slow, senile, and full of medical afflictions. Portrayals of seniors as slow and senile are definitely on the decline.

Advertising to Children

Those who favour regulating children's advertising are concerned that children do not possess the skills necessary to evaluate the advertising message and to make informed purchase decisions. They also believe that certain advertising techniques and strategies appropriate for adults are confusing or misleading to children.

Advertising to children has been a hotly debated topic since the 1970s, when experts estimated that the average child was exposed to over 20 000 commercials.[20] Issues subject to debate include: at what age do children understand the intent and content of advertising messages; should advertising directed at children be permitted?; to what extent it should be regulated?; should restrictions apply to specific media?; and should advertising of those products inherently appealing to children—toys, video games, branded clothing fashions—be banned?

As life expectancy and quality of life for senior citizens increase, the stereotypes of seniors no longer apply. This V8 ad shows how one senior defies aging, living an active, healthy life.

In the United States, legislation has been passed to limit the practice of advertising to children. For example, the 1990 Children's Television Advertising Practice Act limits ads directed to children to 10.5 minutes per hour for commercials in weekend children's television programming and 12-minutes per hour for weekday programs. More recently, President Clinton signed the Telecommunications Act into law in 1996. That act mandates that the broadcast industry develop a program ratings system compatible with the V-Chip, a blocking device for programs that are identified as violent, sexual, indecent, or otherwise objectionable for minors.[21] The industry has been working to comply with the act since its passage into law.

In Canada, Quebec's Consumer Protection Act has strictly banned all advertising directed to children (defined as those under age 13) since 1980. To advertise product of inherent interest to the children's market, advertisers must direct their message toward parents and place the ad in TV programs watched by few children. In addition to this provincial legislation, self-regulation of advertising to children is practised via the Canadian Association of Broadcasters (CAB), in co-operation with Advertising Standards Canada (ASC). The CAB's Broadcast Code for Advertising to Children serves as a guide to advertisers and agencies in preparing messages that adequately recognize the special characteristics of the children's audience. This code is designed to complement the general principles for ethical advertising outlined in ASC's *Canadian Code of Advertising Standards*.[22] According to this code, advertising that is directed to children must not exploit their credulity, lack of experience, or their sense of loyalty, and must not present information or illustrations that might result in their physical, emotional, or moral harm.[23]

Self-Regulation of Marketing Communication

One reason for the heavy regulation of marketing at both the federal and provincial levels is the long-standing assumption that marketing involves illegal and unethical activities. Marketing communication has unfortunately caught the brunt of this criticism. Consequently, professionals working in marketing communication have developed guidelines and codes of ethical conduct so that marketing communication managers and their companies can both avoid violating the law and can act in a socially responsible manner.

For instance, the alcohol industry (except beer and wine) initiated a self-imposed ban 48 years ago to keep liquor ads off U.S. radio and television. The ban lasted for nearly half a century. Then in 1996 Edgar Bronfman, Jr., president and chief executive of Seagram Co. broke the ban by airing a 30-second commercial for its Crown Royal whiskey on an NBC affiliate in Texas. Since then Seagram has purchased advertising time in several markets and has prompted several other distillers to consider breaking the ban. For instance, Hiram Walker & Sons Inc. followed suit, placing ads for Mudslide, a Kahlua-based drink, in 22 local markets.[24]

The Marketing Communication Clearance Process

In addition to external regulation, most companies, agencies, and media have an elaborate network for reviewing marketing communication efforts. Although this review process tends to differ from company to company, it typically starts with the creative team and ends with the medium that carries the marketing communication, such as TV, magazines, the package, or the Internet. Virtually every major medium has guidelines for acceptable marketing communication. *Reader's Digest*, for example, has a long list of unacceptable product categories and message appeals.

At each step in the clearance process, the marketing communication piece is critiqued from a number of different perspectives to ensure that it meets all reasonable standards of ethics and good taste as well as legal requirements. Lawyers may review the piece at several different stages. The marketing communications firm often has a set of standards against which it measures and scores all work. Marketing communication efforts that receive scores below a certain level are rejected. Figure 7.1 shows one example of a marketing communication review process.

Marketing communication managers believe that a vigorous internal review process is beneficial. The risks of allowing an unethical or illegal promotion to be seen or heard by the public are simply too great.

Self-Regulation by Professional Groups

To date there are very few, if any, universal standards by which to judge marketing communication activities. Marketing communicators do not agree among themselves as to what is legal or ethical, and critics apply their own ethical standards. Despite the lack of consensus, uncertainty about what is permissible has decreased during the last two decades. Most of this change comes as a result of the activities of independent organizations that impose regulation through public pressure, and codes developed by groups within the marketing communication industry that are attempting self-regulation. These codes are usually area-specific and deal with topics such as advertising, personal selling techniques, or direct marketing practices.

Advertising Standards Canada

Advertising Standards Canada
www.adstandards.com

Advertising Standards Canada (ASC) (formerly the Canadian Advertising Foundation) is the ad industry's self-regulatory body. Its membership is composed of more than 200 media outlets, ad agencies, and advertisers.

ASC administers the *Canadian Code of Advertising Standards*, which has been developed to promote the professional practice of advertising. This code is widely endorsed by advertising agencies, advertisers, media organizations, and suppliers to the advertising process.

ASC is an extremely powerful organization. If a single consumer complaint to ASC is found to violate the *Canadian Code of Advertising Standards* or gender portrayal guidelines, ASC will ask the advertiser to remove or amend it. In situations where advertisers refuse an ASC request, ASC will instruct media outlets to pull the offending spot. Advertisers that do not co-operate risk having their names published in the ASC bulletin.[25]

Although the Canadian Code of Advertising Standards is ASC's principal instrument of advertising self-regulation, it also administers other advertising self-regulation codes; provides broadcast advertising commercial clearance services for food and non-alcoholic beverage, cosmetic, and child-directed advertising, and broadcast and print clearances for tobacco advertising; and provides consultative services to the advertising industry. ASC also administers the industry's trade dispute procedure. Table 7.2 provides a list of industry codes and guidelines administered by ASC.[26]

Figure 7.1 CHART OF INITIAL AND FINAL CLEARANCE PROCESS

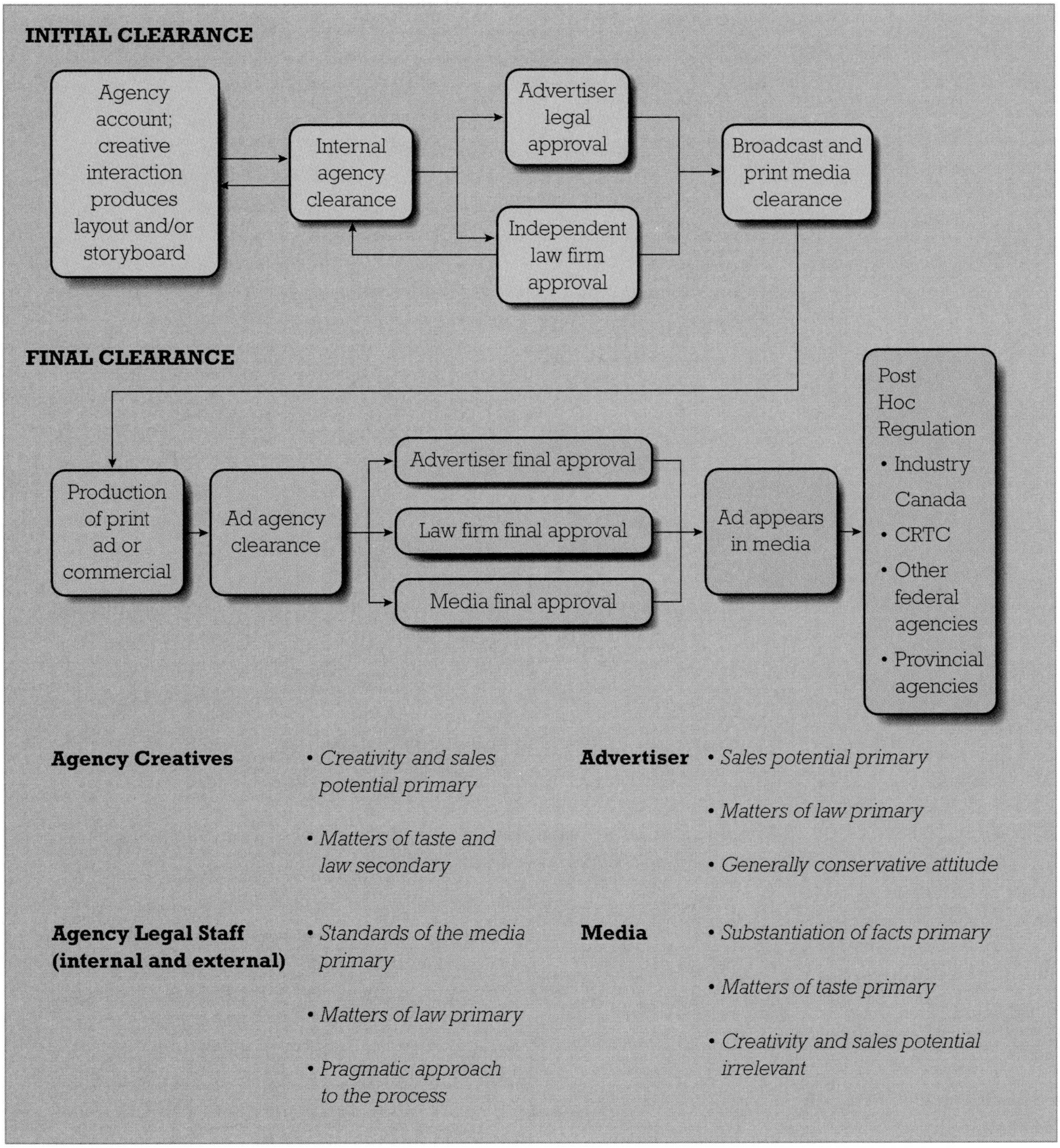

Agency Creatives
- *Creativity and sales potential primary*
- *Matters of taste and law secondary*

Agency Legal Staff (internal and external)
- *Standards of the media primary*
- *Matters of law primary*
- *Pragmatic approach to the process*

Advertiser
- *Sales potential primary*
- *Matters of law primary*
- *Generally conservative attitude*

Media
- *Substantiation of facts primary*
- *Matters of taste primary*
- *Creativity and sales potential irrelevant*

Canadian Marketing Association
www.cdma.org

OTHER AGENTS OF SELF-REGULATION

Several other professional groups actively promote self-regulation of the marketing communications industry in Canada. Many of these groups and their self-regulation efforts are discussed in brief later in this text. These include the Canadian Marketing Association's (CMA) administration of its compulsory *Code of Ethics and Standards of Practice* (Chapter 12). The CMA represents

Table 7.2 INDUSTRY CODES AND GUIDELINES ADMINISTERED BY ADVERTISING STANDARDS CANADA (ASC)

- Canadian Code of Advertising Standards
- Gender Portrayal Guidelines
- Broadcast Code for Advertising to Children
- Advertising Code of Standards for Cosmetics, Toiletries & Fragrances
- Guidelines for the use of Comparative Advertising in Food Commercials
- Guidelines for the use of Research & Survey Data in Comparative Food Commercials
- Trade Dispute Procedure
- Tobacco Voluntary Packaging and Advertising Industry Code

information-based marketers, most of whom use direct marketing techniques. The Canadian Professional Sales Association (CPSA) is another professional organization that represents the interests of marketing communicators. The CPSA administers a *Code of Ethics*, which those who earn the organization's Certified Sales Professional (CSP) designation must agree to abide (Chapter 13).

Self-regulation has also been supported by the Better Business Bureau (BBB), local advertising review boards, advertising agencies, advertising media, and public relations firms. Supported by local businesses, the BBB system of more than 150 Bureaus located throughout the United States and Canada investigates complaints, attempts to persuade offenders to stop unfair practices, and, if necessary, employs legal restrictions on advertising.

The Better Business Bureau urges businesses to adopt the following three principles of advertising self-regulation:

1. My organization will take primary responsibility for truthful and nondeceptive advertising.
2. My organization will make available to the media, or the BBB, evidence to substantiate advertising claims.
3. My organization will ensure that the overall impact of its advertising is not misleading, even though every statement may be true when viewed separately.

Better Business Bureau
www.bbbonline.org

Additionally, the BBB has established the BBBOnline Program to build consumer confidence in the online marketplace. One aspect of this program is the BBBOnLine Reliability seal. Display of this seal indicates to consumers that the business operating the Web site has agreed to stand behind its products and services and has made a commitment to resolve disputes with customers.

MARKETING COMMUNICATION AND THE GLOBAL ENVIRONMENT

Just as legal and social issues affect marketing communication, so does the dynamism of the international environment. In this section we explore five key factors that affect marketing communication directly. First, to compete

concept review

Marketing Communication's Responsibility To Society and Self-Regulation

1. Marketing communicators must be responsive to societal issues, especially the following:
   - Manipulation and subliminal messages
   - Puffery
   - Privacy
   - Offensive products and appeals
   - Stereotyping
   - Advertising to children
2. Marketing communicators engage in self-regulation to prevent violation of laws and to adhere to their social responsibility.
   - Each organization has its own clearance process of evaluating its marketing communication
   - Industry codes and review boards also exist to evaluate marketing communication practice

effectively, more industries are locating manufacturing, assembly, or other facilities close to customers in important world markets. Second, the international community has created a forum to resolve disputes between trading partners—the World Trade Organization. Third, established trade blocs such as the European Union are working to lower barriers to international trade. Fourth, with the disintegration of the communist Soviet Union, huge new markets opened as the nations of Central and Eastern Europe embraced democracy and capitalism. Finally, technological breakthroughs have spawned a number of products and services—fax machines, pagers, cellular telephones, and the Internet among them—that have fostered fast-paced marketing communication unlimited by national boundaries.

Counterbalancing the forces that are shrinking the globe, however, is a growing sense of nationalism among citizens who are concerned about losing their national identity in a borderless world. To reach target audiences that have such concerns, marketing communicators must "think global and act local," or risk alienating large markets.

Globalization of Industries

In industries with international customers, failure to develop global strategy can harm a company's competitiveness. To better serve an integrated market, for instance, a company should not limit itself to obtaining raw materials or locating manufacturing facilities, or offering customer services in the home country (the country where the business is based). Examples of industries that have globalized include housewares, automobiles, computers, pharmaceuticals, soft drinks, and telecommunications.

The globalization of industries has a direct impact on marketing communication. For example, automobile manufacturer Toyota no longer simply builds cars in Japan for export to other countries. Toyota has manufacturing and assembly plants worldwide to better serve its markets and to offset a bias against foreign-made products. In its marketing communications in North America,

This Toyota Echo ad designed for Canadian based print media highlights that Toyota dealers are proud sponsors of the Canadian Special Olympics.

Toyota often stresses the fact many of its best-selling models are built by North American workers using a high proportion of North American-made parts. Also, Toyota will often highlight a sponsorship relevant to the target consumers' country of residence. Such communication strategies help consumers overcome reservations about buying a foreign brand automobile.

The World Trade Organization and Trading Blocs

The World Trade Organization (WTO) provides a forum in which international trading partners can resolve disputes related to unfair trade practices and other issues (including advertising, distribution, or pricing disputes). Based in Geneva, Switzerland, the WTO has a Dispute Settlement Body (DSB) that mediates complaints concerning disputed issues among the WTO's 130 member countries that account for over 90 percent of world trade.[27] During a 60-day consultation period, parties to a complaint are expected to engage in good-faith negotiations and reach an amicable resolution. Failing that, the party that brings the complaint can ask the DSB to appoint a three-member panel to hear the case behind closed doors. The DSB is empowered to act on the panel's recommendations. The losing party has the option of turning to a seven-member appellate body. If, after due process, a country's trade policies are found to have violated WTO rules, it is expected to change those policies. If changes are not forthcoming, the WTO can authorize trade sanctions against the loser.

The WTO can have a direct effect on international marketing communication activity, as shown by a dispute between Canada and the United States over Canadian legislation to ban split-run magazines, such as *Sports Illustrated*. According to the Canadian position, split-run magazines would run a limited number of Canadian stories but sell a large amount of ad space for Canadian advertisers. Thus limiting the market success of more "truly" Canadian publications. The You Decide feature in Chapter 14 discusses this trade dispute in more detail.

Trade barriers in different parts of the world are being reduced or eliminated as countries forge economic agreements with neighbours on a regional basis. One of the most well-known of these trading blocs is the European Union (EU). Member countries include Belgium, France, Holland, Italy, Luxembourg, Germany, Great Britain. Denmark, Ireland, Greece, Spain, Portugal, Finland, Sweden, and Austria. Implementation of the Single European Act at the end of 1992 meant that citizens of the 15 countries were free to cross borders within the Union. Marketing conditions have been improved because content and other product standards that varied among nations have been harmonized. Further EU enlargement has become a major issue. In December 1991, Czechoslovakia, Hungary, and Poland became associate members. The Baltic countries—Latvia, Lithuania, and Estonia—are also hoping to join and thus lower their vulnerability to Russia. There is no doubt that marketing communication in the region should be adjusted to reflect a European audience that, despite cultural differences and a dozen different languages, is becoming more unified.

Developing Nations in the Global Spotlight

Even as the importance of regional trading blocs grows, individual nations are also commanding attention—not all of it flattering. Four Asian countries—South Korea, Taiwan, Singapore, and Hong Kong—are sometimes collectively referred to as "tigers." Fuelled by foreign investment and export-driven industrial development, these four countries have achieved stunning rates of economic growth. Another four countries—Thailand, Malaysia, Indonesia, and China—are also showing signs of industrial take-off. China's population of 1.2 billion offers both a huge potential market for many products as well as a massive low-wage labour force for manufacturing.

However, even as these countries become more fully integrated in the world economy, a number of concerns are surfacing. One is the issue of poor working conditions and the use of child labour in the toy, athletic shoe, and apparel industries. Allegations reflect poorly on both the countries in which abuses occur and the well-known companies whose products are produced in those countries. Increasing numbers of consumers are well informed about where, by whom, and under what conditions their favourite brand-name products are manufactured.

Another problem linked to developing countries is piracy of computer software, videos, recorded music, and other forms of intellectual property. The International Intellectual Property Alliance estimates that Chinese counterfeiting of copyrighted material alone costs U.S. companies $800 million annually. Experts estimate that 98 percent of the computer software used in China is pirated. Factories in China also produce counterfeit Levi's jeans for about $5 per pair and sell them to people who falsely claim to be legitimate Levi representatives.

This billboard in a railway station in Warsaw reminds consumers that Colgate is the "Number 1 Toothpaste in the World." Its image and copy is purposefully simple because Poles distrust ad blitzes and regard Yuppie images as propaganda.

Chrysler Corporation has even discovered sports-utility vehicles on the streets of Beijing that are nearly identical to Jeep Cherokees. Such revelations reflect poorly on China. Notes Hong Kong businessman Barry C. Cheung, "China lacks skills in public relations generally and crisis management specifically, and that hurts them."[28] Part of the problem stems from the unwillingness of China's leaders to publicly explain their views on these issues, to admit failure, and to accept advice from the West.

Central and Eastern Europe after Communism

According to studies conducted by Freedom House, 117 of the world's 191 nations are now democratic—an increase of 20 percent during the past decade. Democracy's accession is especially striking in Eastern and Central Europe.[29] In the early 1990s the extraordinary political and economic reforms that swept the region focused the world's attention on a market of more than 400 million consumers. With wage rates much lower than those in Spain, Portugal, and Greece, the countries of Eastern and Central Europe represent attractive locations for low-cost manufacturing. The transition from centrally planned economies to market-based systems has been accompanied by a realignment of regional power. In 1992 Hungary, Poland, and Czechoslovakia signed an agreement creating the Central European Free Trade Association (CEFTA). The signatories pledged cooperation in a number of areas, including telecommunications, tourism, and retail trade.

Marketing communication will play a key role in promoting economic development throughout the region, although several decades may pass before marketing practices reach a level of sophistication comparable to Western Europe. Having thrown off the yoke of communism, the citizens of the former Soviet bloc must learn about democracy and capitalism and the marketing ommunication tools that are available in such systems. In Hungary, for example, the practice of public relations was restricted under communism, and there were no advertising agencies or media organizations. However, as a 1991 headline in *The Hungarian Observer* proclaims, "PR is Back: Hungary has to learn how to sell itself all over again." Formed in 1990, the Hungarian Public Relations Association has seen its membership grow dramatically in recent years.[30]

Many consumers in the region are familiar with Western brand names and view them as being higher in quality than domestic products. This situation creates an environment in which marketing communications are likely to be perceived favourably. In Russia, L'Oréal SA, Calvin Klein, and Estee Lauder, Inc., are among the companies moving quickly to tap burgeoning demand for consumer products. Russian editions of well-known Western women's magazines such as *Cosmopolitan, Harper's Bazaar,* and *Good Housekeeping* provide ideal media vehicles for upscale advertisers.

Global Technological Change

Technological change has dramatically impacted marketing communication over the past two decades. Pagers, cellular telephones, fax machines, laptop computers with modems, and satellite television have improved communication throughout the world. In addition to these communication changes, the explosion of Internet access and use means that marketing communicators can operate around the world, 24 hours a day. The World Wide Web portion of the Internet and commercial online services offer organizations and companies new ways to interact and conduct business with customers throughout the world. Internet experts believe that the Web will become a truly global mass-communication medium. Predicts CEO Hal Krisbergh of WorldGate Communications, "Just imagine if 60 percent of the population—roughly the number of cable subscribers—has access to the Internet. You'll see a whole shift in communications, shopping—every aspect of how we see the world. It will have a major, universal impact.[31]

The growing popularity of the Internet also creates a number of marketing communication challenges. First, as people spend more time online, they view less television and cut back on reading and other leisure-time activities that represent traditional marketing communication channels. Second, the cost of setting up Web sites can be prohibitive. For example, it can cost several millions of dollars a year to set up and run a Web site for selling goods and services. The third issue is privacy. As more transactions are conducted online, consumers will

concept review

Marketing Communication and the Global Environment

1. The globalization of industries has a direct impact on marketing communication.
2. Two important global organizations include the World Trade Organization (WTO) and regional trading blocs, such as the European Union (EU).
3. Developing nations affect IMC around the world.
4. New technology has changed global marketing communication.

need guarantees that credit card numbers and other personal information are secure. Besides wanting data protection, some computer users and regulators also want to block access to certain types of online content—pornography, for instance. In Singapore, government regulators have the authority to censor the content that reaches the country's Internet users.[32]

A Closing Thought:

All Actions and Communications Must be Fair

If an integrated marketing communication strategy is to work, it is critical that every message, every medium, and every contact point is both legal and ethical. Making a mistake in one area of the strategy may have dire consequences for all the other strategic elements. An unsafe package, an overly aggressive sales force, or a deceptive ad can negate every other element of the marketing communication program. Therefore, marketing communicators should create a review mechanism that considers the entire marketing communication program.

To review the program as a whole, marketers may need to reorganize, to change their business philosophy, or to enlist additional resources. The IMC in Action feature illustrates how several companies within an industry violated this integrated approach and confused consumers as a result.

Giving the Consumer a Headache

Talk about splitting headaches. Since the fall of 1995, the two over-the-counter painkiller giants, Johnson & Johnson's Tylenol and American Home Products' Advil, have been giving consumers a migraine with their constant fighting. Somehow, both have lost sight of the fact that their integrated communication strategies are being negatively affected by their public warfare.

The pounding began when Johnson & Johnson launched a television attack ad that soon had the two companies decrying the side effects of each other's products. The confusing charges and countercharges prompted the major TV networks to pull the harshest spots. ABC went so far as to ban all drug commercials that take potshots at rival remedies.

Undaunted, the combatants continued their fight in print, where Advil launched an assault on Tylenol through a full-page ad in a number of major U.S. newspapers that featured an open letter written by Antonis Benedi, who blames Tylenol for the liver failure that forced him to have an emergency transplant in 1993. Johnson & Johnson was furious, not just about the letter but also at the fact that the newspaper published it without labelling it advertising. Worse, in Johnson & Johnson's view, at the bottom of the ad was a message that Whitehall-Robin's Healthcare was underwriting the letter reprint "as a public service." Not exactly, as it's the unit of American Home Products that makes Advil.

The latest attack led industry watchers to warn that the infighting could become suicidal. "This has exploded out of control," says Paul Kelly, president of Silvermine Consulting, which advises consumer-products companies. "Sooner or later people are going to get concerned about the whole category [of painkillers] and stay away."

Both companies continue to be outstanding strategic marketing communicators who have a clear understanding of how the tools can be synchronized to produce a beautiful melody. They don't seem to understand the risk they take with a sour note.

Source: John Greenwald, "Bitter Ads to Swallow," *Time*, April 1, 1996, 48-9.

summary

1. Identify the government bodies that control the efforts of marketing communicators.

   Marketing communication is the most legislated and scrutinized element of marketing. Because of its visibility, legislators regulate many marketing communication activities. Industry Canada and the Canadian Radio-television and Telecommunications Commission (CRTC) are the primary federal regulatory bodies that affect marketing communications. Other regulatory bodies that impact marketing communication practice include the Canadian Transport Commission, provincial and local governments, marketing boards, and trade associations.

2. Identify the major legal issues that affect marketing communication.

   Advertising legal issues involve misleading advertising practices, such as making false claims, use of tests and testimonials, comparisons, and bait advertising. Legal issues affect each area of marketing communication. In conducting sales promotions, managers must pay particular attention to contests, lotteries, sweepstakes, and warranties. Legal issues relevant to public relations include defamation, violation of privacy, copyright violation, trade-mark infringement, and contractual obligations. Direct marketers must be cognizant of laws governing direct mail, telemarketing, and the Internet. In personal selling, key legal concerns include bid-rigging, price fixing, and tying arrangements.

3. Analyse the social responsibility issues that affect marketing communication.

   The key social responsibility issues that affect marketing communication are manipulation and subliminal advertising, puffery, privacy, offensive products, stereotyping, and responsible advertising to children. Marketing communicators must make a reasoned decision about how to send messages in a socially responsible manner.

4. Discuss the role of self-regulation in marketing communication.

   Marketing communicators self-regulate to prevent violation of provincial and federal laws and to adhere to their social responsibility. They may also self-regulate to prevent laws from being enacted that might be more restrictive than the self-regulatory measures. Self-regulation can occur both within the organization via a formal clearance process and through professional organizations that administer codes of conduct such as the Advertising Standards Canada's (ASC) Code of Advertising Standards.

5. Outline the key global factors that affect marketing communication.

   Several critical issues affect marketing communication. First, numerous industries are becoming international, locating services and plants closer to the customers they serve. Marketing communicators in such industries must strike a balance between thinking globally and acting locally. Second, the World Trade Organization (WTO) resolves disputes between trading partners, many of which relate to marketing communication issues. For instance, a WTO dispute can result in negative public relations to which marketing communicators must be able to respond. Third, several multi-country blocs, such as the European Union (EU), regulate issues among countries. Marketing communicators must be aware of how these blocs affect their ability to promote products in various regions. Fourth, markets in developing nations are opening up as never before, but companies that do business with such nations must be aware of stakeholder reaction to such issues as human rights and environmental concerns. Target audiences in industrialized nations often react negatively to perceived violations of social standards when dealing with developing nations. Fifth, the opening of markets in former communist countries has spurred new marketing activity. However, because of differences in cultural values, economic systems, and attitudes toward Western countries, marketing communicators must proceed with caution to deliver messages that will persuade audiences in those markets. Finally, technology has affected the pace and reach of marketing communications around the world.

points to ponder

Review the Facts

1. Provide an overview of the most important laws affecting marketing communication strategies and tactics.
2. What are the requirements for a misleading advertising conviction to occur under the Competition Act?
3. Define subliminal messaging.
4. Discuss the role of the World Trade Organization (WTO).

Master the Concepts

5. What advice would you give to a person who is developing a claim for an advertising message?
6. What is being done to develop ethical codes for self-regulation of marketing communication? Do you think these activities are sufficient? Explain.
7. How can the marketing communication manager avoid stereotyping?
8. Should businesses engage in subliminal advertising? Why?
9. Why does the development of a marketing strategy or program require an understanding of the global environment?
10. Why do you think it is important for marketing communicators to think globally and act locally?

Apply Your Knowledge

11. Assume that you are a judge. What factors would you use to determine whether a retailer was indeed practising bait-and-switch advertising?
12. Suppose you were the marketing communication director for a clothing designer trying to target the teenage to young adult markets. Your creative team devised a series of print ads and billboards using images of notorious criminals, such as Charles Manson. The initial market research suggests that most people in your target audience like and remember the campaign, but some are offended because they feel the ads elevate mass murders to cult status. Is it socially responsible to run the ads and billboards? Is it a good business decision? Consider the IMC implications. Explain your answer.
13. Assume you are in charge of a cellular phone company's new integrated communication program in Central and Eastern Europe. What parts of the marketing communication program would have to differ from the firm's North American and Western European program? What could stay the same?

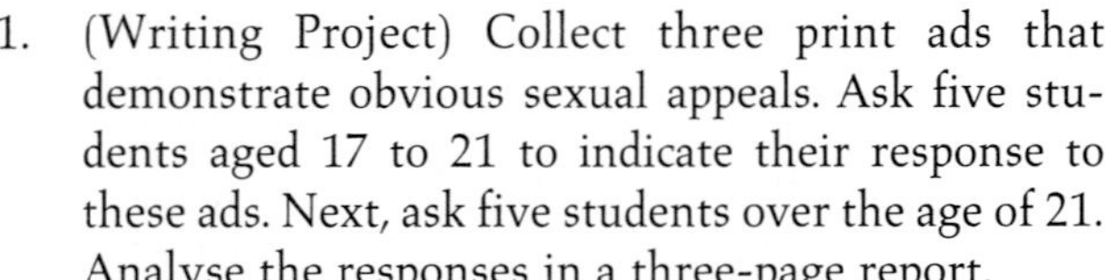

1. (Writing Project) Collect three print ads that demonstrate obvious sexual appeals. Ask five students aged 17 to 21 to indicate their response to these ads. Next, ask five students over the age of 21. Analyse the responses in a three-page report.
2. (Team Project) Divide the class into groups of four to six students. Ask each person in your group to research a different company that offers facilities or services in countries other than the company's home country. The research should focus on the pitfalls and benefits of conducting business in countries other than the home country. Meet in the small group to discuss the research findings. As a group, compile a list of the advantages and disadvantages of locating facilities or services in countries other than the home country, and draw up guidelines for companies that plan to globalize. Be prepared to present your findings to the class.
3. (Internet and Writing Project) You are convinced that a major company is making false claims in its advertising, sales promotion, and Internet direct marketing activities. You want to make a formal online complaint about these activities to the appropriate regulatory agencies. Explore the Internet for regulatory agency sites. Write a brief memo (two to three pages) about the online complaint filing process (if any) at each agency, which agencies you feel would be most responsive to your complaint (or certain portions of your complaint), and why.

Will Power's Surveys Lose Their Punch?

Consumers shopping for a car are in a difficult position, especially if they are interested in new models. Dealers, of course, sing the praises of their brands, but other than such things as fuel efficiency ratings, consumers have very few objective metresticks by which to measure one manufacturer's cars against another. Many eagerly await ***Consumer Reports'*** yearly car-buying guide, which indulges the magazine's ratings of new cars and its subscribers' ratings of cars they own. But although salespeople may be eager to tell prospective customers about the magazine's ratings, ***Consumer Reports*** refuses to let manufacturers use its ratings in advertisements.

The Surveys

So to provide consumers with objective evidence of their products' quality, car manufacturers turn to J.D. Power & Associates. Power publishes four major surveys each year, based on information collected from some 30 000 car owners. Consumers' satisfaction with the buying process is reflected in the Sales Satisfaction Survey. The Initial Quality Survey measures how owners feel after they've had their car three months, the Customer Satisfaction Survey rates customers' assessments of car quality and dealer service a year after purchase, and the Vehicle Dependability Index indicates how owners feel after five years.

Only Good News

Consumer advocates generally approve of the way that Power gathers its information, but some criticize what the company does once it has compiled its surveys; they are, in effect, Power's clients. Until 1986, Power released all its findings, positive and negative. But the manufacturers—also Power's clients—complained that a poor rating from Power could hurt car sales, so now Power makes public only positive ratings. The surveys also rate entire car lines—all Buicks, for instance—rather than individual models, which makes it more difficult for consumers to know how good a particular model is likely to be.

The Bad News

What threatens Power's credibility is the proliferation of ads that use the results of Power's surveys. As many as a dozen different cars may be promoted with Power's rankings at one time. These ads aren't lying; they're just using isolated pieces of the surveys. The major surveys include 20 or more categories, so it is relatively easy for a manufacturer to say that its product was rated "highest in its class" or "tops among North American cars in its class," even though the car in question may in fact have done poorly in the overall ratings or when compared to imported models. The Chevrolet Lumina, for instance, was advertised as "the most trouble-free car in its class," according to Power's Initial Quality Survey. What the ad didn't say was that the Lumina had actually scored below average in the survey; it's just that the other cars in the "midsize specialty class" did even worse.

J.D. Power himself, who started his company in 1971, recognizes the risks of his name being overused. In 1986 he began reviewing—for a hefty fee—all ads that referred to his company's surveys. Policing ads for their validity is a good step, critics say, but it alone won't stop the devaluing of Power's survey results. It seems that car buyers may still have to do their own research just to find out what the Power survey results mean.

Case Questions

1. What are the possible legal and/or social problems faced by auto makers who use the J.D. Power survey data?
2. What are some of the long-term risks the marketing communication manager takes in using data provided by J.D. Power?
3. What would you recommend J.D. Power do to maintain the value of its surveys, given the legal and social concerns?

Sources: "Rating J.D. Powers Grand Plan," ***Business Week***, September 2, 1996, 75–6; Kim Foltz, "J.D. Power's Big Problem: Popularity," ***New York Times***, 17 August 1990, C-5; Barry Meier, "A Car Is Rated Most Trouble-Free, But How Good Is That?" ***New York Times***, 13 October 1990, 16.

CBC VIDEO VIGNETTES

CBC

Prescription Drug Promotion: How Far Should It Go?

Have you noticed an increase in the number of prescription drugs being pitched in the U.S. media? In recent years the Federal Drug Administration loosened the rules that restricted direct-to-consumer advertising of prescription drugs. The result? It's hard to watch your favourite sitcom or skim the pages of popular magazines without noticing ads for prescription drugs that suggest a solution for ailments such as depression, heart disease, baldness, and obesity.

Given the volume of drug advertising, it seems drug manufacturers must be satisfied with the results of these communication efforts. But is prescription drug advertising a surefire means of building brand awareness, and ultimately having a positive impact on profit? Under current rules in the United States, drug advertisers must communicate significant side effects. Given that even some of the safest medications on the market can have potential serious, even life-threatening side effects, ads could ultimately scare off consumers. Moreover, direct-to-consumer advertising is not cheap. This fact leads to claims that direct-to-consumer drug promotion elevates the price of new medications making some medications out of reach to those who cannot afford them.

The Canadian drug lobby wants the Health Protection Branch of Health Canada to loosen its restrictions that prevent prescription drug advertising. The lobby claims the public would be well served by direct-to-consumer drug education. Consumers need information. Opponents argue the public would not be well served. Of particular concern is brand-specific promotion. According to the opponents, this type of marketing communication could alter the patient-doctor consultation relationship in that patients will be more likely to demand specific brands that may or may not be the best from both a therapeutic and cost perspective.

Some opponents believe the rules have already been relaxed too far. At present, manufacturers are restricted from naming specific brand names in their marketing communications. However, these communications can include 1-800 numbers and other direct-response options for those potential consumers who want more information. This practice leads to what could be called "rule-bending"—follow-up communications to non-product information ads that suggest the solution is the ads sponsor's drug brand.

Regardless of whether you support strong restrictions on prescription drug advertising, it seems some drug manufactures are willing to find creative ways to directly promote their products to consumers.

QUESTIONS

1. Are drug manufactures acting in a socially responsible manner when they advertise prescription drugs direct-to-consumers? What are the ethical issues?
2. Should Health Canada loosen its restrictions? If so, to what extent? Specify where you would draw the line on what should and should not be allowed.

Video Resources: Based on "Pushing Pills", ***Undercurrents***, Episode # 99 (October 18, 1998)

8

The Marketing Communication Process

chapter objectives

After completing your work on this chapter, you should be able to

- Define and outline the communication process.
- List five different types of communication systems and explain why they differ.
- Explain why marketing communicators use persuasive communication.
- Discuss how the source, the message, and the audience affect persuasive communication.

The Communication Revolution

We've only begun to see how converging technologies may transform the TV medium so completely that it may scarcely be recognized. TV is a one-way viewing device that demands viewers receive the information passively. The TV is morphing into a medium that combines features currently offered via television, personal computers, and the telephone. The medium will no longer offer just one-way communication, but will instead offer interactivity. As shown here on Toronto-based iCraveTV's Web page, technology is now available that lets us watch our favourite TV programs while sending e-mail or surfing the Net.

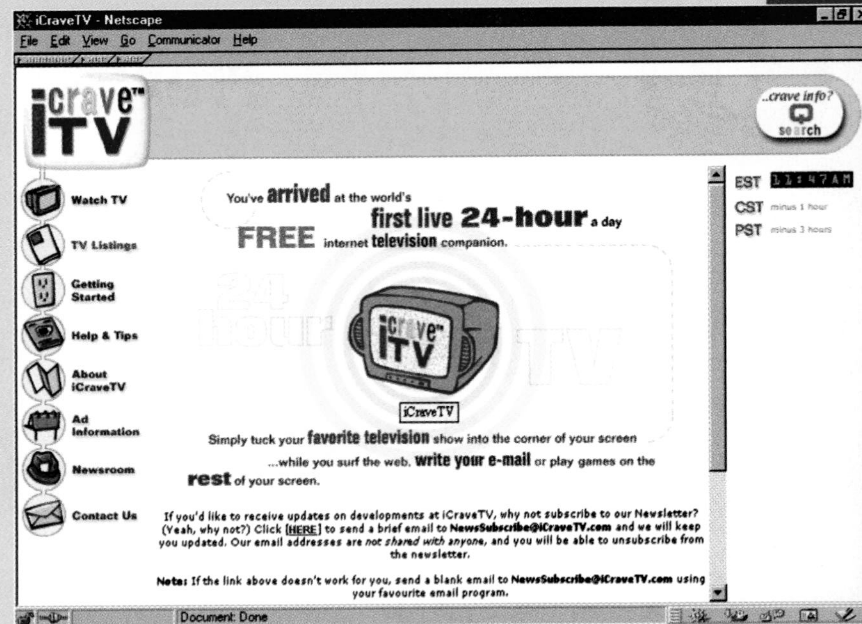

The future of this technology is definitely fraught with uncertainty. No one involved has a precise idea of what the new world will be or how audiences will react to it. When TV offers custom selections to suit every narrow interest, will mass-audience programming disappear? What will happen to CBC and CNN ratings when the 60 or more cable channels become a million or more on the Web? Will the interactive offerings appeal mainly to a select audience of technical gurus, while the rest of us stick with our regular favourites? What about commercials, local affiliates, and video stores? Will we wind up watching more TV or less?

Some businesses are betting that television will become the main access point, or "on-ramp," to the information superhighway. Electronics manufacturers such as Philips Electronics, Sony Corp., Thompson Consumer Electronics, Bandai of Japan, and Funai Electric Company of Taiwan sell a set-top box and remote keyboards to fit on televisions. The box gives access to the Internet and the ability to receive and send e-mail. But computer companies tend to see television access to the information superhighway as a glorified extension of today's personal computer. They're betting that consumers will access the Web and view their favourite TV shows on big-screen PCs.

Still others are hedging their bets, investing in many different media, and waiting to see what will happen. Netscape, an Internet browser provider, is putting its browser software on almost anything with a screen and a modem—an Internet TV, followed by a $700 network computer, online video gaming machines, and Net-surfing cell phones. Sony, NEC, Nintendo, and IBM are joined in the venture. Microsoft purchased Web TV Networks Inc., a company that delivers Internet information directly to TV viewers. In a venture with Compaq and Intel, Microsoft also plans to develop a digital interactive computer—TV that will use Microsoft's Windows operating system.

No matter what services are eventually offered, consumers will drive the development of the television medium. As the system unfolds, companies supplying the hardware and programming will keep track of which services users favour. If users watch a lot of news, documentaries, and special-interest programming, those offerings will expand. If video-on-demand is popular, that area will grow. If services such as videoconferencing, interactive yellow pages, or electronic town meetings are widely used, these services will spread.

Clearly, technology is changing the nature of how we communicate with one another. Even the experts are unsure how the picture will look five, ten, or twenty years from now. Major communication delivery companies such as NBC, Disney, AT&T, Rogers Communications, and a host of others are betting billions of dollars on the possibility that their strategy is best. Regardless of the delivery method, however, audiences still care about the underlying message, the source of the message, and how the message affects their lives.

Sources: John Markoff, "Microsoft Deal to Aid Blending of PC's, TV's and the Internet," *New York Times*, April 7 1997, C1; Frank Rose, "The End of TV As We Know It," *Fortune*, December 23, 1996, 58B68; Lawrence M. Fisher, "2 Companies to Make TV-Top Internet Links Using Oracle Systems," *New York Times*, November 5 1996, C4; Joshua Cooper Ramo, "Winner Take All," Time, September 16, 1996, 59; Michael Krantz, "Voice of America Upgrades Service," *Adweek*, January 2, 1995, 14; Frederick Elking and Amelia Kassel, "A Marketer's Guide for Navigating the Information Superhighway," *Marketing News*, July 31, 1995, 2–3; George Gilder, "Telecom Angst and Awe on the Internet," *Forbes ASAP*, December 4, 1995, 113B216.

Chapter Overview

Marketing communication is the way a marketer blends all communication efforts to create an understandable, credible message that addresses the needs and wants of the audience. Marketing communication attempts to convince listeners to prefer the sponsor's brand, idea, or service to other alternatives.

To succeed, marketing communicators must understand how to communicate persuasively. In this chapter we explore the flow and purpose of marketing communication, the communication process, and types of communication. We also analyse persuasive communication. We then examine the communication source, the message, and the audience. Let's now explore the basic marketing communication features.

Basic Features of Marketing Communication

The role of marketing communication is to support the marketing plan and help key audiences understand and believe in the marketer's advantage over the competition. As Figure 8.1 illustrates, marketing communication has an external and an internal flow.

External flow
Marketing communication that is directed outside the business.

The **external flow** is directed at those outside the business: past, present, and potential customers; resellers, both wholesalers and retailers; other companies;

Figure 8.1 THE FLOW OF MARKETING COMMUNICATION

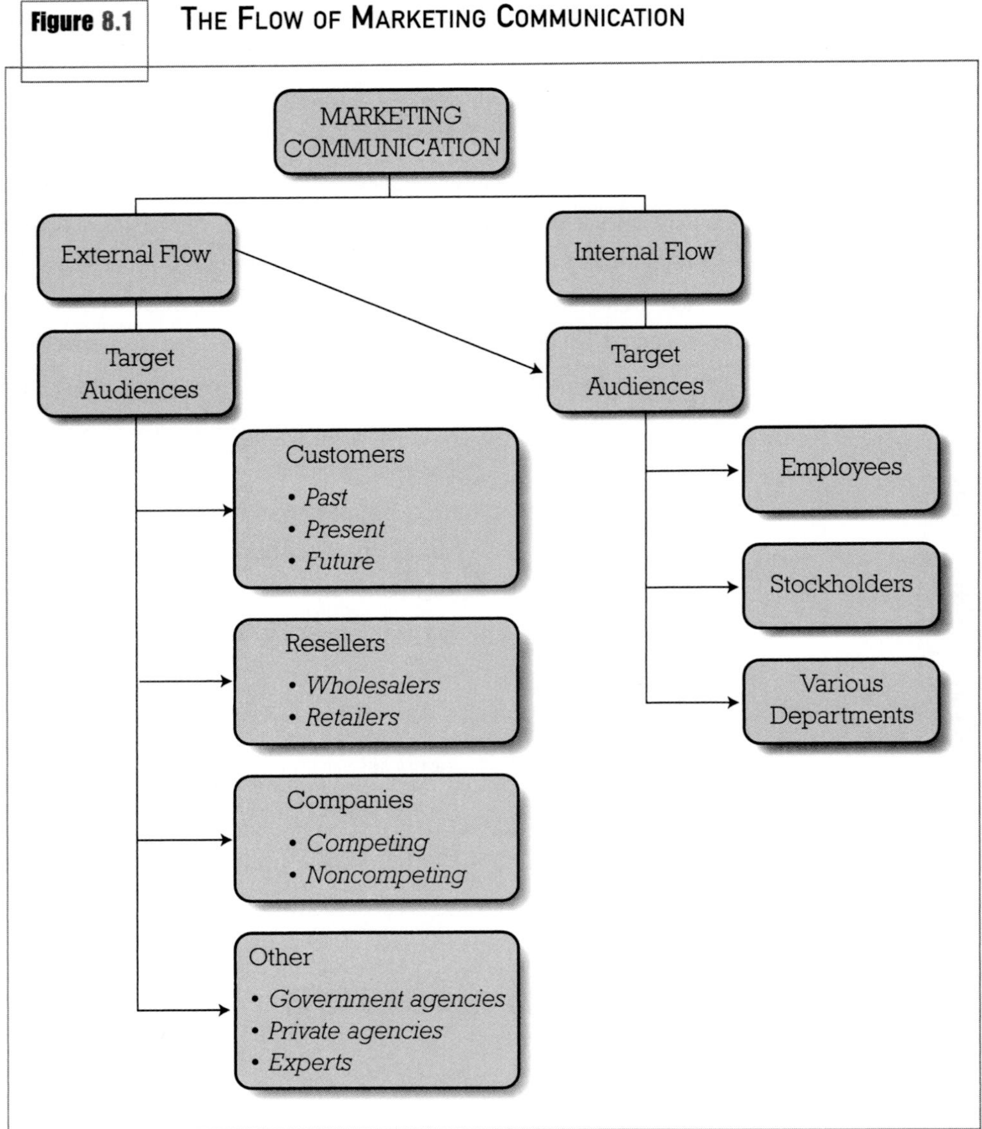

Polaroid Corp.
www.polaroid.com

and government agencies, private agencies, and experts in the field. A large, multinational company such as Polaroid Corp., for example, maintains an elaborate network of external communications. It communicates with past customers through advertising and direct mail; with current customers through advertising, warranties, product updates, and material on how to use its products; and with potential customers through advertising, point-of-purchase displays, salespeople, and so on. Through direct mail and its sales force, Polaroid also communicates information about its products, pricing, and promotion to resellers. It exchanges similar information with competitors and with companies that sell complementary products such as photo albums. Finally, Polaroid keeps government agencies and consumer interest groups (for example, photography clubs) informed about its efforts.

Internal flow
Marketing communication that occurs within the organization.

The **internal flow** of marketing communication is directed at those who are members of the organization. The internal communication may differ according to each internal audience. For instance, employees often need to know what marketing is doing, especially when the organization is introducing new products or deleting old ones, changing prices, or distributing the product in new outlets or markets. By influencing how employees perceive their organization, marketing communication can help shape their morale and performance. If employees feel they are working for an innovative market leader that produces highly regarded ads, for example, they are likely to work harder, stay with the company longer, and become positive opinion leaders in public. Marketing may communicate in more detail with certain departments. Research and engineering departments, for example, share product information with marketing, and vice versa. Through sales forecasts, marketing determines the day-to-day level of production. Stockholders also need to be informed about marketing activities. If they are going to buy stock and recommend the company to other buyers, they must be convinced that the firm's marketing decisions are in their best interest.

Marketing must also communicate with members of the firm in different locations. Ensuring that employees in different cities and regions receive the same messages and understand them in a similar way is critical for the cohesion of the organization and for the coordinated implementation of the business strategy. Of course, this task becomes even more difficult when a company must communicate internationally. On an international level the flow of vital intrafirm information can easily be distorted by factors such as cultural differences and physical distance. For example, Snapple found it hard to convince consumers in the United Kingdom to buy a drink that is not served hot or with milk.

Integrated strategy
The combination of the right information, the right people, the right sources, and the right time into marketing communication strategy.

Whether the flow is internal or external, effective communication means reaching the right people with the right information through the right sources at the right time. It requires an **integrated strategy**, as follows:[1]

1. *The right information*. Assess the relative importance that audience members place on information. Do audience members want objective information, replete with facts and comparisons? Or do they prefer emotional appeals? What do they already know?
2. *The right people*. Select the best way to deliver information. Which delivery methods do audience members prefer? Do the members turn to different methods for some purposes, such as an expensive purchase?
3. *The right sources*. Gauge where the communicator stands in relation to competing sources. Is the audience committed to a particular source, such as friends or *Consumer Reports*? Is the audience open to new sources? What are they?
4. *The right time*. Provide guidelines to determine what mix of communication techniques to use, when to use them, and how best to allocate funds. These guidelines should be based on the communication objectives and available resources.

Implementing a strategy requires a thorough understanding of the needs and wants of the various audiences, a working knowledge of the available communication techniques and how they blend together, and an awareness of competing communicators, including other companies, friends, the government, the news media, and so forth.

Marketing communication strategy is part of the firm's overall persuasive marketing effort. The more that business managers understand about communication, the more they can contribute to a marketing communication program. In the rest of this chapter, we discuss basic ideas about how people communicate and present some keys to effective communication.

concept review

Basic Features of Marketing Communication

1. The role of marketing communication is to support the marketing plan by helping target audiences understand and believe in the marketer's advantage over the competition.
2. An integrated communication strategy should reach the right people with the right information through the right sources at the right time.

The Communication Process

Communication

A process in which two or more persons attempt to consciously or unconsciously influence each other through the use of symbols.

What is meant by *communication*? The communication process has a beginning, middle, and end, and is guided by the communication objectives of the participants. In this text we define human **communication** as a process in which two or more persons attempt to consciously or unconsciously influence each other through the use of symbols.

Figure 8.2 illustrates the basic elements of the communication process. Note, however, that these elements are all closely related. In fact, even something as complex as communication within a large factory can be viewed as a single process, with components and interrelationships within it. If one element is changed, each of the others is altered. In other words, senders, messages, and receivers together form a system of communication.[2]

First, consider the communicators, a component of every communication system. In traditional communication the two communicators are referred to as the sender (or encoder) and the receiver (or decoder). The *sender*, or *source* of

Figure 8.2 A Model of Human Communication

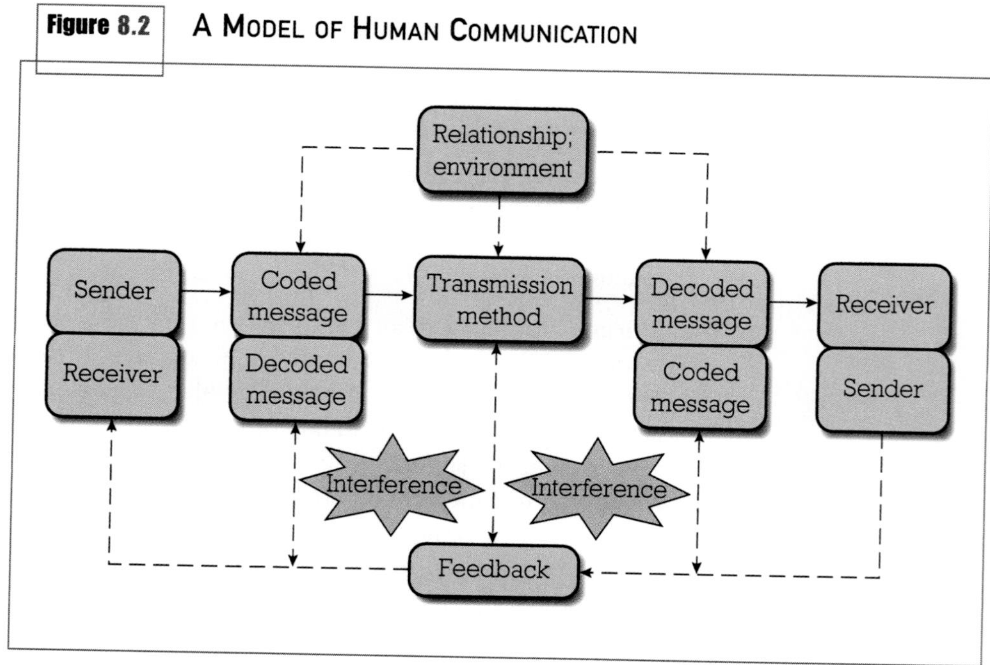

the message, can be an individual, a group, or an institution that wishes to transmit a message to a receiver (or target audience). The receiver, the recipient of a message, can also be an individual, group, or institution.

The sender/source accomplishes the transmission of the message by selecting and combining a set of symbols to convey some meaning to the receiver. The greater the similarity or overlap between the sender and receiver, the more likely that communication will be effective and the less likely that miscommunication will take place. If the sender does not have much in common with the receiver, the sender should learn as much as possible about the receiver to bridge the gap.

Encoding
The process of transforming thoughts into a sequence of symbols.

The process of transforming thoughts into a sequence of symbols is called encoding. When **encoding,** the source should consider the characteristics and capabilities of the receiver. The symbols the sender uses should be familiar to and viewed positively by the receiver. Just as important, the message must be delivered through a medium that the receiver uses and at an opportune time. Delivering the same message through two different media can produce very different results. Receiving a message in person versus through the radio is an everyday example. The message received face-to-face will seem much more personal than the radio message.

Possible media may be classified as either personal or nonpersonal. Personal media refer to message-delivery devices that tend to be one-on-one. Examples include word-of-mouth or personal selling. Nonpersonal media are also called "mass media," and include broadcast, print, catalogues, and so forth.

Although the receiver does not initiate the communication process, the receiver is just as much a communicator as the sender. The receiver communicates with the sender through feedback using the same set of symbols the sender used to communicate. When the receiver provides feedback to the sender, they reverse roles—the receiver is now the sender. Sometimes feedback is explicit: It entails words, pictures, overt signs, or gestures. On other occasions feedback is given implicitly through the use of nonverbal expressions.

Feedback
Process through which the receiver communicates with the sender.

Decode
To interpret a message.

Mass communication, especially advertising, often involves implicit, delayed feedback from target audience members. Advertisers, for instance, usually receive **feedback** in the form of customer reaction, or lack of reaction, to the products or services advertised. When feedback is implicit and delayed, it is difficult to gauge whether the sender has effectively communicated. The nature of the feedback is determined by how well the receiver **decodes**, or interprets, the message delivered by the sender.

Two main factors affect decoding: the communicators' relationship and the environment. The nature of the relationship between the sender and receiver can affect how the message is delivered and how the receiver interprets the message. For instance, a family member could write a short, informal note that another family member could interpret clearly but a potential customer would find confusing. Another factor that can affect decoding is the environment in which the communication takes place. Both the external environment—the weather, time of day, competing messages, and so on—and the internal environment—experiences, attitudes, values, and biases—can often influence the decoding process.

Interference
Environmental factors that distort the communicators' relationship or the communication process.

Whenever environmental factors distort the communicators' relationship or the communication process, this distortion is called **interference** (or "noise").[3] For the marketing communicator, one growing source of noise is competing messages. Experts estimate that the typical North American is exposed to more than 12 000 messages each day.

concept review

The Communication Process

1. Communication is a process in which two or more persons attempt to consciously or unconsciously influence each other through the use of symbols.
2. In the communication process two or more parties are simultaneously sender and receiver, who encode and decode messages and provide feedback.
3. The decoding process can be affected by two factors:
   - The relationship between the communicators
   - The environment

Types of Communication Systems

Several types of communication systems exist. They vary in complexity, the amount of contact between communicators, the timing of feedback, and the communicator's ability to adjust to feedback. Next, we investigate five types of communication systems: interpersonal, organizational, public, mass, and interactive. Figure 8.3 summarizes the characteristics of each of these systems.

Interpersonal communication system
Communication system that may consist of as few as two people and as many as can interact face-to-face so that the participants have the opportunity to affect each other.

Dyad
Two people of two distinct groups.

Interpersonal Communication Systems

The most basic communication system is interpersonal communication. An **interpersonal communication system** is a communication system that may consist of as few as two people and as many as can interact face-to-face so that the participants have the opportunity to affect each other. When the system consists of just two people of two distinct groups, it is called a **dyad**. As the system becomes more complex and more people are added, the small group emerges. The upper limit of the small group is usually between 15 to 20 people.

Figure 8.3 Types of Communication Systems and Their Characteristics

	Characteristics			
Types	Complexity	Contact	Timing of Feedback	Adjustment to Feedback
Interpersonal	Low	High	Short	High
Organizational	Moderate	Moderate	Moderate	Moderate
Public	High	Low	Long	Moderate
Mass	High	Low	Long	Low
Interactive	High	High	Short	Moderate

Interpersonal communication is also affected by the use of supplementary message delivery media. That is, a salesperson talking to a customer is engaging in direct communication. The same salesperson who delivers part of the message through less direct media—such as the telephone, letter, fax, or e-mail—changes the nature of the communication and may diminish the benefits of direct interpersonal communication. The close, direct contact between communicators allows the salesperson to customize the sales message to suit the audience, receive immediate feedback, and adjust the message accordingly. The message itself can be complex because explanation is possible.

Unfortunately, communicating interpersonally also brings disadvantages. It is so time-consuming that some members of the target audience will be missed because there is not enough time to call on all customers.

Organizational Communication Systems

Organizational communication system
A system composed of a large collection of subsystems organized around common goals.

In a bank, factory, retail store, or government agency, communication is much more complex than in an interpersonal system. Each institution has an **organizational communication system**, which is a system composed of a large collection of subsystems organized around common goals. The subsystems all exist as separate entities yet interrelate with each other. Consequently, both a formal and an informal network of communication is often required, making it more difficult to communicate because feedback is often delayed and incomplete.

To communicate effectively in an organizational system, managers must learn as much as possible about the organizations with which they communicate. Simply using the correct technical jargon is an important consideration. Furthermore, their messages should include important benefits the organization desires. Benefits such as reliability, speed of delivery, and high quality are valued by most organizations.

Public Communication Systems

Public communication system
A verbal exchange from one person to a large group of people, as occurs when a person gives a speech to an audience.

Tupperware
www.tupperware.com

A **public communication system** usually involves communication from one person to a large group of people, as occurs when a person gives a speech to an audience. Although everyone affects everyone else to some degree in every communication system, in public communication the speaker generally has the strongest effect on the group. The feedback listeners give to the speaker is less obvious and more subtle than the feedback provided in interpersonal and organizational systems. The speaker needs considerable sensitivity to detect this feedback, which is frequently limited to nonverbal cues such as facial expression, body posture, or eye contact.

Certain types of personal selling use public communication. Party selling such as that of Tupperware Home Parties is an example. Company executives also find themselves giving speeches to local groups, stockholders, and other stakeholder-groups.

Mass Communication Systems

Mass communication
A system of communication characterized by delayed feedback and no direct contact.

Compared with public communication, **mass communication** offers even less opportunity for people to interact or to affect one another. Although there is feedback in mass communication (through such means as e-mail, 800 phone calls, letters, and coupon use), the distinguishing characteristics of this system are delayed feedback and no direct contact. In such a system the source of the

Titleist
www.titleist.com

mass message does not face the audience nor can the source possibly receive feedback from all the people who receive the message.

Marketing communication managers must establish a mechanism to compensate for this lack of personal contact and provide a formal feedback system to gauge audience response. The Titelist sporting-goods manufacturer, for example, connects with customers through the use of Tiger Woods as its spokesperson. Feedback is provided through focus groups, phone surveys, and intermittent in-depth interviews. However, as explained in the next section, the need for a formal feedback system may change with the emergence of interactive technology.

Interactive Communication Systems

Interactive communication system
The use of computer technology, allowing marketing communicators to send persuasive messages while simultaneously allowing the receiver to react, modify, and customize the message and the response.

Interactive communication systems use computer technology that allows the marketing communicator to send persuasive messages while simultaneously allowing the receiver to react, modify, and customize the message and the response. For example, Ford ran basic interactive ads on Interactive Channel-Europe. The first 60-second spot was a corporate ad listing various features available in Ford cars. Viewers could use their TV remote controls to name how many features were mentioned in the spot. The ad would then congratulate viewers on a correct response. If the viewers answered incorrectly, the ad would tell them so and supply the right answer.

The second Ford commercial let viewers find out more about the new Mondeo model. Again using the clicker, viewers could select one of four commercials: a conventional car commercial, one that stressed the Mondeo's technical specifications, one that listed the model's U.K. distribution, or one that showed various press comments about the Mondeo. As this example shows, interactive technology delivers messages to the masses while providing the benefits of interpersonal communication. Still, it is not face-to-face communication, and the number of options available to the receivers is limited and may not always be what the receiver wants to hear or see.

Experts agree that interactive technology will revolutionize marketing communication. But before this can happen, some problems need to be solved. First, interactive systems need to be established in consumer homes at an affordable rate. Second, they need to be as simple as possible so that people like to use them. Many consumers find PCs too complicated, so developers are trying to design devices that are as easy to use as the TV or telephone.[4] Finally, a high level of security is needed.

Persuasive Communication Systems and IMC

Even if an individual ad or sales promotion piece is intended to deliver information, remind, or build awareness, the explicit goal of the IMC strategy is to persuade. The attempted persuasion may take several forms, including providing believable, accurate information; changing attitudes or beliefs; convincing audiences they need to change attitudes or behaviour; and motivating audiences to take a particular action. Consider some marketing communication tools to see the forms of persuasion they use. Advertising and PR tend to be most effective in persuading audiences that information is accurate and attitudes need to change, whereas sales promotion and personal selling, by definition, are a call to action.[5]

Recall that in integrated marketing communication, all marketing communication mix elements should work together to promote the firm's marketing objectives. Together, the elements should provide sufficient motivation to the audience to prompt a change in behaviour. The marketing communication objectives, then, tend to be sequential as shown in Figure 8.4, beginning with name or brand awareness, moving to providing meaningful information, then changing attitudes and perceptions, and ultimately creating conviction and behavioural change. An overtone of persuasiveness permeates all these objectives.

Figure 8.4 THE SEQUENCE OF PERSUASIVE OBJECTIVES FOR MARKETING COMMUNICATION

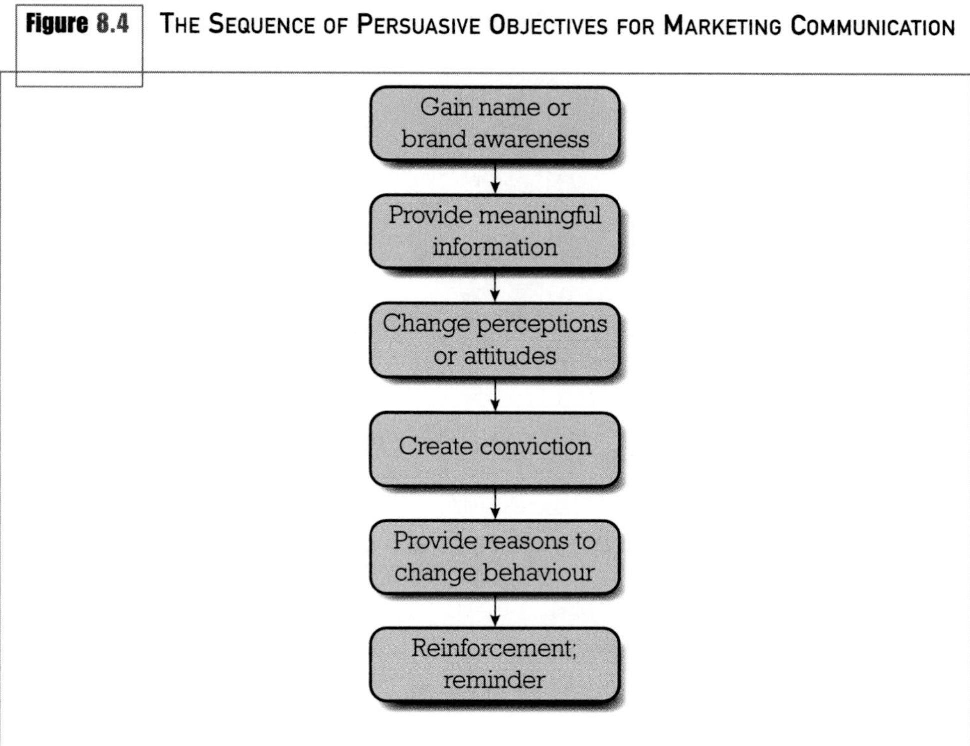

concept review

Types of Communication Systems

1. Several types of communication systems exist that vary in complexity, the amount of contact between communicators, the timing of feedback, and the communicators' ability to adjust to feedback.
2. The five main types of communication systems are interpersonal, organizational, public, mass, and interactive.
3. Persuasive communication is critical in an IMC strategy and may take different forms to accommodate reaching the various communication objectives.

Characteristics of the Source

The source of a message is the communicator or endorser—the person or business whose message is directed at the target audience. Three types of sources

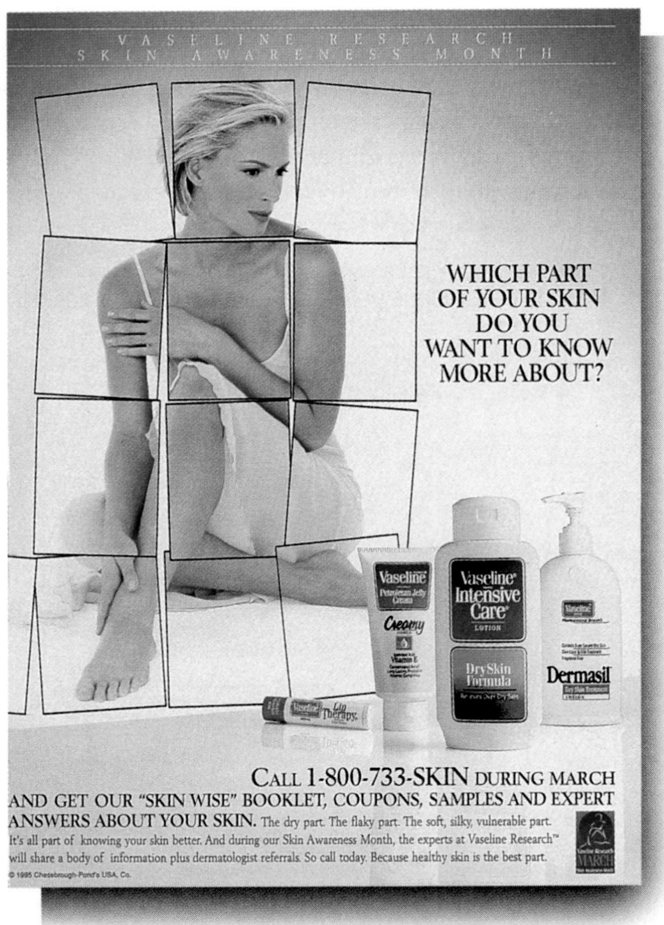

This ad features the sponsor source, Vaseline Research.

exist. The sponsor source is the manufacturer who pays for the message delivery and is usually identified somewhere in the message itself. The ad for Vaseline products not only is a sponsor ad but also includes several integrated components such as an 800 number and sampling.

The reseller source is either a wholesaler or retailer who has associated with the message, often through manufacturer products. Ads produced by Sears represent a retail and wholesale source, respectively. The **message presentation source** is the person, animated character, or voice-over who delivers the actual message. The Energizer Bunny and Snoopy for Met Life represent a presenter source.

Message presentation source
The person, animated character, or voice-over who delivers the actual message.

What makes one source more effective in persuasive communication than another? One of the most successful matchups in recent years is Sprint and actress Candice Bergen, who has filmed more than 75 spots since 1990 and who, the company claims, is directly responsible for Sprint's increased market share. Candice Bergen had three characteristics that contribute to persuasiveness: credibility, attractiveness, and power.

Sprint Canada
www.sprint.ca

This ad shows Snoopy, Met Life's message presentation source.

CREDIBILITY

Credibility
The extent to which the receiver perceives the source to be truthful or believable.

Canadian Medical Association
www.cma.ca

Credibility is the extent to which the receiver perceives the source to be truthful or believable. Highly credible sources tend to create an immediate change in attitude. Highly credible groups (such as the Canadian Medical Association) are even more effective sources than highly credible individuals.[6]

Credibility depends on two related factors. The first is the expertise attributed to the source. Characteristics such as intelligence, knowledge, maturity, and professional or social status all lend an air of expertise to an individual or group. For example, Wayne Gretzky could be considered an expert on hockey equipment. The second factor determining credibility is the objectivity attributed to the source. In other words, does the receiver believe the source is willing to discuss the subject honestly? For example, Michael Jordan is a highly credible source for athletic shoes, and a lung cancer patient can be a highly credible source in a public service announcement advising people to stop smoking.

Objectivity seems to be less important than knowledge or expertise, however, perhaps because most people do not expect the sponsor of a message to be objective. Obviously, Michael Jordan is being paid to promote Air Jordans, so he is not completely objective.

ATTRACTIVENESS

The greater the perceived attractiveness of the source, the more persuasive the message. Cindy Crawford, who acts as a spokesperson for Pepsi-Cola, for example, is an attractive source to many audiences. However, it is not just because she is beautiful and wears expensive clothes, although these characteristics may be part of the attractiveness equation. Source attractiveness is the extent to which the receiver identifies with the source. It results from similarity, familiarity, or likeability. For many who have watched Cindy for several years, she represents all these components.

Research suggests that the more receivers feel that a source is similar to themselves, or how they would like to think of themselves, the more likely they are to be persuaded. This similarity, or perceived similarity, can be exhibited through ideologies, attitudes, and behaviours. Many political candidates are experts in saying the right things to various audiences to make each audience believe its ideology is similar to the candidate's.

The second source of attractiveness, familiarity, is normally created through past association. People have been seeing Bill Cosby for many years. He appears in concerts, on television, and in charity fundraisers. Children especially relate to him because he is funny and one of the most patient, loving, and unusual fathers ever to appear on television. For Jell-O and its pudding and gelatin desserts, Bill Cosby is the ideal spokesperson. By association, Jell-O is fun too. It is not surprising that this well-established familiarity with Cosby has made him one of the most attractive sources in marketing communication history.

The more we like a source, the more attractive that source is to us. Liking, however, is hard to measure and tends to be a transitory feeling that changes quickly. In the end, empirical studies of celebrity spokespersons have yielded mixed results in terms of believability, overall effectiveness, and purchase intention. There are, of course, serious risks associated with using celebrities. Canadian sprinter Ben Johnson, for example, became embroiled in a scandal after testing positive for use of a banned substance. And Bill Cosby's image suffered when a woman claimed she was his illegitimate child.

POWER

In addition to credibility and attractiveness, power can make a source effective. Power depends on the receiver's perception that a source has the ability to administer rewards or punishments. It has three components: perceived control, perceived concern, and perceived scrutiny.[7] For example, salespeople gain perceived control over prospective customers through their knowledge of the product or their ability to offer customers important benefits not otherwise available. Many public relations efforts try to create the idea that the sponsoring company feels concern for members of the audience. Government agencies, banks, employment agencies, and other organizations attain power through their perceived ability to scrutinize our lives. A letter from Revenue Canada is quickly opened and carefully read.

WORD-OF-MOUTH: AN INDIRECT SOURCE

Conference Board of Canada
www.conferenceboard.ca

Most individuals seek information from a variety of sources outside the sponsoring organization. These external sources may organize formally to distribute such information (for example, articles from the Conference Board of

Canada or *Consumer Reports*), provide information in line with their expertise (for example, reports from doctors, investment analysts, and auto mechanics), or may offer individual opinions that are trusted on a particular topic (such as the opinions of family, friends, neighbours, or coworkers).[8]

Experts and trustworthy individuals often provide what is commonly called word-of-mouth information. Unlike the producer, reseller, or spokesperson, word-of-mouth sources do not benefit from the acceptance of the message and are not under the control of the sponsor. The importance of word-of-mouth is well documented. Marketing communicators must therefore attempt to influence those who may create word-of-mouth communication.

The impact of negative word-of-mouth communication has also been well documented. When Microsoft faced word-of-mouth criticism for Windows 95, it immediately conducted consumer research, tested the product, and resolved technical problems. Not all problems generate negative word-of-mouth. When is it likely? Albert Hirschman proposed a model that suggests some answers. According to Hirschman, a dissatisfied customer may make one of three responses:[9]

1. *Exit*: voluntary termination of the relationship
2. *Voice*: any attempt to change, rather than escape from an objectionable state of affairs, by directing dissatisfaction at management or anyone willing to listen
3. *Loyalty*: the customer continues with the dissatisfying product or seller and suffers in silence, confident that things will soon get better

The response a customer selects depends on characteristics of both the individual and the industry. The key individual characteristics are (1) the perceived probability that complaining would help, (2) the costs and benefits of complaining, and (3) the sophistication of the consumer, such as his or her awareness of how to make a complaint.

The industry characteristics are essentially structural. Is the industry concentrated, highly competitive, or a loose monopoly? Negative word-of-mouth is most likely in concentrated industries and least likely in loose monopolies.[10]

concept review

Characteristics of the Source

1. The source of a message is the speaker, communicator, or endorser. The persuasiveness of the source is affected by three characteristics:
   - Credibility—the extent to which the receiver perceives the message source to be truthful or believable—depends on the perceived expertise and objectivity of the source.
   - Attractiveness—the extent to which the receiver identifies with the source—is determined by similarity, familiarity, and liking.
   - Power of the source is determined by perceived control, perceived concern, and perceived scrutiny.
2. Word-of-mouth—messages distributed by individuals not under the control of the sponsor—is a powerful indirect source of information.

For example, a great deal of negative word-of-mouth exists in the automobile industry (see the IMC in Action feature), but little in the nursery plant industry, where three or four growers control the entire output of houseplants sold in North America. Hirschman's model has been empirically tested and appears to accurately portray the likelihood of negative word-of-mouth.

Word-of-Mouth Helps Chrysler

To gauge the success of Chrysler Corp.'s test-drive program for the launch of its LH models, all Tom McAlear needed to do was get a haircut. Shortly after Chrysler had community opinion leaders test-drive its LH line of cars, McAlear, one of Chrysler's zone sales managers, was shooting the breeze with his regular barber. "He said to me, 'I drove an Intrepid for three days. It's terrific, and I'm going to buy one.'" McAlear recalled. "That's the type of great PR we want. A barber talks to a lot of people every day. We didn't just pick CEOs [for the test-drive program]. These cars are not just for them." This chance conversation was the type of positive word-of-mouth Chrysler hoped for.

The introduction of Chrysler's LH cars—the Dodge Intrepid, Chrysler Concorde, and Eagle Vision—was touted as the most important in company history, and Chrysler wasn't satisfied to rely on only the usual advertising and promotion to get the message out. To spur word-of-mouth support, Chrysler embarked on the most ambitious example to date of a growing trend in auto marketing: putting consumers into new cars away from the dealership, often for days at a time. From October through January, Chrysler dealers in 25 regions offered an LH model for a weekend to influential community leaders and businesspeople. More than 6000 primary drivers took the automaker up on the offer, and 90 percent of them responded to a survey afterward. Based on survey results, Chrysler estimated the cars received 32 000 exposures in the three months, including secondary drivers and passengers.

The results were "nothing short of phenomenal," said John Damuse, vice president of marketing for Chrysler. More than 98 percent of those responding said they'd recommend the car to a friend, and 90 percent said their opinion of Chrysler had improved.

In January, Chrysler also placed an LH vehicle at 19 different luxury resorts for free use by guests. A third facet to the Chrysler plan earned further upscale exposure: the Chrysler Concorde Cultural Tour, a sponsorship of charity balls in eight major markets, organized by PR agency Anthony M. Franco, Inc. "People in evening gowns and tuxedos with tails crawled into the cars and kicked the tires," says Peg Tallet, vice president of Fundraising and Corporate Philanthropy at Franco. Tallet estimates more than 7500 people had direct contact with the vehicles, and another 200 000 received information about the car through the foundations involved.

"People are now talking about Chrysler as a luxury car again, something they haven't done in decades," says John Bulcroft, president of Advisory Group. "Word-of-mouth can make or break a car manufacturer, particularly in the luxury segment."

Sources: Bill Vlasic, "Can Chrysler Keep Up?" ***Business Week***, November 25, 1996, 108û20; John P. Cortez, "Put People Behind the Wheel," ***Advertising Age***, March 22, 1993, S-28.

Message Variables

Message variables The specific elements used to convey an idea and the way they are organized.

The specific elements used to communicate an idea and the way these elements are organized constitute the **message variables**. The role of the marketing communication manager is to take marketing information and translate it into the most effective message format. Message variables are divided into two categories: structure and content.

Message Structure

The structure of a message depends on several items: whether the message is a verbal or nonverbal message, readability, ordering effect, repetition, and the presence or absence of counterarguments.

VERBAL VERSUS NONVERBAL

When we think about delivering a message, we think about using words, or verbals. Verbals can be powerful. They can make us laugh, cry, or feel terrified. Nike tells us to "Just do it!" and Allstate Insurance tells us we're "in good hands. . . ." Still, nonverbals also play an important role in effective communication. Is a picture worth a thousand words? According to a study conducted by Ogilvy and Mather, in a given message the words create 15 percent of the impact, the tone creates 25 percent, and the nonverbals create 60 percent of the impact. In his book, *Nonverbal Communication*, Stephen Weitz develops five categories of nonverbal communication:[11] (1) facial expression and visual interaction (for example, eye contact), (2) body movement and gestures (such as muscle tightening and movement toward or away), (3) paralanguage (for example, loudness, pitch, and tremor of the voice), (4) proximity behaviours (appropriate distance between people for certain activities, for instance), and (5) multichannel communication (simultaneous interaction between various factors operating in a communication, such as people and activity).

Ogilvy and Mather
www.ogilvy.com

For persuasive appeals, the most effective nonverbal cues are facial expressions, paralanguage, and timing of phrases; the message designer clearly controls these elements. More specifically, one study of several nonverbals used

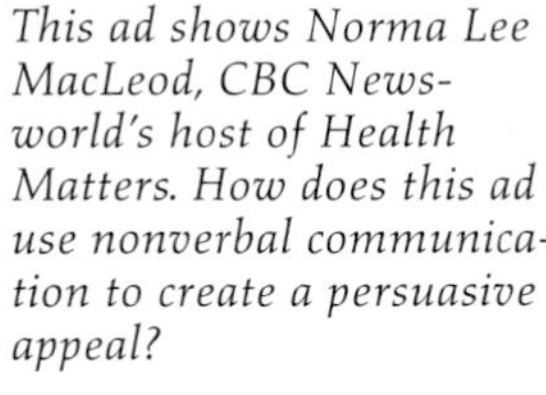

This ad shows Norma Lee MacLeod, CBC Newsworld's host of Health Matters. How does this ad use nonverbal communication to create a persuasive appeal?

Canadian Broadcasting Corp.
www.cbc.ca

in a television commercial found that people who communicated simplicity or single-mindedness were positively associated with persuasion. For instance, nonverbals that correlated strongly with persuasibility included the characters' hands at their sides, the principal character expressing contentment, a likeable spokesperson, a humorous mood, a busy setting, and a wink.[12] The CBC Newsworld ad demonstrates the use of nonverbal cues for persuasive appeal.

Some messages should emphasize words and others should limit words and show pictures. Elizabeth Hirschman concludes that "for product categories (for example, financial institutions, legal services, medical organizations) that generally desire to create an impression of heightened rationality and factualness, the use of all-text or predominantly text would appear best. In contrast, when introducing new products, particularly true innovations, visual images will provide the consumer with perception of greater familiarity."[13] "New and improved" Cheer and its associated campaign used a totally visual message strategy. A man silently hand-washing a dirty handkerchief in cold-water Cheer and displaying the successful results told us all the benefits we needed to know.

Readability

If we concentrate on the verbal elements of a message, it is critical that the message be readable. Readable messages are understandable to the audience and have a very good chance of being persuasive. What makes a message readable? Important factors include its arrangement of words in the core message, word frequency, and sentence length. In addition, the number of ideas used to construct the core message should be kept to a minimum, and these ideas should be restated throughout the message.[14] In a recent Nissan spot, a GI Joe-type character sped over in a toy Nissan sports coupe to win "Barbie" from her preppy boyfriend. Barbie quickly joined GI Joe to take a ride, leaving Ken to watch from the toy house. Then, a quirky Asian man, the Nissan spokesperson, turned to viewers with a smile. The tagline confirmed that "Life's a journey, enjoy the ride." It's a simpler message than discussing features but still understandable.

Nissan
www.nissan.com

Sometimes readability depends on the target audience. Different regions of the country have their own colloquialisms, as do groups of people. Some guidelines for making messages readable and persuasive are listed as follows:[15]

- Use metaphors, such as Revlon's Redline for Revlon Nail Enamel, "Drop-Dead Nails."
- Use low-intensity language, such as the Business Development Bank of Canada's tagline, "For everyone who believes nothing ventured, nothing gained."
- Choose concrete words to make your point, such as the L'Oreal tagline, "Because I'm Worth It."
- Select simple words to explain complex topics, such as Pioneer stereo telling us "For a Great Sound in a Space You Can Live With."
- Include rhyme to make your message more memorable, such as the Oscar Mayer bologna song.
- Use common words, such as "That's Refreshing" and "Just Do It," that are easy to relate to and grasp.
- Keep your heading length short, with five to eight words being the norm.

This Business Development Bank of Canada ad combines a colourful technology generated image and a low-intensity language tagline. Is it effective?

Ordering Effect

Should key ideas be presented at the beginning, middle, or end of the message? Research indicates that the earlier the key message points are presented, the better they will be remembered.[16] Specifically, experts suggest keeping the following tips in mind when ordering your message:

1. When contradictory information is provided in a single message by a single source, disclaimers at the end of a message will generally be ineffective.
2. If people already feel a strong need for a product or service, supportive information should be provided first.
3. Points that are most valued by the receiver should be listed first.
4. Unfavourable information should be placed last.

Repetition

Repetition can take place within a message (repeating a key word or phrase), or it can be the entire message. Research suggests that repeating a message increases its believability, regardless of its content.[17] For audience members who pay attention and understand a message, one exposure is effective. After three repetitions, effectiveness quickly falls. However, in today's world of information overload, no one can guarantee audience attention. Therefore, the number of times a marketing communication manager should repeat a mass communication message is still uncertain.

Too much repetition can even be harmful. The results of one study suggested that repetition actually reduced comprehension.[18] Excessive repetition may create wearout. In the case of humorous messages, *wearout* tends to occur much faster than with serious messages.[19] Perhaps this is one reason why the characters delivering the humour in the milk ads change so often. Changing the people and the context makes a tired punchline less wearing.

Repeating a point within a single message also seems to have a positive effect on persuasion. Several studies have shown that repeating the same point in a message aids retention and increases believability. Marketing communication managers must use both judgment and market feedback to balance the benefits of repetition against the possibility of message wearout.

Arguing and Counterarguing

One-sided message
Presents an argument for the sponsor without mentioning counterarguments.

A **one-sided message** presents an argument for the sponsor without mentioning counterarguments. Using this approach is beneficial when the audience is generally friendly, when the advertiser's position is the only one that will be presented, or when the desired result is immediate opinion change. One-sided arguments tend to reinforce the decision of the audience and do not confuse them with alternatives. McDonald's, for example, only talks about its products and benefits in its advertising.

In contrast, a *two-sided message* includes counterarguments. In general, a two-sided argument is useful with better-educated audiences, who view counterarguments as more objective and thus more honest. Educated audiences are aware of opposing points-of-view and expect communicators to acknowledge and refute these views. Also, if an audience member has multiple opinions about topics that are important to him or her, counterarguments improve persuasibility.

Message Content

Rational appeal
A message that contains both factual and logical appeal.

Emotional appeal
A message directed toward the individual's feelings and intended to create a certain mood, such as guilt, joy, anxiety, or self-pride.

The specific words, pictures, music, and other communication devices, along with the overall appeal, compose the content of the message. We can divide message content into two categories: rational appeals and emotional appeals. A **rational appeal** tends to be factual and logical. In contrast, an **emotional appeal** is directed toward the individual's feelings and is intended to create a certain mood, such as guilt, joy, anxiety, or self-pride. The rational and emotional distinction is somewhat misleading, however, because emotions and thoughts are not tangible things we can place in locked boxes. When someone appeals to our emotions, our cognitive processes still affect our reactions. And even nonemotional appeals may arouse strong feelings in some people.

To fashion emotional appeals, marketing communicators can use many specific types of content. They might use eerie music to create a mood. They might use funny stories or sexy pictures. The choice of appeals is limitless. No one type of content is always persuasive; each choice brings potential risks and benefits. We discuss the primary appeals in the following sections.

Shown in Table 8.1 is a list of the most popular types of appeals used in television, broken down by gender.

Table 8.1 GET THEIR ATTENTION

Type of Commercial	% Women	% Men
Humour	57	68
Children	61	44
Celebrities	39	34
Real-life situations	34	30
Brand comparisons	32	23
Product demonstrations	17	26
Expert endorsements	17	13
Company presidents	6	12

Source: Video Storyboard Tests Commercial Break.

FEAR APPEALS

Intuitively, one might expect that the more fear the message causes, the more persuasive it will be. But research suggests that fear is effective up to a certain level. Beyond that level a"boomerang effect" takes place and negative results occur. As indicated in the You Decide feature, sometimes a fear appeal can go too far.

The relevance of the message to the audience helps determine the impact of a fearful message. For instance, many university students are not motivated to purchase life insurance because death is not that relevant to those so young. However, by the time they reach age 30 and have two kids, the fear of death capitalized on in insurance messages will find more accepting listeners.

The effect of fear may also depend in part on whether the message pertains to physical harm (such as sickness, injury, or death) or to social anxiety (such as streaked dishes or body odour).

The effectiveness of fear appeals also depends on audience demographics, such as age, sex, race, and education.[20] Personality differences are also significant. For instance, people with high self-esteem react more favourably to high levels of fear than do people with low self-esteem, who are more persuaded by low levels of fear. Similarly, the more vulnerable receivers feel, the less effective a fear appeal will be, particularly if it uses high levels of fear. The appeal may terrify them into inaction. In short, marketing communication managers must keep in mind that effective fear appeals depend on many variables.

HUMOUR

Humour can be expressed visually or verbally through puns, jokes, riddles, and so on. Humorous appeals can create four positive effects:[21] they can enhance source credibility, attract attention, evoke a positive mood, and increase persuasion. Using humour may also increase attention paid to the commercial, reduce irritation at the commercial, improve its likeability, and increase product likeability.[22]

The use of humour brings risks, however. Not everyone finds the same things funny. Humour also can be distracting. An audience may enjoy a

Scared to Health

The image is chilling: a series of menacing bear traps laid out like footsteps. "Is a bear trap snapping shut on a human foot, your foot, a scary thought?" reads the copy. "Good. . . ." A promotion for the latest Hollywood horror blockbuster? How about an ad for the Diabetic Foot Care Centres? Now running in newspapers and on radio, the campaign is just one example of the growing use of scare tactics by drug and health-care marketers. "It's shock jock advertising, a bit of desperation on the part of marketers who are faced with new challenges," notes Burt Flickinger, manager of consultancy A.T. Kearney, New York.

There are no hard numbers to illustrate the trend, but observers say fear marketing is definitely on the rise. The issues came to a head in California where Abbott Sales' Ross Products division used heavy print and radio advertising to push its Advera nutritional drink for HIV-positive and AIDS patients. The print ad showed a handsome, seemingly healthy young man with a pair of running shoes and a glass of Advera nearby. AIDS groups criticized this ad, saying it used an implicit scare tactic because anyone as healthy looking as the ad's model wouldn't need the product. Dr. John Stansell, director of San Francisco General Hospital's AIDS clinic, calls the ads "disgusting."

Drug and health-care marketers may have a special temptation to use fear marketing because they deal with people when they are most vulnerable. "We've tried positive-type ads in the past and they did nothing," says Dr. Vincent Giacalone, medical director of the Diabetic Foot Care Center. "We've gotten a much greater response from our new ads." But, notes Paul Barthelemy, account executive for McDonald David & Associates, "That kind of approach can backfire. You don't want to terrify. You need to stay as close to the public mind-set as you can."

You Decide

1. What are the potential strategic problems with the fear messaging described?
2. What are the potential ethical problems?
3. Assume you were the new marketing communication director for Advera. Would you recommend that the campaign use or avoid fear tactics? Explain your answer.

Sources: Peter Galuszka, "Humana Heal Thyself," ***Business Week***, October 14, 1996, 73û74; Joseph Weber and Nanette Byrnes, "A Fat Pill with a Big Fat Problem," ***Business Week***, September 9, 1996, 50; Emily DeNitto, "Healthcare Ads Employ Scare Tactics," ***Advertising Age***, November 7, 1994, 12.

humorous message but may miss the main points of the message, including the name of the sponsor. Humour aids awareness and attention, but it may hinder recall. Finally, humour wears out. Once the audience tires of the humour, they may become indifferent to the message or even irritated by it.[23] For instance, no one knows how much longer people will find the Energizer Bunny amusing.

Despite the risks and uncertainties of using humour, it is likely to remain the favourite strategy of many advertisers. For one thing, humour creates strong memorability, a measure of success that ad agencies consider vital. A 1989 poll indicated that 88 percent of the viewers still remembered Wendy's "Where's the beef?" campaign, which stopped running in 1984. Ad executive Cliff Freeman explains advertising's love affair with humour as follows: "There's an actual physical thing that happens in the body when you laugh. You give off certain chemicals; it's a very positive thing. Therefore, the association with a product is extremely positive. . . . And if your product is good and your advertising is of that nature, it'll really begin to develop an emotional bond between the consumer and the product."[24]

Pleasant Appeals

Pleasant appeal
A message that creates a positive experience and product likeability.

Most people would rather feel good than feel bad. Taking advantage of this desire is the rationale behind **pleasant appeals**, which create a positive experience and product likeability. A pleasant appeal can take several forms. It can use expressions of fun and entertainment, perhaps by showing people dancing, singing, or simply having a good time. Warmth is an emotion considered synonymous with liking. Homecomings, nostalgic situations, and loving relationships all connote warmth. Babies, puppies, and kittens seem to guarantee a feeling of warmth. People cannot resist the Kodak ads that string together heart-warming scenes of childhood, old age, and ordinary family life.

Evidence supporting the effectiveness of pleasant appeals is strong. Warm, entertaining messages are noticed more, are remembered more, increase source credibility, improve attitudes, and create feelings that are transferred to the sponsor. The Ogilvy Center for Research and Development reported a direct link between pleasant appeals and persuasiveness. After showing 73 prime-time commercials to 895 consumers, the Center discovered that people who enjoy a commercial are twice as likely to be convinced that the advertised brand is best. "Now we can say likeability enhances persuasion and that, at the very least, you don't pay any penalty if people enjoy your ad."[25]

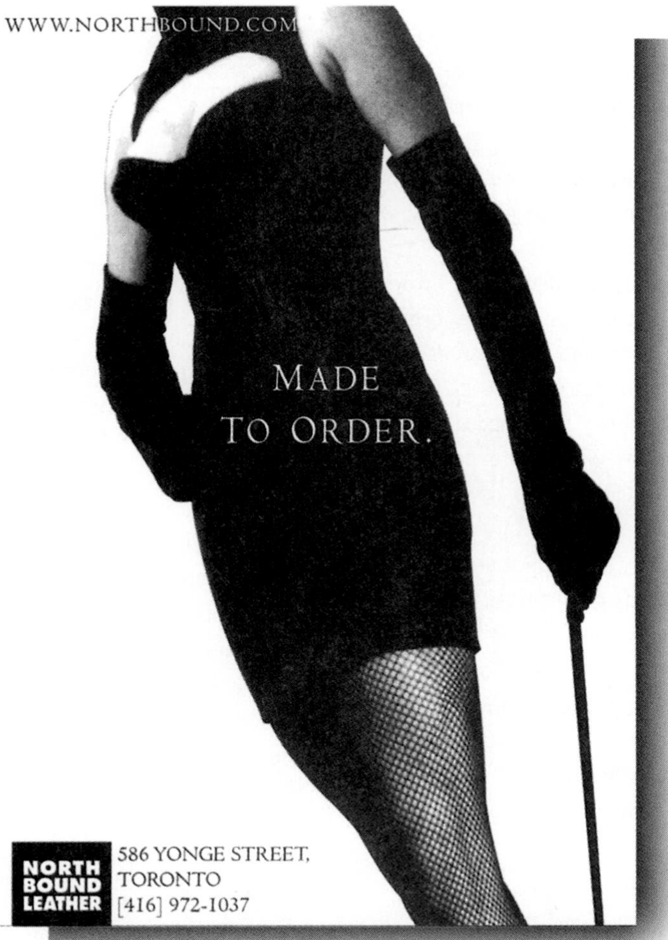

This ad for North Bound Leather uses a strong sex appeal. Is it effective?

Jennifer Nagle

Account Executive
Fresh Advertising Inc.

Academic Background and Career Track

I graduated from McMaster University with an Honours B.A. in Environmental studies in 1994. After travelling and volunteering in Australia, New Zealand, and Southeast Asia for a year, I returned to Toronto and signed on with a temp agency in order to get some real experience and direction. I was immediately placed at Cossette Communication-Marketing and was impressed with the young, enthusiastic work environment. I worked on various accounts, filling in for people as they were on vacation. Unfortunately, nothing permanent was available at the time, and shortly after I was offered a position at an investment company.

Although finance was indeed a digression, I worked in a marketing and sales capacity and quickly acquired transferable skills. Over three years, I increased my responsibilities and knowledge greatly; however, my keen interest in the advertising industry remained undaunted. Fortunately I had kept in contact with several people from Cossette, and by networking I started a new career in advertising.

Fresh is a small company (three partners plus three employees), so it required some getting used to. We started in an open-concept office, where I had the advantage of observing everyone's responsibilities and how they handled certain situations. I immediately started attending meetings and as I became more comfortable, gradually increased my level of participation. From my experience, the best way to learn is by being thrown into the fire.

Typical Day

There is no typical day at a small agency, as anything may happen to send you spinning off on a new project. As a small company, we have the advantage of defining ourselves based on consumer demand. We specialize in the area of technology and Internet-related products, but our clients range from real estate to snowboard packaging. Therefore, my learning not only involves the advertising industry in general, but also requires a lot of personal reading to stay current with different market trends.

Mondays usually begin with a status meeting so that we get a feel for the week's schedule. My week consists of meetings, preparing budgets and creative briefs, contacting media, making sure deadlines are met (both internally and on the client side), and ensuring that the creative is on strategy before it is presented to the client. Teamwork is key and sometimes we will all brainstorm a creative project together. We also like to stay motivated and passionate about our jobs, and have been known to sit around our carpet and discuss something particularly creative that we had seen. It is important to try and have some fun, so that the stress doesn't wear you out.

Most days wrap up around 5:30 or 6:00, but you have to be willing to stay late at a moment's notice if a rush deadline has to be met. It is also very important to stay involved in related extra-curricular activities. I am currently taking the two-year CAPP course (Canadian Advertising Practitioners Program) and attend events, information seminars, and client functions whenever possible.

Advice

For someone interested in working on the account side of advertising, I would say if it doesn't happen right away, be patient. Continue to obtain related experience, even if it is in another industry. Like copywriters, it is actually a benefit for account personnel to have a well-rounded background, as each client expects you to have some insight into their industry. Try to get an internship or temp position, because your chances of getting hired are far greater if you make yourself known and do a good job. If at all possible, spend a week as a volunteer at a large agency and at a small agency. The dynamics are very different and you need to know which sort of atmosphere you thrive in.

Sex Appeals

Sex appeals in marketing communication range from nudity and obvious double entendres to devices so subtle that it takes a trained observer to recognize them.

Even if the ethical questions raised in Chapter 7 are not considered, the effectiveness of sex as a persuasive device is questionable. There is little doubt that sex is an effective, attention-getting device for both men and women. Nevertheless, many people believe that the use of sexual appeals is simply not good marketing. For example, several studies have examined the ability of nudity to enhance brand recall. In every case neutral or nonsexual scenes produce higher brand recall.

Other researchers conclude that sexual appeals in the correct context produce higher attention and recall. That is, there are situations in which the use of a sexual appeal is appropriate, whereas in other instances the use of a sexual appeal is included for its shock value and has nothing to do with the context. Examples of correct context are messages that provide fantasy fulfilment (such as travel), functional fulfillment (for example, fashion), or symbolic fulfilment (for example, romantic setting). In sum, sexual appeals in the correct context can produce powerful results; sex outside of this context can be disastrous.

Music

Prominent singers and musicians, background singers and instrumentalists, and jingles have all been used to deliver persuasive messages. The general consensus is that the right music can make a significant difference in the effectiveness of a particular message, but the amount of empirical evidence supporting this assumption is limited. Recent work suggests at least three potential effects of music.

First, music, especially "distinctive" music, can attract consumers' attention. Certain songs and performers immediately spark the attention of different target audiences. Second, music can influence consumers' processing of the messages. Music can affect learning and persuasion by creating excitement, relaxation, empathy, news, and imagery, and can enhance the perceived benefits of the message.[26] Finally, music can complement other elements in the ad, such as words, colour, pictures, background, and so forth. Music can create a mood that encourages certain types of attitudes and behaviour.

concept review

Message Variables

1. Message structure factors that influence persuasiveness include the following:
   - ***Verbal versus nonverbal:*** Verbals should be emphasized when unique, meaningful messages can be delivered about the product.
   - ***Readability:*** Writing should be clear, concrete, and accessible.
   - ***Ordering effect:*** Key ideas should be presented first.
   - ***Repetition:*** The key point of the message should be repeated, though no fixed number of repetitions is best. Too many repetitions may cause wearout.
   - ***Arguing and counterarguing:*** The effectiveness of the one-sided versus two-sided message depends on the audience and strength of the argument.
2. Message content may consist of a rational or emotional appeal. The content may include fear, humour, pleasant appeals, sex appeals, and music.

Audience Factors

Are some people easier to persuade than others? We all know gullible individuals who will believe anything. Yet there is little solid evidence to support the notion that some personalities are more susceptible to persuasion.

Various personal characteristics, however, can affect persuasibility. William McGuire suggests that personality factors influence persuasibility by affecting the *comprehension* of a message and *willingness to comply* with a message.[27] Self-esteem is an example. For reasons yet to be explained, people with low and high self-esteem differ in their ability to cope with simple and complex information. That is, people with low self-esteem may do better with simple information and people with high self-esteem may handle complex information better.

Gender is the one demographic trait related to persuasion.[28] Women seem more persuadable than men, especially when the source is a female. Some evidence suggests that males and females differ in their information-processing strategies. For example, some studies conclude that females are more sensitive to external cues, with the possible exception of smell.[29] Moreover, it appears that females are willing to take more effort in deciphering complex messages.

As noted in Chapter 7, children are viewed as very vulnerable to the effects of persuasive communication. Children's vulnerability to persuasive communication raises many important questions. Do children pay attention to advertising? Do they understand its purpose and its content? How do children process advertising messages? What is the effect of factors such as age, race, or parental education on these process effects? What is the impact of advertising on children's attitudes and behaviours? What effect does advertising have on the socialization process of children, that is, their learning roles as consumers?[30]

Although the answers to most of these questions remain unresolved, the evidence does suggest that children of all ages are capable of distinguishing commercials from programs, but that young children (preschool age) are not able to discern the intent of commercials,[31] nor do they understand the disclaimers used in many ads. Further, advertising has a moderate impact on children's attitudes toward the advertised product, though the content of commercials does affect children's preferences and choices, as revealed by studies in the area of food advertising to children.[32] Finally, advertising encourages children to request products from their parents, a situation that often leads to child-parent conflict. Parental education, family interaction, and peer integration, however, may reduce these effects.[33]

Are senior citizens more susceptible to persuasive communication? The stereotype of senior citizens who are senile and believe everything they are told seems to suggest they are, but this stereotype is flawed. Senior citizens are not a homogeneous group.[34] The majority of senior citizens are not institutionalized or living under the care of others. As to the persuasibility of seniors, the evidence to date is inconclusive. No clear link has been established between membership in senior-citizen market segments and the degree to which individuals respond to the persuasive content of a message.

Persuasiveness reflects interactions between the personality and culture of members of the audience, the situation, and characteristics of the source and message. To be persuasive, a marketing communicator should keep in mind the interests, attitudes, and values of the audience.

Communicating to Foreign Markets

Marketing communication strategies often need to be tailored to specific foreign markets or countries. For instance, the ad copy should be adapted to differences in customers' perceptions and response patterns. For many marketing communicators, adapting has proven quite difficult. Any book or article on international marketing offers numerous examples of how some marketer (usually North American) made a horrible advertising blunder by using a word that translated negatively, a colour that connoted evil, or a song that was perceived as too sensual. Every facet of a message—words, tone, pictures, context, spokesperson, and appeal—must be carefully screened. As noted in the IMC Concept in Focus feature, providing an integrated marketing communication approach is more difficult when considering other countries.

Concept in Focus

Communicating Across Borders

Global advertising campaigns have long romanced the marketing imagination with their seductive promise of "one world" executional elegance. But the logic they are based on—that global campaigns offer economies of scale and consumers the world over are becoming increasingly more homogeneous—is flawed. If the campaign fails, the economies of scale aren't realized. And consumers' tastes, needs, and wants still remain diverse.

Chanel is an example of a company that failed in its attempt to deliver a global message. Its problems stemmed from taking a top-down, manufacturer-centred approach to advertising instead of using a more consumer-oriented approach. Chanel may well market "global" brands, but consumers live, buy, and consume in "local" environments.

Does this imply that using the same marketing communication concept in diverse multinational markets is impossible? Or that fragrance concepts and advertising campaigns don't travel well across borders? Au contraire! To borrow from Eric Clapton, "It's in the way that you use it."

For Impulse Body Spray, the deodorant-and-fragrance-in-one mass market brand, parent company Unilever uses the same advertising concept (boy meets girl) in almost every market. At last count, the brand was doing quite well in 40 countries—primarily due to the fact that the two-in-one brand concept is unique, and the advertising concept is universally relevant and meaningful, rooted deeply in the human condition.

The moral? Marketers such as Chanel run into trouble because they're primarily concerned with standardizing the marketing communication message. But in a world filled with diversity, marketing communicators should instead figure out how people from many cultures and countries respond to products, and use and develop relationships with parent brands and companies.

Sources: Geoffrey Lee Martin, "Ad Doesn't Measure Up to Council's Standards," *Advertising Age* International, January 15, 1996, 16; Ashish Banerjie, "Global Campaigns Don't Work; Multinationals Do," *Advertising Age*, April 18, 1994, 23.

Obviously, the marketing communicator must use the language of the country, but the words must be more than technically accurate and perfectly translated. They must reflect the tone and emotion of the language. A key to successful communication in a foreign market, then, is to intimately understand the nuances of the culture, especially the language, values, and attitudes of its consumers. The process of designing the message must therefore begin with the cultural context, as the following questions show:

1. *Is the product used for the same purpose in all countries?* Campbell Soup Company learned that its soups are used very differently in Canada and in Eastern and Western Europe. Consumers in France, for example, would never consider using canned soup as the base for a sauce.

2. *What is the motivation for purchasing the product?* The same product may be purchased for a mixture of functional, convenience, and status reasons, with a different combination of motivations in each country. In underdeveloped countries, for example, McDonald's provides status rather than convenience.
3. *Who is the key decision maker?* In patriarchal cultures the father makes most purchase decisions. In the case of certain products (for example, cereal, toys, fast food), children take a very active role. However, the influence of children on a product purchase varies a great deal from country to country, and marketing communicators must examine this purchase pattern closely before making any generalizations.

Cultural mores represent a key factor that affects message design. For example, in Germany and France many women do not shave their legs or underarms. Thus, razor blades are positioned as a special occasion purchase. The Japanese view deodorant differently, so Feel Free deodorant described its product as youthful and chic rather than as a solution to odour problems.

The presence or absence of market segments also dictates message appeal in foreign countries and represents one of the more successful ways of standardizing promotional strategies. For example, a market segment such as university students may be fairly similar from country to country. Levi's uses the same basic appeal to the worldwide youth market for its 501 jeans.

International jet-setters respond similarly to appeals for fine jewellery, luxury cars, and expensive cosmetics. Similarly, when countries join together to share economic resources, transportation networks, or technologies, they create common interests that can also serve as the basis for promotional appeals.

A marketing communicator must decide whether to run a message in one or several local languages. For example, similar to the French- and English-language issue in the Canadian market, some citizens of Switzerland speak mostly German, others speak mostly French, and most speak English. The Snickers billboard illustrates how Mars Inc. customized its marketing communication to fit a particular country.

Mars Inc.
www.mars.com

Figure 8.5 summarizes the factors that affect persuasive communication.

Figure 8.5 FACTORS THAT AFFECT PERSUASIVE COMMUNICATION

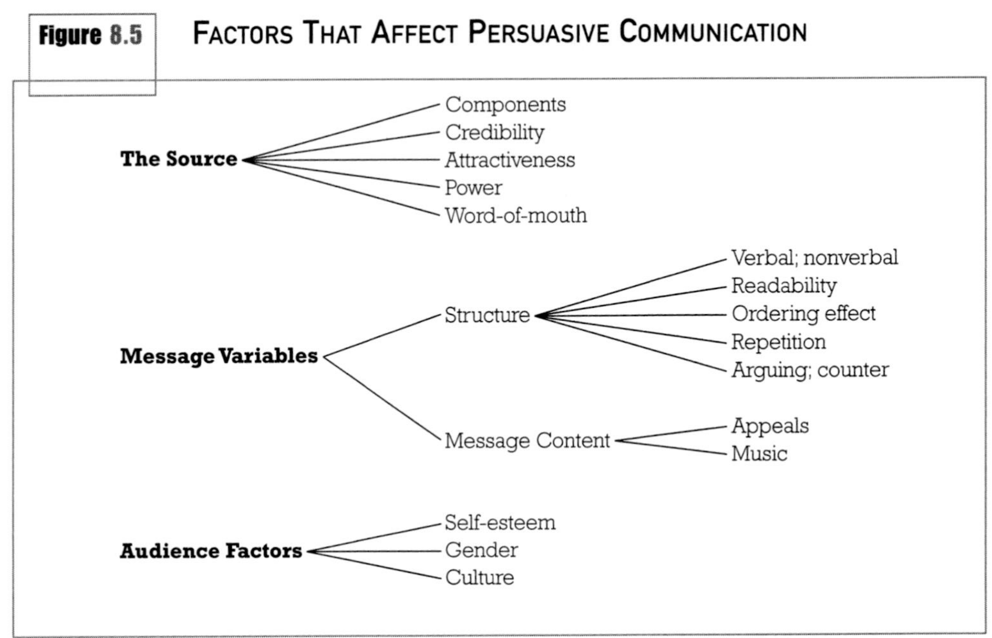

concept review

Audience Factors

1. Audience factors that affect persuasive communication include the following:
    - Comprehension of a message
    - Willingness to comply
    - Self-esteem
    - Gender
    - Age
2. Communicating to foreign markets means more than just using the appropriate language.

Mars Inc. campaigned heavily in Russia to create brand identity for its Snickers candy bar. Promoting Snickers in Russian billboards, ads, and retail displays resulted in a name recognition increase from 5 percent to 82 percent.

A Closing Thought:

Make the Communication Relevant

Consumers no longer tolerate irrelevant communication. They demand messages that speak to their needs and wants and are irritated by messages that don't. With the growth of interactive technology, this trend will increase the demand for one-on-one communication. Nonetheless, the fundamental principles of good communication still apply. Although the means and timing of delivery may change, markets capable of delivering a clear, concise, persuasive message will tend to be most successful.

summary 

1. Define and outline the communication process.

   Communication is a process in which two or more people try to influence each other, consciously or subconsciously, through the use of symbols. Steps in the process occur simultaneously. The basic elements of the process include the communicators (the sender and receiver), the encoding and decoding of messages, a medium of transmission, relationships between communicators, feedback, the environment, and factors that interfere with effective communication.

2. List five different types of communication systems and explain why they differ.

   Five types of communication—interpersonal, organizational, public, mass, and interactive—differ in complexity, form of contact, and ability to adjust to feedback.

3. Explain why marketing communicators use persuasive communication.

   Marketing communicators use persuasive communication to inform, remind, and build awareness so that receivers will change attitudes, perceptions, and behaviours.

4. Discuss how the source, the message, and the audience affect persuasive communication.

   Variables that influence the effectiveness of persuasive communication fall into three groups: (1) source factors, (2) message factors, and (3) audience factors. Manipulation of the credibility, attractiveness, and power of the source can affect the ability to persuade. Message variables (that is, structure and content) show little consistency in their effect on persuasiveness. Each message-related factor must be viewed in context. The effect of audience factors is even less predictable, so marketing communicators must use their judgment to send messages that will be relevant to target audiences.

points to ponder 

Review the Facts

1. Outline the communication process.
2. Define word-of-mouth sources of communication.

Master the Concepts

3. Discuss how the communicator can be both the sender and the receiver.
4. What are the differences between verbal and nonverbal communication?
5. What is the result of interference in human communication? List some ways to reduce interference.
6. Contrast general communication with persuasive communication. What should be the outcome if persuasion is successful?
7. What are the advantages and disadvantages of using music in advertising?
8. Sources can be considered attractive in terms of similarity, familiarity, and liking. Give an example of each.
9. "I really enjoy funny ads. I wish all ads were like that." Comment on these statements.

Apply Your Knowledge

10. Write a 500-word essay expressing why you feel communication must be either intentional or unintentional.
11. Describe the characteristics of a communication source that would appeal to (1) university students and (2) their parents.

suggested projects

1. Collect ads from magazines to locate examples of the following: high source credibility, high source attractiveness, nonverbal appeal, high fear appeal, and high humour appeal. Explain the criteria you used in each case.
2. (Oral Communication) Ask two friends to allow you to observe their conversation. Note the kinds of nonverbal cues each person uses. Quiz them afterward as to whether they are aware they use these nonverbals.
3. (Internet and Team Project) Break into small groups of four to six people. Choose a product or service that your group wants to research. Each group member should search the Internet, find three companies that offer the product or service, and visit the home page of each company. Take notes about how well each company communicates persuasive messages about the product. (Is information easy to understand, memorable, clear, and visually appealing? Is the information static or offered in an interactive format that allows for two-way communication?) Meet as a group to discuss your findings, then select the two best examples of persuasive marketing communication. Choose a spokesperson who will present and explain the reasons for your choices in a five-minute oral presentation to the class.

Doneghel Speaks Up

Background

The Doneghel Furniture Company is a small, regional furniture manufacturer. During the last 32 years, the company has produced custom-made furniture for consumers living within a 320-kilometre radius of the plant. Its major customers, however, are large furniture manufacturers that contract with Doneghel to make hardwood components of the larger pieces sold by companies such as Ethan Allen and Thomasville. Until recently, the management of Doneghel had been very satisfied with this arrangement. However, two occurrences have changed the future of Doneghel. First, due to the general decline of the furniture industry, several of Doneghel's manufacturer customers reduced their orders, some by as much as 50 percent. Second, the reputation of Doneghel's custom-furniture line seems to have extended beyond the immediate market. Consumers from as far away as California have written to request catalogues and general product information. Most of this interest appears to stem from positive word-of-mouth from satisfied customers who have moved out of the region. Doneghel does no advertising.

John Doneghel, president of the company, along with Carol Doneghel, vice president, and their two sons, Jamie and Frank, are faced with the possibility of changing the way they do business. John, Jamie, Frank, and 20 other craftspeople represent the total workforce. Carol takes care of the books and pays the bills. The family loves to work with wood and to create beautiful furniture. Unfortunately, the Doneghels have little experience or interest in doing much else. Last year Doneghel's sales were $1.6 million, of which $280 000 resulted from the custom-furniture business. The only element that even resembled marketing was a 10-page catalogue that described the general kinds of pieces Doneghel makes and gave approximate prices. This catalogue was mailed only to people who requested it.

The dilemma facing the Doneghel family is obvious. Do the Doneghels maintain the status quo and hope the market for large manufacturers improves? Or do they expand their custom-furniture business and learn all they can about marketing as quickly as possible? After agonizing over this problem for several days, the decision was made to hire a consultant.

The Market

Tony Wingler is a marketing professor at a nearby university. He has conducted research for several furniture manufacturers and is thoroughly familiar with the industry. It is his recommendation that Doneghel pursue the custom-furniture business. Because it would be unprofitable for the company to offer total customization, Doneghel should develop a product line that is somewhat standardized and offer two or three modifications of each piece. Wingler further indicates that the upscale customer (that is, someone whose income is higher than $100 000) should be targeted. This person would be willing to pay the higher prices charged for customized furniture. Finally, Wingler feels that distribution represents the most difficult problem facing Doneghel. Because it is unlikely that Doneghel would be able to place its furniture in stores throughout the country, direct marketing offers a better alternative. Direct mail combined with print ads in magazines such as ***Southern Living*** and ***Town and Country*** would represent the primary communication vehicles. Direct mail would also serve as a mechanism for ordering and receiving the furniture.

A meeting was set up with an advertising agency to discuss the marketing communication strategy appropriate for Doneghel. The agency determined that the two main benefits Doneghel offered were excellent craftsmanship and the use of hardwoods. The primary limitations were twofold. First, the public could not experience the furniture firsthand. Would people buy furniture they could not touch? Second, the selection was limited to between 70 and 75 different pieces. The agency felt that combating these limitations would be difficult and that many potential customers would be lost because of them.

Case Questions

1. What are the communication problems facing Doneghel if it uses a direct-marketing approach?
2. (Writing Project) Suggest an initial communication strategy for Doneghel, including specific structure and content recommendations. Make your recommendations in a one- to two-page memo.

The Tools of IMC

9

Advertising

chapter objectives

After completing your work on this chapter, you should be able to

- Define advertising.
- Identify the strengths and weaknesses of advertising.
- Explain how advertising works.
- Outline the three phases in creating an advertisement.
- Describe what makes advertising effective and how to evaluate effectiveness.

Sunlight Gets Down and Dirty

When Unilever Canada decided to take a long hard look at its Sunlight laundry detergent brand, what it found wasn't pretty. The brand's advertising was okay with its soft, diffused lighting, bright white clothing, and lemon-fresh imagery. The trouble was, Sunlight's key target market of women aged 25 to 54 with kids at home, did not have much confidence in Sunlight's cleaning power. They felt the brand's personality was "nice," but when spit-up, spills, and grass-stained knees became the order of the day, it was time to switch to a tougher detergent. "To be blunt," says Ian Gordon, director of home care at Unilever in Toronto, "everybody loved the brand, but they had to buy Tide, because we weren't delivering on the function benefit."

Unilever knew a total overhaul was in order. Sunlight at the time was a "weak" number two player, with around 13 percent of the Canadian laundry detergent market. Procter & Gamble-owned Tide's robust market share was 45 to 50 percent. To engineer the overhaul, Unilever set out to systematically remake the Sunlight brand—from the inside out.

The first order of business, and the most crucial one, was a product reformulation to ensure Sunlight could realistically compete with Tide on the cleanliness front. Unilever then turned to the product's packaging by introducing a new, "modernized" design with brighter, bolder graphics, created through the Marovino Design Group of Toronto. Unilever ad agency, Ammirati-Puris Lintas (APL), then conceived a tactical TV advertisement dubbed "evolution" to introduce the new Sunlight formulation. Around the same time, Unilever and the agency also began to explore the long-term communication possibilities for the brand.

The new formulation meant that Sunlight did not have to be afraid of stains anymore. The challenge was figuring out how to communicate the can-do message without appearing to follow the competition. As Jane Tucker, an APL account director put it, "We needed to have a different voice, and to be credible in our own way."

To help Sunlight find its own "voice," APL took the brand through an in-house planning method. This involved a significant amount of qualitative research, and was designed to help uncover a key concise, focused "brand idea" for Sunlight and to bring it to life. The result: "Go Ahead. Get Dirty."

The first "Go Ahead. Get Dirty." creative ran in the form of a 30-second English-language TV spot titled "Magnetic Mud." The spot features a little boy, who, despite his mom's warning not to get his clothes dirty, gets sucked into a mud puddle, and clearly loves every minute of it. A voiceover asks "Ever met a kid who could resist a mud puddle?" Since then additional spots have aired; one being "Embrace," which depicts two lovers racing through a field—and a huge mud puddle—into each other's arms.

The Sunlight launch was a classic case study of integrated marketing communication. The brand idea has also been carried through to the Sunlight package and the scoop found inside the box, which both now feature the catchy slogan. Additionally, Unilever hired Calgary's The Venture Group to co-ordinate a series of Sunlight sponsorships in western Canada, which involve appropriately dirty sports like bull riding and mountain biking. "Go Ahead. Get Dirty." has also popped up in grocery stores—both on scratch-and-sniff cards available at shelf and in the image of a huge mud puddle set into stores' floors.

Perhaps the most eye-catching appearance of "Go Ahead. Get Dirty." thus far is a five-page ad that ran in issues of magazines such as *Chatelaine, Flare,* and *Elle Québec.* A far cry from the standard one-page magazine execution, the Sunlight ad is set up as a spring fashion spread, complete with the latest looks, as well as clothing prices and credits for the stylists and photographer. Only here, the models are splattered with mud.

The results? Unilever is seeing results in sales, and market share and penetration. But perhaps the most obvious indication that "Go Ahead. Get Dirty." is on the right track is the fact that Unilever is sticking with the campaign. According to Unilever Ian Gordon, "We think we have a keeper, and we think it's having an impact with the consumer. Ultimately, they're the ones who have to make the decision."

Source: Lara Mills, "Down and Dirty," *Marketing*, (April 9, 1999), p. 12, 16.

Chapter Overview

The Sunlight "Go Ahead. Get Dirty." campaign mentions many of the key marketing communication tools we discuss in Part III of the text. In this chapter we focus on advertising, the first of those communication tools. First, we explore advertising basics, including its strengths and weaknesses. Then we investigate how advertising works, focusing on attention, awareness, and memorability. Finally, we examine how marketing communicators create and execute an advertising strategy and how they determine what makes an effective ad.

What Is Advertising?

A flyer on dozens of doorsteps urges consumers to try the new restaurant down the street. Unilever offers consumers a coupon to try the newest version of Sunlight laundry detergent. A full-page ad in the newspaper announces that a local bank is offering reduced interest rates for home mortgages. And at Super Bowl time, networks rake in close to $1.8 million for each 30-second television advertisement. Pre- and post-game ads command $500 000 to $800 000.

Marketing communication managers must understand where advertising fits in the overall marketing communication strategy. Some large marketers (for example, Case Office Equipment, McCain Foods Canada, the Disney theme parks) use very little advertising, and others, such as Procter & Gamble, spend over a billion dollars annually on advertising. Regardless of the emphasis, managers should apply a careful analysis when making advertising decisions that parallels their decisions about other components of the marketing communication mix.

Defining Advertising

Advertising is any paid form of nonpersonal presentation and promotion of ideas, goods, and services by an identified sponsor to a targeted audience and delivered primarily through the mass media. The American Marketing Association has a more expanded definition of advertising: "Paid, nonpersonal communication through various media by business firms, nonprofit organizations, and individuals who are in some way identified in the advertising message and who hope to inform and/or persuade members of a particular audience. Advertising includes the communication of products, services, institutions, and ideas."[1]

Advertising
Any paid form of nonpersonal presentation and promotion of ideas, goods, and services by an identified sponsor to a targeted audience and delivered primarily through the mass media.

The purpose of advertising depends on your vantage point—that is, whether you are a marketer or consumer. Advertising helps identify the meaning and role of products for consumers by providing information about brands, companies, and organizations. To most business managers and marketers, advertising helps sell products and builds company and brand reputation.

The Strengths and Weaknesses of Advertising

Marketing communication managers, like those planning Sunlight's advertising, need to keep in mind both the powers and the limitations of advertising. Some advertising is more effective than others in certain situations, and some types of advertising seem to work better with certain types of products. Some consumers will not buy in spite of extensive advertising, and some will buy without any advertising. Many other marketing issues may affect product and institutional advertising success, such as the price of the product and the convenience with which you can buy it. The effect of specific ads may also vary widely from consumer to consumer and from time to time.

Advertising's primary strength is that it reaches a large mass audience to intensify broad-based demand for a product. It can build brand awareness, create long-term brand images and brand positions, and increase brand knowledge effectively. Advertising also serves as a reminder of a product or brand with which a

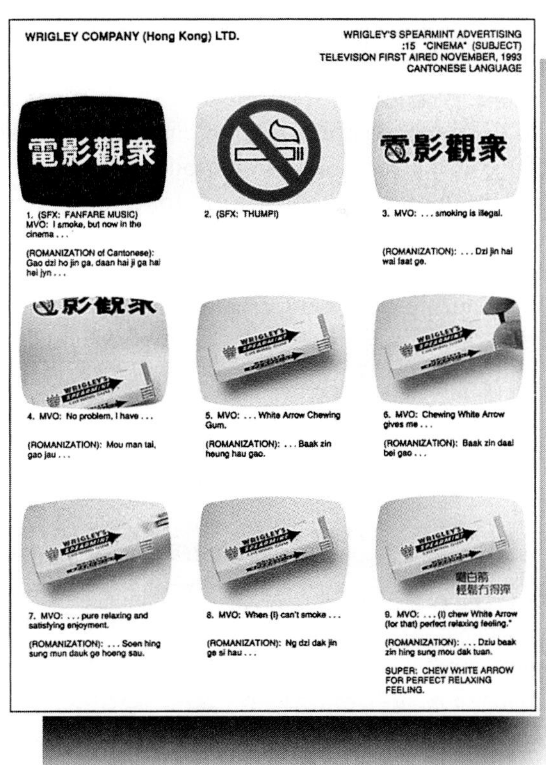

This Wrigley's ad helps remind consumers of a durable, well-known brand.

consumer has had a positive experience. Finally, advertising provides message repetition, an important factor in memorability as described in Chapter 8.

Advertising has limits, however. Consumers often perceive it as intrusive. In turn, consumers may avoid advertising by turning the page, changing the channel, muting the sound, or using other technology to screen out an ad. Because of the large number of competing ads in most media, advertising is also perceived as cluttering the media environment, particularly on television where consumers complain about the number of commercials. Another problem with advertising is the opposite of one of its strengths—it may reach a large audience, but many of those audience members are likely to be nonusers of the advertised product. As a result, advertising wastes a large number of impressions.

In the final analysis advertising is only valuable to businesses if it creates easy consumer identification of the advertised brand or institution. Although advertising may help consumers identify the brand they wish to buy, it may also help them identify those brands they wish to avoid because of bad reports or experiences. Ideally, the continued advertising of a particular brand or institution over several years is an implied warranty to the consumer that the product has met the test of quality and that is why it is still being used. The measure of success for any product is repeat purchase.

How Advertising Links to Other Marketing Communication Areas

Advertising does some things well, like build brand images and reach a wide audience through the mass media. It can also help companies screen consumers for more personal marketing, or make it possible for prospective customers to identify themselves to the marketer. For example, when Procter & Gamble

Proctor & Gamble
www.pg.com

developed Cheer Free, a detergent for people with allergies and sensitive skin, it announced the product in magazine ads with a coupon for a free sample. When people returned the coupon, they included their name and address. From that information, Procter & Gamble was able to build a database of interested customers to target in a direct-mail promotional effort, a more cost-effective means of communicating than mass advertising for a niche market.

Advertising's strengths and weaknesses should be analysed relative to the strengths and weaknesses of the other marketing communication tools. Because marketing communication resources are limited, marketing communication managers must plan a communication mix in which advertising is used to

IMC Concept in Focus

Tensions in the Mix

The adversarial relationship between advertising and the other marketing communication mix components has existed for decades. Because of its high profile, advertising traditionally received all the attention from top management and from those outside the organization. As a result, personal selling, sales promotion, and public relations sometimes took a back seat to advertising. As this situation is gradually changing, advertising is learning to work with these other marketing communication activities as did Ammirati-Puris Lintas in the Sunlight story in the opening vignette.

This change has not been necessarily by choice. Marketers' demand for greater accountability has led to a de-emphasis on image-building advertising; they prefer instead to focus on tools that deliver sales as an immediate result. Price discounts and coupons, for example, give sales a quick, easily measured boost.

As a result of this bottom-line focus, many companies now spend about 70 percent of their marketing communication budgets on sales promotion, leaving just 30 percent for advertising. The link between advertising and sales promotion can be highly successful if they reinforce one another. As the Cheer Free example illustrates, advertising can serve as a vehicle for delivering sales promotions such as coupons, samples, and discounts. Advertising can also serve as a communication device for supporting sales promotion offers such as sweepstakes, special events, and sponsorships. A similar relationship exists between advertising and public relations (PR). In addition to public relations advertising, which carries PR messages through paid-for media, advertising also carries a variety of PR messages. For example, an event such as a marathon or a parade is announced through advertising as well as news releases. New product introductions often require public relations and advertising to work together in a marketing public relations (MPR) program, which we will discuss in Chapter 11.

The most difficult relationship to establish is often between advertising and the sales force. Although advertising can simplify the job of the salesperson, salespeople often believe that the advertising team doesn't understand their problems or their job on the front line. Conversely, advertising people complain they don't get feedback from sales that would help them plan more effective advertising. When the relationship between advertising and sales is harmonious, the sales force can provide ideas for advertising appeals and copy. In turn these ads help familiarize consumers with the brand and its features, giving the salesperson a distinct competitive advantage. This kind of customer preparation saves the salesperson time and energy, reduces anxiety, and increases the likelihood of a successful sale.

Food for Thought

1. Do you have insights into any company—one where a family member or friend works or where you have worked—where tensions exist between advertising and other marketing communication areas? Explain.
2. How would you recommend a business alleviate any tensions between advertising and other marketing communication areas? Why do you think it is important to alleviate such tensions?

Sources: Stuart Elliott, "Warning: The Merry Pranksters of Madison Avenue Are Out Today," *New York Times*, 1 April 1997, C2.

maximize its strengths, not because it's considered glamorous or because the ad agency only wants to do big-budget television commercials. Advertising, in the past, has been seen as the dominant marketing communication area, and that has created some jealousy, as the IMC Concept in Focus feature discusses.

concept review

What Is Advertising?

1. Advertising is the nonpersonal communication of marketing-related information to a target audience, usually paid for by the advertiser and delivered through mass media.
2. Advertising's strengths include its ability to
   - Reach a large mass audience
   - Stimulate broad-based demand
   - Create brand awareness
   - Position a brand or product
   - Increase brand knowledge
   - Provide message repetition
   - Serve as a reminder
3. Advertising has three main weaknesses:
   - It may be perceived as intrusive and, in turn, avoided.
   - It clutters the message environment.
   - It wastes a large amount of impressions because of its mass appeal.
4. Advertising should be used in the marketing communication mix to maximize its strengths, which should be analysed relative to other marketing communication tools.

What Does Advertising Do?

Benetton
www.benetton.com

Most businesspeople advertise because they expect an ad to create a sale. In the case of direct-action advertising, which uses techniques to stimulate immediate action such as toll-free numbers and coupons, this view may be reasonable. However, most advertising is indirect—that is, it creates demand for a product in the long run through indirect methods. Usually, ads try to change mental states to stimulate consumer awareness and interest. Though the ad may not lead to an immediate sale, it may predispose the audience toward the purchase of the advertised product. Benetton campaigns have achieved high levels of awareness using highly controversial advertising that makes little or no effort to sell a product (see the You Decide feature).

Even though advertising's primary objective is to create demand, establishing the link between a specific ad and a particular sale is often difficult, if not impossible. However, a correlation between money spent on advertising, sales, and profitability does seem to exist. In a study of the relationship between advertising expenditures, sales, and profits, researchers found the following:

1. Businesses with higher relative advertising-to-sales ratios earn a higher return on investment.
2. Advertising expenditures and market share are related.[2]

In addition, other studies show that businesses that do not cut advertising during severe economic downturns have the highest growth in sales and net income. In contrast, companies that cut advertising during downturns have the lowest sales and net income increases.[3]

Benetton Shows Its Colours

Many companies combine their advertising campaigns with social issues such as the environment, education, and tolerance. But Benetton, the Italian clothing company that targets the international youth market, has moved beyond combining product and issues in an advertisement. It focuses primarily on social issues that range from racism and world peace to AIDS. The ads have aroused strong reactions and controversy.

The controversial advertising routinely attracts more attention than its relatively modest budget would suggest, which shows how advertising and publicity can be interwoven to create high impact. The creative director of Benetton, Oliver Toscani, claims that the purpose of its focus on social issues is to increase worldwide attention on the issues. Toscani has featured pictures of a dying AIDS patient, a human arm tattooed with the words "HIV POSITIVE," a terrorist car bombing, Albanian refugees, a Catholic nun and priest kissing, a bloody newborn baby, pastel condom sheaths, a black woman breastfeeding a white baby, and a bloody soldier's uniform. In contrast, one ad showed three hearts labelled white, black, and yellow—a less obviously controversial ad.

The divisive advertising triggered some consumer and retailer complaints. Arnie Arlow, executive vice president and creative director at TBWA, an international advertising agency, is one of Benetton's critics: "To place a Benetton logo on the picture of [AIDS victim] David Kirby's deathbed is awful. . . ." Advertising critic Barbara Lippert also takes exception to several Benetton ads. She challenged a Benetton print ad that showed a boatload of refugees desperately swarming in the water, claiming that it was "almost pornographic to use such abstract suffering" for commercial gain. Benetton was also sued by several of its German retail outlets who believed that the provocative ads drove away customers. Benetton won the cases.

Some Benetton ads are more traditional and demonstrate that the company can tone down its controversial approach. Toscani, however, believes his provocative photographic work shows the reality of the world. And that realistic, social-issue focused imagery, according to Toscani, is what moves young people today.

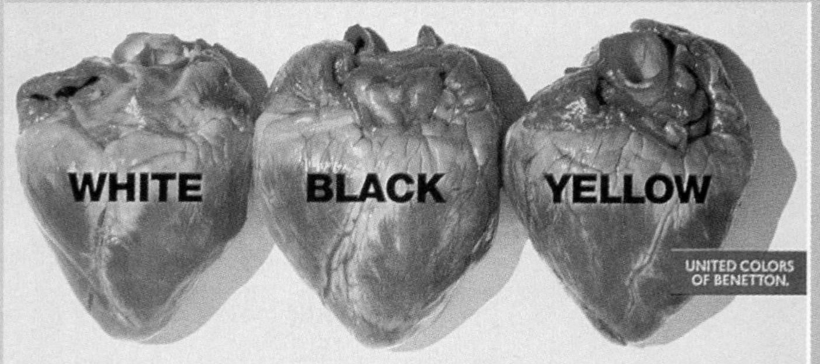

You Decide

1. What do you think? Do Toscani's images speak to young people? Do you feel they appeal to Benetton's target audience?
2. Should controversial photos of others' personal suffering be used to build an image of social concern for a company that sells upscale fashions? Do the controversial visuals contribute to a social-concern image?
3. Assuming the controversial ads seem to generate more awareness, leading to high sales, how should businesses balance their responsibility to society versus the corporation and its shareholders?

Sources: Brad Wieners, "Keep Your Bloody Hands Off Benetton: In Praise of the Yuppie Sweater Company's Sensationalistic Ad Campaign," ***Media Circus, Salon Daily Clicks***, July 4, 1996; "SOS Racisme International Convention Prepares for World Anti-Racism Day," Benetton press release, Benetton home page (July 10, 1996): Internet (Benetton.21Network.Com Benetton/pressreleases/SOS Racisme.html); Christina Lynch, "The New Colors of Advertising: An Interview with Luciano Benetton," ***Hemispheres*** (September 1993): 23û7; Barbara Lippert, "Mixing Politics and Separates," ***Adweek***, February 17, 1992, 30; Noreen O'Leary, "Benetton's True Colors," ***Adweek***, August 24, 1992, 27B32.

How Advertising Works

How does advertising work? In the following section we answer this question by examining three basic features of effective advertising: attention, memorability,

The strong visual coupled with the enticing description of this vacation spot helps create interest and awareness.

Glitz, zero. Unspoiled tranquillity, everything.

In the British Virgin Islands, we've got yachts. Not slots.

We're big on small hotels. Villas terraced down a hillside.

(Even our biggest luxury resorts have maybe a hundred rooms.)

Restaurants open to the soft-scented air.

Beaches as white as powder, and as fine.

Snappers that bump into your mask, they're so unafraid.

Why do experienced yachtsmen and divers from all over the world consider Tortola, Virgin Gorda, and the 60-plus British Virgin Islands to be the water sports capital of the Caribbean? You'll see.

Call 1-800-888-5563, ext. 310 for our Vacation Kit with our Vacation Packages Brochure and our Intimate Inns and Villas guide.

NATURE'S LITTLE SECRETS

and persuasion. Understanding how an ad grabs attention and lodges in memory can help you design a persuasive message strategy.

ATTENTION

One of the biggest challenges for advertisers is to get consumers to notice their messages. To have impact, advertising must break through a cluttered environment, consumer distrust, and catch consumers' attention in a positive way.

Few advertisements actually get read or watched. Consumers often scan the stories and ads in the newspaper, but with limited concentration. Less than half of all ads are paid attention to—that is, noticed on a "thinking" level. Perhaps 20 percent are read a little. Very few are read thoroughly.

Awareness
Implies that the message has made an impression on the viewer or reader, who can later identify the advertiser.

Once advertising grabs the attention of the audience, it should then create awareness. **Awareness** implies that the message has made an impression on the viewer or reader, who can later identify the advertiser. Ads that grab attention are usually high in intrusiveness, originality, or relevance. Relevant advertising creates awareness because the ad is more involving if it speaks to the audience's wants and needs. Ads can address our wants and needs by providing information about such personally relevant concepts as work, hobbies, roles, and relationships.

People for the Ethical Treatment of Animals parodied the milk mustache campaign in this ad that shows comedian Sandra Bernhard sporting a yellow mustache. The ad slams Wyeth-Ayerst Laboratories for its post-menopause product, Premarin, which is made from the urine of pregnant horses.

People for the Ethical Treatment of Animals
www.peta-online.org

Involvement
Refers to the intensity of the consumer's interest in a product, medium, or message.

Interest helps move the audience from attention to awareness. Different product categories, for instance, might arouse different interest levels. Usually, food and vacations are more interesting to most people than are toilet cleaners. Some products are of interest to specific groups of people. A balding person might look at an ad for Rogaine and avoid an ad for hair spray. An ad for a post-menopause product, Premarin, sponsored by People for the Ethical Treatment of Animals, appeals to two different audiences—post-menopausal women who may be considering using the drug and people who are concerned about animal rights. In addition to the built-in interest of the topic for these two groups of people, the ad's creators intensified the interest level by using a visual parody of a well-known campaign for milk that uses celebrities with a milk "mustache."

An interesting message is usually created by one of two things—personal involvement or curiosity. If a message applies to topics that are on your list of interests, then the message has personal relevance. Most people also respond to general "human-interest" items—such as babies and puppies and tragedies and success stories. Ads that open with questions or dubious statements can also build interest and create curiosity.

Attention is the stopping power of an advertisement. Interest is the pulling power of an ad—it pulls readers or viewers through to the end of the message by keeping them involved. Interest is a momentary thing, however; it dies easily as attention shifts. To sustain interest in an advertisement, the message must involve the audience.

Involvement refers to the intensity of the consumer's interest in a product, medium, or message. Recall that high involvement means that a product—or information about it—is important and personally relevant, such as a car commercial when you are shopping for a new car. Low involvement means that the product or information is relatively unimportant. Advertising for high-involvement products provides information about the product. In contrast, an advertisement for low-involvement purchases such as chewing gum, toothpaste, and toilet paper often focuses on simple slogans or memorable images.

Sometimes irritating strategies are used deliberately to intensify attention. Certain product categories—feminine hygiene, jock itch, condoms—are difficult to advertise because the categories are unpleasant and cause consumers to turn away. But there are other types of irritation that are caused by the advertising itself, such as obnoxious characters (used-car salespeople and furniture dealers in some local advertising) and sounds (hammers, buzzers, loud ringing phones) that are used to get attention.

Mean-spirited product comparisons are another source of irritation and are even outlawed in many European and Asian countries. Though not outlawed in Canada or the United States, when Tylenol and Advil moved away from touting their products' potency to attacking each other in 1996, U.S. networks refused to run the ads. The reason? The networks claimed the ads overstated the dangerous side effects of each others' products. Marketing experts predicted that if the two didn't stop sniping at each other, people would be too scared or disgusted to buy either product.

MEMORABILITY

Whereas attention is a function of stopping power, and maintaining interest is necessary for pulling power, effective advertisements also have locking power—they lock their messages into the mind. If you can't remember seeing the ad, or if you can remember the ad but not the brand, then the sponsor might as well not have created it. Let's say a store advertised a sweater sale for a select brand. When you go to a clothing store, it is important that you remember which brand was on sale. How does that process happen?

Our memories are like filing cabinets. We watch a commercial, extract those parts of it that interest us, and then find a category in our mental filing cabinet to store that fragment of information. The fragment, incidentally, may not look much like the original information because the mind modifies it to fit into our own system of concerns and preconceptions. A week later we may not remember that we have a fragment labelled "sweater sale" filed away, or we may not be able to find it in the file. Most of us have messy mental filing systems. A cue, such as a holiday party invitation, may remind you of the sweater sale because you planned to wear a sweater to the party. Cues trigger memory, pull items out of the file, and place them in the forefront of our memory. When you need batteries, for instance, a copper top reminds you to buy the Duracell brand.

This print ad for legal services uses a key visual to reinforce its "We Speak Your Language" tagline.

Recognition
To remember having seen information about some product creating top-of-mind awareness.

Recall
To remember the content of the advertising message.

Taglines
A phrase used in a memorable way at the end of an advertisement to summarize the point of the message.

Key visual
An image that conveys the essence of the message and can be easily remembered.

Advertising research focuses on two types of memory—recognition and recall. **Recognition** means we can remember having seen information about some product creating top-of-mind awareness. **Recall** is more complex. It means we can remember the content of the advertising message. As discussed in Chapter 8, repetition aids recognition and recall.

Several other techniques can enhance message memorability. Jingles and clever phrases are useful because they catch attention and can be repeated without boring the audience. Advertisements use slogans such as "The breakfast of champions" and "The real thing" for brands and campaigns. **Taglines**, which are used at the end of an ad to summarize the point of the ad's message, can be phrased in a memorable way, such as "Nothing outlasts the Energizer. It keeps going, and going, and going." Advertisers that create jingles, slogans, and taglines often use methods to improve memory such as rhyme, rhythmic beats, and repeating sounds.

In addition to verbal memorability devices, many print ads and most television commercials feature a **key visual** that conveys the essence of the message and can be easily remembered. This image is one that the advertiser hopes will remain in the mind of the viewer, such as the finger that gently pokes the doughboy in the stomach at the end of Pillsbury commercials.

PERSUASION

Advertising attempts to develop and change attitudes by providing information or touching emotions to persuade consumers to act. As mentioned in Chapter 8, persuasion is the conscious intent on the part of one person to influence or to motivate another through the use of reason, emotion, or both. Advertising that relies on expert opinion also uses reason to persuade. Advertisers often use emotion to intensify the persuasiveness of a message, such as an appeal to joy, nostalgia, or sorrow.

One persuasive advertising technique that has long been controversial is puffery, the ability of advertisers to make bold statements without substantiation, such as Folger's campaign slogan, "The ultimate one cup coffee machine." Such claims can be made by companies without being sued by consumers because the courts have determined that sophisticated consumers will not take

concept review

WHAT DOES ADVERTISING DO, AND HOW DOES IT WORK?

1. The purpose of advertising is to create demand for a product, though it may do so indirectly.
2. Advertising may not lead to a direct sale, but advertising expenditures seem to correlate to profitability.
3. There are three critical elements of effective advertising: attention, memorability, and persuasion.
   - Attention means that the target audience notices a message. Awareness, which results from attention, means the message has made an impression on the viewer or reader.
   - Effective advertisements are memorable. Recognition and recall are two memory techniques used to lock messages into the mind. Recognition means you can remember having seen something before. Recall means you can remember the information content of the message.
   - Persuading through reason or emotion is essential to motivate consumers to act.

Adese
The use of hyperbole by advertisers to pump up their claims with such terms as "astounding," "stupendous," and "amazing."

such exaggerations literally. Usually you see puffery in **adese**, the language of hyperbole used by advertisers to pump up their claims with such terms as "astounding," "stupendous," and "amazing."

CREATING THE ADVERTISEMENT

The three-phase process of creating an advertisement begins with an analysis of the marketing and advertising strategy to plan a specific creative strategy. In phase two, the execution phase, copywriters and art directors execute creative strategy by writing and designing the ads. The final phase is the production phase. We explore each stage of the process in the sections that follow.

PHASE I: STRATEGY

The marketing communication strategic planning process outlined in Chapter 4 is also used for advertising planning. Two of the most important parts of the advertising strategy are stating the communication objectives and identifying the target audience. Both of these decisions guide the advertising plan—from the creative strategy to the media plan.

Advertising objectives specifically state what the advertising is supposed to accomplish. In Chapter 4 we introduced the Domains Model as a guide for developing objectives (see Table 4.1). The model identifies the effects of three marketing communication message strategies: perception, education, and persuasion. Perception leads to attention, awareness, interest, and recall. Education involves learning and comprehension, association, positioning, and differentiation. Persuasion creates emotional responses, rational responses to reasons and arguments, and attitude and behaviour change. The advertising objectives must be consistent with the message strategy.

Gillette Company
www.gillette.com

For example, let's assume you are the advertising director in charge of a new product launch of the newest Gillette razor for women. You want to set your advertising objectives so they complement your message strategy of developing audience perception, educating consumers, and persuading them to buy your product. First, to ensure that consumers perceive your advertising message, you identify building product awareness and generating interest as your first two objectives. The advertising, then, could try to spur interest by explaining to women how the engineering pioneered in the men's SensorExcel had been modified for women. Second, to implement your strategy of educating consumers, you set an objective to provide information that teaches the target audience to comprehend and differentiate the new Gillette product from its competition. Finally, to persuade the audience to buy the product, your stated objective is to get interested women to try the product through the use of coupons and other promotional techniques.

Copywriters
Those responsible for creating the copy for an advertisement.

Copy
The text of an advertisement or the words that people say in a commercial.

Targeting an audience is another critical part of the advertising strategy. Advertising is most effective if it is written to a specific audience. **Copywriters** are those responsible for creating the copy for an ad. **Copy** is the text of an ad or the words that people say in a commercial. Good copywriters not only work from a profile of the targeted audience but also develop a picture in their minds of someone who fits the profile.

From a strategic standpoint, advertising—and marketing communication in general—moves toward tighter and tighter targets as products are designed for niche markets or customized for individuals. That means messages that may have been designed for mass audiences in the past, such as Coca-Cola's "It's the real thing," are now being more tightly targeted by consumer interest and contact points. The "Always Coca-Cola" campaign, for example, had messages designed specifically for the Gen-Xer audiences, as well as for older consumers. That means every element of the ad's message—tone, style of writing, music, setting, characters, and the storyline—had to be adapted to fit the characteristics of the audience.

Niche markets make it easier to write personal, intelligent copy. An increasing number of Canadian marketers are developing special advertising programs for large ethnic groups such as Toronto's Chinese community (see the Consider This feature in Chapter 5).

Copy platform (workplan)
In advertising, the translation of the creative strategy into a document that specifies what will be said to whom and with what effect and that gives directions about the executions.

A document that outlines the advertising strategy is called a **copy platform**, or **workplan**. The copy platform can vary in format and content. For instance, Karsh & Hagan advertising agency requires that its copy platform answer the following set of questions:

What is the problem or opportunity?

What net effect do we want from advertising?

Who are we trying to reach?

What is the doubt in the mind of our prospect?

What or who is the competition?

What is our key point of persuasion?

How do we support the above?

How will we measure effectiveness?

Are there any obligatory elements to consider?

This copy platform touches on most of the important factors in a creative strategy. Other factors include the product's position, the psychological appeal, the creative approach or "big idea," and the selling premise.

Message Strategy

Message strategy (or creative strategy)
A strategy that outlines what type of message needs to be developed

An agency's creative effort is guided by a **message strategy** (or creative strategy) that outlines what type of message needs to be developed. Table 9.1 outlines seven advertising message strategies, classified by marketing situation. The table shows that by analysing the advertising situation, we can determine what type of message strategy to use. To illustrate, until Glass Plus entered the market, Windex owned the market and could use a generic strategy. Glass Plus, however, realized that Windex was being used for things other than just glass, and used a pre-emptive strategy that focused on all the other uses to undercut Windex.

Selling Premises

Selling premises also affect the advertising creative strategy. In the industry vernacular these are called the "hot buttons," the ideas that touch people's lives and feelings. We discuss two selling premises next: benefits and unique selling propositions.

Benefit
Identifies the basis on which the product can best serve a consumer to fill a need.

The most common selling premise is a **benefit**, which identifies the basis on which the product can best serve a consumer or fill a need. To develop a benefit,

Table 9.1 MESSAGE STRATEGIES

Type of Strategy	Description
1. Generic	Makes no effort at differentiation; claims could be made by any in the market; used in monopolistic situations
2. Preemptive	Uses a common attribute or benefit but gets there first; forces competition into "me too" positions; uses categories with little differentiation, or in new product categories
3. Unique selling proposition	Uses a distinct differentiation in attributes that creates a meaningful consumer benefit; appropriate in categories with relatively high levels of technological improvements
4. Brand image	Uses a claim of superiority or distinction based on extrinsic factors such as psychological differences in minds of consumers; used with homogeneous, low-technology goods with little physical differentiation
5. Positioning	Establishes a place in the consumer's mind relative to the competition; suited to new entries or small brands that want to challenge the market leaders
6. Resonance	Uses situations, lifestyles, and emotions that the target audience can identify with; used with highly competitive, nondifferentiated product categories
7. Anomalous/affective	Uses an emotional, sometimes even ambiguous, message to break through indifference and change perceptions; used where competitors are playing it straight

Source: Charles Frazer, "Creative Strategy: A Management Perspective," *Journal of Advertising* 12, no. 4 (1983): 40.

Promise
A type of benefit statement that looks to the future and pledges that something good will happen if the consumer uses the product.

Reason why
Another form of a benefit statement that explains with logic or reasoning why the user will benefit from a product feature.

you must be able to translate an attribute or product feature in terms of what it can do for the user. To illustrate, Du Pont's use of cordura nylon is a feature that benefits users of its backpacks because the nylon allows packs to be light, yet tough. A **promise** is a type of benefit statement that looks to the future and pledges that something good will happen if you use the product. If you use a certain type of toothpaste, for example, then your breath will smell better or your teeth will be whiter.

A **reason why** you should buy something is another form of a benefit statement that explains with logic or reasoning why the user will benefit from a product feature. An ad for Neutrogena Shampoo, for instance, starts with a headline that states, "Why your favourite shampoo will work better if you stop using it for 14 days." The copy explains the reasons why. In many benefit strategies, the reasoning is unstated, implied, or assumed.

Proof is important for benefit selling premises, such as promises and reasons why. For example, Remington wanted to develop a campaign that proved its long-time promise that a Remington electric shaver "shaves as close as a blade

Remington
www.remington-products.com

or your money back." Remington turned to database company Polk, which collects product registration card data.[4] From the data Remington learned about consumers' previous and current shaving methods and their former and current shaving problems. When Polk examined the data, Remington found that users of other electric shavers were significantly more likely to have complaints than Remington users, and twice as many former blade users had problems with nicks and cuts. Remington users complained much less than those who used other shaving methods. Armed with this information, Remington renewed its claim with convincing proof.

Unique selling proposition
A selling premise based on a product formula, design, or feature that is both unique and important to the user.

A **unique selling proposition** (USP) is a selling premise based on a product formula, design, or feature that is both unique and important to the user. If some aspect of the product is special, particularly if protected by a patent or copyright, then the advertiser can be assured of uniqueness. That is why a USP is frequently marked by the use of an "only" statement: "This camera is the only one that lets you automatically zoom in and out to follow the action."

To review, the strategy phase of creating an advertisement involves, first, deciding on the advertising strategy; and second, deciding the specific message strategy and the appropriate selling premises. These steps are summarized in Table 9.2. The next step involves the execution of the strategy.

Phase II: Execution

Executing the message strategy is the next step in the process of creating an ad. The execution phase is where the ad is actually written and designed for production. This phase involves three stages: devising a creative idea, applying that idea so that it is consistent with the creative strategy, and adapting the idea for different types of media. We investigate each of these stages next.

The Creative Concept

To execute the message strategy, advertisers build on a creative idea that is called either the *creative concept* or the *big idea*. The creative people—the copywriter, art director, and other team members such as a creative director or creative supervisor—take the strategy outline from the copy platform and express the strategy in a way that is imaginative, attention-getting, memorable, and persuasive.

This big idea is usually created through a process of brainstorming, a creative problem-solving technique in which ideas are listed as they come to mind. Often one idea leads to another until a large collection are available to sort through. Brainstorming is usually done in a group, but copywriters and art directors also do a form of individual or team-based brainstorming in which they develop thumbnail sketches, which are rough drawings of an ad or key visuals that try to capture the essence of the big idea.

Table 9.2 Creating the Advertisement

Phase I: Strategy
Decide the advertising strategy.
Decide the message strategy.
Identify the selling premises.

Copywriting and Art Direction

A writer and art director usually make up the creative team. They devise the creative concept jointly and then the copywriter expresses that concept in words—either for print, broadcast, or other media. Copywriting is an art form of its own. Writers are expected to develop captivating, powerful ideas that are easy to understand; can be presented succinctly; and lock in the mind, such as the "catchy phrases" in Table 9.3.

Pepsi
www.pepsi.com

The history of Pepsi slogans also gives some insight into how catchy phrases may evolve over time. The most recent Pepsi slogan, "The Joy of Cola," replaced "Nothing Else is a Pepsi," (launched in 1995). Before that, Pepsi used "Be Young, Have Fun, Drink Pepsi" (1994–95), "Gotta Have It" (1992–93), "The Choice of a New Generation" (1989–92), "Pepsi Now" (1984–88), and "Come Alive! You're in the Pepsi Generation" (1967–69). Which ones strike you as the most captivating and memorable? Which ones are forgettable?

Art
The visual elements, which include illustrations or photographs, the type, logotypes (logos, or brand symbols), signatures (how the brand name is written), and the layout (how all the elements of the ad are arranged) in print.

The art director designs print ads and other printed forms such as outdoor, collateral materials, posters, and brochures and establishes the "look" for television commercials. **Art** refers to the visual elements, which include illustrations or photographs, the type, logotypes (logos, or brand symbols), signatures (how the brand name is written), and the layout (how all the elements of the ad are arranged) in print.

Because advertising is a highly visual communication form, the visuals are a crucial part of the message design. Pepsi ads, for instance, use a dynamic graphic element—the logo on the can—in its ads to create a visual reminder.

Table 9.3 Slogans and Catchy Phrases

See how many of these phrases—product and campaign slogans, taglines and catchy phrases from ads—you remember. Match the phrase to its brand.

____	a. "Don't leave home without it."	1. Maxwell House
____	b. "Where's the beef?"	2. Allstate
____	c. "Builds strong bodies 12 ways."	3. McDonald's
____	d. "Melts in your mouth, not in your hand."	4. Hallmark
____	e. "How do you spell relief?"	5. United
____	f. "When it rains it pours."	6. General Electric
____	g. "Reach out and touch someone."	7. Yellow Pages
____	h. "Takes a lickin' and keeps on tickin'."	8. Rolaids
____	i. "99 44/100 percent pure."	9. Wonder Bread
____	j. "Fly the friendly skies."	10. Timex
____	k. "Let your fingers do the walking."	11. AT&T
____	l. "You're in good hands."	12. M&Ms
____	m. "You deserve a break today."	13. Morton Salt
____	n. "We bring good things to life."	14. American Express
____	o. "When you care enough to send the very best."	15. Ivory Soap
____	p. "Good to the last drop."	16. Wendy's

Answers: a. 14; b. 16; c. 9; d. 12; e. 8; f. 13; g. 11; h. 10; i. 15; j. 5; k. 7; l. 2; m. 3; n. 6; o. 4; p. 1.

The Effects of Advertising Media on the Creative Process

Often the creative idea will be communicated through a variety of advertising media that require message adaptation. Thus, creative people must know the advertising medium that will be used and its peculiar characteristics before they can plan an ad. Let's review the key creative requirements of the more common advertising media.

Print Advertising. Print advertising includes printed advertisements in newspapers, magazines, brochures, and flyers. The key elements of print advertising are copy and art. The copy elements include headlines, subheads, body copy, captions, slogans, and taglines. The use of type in print makes it possible to write a clear and extended explanation. Print advertising tends to be visually intensive, with the message being communicated as much by the pictorial elements as by the words. Visuals that are easy to understand and remember communicate fast and speak to the busy reader who often doesn't want to take the time to read a lot of copy. Copy-heavy advertising, however, is appropriate when there is an interesting story to be told or when the reader is presumed to be interested in acquiring information.

Broadcast Advertising. Ads that are broadcast are heard in one of two formats—radio or television—and they tend to be 15, 30, or 60 seconds in length. This short length means the ads must be simple enough for consumers to grasp, yet intriguing enough to prevent viewers from switching the channel. Interesting and entertaining commercials can hold viewer attention.

Mazda
www.mazda.com

Television is a visual medium of moving images, so action is the component that separates TV commercials from other forms of advertising. Certain types of commercials are particularly effective in television, such as storytelling, demonstrations, sight and sound spectaculars, and real-life situations that touch emotions. A riveting Mazda ad from the Netherlands, for example, showed a man driving at night on a dangerous two-lane highway when he was clearly fighting to keep awake. At the end of the action in the spot, he deliberately drove off the road and rammed a post. The objective of this curious action was to make his airbag inflate, at which point he went to sleep using it as a pillow.

Video
The images (within a commercial).

Audio
The sound (within a commercial).

Talent
The people or animals in the commercial.

Pacing
The speed at which the action develops.

The components of a television commercial include the **video,** or the images; the **audio**, or the sound; the **talent**, or the people or animals in the commercial; and other stagecraft elements such as props, setting, and lighting. Graphics can be generated on the screen as well. These components of a commercial are held together by **pacing**, the speed at which the action develops.

A growing advertising tool is the infomercial, a program-length television commercial. The infomercial business is currently a $1.4 billion industry in North America. It is used by such big-name advertisers as Microsoft, Sony, Lexus, Nissan, Procter & Gamble, and Apple Computer. Fitness products are the leading product category.[5]

Infomercials are successful because they give consumers more information, more education, and more time to understand the product and its message. Effective infomercials provide how-to information that consumers in the target market are eager to receive. Nissan, for example, produced *The Art of Buying a Car*, an infomercial targeted at female car viewers that delivered many leads, given its total cost.

The logo on Pepsi products is designed to be a memory cue. Using the logo in ads creates a powerful reminder.

Infomercials can also be used to tie in with other marketing communication efforts. Excedrin, for example, used a trio of direct-response spots—that is, infomercials that gave viewers the chance to call in during the ad and respond to the offer—to generate a database of headache sufferers who then received a free sample, coupons, and a quarterly newsletter.

Radio advertising relies on attention-getting sound effects and highly memorable music. Radio advertising is often called the "theatre of the mind" because it depends so much on listeners' imaginations to fill in the missing visual element. Listeners, in other words, are active participants in the construction of the message, and that makes radio a very involving medium. Radio, because it is limited to sound, depends on voices, sound effects, and music to create a story.

Even though people often listen to the radio while they are doing something else, strategies in radio advertising have found three ways to heighten the impact on the listener. The first is repetition, particularly for jingles that are so simple and easy to remember that they become sing-alongs. A second technique is to present the creative strategy with either music or humour, both of which grab attention and inspire memory. Finally, timing the ad to correspond to an immediate need works well. Restaurant ads, for example, are often played while the listener drives home from work.

Out-of-home advertising
Advertising that reaches audiences in their daily external environment.

OUT-OF-HOME ADVERTISING. Advertising that reaches audiences in their daily external environment is called **out-of-home advertising.** It includes painted walls, telephone kiosks, truck displays, bus benches, shopping mall displays, in-store merchandising, aisle displays, and billboard advertising. Blimps, airplanes, towing messages, and the scoreboards in sports arenas are also types of out-of-home advertising. This type of advertising is a good way to target groups of people with specific messages at a time when they are most susceptible to its impact. Out-of-home advertising has enjoyed great success because more advertisers are

This eye-catching ad for Yellow.ca grabs the attention of businesses interested in being included in a national online business directory.

looking to alternative media to carry their messages to more tightly targeted audiences.

Transit advertising
Primarily an urban advertising tool that uses vehicles to carry the message throughout the community.

Transit advertising is primarily an urban advertising tool that uses vehicles to carry the message throughout the community. Occasionally you might see trucks on the highway that also carry messages. Transit advertising is of two types—interior and exterior. Interior is seen by people riding inside buses, subway cars, and some taxis. Because such advertising sends messages to a captive audience that has time to read, there is often more copy on the ads. Exterior transit advertising is mounted on the sides, rear, and top of these vehicles, and it is seen by pedestrians and people in nearby cars. Transit messages can be targeted to specific audiences if the vehicles follow a regular route, such as buses. Most of these posters must be designed for quick impressions, and they serve as quick reminders. Transit advertising also includes the posters seen in bus shelters and train, airport, and subway stations. Like interior cards, these posters may be seen by people waiting for transit, and therefore they can be more detailed than messages that are seen quickly by people passing by.

Yahoo! Canada
www.ca.yahoo.com

ONLINE OR INTERNET ADVERTISING. Online advertising may be seen on commercial information online services such as America Online (AOL), and Sympatico; on electronic bulletin board systems; and on Internet directories such as Yahoo! Canada and free search engines such as Excite, HotBot, and SNAP. The IMC in Action feature gives a number of tips for Internet advertisers.

Doing Business and Advertising on the Internet

The hottest trend in retailing is electronic commerce but Canadian merchants do not yet have a significant presence on the Internet. There are, however, indications that more retailers are slowly venturing onto the Internet. A survey released by Ernst & Young Canada Services Inc. and IAB Canada found that more retailers are using the Internet to advertise but, for the most part, are focusing on trying to channel consumers to their brick-and-mortar stores.

How should these retailers design their Internet advertising messages? The creative frontier is figuring out how to lure potential customers in your area. First, you must inform people where your site is by promoting it in other areas of the Internet and in other media. Those who abide by Internet etiquette ("netiquette") frown on unsolicited mass e-mailing, so many businesses announce their Web site address in print or broadcast ads.

To make a good impression on electronic visitors, a company should consider the following tips:

- Stop surfers in their tracks. Offer a deal or use an involvement device such as a challenge or contest that offers a discount or a "freebie" as a prize.
- Change your offer frequently, perhaps even daily. One of the reasons people surf the Net is to find out what's happening now. Good ads exploit "nowness."
- Keep your executions short and succinct. Most browsers have a short attention span. Graphics make a page slow to set up, so use them sparingly on the home page.
- Find ways to keep your browsers' attention focused. Ask provocative questions, make the time they spend with your site worthwhile, give them something even if it is only a piece of knowledge they can use.
- Find ways to use the advertisement to solicit information and opinions. For example, reward browsers for sharing their opinions with you by offering them three free days of a daily horoscope or something else they might find fun or captivating.

Design is the big challenge. When you couple interactivity with the volume of information offered on each home page, advertisers must ensure that their site can be navigated easily. Information-design practitioners help companies design user-friendly sites that people can visit without getting lost or frustrated.

Examples of successful sites include New Balance Athletic Shoes (www.newbalance.com). Targeted at athletes, this site provides tips on exercise, diet, running, and events. It even asks the magazines in which it advertises to provide material for the site. Billed as Canada's first e-commerce site devoted solely to gardening, GardenCrazy. COM Ltd. of Saint-Timothe, Quebec (www.gardencrazy.com) sells seeds and offers gardening advice online. Tambrands has created Troom (www.troom.com) as a place for female teens to get advice on many issues in their lives such as music and makeup. The site is elaborately constructed to resemble a teenage girl's room.

Food for Thought

1. What message do you think advertisers send to stakeholders if their site is hard to navigate?
2. How would you communicate the home page address for a popular soft drink?

Source: "E-Commerce: Smaller Retailers Cash in Online," *The Daily Gleaner*, 14 August 1999, A10; Denise Caruso, "Digital Commerce: Simple is Beautiful, Especially in a Place as Confusing as Cyberspace," *New York Times*, 16 August 1996, C5; Jeffery D. Zbar, "Blurring the Ad-editorial Line," *Advertising Age*, November 13, 1995, 14; Herschell Gordon Lewis, "Cruisin Down the 'Hype-er Space' Road: How to Write Copy for the (Gulp!) Internet," *Direct Marketing* (November 1995): 36-7; Larry Chase, "Crossroads: Advertising on the Internet," *Marketing Tools* (July/August 1994): 60-1.

This home page for The NET IDEA, a Nelson, B.C.-based Internet service provider, incorporates a banner advertisement with a balance of vivid colours and a clear copy to capture attention.

The NET IDEA
www.netidea.com

The commercial services have electronic shopping malls where businesses can offer their products and services to users. Companies can also sponsor conference areas where they are able to participate in dialogues with present and potential consumers. The commercial services also make available space for "banners," lines of copy relating to a product that invite viewers to "click" on the ad to link to more information. These banners run in conjunction with some other page of information that the viewer has consulted. Effective banners must arouse the interest of the viewer who is often browsing through other information on the computer screen. The key is to balance vivid graphics and clear copy. An example is found on the home page of The NET IDEA, a Nelson, British Columbia Internet service provider.

Internet banner advertising is developing rapidly as new technologies from companies such as Sun Microsystems' Java, Netscape, and Microsoft make it possible to incorporate sound, animation, and video. For example, the Java-driven ScorePost on ESPNet Sportszone scrolls through sports scores, and as it does so it moves through a series of ads, much like the rotating signs at basketball games. Duracell uses a drawing of a battery breaking through a page instead of a conventional banner. Curious viewers who click on the battery see an image of the back of the page covered with electrical circuits along with the message "Powered by Duracell."

Netscape also can run multiple window-like frames simultaneously, which allows an ad to run in one window while viewers are surfing to other pages. Viewers can read other pages while watching animation or even video ads in a split-screen arrangement. Netscape's "cookies" tool allows a Web server to download ads tailored to specific types of consumers. A 15-year-old teenager, for example, would receive a different style of Levi's ad than would a 40-year-old woman.

Online advertising is so new that methods of evaluation have yet to be developed. AdLab, a tracking service from Competitive Media Reporting, however, reports that the top advertisers use a print magazine format at their Web sites. Its "ad activity index" ranks advertisers on the number of such ads, the size of ads, and the number of active links the advertiser has.[6]

OTHER ADVERTISING MEDIA. There are a variety of other ways to reach audiences with advertising, including direct-mail advertising to the home or business. Let's briefly review other forms such as direct-mail, directory, and movie advertising.

Direct-mail advertising
Ads in print and broadcast media that offer a product and a means to respond to the ad with an order.

Directory advertising
Occurs in books that list the names of people or companies, their phone numbers, and addresses.

Direct-mail advertising refers to ads in print and broadcast media that offer a product and a means to respond to the ad with an order. The copywriting must be very strong because it has the sole responsibility to motivate the target audience to respond without other assistance such as personal sales or a store display. This type of advertising crosses over between advertising and direct marketing and will be discussed in more detail in Chapter 12.

Directory advertising occurs in books that list the names of people or companies, their phone numbers, and addresses. The most common directories are produced by a community's local phone service. The Yellow Pages is a major advertising vehicle for local retailers. Yellow Pages advertising is described as directional advertising because it advises people where to go to get the product or service they are looking for. Directory advertising's greatest strength is that it reaches prospects who already know they have a need for the product or service. But Yellow Pages are just the beginning of the directory business. There are an estimated 7500 directories available, and they cover all types of professional areas and interest groups.

Trailers
Filmed commercials shown in movie theatres before the feature. These advertisements are similar to television commercials but are generally longer.

Product placement
The practice of having a product appear in a news show or movie to generate valuable visibility.

Most movie theatres will accept filmed commercials to run before the feature. Called **trailers**, these advertisements are similar to television commercials but are generally longer. In addition, movie advertising also includes **product placements** in films. This is a relatively new medium for advertisers, but they have found that having an easily identifiable product that a character in a movie uses can have tremendous impact on the product's acceptability.

INTERNATIONAL STRATEGIES

Once a strategy has been developed, then advertisers need to evaluate how to execute it across social, cultural, and political boundaries. Advertising for international clients offers a challenge: How can advertisers develop advertising that will succeed around the globe? In rare cases advertisements may be taken from one country to another, but in most cases there has to be some modification, if only to the language. Usually, the advertising strategy is the easiest to standardize from country to country, followed by the message strategy and selling premises, and finally the executions.[7] In most cases the executions have to be modified for local audiences.

The same considerations apply to multi-ethnic advertising within a country. As illustrated in Chapter 5, Canadian advertisers often develop separate campaigns for ethnic audiences. In Malaysia, advertisers may adapt their strategies to fit the native Malaysian population, which is primarily Muslim; a large Chinese population; and a smaller Indian population, which is primarily Hindu.

Rolex
www.rolex.com

Whether a strategy can be globalized depends on product category. Certain business products, computer products, status products like Rolex and Montblanc, and soft drinks are used the world over. The target audience may also affect whether the advertising strategy may be globalized. Certain types of people are

Masaru Ariga

Senior Strategic Planner, Marketing Management Division

Dentsu Inc.

Dentsu is an international marketing communication agency. Masaru Ariga is responsible for planning international marketing communication strategies for Dentsu's client companies. He travels extensively and works with planners in overseas Dentsu offices. He frequently takes charge of marketing communication campaigns on a pan-regional basis, particularly in Asia. He explains, "Coming from headquarters, I consider my responsibility to be identifying what can be used across the countries and what needs to be country-specific."

Ariga is also in charge of developing new marketing methodologies to cope with various timely issues. For example, how can national brands compete effectively against private labels? How to use database marketing? How to implement integrated marketing communication? In this role he has been interviewed as an expert on advertising and marketing communication by such international media as CNN.

In addition to his client-based work, Ariga also gives lectures and writes articles on marketing-related topics. He is a lecturer of marketing at the International University of Japan and, from time to time, is asked to give lectures for such organizations as the Japan Marketing Association (JMA) and Japan Advertising Agency Association (JAAA). Some of his articles that have appeared in professional publications include the following:

- "Seven Crucial Viewpoints to Understand Japanese Consumers"
- "Mass Retailing to Japanese Consumers"
- "Changing Marketing Environment and Integrated Marketing Communications"
- "Database Marketing in Singapore"

Academic Background

Ariga graduated with a B.A. in political science from Waseda University in Tokyo in 1985. During the 1981/82 academic year, he earned a scholarship and studied at Macalester College in St. Paul, Minnesota, as an exchange student.

In 1991 he returned to the United States to get his master's degree from Northwestern University. He graduated in 1992 from its new IMC program. His graduate education was sponsored by Dentsu, for whom he had been working since 1985.

Advice

Ariga has found that travelling abroad has been his most helpful experience. He had already visited 30 countries before graduating from college and now can claim 40 countries. He explains, "Having visited new places and exposing myself to different cultures at a young age helped me develop diverse ways of looking at things."

similar in their interests regardless of where they live (business travellers, teenagers, computer techies). Pampers executives have observed, for example, that mothers around the world have similar needs for diapers for their infants. Ads for products and consumer groups that cut across national boundaries, therefore, can be fairly standardized in their strategies.

Sometimes the creative concept can also carry across borders. The Marlboro cowboy works even in countries where cowboys are unknown, probably because of the worldwide fascination with the idea of the West and the rugged independence that the character represents. The Snuggles bear also works well in just about every country in the world.

The execution of an ad, which we discuss in the next section, may need to be modified for individual countries to maximize effectiveness. The creative concept for Impulse Body Spray, for instance, uses the image of a man stopping a woman on the street to give her flowers. That idea works almost everywhere, but the ads are filmed locally so the settings and physical characteristics of the people seem familiar.

There are some parts of the world where advertising messages need special care. Some Asian countries are particularly concerned about "cultural imperialism" and resent the incursion of Western values through advertising. Consequently, some countries severely restrict Western advertising. Malaysia, for instance, requires that all advertising be locally produced. Muslim countries forbid advertising for "sin" products (cigarettes, alcohol), and the women's images in the visuals must conform to Muslim notions of propriety, which can vary from country to country.

The execution phase of creating an advertisement is summarized in Table 9.4.

Phase III: Production

The production requirements for print and broadcast ads are entirely different, but both are complex and demand the specialized skills of expert technicians. Brochures, posters, outdoor boards, the World Wide Web, and all other advertising usually require specialized skills.[8]

Getting a print ad produced, for instance, requires knowledge of the graphic arts industry and specialized information about typography (how the type is chosen and typeset) and art production. Photography, in particular, is difficult to reproduce in printing and demands a number of technical operations.

Storyboard
A drawing of the key scenes in a commercial

A radio ad is produced by recording the sound effects, voices, and music as detailed in the script written by the copywriter. A television commercial uses audio and video recording techniques. Shooting a TV commercial is a complex event that involves characters, sets, lighting, props, and an audio track. All of these elements are assembled according to a script written by the copywriter and a storyboard drawn by the art director. A **storyboard** is a drawing of the key scenes in the commercial. A producer manages the videotaping and directs the shooting of the script, which usually results in a lot more footage than is actually needed in a typical commercial. A film editor assembles the best footage into a series of scenes that follows the script and lasts the correct length, such as 10, 30, or 60 seconds.

Table 9.4 Creating the Advertisement

Phase II: Execution
Develop the creative concept or big idea.
Write the copy and design the look of the ad.
Adapt this creative approach to all of the media used in the creative mix: print, broadcast, infomercials, out-of-home ads, transit, online ads, and other advertising forms and tools.
Adapt the creative approach to cross-cultural and international marketing situations.

The production phase in creating an advertisement begins after the strategy has been decided and the creative ideas for the ads have been developed. Table 9.5 summarizes all three phases in the process of creating an advertisement.

Table 9.5 CREATING THE ADVERTISEMENT

Phase I: Strategy

Decide the advertising strategy.
Decide the message strategy.
Identify the selling premises.

Phase II: Execution

Develop the creative concept or big idea.
Write the copy and design the look of the ad.
Adapt this creative approach to all of the areas used in the creative mix: print, broadcast, infomercials, out-of-home ads, transit, online ads, and other advertising forms and tools.
Adapt the creative approach to cross-cultural and international marketing situations.

Phase III: Production Phase

Work with experts to produce the materials used in all areas of the creative mix.

concept review

CREATING THE ADVERTISEMENT

1. Advertising strategy involves stating the communication objectives and identifying the target audience; the message strategy identifies the strategic creative approaches and the selling premises.
2. In the execution phase the strategy is transformed into concrete ideas for actual ads for all types of media. The creative team does the following:
   - Develops a big idea, writes ad copy, and designs ads that dramatize the big idea
   - Adapts the idea, ad copy, and design to match the needs of the media tools or the form of advertising
   - Considers any adaptations that might need to be made for cross-cultural or international marketing situations
3. Production is a very technical operation for all media that usually requires many specialized skills.

WHAT MAKES AN EFFECTIVE AD?

Like most viewers you probably have a love-hate relationship with television commercials. On the one hand, you may have a favourite commercial or campaign; on the other hand, you can probably identify a dozen commercials that you resent so much you change the channel or leave the room when they

This CMA Canada ad persuades its target market with attention-getting devices—an action photo and a reminder of the benefits of a CMA's vision.

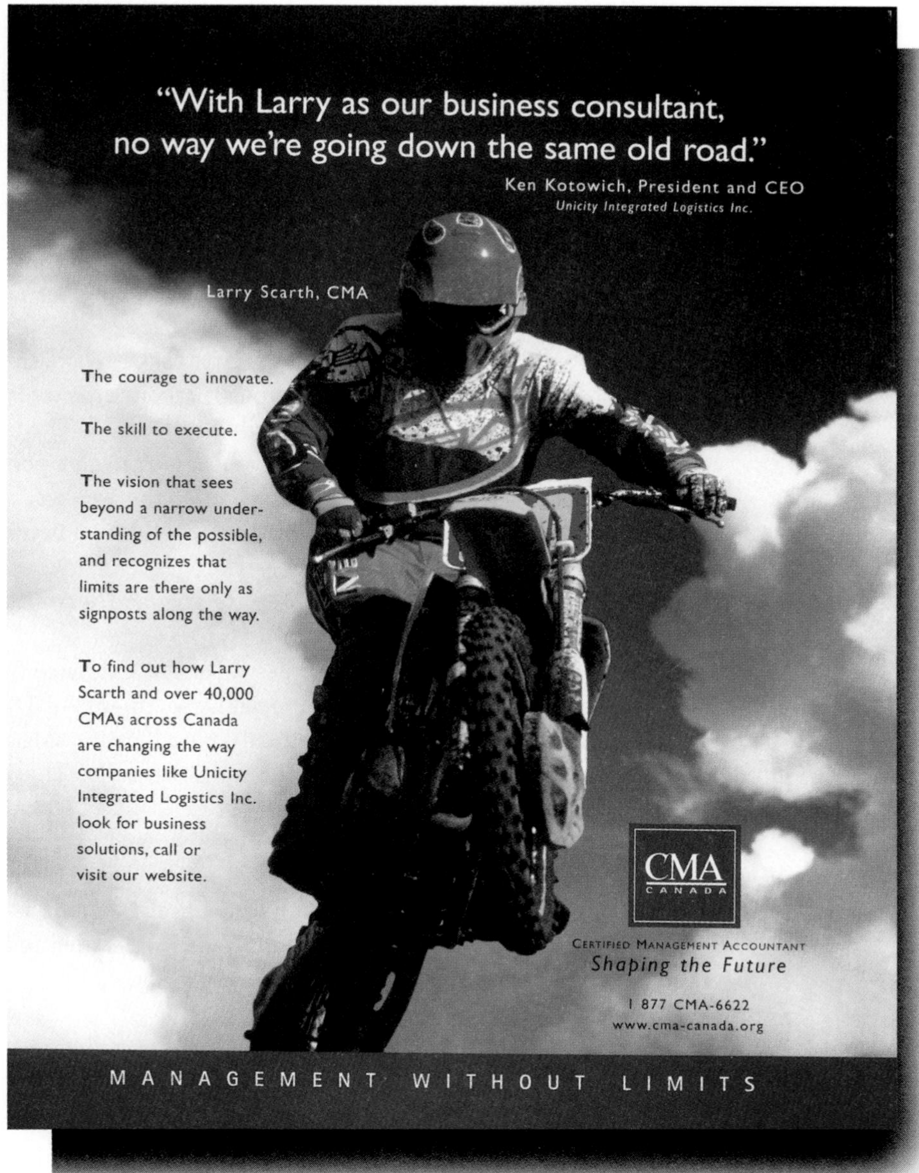

appear. You might hate the product, dislike the characters, and consider the message insulting. Your evaluation of the ad may be based on personal taste—different people like different things. It may be that you aren't part of the target audience so the message doesn't interest you. Or it may be rational judgment—there are, after all, poorly conceived commercials on television and in print. This simple example demonstrates a key point. There are many ways to evaluate an effective ad. Keep in mind that effective advertising must grab attention, be memorable, and persuade. It must also target its audience and meet the advertising objectives.

Ways to Judge Effectiveness

Is effectiveness based on how much consumers like ads? In Canada and the United States various magazine publications and research firms publish consumer ratings of advertisements. One such firm, Video Storyboard Tests, is a U.S.-based organization that monitors consumer reaction to ads. As opposed to consumer ratings, advertising effectiveness also can be judged through a number of competitions that consider creative dimension (the One Show, the Clios, the Cannes awards) or the ads' sales impact (the Effies or the Cassies). Many Canadian creative directors view Cannes as the most important of the major international advertising contests.[9]

A.C. Nielsen Co.
www.acnielsen.com

Advertising effectiveness is being measured using *single-source data*, information gathered by the A.C. Nielsen Co. that compares in-store purchases with exposure to television advertising. In a study based on such data, John Philip Jones reported in his book, *When Ads Work*, that it is possible to persuade people to buy a product through single exposure to an effective advertisement.[10] In exceptional cases advertising can actually triple sales. The advertisements that were the most effective in stimulating short-term sales generate six times the amount of sales as the weakest ones. Some of the weakest advertising actually caused sales to fall. Jones also found a strong correlation between advertising and sales promotion when both activities work together. However, the most successful campaigns made advertising more effective and lessened the need for promotions, particularly price promotions.

Seagram Canada
www.seagram.com

Public service advertising provides different evidence of advertising effectiveness. For instance, Canada's provincial Departments of Transportation collectively spend millions of dollars annually to advertise safe driving behaviours such as usage of children's car seats and seat belts. These dollars are spent because it is believed these campaigns prevent injuries and save lives. It can also be the case that public service advertising is viewed as a communications vehicle for the delivery of a positive message that enables an organization to fulfil its ethical obligation to society. For example, Seagram Canada's "How to Talk About Alcohol" campaign is a communications vehicle designed to help parents talk to their preteen children about responsible use of alcohol.[11]

Evaluation

Advertising can be considered effective only after it has been evaluated in some way. For instance, to better assess advertising effectiveness, General Motors announced that it is developing a standardized approach to evaluate—and learn from—its advertising successes and failures. Its three-part process involves:[12]

1. *Strategic development*, through which creative ideas are tested using a toolbox of techniques such as focus groups, image studies, and positioning studies
2. *Copytesting* using various methods to diagnose the effectiveness and problems of ads as they are being produced
3. *Market tracking*, which will tie the advertising to sales impact

Evaluation research can occur at several points in time. The first opportunity is before the ad has been aired. Pretesting, testing done during concept development, helps assess whether the ad will accomplish what the strategy calls for before making a big investment in production, time, and money. The second point in time, known as posttesting, is while the advertising is running or shortly thereafter. This testing gives real-life feedback about how well the advertising met its objectives and provides information for future ad strategies.

Copytesting
Research in advertising used to decide whether an ad should run in the marketplace and to help guide execution decisions.

Copytesting is formal evaluation research in advertising used to decide whether an ad should run in the marketplace and to help guide execution decisions. It is focused on persuasiveness, recall (awareness), and message understanding. Advertisers who use copytesting at the concept stage hope that it will provide a valid measure of effectiveness and that it will eliminate the risks and conflicts inevitable when decisions are based on judgment alone.

Copytesting is an important research tool because the stakes in advertising are high. By the time an average 30-second commercial is ready for national television, its production may have cost as much as $280 000. And if it is run nationally, it may cost more than a million dollars in air time. Ideally, the results of copytesting would be available before large sums of money have been invested in the finished work.

In general, advertisers must use copytesting carefully. Tests that are fast and affordable often have obvious flaws and provide data that may not be reliable. Furthermore, creative people within agencies distrust many copytesting methods because they believe the tests don't really measure the impact of the advertising as it plays out in a real-world situation. When decisions are difficult, research cannot always tell the decision maker what to do, so there is still a need for insight and professional judgment. Copytesting and other evaluation techniques are discussed in more detail in Chapter 17.

concept review

What Makes an Effective Ad?

1. Effective advertising is attention-getting, memorable, and persuasive. It also must target an audience and meet stated advertising objectives.
2. Advertising is evaluated at two points in time: before an ad has aired or been published (to test effectiveness before a large investment has been made) and during or shortly after an ad has run (to test impact). The former type of test is a pretest; the latter is posttesting.
3. Most copytesting measures persuasion, recall (awareness), and understanding of key copy points.

A Closing Thought:

Clutter Busting

Good creative people know that every advertising message must compete in a cluttered environment for the attention of an indifferent audience. The only way to break through is to express the selling message in an original, fresh way. Though dull advertising can be persuasive, it will rarely get the attention of the audience. Breakthrough advertising should be both persuasive and creative. It can be risky, though, because it is often difficult to evaluate; it doesn't perform like the traditional advertising with which most consumers are familiar.

Another way to break through the clutter is to integrate the advertising with a wide range of other communication tools that reinforce the same message or big idea. When a captivating idea is repeated at different times in different ways, the synergy adds more power to an already strong concept. That is why it is so important in IMC planning to have consistency at the heart of all the different messages stakeholders receive from a company.

summary

1. Define advertising.

   Advertising is any paid form of nonpersonal presentation and promotion of ideas, goods, and services by an identified sponsor to a targeted audience and delivered primarily through the mass media.

2. Identify the strengths and weaknesses of advertising.

   Advertising has many strengths. It can reach a large mass audience to intensify broad-based demand for a product, build brand awareness, create long-term brand images and brand positions, and increase brand knowledge effectively. Advertising also serves as a reminder of a product or brand with which a consumer has had a positive experience. Finally, it can enhance memorability through message repetition. Advertising has several weaknesses also. It is perceived as intrusive and as cluttering the environment.

3. Explain how advertising works.

   To be effective advertising must accomplish three tasks. It must create attention, be memorable, and deliver a persuasive message. Attention, the act of noticing a message, is the first step toward developing awareness, which means the message has made an impression on the viewer or reader. Advertisers use recognition and recall to enhance memorability. Recognition is the ability to remember that you have seen something before. Recall means you can remember the information content of the message. Finally, to motivate consumers to act, advertisers must persuade audiences through reason or emotion.

4. Outline the three phases in creating an advertisement.

   The first phase in creating an advertisement analyses the marketing and advertising strategy and identifies the message strategy for a particular ad. Advertising strategy focuses on the target audience and the communication objectives. Copy platforms outline the message strategy and selling premises. The second phase is the execution: the development of the big idea, the copywriting, and how to design the ad for the creative mix of different media—print, broadcasting, outdoor, and other types of advertising such as directory, transit, movies, and electronic. The production phase identifies the experts who know how to produce the advertising for a particular medium.

5. Describe what makes advertising effective and how to evaluate effectiveness.

   Effective advertising is attention-getting, memorable, and persuasive. It also must target an audience and meet stated advertising objectives. To evaluate advertising effectiveness, businesses may use such research methods as focus groups and image and positioning studies, consumer ratings, or market tracking to test the sales impact of advertising. Copytesting is often used to diagnose the effectiveness and problems of ads in the development stage and during or shortly after an ad has run. Evaluation research before the ad has run is pretesting. Such research during or after the ad has run is posttesting.

points to ponder

Review the Facts

1. Define advertising and explain its basic function.
2. What are advertising's primary functions? What are its limitations?
3. Define persuasion and explain how it is used in advertising.
4. Explain the difference between advertising strategy and message strategy.

Master the Concepts

5. Think of two television commercials that stick in your mind. Analyse them to determine why they are so memorable.
6. Find an advertisement that illustrates each of the selling premises described in this chapter.
7. Find a magazine ad that crosses cultures and could be used in international advertising with only

minor changes. Also find an ad that you think is culturally bound and could not be used for cross-cultural or international advertising. Explain your reasoning.

8. "Every ad should generate sales." Comment on this statement.

Apply Your Knowledge

9. You are writing ad copy for a new bicycle shop named Pedal Power that will open in a couple of months in your community. Brainstorm with your friends and develop a list of at least 10 slogans that the owner might consider.
10. Spend some time on the Internet and find three advertisements that you believe are either highly effective or ineffective. Critique the ads by examining whether they grab attention, are memorable, and persuade.
11. Why might there be conflict between agencies and their clients on the evaluation of advertising ideas?

suggested projects

1. (Oral and Written Communication) Assume that you have been charged with organizing an in-house advertising department for a growing consumer products company. The first task is to hire an advertising manager who will have ultimate responsibility for the company's advertising. Interview advertising managers at companies in your community to find out how they perceive their job responsibilities. What responsibilities do you believe should be mentioned in the job description for this position? Write the job description.
2. (Oral Communication) Divide the class in half. Debate the two sides of the following question: "Is advertising worth the money?"
3. (Internet Project) This chapter discussed Benetton's recent print ads. Now explore the company's Web site (www.benetton.com) to see if it sends marketing communication messages that are consistent with the advertising messages. (Be warned: The "Fan and Hate Mail" link posts uncensored letters that may contain explicitly and graphically sexual material.) Explain your conclusions about the consistency between Benetton's print and Web site marketing communication messages in a brief memo. Be sure to support your conclusions with specific references to the Web site's content, design, and accessibility to its target audiences around the world.

   Now review the entire gallery of Benetton ads by following the links from the home page to the United Colors Divided Opinions page. Select one ad of your choice—other than one of the ads we discussed in the chapter—and evaluate its effectiveness using the criteria described in this chapter. (For instance, is the ad attention getting, memorable, and persuasive? Does it communicate to its target audience? Does it reinforce or hurt Benetton's image?) Prepare a brief memo of your evaluation criteria and your final assessment.

Case 9 CHOOSING AN AGENCY

It is 5:30 p.m. and you have just come from an executive meeting where the performance of your current advertising agency was being reviewed. The consensus at your meeting was that your company should look at alternative advertising agencies for the coming year. Your boss has reassigned your duties and you are now in charge of recommending an advertising agency to handle your firm's new product launch. Since the new product is expected to hit the market in less than eight months it is imperative that a new advertising agency be identified as quickly as possible. You are just about to leave for the day when your boss stops by and suggests that you look at a direct mail piece that she received a few weeks ago from the Institute of Canadian Advertising. She suggests that this might be a good place for you to start your assessment of the suitability of potential advertising agencies. You take note of the Web address listed on the direct mail piece and decide that first thing in the morning you will visit the Institute's Web site (www.ica-ad.com).

Case Questions

1. Assess the suitability of the advertising agencies listed on the ICA Web site, keeping in mind the needs and characteristics of a firm operating within the industry assigned to you by your instructor.
2. Prepare a report for your firm's executive group recommending an advertising agency to handle the impending product launch and detailing the decision criteria you used to make your choice.
3. How confident are you in the integrity and professionalism of the Institute of Canadian Advertising? Explain your answer providing justification for your position.

Source: This case was prepared by Dr. Shelley M. Rinehart, University of New Brunswick in Saint John. Used with permission.

10

Sales Promotion

chapter objectives

After completing your work on this chapter, you should be able to

- Define sales promotion and discuss its purpose.
- Explain how sales promotion fits in the marketing communication mix and how it can be used in an IMC program.
- Outline how sales promotion strategies differ for the trade and consumer target audiences.
- Compare and contrast the techniques used for and the objectives of reseller, sales force, and consumer promotions.

Colour My World

One company that knows how to offer exciting promotions for all ages is Binney & Smith, maker of Crayola products. Take, for instance, its contest to name new Crayola colours. The contest objectives included generating 50 percent awareness in the target market, getting 20 percent of kids aged three to seven to try Crayola's "Big Box" set of 96 crayons, and building a database of 60 000 Crayola consumers of all ages. Here's how Crayola met its objectives. The contest was aimed at parents and children. Prizes included 16 all-expense-paid trips for four to Hollywood, California, and induction into the Crayola Hall of Fame. The promotion was supported by advertising, in-store displays, and a strong publicity program. A parallel retailer contest offered prizes to retailers who supported and generated the most excitement for the consumer contest.

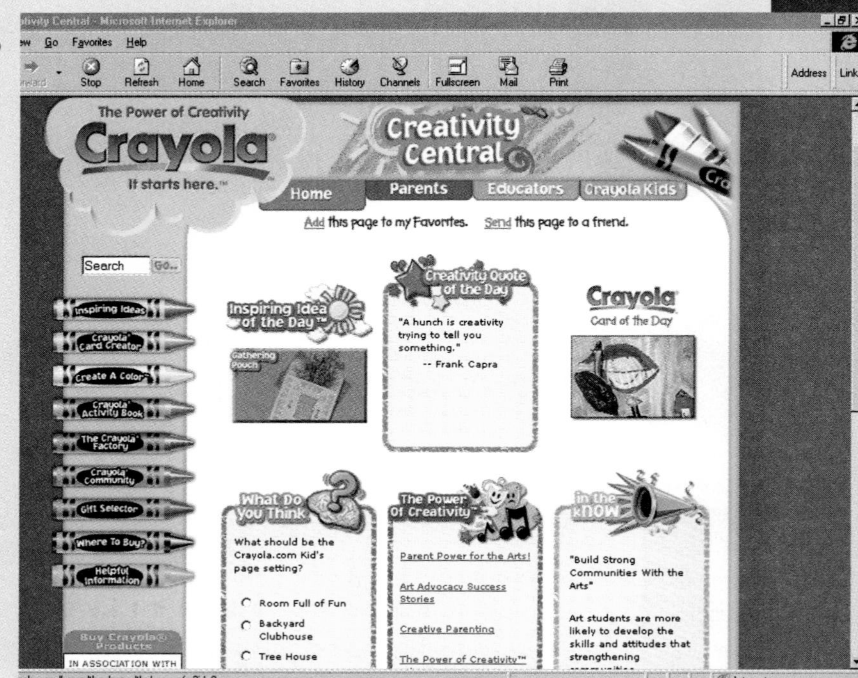

The colour-naming contest was a huge success. Crayola received more than two million colour-name submissions from 122 000 entries. Media coverage resulted in about 1000 print articles and 700 television news stories. Colour winners included: purple mountain's majesty, macaroni & cheese, granny smith apple, pacific blue, tropical rain forest, timber wolf, tumbleweed, tickle me pink, robin's egg blue, cerise, asparagus, denim, shamrock, razzmatazz, wisteria, and mauvelous.

Crayola followed the name-the-colour contest with the Crayola Big Kid Classic adult-colouring contest, which it announced on its Web site. The prizes included $35 000 in silver and gold bullion. In an unusual twist Crayola selected judges for the drawing contest by holding a writing contest in which kids explained why they would make good judges.

To support worthy causes and to promote its Web site, Crayola sponsored an Internet auction of crayon and marker artworks created by more than 30 celebrities such as Whoopi Goldberg, Martin Sheen, Mario Andretti, and Phil Collins. In the first two days, the auction generated more than 50 000 visits to the Web site and to the art gallery where the works were exhibited. Proceeds were donated to the Very Special Arts, a nonprofit organization that promotes learning through the arts to the disabled.

Crayola's sales promotion efforts continue. The sales promotions have heightened consumer awareness of Crayola's new products, reminded customers of its old products, and strengthened its brand image of wholesome fun.

Crayola
www.crayola.com

Sources: "A Room Full of Fun Contest," Crayola home page (January 1, 1997): Internet (www.crayola:80/roomful.com); "Crayola Goes Crayon-line," *Promo* (August 1995), 12; "Name the Crayola Colours Contest," *Brandweek*, April 4, 1994, 32.

Chapter Overview

This chapter introduces the second element of the marketing communication mix—sales promotion. First we examine the strengths and weaknesses of sales promotion and how it fits in the marketing communication mix. Then we outline a framework for planning promotions. Finally, we examine specific techniques aimed at resellers (including retailers, wholesalers, and distributors), the sales force, and consumers.

Defining Sales Promotion

Originally, sales promotion was used as a support tool that was seen as less important than advertising and personal selling in the marketing communication mix.[1] This perspective is no longer valid. Today, sales promotion can support or complement other marketing communication tools, or it may serve as the main tool.

Sales promotion A tool of marketing communication that offers sales-related incentives to produce a measurable action or response for a product or service.

A **sales promotion** has been defined as a marketing communication tool that offers sales-related incentives to generate a specific, measurable action or response for a product or service.[2] Sales promotions may be targeted at any or all of the consumer and trade audiences. The trade audience includes retailers and wholesalers, distributors, and brokers in the distribution channel. The trade audience can also refer to the sales force and other employees. We can better understand sales promotion by examining what sales promotion can accomplish and its strengths and weaknesses.

Stimulate Immediate Action

The main purpose of sales promotion is to offer consumers and trade members (such as sales staff, resellers) an "extra incentive" to act. Sales promotion stimulates sales by offering an extra, short-term incentive to motivate action as is illustrated in the Shaq Mac Attack box (see the IMC in Action that accompanies this chapter). Although this extra incentive is usually in the form of a price reduction, it may be offered in the form of additional product, cash, prizes, premiums, and so on. The Crayola contest prizes are examples of incentives. This extra motivation is what distinguishes sales promotion from the other marketing communication mix tools.

Sales promotion is based on the premise that each brand or service has an established perceived price or value and that sales promotion changes this accepted price-value relationship by increasing the value, lowering the price, or both. Thus, sales promotion offers consumers an immediate inducement to buy a product by the simple step of making the product more valuable. Promotion

IMC Concept in Focus

The Shaq Mac Attack

Though many were sad to see 7'10, 135-kilogram Shaquille O'Neal leave Orlando to move to the Los Angeles Lakers, McDonald's breathed a sigh of relief. Why? The McDonald's in Orlando could finally end a special promotion with the Orlando Magic that had turned out to be a nightmare. When Shaquille O'Neal arrived in Orlando in 1993, McDonald's began redeeming home-game tickets as a coupon for a free Big Mac or Egg McMuffin every time the team hit 110 points or more. It seemed like a good idea at the time.

In 1995, however, the NBA made it easier for teams to run up big scores. First, the NBA moved the three-point line closer to the basket. Second, it eliminated hand checking, the defensive technique of placing hands—sometimes in an ironlike grip—on an offensive player as he tried to move the ball down the court. The Magic also improved its team by adding Horace Grant from the Chicago Bulls and developing Penny Hardaway into an outstanding point guard. The result? Magic fans wolfed down Big Macs at an alarming rate because in 80 percent of the 1995 home games, the Magic team scored 110 points or more.

A perfect example of integrated marketing, the ticket became a coupon that highlighted McDonald's and its sponsorship of the team in a positive way. Winning the free Big Mac had all the excitement of a game. From a sales promotion viewpoint, then, the ticket was a coupon, the redeemed Big Mac was a sample designed to encourage repeat business, and the basketball game was a special event sponsorship. For McDonald's bottom line, however, it turned into a loss because that kind of a winning record gave the 16 000 fans 36 chances to trade in their tickets for a free Big Mac. As you can well imagine, the vision of so many thousands of Big Macs leaving McDonald's free gave the company heartburn.

And backing out of the promotion wouldn't have been simple: At one board meeting a board member suggested raising the barrier to 115 points, but others voiced the concern that McDonald's would then appear stingy. Fortunately, Shaq's departure to the West Coast solved the dilemma.

Food for Thought

1. Assume Shaq had not left Orlando. What sales promotion plan would you have recommended to the Orlando McDonald's?
2. If you were a marketing communication director for the McDonald's in Los Angeles, would you recommend a similar promotion with a 115-point requirement? Explain the advantages and disadvantages of such a promotion.
3. Suppose McDonald's of Los Angeles decided to do a promotion similar to Orlando's and put you in charge of implementation. What should the promotion rules be, and what precautions, if any, would you take before starting the promotion to avoid hurting the company's bottom line?

Sources: "Lakers Sign Shaquille O'Neal," Starwave Corp and ESPN Inc. (October 7, 1996): Internet (www.nba.com/Court/shaq_lakers); Rance Crain, "Big Shaq Attack Giving McDonald's Heartburn," ***Advertising Age***, January 9, 1995, 14.

can prompt consumers who know nothing about the product to try it, and it can persuade them to buy again.[3] Unplanned purchases, for example, can often be directly traced back to one or more sales promotion offers.

To entice customers to try a new product, companies such as Del-Monte Corp., Ralph Lauren, and Wilkinson Sword distribute more than 500 000 free samples in Daytona Beach each spring break. In France, Orangina (the tangerine-flavoured soft-drink maker) joined forces with a fast-food chain to offer music-related premiums to consumers who ordered the drink in the fast-food stores. Orangina sales rocketed as a result.

Sales Promotion Strengths and Weaknesses

Sales promotion techniques can accomplish certain communication goals that the other elements in the marketing communication mix cannot. For instance, sales promotion can turn around a sales trend in the short term. It can help introduce a new product, reinforce advertising images and messages, and generate positive brand experiences among buyers at many stages of the consumer decision-making process. It can also provide new channels for reaching audience segments, such as in-store merchandising materials and special events.

Research suggests, however, that sales promotion cannot accomplish certain goals. For example, sales promotion cannot create a brand's image, change negative attitudes toward a product, or reverse a long-term declining sales trend. In the following sections we discuss the strengths and weaknesses of sales promotion in more depth.

Strengths

The most important strength of sales promotion is its ability to stimulate people to act—to try or to buy something. It does this by adding extra value through special pricing or some other kind of special deal, a practice called changing the price/value relationship. In other words, in the eyes of the consumer it adds a tangible value to the product, such as cents off or a premium.

Sales promotion also offers businesses the flexibility to meet many different marketing communication objectives and to reach any target market. Because of the wide range of promotion techniques, all kinds of businesses—small and large, manufacturers and services, profit and nonprofit groups—can use sales promotion.

A word of caution, however. Although sales promotion is an effective strategy for creating immediate, short-term, positive results, it is not a cure for a bad product, poor advertising, or an inferior sales force.

Sales promotion activities directed at sales forces and resellers can motivate these important trade members to "push" the product by supporting promotions and giving the product more sales attention. Sales force promotions such as rewards and cash bonuses can motivate the sales team to increase sales contacts and overall sales. For instance, a business might give salespeople with the top three sales revenues a $1000 bonus. Promotions aimed at resellers can offer incentives—such as special price deals and gifts of related merchandise—to encourage the trade audience to provide merchandising support to retailers and to create excitement among those responsible for distributing or selling the product. For example, a special promotion on iced tea might offer all participating retailers the coolers used in the display and retailers with product sales above $25 000 the chance to win a trip to Hawaii.

Coupons offer money off products and add extra value for consumers, stimulating them to buy products.

Finally, sales promotions that require customers to fill in name and address information, such as a rebate or mail-in coupons, enable businesses to build databases of customer information. The database information is useful for tracking consumer behaviour and for targeting customers with direct mail. To illustrate, Nabisco built a database of 200 000 cookie and snack purchasers from information collected during a promotion in which consumers sent in proofs of purchase to acquire autographed baseball cards. The company used that database for more individualized direct-marketing efforts.

Weaknesses

Sales promotion activities may have negative consequences. The main weakness of sales promotion is its contribution to clutter. Promotions try to be more creative, shout louder, or deliver ever-increasing discounts to get the attention of consumers and the trade. Another weakness of sales promotion is that repeated use of price-related techniques may reduce the perceived value of the product or brand. In fact, couponing is now so pervasive that some consumers will not buy the product without a coupon. Further, consumers and resellers have learned how to take advantage of sales promotions. Most notably, consumers now wait to buy certain items until they are reduced in price. Resellers may also use forward buying (which means stocking up) when the price is low to improve their bottom lines rather than passing on the savings to their customers.

Also, some sales promotion techniques lend themselves to abuse. Many consumers, for instance, redeem coupons for products they haven't purchased. Theft of premiums (special gifts that reward purchase) is also a problem, especially when easily removed from a package. These fraudulent practices cost businesses millions of dollars.

A key weakness of trade promotion is that it is difficult to get busy trade members, including a company's own sales force, to cooperate. Promotion planners, then, should work closely with the trade audience to provide incentives that will inspire cooperation. Even if trade members such as distributors or salespeople cooperate, however, promotional materials may be wasted if retailers refuse to use the merchandising materials.

If not used carefully, sales promotion may also contribute to declining brand loyalty by shifting consumer focus from brand value to price. Procter & Gamble's division manager of advertising and sales promotion, V. O. "Bud" Hamilton, describes the situation as follows: "Too many marketers no longer adhere to the fundamental premise of brand building, which is that franchises aren't built by cutting price but rather by offering superior quality at a reasonable price and clearly communicating that value to consumers. . . . The price-cutting patterns begun in the early 1970s continue today, fostering a short-term orientation that has caused long-term brand building to suffer."[4]

Some critics believe that the move from brand-building advertising to trade promotions and couponing has created a brand-insensitive consumer who views all products as commodities. In support of their claim, critics cite the price-cutting strategies followed by Coke and Pepsi as an example of two brands that many consumers now view as interchangeable. On any given weekend, especially holiday weekends, Coke and Pepsi products are located on end-of-the-aisle or in-island displays featuring twelve-pack prices as low as $1.99. People buy the cheapest brand and stock up with enough twelve-packs to last until the next sales promotion. The strengths and weaknesses of sales promotion are summarized in Table 10.1.

Sales Promotion in the Marketing Communication Mix

In this section we explore how sales promotion can help implement *push* and *pull strategies*. Then we investigate how sales promotion can aid two specific marketing communication strategies: introducing new products and building brands.

Table 10.1 STRENGTHS AND WEAKNESSES OF SALES PROMOTION

Strengths	Weaknesses
Gives an extra incentive to act	Adds to clutter
Changes the price/value relationship	Can set false retail price
Adds tangible value to product offering Gives sense of immediacy to purchase	Some consumers won't buy unless there is a price deal
Adds excitement, spectacle Stimulates trial	Leads to forward buying by trade members
Stimulates continuity of purchase or support, repeat purchases	Fraudulent redemption of coupons and theft of premiums
Increases purchase frequency and/or quantity Promotes reminder merchandise	Can be difficult to get trade cooperation
Motivates trade support Builds databases	Can undercut brand image, create brand insensitivity

concept review

DEFINING SALES PROMOTION

1. Sales promotion is a marketing communication tool that uses a variety of incentive techniques for consumer and trade audiences to generate a specific, measurable action or response.
2. Its main purpose is to stimulate immediate action—to prompt consumers and trade members to act.
3. The primary strength of sales promotion is that it offers an "extra incentive" for consumers to act. Its primary weaknesses include clutter and the potential to undercut branding.

In many cases sales promotion is used with other types of marketing communication. For example, trade promotions often augment personal sales, advertising may announce special promotions for consumers, and sales promotions may help build databases for later direct-mailing programs.

Table 10.2 reflects a synthesis of the contributions of the various marketing communication tools. These contributions may become blurred when sales promotion is used with other marketing communication tools, such as advertising, because the combined efforts create synergy. The synergistic effect of sales promotion can be a powerful addition to a marketing communication effort. Note the last row of the table. That row shows the contribution to profitability, which is the ratio between what is spent on a promotion compared with the profits generated by that expenditure. We see that sales promotion has a high contribution to profitability, relative to advertising and public relations.

Table 10.2 A Comparison of Sales Promotion with Other Marketing Mix Tools

	Sales Promotion	Advertising	Public Relations	Direct Response (Interactive)	Personal Selling
Time Frame	short term	long term	long term	short term	both
Primary Appeal	both emotional and rational	emotional	emotional	rational	rational
Primary Objective	sales position	image/brand	goodwill	sales	sales relation-ships
Contribution to Profitability	high	moderate	low	high	high

Stimulate Push or Pull Demand

Pull strategy
A promotional strategy that directs most marketing efforts at the ultimate consumer and is usually implemented with large advertising expenditures.

Push strategy
A promotional strategy that directs most marketing efforts at resellers and the sales force to stimulate personal selling efforts.

Promotional strategies can be broadly classified as push or pull strategies, depending on whether the focus is on the consumer or the trade. A **pull strategy** directs most marketing efforts at the ultimate consumer and is usually implemented with large advertising expenditures. It may include additional incentives for the consumer through the use of coupons, rebates, samples, or sweepstakes. These efforts create consumer demand to "pull" the product through the channel of distribution. Thus, a pull strategy requires little promotional effort from resellers.

In contrast, a **push strategy** directs most marketing efforts at resellers and the sales force to stimulate personal selling efforts. The business "pushes" the product through the channels of distribution by asking resellers to demonstrate products, to distribute in-store promotion devices and merchandising materials, and to sell the product. If the product is relatively new, or complex, or if many acceptable substitutes exist, then a push strategy may be more appropriate.

A pull strategy is used when demand for the product is high and when there is high differentiation among products' real or perceived benefits. Some markets, such as children, respond well to a pull strategy. Occasionally, a novelty product or fad can create this overt and assertive behaviour on the part of the consumer. Healthy Choice frozen dinners is an example of a product that was successfully launched by a pull strategy. However, examples of companies that have solely relied on a pull strategy are rare.

Most companies use a combination of push and pull. Marketing representatives for Fruitopia call on supermarkets, discount stores, convenience stores, drugstores, and even specialty stores such as coffee shops and bakeries. As the sales representatives restock the product, they also announce special promotions, offer trade deals, and negotiate for the best possible position for product displays. The company also spends a great deal of money on a consumer marketing communication program to inspire its customers to ask for their favourite beverage. Figure 10.1 outlines the push, pull, and combination strategies.

In addition to stimulating push and pull conditions, there are two specific areas where sales promotion can contribute to a marketing communication strategy—introducing a new product and building a brand.

Figure 10.1 PUSH, PULL, AND COMBINATION STRATEGIES

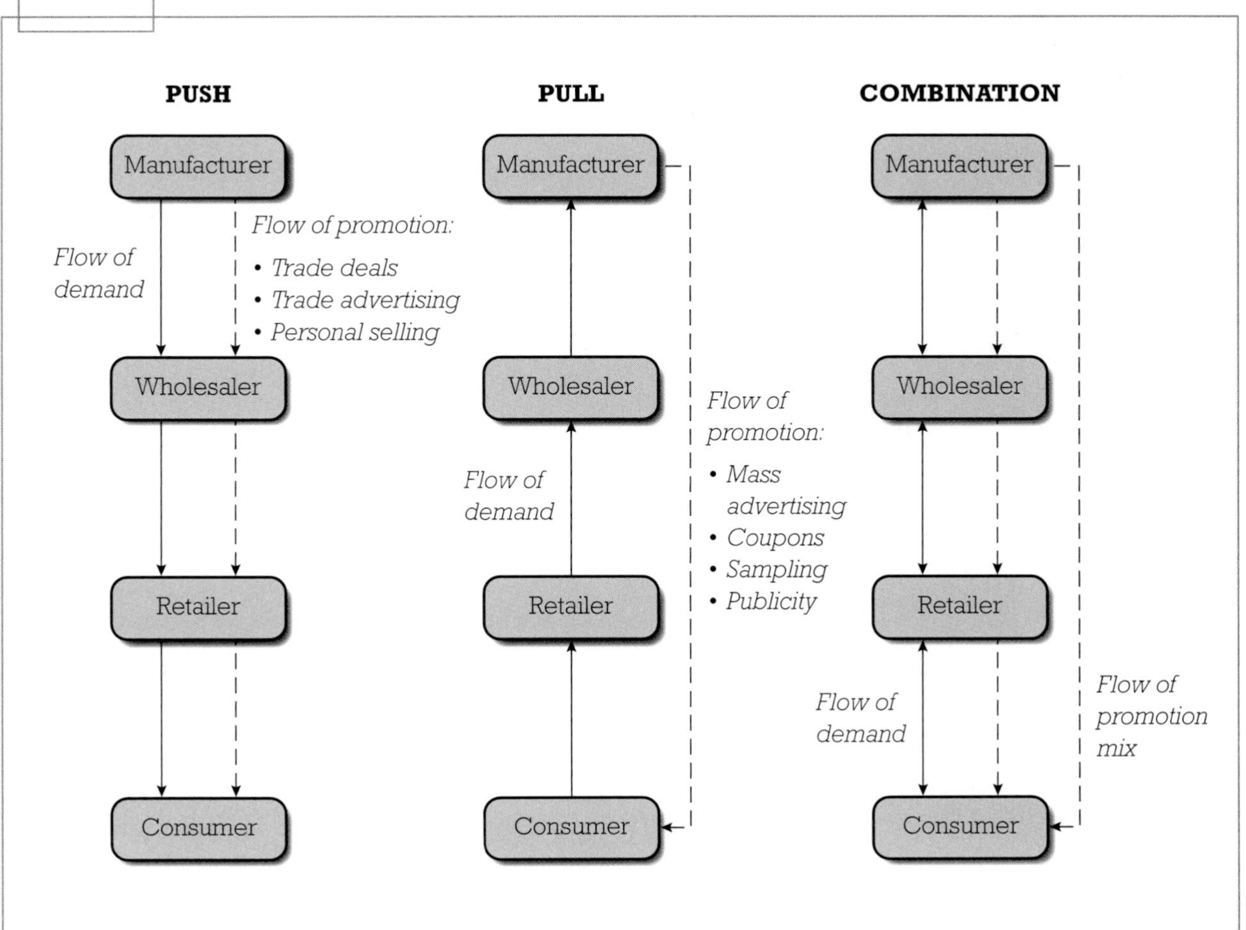

INTRODUCE A NEW PRODUCT

One area in which sales promotion is particularly useful is the introduction of new products and services. Suppose we were in charge of introducing a new corn chip named Corn Crunchies. Our first marketing challenge would be to create awareness of this product. Although advertising can often do this effectively, sometimes sales promotion can call attention to advertising and the brand name. Possibilities include a reduced introductory price, in-store sampling, and a special tie-in with a well-known salsa company.

Creating awareness will only take the product so far. Corn Crunchies must also be perceived as offering some clear benefit compared with the competition. We could use sales promotion to enhance the marketing communication message by offering coupons as a means of advertising. The coupons should stimulate product trial—that is, consumers should try the product. We might also mail free samples of Corn Crunchies to households and offer reduced prices in stores. Conducting a contest in conjunction with the product introduction could also create interest and intensify desire. If we successfully implement this consumer strategy, consumers who are convinced of the value of Corn Crunchies will demand that the product be stocked in their favourite stores. By asking for it, they will pull it through the channel of distribution.

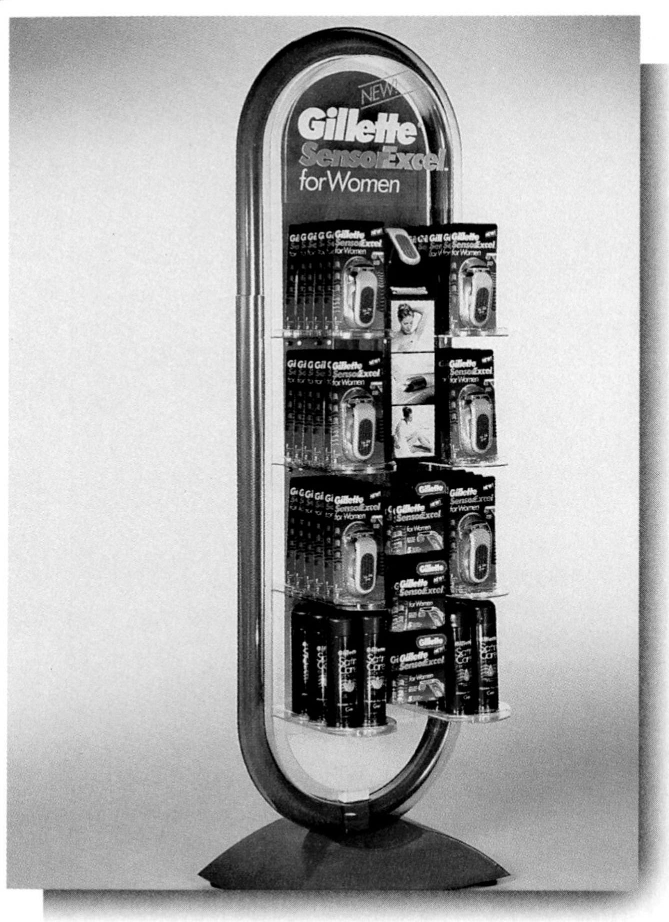

This eye-catching P-o-P display helps Gillette gain valuable shelf space.

Unfortunately, creating awareness and desire means nothing unless the product is available. A push promotional strategy is used to convince members of the distribution network to carry Corn Crunchies. Resellers must be convinced that the product will move off the shelves before they will stock it. Trade advertising directed at wholesalers and retailers can be effective in providing these resellers with important information. In addition, trade sales promotion techniques, especially price discounts, point-of-purchase (P-o-P) displays, and advertising allowances, help to gain shelf space.

After the initial purchase, we want the customer to repeat the purchase, and we also want retailers to allocate more shelf space to Corn Crunchies. To prompt such actions, we must change the advertising copy to remind customers about the positive experience they had with the product and use sales promotion to reinforce customer loyalty with coupons, rebates, and other rewards. For those retailers that carry the product, repeat purchase promotions can also reward them because customers who buy the product are likely to purchase other products while in the store.

Build a Brand

In contrast to the criticism that sales promotion destroys brand loyalty, many sales promotion experts believe it can build brand loyalty. HPD Group, a research firm, conducted a 17-year tracking survey of brand equity in which the results show that loyalty to top brands has been steady since 1987.[5] Marketing communication strategist Michael Schrage notes, "Traditional advertising no longer has the responsibility of maintaining brand equity. Product value is no longer created through advertising imagery, it is determined by the price/performance relationship."[6]

Experts in sales promotion respond to the criticism about branding in two ways. First, they argue that the claim that sales promotion destroys brand image is greatly exaggerated. They refer to many cereal brands, rental car companies, airlines, and hotels that have used a variety of well-planned sales promotion strategies to enhance brand image. Second, sales promotion experts acknowledge that continuous promotion—particularly continuous price promotion—does not always work. However, sales promotion can and does work if it is part of a well-executed strategy to build brand trial and familiarity—especially if it is part of an integrated marketing communication plan.

IBM Canada
ww.ibm.ca

IBM sales promotions for its PC line provide an example of brand-building promotions. IBM uses relatively low-profile promotions, such as giving away a free CD-ROM with lots of software on it to people who buy a new home computer.[7] The company also uses tie-in (or cosponsored) promotions with other marketing partners, such as retailers or suppliers. This type of promotion is designed to help cement relationships with its partners and customers.

concept review

Sales Promotion in the Marketing Communication Mix

1. Marketing communicators often combine sales promotion with other marketing communication tools to create a powerful synergy.
2. A pull strategy is a sales promotion that incites consumers to demand a product; a push strategy tries to convince trade members that the product will sell. If the push strategy is successful, the product is given retailer support and shelf space.
3. Sales promotion is useful in new product introduction because it offers reasons to try the product.
4. Although continuous price promotion can hurt a brand, sales promotion can contribute to brand building if it is part of a well-executed, integrated strategy to build brand familiarity, trial, and loyalty.

Sales Promotion Strategy

Trade promotion
A promotion directed at resellers and sales forces.

Consumer promotion
A promotion directed at consumers.

Recall that sales promotion can be targeted at either consumer or trade audiences. **Trade promotion** is promotion directed at resellers and sales forces; **consumer promotion** is promotion directed at consumers. The target audience dictates both the promotion objectives and the mix of sales promotion tools used.

Objectives

To create sales promotion objectives, planners need to consider two factors: who the audience is and whether the approach will be proactive or reactive. First, different objectives apply to each of the target audiences. Sales promotion is intended to stimulate the consumer to act, motivate the sales force, and gain the cooperation of resellers. Second, sales promotion tends to be either proactive or reactive. The proactive, long-range objectives tend to accomplish the following goals:

1. Create additional revenue or market share
2. Enlarge the target market
3. Create a positive experience with the product
4. Enhance product value and brand equity

Reactive objectives are responses to a negative or short-term situation. They try to accomplish the following goals:

1. Match competition
2. Move inventory
3. Generate cash
4. Perhaps go out of business

Table 10.3 provides examples of both consumer and trade sales promotion objectives. Identify the ones that seek to accomplish proactive and reactive types of objectives.

The Sales Promotion Mix

Promo, the magazine of the promotion marketing industry, reports that the sales promotion industry is growing rapidly for many reasons. It offers the manager short-term solutions; its success in meeting objectives can be measured; it is less expensive than advertising; and it speaks to the current needs of the consumer to receive more value from products.

The most difficult step in sales management is to decide which sales promotion tools to use, how to combine them, and how to deliver them to the two target audiences. Each tool has its own advantages and disadvantages that may change when used in combination with other marketing communication tools. Sales promotion planners should consider several questions when mixing sales promotions:

Overlay
A sales promotion combined with other marketing communication tools and delivered together.

Tie-in
A promotion linking one product to another, using the brand strength of the other product to its advantage.

- *How should the various sales promotion tools be combined physically?* Will the sales promotion tools be delivered separately or will they be designed as an **overlay**—that is, a sales promotion combined with other marketing communication tools and delivered together? Crayola's "Big Kids" promotion, for example, used a contest to attract people to its new Web site. Will the promotion be a **tie-in**, a promotion that links one product to another to take advantage of the brand strength of the other product? Kingsford Charcoal, for example, did a tie-in with a well-known national hot dog brand by offering a price reduction on the hot dogs with a purchase of the charcoal.

Kingsford Charcoal
www.kingsford.com

Table 10.3 Sales Promotion Objectives

Consumer	Trade
• Prompt trial by new users	• Introduce new or improved products
• Stimulate repeated use of the product	• Reduce selling costs
• Encourage more frequent purchase or multiple purchases	• Improve working habits
• Counter competitors' activities	• Offset competitive promotions
• Encourage trade-up in size or cost	• Increase sales volume
• Keep customers by providing an implied reward	• Control inventory
• Reinforce advertising or personal selling	• Stimulate in-store support
• Stimulate trade support • Introduce a product to a new distribution area	• Create a high level of excitement among those responsible for its sale

- *Can or should sales promotion be integrated with other elements of the marketing communication mix?* A coupon, for example, is often used as part of an advertising campaign. A final strategic decision is choosing the type of media to deliver the promotion. Coupons are typically delivered through print media such as newspapers, magazines, direct mail, and **freestanding inserts** (FSIs). FSIs are a separate section of a newspaper that carries coupons.

Freestanding inserts
A separate section of a newspaper that carries coupons.

Taco Bell
www.tacobell.com

Contests and sweepstakes are often more exciting if they are announced on television rather than in print. An example is Taco Bell's Double Decker campaign featuring a one-on-one match-up between basketball greats Shaquille O'Neal and Hakeem Olajuwon. The television spots ran for only four weeks but garnered high effectiveness ratings by research company Ad Track—42 percent of those who knew the ads called them very effective. In addition, the competition generated substantial free media publicity.

Next we will discuss the reseller, sales force, and consumer sales promotion tools in more detail.

concept review

Sales Promotion Strategy

1. Sales promotions are directed at consumer and trade (resellers and the sales force) audiences. To set sales promotion objectives, planners need to consider two factors: who the audience is and whether the approach will be proactive or reactive.
2. Consumer sales promotions are directed at the ultimate users of the product so they "pull" the product through the channel.
3. Trade promotion uses a push strategy. Reseller promotions are directed at the distributors, wholesalers, and retailers whose support is needed to "push" the product. Sales force promotions are aimed to motivate salespeople to give products more sales attention and to meet higher sales goals.
4. Planning the sales promotion mix involves deciding how to combine sales promotion tools physically and how to integrate them with other elements of the marketing communication mix.

Trade Sales Promotion: Resellers

A reseller sales promotion is a trade promotion directed at resellers who distribute others' products to the ultimate consumers or to the sales force. Resellers (also known as intermediaries) distribute goods and services to other resellers and ultimate users. Manufacturers cannot succeed unless resellers are willing to distribute their products. Manufacturers, then, use sales promotion to gain reseller support. Service providers also use trade sales promotion to push their products. Fast-food companies and hotel companies, for instance, use trade promotions to involve their franchise owners and local employees in push programs.

The actual size and worth of reseller promotions are difficult to determine. Although this category represents approximately 50 percent of total promotional spending, expenditures vary by industry and size of business.[8] Moreover, there are millions (or perhaps billions) of promotion dollars that are difficult to trace. Businesses seem to be making a shift, however, from trade promotion (a push strategy) to consumer promotion (a pull strategy).[9]

IMC Concept in Focus

Co-Marketing

Co-marketing is a process whereby leading manufacturers develop marketing communication programs with their main retail accounts, instead of for them. Co-marketing programs are usually based on the lifestyles and purchasing habits of consumers who live in the area of a particular retailer's stores. The partnership means that the advertising and sales promotions build equity for both the manufacturer and the retailer. For example, Procter & Gamble and Wal-Mart might develop a spring cleaning promotion directed at Wal-Mart shoppers. The program could feature P&G cleaning products sold at reduced prices in Wal-Mart stores.

In co-marketing the manufacturer usually initiates the joint venture. In exchange for the manufacturer's brand marketing expertise (consumer knowledge, advertising, sales promotion, and other marketing communication tools), the retailer provides resources, such as personnel and marketing funds, to generate incremental category sales and profits. The manufacturer's brand equity helps drive the promotion. A study of co-marketing strategies found that the two most important requirements were cooperation between partners and a willingness to share information.

Co-marketing usually involves a cross-functional team of people, including such people as a sales promotion agency account manager, the manufacturer's representative, and a representative from the retailer. Companies actively involved in co-marketing ventures include Procter & Gamble, Oscar Mayer, Kraft Foods, Hershey's, Duracell, and Nestlé.

Food for Thought

1. Explain why co-marketing programs are particularly important for companies that have adopted a relationship marketing approach.
2. You're in charge of designing a co-marketing program for your company, Zephyr In-Line Skates, for the store owners who carry the skates. What kind of consumer promotions might you jointly sponsor? What kinds of information do the two companies need to share? Who should be on the cross-functional team that manages the effort?

Sources: Karen Benezra, "McMenu Expands," ***Brandweek***, April 22, 1996, 1, 6; "Promotion . . . By the Numbers," ***Brandweek***, March 13, 1995, 34; Christopher W. Hoyt, "Co-Marketing: What It Is and Is Not," ***Promo*** (March 1995): 34.

Reseller spending currently represents the largest component of a manufacturer's marketing investment.[10] Some studies show that such spending does little to build brand loyalty. It does, however, build stronger relationships between manufacturers and retailers, a trend described as "co-marketing" (see the IMC Concept in Focus feature).

Many promotional devices can motivate resellers to support a product. Here we examine four techniques: dealer contests, trade coupons, dealer loaders, and trade deals including allowances. These techniques are summarized in Table 10.4. Other reseller promotion techniques that may be used to support sales promotion programs, such as trade shows and point-of-purchase displays, will be discussed in Chapter 14.

Dealer Contests

Sales promotion practitioners can develop contests and sweepstakes to motivate resellers. Contests are far more common than sweepstakes, primarily because contest prizes are usually associated with the sale of the sponsor's product. A sales quota is set, for example, and the company or individual who exceeds the quota by the largest percentage wins the contest.

To create enough excitement and motivation to galvanize resellers in a crowded marketing environment, designers have been forced to devise

Table 10.4 TRADE SALES PROMOTION TECHNIQUES FOR RESELLERS

Technique	Objective	Method of Distribution
Dealer contests	Encourage quantity purchases; create enthusiasm; support other marketing communication "big ideas"	Direct mail; trade advertising; sales force
Trade coupons	Increase frequency and amount of purchase; prompt quick trial; promote local store and manufacturer's product	Local advertising; in-store dispensers
Dealer loaders	Reward purchasing at a certain level; reward reseller for supporting a promotion with a gift; create goodwill	Sales force; trade advertising
Trade deals	Reward reseller financially for purchase of product or support of a promotion; stimulate frequency and quantity of purchase; encourage cooperative promotional efforts	Sales force

spectacular contests with impressive prizes and incentives. According to a survey sponsored by *Business & Incentive Strategies* magazine, 46 percent of women and 51 percent of men opt for cold cash, followed by merchandise worth $1000 or more, and travel.[11]

If conducted properly, contests can provide short-term benefits (such as encouraging larger reseller purchases) and can improve the relationship between the manufacturer and the reseller.

This Vanilla Fields promotion, displayed in an Osco coupon booklet, is a sample of a trade coupon.

TRADE COUPONS

Retailers redeem consumers' coupons and must wait for reimbursement from the manufacturer who issued them. Trade coupons differ from consumer coupons in that the manufacturer or service provider offers them to the local retailer to be carried in the retailer's ads or fliers. The manufacturer pays for the advertising and gives the retailer an allowance that covers the upper limit of the estimated redemption. The redeemed trade coupons, then, usually do not have to be returned to the manufacturer.

Trade coupons are often used to stimulate trial of new products quickly. Typically, trade coupons must be redeemed within a few days. The time limit is intended to prompt a quick response. Trade coupons can be a cost-effective tool because they offer the retailer an inexpensive way of promoting the store and help marketers move products into new or difficult markets. Trade coupons can increase both the frequency of purchase and the amount of products purchased.

Dealer loader
A premium that is given to a retailer by a manufacturer for buying a certain amount of a product.

Buying loaders
A gift given for buying a certain order size.

Display loaders
A display that is given to the retailer as a reward after supporting a promotion.

Trade deals
Allowances, discounts, goods, or cash given to a retailer in return for handling a special promotion.

Buying allowances
A type of trade deal in which a manufacturer pays a reseller a fixed amount of money for purchasing a certain amount of the product during a specified time period.

Dealer Loaders

A **dealer loader** is a premium that is given to a retailer by a manufacturer for buying a certain amount of a product. These types of promotions build goodwill with resellers. The two most common dealer loaders are **buying loaders**, typically a gift given for buying a certain order size; and **display loaders**, a display that is given to the retailer as a reward after supporting a promotion. Both techniques can be effective in getting sufficient amounts of a new product into retail outlets or in getting a point-of-purchase display into a store.

Trade Deals

Trade deals (also referred to as trade allowances), which are usually special price concessions, are the most important reseller sales promotion technique. Retailers are "on deal" when they agree to give the manufacturer's product a special promotional effort. These promotional efforts can take the form of special displays, extra purchases, superior store locations, or greater promotion. In return retailers receive special allowances, discounts, goods, cash, or credit on an invoice.

Some industries—such as grocery products, electronics, computers, and automobiles—expect trade deals. In fact, a manufacturer would find it impossible to compete in these industries without offering trade discounts, which often provide the primary incentive for retail support.

There are two general types of trade deals. The first, referred to as **buying allowances**, is a type of trade deal in which a manufacturer pays a reseller a fixed amount of money for purchasing a certain amount of the product during a specified time period. All the retailer has to do is meet the purchase requirements. The payment may be a cheque from the manufacturer or a reduction in the face value of an invoice. The second category is *advertising and display allowances*, which we discuss in more detail in a moment.

Forward buying
When retailers buy more merchandise at the discounted price than they need during the deal period.

Slotting allowance
A fee that retailers charge manufacturers for space the new product will occupy on the shelf.

Free goods allowance
A certain amount of product offered to wholesalers or retailers at no cost if they purchase a stated amount of the manufacturer's product.

Advertising allowance
A common promotion technique in which the manufacturer pays the wholesaler or retailer a certain amount of money for advertising the manufacturer's product.

Buying Allowances

One problem with buying allowances is **forward buying**. This practice, common in grocery retailing, means retailers buy more merchandise at the discounted price than they need during the deal period. They store the extra merchandise and bring it out after the sale period, selling it at regular prices.

Two types of buying allowances include the slotting allowance and the free goods allowance. The **slotting allowance**, a fee that retailers charge manufacturers for space the new product will occupy on the shelf, has become the most controversial form of buying allowance, as discussed in the You Decide feature. A **free goods allowance** is a certain amount of product offered to wholesalers or retailers at no cost if they purchase a stated amount of the same manufacturer's product. The reseller that buys the required amount of product is given free merchandise instead of money.

Advertising and Display Allowances

The two main types of advertising allowances are standard advertising allowances and cooperative **advertising allowances**. Used mainly in the consumer-products industry, an advertising allowance is a common promotion technique in which the manufacturer pays the wholesaler or retailer a certain amount of money for advertising the manufacturer's product. This allowance can be a flat dollar amount or it can be a percentage of gross purchases during a specified time period.

Do Slotting Fees Mean the Big Guys Always Win?

Are retailers ripping off marketers? Manufacturers feel that it doesn't matter anymore how good the product is or isn't. The only way a retailer will place a product on its shelves is if the manufacturer pays a slotting fee. That particularly limits small start-up companies who may not have the financial wherewithal to pay these fees. Manufacturers of all sizes, however, feel they are being held up for ransom by retailers. They also feel the balance of power in the manufacturer-retailer relationship has slipped too far in favour of the retailer.

Retailers argue that they must charge these fees because of small profit margins and product promotion costs. They claim also that introducing new products requires money to redesign shelves and reprogram computers. But grocery manufacturers accuse retailers of peddling their shelf space for extra money—trade deals pay for all the costs of shelving a product. For example, in the grocery industry approximately 60 percent of all manufacturers' sales are accompanied by a trade deal averaging about 12 percent of the manufacturer's recommended price.

So how is the money from slotting fees used? One food industry source estimated that 70 percent of all slotting fees go directly to retailers' bottom lines. In other words, some retailers pocket the money instead of passing it on as savings to the consumer. Even if untrue, retailers suspected of pocketing the allowance money risk jeopardizing key relationships with resellers, such as retailers and manufacturers. They also risk jeopardizing relationships with customers.

Marketers are slowly seeking ways to balance power more equally with retailers. Many manufacturers and service providers are putting together promotional programs and pitching them directly to local store managers. Some are also proposing co-marketing programs to foster cooperation with retailers and are trying to manage retailing promotions more effectively. For instance, Procter & Gamble now has managers in charge of coordinating promotions for similar brands, such as Dash and Tide detergents, so that such promotions help retailers generate more business because they are well timed and don't compete. Maybe the knots in the retailer-manufacturer relationship created by the slotting allowance will diminish through these efforts.

You Decide

1. What do you think? Should retailers be permitted to charge slotting fees? Should manufacturers refuse to pay them?
2. Do you think it's ethical for retailers to use the slotting fees to help their bottom line, rather than to pass savings on to consumers?
3. Slotting fees often stifle smaller, start-up businesses because many of these businesses can't afford to secure shelf space. Do you think that's simply the cost of doing business? Or do you think it's unfair discrimination? Explain.

Sources: Betsy Spethmann, "Trade Promotion Redefined," *Brandweek*, March 13, 1995, 25032; Judann Dagnolie and Lauri Freeman, "Marketers Seek Slotting-Fee Truce," *Advertising Age*, February 22, 1988, 132; Keith M. Jones, "Held Hostage by the Trade?" *Advertising Age*, April 27, 1987, 18.

Cooperative advertising allowance
A contractual arrangement between the manufacturer and the retailer in which the manufacturer agrees to pay part or all of the advertising expenses incurred by the retailer.

Display allowance
A direct payment of cash or goods to the retailer if the retailer agrees to set up the display as specified.

A **cooperative advertising allowance** is a contractual arrangement between the manufacturer and the retailer in which the manufacturer agrees to pay part or all of the advertising expenses incurred by the retailer.

A **display allowance** involves a direct payment of cash or goods to the retailer if the retailer agrees to set up the display as specified. Why would manufacturers pay retailers for display space? Such space is a scarce resource. One trade publication reported that "it's very expensive real estate, and retailers have learned to use that real estate wisely by getting manufacturers to pay for it."[12]

Trade deals have several advantages: They are flexible and can be changed from day to day, if necessary. They also can be combined with other promotional strategies to provide great impact. Ultimately, the willingness of retailers to carry and support a manufacturer's brands depends on the combination of the direct incentives offered to retailers and the promotions offered to consumers.

concept review

Trade Sales Promotion: Resellers

1. A trade sales promotion is directed at resellers who distribute products to ultimate consumers.
2. The most common trade sales promotion techniques include:
   - Dealer contests
   - Trade coupons
   - Dealer loaders
   - Trade deals

Trade Sales Promotion: Sales Force

Sales promotion targeted at the sales force is a crucial competitive weapon. It can help businesses introduce new products successfully, gain shelf space, and motivate resellers and sales personnel. Sales force promotions are intended to motivate salespeople to increase overall sales. Short-term goals may include securing new dealers or retailers, promoting sales of new or seasonal items, communicating special deals to retailers, and increasing order size.

In general these activities build enthusiasm. Often they are aimed as much at raising the morale of the sales force as at creating a sale. Why? Enthusiastic salespeople usually work harder at supporting the marketing effort.

Sales promotion activities directed at the sales force are classified into two categories: **supportive programs** that prepare salespeople to do their jobs and **motivational promotions** designed to encourage salespeople to work harder.

Supportive programs
Programs that prepare salespeople to do their jobs.

Motivational promotions
Promotions designed to encourage salespeople to work harder.

Supportive Programs

Supportive programs are used in training or are used to educate experienced salespeople and to equip them with materials for sales presentations. Examples of such materials include sales manuals, portfolios, models, slides, films, videos, and other visual aids.

One of the most common supportive programs is the **sales meeting**, an educational meeting that can bring together a local, regional, national, or international sales force. The meetings mix business and pleasure in varying proportions. Although social elements are important and can motivate people, training and educational elements tend to be more meaningful. In-house publications such as a newsletter are also useful in relaying information about new products, meetings, awards, schedules and deadlines, announcements, and sales ideas.

Sales meeting
An educational meeting that can bring together a local, regional, national, or international sales force.

Sales kits contain sales manuals with background information, details about other elements of the promotional effort, or detailed product specifications. Sales kits are critical promotional tools that educate and assist salespeople with product presentations. Sales information is often computerized so that sales representatives can access it any time by modem through a groupware software program shared by the salesperson and the organization. Computerized sales kits make it possible for the sales representative to custom-design presentations for customers.

Sales kits
Packages containing sales manuals with background information, details about other elements of the promotional effort, or detailed product specifications.

Motivational Programs

Contests dominate motivational programs. The incentive in a contest is generally a prize or award for those who demonstrate excellent sales performance.

Travel vacations, honorary clubs, and cash awards are frequently used to motivate the sales force. A "sales honours club" may reward teamwork, such as a president's club, which is used in a number of industries to reward sales teams and increase sales. Push money is an extra payment given to salespeople for meeting a specified sales goal. For example, a manufacturer of air conditioners might offer a $10 bonus for the sale of model EJ1, $20 for model EJ19, and $25 for model EX3 between April 1 and October 1. At the end of that period, salespeople send in evidence of total sales to the air conditioner manufacturer so they can receive a cheque for the appropriate amount. Although push money has a negative image because it hints of bribery, many businesses offer it as an incentive to the sales staff and to motivate outside salespeople and resellers.

concept review

Trade Sales Promotion: Sales Force

1. Sales force promotions are used to support and to motivate salespeople to increase overall sales.
2. Sales force promotions include:
   - Supportive programs that include sales kits and sales meetings
   - Motivational programs such as contests, honorary clubs, and push money

Consumer Sales Promotion

Consumer sales promotions are directed at the ultimate users of the product. Users can be consumers or businesses. The "Colour of Money" case at the end of this chapter, for example, illustrates how sales promotion is used in business-to-business marketing.

NCH Promotional Services
www.wattsgroup.com

Typically, these promotions focus on products used by individuals, especially products sold in the local supermarket and drugstore. Consumer sales promotions are intended to "presell" consumers so that when people visit a store they will look for a particular brand. A survey conducted by NCH Promotional Services among Canadian packaged-goods companies (i.e., food, household good, personal care products, and pet food manufactures) revealed that 77 percent of the manufacturers viewed coupons as their most important form of consumer sales promotion. Following in order of importance, were samples, contests, cash refunds, and premiums.[13] Table 10.5 identifies some common consumer sales promotions, their objectives, and their methods of distribution. The following section describes some of the key techniques used to encourage people to take action.

Price Deals

A consumer price deal saves customers money when they purchase a product. Price deals are commonly used to encourage trial of a new product, to persuade

Table 10.5 CONSUMER SALES PROMOTION TECHNIQUES

Technique	Objective	Method of Distribution
PRICE DEALS		
Price discounts	Stimulate incremental and trial purchases, increase purchases per transaction	Point of purchase, mass media, cents-off deal, bonus pack, banded pack
Coupons	Stimulate trial purchases, increase frequency of purchases, encourage multiple purchases, motivate resellers, encourage consumer trade-up	Sales force, direct mail, newspapers, magazines, FSIs, in-pack or on-pack
Refunds and rebates	Stimulate trial purchases, encourage multiple purchases	Sales force, direct mail, mass media, in-pack or on-pack
CONTESTS AND SWEEPSTAKES	Encourage multiple purchases, enhance brand image, create enthusiasm	Sales force, mass media, direct mail
PREMIUMS	Add value, encourage multiple purchases, stimulate trial purchases	Store premiums, in-pack or on-pack, proof of purchase, container premiums, self-liquidator, continuity-coupon plan, free-in-the-mail premium
SAMPLES	Stimulate trial purchases, encourage consumer trade-up	In-pack or on-pack, direct mail, magazines, point of purchase
CONTINUITY PROGRAMS	Maintain consumer loyalty	Sales force, mass media, direct mail

existing users to buy more or at a different time, or to convince new users to try an established product. They are effective only if price is an important factor in brand choice or if consumers are not brand loyal. For instance, soft drinks, laundry detergents, paper products, and diapers are types of products that use price promotions effectively. We explore three kinds of price deals: price discounts, coupons, and refunds and rebates.

PRICE DISCOUNTS

Cents-off deal
A reduction in the normal price charged for a goods or service.

Price-pack deal
A method of price discounting that provides the consumer with something extra through the package itself.

The two main types of consumer price discounts are cents-off deals and price-pack deals. A **cents-off deal** is a reduction in the normal price charged for a good or service (for example, "was $1000, now $500," or "50 percent off"). Cents-off deals can be announced at the point of sale or through mass or direct advertising. Point-of-sale announcements include the package itself and signs near the product or elsewhere in the store. The manufacturer, the wholesaler, or the retailer can initiate both types of cents-off deals.

Price-pack deals provide the consumer with something extra through the package itself. There are two types of pack deals: bonus packs and banded packs.

Bonus packs
Contain additional amounts of the product free when the standard size of the product is purchased at the regular price.

Banded pack
A pack that offers one or more units of a product sold at a reduced price compared with the regular single-unit price.

Coupons
Legal certificates offered by manufacturers and retailers that grant specified savings on selected products when presented for redemption at the point of purchase.

Bonus packs contain additional amounts of the product free when the standard size is purchased at the regular price. For example, Purina Dog Food may offer 25 percent more dog food in the bag. Often this technique is used to introduce a new large-size package of the product. A **banded pack** is a pack that offers one or more units of a product sold at a reduced price compared with the regular single-unit price. Sometimes the products are physically banded together. Bar soap, such as Dial, is often offered this way.

Coupons

Legal certificates offered by manufacturers and retailers that grant specified savings on selected products when presented for redemption at the point of purchase are called **coupons**. Manufacturer-sponsored coupons can be redeemed at any outlet distributing the product. Retailer-sponsored coupons can only be redeemed at the specified retail outlet. The primary advantage of the manufacturer-sponsored coupon is that it allows the advertiser to lower prices without relying on cooperation from the retailer.

The method of delivery is an important factor that influences the rate of coupon redemption (or usage). As the data in Table 10.6 indicates, coupon redemption rates in Canada are largely dependent upon the method of coupon delivery. Instantly redeemable coupons, in-store coupons, and in-pack self coupons have the highest average redemption rates among coupon offers.

Other factors such as the face value of the coupon and the frequency of consumer purchase also influence the rate of coupon redemption. Table 10.7 provides a comprehensive list of factors that influence the rate of coupon redemption.

The latest trends in retailing are online coupons and in-store coupons delivered from shelf dispensers or on the back of the sales receipt. The receipt

This coupon for Healthy Choice's Hearty Handfuls is a manufacturer's coupon that was distributed in a Healthy Choice product package.

Table 10.6 COUPON REDEMPTION RATE BY METHOD OF DISTRIBUTION

Media	Range	Median
IN & ON PACKAGE COUPONS		
In Pack-Self	2.8%-35.4%	12.7%
On Pack-Self	1.7%-34.7%	6.6%
On-Pack Cross	1.1%-12.5%	3.67%
On-Pack Cross	0.3%-7.8%	2.3%
Instantly Redeemable	3.8%-74.8%	29.7%
REGULAR DIRECT-TO-CONSUMER COUPONS		
Free Standing Inserts	0.7% -5.2%	2.5%
Co-op Direct Mail	0.6%-8.2%	2.5%
Selective Direct Mail	3.0%-54.8%	12.5%
IN-STORE COUPONS		
In-Store Handout	1.8%-49.8%	15.5%
In-Store at Shelf	3.1%-42.0%	15.3%
Retailer Booklets	0.1%-5.2%	0.4%

Source: NCH Promotional Services LTD. Used with permission.

coupons often link the consumer's purchases to coupons in related product categories. Online coupon services such as Money Mailer, a company that mails coupons to homes, offer coupon databases. The Money Mailer site, H.O.T! Coupons, contains a database of millions of coupons for local, regional, and national consumer products and services. Check it out to see if there are coupons available for your hometown.

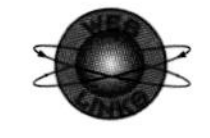

Money Mailer
www.hotcoupons.com

Marketers are finding ways to target coupons more carefully.[14] In fact, coupons are becoming the cornerstone of some of today's database marketing programs. Using some of the more sophisticated data-tracking programs, marketers can determine who in a given household bought which product when and at what store—and sometimes even which TV commercial prompted the purchase.

There are several disadvantages associated with coupons. Although more than 90 percent of consumer product marketers use coupons, the redemption rate is only 2.3 percent for those delivered through FSIs, and 4 to 6 percent for those delivered through direct mail. Depending on the product category, 60 to 90 percent of coupons are delivered through freestanding inserts, however, insert fees (the fees newspapers charge for inserting FSIs) are increasing dramatically, making coupon distribution very expensive. Another problem is misredemption (accidentally or intentionally misredeeming coupons) and, finally, fraud (counterfeit coupons).[15]

Refund
An offer by the marketer to return a certain amount of money to the consumer who purchases the product.

Rebate
Essentially, a refund.

REFUNDS AND REBATES

Simply stated, a **refund** is an offer by the marketer to return a certain amount of money to the consumer who purchases the product. A **rebate** means essentially the same thing as refund. Unlike price discounts, evidence suggests that consumers consider refunds and rebates a reward for purchase. This after-the-fact experience appears to build brand loyalty rather than diminish it.

Table 10.7 FACTORS INFLUENCING COUPON REDEMPTION RATES

Coupon redemption rates are influenced by many factors, including:

- The method of coupon distribution
- The frequency of product purchases by a typical user—this is effectively categorized as the size of the product category in terms of total dollar sales at retail.
- The coupon's value term as determined by the use or non-use of an expiry rate.
- The couponed product's market share.
- The extent of a brand's consumer franchise.
- The coupon's face value.
- The percentage discount offered by the coupon, in terms of face value as a percent of the product's retail price.
- The geographical area in which a coupon is distributed.
- Whether or not the coupon offers a discount on a single or multiple purchase.

Other factors such as coupon design and competitive activity tend to have less impact on redemption rates. Competitive couponing or refunding, however, may affect the redemption pattern of an offer by delaying its use, particularly if the competing offer has a much higher value.

Source: NCH Promotional Services LTD. Used with permission.

Refunds are attractive because they stimulate sales without the high cost and waste associated with coupons.

Most refunds encourage product purchase by creating a deadline. General information of the refund program may be delivered through broadcast media. Details are usually distributed through print media or direct mail. The refund may take the form of a cash rebate plus a low-value coupon for the same product or other company products, a high-value coupon alone, or a coupon good toward the brand purchased plus several other brands in the manufacturer's line.

The disadvantage of rebate and refund programs is that consumers may view them as a nuisance. In one study 85 percent of the survey respondents stated that they would rather use a coupon valued at $1 than send in for a refund worth $2. Furthermore, only 40 percent had taken the time to mail in a refund over the past year, compared with more than 70 percent who regularly use coupons.[16]

Contest
Promotion that requires consumers to compete for a prize or prizes on the basis on some sort of skill or ability.

Sweepstakes
A random drawing that only requires participants to enter their names in another drawing or chance selection.

Game
A type of sweepstakes that differs from a one-shot sweepstakes drawing because the time frame is much longer.

CONTESTS AND SWEEPSTAKES

The popularity of contests and sweepstakes grew dramatically during the 1980s and 1990s. These strategies create excitement by promising "something for nothing" and offering impressive prizes. Consumer **contests** are promotions that require consumers to compete for a prize or prizes on the basis of some sort of skill or ability; that is, participants must perform some task. A **sweepstakes** is a random drawing that only requires participants to submit their names for inclusion in a drawing or other chance selection. A **game** is a type of sweepstakes. It differs from a one-shot sweepstakes drawing in that the time frame is much longer. A continuity is established, requiring customers to return several times to acquire additional pieces (such as bingo-type games) or to improve their chances of winning.

The toy in the Cracker Jacks box is an example of a premium, a tangible reward for the person who buys the product.

A good contest or sweepstakes generates a high degree of consumer involvement that can revive lagging sales, provide merchandising excitement for dealers and salespeople, give vitality and a theme to advertising, and create interest in a low-interest product. If handled improperly, contests and sweepstakes can tarnish a company's image.

PREMIUMS

Premium
A tangible reward given to consumers for performing a particular act, usually purchasing a product or visiting the point of purchase.

A **premium** is a tangible reward given to consumers for performing a particular act, usually purchasing a product or visiting the point of purchase. The premium may be free. If not, the amount the consumer pays for it is well below market price. The toy in Cracker Jacks and the offer of a free atlas with the purchase of insurance are examples of premiums.

Direct premiums
A type of premium that provides an immediate incentive at the time of purchase.

Direct and mail premiums are the two general types of consumer premiums. **Direct premiums** provide the incentive immediately, at the time of purchase. The four categories of direct premiums include:

1. Store premiums: premiums given to customers at the retail site
2. In-packs: premiums inserted in the package at the factory
3. On-packs: premiums placed on the outside of the package at the factory
4. Container premiums: the package is the premium

Mail premiums
A type of premium that requires the customer to take some action before receiving the premium, such as sending in proof-of-purchase seals.

In contrast, **mail premiums** require the customer to take some action before receiving the premium, such as sending in proof-of-purchase seals. Bausch & Lomb generated trial and purchase of its contact lenses by giving away sunglasses as premium incentives. The company gave eye-care practitioners sunglasses certificates to distribute to consumers who purchased Bausch & Lomb contact lenses. Consumers then sent their certificates to Bausch & Lomb to redeem the free sunglasses.

Self-liquidator
A type of premium that requires consumers to mail in a payment before receiving the premium.

A **self-liquidator** is a type of premium that normally requires consumers to mail in a payment before receiving the premium. Star-Kist Foods, for example, offers a Morris-the-Cat T-shirt. The payment is usually sufficient to cover the cost of the item, handling, mailing, packaging, and taxes, if any. Generally, a self-liquidator costs the marketer very little. The food industry is the largest user of self-liquidating premiums, as are industries that sell detergents, cleansers, toiletries, and beverages.

Continuity-coupon plan
A type of mail premium that requires the customer to save coupons or special labels attached to the product that can be redeemed for merchandise.

The **continuity-coupon plan** is another type of mail premium. It requires the customer to save coupons or special labels attached to the product that can be

Canadian Tire's cash bonus coupons are an example of a continuity-coupon plan.

redeemed for merchandise. Cigarette and diaper manufacturers have used continuity-coupon plans.

Retailers can use a variation of this type of premium that requires redemption of a coupon for a cash discount on a subsequent purchase. For example, Canadian Tire's rewards program for shopping at Canadian Tire and for using cash, cheque, or debit card provides consumers with Canadian Tire 'Money' ™ that can be used as cash on a subsequent purchase.

The final type of mail premium is the **free-in-the-mail premium**. With this type of premium, the customer mails the advertiser a purchase request and proof of purchase. For example, Procter & Gamble offered a premium that was a discount on a down comforter with a proof of purchase of White Cloud toilet paper. An advantage of free-in-the-mail premiums is their ability to enhance an advertising campaign or a brand image by association with a desirable product or brand name.

Free-in-the-mail premium
A type of premium that requires the customer to mail the advertiser a purchase request and proof of purchase.

Sampling
Allowing the customer to experience the product or service free of charge or for a small fee.

Sampling

One of the keys to success for many marketers is getting the product into the hands of the consumer. Allowing the consumer to experience the product or service free of charge or for a small fee is called **sampling**. It is a very effective strategy for introducing a new or modified product or for dislodging an entrenched market leader. To be successful, the product sampled must be able to create a positive impact with minimal trial experience.

Samples can be distributed to consumers in several ways, such as through the mail or door to door. Advertisers can design ads with coupons for free samples, place samples in special packages, or distribute samples at special in-store displays. The Body Shop has taken its health and beauty products on the road with an 18-wheeler containing a miniature Body Shop that travels to university campuses, malls, and various socially responsible events. Salespeople on the truck give out coupons and catalogues and do makeovers and massages to demonstrate the products.[17]

In general retailers and manufacturers maintain that sampling can boost sales volume as much as five to ten times during a product demonstration and 10 to 15 percent thereafter. Sampling is generally most effective when reinforced at the same time with product coupons. Most consumers like sampling because they do not lose any money if they do not like the product.

Continuity Programs (Loyalty Programs)

The intent of a continuity program is to keep people using a brand by offering ongoing incentives that reward them for their loyalty. A continuity program such as an airline frequent-flyer program requires the consumer to continue purchasing the product or service to receive the benefit or reward. Typically, the higher the purchase level, the greater the benefits. Continuity programs are synonymous with the word "frequent." Frequent-flyer clubs sponsored by airlines are the model of a modern continuity program. They offer a variety of rewards, including seat upgrades, free tickets, and premiums based on the

CIBC's AeroCorporate™ VISA card from CIBC and Air Canada is a sample of a continuity program. This program offers card users to earn Aeroplan® miles that can be redeemed for free travel on Air Canada and its airline partners.

number of frequent-flyer miles accumulated. Continuity programs work in very competitive situations where the consumer has difficulty perceiving real differences between brands.

There are other techniques that are sometimes referred to as sales promotions such as event sponsorship and cause marketing. These are cross-over marketing communication methods that are also used as part of other programs, such as advertising or public relations. We will discuss them in more detail in Chapter 11.

Although price deals, contests and sweepstakes, premiums, sampling, and continuity programs can be effective alone, they can also be combined to create tremendous impact. For instance, Nestlé positioned three of its products—Raisinets, Goobers, and Crunch—as the "Home Video Candy" in a promotion where consumers could redeem a mail-in certificate with any VCR movie rental receipt along with proof of purchase and receive a $2 cash rebate. The certificate was available in freestanding inserts and at point-of-purchase displays, and the three candy products were packaged in a take-home pack.

concept review

Consumer Sales Promotion

1. Consumer sales promotions are directed at the ultimate users of the product.
2. The most common consumer sales promotion techniques include:
   - Price deals
   - Contests and sweepstakes
   - Premiums
   - Sampling
   - Continuity programs

A Closing Thought:

Working the Promotion Puzzle

Sales promotion is a diverse area of marketing communication. Trying to become an expert on all aspects of sales promotion may be unrealistic, and special skills in certain areas may be best learned on the job. In integrated marketing communication programs, sales promotion skills remain the most difficult for advertising specialists to master. Of course, this difficulty may be due partly to the historical differences in the creative philosophies between the two marketing communication areas. As long as advertisers feel that sales promotion denigrates the brand and steals dollars from them, cooperation and synergy are unlikely. Yet, sales promotion will continue to grow as a marketing communication alternative. Whether it will diminish the importance of advertising is still debatable, but certainly the variety of sales promotion options have changed the marketing communication landscape.

summary

1. Define sales promotion and discuss its purpose.

   Sales promotion is a marketing communication tool that uses a variety of incentive techniques for consumers, trade, and the sales force to generate a specific, measurable action or response. It is designed to offer an extra incentive to consumers or resellers, something that gives the product or service additional value, and stimulates immediate action.

2. Explain how sales promotion fits in the marketing communication mix and how it can be used in an IMC program.

   Sales promotion is used in the marketing communication mix to help implement push and pull strategies, to introduce new products, and to build brands. Integrated marketing communicators often combine sales promotion with other marketing communication tools to create a powerful synergy.

3. Outline how sales promotion strategies differ for trade and consumer target audiences.

   Sales promotion strategies may be directed at consumer audiences or trade audiences that include resellers and the sales force. Trade promotions designed to build support among resellers and the sales force help "push" the product. Consumer sales promotions directed at the ultimate users of the product are designed to "pull" the product through the channel of distribution.

4. Compare and contrast the techniques used for and the objectives of reseller, sales force, and consumer promotions.

   Promotions designed for trade and consumer audiences use different techniques to accomplish different objectives. Techniques used in trade promotions for resellers include point-of-purchase materials, dealer contests, trade shows, dealer loaders, and trade deals of various types. These techniques help garner support for a product and can build a relationship with the manufacturer or service provider. Sales force promotions are intended to increase the productivity of the sales staff through motivation (contests, prizes, and push money) and support for sales force efforts (training, sales meetings, sales manuals, visual aids, newsletters). Sales promotions directed at consumers include price deals (price discounts, coupons, and refunds and rebates), contests and sweepstakes, premiums (direct and self-liquidating), sampling, and continuity programs. The objectives of these promotions are to stimulate trial or repeat purchase, increase the number of purchases, enhance brand image and consumer loyalty, and add value to the product.

points to ponder

Review the Facts

1. What is sales promotion?
2. Define trade members.
3. List the main strengths and weaknesses of sales promotion techniques.
4. How do the objectives of trade and consumer sales promotions differ?
5. Describe the various consumer price deals and the role they play in promotion.

Master the Concepts

6. What are the broad goals of sales promotion for each of its target audiences, and how do these goals differ from those of advertising? How are they the same?
7. When should sales promotion and advertising be used in combination?
8. One agency executive was quoted as saying: "Advertising is on its way out. All consumers want is a deal. Sales promotion is the place to be." What do you think this executive meant? Do you agree or disagree?
9. Your promotional strategy professor is covering some sales promotion methods. Your professor explains that when selecting consumer sales promotions, planners must know the brand situation and objectives before choosing techniques, because some increase product use and others increase new consumer trial. Which methods do you think increase product use, and which increase new consumer trial? Explain.

10. Under what conditions should price deals be used?
11. What types of sales promotion are available to a small manufacturer that must develop a cooperative channel of distribution?
12. Explain the problems associated with slotting allowances. How can businesses avoid paying slotting fees?
13. Which type of sales incentive is best? Explain your answer.

Apply Your Knowledge

14. Allison Wilson is a brand manager for a new line of cosmetics being introduced by Sears called Circle of Beauty. She is about to present her planning strategy to division management. Wilson knows her company has been successful in using sales promotion plans, but she has strong misgivings about following the company trend. "This new line must develop a strong consumer brand identity—and promotion isn't the best way to do that," she thinks to herself. What is a weakness of sales promotion in "developing brand identity"? Should Wilson propose no promotion, or is there a reasonable compromise for her to consider?
15. Alltech Product's sales promotion manager, Mary Lincoln, is calculating the cost of a proposed consumer coupon for March. The media cost and production charges for the freestanding coupon insert are $125 000. The distribution will be four million coupons with an expected redemption of five percent. The coupon value is 50 cents, and Lincoln has estimated the handling and retailer compensation costs to be 8 cents per redeemed coupon. Based on these estimates, what will be the cost to Lincoln's budget?

suggested projects

1. (Oral and Written Communication) Review your local newspaper to identify a retailer who is engaging in cooperative advertising. Interview a store manager for that retailer and determine the specific arrangements that exist between the advertiser and the retailer. What is the attitude of the retailer toward this arrangement? Write a two-page report on the effectiveness of cooperative advertising for this retailer.
2. You have just been named product manager for Puffs toilet paper, a new line-extension product that will be introduced to the market within the next six months. What type of sales promotion strategy would work best for this product? Outline a sales promotion plan for the launch.
3. (Internet and Team Project) Form small groups of two to four students. Assume your group has been asked to create an online sales promotion strategy for the Puffs toilet paper product mentioned in Project 2. Each team member should visit two sites to analyse how effectively businesses use couponing, sweepstakes and contests, and other sales promotion techniques. Meet to discuss your findings and plan a basic online sales promotion strategy.

The Colour of Money

A.B. Dick, a manufacturer of duplicating machines, used an integrated marketing communication program to launch itself into the full-size printing press market. Its integrated marketing communication program combined every possible tool from sales promotion to specialties to product videos.

The problem was that the company was considered a leader in duplicating equipment, not as a printing-press manufacturer. To succeed it had to make its audience aware of its printing-press business by changing consumers' perceptions. Change in this market was an uphill battle. A.B. Dick made its move in late 1992 into the new market with its Century 3000 two-colour printing press. The company targeted three markets for the Century 3000: small printers moving into colour printing, in-plant printers who do printing jobs in-house for their companies, and large commercial printers who wanted a press for short-run colour printing. The Century's position was to handle jobs that were either too large for a small printer or too small for a big one.

Using an IMC agency that serves mid-size and large business-to-business marketers, the company launched a high-profile campaign. All the pieces shared a creative theme adapted from the Paul Newman/Tom Cruise movie, ***The Color of Money***. Why this theme? Tucker president, Bob Tucker, explained that the idea of colour ties in with printers who are tremendously concerned about the quality of colour reproduction. In addition, it carried the timeless business-to-business appeal of making money. The theme promised a product that could generate new revenue streams in return for a relatively modest investment.

In an unusual move the centrepiece of Tucker's integrated campaign was a six-minute video that illustrated the capabilities of the Century 3000. Although Paul Newman didn't star in the video, it did effectively associate the campaign with the movie. The new printing press was introduced to trade reporters at a special Colour of Money press event and was also introduced to trade audiences at subsequent in-office sales presentations.

Tucker kicked off a two-year trade ad campaign with a two-page spread in industry publications. The ads carried a direct-response form offering the free video. After the product was launched, the print campaign moved to testimonials with printers describing new uses they found for the press. These word-of-mouth success stories were relayed to the A.B. Dick marketing manager by field salespeople.

Direct mail with promotional offers was used to highlight the video. Printers received a ***Colour of Money*** poster the first week of the direct-mail campaign. The next week they got an oversized $100 bill accompanied with copy about making "big bucks." The third week they received the video along with a package of microwave popcorn and a business reply card that read, "The movie was great, but I want to see the Century 3000 in action." Those who replied received a live demonstration from a salesperson. The field salespeople knew when the direct-mail campaign began, and were given copies of each mail piece to take on sales calls. A.B. Dick mailed 12 000 copies of the video during the three-year campaign. At the request of the sales staff, the marketing department also customized direct-mail pieces for targeted individual prospects. For example, one salesperson used a custom mailing to the schools in his territory and another to churches.

A ***Colour of Money*** newsletter was distributed to salespeople and customers to promote success stories and new uses of the press. In keeping with the movie-inspired theme, A.B. Dick sent out sunglasses to the "star" printers featured in the newsletter and the ads.

The payoff from the continuing ***Colour of Money*** campaign is the development of a sophisticated database of prospect information. The leads come from the reply card on the video and from incoming faxes responding to direct-mail and advertising pieces. These leads were then sent to the telemarketing department where telemarketers called the prospects, asked more about their needs, and identified the key decision makers. This information was entered into the database and then given to the field sales representatives. The loop was closed when the salespeople responded on the status of the leads and fed more specific customer information into the database that could be used to polish the marketing efforts.

What this integrated program all added up to was the colour of new money for A.B. Dick's business.

Case Questions

1. Develop a proposal for additional trade promotions that could tie in with the ***Colour of Money*** theme.
2. What would you recommend as a sales force promotion that would support this ***Colour of Money*** theme?
3. This is a business-to-business case, but it still uses customer sales promotion as part of its integrated marketing communication strategy. What are the customer sales promotions used in this case, and what others would you recommend for next year's campaign?
4. How many different areas of marketing communication are included in this campaign? Which ones are missing?

Sources: "Printing Money," ***Sales & Marketing Management*** (February 1995): 64–09; Bill Robinson and Alan Maites, "Promotion vs. Direct: Who Should Win?" ***Potentials in Marketing*** (May 1995): 70–02.

11 Public Relations

chapter objectives

After completing your work on this chapter, you should be able to

- Define public relations and explain its purpose.
- Identify the strengths and weaknesses of public relations.
- Distinguish between internal and external stakeholders.
- Explain seven types of public relations programs.
- Outline the steps in the public relations research and planning process.
- Discuss the role of public relations in an integrated marketing communication program.
- Describe the tools used in public relations programs.

Gillette Launches Sensor with an Explosion of Publicity

Gillette is an excellent example of a marketer that understands the effectiveness of integrated marketing communication. Gillette's product launches also illustrate the important role public relations plays in an IMC program. The Porter/Novelli public relations agency leads most Gillette product launch campaigns and works closely with other agencies such as BBDO advertising to establish the market. The coordination between marketing communication agencies coupled with an integrated approach have helped secure Gillette's position as market leader in the shaving industry.

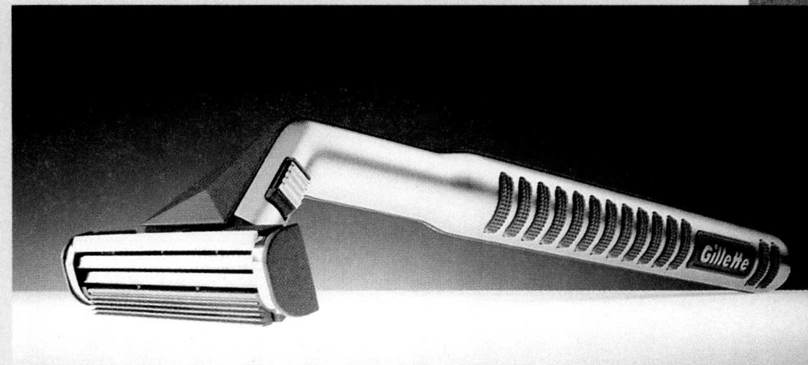

After Gillette succeeded in repositioning its brand under the "Best A Man Can Get" campaign, it continued to have success throughout the 1990s, introducing several new products—the Sensor, the Sensor Prestige Series in sterling and platinum, the Sensor for Women, the new SensorExcel, and Cool Wave and Wild Rain men's toiletries. All these products were launched first with public relations campaigns, supported by advertising, and, followed in some cases, by sales promotion and direct-marketing campaigns.

Let's look inside the Sensor launch, which was the pioneering effort, to see how public relations was used to drive a successful integrated international program. After months of joint planning meetings and idea sessions, Sensor was introduced on Super Bowl Sunday in January 1990 with the launch of its advertising campaign. Before that, however, massive publicity generated announcements and special stories on such major programs as *CBS News*, the NBC *Today* show, and the *Tonight Show*, and hundreds of stories in newspapers and magazines around the world and in Europe. The launch was handled simultaneously in 19 countries. The Sensor shaving system had been more than 10 years in development and cost more than $280 million to create. Because of Gillette's takeover battles in late 1980, the media covered both the corporate and the new product stories heavily, keeping Gillette and its brands in the public eye.

According to an analyst for Prudential-Bache, the Sensor was "the single most successful consumer non-durable product introduction in the history of the planet." They may sound like hyperbole, but Sensor claimed six percent of the market in a little more than six months, selling some 17 million razors in that period, which was twice what the company had forecasted. Gillette stock soared almost 30 percent in the same six months. Surprisingly, the marketing communication had to be cut back because Gillette had trouble meeting demand.

The reason the PR campaign worked so well, according to Bill Novelli, president of Porter/Novelli, was because of the number of different story angles. "The financial media was interested in the corporate story; the marketing press was interested in the marketing story because of the size of the budget and the fact that it was an integrated international launch; the technology writers were interested in the technology because Gillette had taken out 22 patents to make the Sensor work; and the consumer media was interested in the consumer story."

Gillette worked with Porter/Novelli, BBDO, and other Omnicom agencies that specialized in direct mail, sales promotion, packaging, and sales meetings. It also worked with 17 of these agencies' international affiliates. The Gillette marketing manager concluded that "PR was a key part of our strategy," but, he says, "we were not really prepared for the level of success it achieved."

Sources: Pablo Galarza, "Nicked and Cut," *Financial World*, April 8, 1996, 39; "To Launch in the United States, European Success Fuels U.S. Introduction," Business Wire, October 4, 1994; "The Best a Plan Can Get," *The Economist*, August 15, 1992, 59û61; Gary Levin, "Direct Mail Program Helps Gillette Drive Growth of Sensor Razor," *Advertising Age*, October 21, 1991, 24; "After a Close Shave, Cutting Edge Technology," *Inside PR*, September, 1990, 2; "Gillette Mocks Critics with Sensor Sales," *USA Today*, 12 August 1990, 1B; "Gillette Sensor," campaign handout from Porter/Novelli.

Chapter Overview

As the chapter opener shows, public relations (PR) is a vital element in marketing communication. We begin by exploring what public relations is and the way it analyses its "publics." Then we examine types of public relations programs, how managers plan an effective public relations program, and PR's role in a comprehensive marketing communication program. Finally, we discuss the many tools of public relations, which include three specific types of sponsorships—event, sports, and cause marketing.

What Is Public Relations?

Publics
All audiences that a marketing communicator targets to receive messages about the company or who are thought to influence opinions about the company.

The concepts of "public" and "relations" are both important to public relations. **Publics** are all the audiences that the marketing communicator targets to receive messages about the company or who are perceived as influencing opinions about the company. The term *relations* signals that these publics are involved in a relationship with the company. That relationship should be positive to ensure an effective business operation.

Most companies are unwilling to leave their corporate image and reputation to chance. Instead, they try to create goodwill and control their image through public relations activities. As Walter W. Seifert, a public relations expert, noted many years ago, "The public relations expert is as necessary as any other firefighter. But long before the fire begins, he [or she] is needed to build a backlog of goodwill that minimizes misadventures."[1]

The growth of public relations during the last seven decades has been tremendous. PR emerged as a distinct vocation in North America by the early 1920s. Since then, due in part to the efforts of Canadian pioneers of PR like

Herbert Lash, Charles Vining and Rielle Thompson, PR has blossomed as a growing and evolving occupation.[2]

Canadian Public Relations Society
www.cprs.ca

Many of today's PR practitioners seek to earn the APR (Accredited in Public Relations) designation that demonstrates a measure of experience and competence in the professional practice of public relations. The Canadian Public Relations Society (CPRS) and Public Relations Society of America (PRSA) have a reciprocal agreement recognizing each other's APR designation. To earn the APR designation candidates must satisfactorily complete a three-part accreditation examination and subscribe to a Code of Professional Standards. For more information on the CPRS, its Code of Professional Standards, and the APR designation, check out CPRS's Web site at www.cprs.ca.[3]

In Canada the public relations occupation will continue to grow because of PR's power as a communications tool. This communications tool places a strong emphasis on public opinion, relationships, and corporate credibility—and it is cost-effective. The critical issue is no longer whether to do public relations, but how to do it well.

The Role of Public Relations

Public relations tells an organization's story to publics to foster goodwill and understanding. Public relations practitioners help shape the company's practices by counselling top management on public opinion and issues, and on the positive and negative implications of certain behaviours. They also monitor the concerns and expectations of the organization's various publics and explain them to senior management. In summary, **public relations** is the use and communication of information through a variety of media to influence public opinion.

Public relations
The use and communication of information through the media to influence public opinion.

Another function of public relations is to plan how to handle communication about crises before they occur or how to handle unpredictable crises in a quick and careful way. For example Odwalla faced serious public relations challenges in 1996 when the *E. coli* bacteria was traced to its apple juice products. It had no plan for dealing with the huge volume of inquiries from customers, retailers, and the media, but quickly established a Web site and hotline to respond to questions. It also held informational press conferences and responded carefully and speedily to regulators and to victims and their families.

Strengths of Public Relations

Public relations has a number of strengths. First, public relations targets and manages relationships with important stakeholders. Second, public relations can reach difficult-to-reach audiences, such as opinion leaders and upscale consumers. Many of these people devote time to reading publications and watching or listening to news programs, but they are uninterested in advertising, are highly likely to dispose of direct mail, and have assistants who screen out sales calls. Publicity presented through the news media can more effectively reach this group.

Third, public relations professionals, ever-sensitive to public opinion, can advise clients and companies on the implications of trends and corporate activities. Fourth, public relations specialists can present the company as a good citizen through careful relationship management and monitoring of an organization's reputation and corporate image. Fifth, they can plan how to handle crises, thereby minimizing negative effects on the organization's reputation. Sixth, public relations offers a business more message flexibility compared with advertising and sales promotion because the laws governing news releases are less strict than for those regulating advertising of all forms.

Seventh, PR adds credibility and believability because target audiences usually consider news stories to be more objective than other marketing communications that are developed, presented, and paid for by a sponsor. Eighth, public relations breaks through clutter more effectively than other marketing communication areas because people are more willing to believe a news message than a commercial message. Finally, public relations is relatively cost-effective because news coverage, if warranted, is free.

Weaknesses of Public Relations

Public relations also has three main weaknesses. First is the lack of control over how stories are covered. Business information released to the media may not be used by the press as the company intended, especially because the press has access to other information sources. Second is the inability to control which stories receive coverage. Editors and producers act as "gatekeepers," which means they decide what gets into the newspaper, magazine, or news program. If editors or producers feel that a story released by a company doesn't have enough news value, they don't have to use it. For instance, on a day during which many newsworthy events happen, the business story may not get covered.

Another weakness of public relations is that it is hard to evaluate its effectiveness. Public relations is monitored in terms of the extent of the media coverage that a story generates, but that doesn't really measure its impact on public opinion or other stakeholder relationships. In short, the problem is measuring its effect on opinions, as well as on the bottom line. Table 11.1 summarizes public relations' strengths and weaknesses.

Table 11.1 Strengths and Weaknesses of Public Relations

Strengths	Weaknesses
Reaches stakeholders other than consumers—employees, community leaders, legislators and regulators, financial community, and special-interest groups	Lack of control over how the story gets covered
Reaches hard-to-reach targets, such as upscale opinion leaders	Subject to others' approval for news story to run
Can advise company/client on image issues Establishes corporate-citizen role	Bottom-line impact is difficult to measure
Proactive—can plan for crises	
More message flexibility due to fewer legal restrictions	
Adds credibility/believability	
Can break through "ad clutter"	
Low costs	

concept review

The Role of Public Relations

1. Public relations is used to create and maintain goodwill and control a corporate or brand image.
2. Public relations is the use of information and the communication of that information through a variety of media to influence public opinion.
3. Public relations has many strengths, including its wide reach, credibility, message flexibility, and relatively low costs. Its weaknesses are the lack of control over how and which stories are covered and the difficulty in measuring effectiveness.

Understanding PR's Publics

Internal publics
People with whom an organization normally communicates in the ordinary routine of work, such as employees, investors, suppliers, dealers, and regular customers.

External publics
People with whom an organization communicates but does not have regular or close ties, such as community neighbours, government officials, regulators, special-interest groups, media, and financial communities.

A public exists whenever a group of people, drawn together by specific interests, has opinions about those interest areas or issues. Individuals are frequently members of several publics, which may result in overlapping roles and conflicts of interest.

Public relations must be sensitive to two types of publics: internal and external. **Internal publics** are the people with whom an organization normally communicates in the ordinary routine of work, such as employees, investors, suppliers, dealers, and regular customers. **External publics** are the people with whom an organization communicates but does not have regular or close ties, such as the local community neighbours, government officials, regulators, special-interest groups, media, and the financial community. Table 11.2 lists the internal and external publics. All these groups are referred to collectively as stakeholders because in some way they have a stake in what the company does.

Table 11.2 The Publics of Public Relations

Internal Publics (Stakeholders)

Employees
Shareholders
MPR Publics: Suppliers, distributors, brokers, wholesalers, retailers, dealers
Regular or loyal customers

External Publics (Stakeholders)

The media
Local community neighbours
Municipal, provincial, and federal government bodies and regulators
The financial community
Special-interest groups
Prospective customers, employees, and shareholders

Internal Publics

The most important internal audience is employees. As Figure 11.1 shows, companies rely on a combination of downward, upward, and horizontal communication to foster employee relations. Downward communication from management to employees keeps people informed about programs and policies. It is handled through employee newspapers and magazines, video news broadcasts, bulletin boards, posters, films, reading racks, letters, and ceremonies. Upward communication from employees to management is usually much less developed, relying on informal feedback, suggestion boxes, surveys, group meetings, and open-door policies. Horizontal communication across department lines is usually structured through teamwork projects, networking programs, or team meetings.

External Publics

Publicity
A tool of public relations that is used to provide the media with information disseminated as news stories or mentions in news stories.

In external relations the first concern is usually with the press because it can have tremendous influence over public opinion. **Publicity** is a tool of public relations that is used to provide the media with information. In publicity, information is disseminated through the media as news stories or mentions in stories. Some people use the term "publicity" as a synonym for public relations. However, the terms are not interchangeable. As we see later in this chapter, public relations includes many more activities than publicity.

Consumers are a large external public. They are reached directly through advertising and sales and indirectly through media publicity. Another important external public is the government. Frequently, governmental interests overlap with consumers, particularly consumer activist groups. Special programs may be necessary to develop positive relationships with activist groups if the company is working in sensitive areas that affect public health, safety, or the environment.

The financial community—investors, stockbrokers, and the financial press—is another important audience for publicly held companies. Financial relations experts must have a basic understanding of business law, economics,

Figure 11.1 Downward, Upward, and Horizontal Employee Relations Communications

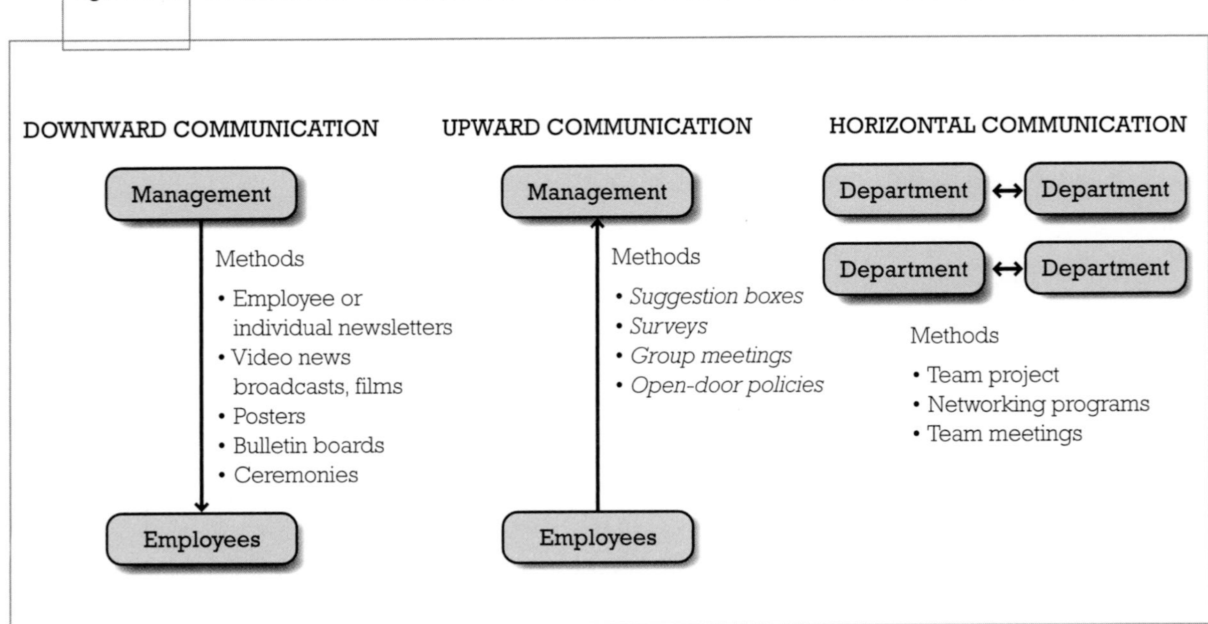

corporate finance, and investment practices. They must understand how corporate and external activities affect stock prices and changes in the company's bond rating. These highly skilled specialists develop the company's annual report and handle media relations with the financial press.

There can be interaction and overlap between internal and external publics. The trade, for example, is an internal public in that suppliers, vendors, and resellers usually work in partnership with a business. However, trade associations and other people in the industry are an external audience because they are not directly involved with the company's business.

The Importance of Stakeholders

IMC relies heavily on the idea of targeting stakeholder publics as part of the marketing communication strategy. This concept of stakeholders radically expands the traditional notion of the customer as the target audience in a marketing communication program.

The task of targeting stakeholders successfully is not easy because many consumers do not believe businesses treat stakeholders well. To illustrate, a Pew Foundation survey found that the public perceives big business to have concern primarily for investor and senior management stakeholders, though it should have more concern for other stakeholders.[4] The survey results show that 46 percent of the respondents believe businesses put investors' interests first; 34 percent believe big business puts executives' interests first; and only 4 percent believe big companies put the interests of their employees first. However, when asked whose interests should come first, 31 percent of the respondents answered customers and 30 percent answered employees. These findings identify a serious gap in public perception about what does happen and what should happen with stakeholder interests.

In a stakeholder-focused program, all publics associated with corporate communication are important. These publics include financial industry publics, such as analysts, stockbrokers, and the financial media; employees; customers; suppliers and vendors; resellers, such as brokers, dealers, wholesalers, and retailers; the local community, including local officials and neighbours; special-interest groups; and government regulators at the federal, provincial, and local level.

Why are these stakeholders important? Consider these possibilities. If employees are not part of the team, they can sabotage production, contribute to quality control problems, or conduct a negative word-of-mouth campaign against the firm. If special-interest groups are not listened to and their concerns addressed, they can take legal action that stops production or expansion. If the media are not treated as partners, then the first time the company has a product crisis the media will be more willing to look for irresponsible behaviour rather than to explain the company's perspective.

These possibilities become more likely when members of the stakeholder groups overlap. An employee may be an investor, so what a company says to its investors had better be consistent with the messages it sends to its employees. For instance, the financial relations department can't tell investors that it's been a great year while human resources tells employees that costs are so high that staff must be cut. An employee-investor who hears both messages will not only be confused but also distrustful. Integrated marketing communication minimizes contradictory messages, which helps organizations to develop more positive contacts with all stakeholders.

concept review

Understanding PR's Publics

1. Internal publics have communication with the organization in the ordinary routine of work. These publics include employees, investors, suppliers, dealers, and resellers.
2. External publics do not have close ties with the organization, but their interests overlap occasionally. Examples include the press, consumers, activist groups, government, the financial community, and trade associations.
3. Stakeholders are all those who have a stake in the activities of a company and who can affect its business. They are important because they can influence the quality of the product and perceptions about the business or product.

Types of Public Relations

Public relations can perform many functions. In this section we explore seven types of public relations: media relations, corporate public relations, crisis management, employee relations, financial relations, public affairs and community relations, and marketing public relations.

An annual survey of PR agency clients by the Thomas Harris company gives insight into what clients value in a public relations agency.[5] Ninety-seven percent of the client-respondents feel media relations is the most important PR capability, which we turn to first.

Media Relations

Media relations
The public relations function primarily responsible for publicity.

The public relations function that is primarily responsible for publicity is **media relations**. Media relations specialists develop personal relationships with the media covering their industry or company. They provide information in the form of story ideas, press releases and other publicity materials, serve as a source or find an expert when reporters need to talk to someone knowledgeable, and train other corporate executives in how to be interviewed and how to handle questions from the media.

The relationship between the news media and the PR professional can be both cooperative and adversarial. The reporter is motivated by the public's right to know, and that sometimes challenges the PR person's loyalty to the client or the organization's best interests. Successful public relations is built on reputation; once this reputation is lost, the PR person cannot function with any effectiveness. Thus the road to media respect is honesty, accuracy, and professionalism. The issue of what is expected of media relations professionals is discussed in this chapter's You Decide feature.

Corporate Public Relations

Corporate public relations
High-level counselling with senior management about the company's overall reputation, its image in the eyes of various stakeholders, and its response to issues that may affect the success of the company.

Corporate public relations is the term for high-level counselling with senior management about the company's overall reputation, its image in the eyes of its various stakeholders, and its response to issues that may affect the success of the company. The corporate public relations practice of planning a company's

Canadian Media Trends: What's Expected of Media Relations Professionals?

After experiencing significant budget cuts and waves of downsizing, the Canadian media industry is alive and well. In fact, it's growing—hiring new staff, adopting new technologies, and even enjoying a renewed sense of pride. These were some of the findings revealed in Angus Reid Group's *1998 Canadian Media Review: Alerts Bulletin.*

Angus Reid surveyed 106 print and broadcast journalists to determine how the industry is changing and what they (the journalists) expect from media relations professionals. It seems the audience is the most important consideration in producing news. More than half the journalist surveyed said a story's newsworthiness is based on the things that affect their readers or viewers. Economy and business is the leading "hot" topic that media organizations expect to track in the near future, followed by politics and government, and health care and medical issues.

For media relations professionals attempting to get press releases noticed, the survey results indicate that managing editors are the ones to chase. Twenty-one percent of respondents said managing editors have the most influence as to which stories are covered, while a mere three percent listed reporters. Also of note, the survey findings indicate that media relations professionals should ensure that information is honest and on time; more than 40 percent of journalists indicated that media-relations professionals are not honest or forthcoming with information, while almost 20 percent believe they are not timely enough.

You Decide

1. What factors might account for the reported belief of 40 percent of the surveyed journalists that media-relations professionals are not honest or forthcoming with information?
2. If you were a marketing communication director, how would you make sure your press releases are honest and on time?

Source: "Trends in Media," ***Marketing*** (June 21, 1999), 34.

Issue management
The corporate public relations practice of planning a company's response to important issues.

Corporate advertising
Advertising used by the company, and managed by corporate public relations, to create positive attitudes and goodwill toward the company.

Advocacy advertising
A type of corporate advertising that expresses the viewpoint of the company on selective issues.

Crisis management
Public relations staff anticipates the possibility of disaster and develops a plan to manage communications during the crisis.

response to important issues is called **issue management**. Corporate public relations practitioners help shape their organizations: They determine the concerns and expectations of the organization's publics and explain these concerns to management.

Corporate public relations manages **corporate advertising**, which is advertising used by the company to create positive attitudes and goodwill toward the company. Although a form of advertising, the corporate public relations department may handle it. Why? Such advertising does not try to sell a particular brand but aims instead to enhance the image of the sponsoring organization. The ad from Kellogg Canada (on the next page) is an example of corporate advertising. The ad communicates Kellogg's involvement with the Centre for Research in Women's Health.

Advocacy advertising is a type of corporate advertising that expresses the viewpoint of the company on some issue. Banks and cigarette companies, for instance, will sometimes run ads that read like editorials and explain their views on issues that impact their industries.

Crisis Management

Crisis management involves planning how to manage communications during crises or disasters—oil spills, plane crashes, management improprieties,

This ad for Kellogg Canada demonstrates that the company is actively engaged in a joint mission with The Centre for Research in Women's Health. Do you think this ad enhances Kellogg's corporate image?

Kellogg Canada
www.kelloggs.com

carcinogens in the product, and challenges to other company operations. Sometimes internal corporate public relations specialists prepare the crisis plan, but some businesses, especially large ones, will hire an outside firm that specializes in developing crisis management plans and training staff to prepare for a crisis.[6]

In almost every corporation's life there will be some event that is perceived negatively by the public. In crisis management a public relations staff anticipates the possibility of disaster and establishes a plan for communicating the bad news to various stakeholder groups. That staff designates spokespeople to describe the damage accurately and to answer questions from victims, their families, the media, lawyers, and government officials. The crisis management team assigns someone to make arrangements for space where reporters can work, transportation, phones and computers, and perhaps even food when necessary. Crisis management public relations is such an integral part of doing business that some insurance policies cover the costs of hiring a crisis management PR firm as part of their corporate liability policy.[7]

As one crisis management expert notes, management people don't judge good guys based on whether they've made mistakes but how they've fixed them. Johnson & Johnson took immediate steps to recall Tylenol after contaminated bottles were found. On the other hand, Intel tried to avoid the cost of recalling its flawed Pentium chip and denied the problem as the company got flamed on the Internet by worried customers.

Exxon
www.exxon.com

One of the most dramatic crises faced by a business was the disaster created by the wreck of the Exxon oil tanker *Valdez*. Exxon may never be forgiven for the damage it did to the environment and wildlife off the coast of Alaska. To make matters worse, Exxon CEO Lawrence Rawl was widely criticized for the way he and his staff handled the crisis. At first, Exxon denied the extent of the catastrophe and responsibility for the cleanup. Later admitting errors in judgment, Exxon provided a great deal of misinformation about the costs of the cleanup. The public response was immediate and dramatic. Over 40 000 Exxon credit cards were cut up by consumers and mailed back to Exxon headquarters.

With careful preparation, a company can weather a crisis with its reputation intact. A crisis plan, however, must anticipate the kinds of crises that the company might face and must detail people's duties in such a situation. Some companies practise dealing with disasters by creating disaster scenarios and acting out their responses as outlined in the crisis plan.

Employee Relations

Employee relations
A company's internal communication to its employees and programs aimed at employee motivation.

Employees are key to the success of any business. **Employee relations**, a company's internal communication to its employees, creates programs designed to motivate employees to do their best work. Such programs may be run by human resources or public relations specialists. Employee relations staff are involved in the development of newsletters, bulletin boards, flyers, and video programs. Table 11.3 offers six keys to a successful employee relations program: security, respect, participation, consideration, recognition, and opportunity. If employee relations are effective, companies are much more likely to have high employee morale, motivation, and productivity. All these factors can help improve the company's bottom line because employees also help produce positive relationships with customers and other stakeholders.

Financial Relations

Financial relations
A public relations field in which specialists who understand finance work with the financial community and comply with government financial regulations for public companies.

Financial relations is a public relations field in which specialists who understand finance work with the financial community and comply with government financial regulations for public companies. Financial relations specialists manage communication with stockbrokers and investors and the financial press. They also deal with a wide variety of financial information, such as company acquisitions, changes in company policies and how those changes may affect stock prices, and changes in the company's bond rating and stock prices. A primary responsibility of the financial relations staff is the production of the company's annual report, a document that must follow strict governmental regulations and present the image and position of the company to its investors.

Table 11.3 KEYS TO AN EFFECTIVE EMPLOYEE RELATIONS PROGRAM

1. Security: How secure is the company and my job within it?
2. Respect: Am I recognized as a person who does something worth doing?
3. Participation: How much do I have to say about the processes of which I am a part?
4. Consideration: Is there an opportunity for me to express my ideas?
5. Recognition: What rewards are given for good and faithful service?
6. Opportunity: Is there a chance to advance?

PUBLIC AFFAIRS AND COMMUNITY RELATIONS

Specialists in **public affairs**, public relations programs that focus on government relations, work closely with federal, provincial, and local government agencies. **Lobbying**, activities aimed at influencing policy decisions of government officials, is a type of public affairs activity. **Community relations** involves managing relations with stakeholders in the local community. Community relations officers arrange community events and sponsorships and handle community issues such as the environmental implications of a company's operations.

Public affairs
Public relations programs that focus on government relations by working closely with federal, regional, provincial, and local government agencies.

Lobbying
A type of public affairs activity aimed at influencing policy decisions by government officials.

Community relations
The management of relations with stakeholders from the local community.

Marketing public relations (MPR)
The public relations field that seeks positive publicity of products.

MARKETING PUBLIC RELATIONS

The public relations field that seeks positive publicity for products is **marketing public relations** (MPR). MPR is particularly important in the launch of a new product, a point illustrated in the Gillette opening story, where the concept of "newness" makes the product newsworthy and thus offers a natural platform for publicity. For instance, a positive review in the newspaper of a new movie, restaurant, or book is an example of successful MPR. But more than that, MPR specialists work closely with marketing people on the design of the product and its strategic positioning in the marketplace. In addition, MPR specialists know how to handle the special events used for major announcements and product launches. They may work closely with an advertising team, as Porter/Novelli worked with BBDO on the Gillette new product launches, and other marketing communication specialists such as those in direct marketing, sales promotion, and event marketing.

Porter/Novelli worked with Gillette to sponsor this Gillette Sensor for Women special event for media specialists.

concept review

Types of Public Relations

The main types of public relations include the following:

1. Media relations
2. Corporate public relations
3. Crisis management
4. Employee relations
5. Financial relations
6. Public affairs and community relations
7. Marketing public relations

Managing Public Relations

Like any business endeavour, successful public relations requires a plan. Like all other areas of marketing communication, a plan requires research. Therefore, before discussing the development of a public relations plan, let's examine the goals and techniques of PR research.

Public Relations Research

Before an organization can communicate an image to others, it should correctly identify that image. Research is used to diagnose the organization's image. The general objectives of PR research include probing basic attitudes, measuring actual opinions, identifying opinion leaders, describing the characteristics of various stakeholder groups, testing themes and media, and identifying potentially troublesome issues before they develop. The role of PR managers is to intelligently assess such findings, puzzle out the contradictions, and identify the relevance for their organization.

Planning Public Relations

Public relations plans are developed like other business and marketing plans. The plan development consists of the following six steps: (1) an assessment of the current situation, (2) a statement of objectives, (3) selection of target audiences, (4) selection of methods of implementation, (5) a determination of costs, and (6) an evaluation of results.

Assessing the Situation

Research helps organizations assess current situations. A key problem often uncovered in research is a confused or an unfocused corporate image. It takes constant vigilance to maintain a positive image and reputation. As an example, Procter & Gamble made an immediate and expensive public relations response to quell negative word-of-mouth surrounding the rumours that the origin of its logo was from a satanic cult.

Objectives and Targeting

Once the current situation has been assessed, PR professionals can develop program objectives that are in concert with the marketing communication program.

Christina Rodmell

Senior Consultant, Environics Communications, Inc.

http:www.environics.net

As a Senior Consultant in the high-technology practice at Environics Communications, Christina Rodmell is responsible for the strategic communications management of tier-one Internet, hardware/software and IT education companies.

Managing five accounts and over $200 000 in annual billings, Christina is never too far from her PC or a telephone.

Environics Communications is a leading North American communications agency that knows what it takes to make news in today's information overloaded society and to strengthen brand equity.

Christina's expertise is in media relations in the high-tech industry and includes a combination of industry experience, strategic insight and creativity—as well as an aggressive proactive approach to building a company's profile with journalists, customers, investors and other key audiences in North America.

Christina works with a team that is rich in experience and committed to results. Everyone hits the ground running—supporting Environics' technology clients' business goals with creative, high-impact public relations activities.

Academic Background

Christina received a B.A. in English from the University of Western Ontario. As part of her final year, she spent two months at Oxford University in Oxford, England studying Shakespeare and the history of Oxford. Following graduation Christina travelled to Europe to broaden her knowledge and to enhance her personal growth.

She then spent an intensive nine months at Toronto's Humber College in the post-graduate Public Relations program to gain practical skills for the business world. Graduating with an honours degree she entered the high-tech industry in 1992. With a passion for public relations and with the determination to succeed in the male-dominated technology industry, Christina worked at three communications agencies and achieved senior consultant status within four years.

Track Record

To date, Christina's achievements include receiving an International Association of Business Communicators' Marketing Award for communications efforts achieved with a leading-edge Internet company; establishing herself as a co-founder of Wired Woman Toronto chapter, a national nonprofit Canadian organization dedicated to creating a comfortable environment for women to learn more about the IT industry; seeking and securing a roster of new high-technology clients; and implementing unique media and internal initiatives that set Environics apart from other communications agencies.

Advice

Christina believes that passion for what one does in both his or her personal and professional life is key to achieving one's dreams. Without a drive to succeed or drive to be different, personal limitations can subconsciously set in that can easily become barriers.

Empowering oneself in a career involves taking risks, continuous learning, and establishing relationships with people you admire and respect. Business skills can be taught and business relationships can be fostered, but business and personal tenacity evolves from experience and a passion to succeed.

For the most part, PR attempts to change some aspect of public opinion. But public opinion is elusive, difficult to measure, and in constant flux. Because the impact of public relations is often difficult to gauge and may take a long time to appear, establishing meaningful objectives is especially difficult. Most PR objectives relate to attitudes, opinions, information, and feelings. Some, however, relate to behaviour. Because researchers can measure how many people attended a company-sponsored event due to event publicity, PR specialists might set an objective of 5000 attendees at a special event.

Gillette's PR objectives for the Sensor launch were fairly straightforward: to communicate that the Sensor razor was a breakthrough new product, to create anticipation and widespread awareness, to generate trial when the product hit the market, to maximize conversion to the new shaving system, to reinforce the Sensor shaving experience, and to generate trade support.

The potential audiences for a public relations effort should be researched just as carefully as the target audiences for an advertising campaign. The more PR practitioners know about each audience, the better the message design will be. Researchers should be able to answer several questions. Who are the people, institutions, or organizations that need to be reached by the PR effort? Where are they located, and what is the most effective and efficient way to make contact? What do they believe and feel about the company, and what does the organization need to say to them?

Gillette relied heavily on consumer attitude research during planning for the Sensor launch. Based on research that showed Gillette's user imagery was almost identical in the United States, Canada, and seven European countries, Gillette decided to treat these countries as one market. It planned to deliver the same message in the same way to virtually every male shaver in this market.

Implementation

Once PR planners decide what they want to do and which audiences to target, they must wrestle with how to implement their plans. Implementation includes the choice of specific public relations tools, decisions about the message strategy, and the method and time of delivery of the message.

Although the intention with the Sensor launch was to keep the theme consistent across the market, some local adaptation occurred because northern European shaving markets differ from southern European markets. In the south complexions are darker, men have tougher beards, and the Latin countries are more open to a romantic angle. In Scandinavia most men have soft blond hair, a fair complexion, and are less swayed by romantic imagery. Even with the adaptations, the European campaign communicated the quality and breakthrough engineering of the product and the Gillette Sensor "Best A Man Can Get" theme.

The publicity also had to be adapted because techniques such as video news releases worked well in countries such as Italy that have flourishing private electronic media but were less effective in the United Kingdom, where a public company, the BBC, still controls access to two of the four channels and avoids commercialization.

Coordinated timing is critical in an integrated PR campaign. In the case of Gillette's Sensor, Gillette decided that the Sensor story could be presented at two different times from two different perspectives. Three months before the product became available, Gillette presented the Sensor as a business story, focusing on the company, the product patents, the development of the product, and the marketing story. Most product publicity (why the shaving system was effective) was timed to take place a few weeks before both the launch and the start of the consumer advertising campaign. This two-step plan made it possible to sustain interest over three-and-a-half months. The amount of actual media coverage far exceeded the goals set for the PR program.

Unfortunately for the Sensor launch, there was so much interest in the story that product information started to leak out to general publications ahead of schedule. In response, Porter/Novelli decided Gillette should hold a press conference simultaneously in six markets 10 weeks before the launch. The coverage from that press event was so heavy in the United States that *Fortune* named the Sensor one of its 10 products of the year—before the Sensor became available in stores.

Budgets and Evaluation

Planners must know—not guess—what things cost. For example, publicity places news stories in the media without a media fee, but it is hardly free. A great many resources are used to prepare a press release and develop the media contacts that result in "free" publicity. The costs of other specific items, such as a brochure, newsletter, video news release, or special event, however, can be estimated. The budgeting question then becomes, What can the business afford? For instance, the most effective way to communicate with a specific audience might be via a prime-time television program, as Hallmark does with its Hallmark Hall of Fame. But the cost of this type of public relations might exceed the budget. To match the needs of the business to the budgetary constraints, PR planners must ask: What can we afford to do to implement the public relations objectives properly?

Despite the difficulty of measuring the results of public relations, a study found that 97 percent of PR executives feel that public relations professionals should routinely measure the impact of their programs.[8] PR is evaluated through both informal and formal research methods. Informal techniques include counting the attendance at an event, hosting informal interviews, or recording the number of requests for speakers.

Formal research methods include focus groups, content analysis, and monitoring public relations activities and public opinion over time. Focus groups can be used to measure the qualitative effects of material or messages on members of a target audience before the material is officially distributed. Content analysis of PR communications can show what is being reported, where, to how many people, over what period of time, in which media, and how the coverage changes over time. Monitoring keeps track of PR activities and public opinion over time. It might include weekly ongoing opinion polls or a count of the number of press releases that appear in print.

concept review

Managing Public Relations

1. Research in public relations is a planned, carefully organized, sophisticated fact-finding effort that focuses on listening to the opinions of others.
2. The six steps in public relations planning are:
   - Assessment of the current situation
   - Statement of objectives
   - Selection of target audiences
   - Selection of methods of implementation
   - Determination of costs
   - Evaluation of results

The Sensor launch was measured by examining sales revenues and monitoring coverage. Gillette's marketing manager estimated the impact of public relations to have added $7 million in publicity to the value of the advertising. The marketing manager based the estimate on the number of PR contacts, which included 403 million media impressions (the number of people seeing the story or mention) that resulted from 840 placements in the media. The continuing success of public relations is highlighted in the IMC in Action feature.

PR Drives Sales for The Sensor for Women

This photo shows how Gillette created a summer day in February for press members.

Given the incredible success the Porter/Novelli public relations firm had with the launch of the Gillette Sensor, it wasn't surprising when, several years later, Porter/Novelli was chosen to lead the launch of Gillette's new razor for women. Using a similar strategy, Porter/Novelli drove pre-advertising sales to more than 50 percent beyond Gillette's own ambitious forecast and established Sensor for Women as the fastest-growing product in the health and beauty category.

Prior to consumer advertising, more than 600 separate stories appeared in high-profile media communicating to women across North America the breakthrough technology and design of the new product. The strategy was to use credible, third-party editorial coverage to inform women about the benefits of the newly designed razor. Objectives were to establish awareness and achieve trial and repeat purchases.

Activities included a two-day media preview. The first day targeted magazine and newspaper editors that required a long lead time to publish articles. The second day targeted general news media with a press conference. This strategy resulted in two peaks of publicity. The first round of coverage appeared in general news, business, and trade publications, and broadcast outlets through the spring. The second round appeared in influential women's magazines and in newspaper lifestyle sections during the summer when the product first became available.

For the magazine and newspaper editors that required more lead time, Porter/Novelli created a summer environment on a dreary day in February to get editors thinking about shaving for summer activities. More than 80 metres of tenting, hundreds of azaleas, tulips, jonquils, daffodils, ficus trees, and even a custom-made waterfall transformed the rooftop of New York's Peninsula Spa into a summer garden. The 57 editors attending received an in-depth product briefing and were offered an opportunity to sample the product in the spa. The press materials were contained in a media resource guide that included an 18-month editorial calendar and extensive background information for the development of feature stories.

On the following day, business, financial, and general news media watched the creation of a dramatic photo of Sensor for Women on a seven-storey wall of water. They also received samples and product information. At the same time, specially packaged product samples were distributed to 1600 female opinion leaders nationwide. The success of this effort in driving sales demonstrated the power of public relations when used as a strategic marketing communication tool.

Sources: "Gillette Sensor for Women," Porter/Novelli handout; "Sensor Gets Big Edge in Women's Razors," *New York Times*, 17 December 1992, B1.

Integrating Public Relations

Successful public relations efforts depend in large part on how well they are integrated with other marketing communication functions. A survey found that of the companies that use public relations, PR executives believe that 70 percent of management want public relations integrated with other marketing communication. It also found that 90 percent of the PR executives feel that public relations professionals should spearhead efforts to integrate PR with other communication areas.[9] For the most part, companies have failed at this task. Historically, public relations has been physically and philosophically separated from the rest of the organization's marketing communication team and, thus, has not had a role in managing or planning the company's total communication program.

This historical isolation has been partly due to the nature of the work performed by public relations and partly due to the attitudes of the people working in it. Because management often does not view PR as a profit generator and has difficulty verifying the effect PR has on the bottom line, profit-oriented - managers may discount its value. This perception is compounded when people working in public relations, often trained as journalists with little background in business, do not view selling or profit generation as a part of their responsibility.

PR expert William Novelli believes these attitudes must change: "All communications can and should stem from common strategies, and the total program should speak with one voice."[10] Another expert, Yustin Wallrapp, suggests: "There must be a real commitment to the legitimacy of PR as a part of the communication mix."[11] For public relations to have an important role in a total communications program, it must be recognized that PR's expertise is in relationship management, which is the heart of a marketing communication program.

Integration is essential, especially in areas where PR overlaps with other marketing communication tools. Corporate advertising, advertising for PR purposes, overlaps with product advertising and can enhance the advertising message and brand image. Research shows that customers do care about a company's social responsibility, and that information gets factored into their buying decisions.

concept review

Integrating Public Relations

1. To be effective, public relations should be integrated into a marketing communication program because it overlaps with other communication activities and its specialists are experts in relationship management.
2. Historically, PR has been isolated from other marketing communication areas because many managers don't view it as a profit generator and many PR specialists don't feel responsible for generating revenues.

News release
A form of publicity that commits a story to paper or video in the style acceptable to the medium for which it was intended.

Press conference
An event held by an organization to make a significant announcement to representatives of the press.

Press kit
A collection of supporting material distributed at a press conference to representatives of the press.

Canada Newswire
www.newswire.ca

Furthermore, the problems and crises that PR people have to manage are often linked to other marketing communication activities, such as Kraft's sweepstakes promotion that, because of a printing error, made the company responsible for giving away an unexpectedly large number of minivans. The Big Mac Shaq story in Chapter 10 is another example of a sales promotion that caused public relations problems—McDonald's knew that if it modified the contest to avoid huge losses, the public would have cried foul for changing the game rules.

Tools of Public Relations

Public relations specialists use many tools to communicate. Some of the most common ones include publicity and news releases, corporate advertising, publications, videos and film, sponsorship, lobbying, fundraising, meetings, and organized social activities.

Publicity

Providing editors and reporters with an organization's story generates publicity. As mentioned earlier, publicity is one of the responsibilities of a media relations program. The credibility of articles in the mass media is much higher than that of advertising because the medium has the choice to run or not run the story and to change it as desired.

Most publicity is delivered in the form of a **news release** (also referred to as a press release) that commits a story to paper or video in the style acceptable to the medium for which it is intended. News stories are usually written one way for newspapers and another way for the electronic media. Newspeople appreciate direct, clear-cut explanations because they themselves are experts in concise writing and are usually hard-pressed for time. A single copy, or exclusive, is sent to a news editor, section editor, or a specific reporter. Multiple copies can be mailed to a mailing list of editors or put on a news wire, such as Canada NewsWire. Table 11.4 provides guidelines for submitting a news release.

To make a significant announcement to representatives of the press, an organization may hold an event called a **press conference**. At a press conference, press representatives listen to the announcement and may also ask questions and interview important people. Busy media will not attend such events unless the announcement is important, such as a candidate announcing that he or she is running for public office. If the news could just as well have been obtained from a prepared release, then the press conference probably should not be held. A collection of supporting materials, known as a **press kit**, provides photographs, releases, copies of speeches, maps, timetables, and other material that might be of use to reporters. Publicity photos in the

This press release from the University of New Brunswick presents the facts early, includes a contact name and number, and suits the newspaper medium for which it was intended.

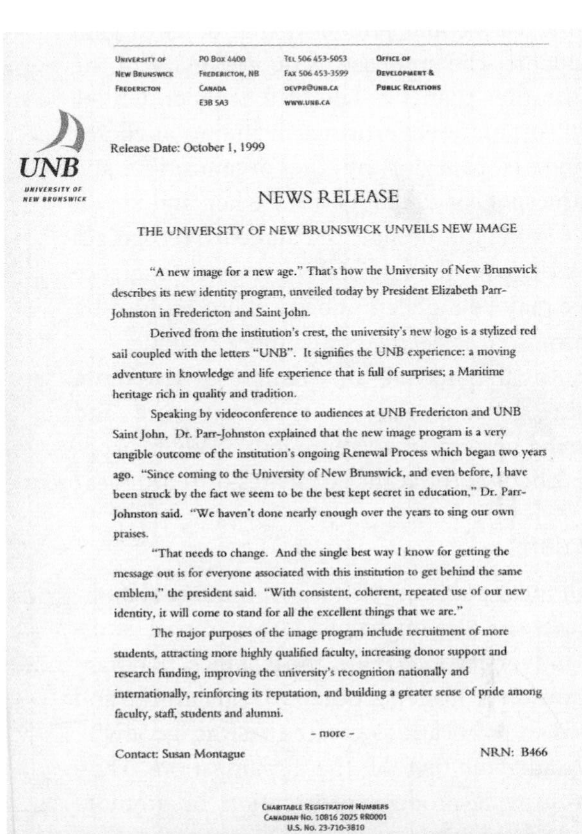

University of New Brunswick Fredericton | PO Box 4400 Fredericton, NB Canada E3B 5A3 | Tel 506 453-5053 Fax 506 453-3599 devpr@unb.ca www.unb.ca | Office of Development & Public Relations

UNB
University of New Brunswick

Release Date: October 1, 1999

NEWS RELEASE

THE UNIVERSITY OF NEW BRUNSWICK UNVEILS NEW IMAGE

"A new image for a new age." That's how the University of New Brunswick describes its new identity program, unveiled today by President Elizabeth Parr-Johnston in Fredericton and Saint John.

Derived from the institution's crest, the university's new logo is a stylized red sail coupled with the letters "UNB". It signifies the UNB experience: a moving adventure in knowledge and life experience that is full of surprises; a Maritime heritage rich in quality and tradition.

Speaking by videoconference to audiences at UNB Fredericton and UNB Saint John, Dr. Parr-Johnston explained that the new image program is a very tangible outcome of the institution's ongoing Renewal Process which began two years ago. "Since coming to the University of New Brunswick, and even before, I have been struck by the fact we seem to be the best kept secret in education," Dr. Parr-Johnston said. "We haven't done nearly enough over the years to sing our own praises.

"That needs to change. And the single best way I know for getting the message out is for everyone associated with this institution to get behind the same emblem," the president said. "With consistent, coherent, repeated use of our new identity, it will come to stand for all the excellent things that we are."

The major purposes of the image program include recruitment of more students, attracting more highly qualified faculty, increasing donor support and research funding, improving the university's recognition nationally and internationally, reinforcing its reputation, and building a greater sense of pride among faculty, staff, students and alumni.

- more -

Contact: Susan Montague NRN: B466

Charitable Registration Numbers
Canadian No. 10816 2025 RR0001
U.S. No. 23-710-3810

Table 11.4 GUIDELINES FOR PREPARING A NEWS RELEASE

1. Learn as much as possible about the particular medium being used and what that medium considers newsworthy.
2. Make sure the story is totally accurate.
3. Make sure the story is timely. Old news is of no use to most editors.
4. Keep the story as succinct as possible.
5. Because newspaper readers are skimmers, present the main facts in the first few sentences when submitting to this medium.
6. Proofread carefully. Any typographic or grammatical mistakes will suggest a lack of professionalism on your part and may result in the news release being thrown in the garbage.
7. Include a name and phone number of a contact person who can answer questions.
8. Don't expect the news medium to use your news release just because you sent it and it is important to your company. News judgments are balanced against the volume of the news and the editor's feel for the audience's interests.

Royal Bank
www.royalbank.ca

press kit are particularly important because the decision to use a story may depend on the availability of a dramatic visual.

Corporate public relations is the focus of this cover to a magazine insert.

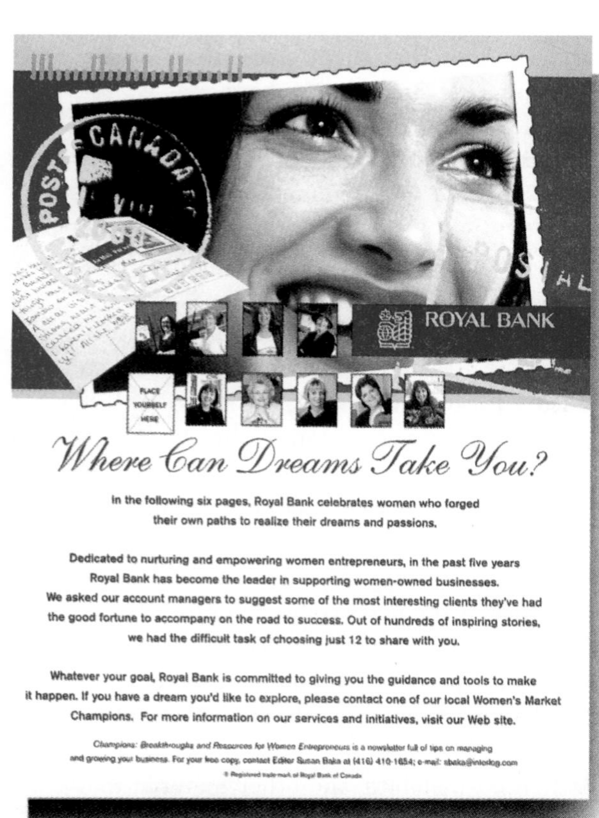

CORPORATE ADVERTISING

As noted earlier, corporate advertising is communication by an organization about its work, views, and problems that aims to gain public support. The emphasis is on the image of the company rather than the sale of a product. Unlike publicity, corporate advertising, including advocacy advertising, is paid for by the organization and enables the sponsor to tell its story when and how it chooses. On the minus side, the audience recognizes that an ad is paid for and self-serving, so audience resistance may be higher. Publicity is not paid for by the sponsor, so it is deemed to be more credible.

The Royal Bank ad, an example of corporate advertising, speaks out on the nurturing and empowering of women entrepreneurs. What corporate image do you think the ad creates or reinforces?

PUBLICATIONS

Although most publications target an internal audience, some are also distributed to external audiences. A university magazine, for instance, may target community leaders, donors, legislators, and alumni. Such publications create prestige, goodwill, and an understanding of the organization. They may also provide product information, or promote products and services.

In addition to internal magazines and newspapers, other publications include brochures, flyers, posters, and other forms of printed materials. PR departments, particularly those for public organizations like hospitals, often produce a variety of brochures that describe specialized programs or products offered by the organizations. Banks, for example, may have a line of brochures that describe their various offerings, investment programs, and financial planning services.

Annual report

An official document required for publicly held companies that contains financial information.

Another type of company publication is the **annual report**. This is an official document required for publicly held companies. The annual report, which is sent to all investors and the financial community, is often used as a statement about the company's financial health and market position. It is an important tool in establishing and maintaining a corporate image.

Videos and Film

Although videos and film are some of the most complex and expensive means of communication, they offer an opportunity to influence viewers in a way that no other medium can match. For instance, businesses may send video news releases to television stations as a type of publicity. Videos can also be used for sales meetings, training, and staff conferences. Some large companies even produce their own news shows that are played for employees during lunch or breaks. **Product placements**—the practice of having a product appear in a news show or movie to generate lots of valuable visibility—is another form of publicity that uses the film medium. *Seinfeld*, for example, highlighted products such as Glide dental floss and Kenny Rogers chicken in select episodes. There are some limitations to video and film, however. First, people are accustomed to quality images and therefore expect to see video and film that are professionally produced. And that means these materials will be expensive. Second, moving images tend to proceed at their own pace and allow little time for viewers to ask questions, so they do not generate two-way conversations.

Lobbying

Lobbying is an area of great sensitivity because it involves contacting government officials with information and persuasive communication. Lobbyists are often former government officers, although some public relations practitioners who are lobbyists work for organizations such as the media conglomerates or power utility companies. Lobbyists work closely with the staffs of federal and/or provincial elected bodies and regulatory offices. The staff often depend on lobbyists to explain the intricacies and implications of proposed legislation and regulation. Lobbyists use their in-depth information to influence and persuade.

Fundraising

Public relations is important for nonprofit associations that rely on goodwill to stimulate memberships and donations. Fundraising is a specialty that involves public relations. Your campus is probably filled with people or groups that help raise funds, such as the alumni association or university foundation, the athletic department, the library, and numerous student groups. Professional fundraisers are skilled at developing campaigns that can bring in large sums of money. They know how to make the initial contacts that inspire other people to participate, how to use other marketing communication tools such as advertising, and how to make the best use of special events and public recognition.

This University of Victoria publication cover helps create prestige, goodwill, and an understanding of the organization.

MEETINGS

Meeting with others to discuss ideas is an often-neglected communication technique in sophisticated communication planning because it seems too simple. Meetings have great power for good or ill because they involve personal, interactive communication rather than the distant, passive communication of a mass-media message. Because meetings are limited by the size of the setting, they should be used to communicate with relatively small stakeholder groups. They are often used for such purposes as an annual report meeting for investors, a meeting with an activist group to hear concerns, an employee meeting to announce a new policy, a public lecture by a visiting scientist, or the showing of a new movie or play to opinion leaders.

A poorly run meeting can send a message of disinterest or incompetence. To avoid such an image, meeting planners should select the setting with care, plan for audiovisual materials, provide equipment, invite participants in a timely and gracious manner, organize social activities before and after the event, and attend to countless details.

Social Activities

Company picnics, holiday parties, bowling and baseball leagues, and golf tournaments are all tools of public relations. Public relations specialists use these events to create a pleasant atmosphere for employees and to convey the impression that management is thoughtful and interested. PR specialists may also use social activities to build relationships with major customers, dealers and retailers, donors, investors, and other important stakeholders.

Sponsorships (Event, Sports, and Cause)

Sponsorship
A company's financial support of an event or cause in exchange for an affiliation with the organization or event sponsored; can create goodwill and positive associations that companies can feature through other communication tools such as advertising.

A **sponsorship** is the provision of financial support for an activity or organization—sports, art, entertainment, a good cause, or fairs and festivals—so that it can survive. The aim is to polish the sponsor's image in ways that reflect positively on the bottom line. In most cases the company wants to be associated with the positive social values reflected by the person, activity, or organization it sponsors. We'll discuss three specific types of sponsorships—event, sports, and cause marketing.

A stadium sponsorship is one of the newest types of sponsorships. For a million bucks or so a year, as Table 11.5 illustrates, marketers buy the opportunity to reach tens of thousands of consumers at every sports event and concert held in the stadium, week after week. That compares favourably with 30 seconds of advertising on *ER* for $700 000 to $800 000 or half a minute on the Super Bowl for $1.7 million.[12] And the newest corporate drive is to have a stadium or arena named after the company.

Fleetcenter
www.fleetcenter.com

For signage sponsors, if the local team is strong enough to get national TV coverage, then the sponsor gets national visibility as a bonus. Sponsorships of executive suites—sometimes called skyboxes—in the stadiums are also big business. The new FleetCenter in Boston, for example, has 104 suites that cost about $300 000 a year for a total of $29 million split between the team and the Center's owners.

Table 11.5 The Stadium Game

Stadium	Location	Sponsorship Terms
Pepsi Center	Denver	$70 million plus over 20 years
3Com Park	San Francisco	$6 million over 4 years
Air Canada Centre	Toronto	$20 million over 20 years
Trans World Dome	St. Louis	$36 million over 20 years
GM Place	Vancouver	$28 million over 20 years

Sources: Mark Lewyn, "See a Game, Shop for a Car, Surf the Net," *Business Week*, January 29, 1996, 53; Wendy Tanka, "High-Tech Firms Lift Their Profiles at Sports Venues," *Rocky Mountain News*, 15 August 1996, 16B.

Although many people think sponsorships are used mainly for big-time sports or major causes, sponsorships can be used in other ways. Companies sponsor children's programs at the local symphony, provide materials for schools, and award scholarships for students. Businesses give grants to artists to support their creative work. Some major advertisers, like Hallmark, sponsor their own TV programming, the Hallmark Hall of Fame.

Under this general heading of sponsorships, companies may affiliate with events, sports and athletes, and good causes in myriad ways. In all cases the bottom-line value of the sponsorship depends on the fit of the business to the affiliation. Does it make sense for a pantyhose manufacturer to sponsor men's tennis? Probably not. It does make sense for Subaru, with its four-wheel-drive feature and its underdog image, to sponsor a women's ski team.

Let's now turn to the strategic aspects of the three main types of sponsorships: event marketing, sports marketing, and cause marketing.

Event Marketing

Columnist John McManus estimates that the beer, soft drink, car, camera, film, and computer marketers who have pioneered event marketing have made it into a $6.6-billion industry in North America.[13] The objective of event marketing is

Support of figure skating events allows the Bank of Montreal to reach audiences in communities across Canada.

to cut through the clutter of mass media and gain higher levels of awareness by linking with some cause, entertainment, or activity that creates a positive association for the company. Coca-Cola, for example, is involved in about 5000 local, regional, national, and international events a year across North America.

Public relations programs use special events to celebrate major happenings such as a groundbreaking, a ribbon-cutting, or an open house after a new building is finished, a political candidate announcement, or a reception for a winning sports team. In marketing public relations (MPR), special events are used to link companies and brands to public events, issues, or ideas that engage the interest of the public.

Special events are not tied only to public relations or to any one marketing communication area. Instead they combine many traditional marketing communication activities—advertising and sales promotion among them. Furthermore, there are two levels of marketing communication involved in most events—the event itself and the media coverage of the event. In cases like the Olympics, sponsors can also generate communication through company publicity, advertising, and other forms of tie-in promotions.

The growth in event marketing in recent years has been tremendous. Three main reasons explain such growth. First, events tend to attract a homogeneous audience that is appreciative of the sponsors of the event. Second, event sponsorship builds support from trade members and employees. The employees who manage the event may receive recognition, and trade members often participate in the event. Finally, compared to producing an advertising campaign, event management is simple because many of the elements can be prepackaged. An organization such as MCI Communications Corp. can use the same group of people and the same plan to manage many different events.

Another strength is that event sponsorship can go where other marketing communication functions, such as advertising, are forbidden or undeliverable. For many companies marketing in countries abroad, sponsorship of sports or the arts is a requirement as a way of proving commitment to the local culture. In England, where there are only four channels and tremendous demand for advertising space on them, event sponsorships are an important alternative to build corporate or brand visibility. These sponsors are reaching a market that is hard to reach via traditional tools such as advertising.

Three pitfalls to event marketing exist. First, if the match between the event and the company is poor, the benefit to the company may be small compared to the cost. Second, many uncontrollable factors such as weather can influence an event. Third, special events generally reach a smaller audience than mass-media advertising. The events effectively build awareness in a tightly targeted, committed market but are less effective at creating awareness in a broad-based audience.

Companies that jump into event marketing because they have a passion for a sport or a cause, but don't plan or analyse the costs and benefits before providing the sponsorship, often encounter problems. Drew Sheinman, Coca-Cola's event marketing director, observes, "We see more and more people start to foray into event marketing programs that are not founded on a strategic plan [to build] their brands."[14] He concludes that many do not understand how to leverage the value of the association with the brand.

Sports Marketing

The fastest-growing sponsorship category is sports marketing. A company can be engaged in sports marketing in many ways. It may sponsor a sporting event such as the Olympics, a bowl game, a golf tournament, a stockcar race, or a 10K run. Alternatively, a company may sign up a star athlete such as Elvis Stojko, Katarina Witt, or Tiger Woods. These athletes use the company's products and appear in its ads and other marketing communication programs. A company may also sponsor a participant in a sporting event, such as Valvoline's sponsorship of a race-car driver, or it may sponsor a team. Finally, sports equipment manufacturers who promote their products are also considered sports marketers.

Roots Canada
www.roots.com

Sports marketing involves a variety of marketing communication activities, ranging from celebrity endorsements to licensed premiums to advertising and public relations activities. There are a number of factors to consider before agreeing to sponsor a sports marketing event. Table 11.6 identifies some considerations.

Being associated with sporting events can create a positive brand image, but it does more than that. It heightens awareness, improves attitudes about a company and a brand, adds credibility to the company's message, and creates higher levels of confidence in the company.[15] For instance, Roots Canada was one of the official clothing providers for the Canadian Olympic team in Nagano. This sponsorship heightened worldwide awareness of Roots Canada. It also had a tremendous impact on sales of its red Olympic poor boy hat that was worn by the Canadian Olympic team.

Table 11.6 Sports Marketing Considerations

The following should be considered before making a deal to sponsor a sport:

- *Does the product match the audience demographic at the sporting event?* Marketing beer at a basketball game makes sense; marketing perfume at a wrestling match doesn't.
- *Does the timing of the promotion match the selling season?* It wouldn't make sense to launch a suntan lotion at a January ice hockey event.
- *Match the locale of the event to the geography of the market.* Don't use a national event for a product that is marketed in only a few regions of the country.
- *Should the promotion be a single event or occur many times in multiple markets?* If the event can go on the road, then it can reach a far larger audience.
- *Match your goal to the audience of the sport.* Do you want stronger trade relations, broader distribution, increased awareness of the brand, or sales increases? Know your goals and make certain the event audience matches your target audience and can deliver on the objectives.
- *Will your sponsorship be a stand-alone effort or integrated into a total communication program?* If so, make it clear who will manage the integration.
- *Do you have the time in the schedule to allow adequate time for merchandising support?* Plan and announce the program at least three months in advance because retailers usually need a 13-week window.
- *Determine what you need to get out of the program before spending anything.* In other words, what is your payout and at what point does it make financial sense—or not make financial sense?

Source: Adapted from Blair R. Fischer, "The Rules of the Game," *Promo* (December 1995): 53û7.

The Canadian Olympic team, in Nagano, popularized Roots Canada's red Olympic poor boy hats.

Another reason to value sports marketing is the boost such programs give to trade and employee motivation. Visa, for example, uses its sponsorship of sports events such as the Olympics to anchor merchant programs (programs in which local retailers cosponsor Olympic tie-in promotions with Visa) and a program for the 18 000-member financial institutions that promote and market Visa cards.[16]

Because of the effectiveness of sports marketing, major companies invest tremendous sums in it. For example, Nike has an all-sports agreement with a number of major U.S. universities—Alabama, Colorado, Florida State, Illinois, Michigan, North Carolina, Penn State, USC, Miami, and Michigan. Nike provides the teams with $7 to $8 million in apparel and contributions. In exchange, the teams are required to display Nike's trademark swoosh logo and use Nike shoes, uniforms, and training apparel. Michigan reportedly has the largest deal, worth about $8.8 million over six years. Analysts estimate Nike will likely make back two or three times that amount in exposure, merchandising, and the future endorsement potential of star athletes who move from university to professional ranks.[17]

Sports marketing does have some drawbacks, however. First, not everyone is interested in sports or a particular sport, so finding a match between the target audience and the sports activity audience may be difficult. To avoid this drawback, the sports marketer must understand the company or brand's target audience. That audience must have sufficient interest in the sport to justify the sponsorship.

In addition to understanding the target audience, marketers must also understand the size and type of the sports event audience. Only then will they know whether reaching that audience supports the company's marketing communication objectives. A multinational company trying to reach a worldwide audience might sponsor the Olympics instead of a local 10K run. Sports marketers must also consider the type of audience at sporting events. Some sports reach a spectator audience, such as football. Others reach audiences of mainly participants, such as a mountain biking or snowboarding event. Although the participatory sports may reach smaller audiences, those audiences

Nike's sponsorship of Tiger Woods requires him to wear the Nike swoosh on his hat or clothing to give the company added exposure and credibility.

tend to be more committed to the products associated with the sport than are spectators.

Cause Marketing

When companies run a promotion with a charitable organization and donate a portion of their business profits to the cause, the practice is called cause marketing. The promotion runs for a period of time, briefly boosting the sales and possibly the image of the company.[18] In exchange for the sponsorship, the company earns the right to tell customers that the more of a company's products they buy, the more the cause will benefit. Companies use cause marketing to do something good for society, associate themselves with a positive cause that will reflect well on their corporate image, break through the commercial clutter, and target a group of people interested in that cause.

Cause marketing campaigns usually involve supporting promotional efforts. For example, companies underwrite national advertising and promotional campaigns for the National Breast Cancer Awareness Month during October.

This Tim Horton's poster illustrates an example of cause marketing. The Tim Horton Children's Foundation is committed to helping kids see what they're capable of achieving.

Basically, cause marketing is sales promotion with a public relations spin. In other words, marketing communication managers have found that doing good can be good for business. In a Roper Starch survey, 2000 adults reported that when given a choice between two products of equal price and quality, 78 percent said they would be more likely to buy the one that supported a cause that they cared about.[19]

Cause marketing has the strengths and the weaknesses of both public relations and sales promotion. Like sales promotion, it can instantly affect sales by offering something extra. The sales boost is aided further by public relations' ability to break through the commercial clutter. Thus cause marketing helps keep a company or brand top-of-the-mind, but only if the cause and the company are related in some way. For example, Crayola sponsors arts education and Seagram Canada supports responsible use of alcohol programs. But cause marketing has limitations. It is often poorly integrated into a company's overall marketing communication program and may, as a result, be ineffective. As practised by many companies, it is relatively short term, opportunistic, and seen by more and more people as self-serving and exploitive.[20]

Ben and Jerry's
www.benandjerrys.com

A more strategic way to improve audience relationships through support for socially responsible causes is an approach professor Tom Duncan has dubbed "mission marketing."[21] This approach integrates a noncommercial, socially redeeming value system into a company's business plan and operations. In other words, the cause is not something that is adopted and then forgotten, but an important part of the company's business. Examples of companies that have built significant business activities on mission marketing are Ben & Jerry's ice cream and The Body Shop.

American Express
www.americanexpress.com

Mission marketing funnels all of a company's "philanthropy" into a single, long-term commitment that is related to the company's expertise and mission. For example, American Express helped develop tourism in Eastern European countries struggling to find ways to attract hard currency. The company sent executives to work with the Hungarian government's tourism staff, set up a foundation that financed university research on effective ways to publicize the region's museums, and funded tourism educational programs in 23 secondary schools to help prepare students to work in tourism and travel-related businesses. Amex enlisted local help for these projects from Hungarians in government and in the airline, hotel, and restaurant industries. These government and business contacts with key people in the travel industry will give American Express a strong base when tourism takes off in the countries it has helped.

This "strategic philanthropy" adds an element of trust to the relationship between the company and its customers and other stakeholders. In addition, it provides a tool to create a truly integrated marketing program because it "fosters synergy among business units."[22] When properly done, mission marketing should promote comments such as: "I want to work for this company—or buy its products—because this company stands for something more than just making a profit."

IMC AND SPONSORSHIPS

Sponsorships of any kind are the ideal place to practise integrated marketing communication because they all involve a variety of messages and media aimed at many stakeholders—all held together by one theme related to the sponsorship. In its sponsorship of World Cup soccer, for example, Sprint's integrated marketing effort used approximately 70 different marketing initiatives targeted at each of Sprint's primary stakeholders: businesses, residences, international customers, business travellers, journalists, and its own employees.[23] Furthermore, sponsorships may affect other areas of the marketing mix as products are designed or redesigned to fit the tie-in, special pricing opportunities are created, and, in some cases new distribution channels are used as part of the event.

Sponsorships are valuable if they provide a meaningful and cost-effective way to build business. They must also fit with the company's mission and help achieve its marketing communication objectives. John Beneath, Visa senior vice president, makes the point that the company's sponsorship of the Olympics would not make sense if the event wasn't integrated into many areas of its communication program beyond just using the Olympic images and symbols. Visa uses Olympic-related activities, for instance, in both employee and trade relations. Employees, customers, and business partners help raise funds for the teams. The key is to leverage the sponsorship throughout the company's business dealings.[24]

A Closing Thought:

Fitting in PR

For public relations to fulfil its promise, it must be integrated as a key part of a total communication program. The public relations team, then, must work closely with the other marketing communication functions, making it a partner rather than a poor relation.[25] If such a partnership is the future of public relations, it holds important challenges for PR practitioners who must be market savvy and sensitive to the bottom-line concerns of business managers. Many public relations programs and practitioners have moved in this direction. They work with clearly stated, measurable objectives that dovetail with the company's marketing communication plan.

concept review

Tools of Public Relations

1. Using publicity as a public relations tool requires the ability to handle media relations, news releases, and press conferences.
2. Corporate advertising focuses on the image of the organization rather than a product.
3. Company publications, another PR tool, can reach both an internal and external audience. They include magazines, newspapers, and newsletters, brochures and flyers, and more formal documents such as annual reports.
4. Videos and film are used for video news releases to television studios, for sales meetings, training, staff conferences, and in-house news programs.
5. Tools used in public relations include lobbying, fundraising, meetings, organized social activities, and sponsorships.
6. A sponsorship is the provision of a company's financial support so that a sport, event, or cause can survive. The purpose of the sponsorship is to bolster the sponsor's image in ways that reflect positively on the bottom line.

Meanwhile, companies are likely to place increasing importance on public relations as they become more aware of the critical role that PR has to play in relationship marketing. With consumers who are demanding better information, higher value, and improved service, companies will have to be aware of and learn to manage the images they portray to all stakeholders whenever possible.

summary 

1. Define public relations and explain its purpose.

   Public relations is a communication activity that tries to change the attitudes and beliefs of stakeholder audiences. It helps build goodwill and strengthen relationships with all stakeholders and develop and maintain a positive company image.

2. Identify the strengths and weaknesses of public relations.

   Public relations has many strengths. First, marketing communicators can use it to manage many different stakeholder relationships (employees, financial community, media, local community, and so forth) and to monitor issues and public opinion related to the organization's concerns. It can also add credibility and believability to a message when it appears in the media. Weaknesses include a lack of control over how and which messages are covered in the media and the difficulty of evaluating effectiveness.

3. Distinguish between internal and external stakeholders.

   Stakeholder publics are the groups of people targeted to receive public relations messages. Internal publics are those with whom an organization normally communicates in the ordinary routine of work, such as employees, investors, suppliers, dealers, and regular customers. In contrast, external publics are publics the organization communicates with but does not have regular or close ties, such as local community neighbours, government regulators, special-interest groups, media, and the financial community.

4. Explain seven types of public relations programs.

   There are seven main types of public relations programs: media relations (working with press representatives and providing them with story ideas and information), corporate public relations (counselling senior management about the company's overall reputation, its image in the eyes of stakeholders, and its response to important issues), crisis management (predicting where and when disasters will strike and planning how to handle the company's relations and communications in times of crisis), employee relations (keeping the employees informed and in the communication loop), financial relations (keeping analysts, stockbrokers, and investors informed), public affairs and community relations (working on local and government issues that affect the organization), and marketing public relations (the use of publicity and other PR tools to launch and promote products).

5. Outline the steps in the public relations research and planning process.

   Research is used to help planners become better informed about the issues and attitudes of stakeholders. The planning process, similar to that used in other areas of marketing communication, consists of the following six steps: (1) assess the situation, (2) set objectives, (3) select target audiences, (4) implement details, (5) determine costs and budgeting, and (6) evaluate results.

6. Discuss the role of public relations in an integrated marketing communication program.

   Public relations contributes to an integrated communication program in several key ways. It helps launch new products because it provides ways to use the news to announce the products in a credible way that generates excitement. It helps organizations identify key stakeholders, analyse the nature of those relationships, and deliver the messages needed to keep the relationships positive and productive. Corporate advertising, an area where advertising and public relations intersect, requires strong coordination with other marketing communication areas. Planning for a crisis is also crucial to an integrated program, especially when the crisis is precipitated by a product or marketing activity, such as a product that fails or a promotion that goes awry. To ensure integration, public relations specialists must be sensitive to the bottom-line concerns of business managers, and companies must recognize the key role PR can play in relationship marketing.

7. Describe the tools used in public relations programs.

PR managers use many tools. These tools include publicity; corporate advertising; publications, videos, and film for internal and external audiences; special events and sponsorships of events to generate publicity and increase enthusiasm; lobbying; fundraising; meetings; and organized social activities.

points to ponder

Review the Facts

1. Distinguish between the terms "public relations" and "publicity."
2. Define a public. Differentiate between internal and external publics. Name several types of publics that are of interest to the PR planner.
3. Explain why the concept of relations is so important to public relations.
4. Define sponsorship and explain how it is used strategically by a company to create positive associations.

Master the Concepts

5. What steps might a public relations person take to prevent a firm from developing a negative public image?
6. What are the pros and cons of using corporate advertising? Under what conditions would it be appropriate?
7. How does public relations differ from advertising and sales promotion? What advantages does public relations offer that are not available through these other two marketing communication functions?
8. What are the similarities and differences between cause marketing and mission marketing?

Apply Your Knowledge

9. You are the public relations director for a company that makes children's clothing. Develop a proposal for a public relations issues and crisis management program. What research needs to be done? What kinds of recommendations would this program be likely to address with top management?
10. Prepare a set of guidelines for developing a healthy relationship between the news media and the firm's PR department.
11. Assume that you are the public relations director for a bank. Suppose that two people were robbed while withdrawing money from one of your bank's 24-hour automatic teller machines. The president wants your advice on what to say to the news media. What would you recommend?
12. Use the robbery as a rationale for developing a crisis plan for the bank. Develop a draft that outlines various types of crisis scenarios and how they should be handled. Identify the key roles of senior management and those of the public relations office.

suggested projects

1. (Writing Project) Review several newspapers and magazines and collect five articles that you feel are based on news releases prepared by a public relations specialist. What do you believe were the objectives of each of these releases? Do you believe the articles helped create or reinforce a positive image of the company? Prepare a one- to two-page memo that describes your findings. Be sure to attach copies of the articles.
2. (Team Project) Divide into small groups of four to six students. Assume that you are the PR team for the athletic program at your university. The police have announced that some hockey team members have been charged with, but not yet convicted of, illegal drug use. Brainstorm ideas and then outline a public relations strategy that will respond effectively to this bad news. Select one group member to present the group's finding to the class.
3. Develop a crisis communication plan for your university, faculty, or department. What are the possible disasters that might affect your program? What decisions need to be made in advance of that happening? Who should do what?
4. (Internet Project) Assume you are the marketing communication director for an upscale hotel chain. The business operates around the world. Recently, press reports in the United States and the United Kingdom claim that business managers in several of your hotels in the Caribbean and Asia have relied on child labour for both cleaning and kitchen jobs. Complaints from potential customers are increasing daily; U.S. bookings are declining. You've set up a toll-free customer hotline in response, but you feel you need to address this issue on your Web site in order to help communicate in a timely manner with customers, travel agents, and other key stakeholders around the world. You decide to turn to an outside agency for help with this site content and the planning and implementation of a comprehensive PR strategy.

   Visit the Web sites of at least three international agencies to see who you would consider hiring. Some suggested sites include the following:

   Fleishman-Hillard (www.fleishman.com)

   Hill & Knowlton Canada Ltd. (www.hillandknowlton.com)

   Canada Porter/Novelli (www.porternovelli.com)

   Explore each company's site. Be sure to note where the agency has offices, how much experience it has in developing Web site content, and whether it has aided other clients with similar situations. Describe your findings and recommendations in a two- to three-page memo.

Shaping Up the Body Shop

The Body Shop operated with an anti-advertising philosophy for years after it was founded in 1976 by marketing maverick Anita Roddick. The company became successful based on its good reputation and its image as a company with a mission dedicated to social change. Roddick believed her high profile would make it possible to keep the company in consumers' minds, relying on public relations rather than traditional advertising. The company's positive image, however, soured when *Business Ethics* ran an article that spotlighted the gap between its image and its practices.

Roddick, the daughter of Italian immigrants, opened her first store in Brighton, England, more than 20 years ago. Within 10 years, some 1100 franchises were operating worldwide. More than 90 percent of the stores are independently owned. Roddick outlined her philosophy as follows:

> When I opened the first Body Shop in Brighton in 1976, I knew nothing about business....Today the Body Shop is an international company rapidly expanding around the world....[M]y passionate belief is that business can be fun, it can be conducted with love and be a powerful force for good. . . . Passion persuades, and by God, I was passionate about what I was selling.

An outspoken critic of traditional marketing, she claimed to have never spent a cent on advertising, which she considers to be hype—that is, until after the ethics scandal. Instead, she relied on free coverage in the media to tell her story. Body Shop also relied on its front line—employees and customers—to spread the news about the company and its philosophy.

The 1994 ***Business Ethics*** article, entitled "Shattered Image," damaged the Body Shop's reputation. The issues? First, the U.K.-based retailer and cataloguer of personal care products was charged with not purchasing as many ingredients from developing countries as claimed. Second, the ingredients used in Body Shop products were not as socially responsible as claimed. The article alleged that Body Shop lotions and creams were not completely natural and that some ingredients were tested on animals. Third, the franchisees complained that the Body Shop treated them unfairly. The company supposedly sold franchisees products at such high prices that the franchisees could not resell products with standard mark-up prices and remain competitive. Franchise owners also claimed they were misled about the earning potential of a franchise.

Until the article, the Body Shop was often cited as a paragon of socially responsible marketing and a paradigm for how to sell to modern consumers. The idea is that customers will be loyal to companies they consider to be responsible corporate citizens.

The Frankly Research Development Corp., one of the largest investment firms focusing on socially responsible investing, gave the Body Shop its top social rating in 1991. After the article ran in ***Business Ethics***, the company eliminated the Body Shop from its roster of rated companies. To compound problems, an Amazon chief featured in Body Shop posters in 1996 sued the company for using his image for publicity purposes without permission—again smearing the image of a company that professed to be interested in doing business with love and concern.

So with the negative publicity, the Body Shop faced the ultimate test of its reputation and credibility. Financial reports in 1995 and 1996 indicated that the company's U.S. business declined noticeably. Company executives claim the decline occurred because of overexpansion and increased competition. However, analysts cite the bad publicity as another factor.

Though the Body Shop saw growth in its Asian market, particularly Japan, revenues continued steady through 1995 but flattened in 1996. Controversy surrounding the company's proposal to introduce Body Shop Direct (a home-shopping-by-party division) triggered bad publicity and strained relations with franchisees in England that fear the division could harm their survival.

The company cannot be considered financially healthy as long as its questionable ethics continue to tarnish the company's super-green image.

Case Questions

1. If you were public relations manager for the Body Shop in 1994, how would you have handled the ***Business Ethics*** article fallout?
2. If you were the public relations manager for another company that emphasized its social responsibility, what would you learn from this case and how would you counsel senior management in your company on what the company needs to do to prevent this kind of situation from happening?
3. Do you believe the Body Shop can rebuild its image? What would you recommend?
4. How would you test the idea that customers who are loyal to companies they believe in will stay loyal in spite of bad news? What could be learned from the Body Shop's experience?

Sources: Ardyn Bernoth, "Roddick Faces Franchise Rebellion," ***Sunday London Times***, 22 September 1996, B1; "{Body Shop Starting to Lose Gentle Touch," ***The Daily Telegraph***, 20 June 1996, 22; Michael Durham and Jan Rocha, "Amazon Chief Sues Body Shop," ***The Observer,*** 3 March 1996, 5; Susan Gilchrist, "Body Blows Wash Over Body Shop," ***The London Times***, 14 October 1994, B1.

Communicating Through Direct Marketing

chapter objectives

After completing your work on this chapter, you should be able to

- Define direct marketing and explain its role in the marketing communication mix.
- Discuss the strengths and weaknesses of direct marketing.
- Outline how to manage, design, and evaluate a direct-marketing program.
- Describe how direct marketers use the tools of direct mail, catalogues, mass media, and telemarketing media.

Teaming Up at Amex Canada for Direct Marketing Success

From data mining to the Internet, new technologies mean direct marketing will remain the pacesetter for the entire marketing communications industry. With the emergence of new technologies, the established methods of marketing communication are being given a new spin and a new life. Technology allows direct marketers to use techniques such as data mining and data warehousing to capture and understand relevant customer information. For instance, as discussed in this Chapter's CBC Video Vignette, new technologies are helping marketers identify their most profitable customers so that marketing strategy can focus on these customers.

When Amex Canada Inc. launched the American Express Air Miles credit card across Canada, it expected to expand its brand image and market share by targeting a new base of potential customers – Air Miles collectors. What it didn't expect was a customer response so overwhelming that it put the company 80 percent beyond its forecast. In addition to winning customers, this launch won Amex the RSVP Best-of-the-Best award presented by the Canadian Marketing Association (formally known as the Canadian Direct Marketing Association).

Why was this product launch so successful? Amex utilized technology and a partnership with The Loyalty Group Canada Inc. of Toronto to enhance the design and implementation of a product launch that integrated several established marketing communications tools, many of which were direct marketing techniques.

Critical to the success of the launch was Amex's access to a quality database of 6.4 million Canadian households through the company's database of existing Air Miles collectors. As noted by Bryan Pearson, President, Consumer Air Miles Program at The Loyalty Group, the collector database is a coalition database for the exclusive use of Air Miles sponsors to help them target their marketing programs.

In addition to effective use of the database, the Amex launch involved a simultaneous PR, awareness TV, and direct-response TV initiative. This was followed by a full-thrust direct mail campaign to the Air Miles collectors. At the same time as the mailing, Amex placed FSIs (free-standing inserts) into a number of newspapers on the West Coast and in Ontario, included an insert in an Air Miles Summary report and offered a take-one campaign in partnership with a number of other Air Miles sponsors.

By all accounts, the launch exceeded all expectations. "No matter what channel we tried, we exceeded our goals," explains Amex's director of card member acquisitions. The advertising campaign generated 80 percent more applications than anticipated at a cost approximately 40 percent lower than historic levels.

Sources: David Chilton, "New Tools Promise No End in Sight for the DM Boom," *Marketing*, (February 2, 1998), 8-9; Leslie McNab, "Dealing a Winning Card," *Marketing*, (February 2, 1998), 10.

American Express Canada
www.americanexpress.com/Canada

Chapter Overview

Few areas of marketing have undergone more dramatic change than direct marketing. Until recently, most consumers viewed direct marketing as junk mail and junk products. As the Amex Canada experience shows, however, direct marketing can strengthen customer loyalty, target and win new customers, provide consumers with better information more quickly, and generate more wealth for the company.

In this chapter we first examine the definition and types of direct marketing. Next we explore the strengths and weaknesses of direct marketing in an integrated marketing communication program. Finally, we investigate how to manage, design, and evaluate a direct-marketing program and examine how direct marketers use direct mail, catalogues, and mass media.

The World of Direct Marketing

Direct marketing
An interactive tool of marketing communication that uses one or more advertising media to effect a measurable response and/or transaction at any location.

Direct marketing is an interactive marketing communication tool that uses one or more advertising media to effect a measurable response and/or transaction at any location. In addition, **direct marketing** uses a database—a customer file.[1] This definition has five key points.

First, direct marketing is an *interactive system*. That is, the prospective customer and marketer can engage in two-way communication. For instance, La Vie En Rose, a Quebec-based lingerie retailer, may send out a mail-order catalogue; the customer can respond by calling for more information, visiting the Web site, or even placing an order. Second, as part of the two-way communication, direct marketing always provides a means for the customer to respond. Because response is possible, the number and characteristics of those who do not respond have a strong impact on planning.

Third, direct marketing can occur any time and any place. The response does not require a retail store or a salesperson. Instead, the order can be made at any time of the day or night and can be delivered without the customer leaving home. In the case of La Vie En Rose, for example, customers can place an order by phone, fax, mail, or Internet and the item can be express-mailed to the customer without a store visit.

Fourth, direct marketing must have a measurable response—the direct marketer must be able to calculate precisely the costs of implementing the strategy and the resulting income. Its measurable response represents the primary benefit of direct marketing and is undoubtedly a reason for its recent growth in popularity.

Fifth, direct marketing requires a database of consumer information. Through the information in databases, the direct marketer can tailor communications targeted at prospective individual or business customers. The information also allows direct marketers to offer benefits to its consumers: convenience, efficiency, and time savings.

Strengths and Weaknesses of Direct Marketing

Many marketing communication activities are better done through direct marketing. To begin with, direct marketing is more targeted than indirect marketing. Direct marketers' ability to tailor a list of prospect names combining several characteristics—for instance, proven mail-order buyers who own VCR machines and take at least two ski vacations a year—allows them to carve out new market segments with profit potential.

Because direct marketers can find out so much more about their prospects and customers, direct marketing is able to address these people in very personal terms. Rather than men or women, marketing communicators can talk to old-movie buffs, duck hunters, and tennis players. Also, every dollar spent in direct marketing is measurable. Each call, mailing, and ad contains a call to action that can be counted. This makes direct marketers accountable for every dollar they spend.

Because direct marketers can generate firm numbers that measure the effectiveness of their efforts, it is possible for them to devise accurate head-to-head tests of offers, formats, prices, payment terms, creative approach, and much more—all in relatively small and affordable quantities.

Direct marketing is extremely flexible. This is especially true in direct mail, where there are few constraints on size, colour, timing, and format. Other than conformance to postal service standards, a direct-mail marketer can sell with a formula ranging from a postcard to a three-dimensional package.

Tremendous growth and poor early management created some problems in the direct-marketing industry. Many of the troubles are symptoms of managerial "nearsightedness"—failure to consider long-term goals and the organization as a whole. Examples of the short-term approach crop up daily in consumer mailboxes: mailings that look like telegrams, air-express packages, legal communications, or government documents. Short-term direct marketing can get a response, for a while, until customers become wary. But at what price? This kind of direct marketing creates short-term, disloyal customers who were really fooled into responding.

In contrast, Amex Canada spends thousands of dollars a year sending "love letters," communications that might typically congratulate customers on their tenth anniversary as card members. The objective of the communication is to reinforce a customer's relationship with Amex Canada over the long term. Thus, if done correctly, direct marketing can be an effective communication tool that has long-term benefits.

Direct marketing has weaknesses, then, in part because too many aren't using it correctly due to poor training. Companies that would not dream of running an ad in *Hardware Age* or another trade publication without getting professional help let their in-house trainee design their direct-mail piece. Unless direct marketers make the critical changes in strategy, media planning, and creative execution that direct marketing requires, they will fail.

Poorly executed direct marketing creates an environment of distrust. The personalization of direct marketing through sophisticated databases is a case in point. People pay attention when marketers call them by name, and they are flattered if marketers know a little bit about their needs, tastes, and preferences. However, people become upset if they think marketers know too much about them or if marketers seem to be misusing this personal information. The sponsor of such intrusive direct marketing will develop a poor image in the eyes of target audience members.

All too often, direct marketing does not mesh with a company's operations, its distribution systems, communications, research, overall strategy, or even its culture. For example, direct marketers have been part of programs that have failed because they are so successful: catalogue companies run out of inventories, costing them not only short-term sales but also long-term goodwill, or financial firms generate too many leads for their salespeople to follow up.

Another common weakness is direct-marketing messages that conflict with other marketing communication messages, especially advertising. Conflicting messages occur because the direct-response marketers are not integrated with other marketing communicators, such as those who do indirect advertising.

concept review

Strengths and Weaknesses of Direct Marketing

1. Direct marketing has the following strengths:
   - More targeted than other forms of marketing communication
   - Ability to personalize approach
   - Results are measurable
   - All elements of a direct-marketing piece are testable
   - Elements are extremely flexible
2. Several weaknesses of direct marketing follow:
   - Ineffective unless used as a long-term strategy
   - Poorly executed direct marketing creates distrust and a poor image
   - Failure to coordinate with operations, distribution, or corporate strategy can lead to decreased goodwill
   - Direct-marketing messages may conflict with other marketing communication messages

Direct Marketing and the Marketing Communication Mix

Direct marketing differs from other marketing communication tools. First, those who use direct marketing go straight to the customer, not to resellers or retailers, for product distribution. Companies such as Kraft Canada, Ford Canada, and Compaq, for instance, distribute their products through resellers (wholesalers and retailers) who make these companies' products available to customers. Direct marketers tend to skip resellers and contact customers directly. Some direct marketers, such as L.L. Bean, have retail stores, but those stores represent a very small part of their business.

Second, direct-marketing communication is designed to generate a response, not create awareness or enhance the company image. Most ads for Coca-Cola,

Levi's 501 Jeans, and Pert shampoo are not intended to cause an immediate change in behaviour. Known as awareness advertising, the primary purpose of such ads is to create and maintain brand awareness. Awareness ads reinforce the positive elements of the brand in consumers' minds and can deliver extra value through coupons, rebates, and sweepstakes.

In contrast, direct-marketing communication usually involves **direct-response advertising**, that is, advertising designed to motivate customers to respond with either an order or inquiry. Also, direct marketing communicates directly with customers through targeted media rather than mass media. Examples of such media include direct mail, telemarketing, and point-of-purchase displays.

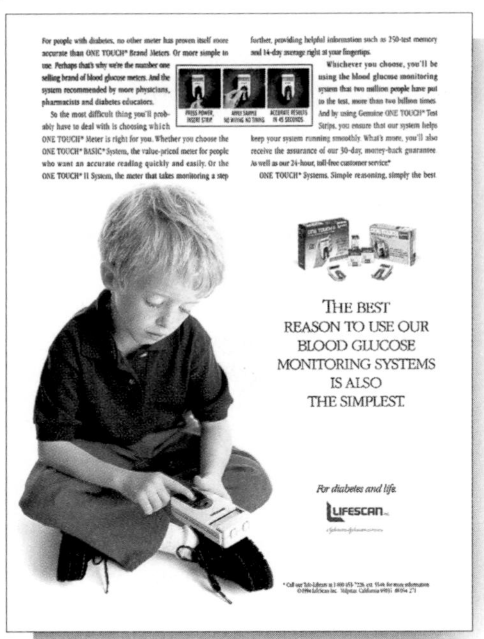

Here is an example of a direct-response ad designed to motivate a response—an inquiry about the product.

Direct marketing also differs from personal selling, a marketing communication tool often used to supplement indirect marketing efforts. Direct marketing does not rely on the sales force to spread the sales message. With indirect marketing, the sales force plays a pivotal role by informing and selling to resellers or end users. In contrast, direct marketing primarily relies on media, not a salesperson, to generate a sales lead. It is critical, then, that the direct-marketing piece—such as an ad that contains a toll-free number, a Web site that offers an e-mail response feature, or a letter that includes a blank order form—contains all the necessary information for the customer to respond.

In direct marketing the message communicated in nonpersonal media makes a measurable contribution to selling. Salespeople, however, are often necessary to complete the sale or provide information in response to inquiries triggered by the direct-mail piece.

The inclusion of an 800 number and other means of contact in this ad provides solid sales leads for this product.

For example, the advertisement for Commport Communications contains a toll-free number to call for further information and to subscribe to the publication. Salespeople, then, receive the calls and sign up interested educators. This type of direct-marketing advertising has become the primary lead-generating device for many sales forces.

A final difference between direct and indirect marketing is the ease with which various elements of the media piece can be tested. Because direct marketing leads directly to sales rather than recall or attitude change (typical goals of indirect marketing), manipulating an 800 number, a special discount, or a product featured as part of the direct-marketing communication piece can be quickly noted. As a result, elements that are not working can be readily changed.

Table 12.1 summarizes how direct marketing differs from other marketing communication tools that rely on indirect marketing.

THE STATE OF THE INDUSTRY

The origin of direct marketing goes back many years. Orvis issued its first catalogue, offering fishing equipment, in 1844. Sears entered the field in 1886,

Direct-response advertising
Advertising designed to motivate customers to respond with either an order or an inquiry.

Canadian Marketing Association
www.cdma.org

and in the early 1900s L.L. Bean arrived on the scene. It was after World War II, however, that magazines turned to the mail as the battleground for their mass-circulation wars, and direct mail entered a period of rapid growth and development.

To this day, information technology has spurred growth in direct marketing. Increasing power and decreasing cost of computers, and rapid growth in consumer usage of interactive technologies such as kiosks in retail outlets and the Internet enable businesses to collect and manage databases of information about consumers. This information allows companies to efficiently identify the most likely buyers, segment them, and target them directly. Today marketers can develop or buy sophisticated databases with relevant data about consumers' buying behaviour, lifestyle, names, addresses, and so forth. With these lists, marketers can personalize and vary communications.

According to John Gustavson, president of the Canadian Marketing Association (formally known as the Canadian Direct Marketing Association), most major marketers do some form of direct marketing today and will do even more information-based direct marketing in the future.[2] Rapid advances in

Table 12.1 KEY DIFFERENCES BETWEEN DIRECT MARKETING AND INDIRECT MARKETING

Indirect Marketing	Direct Marketing
Reaches a mass audience through mass media	Communicates directly with the customer or prospect through more targeted media
Communications are impersonal	Can personalize communications By name/title Variable messages
Promotional programs are highly visible to competition because mass media is used	Promotional programs (especially pretests) are relatively invisible to the competition
Amount of promotion controlled by size of budget	Size of budget can be determined by success of promotion
Desired action either unclear or delayed	Specific action always requested Inquiry Purchase
Incomplete/sample data for decision-making purposes Sales call reports Marketing research	Comprehensive database drives marketing programs
Analysis conducted at segment level	Analysis conducted at individual/firm level through personalization
Use surrogate variables to measure effectiveness Advertising awareness Intention to buy	Measurable, and therefore highly controllable

Source: Mary Lou Roberts and Paul D. Berger, *Direct Marketing Management* (Englewood Cliffs, N.J.: Prentice-Hall, 1989), 4. Reprinted by permission of Prentice-Hall, Inc.

This ad for Canada Post touts its ability to help harness the power of direct mail.

information technology could accelerate the growth in direct marketing beyond the already rapid 10 to 12 percent annual growth it enjoys today.

The integrative nature of direct marketing is another factor that could accelerate growth in the practice of direct marketing. Many marketing experts no longer view direct marketing as a discipline unto itself with a unique set of requirements. According to Bill Stanwick, director of corporate services marketing at Amex Canada, "We've experienced real integration throughout all we do . . . whether it's TV with direct response, whether it's posters, whether it's print, or whatever else. Giving customers an opportunity to contact us is a really important outcome of whatever marketing and promotion that we're doing."[3] Amex Canada is not alone. Direct marketing has become a well-integrated aspect of most sophisticated marketing communication plans.

In Canada, the direct marketing industry is well organized, as is indicated by the membership of the Canadian Marketing Association (CMA). The CMA represents information-based marketers, most of whom use direct marketing to reach consumers through media such as the Internet, television, telephone, radio, and addressed advertising mail. CMA has a membership of over 750 organizations and more than 3000 individual members. Its members account for over 80 percent of the annual $13.5 billion in information-based marketing sales in Canada. Corporate members include Canada's major financial institutions, insurance companies, publishers, cataloguers and charitable organizations, relationship marketers, and those engaged in electronic commerce and multimedia marketing.[4]

Types of Direct Marketing

Direct marketing can take three forms: the one-step process, the two-step process, and the negative option.

1. *One-step process.* The consumer responds to an ad in a media vehicle and receives the product by mail. A bounce-back brochure promoting related merchandise may be included with the product.
2. *Two-step process.* The potential customer must first be qualified before ordering the product. Insurance companies use the two-step process when they require a

physical exam before enforcing the policy. Similarly, a company selling high-ticket items, such as land or furniture, may require a preliminary credit check. Or a company may charge a fee for a catalogue of direct-mail merchandise; the fee can be used as credit toward purchases.

3. *Negative option*. The customer joins a plan such as those offered by music or book clubs to automatically receive unrequested merchandise at regular intervals. The initial merchandise is often offered with a free gift or at a discount price.

The Process of Direct Marketing

Direct marketing uses the planning framework suggested throughout this text. It is unique, however, because its primary objectives are sales-related, and it relies heavily on a high-quality database. It also uses special media to deliver messages and employ a unique creative approach. Finally, there is a reliance on a fulfilment company to deliver the product to the customer. The primary components of the direct-marketing process are shown in Figure 12.1. The material addressed in the following sections applies to direct marketing only.

The Database: A Key to Success

Databases
Files of information that include names, addresses, telephone numbers, e-mail addresses, and demographic and buying-behaviour data.

Database marketing
The process of building, maintaining, and using customer databases for the purpose of contacting customers and transacting business.

The *database* is the essence of direct marketing. A **database** contains information about customers and prospects that has been collected over a considerable time.

Database marketing is the process of building, maintaining, and using customer databases for the purpose of contacting customers and transacting business. Typically, a company can expect to invest anywhere from $100 000 to several millions of dollars to build and implement a marketing database.

Most databases are not designed exclusively for marketing but perform several functions within an organization. Although a computer is not required, practically speaking, it is impossible to effectively maintain a database of useful size without one. As an example of questions to ask to build a customer database, Figure 12.2 displays a questionnaire that could be used by a clothing retailer to collect internal data.

In the sections that follow, we explore how companies develop, maintain, and use a database.

Developing the Database

Mailing list
A list of customer or prospect names, addresses, phone and fax numbers, and e-mail addresses if available.

Obtaining a mailing list is the first step toward establishing a database. A **mailing list** is a list of customer or prospect names, addresses, phone and fax numbers, and e-mail addresses if available. It does not contain any behavioural information, such as purchasing history. The mailing list can be generated internally (through warranty cards, for example) or purchased externally. Once the direct marketer obtains a list, managing the database system involves five additional steps:

1. *Capture, organize, and maintain existing marketing data*. Companies buy or develop mailing lists and continually add to the basic data to keep it current.
2. *Convert the data into useful information that has possible application to company strategies*. Suppose Toyota maintained a database of detailed information about Toyota car users. If this year the company hopes to increase sales of a new version of the Camry, Toyota's direct marketers could sort the database

Figure 12.1 THE PROCESS OF DIRECT MARKETING

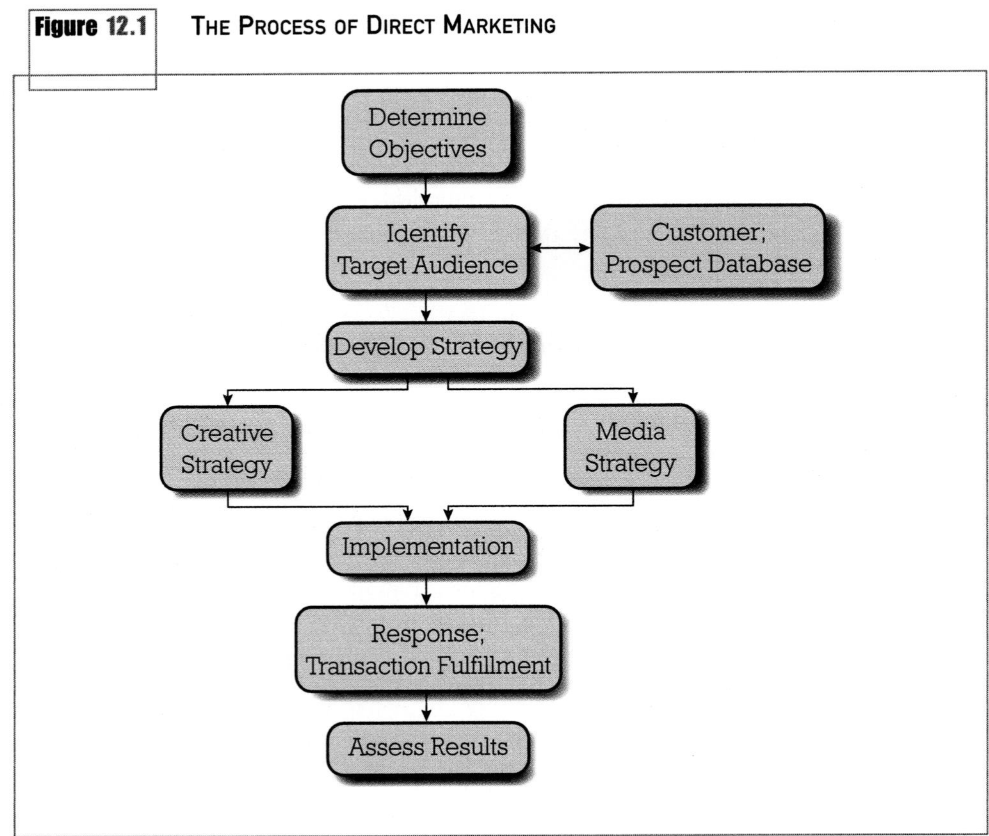

Figure 12.2 PREFERRED CUSTOMER FORM

PREFERRED CUSTOMER

Name ______________________________ Nickname ________
FIRST MIDDLE INITIAL LAST

Home Address ______________________________

City ____________________ Province __________ Postal Code ________

Office Phone ____________________ Home Phone ____________________

Suit __________ ☐ Short ☐ Regular ☐ Long ☐ Extra Long

Trouser Waist________ Shoes ________ Are you married? ☐ Yes ☐ No

Shirt Neck________ Sleeve ________ Spouse's name ____________________

Sweater ________ So Shirt ________ Your birthday Month ______ Day ______

FOR OFFICE USE ONLY

?? to ______ Salutator ______________________________ Date ______

concept review

The World of Direct Marketing

1. Direct marketing is an interactive system of marketing that uses advertising media to effect a measurable response or transaction at any location. Every direct-marketing system must have a database.
2. Direct marketing differs from indirect marketing in the following ways:
   - It skips resellers and retailers; direct marketers contact customers directly for product distribution.
   - It relies on direct-response advertising rather than awareness advertising.
   - It communicates through targeted media rather than mass media.
   - It does not rely on a salesperson to generate sales leads, relying instead on customer response to media for those leads.
3. Due to improved information technology, and the integrative nature of direct marketing, the practice of direct marketing continues to grow in popularity.
4. The three types of direct marketing are one-step, two-step, and negative option.

information into a list of satisfied Camry owners with cars over five years of age as a target market for the new version.

3. *Apply the database to specific strategies*. The satisfied Camry owner list could then be converted to a mailing list for a direct-mail piece on the new version of the Camry that offers a rebate.
4. *Test results*. Direct marketers have the opportunity to test the wording, design, and message in the direct-mail piece before sending it out to the target market. Toyota could test the direct-mail piece with select customers for feedback. Ultimately, sales of Camrys would be the measure of success.
5. *Capture new data and integrate it into the existing database*. Camry buyers would be surveyed six months after purchase to assess their level of satisfaction and response to specific features.

Companies may develop their database internally or externally, or use a combination of internal and external means. Internal, or in-house, databases are derived from customer receipts, credit card information, or personal information cards completed by customers. The internal approach is cost-effective as long as the company has the expertise and resources.

Many companies have neither the resources nor the expertise to develop in-house database systems. These companies can obtain commercial databases from firms whose sole purpose is to collect, analyse, categorize, and market an enormous variety of detail about the consumer. From such information as income, education, occupation, and census data, their databases can describe life in individual neighbourhoods across Canada with amazing accuracy.

Maintaining the Database with RFM

RFM
The recency, frequency, and monetrary value of purchases.

Direct marketers continuously refine their databases with information on the **RFM**—the recency, frequency, and monetary value of purchases. Other relevant information that marketers need to maintain a useful database includes the method of customer payment, where they live, what they purchase, how long they have been customers, and their last date of purchase. Each company must consider its own needs when developing its database, given the objective of finding the most profitable customers and prospects.

Building Relationships Through CLV

Database marketing is most effective if it focuses on building relationships. In database marketing the customer lifetime value (CLV) approach is the equivalent of relationship marketing. The CLV approach recognizes that a new customer means not only an immediate sale but also additional purchases over the customer's lifetime as a user of your product.

Generally, direct-marketing CLV works best when the target market has the means to respond, and the provider supplies sufficient benefits to customers to make it worth their while to respond. The responses can then be measured. The CLV approach requires product research, satisfaction surveys, and personal information to ensure that the target market has both the means and motivation to respond. As indicated in the You Decide feature, direct marketers should adhere to the CMA's guideline code of ethics when collecting personal information from children.

Global Database Management

Before the 1990s database marketing was much more prevalent in Canada and the United States than in the rest of the world. Advances in technology and the growing globalization of marketing operations, however, have spurred growth in database marketing in Europe, Asia, and South America. However, differing cultures around the world may require companies to implement global database-marketing methods that are sensitive to others' cultures. Europeans, for instance, tend to distrust organizations that collect and sell personal information, and several countries have passed privacy laws prohibiting such practices. Asians tend to rely on product quality and reputation in their purchasing decisions. Once they try and are satisfied with a particular product, they are often very brand loyal. This tendency suggests that marketers should use database technology to improve relationships with existing customers rather than to constantly prospect for new, one-time buyers.

Designing a Direct-Marketing Strategy

The direct-marketing strategy details the events and methods needed to complete an objective. It includes decisions in five areas: (1) the offer, (2) the medium, (3) the message, (4) timing and sequencing, and (5) customer service.

The Offer

The proposition made to customers is often referred to as the offer. It is the key to success or failure, and the manner in which it is presented can have a dramatic effect. The offer's message and design should be supported by comprehensive research. When creating an offer, managers must consider numerous factors. Some factors include price of the product, who pays the cost of shipping and handling, what product options to offer, how to motivate customers (greed, fear, goodwill), and how to make it easy for the consumer to respond (for example, use of a toll-free number or postage-paid envelope).

To begin with, there is a price. The correct price must not only include a sufficient markup but also reflect what competitors are charging and what

Tracking Kids Online

A recent study by the Center for Media Education in Washington, D.C. chose 80 of the most popular kids sites to analyse. Of the sites reviewed, which included such well-known brand names as Lego, Crayola, and Barbie, it found that 88 percent collected some kind of personal identification, and 52 sites (74 percent) neglected to obtain parental consent.

It seems, however, that Canadian marketers are much more cautious in their collection of data from children. For example, Irwin Toys of Toronto has a Web site that offers kids the chance to adopt a virtual pet. The site doesn't ask for personal information, and that, says president George Irwin, is as close as the company gets to direct marketing to kids. Lynne DeCew, general manager of Imagination Youth Marketing at Palmer Jarvis DDB in Vancouver, says the agency doesn't do any direct marketing to kids, period. According to DeCew, "The marketplace is very sensitive about the trading of information on children . . . and the other thing preventing many people from investing heavily in database marketing to kids is that while kids are certainly spending a lot in total, their purchases are fairly small. It's not economically viable to send a candy purchaser or a beanie baby purchaser an expensive direct-mail piece."

Concerned with the sheer number of children interacting directly with marketers, the Canadian Marketing Association (CMA) recently amended its guideline code of ethics for Internet marketing to children. The new guidelines define the age of a child as under age 13, raise the level of privacy protection for children, and provide marketers with direction in the areas of marketing language and commercial transactions. The CMA guideline code of ethics highlights the following:

- CMA members will now be required to obtain positive consent from a child's parent or guardian before collecting, retaining, or transferring a child's personal information;
- Language used in marketing directed to children must be clear and simple and take into account a child's inexperience;
- If conducting games, contests, or sweepstakes for children, marketers must have parental consent, unless they are collecting minimal personal information sufficient to determine the winner, deal only with the parents, don't keep the personal information at the end of the contest, make no other use of the information, and do not transfer it to other organizations or individuals.

You Decide

1. As a direct marketer, would you support the recent amendments to the Canadian Marketing Association's code of ethics for Internet marketing to children? Would you recommend further amendments? Explain.
2. Now assume that you are the director of communications for a children's hospital. A direct marketing firm has offered thousands of dollars for the database you maintain of those children cared for at your hospital. By accepting the money for selling your database, you can afford to purchase much-needed medical equipment. However, you're worried about the ethical issues. What are the ethical issues?

Sources: Eve Lazarus, "Tracking Kids Online," ***Marketing***, (October 18, 1999), 20; Eve Lazarus, "Rules Require Parents' Consent," ***Marketing***, (October 18, 1999), 20.

consumers expect to pay. Odd-pricing (for example, $7.95), multiple unit pricing (such as two for $29.95), and giveaways (for example, $49.95 plus free steak knives) are common pricing strategies in direct marketing. The components of the price should be stated clearly and concisely.

The cost of *shipping and handling* can be an important part of the offer. Who should pay these costs? Can they be added to the base price of the product without adversely affecting sales? Increases in postal rates have shifted this cost burden to consumers in several instances.

Optional features are part of the basic offer. Special colours and sizes, personalization, or large-type editions are a few examples. Certain options can dramatically increase sales, whereas others prove unappealing. This is an area in which research is very important.

Many offers contain a *future obligation*. Book clubs and music clubs are two industries that normally ask for a one- or two-year commitment. The system of sending products at regular intervals and billing automatically allows the marketer to charge a very low price for the first order, knowing there will be a long-term payout. The availability of credit may be the most important element of an offer. Research indicates that if either commercial credit (such as Visa or MasterCard) or house credit (for example, an installment plan) is available, the average order size increases 15 percent.

Extra *incentives*, such as free gifts, discounts, sweepstakes, and toll-free ordering privileges, can all increase the attractiveness of an offer. Yet there is also the risk that the customer will have little interest in the incentive or, more important, that the cost of the incentive will inflate the price.

Time and quantity limits create an urgency in the mind of the customer. Suggesting that an offer will end on a certain date or that a product is a limited edition moves the prospect to action. It is important that the time or quantity limits be legitimate. Limits that are repeatedly extended quickly lose their impact.

The *guarantee* is an automatic part of any direct-marketing offer. Whenever people order products by phone, mail, or Internet, they perceive risk. They must be assured that they can back out of a mistake. Sometimes there is a "guaranteed buy-back" offer. Some guarantees even pay "double your money back." The free issue wording says simply: I may cancel my reservation after looking at the premier issue.

The Medium and the Message

The choice of medium and the choice of the message are related decisions. The message strategies should consider the needs of the target audience, the company's objectives, and factors such as repetition, memorability, and clutter discussed in Chapter 8. The writing must grab attention through content and design. The media used in direct marketing have been specially developed to accommodate the unique advantages of direct marketing. More will be said about direct-marketing media later in this chapter.

Direct marketing requires that the writing and visuals grab attention. This ad uses content, an interesting design, and strong copy to arouse readers' interest

Timing and Sequencing

One difference with direct marketing is the emphasis on the timing and sequencing of the direct-marketing pieces. For example, when should a prospect receive a Christmas catalogue or a direct-mail piece? Should the direct-mail piece be followed by telemarketing? Direct marketing must reach the right person at the right time. Direct-marketing experts estimate that 70 percent of the success of direct marketing is contingent on making the correct timing and sequencing decisions.[5] Much of this success depends on the quality of the database and the research behind it.

Customer Service

In direct marketing the importance of service cannot be overstated. The types of customer services offered—toll-free telephone numbers, free limited-time trial, acceptance of several credit cards, and a Web site, for example—are important techniques to motivate consumers to buy via direct-response media. The level of service is equally important. Speed and accuracy in filling orders, careful handling of customer complaints, and guaranteed return policies have been critical to the success of direct marketers such as J. Crew and L.L. Bean.

EVALUATING DIRECT MARKETING

Direct marketing is the most measurable element in the marketing communication mix. The basic philosophy of direct marketing is quite simple: There is no reason to invest resources in a direct-marketing program unless it has a high probability of success. In general, direct marketers evaluate profitability and customer characteristics and response. As indicated in this chapter's CBC Video Vignette, direct marketers cannot afford to extend marketing communications to customers who offer little prospect of profitability.

PROFITABILITY ANALYSIS

The bottom line for direct marketing is profitability. Every decision considers how much profit the direct-marketing campaign will generate. If sufficient, the company will proceed with the activity. Essentially, costs and potential revenues are projected for each activity, and a return-on-investment is calculated.

CUSTOMER CHARACTERISTICS AND RESPONSE

Direct marketers not only want to know if their messages are reaching the right people at the right time, they also want to know if any of the people are responding. Three techniques are used in direct marketing to make this type of assessment: respondent/nonrespondent surveys, tracking studies, and geodemography.[6]

Respondent/nonrespondent survey
This type of survey attempts to identify differences between those who did and those who did not respond to the direct-marketing program.

RESPONDENT/NONRESPONDENT SURVEYS. As the term suggests, **respondent/ nonrespondent surveys** attempt to identify differences between people who did and did not respond to the direct-marketing program. Because the marketer has a list of both respondents and nonrespondents, this technique entails a follow-up survey by telephone or mail to identify the demographic and psychographic characteristics of both groups and the reasons why they did or did not respond. This information serves as a guide for offering products in the future, for modifying the language in a direct-marketing piece, or for modifying the database.

Tracking study
Survey that gathers information from a large number of people by simply counting responses over time and collecting some information from a sample of respondents.

TRACKING STUDIES. **Tracking studies** are usually surveys that gather information from a large number of people by simply counting responses over time and collecting some information from a sample of respondents. The purpose is to assess whether purchase patterns and/or purchasers change over time.

Geodemography
Analyses an existing database on the principle that people who live together in small geographic areas such as blocks and postal-code units tend to share more demographic characteristics than people who live elsewhere.

GEODEMOGRAPHY. This useful technique evolved during the last decade. **Geodemography** analyses an existing database on the principle that birds of a feather flock together. That is, people who live together in small geographic areas such as blocks and postal-code units tend to have more similar demographic characteristics than people who live elsewhere. One system, PRIZM, has given its clusters colourful names such as "Blueblood Estates" and "Bunker's Neighbourhood." Geodemographic systems can track the demographic quality

concept review

The Process of Direct Marketing

1. Database marketing is the process of building, maintaining, and using customer databases for the purpose of contacting customers and transacting business.
2. To manage a database, companies must:
   - Obtain a list of customers or potential customers.
   - Capture, organize, and maintain the existing marketing data.
   - Convert the data into useful information that has possible application to company strategies.
   - Apply the database to specific strategies.
   - Test the direct-mail piece before sending it out to the target market.
   - Capture new data and integrate it into the existing database.
3. Marketers design a direct-marketing strategy by focusing on five components: the offer, the medium, the message, timing and sequencing, and customer service.
4. Marketers use several techniques to evaluate direct marketing, including analysing profitability and assessing response.

of respondents or conduct automatic respondent/nonrespondent studies, using only addresses as resources.

Direct-Marketing Media Tools

Direct marketers use many media tools. The four most common direct media are (1) direct mail, (2) catalogues, (3) mass-media direct marketing, and (4) telemarketing.

Direct Mail

Canada Post
www.mailposte.ca

Direct mail delivers the message and the product through Canada Post or a private delivery organization. Direct mail has been used to generate orders, presell activities before a field salesperson's visit, qualify prospects for a product, follow up a sale, announce special sales in local areas, and raise funds for nonprofit groups.

A number of advantages are associated with direct mail as compared with traditional mass media. First, the medium offers a variety of formats and provides enough space to tell a complete sales story. Second, it is now possible to personalize direct mail across a number of characteristics, such as name, product usage, and income. Finally, direct mail allows the marketer to reach audiences who are inaccessible by other media.

The primary drawback of using direct mail is the widespread perception that it is junk mail. A second disadvantage of direct mail is the high cost per prospect reached. However, a direct-mail campaign may still be less expensive than trying to reach a particular target group through other media. A final drawback is the emergence of new technologies that do the same thing as direct mail. Fax machines are one option. E-mail and voice mail have also emerged as substitutes for direct mail. E-mail is a growing new media for direct marketing. Marketers now send sales announcements, offers, and other messages to e-mail addresses, sometimes to a few individuals, sometimes to large groups. Some marketers have programs that dial a large number of telephone numbers and leave a voice-mail sales message.

As this ad implies, companies such as The Dun & Bradstreet Corp. have become important list providers.

Compiled lists

These lists identify people who share some common interest such as skiing, retirement housing, or gourmet cooking.

Lists

To successfully solicit customer orders, managers need accurate and up-to-date lists. Ideally, the lists should include only those who are in a position to purchase. For example, internal lists should include information such as how customers paid, where they live, what they purchase, how long they have been customers, and when they bought last. External lists can be of several types. **Compiled lists** identify people who share some common interest, such as snow skiing, retirement housing, or gourmet cooking. Lists of inquiry or lists of customers from other companies are provided by both competing and noncompeting companies. Each of these categories can be further refined until the marketer specifies just one characteristic, for example, income or telephone exchange.

Direct-Mail Packages

Everything in a direct-mail package must be designed to work in harmony. The package must stand out from other mail and encourage the receiver to open it. The components of the package should reflect a total design concept. The classic direct-mail package consists of a mailing envelope, letter, circular, response device, and return device.[7]

- *Mailing envelope*: The direct-mail selling process begins with the mailing envelope. Teaser copy of a "flash" (for example, "important, don't delay!") is often used to arouse interest and lead the reader to open the envelope.
- *The letter:* The letter should be personalized, speak to the self-interest of the reader, and elicit interest.
- *The circular*: The circular gives the details of the product—the specifications, colour, pricing, photographs, guarantees, and endorsements. It presents the primary selling message and can take the form of a booklet, broadsheet (an oversized enclosure or jumbo folder), brochure, flyer, or single sheet.
- *Response device*: The response device is the order form, often including a toll-free phone number. It should summarize the primary selling points and be simple to read and fill out.
- *Return device:* This item allows the customer to return the necessary information. It can be an information request form, an order form, or a payment.

Writing Direct-Mail Copy

To write good copy, the direct-mail copywriter needs valid information about the producer, the customer, and competitors. The direct-mail copywriter must know why people buy. Good copy translates selling points into benefits, emphasizes the buyer's self-gratification, and uses crisp, clear language. The offer must be stated immediately and emphatically. Moreover, the writer must convince the customer that what is promised will be delivered. Finally, good copy makes it easy to take the desired action. Requested action should be simple, specific, and immediate.

The large amount of copy space available in direct mail as compared with mass print media presents a temptation as well as an opportunity. There is a tendency to include excess material and use ultracreative formats. But the objective of direct mail is to sell, not to impress. Each word and picture must support that objective.[8] A direct-mail program must often be modified to effectively communicate with different target audiences, as demonstrated in the IMC in Action feature.

Finally, business-to-business direct response and advertising specialist Alan Sharpe lists the eight most common direct-mail mistakes:[9]

1. Wrong list
2. No testing
3. No offer
4. Starting with you, not me
5. Slow in getting to the point
6. Poor follow-up
7. No time limit
8. No call to action

Retail catalogues
Contain merchandise equivalent to that found in the sponsors' stores.

Full-line merchandise catalogue
Contains all the merchandise found in a complete department store plus other products such as appliances and home-related remodelling and installation materials.

Business-to-business catalogues
Contain products that are sold from one business to another to reduce the costs associated with personal selling.

Consumer specialty catalogues
Contain a line of related products that are sent only to those consumers considered potential customers.

CATALOGUES

Catalogues have changed dramatically over the last century. Born out of the need to provide products to people living in isolated locations, the catalogue has become a shopping and purchase vehicle used by virtually all consumers—employed women in particular. Strapped for time, the modern consumer now accepts catalogues as a reliable and trustworthy alternative for the purchase of all types of products, from doormats to computers to trips around the world.

Catalogue developers use sophisticated marketing tools. With the availability of accurate mailing lists, catalogues have become more specialized, both in terms of products carried and consumers targeted. For instance, Sears Canada has begun to distribute well-targeted, cost-effective catalogues in order to face the competition it has been experiencing from the thousands of specialty retailers that aim their catalogues at market niches.

There are four general types of catalogues. **Retail catalogues** contain merchandise equivalent to that found in the sponsors' stores. The intent is to build both store traffic and mail-order sales. **Full-line merchandise catalogues** contain all the merchandise found in a complete department store, plus other products such as appliances and home-related remodeling and installation materials. The Sears catalogue is such a catalogue. **Business-to-business catalogues** contain products that are sold from one business to another to reduce the costs associated with personal selling. Office-supply stores are an example. And finally, **consumer specialty catalogues** contain a line of related products that are sent only to those consumers considered potential customers. For instance, the La Vie En Rose catalogue of lingerie is a consumer specialty catalogue.

Direct Mail to Asian-Canadians

The direct-marketing industry has the ability to target a universe of potential buyers and to customize its messages to a specific culture. Direct mail, then, would seem to be an effective marketing vehicle to Asian-Canadians. Here are some pointers for targeting Asian-Canadians through direct mail. First, learn as much as possible about each distinct Asian-Canadian demographic group in your target market. Second, become thoroughly familiar with their similarities and differences. Language and cultural ties are two of the most important concerns to examine.

Language

- Deliver the marketing message in both English and the native language of the target market. Purchasing decisions in Asian-Canadian homes often involve a bilingual dynamic, so a marketing message in both languages helps reach more of your market.
- Use both English and the native language on the outside of a direct- mail piece. The use of both languages will help break through clutter and increase the chances that a prospect will open the piece.
- Allow prospects to respond in either language. To encourage prospects to make further contact with marketers, remove inhibitions about calling a toll-free number, receiving a sales call, or responding to follow-ups by assuring the market they may respond in the language with which they are most comfortable.

Culture

- Associate the marketing message with traditional symbols, images, and other cultural references. Asian-Canadians have a high regard for their traditions. Traditional symbols and design elements have a high recognition level and will add positive associations to the message.
- If the design includes traditional symbols and elements, ensure that the design is distinctive and tasteful. The distinctive appeal to tradition will separate packages from the "junk mail" category, encouraging prospects to open and read the package. A poorly executed design, however, may offend and result in the package being discarded.
- Traditional Asian holiday and gift-giving occasions should be incorporated into the marketing strategy, with mailings timed accordingly.
- Tie promotions to festivals, celebrations, and other cultural events.

To reach this diverse audience, marketers must do their homework. The effort, however, can be well worth it.

Food for Thought

1. Find an ad that features or targets Asian-Canadians. Evaluate how well it adheres to these suggestions.
2. Now assume you were trying to target Italians in Quebec. How many of the ideas presented in this feature could you apply to target that market?

Everything in a catalogue must make a harmonious contribution to the whole. The cover must immediately attract the prospect's attention. The photography must generate interest. The copy should be easy to read, highly descriptive, and concise yet comprehensive. The merchandise selected for sales must create an optimum mix in terms of quality and depth. The order form should be easy to follow and fill out. Finally, the shipping charges should be consistent with the values of the product. For example, shipping charges of $3.75 on a $5.00 item are out of line.

Undoubtedly, the most important change occurring in the catalogue industry is the emergence of online services, the Internet, as well as other interactive media including CD-ROM and fax-back services. Most catalogue marketers currently have their own home page and are developing the ability to create a different catalogue for each customer they service. Although the adoption of this technology by the catalogue industry is still in its infancy, expertise is quickly being developed.

Mass-Media Direct Marketing

Print, television, radio, and the Internet offer another form of direct-response marketing. The fact that mass media are already classified by demographic and geographic characteristics means that direct-marketing messages can be targeted at certain geographic areas, market segments, or market areas with a history of higher response rates. Direct marketers must weigh the benefit of specific targeting against several disadvantages of using mass media. Unlike direct mail and catalogues, mass media impose time and space limitations on the advertiser. Appeals carried in mass media must compete with the editorial or program content and other ads. And extremely high costs are associated with mass media.

Because earlier discussion considered only these media and the guidelines for effectively creating ads in each, only considerations unique to direct marketing will be discussed here.

Using Print

Print ads can carry a direct-marketing appeal by simply providing information about the product and an order form or a toll-free number for ordering it directly from the manufacturer. The copy tends to be direct and concise with little emotionalism and few claims. There must be a "call to action." If the reader is not asked to order the product, then the copy should cite other actions—filling out a coupon or calling a number, for instance. The copy should be benefit-oriented, and the design should lead the reader through the ad in logical order. Sufficient space for address information and signature should be provided on the order blank. The terms of the offer, including price, must also be clearly stated. The order form should be keyed or coded so marketers can determine the origin of incoming customer orders or inquiries. The key or code is the most important part of the order card because it indicates the source of sales.

Magazine insert
A multipage piece or a reply card bound next to a full-page ad.

Bingo card
Appear in the back of magazines and give consumers an easy way to request information on products and services. The publisher prints a designated number for specified literature, and the consumer circles the number of the desired information.

Newspaper insert
Single-page, direct-marketing pieces, multipage booklets, perforated coupons, or gummed reply envelopes.

In addition to the standard full-page or partial-page formats, other print ad formats are available. A **magazine insert**, for example, can be a multipage piece or a reply card bound next to a full-page ad. **Bingo cards** appear in the back of magazines and give consumers an easy way to request information on products and services. The publisher prints a designated number for specified literature, and the consumer circles the number of the desired information. **Newspaper inserts** include single-page direct-marketing pieces, multipage booklets, perforated coupons, or gummed reply envelopes.

Thanks to new technology, magazines now have some of the same advantages offered by direct mail. Specifically, magazines now offer: (1) selective binding—a computerized binding method to target audience segments with two, three, four, or more ad choices; (2) ink-jet printing—a computerized binding process that can customize individual messages to every subscriber.

Using Television and Radio

Television is well suited to demonstrating a direct marketer's product. Television is used in three major ways: to sell a product or service, to generate leads for a product or service, and to support direct-response advertising in other media (for instance, Publishers' Clearing House). Marketers provide viewers with toll-free numbers to generate immediate response. In direct-marketing television commercials, at least one-fourth of the broadcast time is devoted to ordering information.

Cable television has become the primary broadcast medium for many direct marketers. It is less expensive, more targeted, and allows longer messages than

Home shopping on television is booming. Produce demonstration as well as price. order, and inventory information are all provided in an entertaining way in the comfort of the living room.

Home shopping channel
A television show that presents items for sale, gives the price, and explains how to order.

television. Cable has produced two special forms of direct-message delivery systems. The first is the various types of **home shopping channels,** in which viewers can watch programs that present items for sale, give the price, and explain how to order the item.

Infomercials are the second type of direct-marketing cable delivery system. An infomercial is a "documentary-style" 30- to 60-minute commercial. This format has been criticized because the ads are often written in a manner that makes them sound like regular programming.

Air and production costs are far lower for direct-radio response than for television. Direct radio can be scheduled quickly and, if live, can be revised at the last minute. Radio is also more efficient than television in attracting particular types of listeners. Radio has its own limitations, however, including the lack of visualization and the fact that many listeners are otherwise engaged when hearing the ad. Because listeners often do not have a pencil and paper handy, the response must be easy to remember.

Using the Internet

Despite the relative uncertainty associated with the profitability of this interactive online medium, companies are spending millions of dollars to become players in cyberspace. This trend is likely to continue because often a consumer's first research into a company involves a Web site visit. Although the percentage of Canadian companies that have a Web site is growing, up to 75 percent of Canadian businesses do not have a Web site.[10] The growing number of Internet users are discovering that it allows them to send e-mail, exchange views, research, and shop for products. It also gives direct marketers the chance to reach consumers around the world.

Direct marketers can use the Internet in four ways: create an electronic storefront; place direct-response ads online; participate in forums, newsgroups,

This ad for nGage Electronics Commerce touts its ability to manage the entire online sales process for prospective clients wanting to sell on the Web.

Dell Computers
www.dell.ca

Norstar Mall.ca
www.norstarmall.ca

ShopNow.com
www.shopnow.com

and bulletin boards; and communicate via e-mail. For example, if a person types in Dell's home page address, Dell's home page appears in full colour. It offers several options, including descriptions of its products and Web site solutions, and access to sales and service. The key is to entice browsers to visit and then respond to the company's home page. Web shopping malls are indexes of many product and service providers. Consumer or business shoppers can visit the malls, search via product or service, and link to a company's electric storefront. The shopper can browse offerings and choose the service or product with the click of a mouse. Two examples of shopping malls include the NorstarMall.ca Inc. and Shop Now.com Inc.

Companies such as Budget Car and Truck Rental can place a direct-response ad online with a commercial online service provider: "Rent a car from Budget and get up to 2 days free!" Bulletin board systems (BBSs) are specialized online services that focus on a specific topic or group. Thus, a ski equipment manufacturer might want to participate in a BBS that enjoys "extreme skiing." Finally, a company can encourage prospects and customers to send questions, suggestions, information, and even complaints to the company, using the company's e-mail address.

The mall directory page for the NorstarMall represents one form of online media.

TELEMARKETING

Another marketing medium is *telemarketing*, which is a direct-marketing technique that combines telecommunications technology, marketing strategies, and information systems. It can be used alone or in conjunction with advertising, direct mail, sales promotions, personal selling, and other marketing communication functions.

There are two types of telemarketing: inbound and outbound. An inbound, or incoming, telemarketing call originates with the customer. Calls originating with the firm are outgoing, or outbound.

Inbound calls are customer responses to a marketer's stimulus, whether a direct-mail piece, a direct-marketing broadcast, a catalogue, or a published toll-free number. Because it is almost impossible to schedule customer calls, every effort must be made to ensure that the lines are not blocked. Having numerous lines is costly, however.

Although most inbound telemarketing occurs via toll-free 800 and 888 numbers, the 900 number has also grown in popularity. Media and entertainment companies have been in the forefront of promoting via 900 numbers. For example, Phone Programs created a 900 program to promote HBO's *Tales from the Crypt* horror show. For two dollars callers heard elaborate sound effects and answered horror trivia questions for a chance to win prizes.[11]

Outbound telemarketing is used by direct marketers whenever they take the initiative for a call—for opening new accounts, qualifying, selling, scheduling, servicing, or profiling customers. Wide Area Telephone Service (WATS) is often used as an economic long-distance vehicle. Outbound telemarketing is generally most efficient if the call is directed to a prospect who has been prequalified in some way, because the cost per telephone call is quite high.

Olan Mills Studies
www.olanmills.com

Telemarketing has four main applications: order-taking, customer service, sales support, and account management. Order-taking is the traditional use and also an excellent means of possible cross-selling. Olan Mills Studios uses more than 9000 local telemarketers to sell photograph packages, frames, and related items, with a response rate of three percent. Customer service usually means handling complaints or initiating cross-selling opportunities by informing customers of new features, models, or accessories. To provide sales support for the field sales force, telemarketers schedule sales calls, confirm appointments, maintain supplies, make credit checks, and sell marginal accounts. Account management replaces the personal contact with customers. If well planned, telemarketing sales specialists can maintain an ongoing relationship with certain customers.

Telemarketing is a viable marketing communication tool, but it must be carefully planned and guided by experts. Although the supposed benefit of telemarketing is cost savings because of its ability to segment the market, it is not cheap. Telephone calls range from three dollars to five dollars for consumer market calls and from six dollars to ten dollars for business market calls. Cost-efficient results will be attained only if the prospect list is targeted and the telephone is not used for random attempts.[12]

concept review

Direct-Marketing Media Tools

There are several types of direct-marketing tools:

1. Direct mail delivers the message and product through the postal service or a private delivery service. Its success is based on the quality of the lists, the package, and the copy.
2. Catalogues fall into one of four categories: retail, full-line merchandise, business-to-business, and consumer specialty.
3. Mass media used by direct marketing include print, television and radio, and the Internet.
4. Telemarketing includes inbound and outbound calls.

Janice MacPherson

CEO—The Net Idea Telecommunications Inc.

Web: http://www.netidea.com

As CEO of a regional Canadian Internet service provider (ISP), Janice MacPherson is responsible for the overall operations of the business as well as strategic planning and product innovation.

The Net Idea, founded in 1995, is the leading Internet service provider in the West Kootenays of British Columbia. Operated with headquarters in Nelson, the company offers Internet services throughout the West Kootenays. Being a local business with a reputation for quality customer service and innovation allows The Net Idea to successfully compete against national ISPs on a regional scale.

The Net Idea has two divisions: Internet Access and E-business. For four years the main focus of the company was on the Internet access market. As more businesses have come on-line, the need for E-business solutions found its way as a new service for the Net Idea.

With the Internet access division, Janice's main responsibilities are on new products, new pricing, branding and customer service. In the Kootenays, the Net Idea has become a household name for high-speed access and excellent customer service. The customer-care representatives are knowledgeable and friendly, and ensure that customers receive the "human touch."

E-business is the newest division for the Net Idea and is where creativity becomes an art form. Janice heads a team of programmers and creative designers who consult with clients and offer the best solutions for each. Whether consulting on on-line business plans or creating dynamic database solutions that integrate with the client's current business structure, her team continually demonstrates that the possibilities for small and medium-sized business are limitless.

Academic Background

Janice received a Bachelor of Business Administration degree from the University of New Brunswick in 1992, graduating with honours. During her term at university, she was heavily involved in AIESEC, an international business and economic students' association where she held the position of VP Marketing during her final year.

Career Track

Upon completion of her BBA, Janice worked for a consulting firm for one year before moving to British Columbia. Her consulting experience built her confidence and strengthened her ability to analyse businesses and develop strategic solutions to help them grow.

The Net Idea was created with partner Keith Dunphy shortly after moving to BC. Juggling a full-time job in addition to starting this new business was quite a challenge. The persistence and dedication of the pair have allowed the company to grow from a "mom-and-pop" shop to one of the highest-growth businesses in the region.

Janice has been involved in the industry as well as the business where she held positions as a board member of the Kootenay Internet Communications Society for two years and the British Columbia Internet Association for one year.

Advice

If given the opportunity to run your own business, Janice believes that to succeed you must create a positive, creative work environment. She learned early on in school that those professors who worked with an "open-door" policy were the ones who helped make her who she is today. She in turn operates her business by adopting this same attitude. The company is built of many individuals who bring great strength to the organization as a whole. Providing an open, flexible environment where each employee can share ideas only leads to positive growth for the whole organization.

summary 

1. Define direct marketing and explain its role in the marketing communication mix.

   Direct marketing is an interactive marketing communication tool that relies on a database and uses one or more advertising media to effect a measurable response and/or transaction at any location. It differs from conventional indirect marketing communication tools in two important ways. First, the only way to receive the product is through direct contact with the provider. Second, this direct contact between provider and customer requires some unique adjustments in the marketing strategy, particularly marketing communication techniques.

2. Discuss the strengths and weaknesses of direct marketing.

   Direct marketing has several strengths. It is a highly targeted and personal form of marketing communication. It is also easy to measure and test and is flexible. Direct marketing also has some weaknesses. It is not an effective long-term strategy; used ineffectively it can foster consumer distrust, and it is often difficult to integrate with other marketing communication tools.

3. Outline how to manage, design, and evaluate a direct-marketing program.

   Database marketing is the process of building, maintaining, and using customer databases for the purpose of contacting customers and transacting business. To manage a database, companies must obtain a list of customers or potential customers; capture, organize, and maintain the existing marketing data; convert the data into useful information that has possible application to company strategies; apply the database to specific strategies; test the direct-mail piece before sending it out to the target market; and capture new data and integrate them into the existing database. Marketers design a direct-marketing strategy by focusing on five components: the offer, the medium, the message, timing, and sequencing, and customer service. Marketers use several techniques to evaluate direct marketing, including analysing profitability and assessing response.

4. Describe how direct marketers use the tools of direct mail, catalogues, mass media, and telemarketing media.

   Direct mail offers a choice of formats and provides enough space to tell a complete sales story. It can also be personalized and allows the marketer to reach audiences who are inaccessible by other media. The drawbacks of direct mail are the widespread perception that it is junk mail and the high cost per prospect reached. Catalogues are becoming increasingly more popular and targeted. A shopping and purchase vehicle, catalogues are used by virtually all consumers, especially those pressed for time. Catalogues are available in print format, online, and are offered via other technology such as fax-back services. Direct marketing via mass media is used to reach a wider audience but can be costly. Examples included newspaper inserts, cable home shopping channels, and Internet direct-response ads. Telemarketing is a direct-marketing technique that combines telecommunications technology, marketing strategies, and information systems. It can be used alone or in conjunction with advertising, direct mail, sales promotions, personal selling, and other marketing communication functions.

points to ponder

Review the Facts

1. Discuss the primary difference between direct-marketing advertising and general advertising.
2. Compare and contrast inbound and outbound telemarketing.
3. What is database marketing, and why is it important to direct marketing?
4. What are the main differences between direct and indirect marketing?

Master the Concepts

5. "Direct marketing is junk mail that sells junk products. Its popularity is just a fad." Comment on this statement.

6. What types of databases are available to direct marketers? What are the characteristics of a good database?
7. What are the advantages and disadvantages of direct mail?
8. Discuss four requirements of a successful catalogue.
9. Contrast broadcast and print media in terms of their effectiveness for direct marketing.
10. What are the benefits of using on-line technology for direct marketing? What are the potential risks?

Apply Your Knowledge

11. Select two print ads you consider to be direct marketing, one directed at ultimate consumers and one at businesses. Critique each with respect to how well it makes the offer, includes sufficient information, and provides a mechanism for responding.
12. Select two direct-marketing catalogues and critique each using the criteria you listed in response to question 8. How well does each catalogue satisfy the criteria?
13. As vice president of marketing for a seed company, you are in the process of designing a direct-mail package aimed at experienced gardeners living throughout Canada. Describe the contents of the package and give an example of the copy you might use.

suggested projects

1. Select a consumer product that is not normally sold through direct marketing (for example, over-the-counter drugs, automobiles, pets). Create a direct-marketing plan for this product. Be sure to specify your objectives and indicate the parts of the offer, the medium, and the message.
2. (Writing Project) Contact three mailing-list houses. Compile several consumer profiles and ask for a cost estimate for 100 000 names containing these traits. Also, ask the houses to indicate the guarantees that accompany the list. Write a brief report summarizing your findings.
3. (Internet Project) The Internet provides an ideal environment for marketing music recordings, books, and other entertainment products. The reason is simple: There are too many titles for a single retail store to stock. Visit at least two storefronts that sell in the same industry. For instance, you may want to visit the following sites:

Sam the Record Man	www.samscd.com
Columbia House	www.columbiahouse.canada.com
HMV	www.hmv.com
Amazon.com Books	www.amazon.com
Chapters.	www.chapters.ca
Barnes & Noble	www.bn.com
Indigo	www.indigo.ca

In direct marketing, the offer is crucial. Compare the offers each storefront makes. Which offer is more persuasive? More clear? Does the online store do an effective job convincing consumers that online buying is better than visiting a retail store? Does the site make ordering easy? Secure? Based on what you learned in this chapter, what suggestions would you make to improve the offer? Write a brief critique of the two storefronts.

KISS A PIG, HUG A SWINE

Background

The New Pig Corporation, a company that specializes in producing absorbent cleaning materials to soak up industrial leaks and spills, has one of the most creative approaches to integrated marketing communication of any industrial marketer.

The company's name reflects its origins—the product was created in the "pig pen"—a perpetually dirty area of a warehouse dedicated to new product development. The advertising agency that had been hired to choose a name strongly objected to the "pig" name because of its negative connotations. But none of the names the agency proposed had the same cachet, and when test marketed, customers were very positive. "Pigs are really a lot of fun," says Carl DeCaspers, the company's public relations director.

Communication Strategy

The pig theme has been carried throughout the company. Customers are put on hold when calling so that they can hear Ray Stevens' country-western tune, "Kiss a Pig." The title of its catalogue is Pigalog®; its most popular sales promotion premium is a pig-snout baseball cap; its business cards, stationery, shipping cartons, and fax covers all are pig-embossed; and its notepads are pig shaped. Here are some other ways the theme is carried throughout the company's business:

Company motto:	No yes, ands, or butts about it ... we're out to serve you like no one else!
Address:	One Pork Avenue
Customer fax number:	800-621-PIGS
Customer service survey	Repork Cards
Trade show mascot:	A three-metre Mac-the-Pig balloon

Direct-Marketing Strategy

New Pig sells directly to its end-users, whereas many of its competitors use a network of distributors. Consequently, the company has control of its zany image all the way through the pipeline, and its customers are more likely to appreciate the lighthearted approach than would trade customers in a more traditional distribution channel. Undoubtedly, a few customers are turned off by this approach.

The company markets its products with collateral materials, catalogues, advertising, and trade shows—most of which are produced or managed in-house by its 23-person marketing staff. The company's marketing communication relies mostly on direct mail, where it spends about 85 percent of its total $11.9-million marketing budget. The four-colour 250-page Pigalog® catalogue showcases some 1500 industrial cleaning products. It is mailed three times a year to 85 000 customers and another 100 000 prospects. In keeping with the company's tone, each catalogue also has fun-and-game pages, full-page comic-like photographs, and contests with opportunities to win pig T-shirts and caps. Orders of $70 or more automatically qualify the customer to receive a pig-snout cap.

An important interactive element in the catalogue is a mail-in card for customers to share their product ideas in exchange for a pig T-shirt. In addition, a staff of 30 inbound customer service reps take orders and answer questions. Another 20 outbound telesales reps make sales contacts. The company employs no field salespeople.

In addition to the catalogues, New Pig mails monthly "Slim Lines," which are 40-page or less mini-catalogues that focus on one business area, such as safety products, absorbents, or storage and handling products. Because the company has an excellent database, it is possible to mail Slim Lines to heavy buyers of products in each of the company's sales categories, as well as good prospects. Slim Lines is used to lead prospects to other parts of the company's product lines.

As a continuity program to build relationships with active customers, the company also mails a technical newsletter three times a year. Introduced in 1991 as a value-added service, each eight-page issue gives tips and case studies explaining how New Pig's products can help users minimize waste and meet government requirements. Columns include "Ham and Regs," and "Pig Feats."

In addition to the direct-marketing program, New Pig places about 30 quarter-page ads a year in some 13 technical trade publications. It also buys booth space at three trade shows annually and distributes countless sales promotion premiums such as the pig-snout caps, pig-butt hats, pig-shaped pencils, pig-emblazoned boxer shorts, mugs, colouring books, and, of course, T-shirts.

New Pig's philosophy is based on relationship marketing. It focuses less on mass marketing and more on helping each customer as an individual. The individuality of the company's identity program also helps it stand out from its other bigger competitors such as 3M and is the primary way the manufacturer differentiates itself in an industry filled with practical yet mundane products.

Case Questions

1. How would you evaluate the direct-marketing strategy followed by New Pig?
2. What other direct-marketing techniques could New Pig consider?

Source: Ginger Trumfio, "Hamming It Up," *Sales & Marketing Management* (June 1995): 84–5.

CBC VIDEO VIGNETTES

CBC

Direct Marketers Firing Customers

It seems all customers are not of equal value. Direct marketing analysts estimate that approximately 25 to 30 percent of the customers on a typical retail catalogue mailing list are costing the respective retailers money. These customers are not profitable for reasons such as frequent call-centre inquiries that do not result in a purchase, infrequent purchases of "small ticket" items, and a tendency to only purchase sales items.

With the aid of new computer technologies, direct marketers are learning to analyse data in order to identify those customers who cost money, instead of generating profits. However, the identification of those customers who are having a negative impact on the bottom line presents a new challenge for direct marketers – what do you do with this information? Should strategies be implemented to encourage these customers to spend more? Should steps be taken to reduce the cost of servicing these customers? Should those customers who are not generating profits be fired?

If "firing" the customer is the decision, the most thought-provoking question is – how should customers be fired? Two frequently adopted approaches are to: 1) slowly and quietly reduce interactions (mailings, e-mail offers, etc.) so that customers do not suspect they are being "fired;" and 2) offer a last chance to respond to a specified offer. The latter alternative may involve personalized correspondence that informs these customers of their need to respond to a specific offer to remain a preferred customer.

QUESTIONS

1. Assume that you are the marketing manager for a catalogue retailer. Analysis of your customer database indicates that 15 percent of your customers have not only failed to purchase a single item in the last six months, but each of these customers has also placed at least two calls to your call-centre customer-service representatives. What should be done with these customers? Explain.
2. What are the implications of "firing" customers?

Video Resource: Based on "Firing Your Customers," ***Venture*** # 710 (January 26, 1999).

13

Personal Selling

chapter objectives

After completing your work on this chapter, you should be able to

- Define personal selling.
- Describe the strengths and weaknesses of personal selling.
- Discuss how personal selling fits in the marketing communication mix.
- Outline both the types and the process of personal selling.
- Explain the tasks of sales management that relate directly to marketing communication.

CONSIDER THIS

Technology: A New Dimension of Professional Personal Selling

Will technology replace the need for salespeople? Although we can only speculate about dramatic changes in the nature of personal selling, the role of the professional salesperson will likely remain intact for several decades. Why? Simply because many products will still need to be sold personally by a knowledgeable and trustworthy professional who is willing to devote significant time and effort to discover customer needs and the solutions necessary to earn their loyalty.

Recall the Consider This feature in Chapter 6, in which Blair D. Hayden, a manager with London Life, and James Pinnock, the managing director of Stanley Mutual Insurance, commented on the importance of needs-based selling in the financial services sector. According to these sales professionals, there is no better way to build trust-based relationships with clients than to invest the time necessary to identify their needs and recommend customized solutions.

It seems, however, that some observers speculate that the era of e-commerce and Internet-based communications will fundamentally alter traditional selling methods. At present, salespeople spend much of their time selling face-to-face, via phone, or e-mail. But according to Christopher Lochhead, chief marketing officer for California-based Scient Corporation, by 2002 the primary method of doing business will be the Internet. Lochhead speculates that the "Internet is going to do 70 percent of what a salesperson does today ... and with this new distribution channel opportunity, the salesperson will guide the customer in their shopping experience."

If the Internet will eventually have such a profound impact on what a salesperson does, it is interesting to note that the latest Canadian Professional Sales Association (CPSA) technology study indicates the Internet is not currently being embraced as a replacement for face-to-face selling. Sixty-four percent of respondents said technology helps them achieve their sales goals and close a deal faster—but the study results make it clear that selling is still highly dependent on face-to-face contact. When respondents were asked what is the most important tool when reaching customers, face-to-face meetings ranked highest, followed closely by telephone contact, then faxes, e-mail, and letters.

The CPSA's technology survey indicates that when used properly by experienced users, computers, and all the devices that attach to them, save sales professionals time and can be a major factor in closing a deal. What is equally clear from the CPSA survey, however, is that

technology has not replaced face-to-face contact as a preferred form of communication. And understandably so. Existing technologies cannot convey a sense of responsibility, empathy, and concern for buyers.

Sources: Mary Klonizakis, "How Wired Are We?," *Contact*, Vol. 2(5), September 1999, 6. Christopher Lochhead, "Net Results: The Advent of E-Commerce Spells Change," *Contact*, Vol. 2(2), March 1999, 14.

Chapter Overview

Although face-to-face contact remains the preferred form of communication for salespeople, the most effective way to implement a marketing strategy is to coordinate all marketing communication tools. If advertising, sales promotions, telemarketing, and direct-mail marketing tools are coordinated, the sales job is much easier. Also, customer feedback that salespeople often collect can provide timely and valuable information that marketing communication specialists can use to improve the communication efforts.

In this chapter we investigate what personal selling is, its strengths and weaknesses, and how to integrate personal selling in the marketing communication mix. Then we explore the types and the process of personal selling. We also examine how to manage a sales force effectively. We conclude by analysing personal selling trends.

Personal Selling and the Marketing Communication Mix

Salespeople are often separated from marketing communication specialists because of both the structure of the business and differences in perspective. Advertisers, sales promotion managers, and public relations experts rarely consider the needs and suggestions of salespeople, and salespeople seldom pay attention to information about a marketing communication campaign. As this chapter's IMC Concept in Focus explains, this could change with the increasing professionalization of salespeople.

To integrate personal selling with other marketing communication tools to forge strong customer relationships, top management should lead the integration effort. Unless managers understand what salespeople do, however, integration may not be successful. Before considering how to combine selling efforts with other marketing communication tools, we first describe the job of personal selling.

Understanding Personal Selling

Personal selling is a marketing communication tool that is used to increase sales directly through personal contact. Though the other marketing communication mix elements contribute to sales, their impact is often indirect. In contrast, the impact of personal selling is direct—in fact, the salesperson's livelihood depends on making sales. The importance of this direct impact is demonstrated by the number of people employed in the personal selling field. Thousands of people are employed in advertising, whereas millions are employed in personal selling.

Concept in Focus

Sales Force Certification

Gone are the days of traditional selling, which involved getting in, pushing a product, and moving on to the next account. Marketing experts will tell you that modern professional selling is nothing like that. Today's sales professionals are not the fast-talking, back-slapping, con-game players as depicted in the movie ***Tin Men***. Sales professionals are now considered a vital link between the customer and the organization as they are often given the responsibility to cultivate customer relationships and implement communication strategy.

Given the importance of these responsibilities, organizations expect their salespeople to possess what it takes to be a successful sales professional. Likewise, salespeople understand the need to continuously improve their selling skills. Aware of these expectations and needs, the Canadian Professional Sales Association's (CPSA) Sales Institute is dedicated to maintaining progressive competency standards for sales professionals. To accomplish this mandate, the Sales Institute offers the Certified Sales Professional (CSP) designation to qualified candidates.

To earn the CSP designation, candidates must complete sales-related education, meet a two-year practical work experience requirement, successfully complete a written and oral professional exam, agree to abide by the code of ethics, be a member in good-standing of the CPSA, and be approved by the CPSA–Sales Institute's board of directors. In addition to traditional selling skills such as time and territory management, CSP candidates are tested on other sales competencies such as relationship building, communication, and strategic sales planning.

The demonstrated competencies of CSP-designated sales professionals can help bridge the differences in perspective that have historically existed between sales and marketing communication specialists. CSPs display the strong consultative and interpersonal skills needed to assist in the implementation of an IMC perspective.

Sources: Mary Klonizakis, "The Big Picture," ***Contact***, Vol. 2(5), September 1999, 23. CPSA Web site: http://cpsa.com/html/body_sales_institute.asp. Extracted November 18, 1999. Frederick G. Crane, E. Stephen Grant, Steven W. Hartley, ***Marketing: Canadian Insights and Applications***, Irwin/McGraw-Hill Ryerson Limited, 1997, 417.

Personal selling
The face-to-face presentation of a product or an idea to a potential customer by a representative of the company or organization for the sake of making a sale.

Personal selling is the face-to-face presentation of a product or an idea to a potential customer by a representative of the company or organization. This definition highlights a key difference between personal selling and other marketing communication tools: Personal selling involves one-on-one communication rather than the mass communication that characterizes advertising, sales promotion, and public relations. Personal selling also differs from direct marketing, which uses a nonpersonal media to generate a response. In personal selling, information is presented personally, there is immediate feedback, and adjustments to the message can be made immediately.

Personal selling differs from other elements of marketing communication in two other key ways. First, the task and the problems of selling primarily involve interpersonal relations. In selling, the main task is to build relations—between salespeople and customers, between salespeople and their supervisors, and between salespeople and others in the organization. In other marketing communication areas—advertising, for example—the heart of the task is creating a message. Second, even in companies that house their marketing communication specialists in the marketing communication department, most organizations separate the sales force from the other marketing communication areas of a business.

Strengths and Weaknesses of Personal Selling

Personal selling has several important advantages and disadvantages compared with the other elements of the marketing communication mix. Undoubtedly, the most significant strength of personal selling is its flexibility. Salespeople can tailor their presentations to fit the needs, motives, and behaviour of individual customers. As salespeople see the prospect's reaction to a sales approach, they can immediately adjust as needed.

Personal selling also minimizes wasted effort. Advertisers typically expend time and money to send a mass message about a product to many people outside the target market. In personal selling the sales force pinpoints the target market, makes a contact, and expends effort that has a strong probability of leading to a sale.

Consequently, an additional strength of personal selling is that measuring effectiveness and determining the return on investment are far more straightforward for personal selling than for other marketing communication tools, where recall or attitude change is often the only measurable effect.

Another benefit of personal selling is that a salesperson is in an excellent position to encourage the customer to act. The one-on-one interaction of personal selling means that a salesperson can effectively respond to and overcome objections (customers' concerns or reservations about the product) so that the customer is more likely to buy. Salespeople can also offer many specific reasons to persuade a customer to buy, in contrast to the general reasons that an ad may urge customers to take immediate action.

A final strength of personal selling is the multiple tasks the sales force can perform. For instance, in addition to selling, a salesperson can collect payment, service or repair products, return products, and collect product and marketing information. In fact, salespeople are often best at disseminating negative and positive word-of-mouth product information.

High cost is the primary disadvantage of personal selling. With increased competition, higher travel and lodging costs, and higher salaries, the cost per sales contact continues to increase. Many companies try to control sales costs by compensating sales representatives based on commission only, thereby guaranteeing that salespeople get paid only if they generate sales. However, commission-only salespeople may become risk averse and only call on clients who have the highest potential return. These salespeople, then, may miss opportunities to develop a broad base of potential customers that could generate higher sales revenues in the long run.

Companies can also reduce sales costs by using complementary techniques, such as telemarketing, direct mail, toll-free numbers for interested customers, and online communication with qualified prospects. Telemarketing and online communication can further reduce costs by serving as an actual selling vehicle. Both technologies can deliver sales messages, respond to questions, take payment, and do follow-up.

Another disadvantage of personal selling is the problem of finding and retaining high-quality people. First, experienced salespeople sometimes realize that the only way their income can outpace their cost-of-living increases is to change jobs. Second, because of the push for profitability, many businesses try to hire experienced salespeople away from competitors rather than hiring university graduates, who take three to five years to reach the level of productivity of more experienced salespeople. These two staffing issues have caused high turnover in many sales forces.

Another weakness of personal selling is message inconsistency. Many salespeople view themselves as independent from the organization, so they design their own sales techniques, use their own message strategies, and engage in questionable ploys to create a sale. Consequently, it is difficult to find a unified company or product message within a sales force, or between the sales force and the rest of the marketing communication mix.

A final weakness is that sales force members have different levels of motivation. Salespeople may vary in their willingness to make the desired sales calls each day; make service calls that do not lead directly to sales; or use new technology, such as a laptop, e-mail, or the company's Web site. Finally, overly zealous sales representatives may tread a thin line between ethical and unethical sales techniques. The difference between a friendly lunch and commercial bribery is sometimes blurred. Table 13.1 summarizes the strengths and weaknesses of personal selling.

Table 13.1 STRENGTHS AND WEAKNESSES OF PERSONAL SELLING

Strengths	Descriptions
• Flexibility	• Can tailor presentations to suit needs, motives, and behaviours of individual customers
• Minimizes wasted effort	• Unlike mass-media marketing communication, the marketing message is only offered to a target audience of likely buyers
• Facilitates buyer action	• The one-on-one interaction allows specific requests for action on a repeated basis, if necessary
• Multiple capabilities	• Collection of payment, servicing the product, accepting returned products, and collecting information are all possible
Weaknesses	
• High cost	• Cost per contact is high due to travel, lodging, and salaries
• Finding and retaining salespeople	• Both salespeople and the company look for alternative ways to maximize personal benefits.
• Message inconsistency	• Due to independence of sales force, delivering a unified message is difficult
• Motivation	• Difficult to motivate salespeople to use required sales techniques, make all necessary sales calls, use new technology, and behave ethically

The Role of Personal Selling in the Marketing Communication Mix

In view of the strengths and weaknesses of personal selling, how should managers use this tool effectively in the marketing communication mix? Recall that each marketing communication tool has a unique role to play in reaching communication objectives. For instance, advertising builds awareness, informs the customer about product features, and persuades the customer that the advertised brand is the best choice. Public relations tends to support these objectives indirectly by creating a positive product or company image. Sales promotions, direct marketing, and personal selling all try to prompt immediate action by adding value to the product. Personal selling is the most direct marketing communication tool, enabling salespeople to spontaneously answer questions, establish the key terms of the purchase decision, and make the sale.

As noted in Part I of the text, the IMC approach coordinates the use of all marketing communication tools to create a synergistic effect that optimizes the likelihood of a sale. The best combination of tools depends on several factors. First, it may depend on the market. In general, personal selling is emphasized in industrial markets or in selling to resellers but plays a smaller role in consumer markets. Second, the combination of tools may depend on the type of product. Simple, low-cost products such as cereals and canned vegetables require little personal selling. Mass advertising can provide brand awareness, basic product information, and retail-related information. Sales promotion may provide an extra incentive to buy. In contrast, a technical product such as an automobile or an appliance that requires an explanation, demonstration, or both usually requires a salesperson. Also, products that have a high risk such as real estate or stocks usually need personal selling.

Tetley Canada
www.tetley.ca

The distribution channel can also influence the role of personal selling. For instance, a Wal-Mart supplier may not need to call on each Wal-Mart store. However, when Tetley Canada competes against Thomas J. Lipton for Wal-Mart's business, Tetley knows personal selling is critical to earn the business. The key is to cement the relationship between the Wal-Mart purchasing agent and the Tetley sales representative. Why? Business relationships are based on a bond of trust between people, not between companies. A personal sales call, then, will be much more beneficial than a direct-mail marketing piece in such a case.

Marketing communicators use personal selling when its strengths and the situation prompt its use. In general, when a personal meeting between buyer and seller is important, personal selling dominates. It is unlikely, for instance, that consumers would buy a big-ticket item such as a luxury automobile without a salesperson. Personal selling allows information exchange, adjustments to various types of relationships, and personal persuasive techniques that convince customers to buy.

Ultimately, the marketing director or the marketing communication manager employs four criteria to determine the role of personal selling in the marketing communication strategy:

1. The nature of the information that should be exchanged to promote the product or service
2. The marketing communication objectives
3. The marketing communication mix alternatives available to the organization, with special concern for the firm's capabilities to implement each one

4. The relative cost of personal selling compared with the other marketing communication mix elements

Integrating Personal Selling

Bringing personal selling and other marketing communication mix elements together remains a major frustration in most businesses, as discussed earlier. Despite the difficulties of such integration, under certain circumstances the benefits outweigh the costs of integrating personal selling with other elements. We examine those instances next.

Personal Selling and Advertising

Under what conditions should personal selling be combined with advertising? Advertising can reach large audiences simultaneously with a vivid message. The message must be quite general and the copy relatively short; opportunity for feedback and adjustment is virtually nil. Because personal selling offers the opposite set of strengths and weaknesses as advertising does, advertising and personal selling tend to complement one another. When audience coverage, vivid presentation, explanation, feedback, and the adjustment are all important to the success of the marketing program, combining advertising and personal selling is appropriate. These factors often arise with the introduction of new products. For instance, when Duncan Hines introduced its low-fat cake mixes, the company ran a great deal of consumer advertising to make consumers aware of this new product. However, it was just as important for the sales force to call on every supermarket manager and explain the product's benefits, show market-research results, and offer trade incentives.

Advertising can also provide sales leads when introducing a new product or promoting an existing one. Including a toll-free number or a mail-in coupon in an ad can provide a salesperson with a list of hundreds of prospective customers. Marketers of business-to-business products are particularly effective at this tactic.

In summary, when advertising is needed to create awareness and provide basic information, but personal selling is necessary to complete the exchange process, the advertising–personal selling combination makes sense.

This ad, with its toll-free number and Web site address, helps to generate sales for the company's sales representatives.

Personal Selling and Sales Promotions

Sales promotion is an important tool that can help sales representatives during or in addition to the selling process. Recall from Chapter 10 that salespeople often deliver sales promotion materials to trade members during sales presentations. Price deals, premiums, contests, and other incentives represent part of the repertoire that can make the sales process much more successful. These trade sales promotions are often coordinated with a parallel consumer sales promotion to give both more impact. For example, Dole Pineapple might run a "Trip to Polynesia" sweepstakes with both consumers and resellers.

Sales promotion can work to add additional value to the personal selling process. An IBM salesperson knows that the customer has already been "presold" because the buyer received a direct-mail discount coupon and an opportunity to sample the product. Conversely, salespeople can explain sales promotions more fully or even deliver premiums or prizes to winning customers. Sales promotions add to the value of the product or service. In turn, that extra value makes the product or service easier to sell. The personal selling/sales promotion combination is particularly effective in competitive situations where products are similar and the salesperson needs something extra to create a competitive advantage.

Personal Selling and Public Relations

Some people would argue that the salesperson is the most important public relations strategy in many organizations. If we look at public relations as the shaping and maintenance of goodwill, this is clearly the case. In some instances the role of the salesperson as a public relations provider is informal and revolves around the person's day-to-day activities. The salesperson would probably view activities such as taking a customer out to lunch, remembering the client's birthday, responding to questions or complaints, and treating people with empathy as part of getting the sale rather than public relations.

United Way of Canada
www.unitedway.ca

However, the salesperson can also be involved in more formal public relations activities that help both the salesperson and the public relations manager. For example, salespeople are encouraged to get involved in community activities, head the United Way campaign, join a public service organization, or coach PeeWee hockey. Salespeople are also excellent at explaining the company's products to people or to organizations that request such information. Leading plant tours or hosting open houses are two other PR activities that salespeople do well. Finally, salespeople are usually an integral part of trade shows, customer meetings, and any other event where customers and the company are together in an informal setting.

Personal Selling and Other Marketing Communication Tools

Personal selling can increase in value when combined with other communication tools such as direct marketing, point-of-purchase marketing, and so forth. Special events, for example, are an effective way for salespeople to generate sales leads, and the event is usually more effective if a salesperson is available to answer consumers' questions.

Direct-marketing techniques such as telemarketing, direct mail, and Internet marketing are also useful in screening customers and generating leads. The benefit works in the opposite direction too. The insights of salespeople who know their customers well can guide the design of direct-marketing tools, point-of-purchase displays, packages, and other promotions. For instance, Lactite, a manufacturer of industrial adhesives, surveys its sales force semiannually for feedback on the company's marketing communication techniques.

The World of Personal Selling

Although the sophistication of personal selling has increased over time due to better-educated individuals and advanced technology, the selling process has basically remained the same. It still requires a person who has the courage to sell to current and prospective customers daily. Rejection is part of the process. Most

concept review

Personal Selling and the Marketing Communication Mix

1. Personal selling is the face-to-face presentation of a product or an idea to a potential customer by a company representative.
2. Compared with other marketing communication tools, personal selling has several strengths: flexibility, minimal wasted effort, sales generation, and multiple capabilities. It also has several weaknesses: high cost, finding and retaining high-quality people, inconsistent messages, and different levels of motivation in the sales force.
3. The role that personal selling plays in the marketing communication mix depends on several factors including the product, the market, the distribution channel, and the available marketing communication alternatives.
4. Integrating personal selling with other marketing communication tools can be beneficial when the tools complement each other.

people who try to sell, fail. Successful salespeople, however, probably can sell anything. In the sections that follow, we discuss the types of personal selling and the process of personal selling.

Types of Personal Selling

No two sales jobs are exactly alike—even when two sales jobs have identical titles and job descriptions. Nevertheless, we can describe several general types of sales jobs to give you some idea of the range of opportunities. The six following types of sales differ in some important ways.[1]

Responsive Selling

In responsive selling the salesperson reacts to the buyer's demands. Route driving and retailing are two kinds of responsive selling. For instance, route drivers who deliver products such as soft drinks or fuel oil usually do so at the request of the client. Similarly, clerks in an appliance or clothing store sell when the customer asks for their help.

Trade Selling

As in responsive selling, the salesperson is primarily an order-taker, but the job duties place more emphasis on service. Trade selling involves calling on dealers, taking orders, expediting deliveries, setting up displays, and rotating stock. This type of selling is used often in the food, textile, apparel, and household products industries. Special tasks, such as the assembly of point-of-purchase displays, are performed by this type of salesperson. Often this salesperson plays an integral role in maintaining relationships with trade members.

Missionary Selling

A missionary salesperson's primary responsibility is to explain a new product to the market before the total product is available to the public. The classic example of a missionary salesperson is the pharmaceutical sales representative who calls on physicians to explain about new drugs offered by the drug company. The missionary salesperson gives physicians free samples of the drug and encourages them to give the sample to patients and to note the results. The salesperson hopes that physicians will specify that particular drug when prescribing to future patients.

Technical Selling

This type of salesperson sells a service—the ability to solve customers' technical problems through expertise and experience. Technical selling is common for industrial goods such as chemicals, machinery, and heavy equipment. The salesperson's ability to identify, analyse, and solve customers' problems is essential. Typically, a technical salesperson calls on prospects who have identified a problem and assume the salesperson's company offers possible solutions.

Creative Selling

This type of selling is usually related to new products or to an existing product that is being introduced into a new market. The salesperson must convince prospects that they have a problem or unfulfilled need and that the salesperson's product is the best solution. The salesperson is an "order-getter" who emphasizes and stimulates demand for products. Salespeople working for Procter & Gamble, Compaq Computers, and Arthur Anderson Consulting all sell creatively. For example, a sales representative from the health and beauty aids division of P&G may make several sales presentations to supermarket purchasing managers to demonstrate how a new Head and Shoulders shampoo product satisfies a consumer need better than all other shampoos.

Consultative Selling

This type of selling is a form of relationship marketing. The salesperson first meets with customers, offers little direction, and builds rapport. The salesperson next shifts to directive questions that diagnose customer's needs. Then and only then does the salesperson prescribe the solution with a presentation customized to the customer's needs. She closes the sale, using both direction and support, as she asks for the order and overcomes any of the customer's reservations. After the sale, the salesperson uses support to reinforce the sale, ensure satisfaction, and maintain the relationship.

The Process of Personal Selling

The process of personal selling varies somewhat from company to company, but it typically involves the six steps outlined in Figure 13.1.

Attaining Knowledge

Modern salespeople must be equipped with detailed product information. They need a thorough knowledge of the buyer's motives, characteristics, and behaviour. They also need factual information about their own company and the competition.[2] The amount and kind of information required depend on the type of product, product line, characteristics of the customer, organizational structure, and type of selling. If a company has a simple product and few competitors, the level of necessary working knowledge could be quite basic. In contrast,

Figure 13.1 THE PROCESS OF PERSONAL SELLING

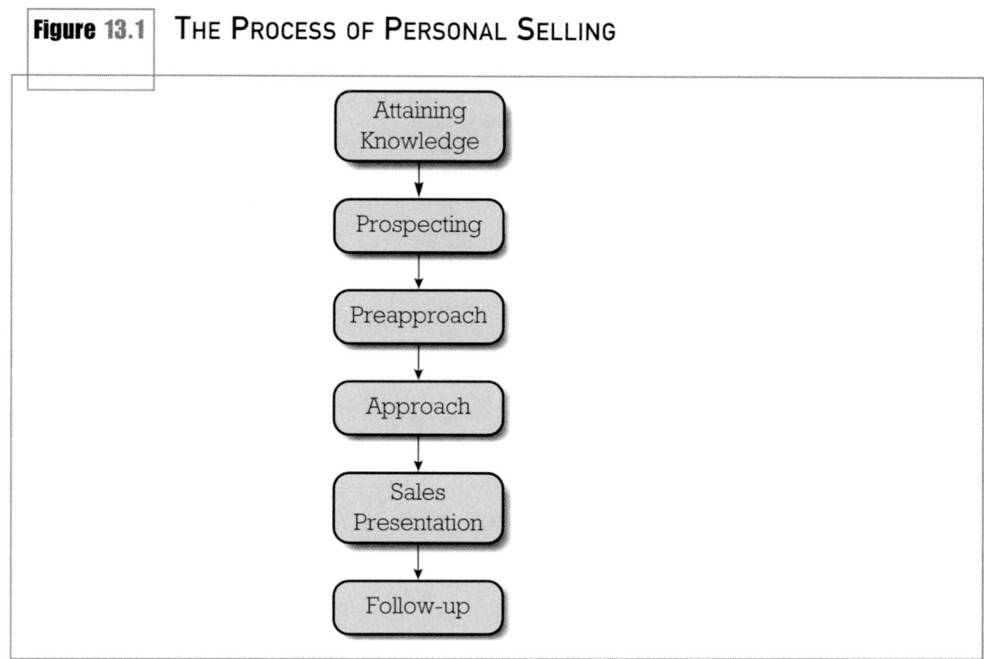

salespeople for companies like Dow Chemical or Dell Computers, which have extensive product lines and many competitors, need technical training to understand their products, how customers use their products, and the strengths and limitations of their competitors' products.

To illustrate how a salesperson attains knowledge, consider Jeff Crown, a 25-year-old who works for Envirotank, a company that makes above-ground storage tanks for oil, gasoline, and used oil products. Jeff spent six months learning about his product and continues to attend seminars about metallurgy and petroleum products. He also collects materials on his four major competitors, visits their Web sites weekly, reads the various trade publications, and contacts prospects and customers as often as possible. He also staffs Envirotank's booth at the two trade shows they attend.

PROSPECTING

Prospecting
The process of locating potential customers and then obtaining permission to present a sales presentation

The process of locating potential customers and then obtaining permission to present a sales presentation is called **prospecting**. Prospecting is a continuous task because existing customers are always lost through transfers, retirement, and competition; meanwhile, new buyers constantly enter the marketplace. Surveys estimate that the typical salesperson spends at least 30 minutes each day prospecting and that 20 to 25 percent of sales visits are with new customers.[3]

Prospecting methods vary for different types of selling. The most common methods of prospecting follow:

1. *Inquiries*: Most companies receive a steady supply of sales leads from their advertising, telephone calls, and catalogues.
2. *Endless-chain method*: The salesperson obtains at least one sales lead from each person interviewed.
3. *Centre-of-influence method*: This method is a modified form of the endless-chain method. Here, the salesperson cultivates people in the territory who are willing to supply prospecting information.

4. *Public exhibitions, demonstrations, and trade shows*: People attending these events are often already interested in the product so they become prospects that the salesperson meets with at or after the event.
5. *Lists*: Individual sales representatives may develop their own lists of potential customers by referring to such sources as public records, classified telephone directories, club memberships, databases, and hits/inquiries on Web sites.
6. *Friends and acquaintances*: These people are often a source of sales leads for new sales representatives.
7. *Cold-canvas method*: The salesperson makes calls on every individual or company in a target group without any knowledge of their interest level.

To illustrate the prospecting process, let's look again at Jeff Crown of Envirotank. He uses three of the prospecting methods listed. Every Friday afternoon he gathers the inquiries he received from the company's toll-free number. He spends Saturday morning scrutinizing these leads and selecting the top 20 that he will call for appointments on Monday. Jeff also receives leads through trade shows. Finally, he generates a great many leads through Envirotank's Web site. This last source is quickly becoming his most productive option.

In support of Jeff's strategy, there is substantial evidence that leads are increasingly generated through marketing communication alternatives. Figure 13.2 shows the results of a survey that asked respondents to estimate the amount of power various communication tools have to generate sales leads. Results indicate that the respondents believe advertising generates 30 to 35 percent of the sales leads, whereas public relations generates 22 to 24 percent.

Preapproach
Learning more about the prospect to establish the best selling approach, identify problem areas, and avoid mistakes.

PREAPPROACH

Once a prospect has been qualified, the salesperson needs to learn more about the prospect to determine the best selling approach, identify problem areas, and avoid mistakes. This part of the selling process is known as the **preapproach.**

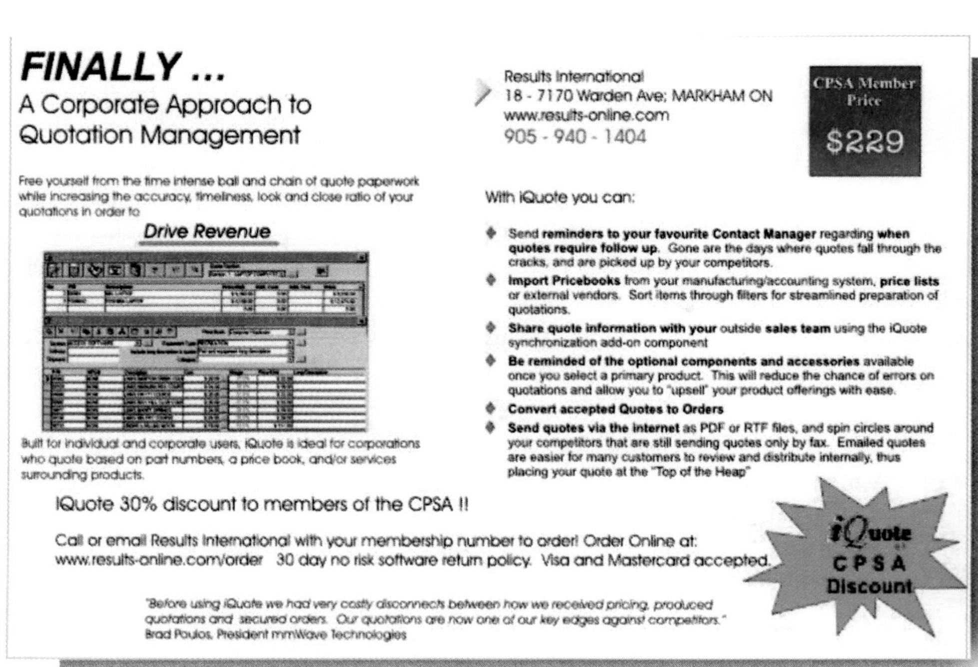

This ad for Results International's iQuote software explains the benefits of a technological product designed to aid the sales process.

Figure 13.2 AN ASSESSMENT OF SALES LEADS THROUGH MARKETING COMMUNICATION TOOLS*

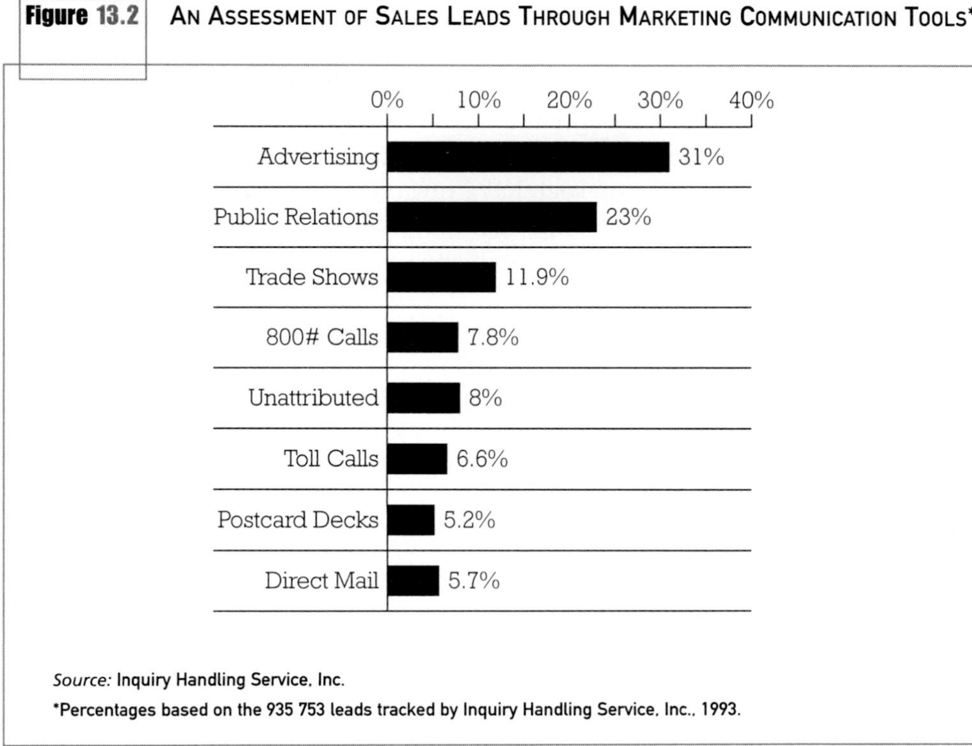

Source: Inquiry Handling Service, Inc.

*Percentages based on the 935 753 leads tracked by Inquiry Handling Service, Inc., 1993.

During this stage, salespeople gather additional personal and business information about prospects to qualify them further—that is, to determine whether a prospect has the resources to buy, interest in the product, any unique buying conditions, history with the firm, and so forth. Some of this information can be gleaned from the prospect directly. Other information may require discussions with knowledgeable people in the industry.

Let's again consider Jeff. He recently evaluated one of his best prospects, DPI Petroleum. DPI would be a new customer with an estimated annual purchase of nearly 500 tanks. Jeff called the DPI purchasing agent, learned that the company is unhappy with its current tank provider, and learned DPI would be interested in receiving a proposal from Envirotank. Further, Jeff had extensive conversations with Jim Barton, a retired engineer/consultant with extensive knowledge of DPI. He also checked the DPI Web site for further information.

APPROACH

Approach
The lead-in to the sales presentation.

Following the preapproach, the salesperson begins the **approach**, the lead-in to the sales presentation. An approach may have several objectives, but essentially it is the strategy used to gain the prospect's attention so the salesperson can make an effective sales presentation. Some salespeople use phone calls or personal letters to approach prospects. Phone calls save time for salespeople because they reduce waiting time. Letters allow salespeople to include other information—drawings and product specifications, for instance—about the products that cannot be easily communicated. Of course, Web sites provide much of the same information, employing a much more colourful format. All of these methods of approaching prospects have the disadvantage that buyers find it fairly easy to say no over the phone, ignore their voice mail, throw away letters, or refuse to view a Web site.

Regardless of the approach method used, the salesperson must immediately establish a rapport. Establishing a rapport can occur in a number of different ways. In some cases comments about unfinished business from previous sales calls will get the buyer's interest. Another approach is one during which the salesperson informs the buyer of the benefits he or she will gain from the product being sold. Jeff Crown has developed what he calls a "marketing incentive kit" that he sends to prospects. It includes an introduction letter, a set of product fact sheets, testimonials from satisfied customers, and a model of the tank Jeff wishes to sell.

Sales Presentation

A successful sales approach is important in making the transition to the sales presentation, the heart of the sales process. The purpose of the sales presentation is to explain in detail how the product meets customer requirements. The salesperson must inform prospects and customers of the characteristics and benefits of the product and must persuade them that the product will satisfy their needs.

Talking about the weather, the Stanley Cup, or business conditions are easy means of starting a sales call. For some salespeople a more effective opener is to start by discussing the organization or person being called on.

Ultimately, every presentation gets to the reason for the salesperson's being there—the product. If the sales presentation is to be effective, the sales representative's claims about the product must be relevant and believable. The salesperson's background knowledge of the account or similar accounts should help establish the most effective presentation.

There are a number of sales presentation categories. All start with an understanding of the customers' needs and wants. They tend to vary in terms of formality. For example, a "fully automated" sales presentation is highly structured, with the salesperson doing little beyond setting up a movie, showing slides, answering questions, and taking orders. This would be used as part of the trade-

Sales presentations vary. Here, we see how salespeople can use visual aids and technology to enhance effectiveness.

show booth. In the "semi-automated" approach, the salesperson reads from prepared aids such as a flip chart or brochure. If necessary, the salesperson can also add comments. A third technique is the "memorized" or "canned" sales presentation. This is prepared by the company, and very few changes are allowed. In "organized" sales presentations the salesperson has complete flexibility to change the wording of the sales presentation. Finally, "unstructured" sales presentations are designed so that the salesperson and buyer together can more fully explore the product and how it fits the needs of the buying firm. This type of presentation is most effective when the salesperson and buyer stay focused on the buyer's problem or need.[4] Jeff Crown typically uses an unstructured sales presentation technique.

Regardless of the type of sales presentation used, objections are inevitable. Sometimes the objections are irrational or nebulous and have little to do with the product, the company, or the seller. There is also the unspoken objection, which is considered but not expressed. Some objections may, of course, be legitimate. In handling objections there are two basic questions to consider: Why do people object? What techniques are available to overcome these objections? Table 13.2 depicts some of the more common objections and how they should be handled. Such techniques are not specific, and salespeople often learn how to handle objections through trial and error.

se
sk for and secure the sale.

The hardest thing for many salespeople to do is **close**—that is, ask for the business. Yet the good salesperson is always closing. Without a close, the time has been wasted. The close is the ultimate test of sales ability, and a salesperson's income is highly correlated to a successful close.

There are several difficulties associated with closing a sale. Many potentially successful salespeople fail because they are afraid to close. If they never have to

Table 13.2 METHODS OF HANDLING OBJECTIONS

Techniques	Description	Example
Direct denial	Defend your company against the criticism.	"Mr. Jones, you simply are wrong about that point."
Indirect denial	Refer to a third party who had a similar objection and state how it was resolved.	"Ms. Smith expressed a similar concern. We called headquarters and had our answer in ten minutes."
Boomerang	The objection is turned back on the user.	"I'm glad you brought that up. That's exactly why I'm here."
Compensation	Admit the validity of the objection and offer compensation.	"Though it's true that we can't promise 72-hour delivery, the quality of our product is twice as good as Brand X."
Pass up	Ignore the objection as invalid.	"Let's go back and talk about some key features."
Question	Ask and listen.	In response to a concern about cost, the salesperson could ask, "How much did you plan to spend?"

ask for the sale, they are never rejected. More often, the close is unsuccessful because the presentation is unsuccessful. Prospects cannot be expected to buy if they do not understand the presentation or if they cannot see how they will benefit as a result of the purchase. Finally, some salespeople do not have good closing skills. They become so fascinated by the sound of their own voice that they talk themselves out of sales they might have had.

A nod of the head, a more relaxed posture, and a smile all may be interpreted as signals of a buyer's readiness to buy. When one of these signals occurs, the salesperson should not hesitate to attempt to close the sale. The basic idea is to incorporate a few trial closes in the sales presentation. A **trial close** should be in the form of a question and should ask for an opinion on the part of the buyer: "Do you think this product is within your price range?" or "Does the quality of the product meet your standards?"

Trial close
A question that asks for the potential buyer's opinion of a product or service.

Ultimately, the primary reason a person buys is because the salesperson has keyed into one or more motivating factors. Factors that motivate vary by person, company, and situation. Product quality may be pivotal in one case, and price or reliable service or delivery may be critical in another. Successful salespeople know they must identify this hot button.

Follow Up with Postsale Activities

An effective selling job does not end when the order is written up. Postsale service (service after the sale) can build customer goodwill and lay the groundwork for many years of profitable business relations. These services can ensure repeat business and generate leads to other prospects. If product installation is necessary, sales representatives should ensure that the job is done properly. Salespeople need to make sure the buyer understands the sales contract and any guarantees fully. In addition, salespeople should reassure customers that they have made the right decision by summarizing the product benefits, repeating why their choice is better than the alternative choices, and pointing out how satisfied they will be with the product's performance. These actions reduce customers' post-decision anxiety (also referred to as cognitive dissonance).

Style of Communication in Personal Selling

Salespeople must do more than present the right information to buyers. To sell in person effectively, a salesperson must choose the right communication style for the situation. We examine five elements of communication style:[5]

1. *Pace*: The speed at which the salesperson moves to close a sale is known as **pace**. A salesperson must adjust this pace so that the buyer does not feel rushed, offended, or bored.
2. *Scope*: **Scope** refers to the variety of benefits, features, and sales terms discussed. Some sales presentations, designed to appeal to all customers, use a broad scope. For high-priced, customized products, the presentation tends to have a narrower scope, focusing on the most important benefit to the buyer.
3. *Depth of inquiry*: The extent of the salesperson's effort to learn the details of the buyer's decision process is the **depth of inquiry**. The appropriate depth is affected by three factors: (a) the salesperson's previous experience with the prospect, (b) the extent to which several people are involved in the purchase decision, and (c) the prospect's feeling about the product before and after the presentation.[6]

Pace
The speed at which a salesperson moves to close a sale.

Scope
The variety of benefits, features, and sales terms discussed.

Depth of inquiry
The extent of the salesperson's effort to learn the details of the buyer's decision process.

4. *Interactive communication*: In personal selling two-way communication must be initiated and maintained. Salespeople must ask questions and listen carefully to match the product with customer needs. They must avoid the temptation to present the product in a manner that discourages customer interaction.

5. *Use of supporting materials*: Many salespeople use materials, such as visual and auditory aids, to support their presentations. Because it is difficult for buyers to visualize intangibles or complex products, flip charts, slides, product demonstrations, written proposals, and the like all help customers visualize product benefits.

concept review

The World of Personal Selling

1. Six common types of selling are responsive, trade, missionary, technical, creative, and consultative selling.
2. The personal selling process typically involves six stages:
   - Attaining knowledge
   - Prospecting
   - Preapproach
   - Approach
   - Sales presentation
   - Follow-up
3. Five communication style elements in personal selling are pace, scope, depth of inquiry, interactive communication, and the use of supporting materials.

Managing a Sales Force

Most sales executives agree that strong sales supervision is a key ingredient in building an excellent sales force. A typical sales force is composed of men and women with diverse backgrounds and experience levels, often separated from headquarters by thousands of kilometres. Through necessity, many salespeople become the primary connection between the customer and the company. Consequently, there is a strong tendency for salespeople to be independent and to act as though they are running their own business. In the recent past sales managers made overt attempts to decrease this independence by requiring salespeople to report for weekly meetings. Because of the high cost of travel combined with the communication capabilities of laptop computers, this pattern has changed.

Today salespeople find themselves walking a thin line, splitting loyalties between customers and the company that pays their salary. Salespeople see their customers regularly but may have little contact with the company. In fact, the sales manager may be the only contact the salesperson has with the company.

The sales manager becomes the key link between the company and the sales force. The sales manager defines and interprets business policy, directs the daily efforts of the sales force, coaches the sales force, and helps salespeople resolve problems. The sales manager's task is far more complex than it was 20 years ago.

Products and services are more diverse and sophisticated. Buyers are more knowledgeable. Consequently, sales managers have had to become proficient at five sets of business activities:

- *Planning*: Planning is the process of forming objectives and strategies for personal selling. Taking into account both internal and external factors, sales managers should organize and plan a firm's personal selling effort so that it is consistent with other aspects of a firm's marketing communication program.
- *Staffing*: Staffing activities are those acts that sales managers take to recruit, hire, train, and maintain a quality sales force.
- *Implementing*: This is the process of taking steps to achieve the firm's sales plans. One step might be to design a program that helps salespeople meet the firm's sales revenue goal.
- *Controlling*: This set of activities is concerned with the performance of salespeople. Performance must be evaluated on a regular basis and must be equitable and consistent.
- *Adapting to change*: Sales managers must develop the ability to adapt to changes in the company, the business world, and technology. Global competition, for instance, may lead to company cost-cutting that forces sales managers to maintain or increase productivity with fewer resources. (The IMC in Action feature discusses cost issues that many sales managers face.) Managers must also quickly master new technology used to support sales efforts. They must often train others and learn to maximize the technology benefits.

Next we examine two sales management tasks that directly support the overall marketing communication effort. These tasks are setting sales objectives and motivating the sales force.

Setting Sales Objectives

The specific objectives for the sales force should be driven by the marketing communication objectives and should complement the stated objectives for the other marketing communication tools (see Figure 13.3). Unfortunately, this coordination of objectives is rarely done. Instead, sales managers revert most often to traditional personal selling objectives, such as targets and quotas.

Sales target
The desired level of sales for a product or product line during a specified time frame.

Sales quota
The share of the overall sales goal that is allocated to a salesperson, territory, or some other segment of the company business.

A **sales target** is the desired level of sales for a product or product line during a specified time frame. A **sales quota** is the share of the overall sales goal that is allocated to a salesperson, territory, or some other segment of the company business. Although these traditional sales objectives are relatively easy to understand and implement, they do not necessarily incorporate an integrated perspective. IMC-based personal selling objectives should consider all the contact points between personal selling and all other marketing communication tools. For example, salespeople could have objectives relative to their performance at trade shows, distribution of coupons, or local organizations to which they belong.

Motivating the Sales Force

We've already discussed how difficult it is to tear down the barriers that separate the various marketing communication divisions. This is even more difficult with personal selling, which has traditionally been isolated. Motivating salespeople to

Balancing the Personal Selling Budget

The personal sales call is no longer the most cost-effective means of satisfying customers' demand for information. It is not unusual for the cost of a single personal sales call to exceed $500.

Because of rising costs, marketing communicators can no longer afford to invest as much in the selling cycle. Some major manufacturers now sell directly to the customer. However, they must demonstrate how a product or service provides a cost-effective, competitively superior solution to a prospect's solution. To do that through a series of personal sales calls (one to assess customer needs, one to present a proposed solution, and usually a third to do lunch and close the deal) is often cost prohibitive. It takes 3.7 personal calls to close a sale—$500 x 3.7 = $1850).

Somehow marketing communicators must find a way to generate leads, gather prospect information, customize presentations, and maintain close contact with the prospect throughout the selling cycle in a cost-effective manner.

Here are some suggestions:

- *Teleprospecting*: If you can define your target audience by industry, size of company, title, or function, you can generate a prospect list and prequalify prospects over the telephone.
- *Electronic sales call*: If your product lends itself to a demonstration on videotape, computer disk, or the Internet, consider sending a cover letter with a brochure, demo tape, or disk as a first sales call. Or you could send an e-mail that explains how interested prospects can visit a Web site for a demonstration.
- *Selling for bunches*: Assembling 10 qualified prospects in a room for a demonstration and sales pitch is a better use of a salesperson's time than calling on them individually.
- *Point-of-sale*: Join forces with other divisions or companies to sell noncompeting families of products. Sharp managers try to maximize sales time and results by giving the sales force a broader base of products that they can sell in one call. The interactive kiosk, for example, may be placed in a central location where prospects can examine alternative sources and seek additional information.

Food for Thought

1. Do you think there will always be some customers who want to talk to a salesperson personally? If so, what are the implications?
2. How could these new cost-effective techniques improve integration of personal selling with other marketing communication activities?

Sources: Andy Cohen, "No Deal," ***Sales & Marketing Management*** (August 1996): 51–4; Nancy Arnott, "Selling is Dying," ***Sales & Marketing Management*** (August 1994): 82–6; Richard Van Gaasbeck, "Marketers Can't Afford to Invest More in Personal Sales Calls," ***The Marketing News*** 27, no. 19 (September 13, 1993): 11.

sell more may often spill over and create a higher level of cooperation between marketing communication groups. One might assume that salespeople who experience some level of personal and monetary success would not need additional incentives to perform well. In fact, providing such incentives is one of the most time-consuming aspects of the sales manager's job. Motivation provides positive incentives; discipline involves the use of negative incentives.

Sales managers use several methods to motivate. Among the most common are financial bonuses, security, opportunity for advancement, a meaningful job, status, personal power, self-determination, and pleasant working conditions.[7]

Financial Incentives

Monetary rewards are still the primary means of motivating salespeople. Financial incentives can be divided into two categories: base compensation and extra compensation. Extra compensation includes incentives such as bonuses, optional programs (for example, stock purchases and profit sharing), prizes, and rewards.

To attract and hold good salespeople, a compensation plan must meet employees' requirements. However, the compensation plan must also be consis-

Figure 13.3 COMPANY OBJECTIVES FOR SALES GROWTH TRANSLATED INTO SPECIFIC OBJECTIVES FOR THE SALES FORCE

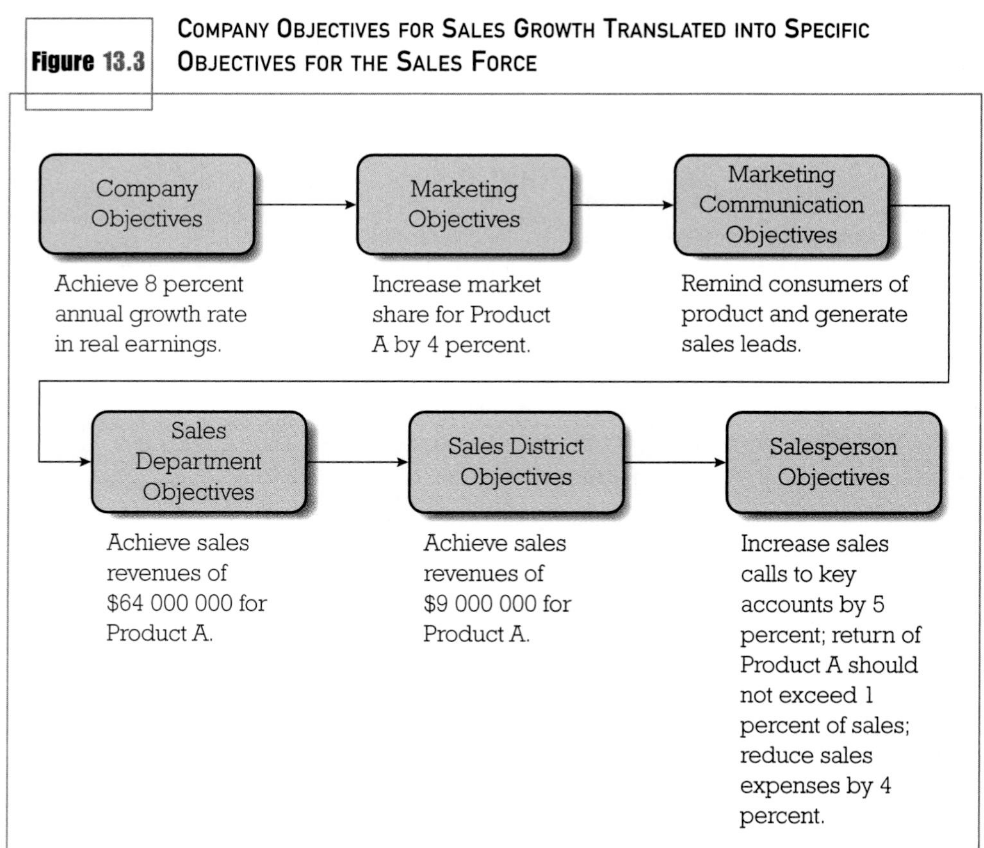

tent with the company's requirements and must support the overall marketing communication program. Balancing employee and company requirements is not always easy.

Straight salary
The compensation of people for time spent on the job.

The three basic types of compensation for salespeople are straight salary, straight commission, and combination. **Straight salary** compensates people for time spent on the job. This guaranteed amount provides financial security but provides no incentive to work harder. It is a fixed cost for the company and is a problem only if sales decline severely.

Straight salary programs are more common in business-to-business than in consumer product selling, as is the case when several specialists on a team sell complex aerospace products to airlines and the government. Salary is also appropriate in situations where products are presold through advertising or sales promotion and the salesperson primarily takes orders.

Straight commission
Compensation paid to salespeople on a fixed or sliding rate of earnings based on their sales volume or profit contribution.

The second compensation approach is **straight commission**. Under a commission plan, salespeople are paid a fixed or sliding rate of earnings based on their sales volume or profit contribution. The commission rewards people for getting orders. It also motivates them to exceed established standards of productivity. Because salary is tied directly to sales productivity, this compensation plan virtually pays for itself. However, it is difficult for salespeople to make a living on a straight commission program if they hit a slow period or take a little longer to get started. For experienced, successful salespeople who wish to have no ceiling on their income, straight commission is a powerful incentive.

Straight commission works best when maximum incentive is needed and when a minimum of aftersale service and missionary work is required. This

Avon Canada
www.avon.ca

Combination plan
The combination of salary and commission program aimed at maximizing its program's particular benefits.

Extra incentives
A variety of awards given to salespeople for achieving specific goals.

situation exists for most organizations that sell housewares and cosmetics door to door. Mary Kay Cosmetics, Tupperware, Avon, and Amway use straight commission compensation programs. Other types of businesses that often use straight commission plans include life insurance, real estate, stock brokerage, wholesale clothing, and printing.

The **combination plan** attempts to eliminate the limitations of the straight salary and straight commission programs and maximize their advantages. The salesperson's base salary is usually high enough to provide the financial security that the employee desires. That salary is also low enough so that its fixed cost does not seriously affect the firm in periods of declining sales. In addition to the base salary, an incentive is paid in the form of a commission—usually on sales greater than a set quota. Combination plans are widely used in industrial firms that sell building materials, machinery, electrical supplies, and paper products. This plan is less popular in consumer product companies.

Virtually all organizations also offer extra incentives to their salespeople. **Extra incentives** include a variety of awards given to salespeople for achieving specific goals. These extra incentives are in addition to compensation. The awards usually fall into three categories: cash, merchandise, and travel. A recent survey by *Incentive* reports that travel remains the award of choice (36 percent); merchandise is second (33 percent); and cash is third (31 percent).[8]

Other Motivators

Security is important to many people. To provide a more secure environment, companies may offer better salaries, better fringe benefits, and an atmosphere that assures salespeople that the company respects and values them.

Opportunity for advancement is another motivating factor. In most companies salespeople tend to follow one of two career paths. Either they want to remain a sales representative with greater compensation and responsibility, or they are using their current job as a stepping stone toward a sales management job. For both career paths, the sales manager must develop a clear and fair set of criteria that a person must meet to be promoted.

Managers also motivate salespeople by making them feel that their job is meaningful. Sales managers must learn to raise the status of selling within the firm on the basis of both its absolute contribution to the firm and to society. In companies where salespeople feel their jobs are meaningful, morale is seldom a problem.

Closely related to the meaning of the sales job is individual status. In many companies status may mean little more than conferring titles and labels that generate personal prestige. Being called a sales representative or a client representative, for example, may seem more impressive than being called a salesperson. Receiving the label CLU (Chartered Life Underwriter) or "member of the million-dollar roundtable" means a great deal to a life insurance salesperson. Status can also be conveyed through the quality of the company car provided or the size of an expense account.

Sometimes the incentives provided to salespeople can prompt them to engage in unethical behaviour. As noted in the You Decide feature, integrating personal selling with other marketing communication activities may solve this problem.

Increasing salespeople's authority may also motivate, such as giving salespeople the right to make decisions that they were not allowed to make before.

A Different Perspective

Few companies are better candidates for a business-school case study on Murphy's Law than the beleaguered Prudential Insurance Co. When the meter stops, the Pru will probably have shelled out more than $2.1 billion to settle claims from 1980s sales of soured Oil and Gas Limited partnerships by its Prudential Securities, Inc., unit. In 1996, after an investigation that had lasted more than a year, investigators concluded that Prudential had improperly urged some customers to cash in or borrow against existing policies to buy new, often more expensive ones.

In accepting the findings Prudential agreed to pay a fine of $49 million and to compensate policy holders—a $196-million tab.

Enter Pru senior vice president Martha Goss, who was tapped in 1993 by chairperson Robert C. Winters for a daunting three-year assignment: Install a top-to-bottom system of integral internal controls in every unit, and, along the way, overhaul the corporate culture.

Goss admits that some controls broke down in the late 1980s. To remedy this the company installed a comprehensive, integrated risk control system with the help of Coopers & Lybrand. Over the next year or so, Goss, with the aid of a small staff, swept through the company, working with managers to identify risks and then building controls to address them. All managers, she said, will be called upon to ask themselves: "What's the worst that can happen, and could I survive it?"

Goss explained that the thrust of the exercise was to ensure that "people know what their jobs are, what's expected of them, and that they're accountable for them." She felt the program could convince employees that they have not only a right but a responsibility to ask questions if they are instructed to do something they don't think is right or don't fully understand. This change in philosophy has a particularly strong bearing on the sales force, who traditionally did what they were told to do, no questions asked. With this integrated approach to the management of Prudential, the risks of salespeople making unethical decisions should have greatly diminished.

However, the 1996 investigation findings indicated that for more than a decade Prudential's representatives had engaged in improper sales practices that harmed customers.

After Prudential accepted the investigation findings, it made attempts to reconcile with its customers. The first program is called the client acquisition process. It attempted to reduce the complexity of the application process by instituting the use of a shortened client information form at the point of sale. It connected the client directly with the underwriter and allowed the salesperson more time to build relationships and less time filling out forms. Prudential also agreed to another program—supervised by insurance regulators and independent auditors—in which the firm contacted each person who felt unfairly treated and tried to work through those issues.

You Decide

1. What effect does the sales force behaviour have on the other communication elements at Prudential?
2. Do you think the activities Goss undertook could still help Prudential? Explain.
3. How likely do you think it is that Prudential can reconcile with its customers? What additional steps, if any, should it take?
4. Do you think that Prudential should consider paying its sales force a different form of salary other than straight commission? Explain your answer.

Sources: Joseph B. Treaster, "Prudential to Pay Policyholders $140 Million for Its Sales Tactics," ***New York Times***, 25 September 1996, C1; Prudential home page, The Prudential Insurance Co. of America, Newark, N.J. (1996), Internet (www.prudential.com); Philip L. Zweig, "Prudential: Making it Rock-Solid Again," ***Business Week***, October 31, 1994, 96.

Sales managers can also motivate salespeople by giving them more autonomy. Individuals tend to enter the sales field because of the independence it provides. They resent being told what they should do and how they should do it.

Finally, good working conditions also tend to improve productivity. Many aspects of the sales job (for example, long hours and extensive travel) are unattractive. Intelligent sales managers allow salespeople to live well while travelling by providing a safe, comfortable car and allowing them to eat at good restaurants and stay at pleasant hotels. It is better to economize in other areas than to limit the work environment of the salesperson.

concept review

Managing a Sales Force

1. Sales managers must become proficient at five sets of business activities:
   - Planning
   - Staffing
   - Implementing
   - Controlling
   - Adapting to change
2. The sales manager must also set personal selling objectives and motivate the sales force. Sales managers motivate salespeople through such means as financial incentives, security, and opportunity for advancement.

A Closing Thought:

The Sales Force of the Future

As discussed in the Consider This feature of this chapter, we can only speculate about changes in the nature of personal selling in the coming decades. However, the need for professional salespeople who embrace technology to aid their application of needs-based selling will likely remain intact for several decades. Why? Simply because many products will still need to be sold face-to-face by knowledgeable and trustworthy persons who are willing to resolve customer problems.

Still major changes in personal selling will occur, in large part due to technology. Though technology has increased selling efficiency, it has also resulted in more complex products that require more sales calls per order in many industries.

Sales teams will continue to gain popularity because customers are looking to buy more than a product. They are looking for sophisticated design, sales, education, and service support. Even today, many organizational buyers are looking for suppliers who will take responsibility for looking after the part of their business that pertains directly to the supplier's product.[9] To meet such expectations, salespeople need to engage several individuals who possess unique expertise and coordinate their efforts to help meet customer needs in every way possible.

Salespeople of the future will have to adjust to new forms of competition. With the increased capabilities and greater use of direct marketing, for example, salespeople must recognize that some customers will buy a product without contact with a sales person. Where appropriate, information technologies will be embraced to enhance marketing communications. Salespeople of the twenty-first century should either integrate direct marketing to support the selling process or offer the customer benefits not available through other marketing communication techniques.

On this very small planet, salespeople will also have to adjust to new sources of competition. Companies in Asia, South America, and Eastern Europe are introducing thousands of new products to industrialized nations every year. The salesperson of the future must know how to respond to foreign competitors and how to enter their markets. A program that integrates personal selling with other marketing communication tools will give salespeople more opportunity to act efficiently and have selling success.

summary

1. Define personal selling.

   Personal selling is the face-to-face presentation of a product to a potential customer by a company representative.

2. Describe the strengths and weaknesses of personal selling.

   Compared with other marketing communication tools, personal selling has several strengths. First, it is more flexible because salespeople can adjust their presentations to suit customers' needs and motives. Second, salespeople target potential customers rather than a mass audience, so personal selling minimizes wasted communication efforts. Third, the interactive nature of personal selling allows salespeople to make repeated requests for action, often resulting in sales. Fourth, salespeople can perform many jobs on behalf of the company, such as taking orders, collecting information, and offering service. Finally, the effectiveness of personal selling is easy to measure. Personal selling also has several weaknesses. Its cost is relatively high, finding and retaining high-quality people is difficult, the sales force often sends messages inconsistent with other marketing communication and with other salespeople, and sales representatives often have different levels of motivation that can affect product sales.

3. Discuss how personal selling fits in the marketing communication mix.

   The marketing communicator must decide how to use personal selling in the marketing communication mix by examining several factors, including the product, the market, the distribution channel, the nature of the information needed to sell the product, the marketing communication objectives, the marketing communication mix alternatives available, and the relative cost of personal selling compared with other marketing communication mix tools.

4. Outline both the types and the process of personal selling.

   The six most common types of personal selling are responsive selling, trade selling, missionary selling, technical selling, creative selling, and consultative selling. No matter what type of selling is used, the personal selling process generally follows a pattern of six steps: attaining knowledge, prospecting (scouting for interested customers), preparing for the sale (known as the preapproach), approaching the sales presentation, making the sales presentation, and follow up with activities after the sale (such as service, oversight of installation).

5. Explain the tasks of sales management that relate directly to marketing communication.

   To manage a sales force, sales managers must accomplish many tasks, such as planning, staffing, implementing sales objectives, controlling, and adapting to change. Two sales managerial tasks relate directly to marketing communication—setting sales objectives and motivating the sales force.

points to ponder

Review the Facts

1. Explain the six steps in the personal selling process.
2. Discuss the strengths and weaknesses of personal selling.
3. The relative importance of personal selling in the marketing communication mix is a function of several factors. What are those factors?

Master the Concepts

4. What styles of communication can salespeople use in personal selling? Explain the key ideas behind each stylistic element.
5. What contributions can personal selling make to a firm that advertising or sales promotion cannot provide?
6. What are the implications of the rapid advances of technology and the high cost of selling on the future of personal selling?

Apply Your Knowledge

7. "Personal selling should be a separate part of the organization. We create the sales, unlike those fools in advertising." Evaluate this statement and explain the problems that result in an organization that has this opinion.
8. What are the problems faced in motivating sales personnel? Identify three types of sales jobs. What type motivation would work best with each?
9. Now suppose you were the sales manager for a firm that wants to integrate personal selling more closely with its other marketing communication activities. The business sells nonprescription sunglasses that use a newly patented sun glare protection device that no other sunglasses manufacturer can offer. You've been assigned to work with the marketing director and the managers of advertising, public relations, sales promotion, and direct-marketing. Describe the steps the firm could take to integrate personal selling with the other marketing communication tools, discuss how you might set sales objectives consistent with the marketing communication objectives, and outline how you could motivate the sales force to support the integrated efforts.
10. Consider the process of personal selling. Identify which marketing communication tools could be useful at each stage of the process and explain how those tools would be helpful.

suggested projects 

1. (Oral Communication) Contact two salespeople (one who sells industrial products and one who sells consumer products). Interview them about the steps they follow in selling their products. How do they differ? How are they alike? Be prepared to present your findings to the class.
2. (Writing Project) Select and research the marketing communication activities of a company of your choice that sells a product or service to other businesses. Write a two-page essay on how personal selling and the other marketing communication techniques could complement one another.
3. (Internet Project) Some experts have predicted that the Internet will replace the traditional sales force. Others claim that the Web can improve the service a salesperson can offer because it can provide additional support, general information, and a means for reaching customers cheaply at any time of day or night. Take a look at the Web site of at least one direct marketer to see whether the site is designed to help its sales force and, if so, how. Alternatively, does the site seem to encourage ordering directly from the company, rather than putting consumers in touch with a sales representative? Explain. Be prepared to discuss your findings in class. Four suggested sites follow:

Amway	www.amway.com
Avon	www.avon.ca
Tupperware	www.tupperware.ca
Pampered Chef	www.pamperedchef.com

INTERPLAK MAXIMIZES SALES

When Interplak was first introduced to the marketplace, Bausch & Lomb traditionally worked with dentists and hygienists to maximize their sales potential. The Interplak was distributed primarily through dentists to patients. A revolutionary tool in dental health care, the electric toothbrush featured 10 tufts of bristles that rotated 4200 times per minute, reversing direction 46 times each second. It cleaned teeth of plaque and reduced gingivitis so effectively that thousands of dental professionals enthusiastically recommended it to their patients.

The Interplak instrument was then made available at retail stores. Bausch & Lomb salespeople knew that a significant number of consumers bought the instrument because of dentists' recommendations. When consumer demand and retail distribution increased, the sales force wanted to strengthen relationships with dentists who would recommend the Interplak to patients.

Robert LeBoeug, director of professional marketing and sales, described the situation: "One of my first challenges when I joined Bausch & Lomb a year ago was to transition our professional sales force. We needed to move from 'unit sales' strategy to a 'recommendation sales' strategy so dentists would continue to strongly recommend our highly effective product."

To maximize sales Bausch & Lomb needed to minimize the amount of time their professional salespeople spent locating dentists with high recommendation potential. Says LeBoeug, "Most of us who work in an office have a place to start each morning. But because salespeople don't have an office, they have to decide each day where to go and what to do once they get there. The more information we can give them, the stronger our company grows."

So Bausch & Lomb enlisted the help of a company named NDL that could identify areas with the greatest potential. NDL helped Bausch & Lomb develop a way to track their success. First, Bausch & Lomb provided NDL with a list of dentists they wanted to track. NDL created maps of Areas of Dominant Influence (ADIs), broken down by postal codes, for each Bausch & Lomb sales territory. On these maps NDL plotted where all dentists were located and highlighted those who were the strongest advocates for the Interplak instrument. Next, NDL developed a consumer profile of existing Interplak users. Finally, by overlaying that consumer profile on NDL's master database, NDL could also map Bausch & Lomb's best prospective Interplak consumers.

What immediate effect did this information have on Bausch & Lomb's professional sales force? "It blew them away," LeBoeug says. "Right away they were impressed that we could give them such detailed information on their territories. That same information also helps Bausch & Lomb motivate its salespeople to increase their productivity. "Before working with NDL, we had a difficult time measuring recommendation sales on a per-territory basis. NDL helped us develop a way to measure the impact of a specific salesperson's efforts, based on the number of recommendations we received within a particular postal code. Tracking these numbers tells us how effective our salespeople are in increasing recommendations for our products."

Case Questions

1. What are the benefits of reaching dentists when the primary distribution channel is retail stores?
2. How else could Bausch & Lomb use their database?
3. Assume you sell Interplak for Bausch & Lomb and you have been placed on a marketing communication committee to analyse how to combat competition, including Braun's Oral-B toothbrush. What suggestions would you make to other members of the committee about how the sales force should work with other marketing communication specialists in tackling the competition?

Source: "Interplak Brushes Up on Productivity," ***Focus*** (Winter 1992): 4–5.

14 IMC Media

chapter objectives

After completing your work on this chapter, you should be able to

- Explain why marketing communicators must understand the comparative strengths and weaknesses of the various media alternatives.
- Describe the characteristics, buying process, and strengths and weaknesses of the primary print media—newspapers and magazines.
- Describe the characteristics, buying process, and strengths and weaknesses of the primary broadcast media—TV and radio.
- Describe the characteristics, buying process, and strengths and weaknesses of the primary out-of-home media—outdoor and transit.
- Explain the role that supplemental and new media play in the overall media strategy.

The Future of Mass Media

The similarities between the early days of TV and the current evolution of interactive media are striking. Some observers view it as part of a natural business cycle. "All radically new technologies are met with huge skepticism. This was true about television and it's true about interactive media," says George Gilder, author of ***Life After Television***. "The people who've learned the old technology are afraid to learn something new. People's knowledge is really their resource." Others see it as being indicative of marketing communication firms' underlying fear of the unknown and unwillingness to encourage companies to take risks.

You know when you were a kid and you had a box full of your favorite stuff?

This is the new electronic version.

Tune into what you're into.

Today, with passive TV a dominant force in people's lives, many question whether viewers will want to interact with TV, or whether they'll want to sit in front of a computer to do tasks, such as banking and shopping, that they now do outside the home. Part of what drew marketers to TV in the early days, despite their fears, was the belief that early adopters of new technologies represent more desirable, affluent, and educated consumers. The same belief is drawing marketers to interactive services today.

Eugene Kummee, chairperson emeritus of McCann-Erickson Worldwide, indicates that advertisers "were reluctant to give up the efficiency of radio and print until they were absolutely sure [TV] was coming.... I think the same thing is happening today." ***Newsweek*** vice chairperson Don Durgin notes, "Nobody's pooh-poohing interactivity, like they did TV. . . . They're simply saying nobody knows how to place the bets on how all of this will come out."

Based on the growth of Web sites alone one would have to assume that interactive media is here to stay and that it is only a matter of time before it reaches critical mass. Already the Internet has become the ultimate narrowcasting vehicle: Everyone from UFO buffs to Vancouver Grizzlies fans have a Web site (or a dozen) to call their own—a "dot-com" in every port. The featured Web-TV Network ad suggests the next stage of evolution: interactivity via your TV.

No one has taken a more aggressive look at interactive media than Edwin Artz, chair of Procter & Gamble. He envisions a P&G–produced CD-ROM, for example, titled: "Are You Getting a Cold?" The CD-ROM's program would follow a cold's average five-day cycle, demonstrating the patient's need each day for a new P&G product, from Vick's VapoRub to NyQuil.

Sources: Richard Zoglin, "The News Wars," *Time*, October 21, 1996, 58–63; Scott Donaton, "The Next 50 Years," *Advertising Age* (Spring 1995): 54; "P&G's Artz: TV Advertising in Danger," *Advertising Age*, May 23, 1994, 34, 40; Mark Rebuchaux, "Despite Many Claims for 500-Channel TV, Long Road Lies Ahead," *Wall Street Journal*, 29 November 1993, A1.

Chapter Overview

Regardless of how well designed and targeted a marketing communication message is, it will not succeed unless it is transmitted through the most appropriate medium. What is an appropriate medium? One that complements the message, one that target audience members use consistently, and one that can deliver the message at the right time—that is, when the target audience is most receptive.

Selecting and combining appropriate media effectively is a complex process. It requires that marketing communication managers plan a comprehensive combination of media suitable for both the marketing communication message and the target audience. This combination of media—known as the media mix—must suit both the message and audience to increase the chance of a successful marketing communication program.

Though media planning—the process of selecting media objectives for the marketing communication program and devising a strategy to reach those objectives—is a key part of marketing communication, few students begin their university careers with media planning in mind. The job requires a penchant for numbers, detail, and organization as well as an ability to see the big picture and to generate creative solutions. Media planning also requires two kinds of knowledge. First, **media planners** (those who make decisions about the media mix and implement those decisions) must have a thorough understanding of all types of media—of their capabilities, limitations, trends, and technology. Second, media planners must understand the media planning process, such as how to select media objectives and evaluate whether the media suits the target markets, the schedule, and the budget. **Media buyers** actually purchase the media selected. This job is usually an entry-level position that leads to media planning.

Media planners
The people who make decisions and implement the media mix that best fits the client's marketing strategy.

Media buyers
The people who actually purchase the media selected.

In this chapter we explore five different types of mass media: print, broadcast, out-of-home, supplemental, and new media. The supplemental category includes merchandising material, specialty advertising, directories, telemarketing, and direct mail. The new media section deals with recent trends, including online technology.

Mass medium
It can reach many people simultaneously, and it requires the use of some technological device to connect the marketing communicator with the audience.

Mass-Media Developments

A **mass medium** must meet two requirements: (1) it can reach many people simultaneously, and (2) it requires the use of some technological device to connect the marketing communicator with the audience. Thus the interactive media discussed in earlier chapters, such as interactive television, is mass media because it can reach many audience members at the same time and uses technology to do so.

Marketing communicators strive to find the most effective mass media for their messages, given the target audience, schedule, and budget. Understanding of the capabilities of each type of mass media can help marketing communicators find the most effective mix. Table 14.1 summarizes the capabilities of many types of mass media. In the following sections we detail the strengths and weaknesses of each media type.

Media planners must also understand the cost of each medium. The tremendous cost and waste associated with traditional mass media, such as network television commercials, have pushed many marketing communicators toward

Table 14.1 STRATEGIC CAPABILITIES OF MASS MEDIA

Tyes of Media	Market Coverage	Cost	Cost per Thousand	Flexibility	Emotional Impact	Targetability	Reputation	Clutter	Message Length	Frequency	Immediacy	Creativity	Reseller's Support	Production
National newspapers	—	—	+	—	0	+	+	—	+	+	+	+	—	+
Local newspapers	+	+	+	+	0	+	+	—	+	+	+	—	+	—
Magazines	—	0	—	—	+	+	+	—	+	0	+	+	+	+
Network television	+	—	+	—	+	0	+	+	0	0	+	+	+	+
Cable television	0	+	+	+	0	+	0	+	+	+	+	+	+	+
Local radio	+	+	+	+	0	+	0	—	—	+	+	0	+	0
Out-of-home	—	+	+	—	—	—	—	—	—	0	—	0	—	0
Directories	0	+	+	—	—	+	+	—	—	—	—	0	—	0
Online	—	0	—	+	+	+	—	0	+	+	+	+	0	+

— Weak Capability 0 Moderate capability + Strong capability

media that is less expensive, better targeted, and easier to track. Media planners are also becoming more aggressive in dealing with the media by dictating rates, demanding greater service, and asking for guaranteed results.

Media alternatives are also being analysed as part of an integrated marketing communication program. Media planners evaluate which combination of media can best deliver the marketing communication message in a way that builds relationships with stakeholders. In integrated programs, then, media intended for the masses are often modified to appeal to the individual. For instance, a media planner might choose to run a print ad in *Maclean's* that includes a toll-free number or Internet home page address, and is placed in its Platinum demographic edition modified to speak to the needs of subscribers with annual household incomes greater than $75 000. Or the media planner for STP might opt for a commercial on ESPN that would not only sell STP gas treatment but would also inform viewers of both local dealers who sell the product and an STP-sponsored racing event.

Throughout this chapter and the next, we view media and media planning as part of an integrated marketing communication program. Media that complement one another and facilitate one-to-one communication usually aid integration more than media that cannot do these things. We look carefully at these types of media, beginning with print media. The order of discussion has nothing to do with the relative importance of the media alternatives. Employing an integrated approach means that a media strategy starts with a blank slate.

PRINT MEDIA

Before the emergence of television and radio, print media dominated our society. However, since that time we have become a broadcast-based society. The nightly TV news has surpassed the daily newspaper as the primary source of information. Catalogues, telemarketing, and infomercials are gradually supplanting magazines as the media through which niche markets learn about products. Still, print media can accomplish some objectives better than broadcast media, as shown in Table 14.1. IMC strategists must understand the capabilities of print compared with other types of media, such as radio and TV. For instance, a recent study of 2000 consumers shows that consumers consider print ads more informative, more entertaining, and less offensive than broadcast commercials.[1]

NEWSPAPERS

Newspapers are changing the way they deliver the news. In the near future newspapers will link customers through telephones and cable-television hookups. Many papers are moving online in more accessible ways, including through the electronic catalogues now in wide use in public libraries. Daily papers are also adding new technology to allow readers to interact in different ways with the papers' information databases. In addition, daily and national papers are adding more phone-accessible fax delivery of articles and special reports. There are even companies like CANOE, Canada's Internet Network, that offer a totally customized daily supply of information. "I'll take the News headlines, please, plus NHL scores, updates on my Investor's Group mutual fund—and my horoscope."

Canoe
www.canoe.ca

THE INDUSTRY AND ITS AUDIENCE

Southam Inc.
www.southam.com

More than 9200 newspapers are published in North America today. In the Canadian market, there are approximately 110 daily newspapers with a total average daily circulation of 4.8 million copies.[2] Southam Inc., a privately held Canadian corporation, is one of Canada's largest publishers of daily newspapers, with an average circulation of about 1.2 million copies. Southam's principal publications are the *National Post, The Vancouver Sun, The Province (Vancouver), The Edmonton Journal, Calgary Herald, Ottawa Citizen,* and *The Gazette* (Montreal). Southam also produces a national consumer Web site, Canada.com, which provides news content and searching capabilities through the Internet.[3] Another major force in the Canadian newspaper industry is The Thomson Corporation. Thomson's principal newspaper publications are *The Globe and Mail* and *The Winnipeg Free Press.*

The Thomson Corp.
www.thomcorp.com

In 1998, Canadian dailies' net advertising volume was $2.379 billion, outperforming television's $2.312 billion by 2.8 percent. Moreover, the dailies' share of net advertising volume in 1998 was almost 25 percent of the $9.543 billion spent by Canadian advertisers across all media.[4] The level of circulation of Canadian newspapers explains, in part, why newspapers are a major generator of advertising revenue in Canada. Other explanations for this medium's attractiveness to advertisers include its credibility as an information source, the flexibility of its market and lead time, a large pass-along audience, and the ability for local promotions to be tied in to national promotions. These strengths are discussed later in this chapter.

Shopper
Publications such as *Real Estate Guide* usually distributed free to certain homes in certain neighbourhoods or through supermarket racks.

Newspapers can be classified in several ways: by their physical size (standard or tabloid), intended audience (for example, financial, French-speaking), and type of circulation (for example, paid or controlled). Most newspapers are "paid," that is, subscribers pay for them. A **shopper**, such as real estate or restaurant guides, are usually distributed free to certain homes in certain neighbourhoods, or through supermarket racks. The primary way of classifying newspapers, however, is based on their frequency of publication, either daily, weekly, or on Sunday.

Various trade organizations and academic researchers provide information that help media planners understand the readership patterns of subscribers. For instance, market research shows that readers have become more selective about what they read in the newspaper. To maintain subscribers many newspapers have become more responsive to the needs and interests of their readers. Such information is quite useful to the marketing communications strategist, who can then determine whether a product would fit the newspaper.

Classified ads
Include all types of messages arranged by classification of interest, such as Help Wanted, Cars for Sale, and so on.

Display ads
Found throughout the newspaper, they generally use illustrations, headlines, white space, and other visual devices in addition to the text copy.

Short rate
A rate higher than the contract rate that is applied if less-than-agreed-upon space was purchased.

Buying Newspaper Space

A newspaper's audience size, demographic characteristics of readers, and advertising rates are among the characteristics media planners must consider. Most daily newspapers offer classified advertising (including regular and display) and display advertising. **Classified ads** include all types of messages arranged by classification of interest, such as Help Wanted, Cars for Sale, and so on. Classified display ads allow more flexibility than regular classifieds because advertisers may use borders, large type, white space, photos, and occasionally colour.

Display ads are found throughout the newspaper and generally use illustrations, headlines, white space, and other visual devices in addition to the text copy. They can be of any size. For display ads the infrequent advertiser usually pays a standard rate per column space occupied. An advertiser who uses significant amounts of space pays a discounted bulk or contract rate based on the total amount of space purchased. Advertisers and newspapers frequently sign annual contracts for a given space commitment. When it comes time for a tally, if less-than-agreed-upon space was purchased, a **short rate** that is higher than the contract rate is applied. If more space was purchased, a rebate is provided.

The Globe and Mail
www.globeandmail.com

Determining Costs. Newspaper space is sold primarily on the basis line space occupied. Media buyers refer to two units of space measurement when comparing the cost of one newspaper with another: Modular Agate Line (MAL) and Canadian Newspaper Unit (CNU). A MAL is a standardized unit of space equal to one newspaper column wide and 1/14 inch deep. Standard newspaper column widths are 1 1/16 inch. CNU is a standardized unit that is one newspaper column wide by 30 modular agate lines deep (2 1/8 inch). Sources such as a newspaper's rate card list the newspaper's line rates. The rates vary depending on circulation, cost of operation, labour costs, qualitative factors, and type of newspaper. Figure 14.1 provides a rate card for *The Globe and Mail.*

Specific Marketing Communication Options. Advertisers can usually order specific pages or positions for an extra charge. For example, if an advertiser using the *Ottawa Citizen* wants to ensure ad placement at the very top of the page and next to reading matter along one of its vertical sides (called full position), the

Figure 14.1 A RATE CARD FOR THE GLOBE AND MAIL

GENERAL RATES

THE GLOBE AND MAIL

2000 ADVERTISING RATES

Effective January 17, 2000

To reach Canada's most sought-after audience, there is no better place than through The Globe and Mail.

Its readers are educated, influential and discerning, with the highest average household income of any newspaper in Canada.*

They are predisposed to spending on a wide variety of products and services for both personal and business use.

Whatever you are selling, The Globe and Mail delivers more of the people who are your best customers daily – in numbers too significant to ignore – more of the people who are helping to build your business.

News and Report on Business

Report on Business appears in National Edition only.

Monday to Friday

	National	Ontario	Metro
Transient	$25.64	$22.13	$20.38
900	24.86	21.48	19.78
1,800	24.23	20.83	19.18
3,600	23.59	20.25	18.62
5,400	22.81	19.58	18.03
7,200	22.43	19.29	17.76
10,000	21.66	18.63	17.16
13,000	21.28	18.31	16.85
16,000	20.90	17.98	16.56
20,000	20.63	17.77	16.36
25,000	20.26	17.44	16.06
32,000	19.87	17.10	15.75
43,000	19.61	16.87	15.55
58,000	19.10	16.42	15.13
75,000	18.58	15.97	14.71
100,000	17.94	15.41	14.19
135,000	17.30	14.86	13.69
175,000	16.53	14.20	13.08

Saturday

	National	Ontario	Metro
Transient	$26.92	$23.24	$21.40
900	26.10	22.55	20.77
1,800	25.44	21.87	20.14
3,600	24.77	21.26	19.55
5,400	23.95	20.56	18.93
7,200	23.55	20.25	18.65
10,000	22.74	19.56	18.02
13,000	22.34	19.23	17.69
16,000	21.95	18.88	17.39
20,000	21.66	18.66	17.18
25,000	21.27	18.31	16.86
32,000	20.86	17.96	16.54
43,000	20.59	17.71	16.33
58,000	20.06	17.24	15.89
75,000	19.51	16.77	15.45
100,000	18.84	16.18	14.90
135,000	18.17	15.60	14.37
175,000	17.36	14.91	13.73

The Globe Review, Technology, Travel and Special Interest Reports

Monday to Friday

	National	Ontario	Metro
Transient	$15.99	$13.86	$12.72
900	15.41	13.35	12.23
1,800	14.94	12.94	11.85
3,600	14.43	12.57	11.36
5,400	14.05	12.15	11.03
7,200	13.87	11.99	10.93
10,000	13.44	11.61	10.59
13,000	13.19	11.40	10.40
16,000	12.99	11.22	10.25
20,000	12.82	11.08	10.11
25,000	12.62	10.90	9.94
32,000	12.39	10.69	9.76
43,000	12.23	10.56	9.63
58,000	11.97	10.33	9.41
75,000	11.70	10.10	9.21
100,000	11.36	9.81	8.93
135,000	11.02	9.51	8.65
175,000	10.53	9.08	8.27

Saturday

	National	Ontario	Metro
Transient	$16.79	$14.55	$13.36
900	16.18	14.02	12.84
1,800	15.69	13.59	12.44
3,600	15.15	13.20	11.93
5,400	14.75	12.76	11.58
7,200	14.56	12.59	11.48
10,000	14.11	12.19	11.12
13,000	13.85	11.97	10.92
16,000	13.64	11.78	10.76
20,000	13.46	11.63	10.62
25,000	13.25	11.45	10.44
32,000	13.01	11.22	10.25
43,000	12.84	11.09	10.11
58,000	12.57	10.85	9.88
75,000	12.29	10.61	9.67
100,000	11.93	10.30	9.38
135,000	11.57	9.99	9.08
175,000	11.06	9.53	8.68

*SOURCE: NADbank 1999, 37 Markets.

On-line Media Kit:
Visit our Web site at
www.globeandmail.com

1/17/2000

THE GLOBE AND MAIL

CANADA'S NATIONAL NEWSPAPER • FOUNDED 1844

advertiser may have to pay a premium price. However, certain advertisers may be able to negotiate for the same position without paying extra.

Newspapers may also offer special production capabilities for additional charges. For instance, colour preprint is a service offered by many daily newspapers. In this process colour ads are preprinted on a roll of paper that is fed into the presses. Colour preprints provide the national and local advertiser with many of the "quality" advantages of magazine colour while allowing each retailer to place imprinted copy next to the national advertiser's four-colour ad on the same page.

Another option offered by newspapers is the supplement. Each of the syndicated supplements is compiled, edited, and printed by a central organization that then sells it to newspapers; it offers group-rate advertising charges. Printed on paper that is heavier and better finished than newsprint, supplements can offer surprisingly low rates.

Newspaper Strengths and Weaknesses

As noted earlier, a primary strength of newspapers is that they serve as a trusted source of local information for many consumers. Sales promotion information (such as price discounts and coupons) and public relations information (such as open house announcements and special events) can all be delivered through newspapers. More important, consumers seek out this information.

Market flexibility is another advantage of newspapers. Gone are the days when one general newspaper served a particular market. Today newspapers have the capability of reaching special-interest groups, unique ethnic or racial groups, or even people living in isolated parts of the world.

Lead-time flexibility is a third advantage of newspapers. Lead time is the amount of time between when an ad must be delivered to the medium and when it is actually run. For example, the lead time for a newspaper ad is quite short, often 48 to 72 hours. Ads can therefore be changed at the last minute, or new ads can be inserted to meet an unforeseen circumstance, such as a dramatic change in the weather.

Newspapers also provide the advantage of a large pass-along audience. Not only do members of a family share the same newspaper, but newspapers are also read by people at fast-food chains, diners, bus and subway stations, and professional offices.

Furthermore, newspapers effectively combine local ads or sales promotions with national promotions. A local retailer can easily tie in with a national campaign by using a similar ad. Newspapers also allow preprinted ads and freestanding inserts (FSIs) to accommodate national promotions.

The most serious weakness of newspapers is clutter. With 65 percent or more of a typical newspaper filled with ads, it is difficult to create awareness. Clutter is also a problem with the freestanding inserts that deliver consumer coupons. FSIs are now so thick and bulky that sorting through them all is a task that many readers reject, choosing instead to remove the entire packet and put it aside.

Other limitations of newspapers include the one-day life of a paper, which means that a message has a very short time in which to work. A final weakness is the technical quality of newspapers. Porous paper and poor reproduction of print and photography often mean that an ad is difficult to read.

Magazines

Today magazines are the most specialized of the mass media, dramatically demonstrating the fact that the mass audience is becoming increasingly segmented. For example, *Writer's Market* lists more than a hundred magazines distributed in North American that deal with farming, soil management, poultry, dairy farming, and rural life. Farming magazines are one example of special-interest publications, which account for more than 90 percent of the total number of magazines published today.

Magazines and Their Audiences

Currently, there are approximately 1400 Canadian magazine titles. Many of these titles are special-interest magazines that have flourished partly as a result

concept review

PRINT MEDIA (NEWSPAPERS)

1. Media planners rely on circulation and rate information as the primary means for determining where to place ads.
2. Classified and display advertising in newspapers are sold on the basis of either a line rate or a bulk or contract rate.
3. The strengths of the newspaper medium are its credibility as an information source, the flexibility of its market and lead time, a large pass-along audience, and the local tie-in to national promotions.
4. The weaknesses of the newspaper medium are clutter, short life, technical quality, and high extra rates for national advertisers.

of the high advertising rates charged by mass-circulation, and general-interest magazines such as *Reader's Digest*, *Maclean's*, and *People*. This division into special- and general-interest magazines is just one of several ways of classifying magazines.

Magazines may also be classified by frequency of publication and the audience to which they are directed. Monthly magazines are the largest category, followed by the weeklies, semi-monthlies, bi-monthlies, and quarterlies. On the basis of the audience served, there are two types of magazines:

1. *Consumer magazines*, which are edited for people who buy products for their own consumption.
2. *Business magazines*, which are directed at business readers. These may be further divided into trade papers (read by retailers, wholesalers, and other distributors), industrial magazines (read by manufacturers and service providers), and professional magazines (read by such groups as physicians and lawyers).

Table 14.2 displays the total circulation of the top general interest and special interest consumer magazines.

The magazine industry applies three other possible classifications to each of the two just discussed. Consumer and business magazines can also be classified by geographic, demographic, and editorial content.

1. *Geographic content:* Regional editions of national publications (for example, *Maclean's*) may be circulated in an area such as the Atlantic Region, a single province, or limited to a single city.

Table 14.2 GENERAL- AND SPECIAL-INTEREST MAGAZINE CIRCULATION

GENERAL INTEREST		SPECIAL INTEREST — NEWS		SPECIAL INTEREST — HOMES	
CATEGORY	CIRCULATION	CATEGORY	CIRCULATION	CATEGORY	CIRCULATION
Reader's Digest	1 537 197	*L'actualité*	180 364	*Canadian House and Home*	153 138
Equinox	107 871	*Maclean's*	502 786	*Century Home*	29 344
Harrowsmith	152 972	*Time*	318 827	*Decoration Chez-Soi*	67 836

Source: Data extracted from ***Canadian Advertising Rates and Data***, December 1999. Printed with permission of CARD, Roger's Media Inc. Reported numbers represent average total paid circulation.

2. *Demographic editions:* Many magazines offer special editions for subscribers of a certain age, income, occupation, and so forth.
3. *Editorial content:* Magazines are defined by interest category such as general editorial, women's services, and business.

A magazine's total circulation, like that in Table 14.2, is just one of the significant pieces of data. For example, some media buyers regard news-stand sales as a good criterion of the quality of a magazine's circulation, because purchases at a news stand are completely voluntary. By paying more per copy and taking the initiative, news-stand buyers are viewed as more serious readers. Information relating to which subscribers renew their subscriptions is also important.

Audience profiles are invaluable to media buyers because reliable buyers can see how closely the magazine audience matches the target audience. In general, magazine readers are better educated, better read, and better paid than other members of the population.[5] However, the trend is definitely moving away from general-interest magazines and toward specialty titles. With consumers having less time to themselves, they're more interested in indulging in their personal interests.

Many magazines provide reader profiles to their advertisers to influence them to buy space. A media buyer may find that the audience profile for a magazine is attractive enough to override the fact that its circulation is smaller than that of a competitor. Careful media buyers need a complete picture of the magazine audience before purchasing advertising space. As a minimum, they should consider the following factors:

- Total circulation
- The percentage of the publication read completely
- Reader loyalty
- Reader demographics
- The magazine's past ability to generate high response in mail-order ads
- Special sections
- Number of pass-along readers

Buying Magazine Space

Besides considering the characteristics of readers, media buyers must also consider the cost of magazine space. Only a handful of marketers can afford to pay $25 000 or more for a full-page four-colour ad in a mass-circulation magazine. As a result, many smaller companies have turned to less expensive special-interest magazines, where their messages will be seen by fewer but more receptive readers.

Advertising Rates. Magazine space is sold primarily on the basis of pages or some increment of a page. For example, the rate card for *Maclean's* national editions is shown in Figure 14.2. Note that the rates are based on the purchase of a full page or some part of a page, converted into columns and some portion of a column. Also, four-colour ads will cost considerably more than black-and-white ads.

Figure 14.2 A RATE CARD FOR *MACLEAN'S* NATIONAL EDITION

ADVERTISING RATES: National

	A 1-5 issues Under 6 pages	B 6-12 issues 6-12 pages	C 13+ issues 13+ pages
Four Colour			
Full Page	$30 565	$29 800	$29 040
2/3 Page Horizontal or 2 Column	24 450	23 840	23 230
1/2 Page Horizontal or Dbl. 3/4 Column	21 400	20 870	20 330
(Junior Page) Banner	18 030	17 580	17 130
1 Column or Square 1/3 Page	14 670	14 300	13 940
Inside Front or Inside Back Cover	33 620	32 780	31 940
Outside Back Cover	36 680	35 760	34 850
Black & 1 Colour*			
Full Page	26 900	26 230	25 560
2/3 Page Horizontal or 2 Column	21 520	20 980	20 440
1/2 Page Horizontal or Dbl. 3/4 Column	18 830	18 360	17 890
(Junior Page) Banner	15 870	15 470	15 080
Column or Square 1/3 Page	12 910	12 590	12 260
Black & White			
Full Page	23 840	23 240	22 650
2/3 Page Horizontal or 2 Column	19 070	18 590	18 120
1/2 Page Horizontal or Dbl. 3/4 Column	16 690	16 270	15 860
(Junior Page) Banner	14 060	13 710	13 360
Column or Square 1/3 Page	11 440	11 150	10 870

Source: Extracted from http://www.macleans.ca/docs/advertise/ratesnational.html, November 23, 1999. Used with permission.

Should Government Subsidize Canadian Magazines?

Ottawa avoided a trade war with the United States by establishing an agreement to resolve a dispute over "split-run" editions of U.S. magazines. At issue was market share of Canadian-magazine advertising dollars. U.S. magazine publishers wanted to print Canadian versions (i.e., split-runs) with up to 100 percent Canadian ads. In an effort to protect the Canadian magazine industry by preventing this practice, Sheila Copps, Heritage Minister, championed Bill C-55. A controversial piece of legislation, Bill C-55 would have made it illegal for Canadian companies to advertise in "split-run" magazines. To avoid the trade war that was threatened by the Clinton administration if Bill C-55 were not abandoned, the two governments reached a compromise agreement.

The compromise involves a three-year phase-in that allows U.S. publishers to access Canadian advertising ranging from 12 percent in the first year and up to 18 percent in the third year. After the three-year phase-in, U.S. magazines wanting more than 18 per cent Canadian advertising content will have to contain a majority of Canadian content. In fact, it would have to be a Canadian magazine within a business established in Canada. To help offset expected financial problems for the domestic industry, the Canadian government proposed a subsidy scheme. The fund for this subsidy scheme is to total $150 million over three years. To be eligible for subsidy, publications must be Canadian-owned and controlled, and must contain 80 percent Canadian editorial content.

Reaction to this compromise seems mixed. Canadian publishers argued that letting U.S. magazines have access to more than 10 percent of the Canadian advertising market would be unacceptable. Sympathetic to Canadian publishers' concerns, the Writers Union of Canada claims that they too will be negatively affected by this practice. According to Christopher Moore, chair of the Writers Union of Canada, "[Canadian] magazines are under serious threat because advertisers can now find a cheaper venue through the dumped American version. So we see our writers will again lose markets for writing stories." Reaction to the compromise agreement has not been all negative. For example, a coalition representing the Association of Canadian Advertisers, Canadian Media Directors' Council, and Institute of Canadian Advertising say the agreement will foster a more vibrant business environment for magazines. Claiming to be supportive of the Canadian magazine industry, this coalition believes the agreement will give advertisers opportunities to reach certain markets and also create opportunities for Canadian publishers to broaden their initiatives.

You Decide

1. Do you think the compromise agreement is appropriate? Should the Canadian government implement a subsidy scheme for Canadian publishers? Explain your position on each of these issues.
2. Assume you are a media buyer for a large Canadian advertising agency. Would you be supportive of Bill C-55? Explain your position.
3. Assume you are the publisher of a Canadian specialty magazine. Would you be supportive of Bill C-55? Explain your position. Would your position on this issue be different if you were the publisher of a mass-circulation Canadian general-interest magazine?

Sources: "Canadian Magazines to Get $150M Subsidy," Ottawa, Dec. 16 (Reuters), extracted from www.canoe.ca/MoneyNews, December 16, 1999; Chris Cobb, "Ottawa Plans $90M Subsidy for Magazines," National Post Online, Monday, August 16, 1999; "Magazine Compromise Angers Canadian Publishers," CBC News, WebPosted Wednesday, May 26 22:30:04 1999; "Canada-U.S. Agreement First Step to Stronger Magazine Industry," (26 May, 1999), Extracted from www.aca-online.com?news1.htm, December 06, 1999; Jennifer Henderson, "Writers 'Discouraged' by Magazine Bill," CBC Radio News, (31 May, 1999), Extracted from www.infoculture.cbc.ca/archives, December 6, 1999. David Chilton, "Onslaught of Split Runs Has Begun," ***Marketing***, November 15, 1999, 4. "Magazines' Future Now," ***Marketing***, September 20, 1999, 11-14.

Remnant space
Publishers, especially those with geographic or demographic editions, sometimes have extra space in some editions when they are ready to go to press. Publishers usually offer this space to advertisers at a big discount.

A number of publishers, especially those with geographic or demographic editions, sometimes find themselves with extra space in some editions when they are ready to go to press. Rather than run an empty space, the publisher often offers this **remnant space** to advertisers at a big discount.

See this chapter's You Decide feature for a discussion of a recent Canada-U.S. trade dispute that raised concerns among Canadian magazine publishers. Canadian magazine publishers and others fear advertisers will find a cheaper venue in Canadian versions of U.S. magazines (i.e., split-runs).

Fractional page space
One-page or double-page ads broken into a variety of units.

Gatefold
A magazine cover or inside page that opens to reveal an extra page that folds out and gives the ad a big spread.

First cover page
Name given to the front cover of a magazine.

Second cover page
Name given to the inside of the front cover.

Third cover page
Name given to the inside of the back cover.

Fourth cover page
Name given to the back cover of a magazine.

Run-of-book
The cheapest magazine rate, which means that the ad can be placed anywhere in the magazine.

Bleed ad
The colour runs to the edge of the page, often costing an extra 15 to 20 percent.

Advertisorial
A set of consecutive pages on a single product or advertiser that is glued or stapled into the magazine.

Breakouts
Messages that will appear only in copies sent to a specific geographic region.

Closing date
This is the last date on which a magazine will accept advertising materials for publication in a particular issue.

Cover date
Date appearing on the issue's cover.

On-sale date
The day the issue goes on sale, which is when it reaches the reader.

MARKETING COMMUNICATION OPTIONS. In most cases the double-page spread is the largest unit of space sold by magazines, although larger books such as *Better Homes and Gardens* and *People* also offer a three-page gatefold. Magazines allow one-page or double-page ads to be broken into a variety of units called **fractional page space**: vertical half-page, horizontal half-page, double horizontal half-page, island position (surrounded by editorial matter), half-page double spread, and checkerboard.

Sometimes a magazine cover or an inside page opens to reveal an extra page that folds out and gives the ad a big spread. Advertisers use these **gatefolds** on special occasions to make the most spectacular presentation in the magazine, usually to introduce a colourful product like a new model car or beautiful flooring. They are an additional expense that requires advance planning.

An example of an unusual gatefold was partnered by *Elle* magazine and Elizabeth Arden Co. *Elle* agreed to split the cover down the middle to hide an ad for Arden's Sunflowers fragrance beneath the flags. To keep the cover from tearing, Elle's wrapped this issue in a clear plastic bag. The wrap also kept readers from seeing the split cover until after they bought the magazine.

The front cover of a magazine is called the **first cover page**. The inside of the front cover is called the **second cover page**, the inside of the back cover the **third cover page,** and the back cover the **fourth cover page**. Depending on the magazine, these covers may cost 10 to 60 percent more than a page inside the book.

The cheapest magazine rate is **run-of-book** (ROB), which means that the ad can be placed anywhere in the magazine. A **bleed ad** means the colour runs to the edge of the page. It often costs an extra 15 to 20 percent.

Many magazines also offer space for inserts. Examples are return cards (usually blown in—that is, unattached), coupons, receipt booklets, product samples, and other kinds of outside material bound or blown into the magazine in connection with an adjoining ad. Inserts are never sold separately. Negotiating and creating such inserts is the job of the marketing communication manager. A special type of insert that appears to be growing in popularity is called an **advertisorial**. It is a set of consecutive pages on a single product or advertiser that is glued or stapled into the magazine. Pick up *Fortune* magazine and you are likely to see an advertisorial of 6 to 12 pages long, sponsored by a foreign country, for example.

Other features are offered by mass-circulation magazines in an effort to meet the competition from special-interest magazines. For example, magazines such as *Maclean's* offer local companies reduced rates for regional **breakouts**, messages that will appear only in copies sent to a specific geographic region. Reduced regional rates give smaller companies a chance to appear in a national magazine at a rate they can afford. *Maclean's* also offers advertisers the opportunity to target subscribers who live in a high-income household, receive their subscription at a business address, or those who are in the 50-plus age category. Editions that are sent to these subscribers are known as demographic editions.

PURCHASING PROCEDURES. Magazine advertisers are ruled by three dates. The **closing date** is the last date on which a magazine will accept advertising materials for publication in a particular issue. The **cover date** appears on the issue's cover. The **on-sale date** is when the issue goes on sale. Thus a magazine with a January cover date could go on sale December 15. The on-sale date is important because it tells when most issues reach the reader.

Desktop publishing and satellite transmission have shortened the lead time for magazines. Computer-processed magazine pages are sent directly to the printing operation via satellite, thus shortening the time it takes to produce the magazine. *Vanity Fair* closes some pages just hours before press time, using totally electronic page composition and satellite transmission to its printer.

MAGAZINE STRENGTHS AND WEAKNESSES. The ability to reach highly segmented target audiences is clearly the main advantage of magazines. As a result, the absolute cost for magazine promotions is fairly low, but not as low as broadcast costs, discussed in the next section. Allowing the ever-increasing audience specialization of magazines, personalized editions are the next logical step.

Through selective binding (a computerized process that allows for the creation of hundreds of editions of a magazine in one continuous sequence and personalization of advertising) consumer magazine publishers will be able to offer ultranarrow targeting previously available only through trade magazines. Ink-jet imaging is a special computer-controlled printing process that allows parts of the message to be changed by the program. Ink-jet imaging also enables the advertiser to address readers personally. You can tell a reader, "If you're interested, Mr. Jones, you can buy this product at Leroy's Hardware at 39th and Elm." Sophisticated database management allows even greater segmentation. Publishers can match subscriber lists against various lists—association membership, catalogue lists, and so forth—and transfer that information to subscriber lists.

Another advantage of magazines is their excellent visual quality. Magazines are printed on good paper and provide excellent photo reproduction in either black and white or colour. Also, thanks to computer software, photocompositing systems can bring together a studio photo and several ad stock photos to create a striking visual.

This Treehouse TV ad shows a colour bleed ad.

Magazines also provide coupon distribution, special editions, and print ads of various sizes. In fact, the willingness of magazines to accommodate advertisers' needs and wants remains one of the main attractions. Recently, magazines have led the way in joint programs with other media. Examples are tie-ins with other media outlets such as direct mail and cable. *Sports Illustrated* and *ESPN*, for example, joined together to entice marketing communicators such as Gatorade and Budweiser to advertise in both media.

Another advantage offered by magazines is reader involvement. People subscribe to magazines because they are interested in their content. The time spent reading the magazine, according to research, is active involvement. Also, readers do not seem to view magazine ads to be as intrusive as ads in other media.

The key weakness of magazines is the difficulty of reaching a mass audience. Advertising in mass-audience magazines, such as *People* and *Maclean's*, leads to wasted circulation, high costs per contact, and limited premium locations.

Also, such magazines often have high clutter. Magazines such as *GQ* and *Seventeen* often will consist of 70 percent ads and 30 percent editorial material. In addition, many of these ads are for direct competitors.

Print Goes Online

Clearly the major trend affecting both newspapers and magazines is their move to online technology. (We have already discussed the online option in the direct-marketing chapter, and will not repeat that information.) Both newspapers and magazines are employing the World Wide Web and online services to create home pages and repackage information. For example, publishing giants Advance, Cox, Gannett, Hearst, Knight-Ridder, Times Mirror, Tribune Co., and the Washington Post Co. formed a consortium called New Century Network that has produced a series of Web sites featuring their various newspapers.[6]

Although there is a great deal of excitement about print going online, many are skeptical about its future. Most point to the "bathroom factor." Simply, you can't take a computer to bed very comfortably. You can't read it in the tub. Critics argue that magazines and newspapers have existed for several hundred years in their current format because they provide interesting reading that is portable and answers the "why" questions. The Web is most certainly not that, which begs the question: Will people really want their newspapers and magazines online in condensed form? This is a question media planners must answer as well.

concept review

Print Media (Magazines)

1. Magazines are the most specialized of the mass media, as verified by the growth of special-interest magazines.
2. The two types of magazines are consumer and business. These types can be further classified by geography, demographics, or content.
3. Careful media planners must understand the complete picture of a magazine's readership before buying space.
4. The primary strengths of magazines are their ability to target the audience, high-reproduction quality, flexibility of services, and reader involvement.
5. The main weaknesses of magazines are that some promotional efforts are wasted, they provide limited premium locations, and are sometimes cluttered.
6. Print media have moved to online technology in the hope that readers will accept this form of media.

Broadcast Media

Historically, broadcast media referred to radio and television—both media that were developed during the mid-twentieth century. Today some experts prefer the term "electronic" in favour of the term "broadcast" because they believe it reflects the technology in a more accurate manner and broadens its scope to include computer-generated messages that are broadcast to mass audiences. However, as is the case with online newspapers and magazines, "electronic" media can also deliver traditional print messages. To avoid confusion, we retain the term "broadcast," recognizing that many of the media we discuss in this section are now delivered electronically.

Television

For most of its brief history, the structure of the television industry was straightforward. However, the industry has been shaken up in recent years by the emergence of new specialty networks, the proliferation of cable television, the increasing penetration of satellite television, and the emergence of interactive television technology.

Local Stations and Networks

Affiliate
A local station that has signed a contract with a network to carry its programming.

CTV Network
www.ctv.ca

Local stations can be either independent or **affiliated** with a network. There are three national networks: the Canadian Broadcasting Corporation (CBC) English-language network, the CBC's French-language network (Radio-Canada), and the CTV Network. Unlike CTV, a privately owned enterprise, the CBC is a Crown corporation. These networks sign contracts with local stations to carry their programming. Each of these stations then becomes an affiliate. The networks either produce or buy programming from a production company, provide a means to distribute the programming through local affiliates, and make their money by selling commercial time to national advertisers.

Network affiliation is crucial to local stations because it allows stations to fill up airtime with diverse, high-quality programming and generates strong lead-ins for local news and syndicated programs. Stations can also piggyback on the considerable promotion and public relations value of the networks and their leading stars.

Clearance
When a local station carries a network program.

When a station carries a network program, this is called **clearance**, because the local station clears the time for the network show. A network should have as high a clearance as possible (that is, from 95 to 100 percent) so it can offer advertisers total market coverage. Affiliates may lose network affiliation if they do not carry enough programming.

In addition to national networks, there are regional and specialty networks. The regional networks operate on a regional basis in Canada. Examples include the Atlantic Satellite Network (ASN), Ontario Television (ONTV), and Saskatchewan Television. French-language networks include Quatre Saisons and TVA. The CBC also divides its national network into four regional networks: Pacific, Western, Central, and Atlantic.

Bravo!
www.bravotv.com

The Discovery Channel
www.discovery.com

In recent years, there has been significant growth in the number of both English and French-language specialty networks that offer commercial time on a national basis. These networks occupy narrow niche markets. Future growth in alternative offerings is expected in areas such as sports, news, and children's programming. Examples of specialty networks include The Weather Network, CBC Newsworld, The Discovery Channel, Bravo!, Le Reseau des Sports (RDS), and MuchMusic.

Cable, Satellite, Pay-per-view, and Interactive Television Services

Shaw Communications
www.shaw.ca

Cable television originated because obstacles such as tall buildings, forests, and mountains prevent normal television broadcast signals from reaching potential viewers. Today cable remains a primary television service with significant market presence across Canada by media moguls such as Roger's Communication and Shaw Communications. Despite cable's market dominance for several decades, wireless direct-to-home satellite is growing rapidly due, in part, to strong marketing efforts by ExpressVu Inc. and Star Choice. These services require the purchase of a small satellite dish, a receiver, and payment of a monthly fee that is competitive with cable subscription fees. Like conventional cable service, satellite television offers pay-per-view service. As the name suggests, pay-per-view service requires a payment (ranging from $1.95 to $29.95) per movie or event. Made available in Canada through a strategic alliance with major U.S. studios, this service provides hit movies, adult entertainment, live sporting championships, and music events.

iMagic TV
www.imagictv.com

The latest communication technology to be introduced in the Canadian market has enabled a convergence of telephone, television, and the Internet into one seamless package. This service offering is commonly referred to as either interactive TV or Web TV. Recent technological breakthroughs by firms such as iMagicTV, a member of the Aliant group of emerging businesses, have enhanced traditional television viewing. As an example, iMagicTV users are able to seamlessly surf both channels and Web sites on their TV. With iMagicTV's software you can watch "Hockey Night in Canada," click over to the winning team's Web site to get more information about the team or one of its players, and once there, you can e-mail a quick note to the team or alternatively you can e-mail your friend, to boast about your team's performance.[7]

Canadian television is changing. Although the future of television and its convergence with telephone and the Internet remains uncertain, it appears that Canadian consumers will continue to enjoy a growth in the number of channels, specialty networks, and services. Likewise, marketing communicators will enjoy the ability to use television to reach specific target audiences. Moreover, the convergence of communication technologies will enable marketing communicators to implement well-targeted IMC tactics that allow interaction with desired target groups.

Methods of Measuring Broadcast Audiences

Different methods of measuring audiences can yield different results. Four basic techniques are used to measure broadcast audiences: audimeter, telephone coincidence, diary method, and roster recall.

Audimeter
An electronic recorder used to measure broadcast audiences.

The first technique uses an electronic recorder commonly called an audimeter. The A.C. Nielsen Company and BBM Bureau of Measurement (BBM) use this technique. **Audimeters** (known in the industry as "people meters") attach to a television set to measure not only which show is being watched but also who is doing the watching. Each member of the household has his or her own button. A remote control makes it possible to make entries from anywhere in the room, and a sonar device sends out an alert to log in or out. The machine measures only which shows people watch.

Telephone coincidence
Households are called at random to discover which programs are being watched.

A second technique uses **telephone coincidence**. An interviewer calls households chosen at random and asks which program is being watched. Up-to-date data can be collected quickly, but not all times of the day or days of the week may be covered completely.

Diary method
Preselected homes are sent diaries in which each viewer writes down the stations and programs watched. A separate diary is provided for each television in the home and a cash award is given for cooperating.

The **diary method** is the third technique. Preselected homes are mailed *diaries* in which each viewer writes down the stations and programs watched. A separate diary is provided for each television in the home and a cash award is given for cooperating.

Information providers such as A.C. Nielsen and BBM can supplement telephone and diary data with people-meter information to compile audience measurement reports. These reports can be used by national advertisers to determine their CPM, or cost per thousand. Thus CPM indicates what advertisers paid for and what they received. The formula is stated as follows:

$$\text{CPM} = \frac{\text{Ad cost} \times 1000}{\text{Circulation (audience size)}}$$

If *Friends* has an audience size of two million and a 30-second spot costs $30 000, then the cost per thousand would be

$$\text{CPM} = \frac{\$316{,}000 \times 1000}{21{,}000{,}000} = 1.5047619$$

Roster recall
Door-to-door interviews whereby the interviewer carries a roster of programs that were broadcast the day before. The interviewee answers questions about these programs and responds to demographic questions.

The fourth method, called **roster recall**, uses door-to-door interviews. The interviewer carries a roster of programs that were broadcast the day before and lets the person look at the roster while answering questions. Several demographic questions are also asked.

The four methods of measuring audiences provide a wealth of information. Perhaps their most significant information is the program rating and share report. A program rating is the percentage of television households in an area tuned to a specific program during a specific time period. Thus if two million people watched *Friends,* of the 10 000 000 total television households, the rating for *Friends* would be

$$\frac{21{,}000{,}000}{106{,}300{,}000} = 19.8$$

A rating point (RP) is extremely important to the media planner because it dictates the price charged per 60 seconds. It also provides a basis for comparing one program with another. This is referred to as cost per rating point (CRP) and is calculated as follows:

$$\text{CRP} = \frac{\text{Cost}}{\text{RP}} = \frac{\$310{,}000}{19.8} = \$15{,}656.57$$

Share
The percentage of households watching a particular program at a particular time.

Share is the percentage of households with their sets on that are watching a particular program at a particular time. It is calculated by dividing the number of households (HH) tuned to a particular show by the number of "households

This frame from a television ad for McCain Foods' punch illustrates television's tremendous dramatic capacity. It can effectively communicate a slice of life and make mundane products appear exciting and interesting

using television" (HUTS). If 70 percent of television sets were on during *Friends*, then 7 000 000 sets were actually on, of which two million were watching *Friends*. The program's share would be 28.6 (2 000 000 ÷ 7 000 000). Typically, the rating services report the two numbers: *Friends*: 20.0, 28.6. Research on the local audience is used to define television markets.

Television market
Rigidly defined geographic area in which stations generally located in the core of the area attract most of the viewing

A **television market** is a rigidly defined geographic area in which stations generally located in the core of the area attract most of the viewing.

Buying Television Time

Television is an extremely costly medium with a prime-time cost as high as $35 000 for a 30-second commercial. Rates are directly related to the rating and share scores discussed earlier. There is also a match-up factor. Some shows, such as the new *7th Heaven*, are a perfect match with companies that have targeted the family audience. Consequently, *7th Heaven* can demand a higher rate even though the scores do not necessarily support this price. There are also alternatives to prime-time network commercials.

Key Purchasing Options

If media buyers decide to use television, they then face many decisions about how to use it well. Among the key choices are whether to buy time on a network or from a local station, what the level of commitment should be, and what time periods and programs should be selected.

Network and Cable Time. For mass coverage, a national network buy is the best option. Placing an ad with CBC, for instance, will reach a mass audience simultaneously. The networks still tend to offer popular programs, and purchasing time on a network is relatively simple. However, the absolute cost of network advertising is very high, as is the waste.

For marketing communicators with limited funds or limited market coverage, two alternatives to network buys may be attractive. First, the major networks offer regional networks; that is, marketing communicators can select a region of the country for their promotion and pay the network a proportional rate plus a nominal fee for the splitting of the network feed. Second, marketing communicators may turn to the smaller regional or specialty networks. These outlets charge less and can provide more targeted coverage than the national networks.

Spot advertising
Advertising time bought directly from local television stations.

National spot advertising
Local advertising time bought by a national company.

Local spot advertising
Spot advertising bought by local firms.

Spot and Local Advertising. Television advertising is divided into three categories: network, spot, and local spot. We have already discussed the advantage of network advertising—simultaneous coverage of a mass market. However, the other two options offer certain advantages as well. When time is bought directly from local television stations, it is called **spot advertising**. Because local stations usually cannot sell time in the middle of network programs, most spot ads occur adjacent to network programs, but local stations also show them during their own programs.

When a national company buys local time, it is called **national spot advertising.** In contrast, spot advertising bought by local firms is called **local spot advertising.** As a result, local advertising is virtually a synonym for retail advertising. The major spenders on local advertising include department and discount stores, financial institutions, automobile dealers, restaurants, and supermarkets. To illustrate, a national car manufacturer such as General Motors Corp. buys network television advertising to reach the entire Canadian market. Chrysler Corp. buys national spot advertising for the Jeep Cherokee campaign because it only wants to reach markets where off-road vehicles are popular. And Wood Motors Ford buys local spot advertising because the Fredericton, New Brunswick market is its primary target audience.

For the marketing communicator, buying time from local stations rather than national networks provides flexibility. An advertiser can select particular markets at particular times on particular programs. National marketing communicators might use spot ads to supplement a regional network campaign; to test new products, a media mix, or a creative strategy; or to obtain a cost-effective alternative in markets with high sales.

Still, using spot promotions has three key drawbacks. First, the likelihood of clutter is increased, because unless network advertisers have bought all of the commercial time on a program, local stations can sell time on network-originated shows only during station breaks between programs. Second, spot promotion is cumbersome for the national promoter. The marketing communicator must communicate with stations in many markets to select a station, determine airtime, negotiate the price, and check the promotion's appearance. And finally, if the cost per thousand is calculated, local television turns out to be much more expensive than national television. Hence, national companies prefer to purchase network time; when necessary, they supplement those purchases with messages on local television.

SPONSORSHIP, PARTICIPATION, AND SPOT ANNOUNCEMENTS. When buying television time, promoters must also determine their level of commitment. In the early days of television, it was very common for a single advertiser to sponsor an entire program, paying for production, salaries, and airtime. The *Hallmark Hall of Fame* is an example of a sponsored program that only shows the ads of the sponsor. Today, *sponsorships* are too expensive for most advertisers who are unwilling to devote most of their budget to one 30- or 60-minute slot. Nevertheless, for highly seasonal products (for example, holiday toys and greeting cards), using sponsorships is still a viable strategy.

Participation
When several advertisers buy spots on a particular program.

Because most advertisers cannot afford sponsorships, they opt for **participation.** It means that several advertisers buy spots on a particular program. An advertiser can participate in a particular program once or several times on a regular or an irregular basis. Advertisers often split major sporting events, leading to an announcement that "this portion of Skate Canada International is brought to you by. . . ."

Spot announcements
Purchased from local television stations, these announcements appear during the adjacent time periods of network programs.

We discussed a third option earlier. National **spot announcements** are purchased from local television stations and appear during the adjacent time periods of network programs.

TIMES AND PROGRAMS. Those who buy television time must consider the time of day and the program broadcast because both affect the size and nature of the audience reached and, as a result, the rate charged for the television time. Although these time frames vary somewhat across time zones, the standard time periods in television are the following:

Early morning	6 a.m.–9 a.m.
Daytime	9 a.m.–5 p.m.
Early fringe	5 p.m.–7:30 p.m.
Prime	7:30 p.m–11 p.m.
Late news	11 p.m.–11:30 p.m.
Late night	11:30 p.m.–1 a.m.

Each time period reflects different audience size and characteristics. For example, early morning audiences are fairly small and represent upscale men and women getting ready to leave for work, children, and specialty audiences, such as viewers of exercise shows. Prime time has the largest audience and represents the family more than any other time.

To schedule purchases of television time, media buyers look at gross rating points, or GRPs. GRPs measure the viewing audience of a group of programs. Nielsen ratings provide the basis for GRPs. We take a close look at GRPs in the next chapter.

Television Strengths and Weaknesses

No medium has a greater potential to create an impression on consumers' minds than television. Combining moving pictures, voices, music, and convincing acting, television has the capability to run the entire gamut of human emotions. Television allows the audience member to learn more about the product, the spokesperson, and the message because the consumer is more personally involved.

Television also offers wide market coverage flexibility. National network television allows the marketing communicator to reach the entire country. Cable, regional networks, and specialty networks bring a message to highly focused markets. As indicated in the IMC in Action feature, cable and satellite also reaches European countries.

A third advantage of television is the important role it plays in our culture. For many people, television is the primary, most reliable source of entertainment, news, and sports. People count on television and hold a favourable attitude toward it.

Another advantage of television stems from its ability to deliver well-defined audiences. Research shows that there are remarkable similarities in the characteristics of viewers. *Traders* delivers the boomer audience to advertisers such as Kraft Foods, Procter & Gamble, and Coca-Cola week after week. MuchMusic delivers an audience of young people.

Television, usually thought of as a medium for delivering advertising messages, can also deliver sales promotion, public relations, and personal selling–related messages. For example, television can make sweepstakes exciting, highlight the value of a premium, or add urgency to a temporary price reduction. Many public relations efforts benefit from advertising. The "Just say no" anti-drug campaign is much more powerful on television than in print. Finally, because of its emotional impact, television does an excellent job of preselling a product, thus simplifying the job of the sales rep.

Television has weaknesses that can deter some marketing communicators from choosing this medium. Television's absolute cost is still high. Clutter,

MTV as an International (Local) Medium

TV Europe's access to 59 million cable and satellite homes has made it one of the few successes in pan-European TV. In 1995 MTV Networks introduced VH1, its first channel with programs tailored to a local market. But it has not abandoned its more than 300 pan-European advertisers, some of whom are also buying airtime on VH1 UK. The latter is aimed at 25 to 49-year-olds in more than three million British cable and satellite homes. VH1 aims to complement MTV Europe, a plan that appeals to jeans marketer Levi Strauss & Co. "Although VH1 is for an older audience, we've learned that one-third of its audience is from the [jeans-buying] MTV age group," says Steve Clark, group media manager at Levi Strauss' agency, Bartle Bogle Hegarty, London.

When the Media Centre, London, buys airtime for Anheuser-Busch's Budweiser beer, it uses VH1 to circumvent regulatory obstacles that could be caused by advertising alcohol on a pan-European network, according to Andrew Smith, Media Centre's head of TV buying.

VH1 UK now claims more than 200 advertisers, including Nestlé, Procter & Gamble, Unilever, Nissan, Volkswagen, and Compaq. MTV's next move will be a tailor-made VH1 channel for other countries. "I see no reason why we won't consider VH1 for other European markets," outside the UK, Smith says. "It would have been difficult to introduce a pan-European version for VH1 because there aren't that many similarities in the lifestyles, culture, or history of TV's older viewers in the different European countries."

The advent of digital compression technology in Europe will enable MTV Europe to transmit different versions of MTV and VH1 using the same signal. Advertisers will be able to run commercials simultaneously in local languages in any combination or assortment of countries. "MTV Europe has been seen to be a very successful blueprint for advertisers in other parts of the world," notes Smith, who is moving to Singapore to introduce MTV Asia and MTV Mandarin.

The success of VH1 and MTV Europe is a rarity. Since the break-up of state-controlled broadcasting monopolies in 1992, the general trend in much of Europe is to develop home-grown programs and shy away from American hits, such as ***Baywatch,*** which once dominated. In Italy the top five shows are all Italian. In France seven of the top eight are French. Part of this trend is cultural, part is economic. Since 1991 American programs have more than tripled in price. That has given independent producers in Europe an opening for their lower-cost—and now more popular—shows.

Media planning in Europe is clearly a mixed bag. No longer should U.S. advertisers assume that European consumers will prefer U.S. programs. Instead, familiarity with local preferences should become the norm.

Food for Thought

1. What are the risks a media planner would assume by concluding that the success of MTV Europe is the norm?
2. Is international MTV possible?

Sources: John Tagliabue, "Local Flavor Rules European TV," ***New York Times***, October 14, 1996, C1, C4; Juliana Koranteng, "MTV: Targeting Europe Market-by-Market," ***Advertising Age***, March 20, 1995, I13, I20.

especially on national network television, exists. As many as 25 separate spots can be shown during 30 minutes of prime-time programming. Finally, television does not work with products that are unattractive (for example, industrial fluids), that cannot be demonstrated (for example, Preparation H), or that do not have inherent emotional characteristics or emotional associations (such as table salt).

RADIO: AN OLD STANDARD

Two types of stations exist: those that transmit signals via amplitude modulation (AM) and those that transmit via frequency modulation (FM). The primary difference is the distance covered by the signal. AM signals can travel up to 1100 kilometres, whereas FM signals travel about 60 to 80 kilometres. However, the clarity of the signal across the maximum FM distance is better for FM stations than for AM.

With the exception of the Canadian Broadcasting Corporation (CBC), which is funded by the federal government, Canadian AM and FM radio stations are

concept review

Broadcast Media (Television)

1. Television comes in multiple forms: local, network, cable, satellite, pay-per-view, and interactive.
2. Television market size is assessed through four techniques: audimeter, telephone coincidence, diary method, and roster recall.
3. When advertising on television, marketing communicators can buy network, spot, or local advertising, or can also opt for sponsorship, participation, or spot announcements.
4. The size of a program audience is assessed through rating points and share. The weight of the schedule is determined by the total number of gross rating points (GRPs) delivered.
5. Market coverage and emotional involvement are the primary strengths of television.
6. High absolute costs and clutter are the major weaknesses of television.

privately owned and depend on advertising revenues to support operations. For these privately owned stations, there are no restrictions on the number or placement of advertisements.

Radio remains an "old standard" for advertisers because it delivers a highly selective audience at a relatively low cost. With radio, the audience that can be targeted depends on the format of the station. For example, a country-format station provides its audience with country music content. This content tends to appeal to a particular target group that is well defined by demographic (usually age and sex) and psychographic characteristics. Marketing communicators often depend on the research services of BBM to gain an understanding of specific radio audiences. Check out BBM's Web site (www.bbm.ca) to learn more about its radio audience research services.

Buying Radio Time

Years ago nearly all radio programming was live. As radio has become a more local medium, there has been a greater use of recorded shows, with little live programming except the news and on-the-spot broadcasts. This change has reduced the costs of commercials while improving the quality.

Advertising Rates. Radio rate cards are usually broken down into six time periods:

Morning drive time	6 a.m.–10 a.m.
Midday	10 a.m.–3 p.m.
Afternoon drive time	3 p.m.–7 p.m.
Evening	7 p.m.–Midnight
Late night	Midnight–6 a.m.

The cost of radio time primarily depends on four classifications:

1. *Drive time:* Drive time refers to the periods in which the population is moving around, in transition between sleep and the activities of the day or in transition from daytime activities to the events of the evening. These are the periods in

which radio listening is at its highest levels and during which the adult population is least likely to be attending to television.

2. *Run-of-station (ROS):* This means that the radio station can move a commercial at will within the time period, wherever it is most convenient; pre-emptible ROS has the lowest rates.
3. *Special features:* This time slot is adjacent to weather signals, news reports, time signals, traffic reports, or stock reports.
4. *Demographics:* Demographics in the listening area also determine the cost or rate charged.

As is true in other media, advertisers pay less per commercial when they purchase spots in larger volume. Radio stations refer to volume purchases in several ways: 6- and 13-week flights, package plans (the station puts together an assortment of times), and scatter plans (a collection of spots in drive time, daytime, evening time, and weekend time).

Who Listens to the Radio?

BBM, the chief measurement service for radio audiences, reports that nearly everyone (94 percent of all persons aged 12 and older) tunes in to a radio station at least once a week. People listen to the radio while cooking, reading, exercising, eating, driving, and working. This unusual participation makes radio a powerful means of reaching lifestyle segments and demographic groups. Age and sex are still the basic demographic measures, and radio stations divide the population by these characteristics.

Young people and older people seldom listen to the same kind of radio stations. Whereas most young people like rock, rap, or country, the stereotypical radio format for older people is "beautiful music"—instrumental versions of favourite songs. But not all mature adults prefer this kind of so-called elevator music. Men and women aged 55 and older are the primary listeners of news and talk stations.

According to BBM research, radio reaches a remarkably consistent number of people across Canada. However, there are some regional differences in the number of hours spent with radio, with Ontario and Alberta residents listening more than average and residents in B.C. and Atlantic Canada listening less.[8]

Radio Strengths and Weaknesses

As discussed earlier, one of the main advantages of radio is that it can deliver a highly selective audience at a very low cost. Therefore, it is one of the few media that can allow market penetration and high repetition. Second, radio is a very flexible medium. A radio station is tolerant of last-minute changes, unusual formats, mobile hookups, and so forth. This adaptability makes radio appealing to a wide variety of companies and businesses. A small manufacturer, a local insurance agent, and a supermarket can all use radio. Third, radio provides immediacy because it is constantly delivering the latest news, time, and weather. The audience actively listens to the radio, so an ad sandwiched between news announcements is given attention. Finally, if the marketing communicator encourages imagination and imagery, radio can do an excellent job of creating high interest and involvement. When using radio, a humorous tactic tends to work best.

Radio has three main weaknesses. First, it is viewed as a passive medium because it provides only sound, and people tend to have the radio on while they are doing other things (driving, eating, or studying, for example). Compared with television messages, people have low recall of radio messages. Recall, however, increases when messages of high interest are on the radio (for example, news, weather, a favourite song, or a popular deejay). Finally, radio is not appropriate with certain products that are difficult to visualize or that are used infrequently (for example, medical products) or to reach a national audience simultaneously.

concept review

BROADCAST MEDIA (RADIO)

1. There are AM and FM radio stations.
2. Radio stations sell their time as drive time, run-of-station, and special features.
3. Radio offers excellent local coverage at a low cost, it is a flexible medium that has immediacy, and it can create high interest and involvement.
4. Radio is a passive medium that does not work well with some products.

OUT-OF-HOME MEDIA

Out-of-home
All media that carry messages where the message or the consumer is on the move or mobile. This includes outdoor and transit media.

The term **out-of-home** includes outdoor (outdoor boards and billboards) and transit media. It refers to all media that carry messages where the message or the consumer is on the move or mobile. It is a relatively minor medium that usually supplements print or broadcast.

OUTDOOR MEDIA

In a sense outdoor advertising represents the oldest medium because it is a distant cousin of the sign. It is virtually impossible to go anywhere in this country without being exposed to outdoor advertising. Perhaps because of this constant overt exposure, outdoor advertising remains the medium most criticized by the public for desecrating the natural beauty of our country.

TYPES OF OUTDOOR VEHICLES

There are three primary types of outdoor advertising: posters, painted bulletins, and electric spectaculars. The advertising message on posters (also referred to as billboards) is usually lithographed on sheets of paper and then posted on some structure. The standard-size posters in Canada is 3 m by 6 m (305 cm by 610 cm).

In some markets smaller posters are available. These posters are generally used for pedestrian traffic and are often placed in shopping-centre parking lots or on the sides of buildings.

Painted bulletins (also referred to as murals) are usually very large. The message is changed two or three times a year. Painted bulletins can be painted on the sides of buildings and other large structures. Wall bulletins cannot be

This eye-catching bulletin was painted on a wall in a high-traffic location.

standardized in size because the shape and area on the side of a building are unpredictable. Some bulletins have cutouts that provide a three-dimensional effect. Most bulletins are illuminated.

Spectaculars are large, illuminated, and often animated signs in special high-traffic locations. Spectaculars are custom designed and are sold for periods of one year or more. Beyond the budget of most marketing communicators, these structures often use attention-getting devices such as flashing lights, electronic message boards, and laser beams.

Because outdoor is such a visual medium, everything must be kept simple. People should be able to grasp the message clearly and completely in a maximum of five seconds. There should be one dominant design; five or so words of copy; bright, warm colours; and crisp lettering. Physical factors are also important. For example, the longer the poster or painted bulletin is visible to passing travellers, the better. Slower traffic is also beneficial. Obviously, it is preferable if the outdoor ad stands alone.

Outdoor Media Strengths and Weaknesses

For certain marketers, such as restaurants, motels, and gas stations, outdoor media can provide some real benefits.

1. By combining colour, art, and short copy, outdoor ads can quickly create an association with a particular brand.
2. This medium provides repetition. If a product or service is advertised at a busy intersection, audiences see the ad again and again. The more often the idea is repeated, the more likely it is to be retained.
3. Billboards also have immediacy and can be located in the neighbourhoods that are most relevant to the marketing communicator. A rural bank branch can be quite sure that the majority of consumers who pass its billboard are potential customers.

4. The cost is reasonable. The cost per billboard in a major metropolitan area is quite low.
5. Outdoor advertising gains attention through sheer size.

Outdoor advertising also has the following limitations:

1. Outdoor copy must be brief because it is perceived while the audience is on the move. For certain types of products, it is impossible to effectively deliver the message or demonstrate the product.
2. A great many uncontrollable factors may lessen the effectiveness of outdoor ads. Signs, trees, structures, traffic signals, or a hazardous part of the highway may distract the consumer. An ad placed next to others that are controversial or in poor taste could damage the image of the company.
3. Good locations may be limited. In some communities there may be just one spot that has a high traffic count.
4. Many people view outdoor ads as an ecological nuisance.

Transit Media

Transit media can be considered a minor medium compared with those already discussed. The consumer has a relatively longer time to look at transit messages compared to outdoor advertising, and the marketing communicator can get a more complete story across. There are three primary types of transit advertising.

1. *Car cards:* Typically, a car card is 28 cm by 60 cm, although widths of 28 cm by 175 cm are often available. These cards are placed inside the vehicle (i.e., buses and subway cars) along each side above the windows. In some vehicles larger, different-shaped cards are placed at the middle or end of the vehicle. Inside displays are purchased on the basis of full-, half-, or quarter-fleet showings.
2. *Outside displays:* Exterior travelling displays are located on buses and taxis. Again, these ads are bought on the basis of showings—100, 75, 50, or 25.
3. *Station posters:* These mini-billboards are located at bus, railway, subway, and air terminals. The most common units are the two-sheet poster (152 cm by 122 cm) but much larger sizes are also available.

Transit media offers several advantages:

1. Most notably, transit posters offer a relatively inexpensive medium for reaching a variety of people, repeatedly, in a variety of locations (for example, sidewalks and shopping centres) closest to the point of sale.
2. Several techniques make the medium flexible and attractive, including backlit displays, curved frames, optical effects, and the take-one poster.
3. Transit promotion can serve as a type of reminder ad in conjunction with other media.

The limitations of transit media, similar to those of outdoor media, follow:

1. Transit cards must carry relatively short and concise messages.
2. Viewers' attention may be hard to attract and retain because of the many distractions (for example, crowded cards, traffic, noise, marked and torn signs).

Transit space is not available in all markets.

concept review

Out-of-Home Media

1. There are three main types of outdoor advertising: posters, painted bulletins, and electric spectaculars.
2. The three transit media include car cards, outside displays, and station posters.
3. Outdoor and transit promotions can reach the market with a reminder message at a low cost.
4. Both outdoor and transit promotions have a relatively short time to deliver their message and must contend with many uncontrollable factors.

Supplemental and New Media

In every media plan several supplemental and new media are used to support primary media such as newspapers, magazines, TV, radio, and out-of-home. Their intent is to reinforce the primary idea and reach the target audience at times when primary media cannot. In many instances these media provide marketing communicators with an affordable, effective, and targeted media supplement. The list is quite lengthy, and many were fads that lasted a very short time. We highlight the dominant forms of supplemental and new media in the following sections.

Supplemental Media

Merchandising material (also referred to as in-store media), specialty advertising, and directories are three of the more popular alternatives of supplemental media. Telemarketing and direct mail are also supplemental and were discussed in Chapter 12.

Merchandising Material

A display designed by the manufacturer and distributed to retailers to promote a particular brand or group of products in the store is a **point-of-purchase display** (P-o-P). These displays are often created to support sales promotions and advertising campaigns. Although the forms vary by industry, P-o-P can include special racks, display cartons, banners, signs, price cards, and mechanical product dispensers. More recently, manufacturers are using up-to-date information via

This transit ad shows how flexible and attractive the medium can be.

computer chips and touch-screen technology. Product visibility is the basic purpose of P-o-P displays. In an industry such as the grocery field, where a consumer spends about three-tenths of a second viewing a product, anything that gives a product greater visibility is valuable. Unfortunately, retailers are often reluctant to use P-o-P displays because they contribute to store clutter.

When all the elements of a sale—the consumer, the money, and the product—come together at the same time, point of purchase is usually the most effective marketing communication technique. As we move toward a self-service retail environment in which fewer and fewer customers expect help from salesclerks, the role of point of purchase will continue to increase. According to the Point of Purchase Advertising Institute (POPAI), 66 percent of purchase decisions are made in the store rather than before entering the store.[9]

This ad shows how effective point-of purchase advertising materials can be.

Point of purchase is a $21-billion business effort that must be well planned to succeed. Marketing communication planners must start by answering two equally important questions: Is P-o-P appealing to the end user? And will it be used by the reseller? Retailers will use P-o-P only if they are convinced that it will generate greater sales. To ensure greater sales, planners should coordinate the P-o-P with the theme used in other marketing communication, such as advertisements. This consistency not only reinforces through repetition, but it also creates a last-minute association between the campaign and the place of decision.

Other merchandising materials designed for in-store use include signage and displays other than P-o-P. Retailers have become experts in the use of store signage (banners, posters, shelf and cooler signs) and window displays.

In retail it is through these signs and displays that customers compare prices and selections. In addition, displays may be the main motivator of impulse buying. Given the limited amount of space available, however, the cost of convincing retailers to use these materials may be as great as the cost of designing and producing them.

One issue is whether the retailer charges the manufacturer for placement of these materials. A study of display allowances (see Chapter 10) found that roughly 70 percent of the manufacturers surveyed did not pay for placement. Another 28 percent, however, did report paying these charges, and some of the costs ranged as high as $400 000 or more.[10]

Retailers also engage in promotional activities, such as theme promotions, in-store demonstrations, sponsorships of community activities, and support for manufacturers' cooperative efforts—called cross-marketing—where several related products are marketed together. The most common type of event is an in-store theme promotion such as Back-to-School days or White Sales. Theme promotions are supposed to excite consumer interest.

Specialties

Sometimes called **specialty advertising**, this tool is also considered a form of sales promotion because it usually involves presenting the company's name on something that is given away as a reminder item—calendars, pens, mugs, pencils, match covers, and so forth. During its virtual reality tour, Bubble Yum used

This P-o-P sign supports the introduction of Tim Hortons' new dessert product.

specialty items such as purple sponge balls and baseball caps with the Bubble Yum logo. The ideal specialty is an item kept out in the open where a number of people can see it for a long period of time, such as a calendar or penholder displaying the company's name. Other items work well because they are attention- grabbing novelties. Unfortunately, the cost of specialty advertising is often quite high, especially in comparison with the actual value derived. A specialty silk-screened baseball hat may cost as much as $15.00.

The 15 000-plus specialty items manufactured by companies are used for a variety of marketing purposes. They offer stakeholders additional value just as premiums do, except that the consumer does not have to purchase anything to receive that value. The company name and promotional message on the items serve as a reminder. Specialties also build relationships, such as items given away as year-end or thank-you gifts (the calendar hanging in the kitchen). They may also generate sales leads.

Some people question the value of specialty advertising, considering it to be a little tacky, particularly low-end items such as pencils and matches. However, professionals know that if you want to keep the name of your company in front of the customer, give them a calendar or a coffee cup. A study sponsored by an advertising organization suggests these techniques work. Consider this:

1. 83 percent of consumers use such products.
2. 94 percent appreciate receiving them.
3. 94 percent have a positive attitude toward the marketer.[11]

Executive gifts and contest prizes are another area related to specialties, although they usually involve more costly items. Instead of a pencil, an executive gift may be a Cross pen-and-pencil set. For a more important recipient, the company may give a more expensive gift—a Waterman or Montblanc set instead. Prizes for consumer and trade contests can include some inexpensive items such as baseball caps. However, prizes intended to motivate or reward extraordinary behaviour are often high-ticket items such as electronics (televisions, CD-players) or vacation trips. Even activities like trips often come with related smaller gifts that carry the company or brand identification such as travel cases, luggage, jewellery, and clothing (kimonos, hula skirts, Hawaiian shirts, and so forth).

Directories

Directories
An important supplemental medium, especially to local businesses. Directories can be industry specific, product specific, or target-market specific.

Directories represent an important supplemental medium, especially to local businesses. Directories can be industry specific, product specific, or target-market specific. The aerospace industry has its own directory, as does the electric motor product category. The *Silver Yellow Pages* are targeted at consumers over the age of 55. The messages often tie in with advertising on television or in the newspaper. Undoubtedly, the *Yellow Pages* is by far the largest directory. Many advertising agencies have specialists who work on their clients' *Yellow Pages* advertising. The primary purpose is to establish the trademark as the reference point and then list all the local dealers under that trademark. The dealer may then run their own ads separately.

Other supplemental media that have achieved a level of acceptance include: ads spliced onto videotaped movies, ads on videocassettes (usually in the form of an infomercial), ads sent via fax, ads shown in movie theatres or in in-flight movies, ads on computer disks or CD-ROM, ads that are implicit by placing a product in a movie or TV show (who can forget Reese's Pieces in *E.T.*?), and ads found in changing rooms, bathroom stalls, and brochures hung on your door knob. All these choices tend to be less expensive than primary media but lack market coverage and, in the case of fax and changing-room placements, may irritate the consumer. They should be considered when there is a need to fill in the blanks and when spending limited dollars on such media makes sense.

New Media

As noted earlier, the most dramatic breakthroughs in media development during the last decade have come through the emergence of digital interactive technology. Early adopters of this technology consider it the wave of the future. To these individuals the "conventional" ad world is becoming irrelevant, and the large ad shops are either dinosaurs soon to become tar pits or, more charitably, are being led by managers who "just don't get it." But most media directors feel that the digital future may be further away than the advocates think. The projection is that interactive advertising will amount to $10.5 billion worldwide ($3.0 billion in the United States) in the year 2000. That amount would represent less than two percent of media spending.[12] Ken Auletta, media correspondent for *The New Yorker*, says the overriding issue today is whether interactive technologies will open up new opportunities for TV as we know it, or will lead to the death of the boob tube.

Still, the technology is not going to stop. For example, the differences between cable television and personal computers are becoming increasingly irrelevant. Some experts suggest that manufacturers will have their own channels, catalogue companies could deliver products almost instantaneously, anyone could sell anything on the Internet or via interactive TV, costs will decrease, and penetration will multiply. New media is being introduced every day. Media planners must be able to gauge its place in the media mix.

concept review

Supplemental and New Media

Supplemental media are used to reach other target audiences or primary target audiences at other times. The supplemental media currently employed are

1. Merchandising material
2. Specialties
3. Directories
4. Ads on videotaped movies, on videocassettes, sent via fax, shown in movie theatres and in in-flight movies, on computer disks and CD-ROMs, and product placements.

Most new media relate to interactive digital systems. It is still uncertain how relevant this media will be in the immediate future.

A Closing Thought:

Putting It All in Perspective

Despite the excitement about interactive digital media, media planners must be aware of the fact that consumers only have 24 hours in a day and old habits die hard. It is more important to view interactive technology as one element in an integrated marketing communication strategy. By combining media into a unified effort that encompasses sales and trade promotion as well as public relations and direct mail, the marketing communicator reaps the benefits of a campaign that provides a coordinated communication effort against his or her target audience.

Historically, agencies viewed media as a "necessary evil." Now it's treated with respect and as an important part of the agency function, and it will become even more important in the future.

summary 

1. Explain why marketing communicators must understand the comparative strengths and weaknesses of the various media alternatives.

   A mass medium reaches many people simultaneously and requires the use of some technological device to connect the marketing communicator with the audience. Media planners must understand the strengths and weaknesses of each medium, as well as its costs, to find the most effective media mixes, especially in light of an integrated approach.

2. Describe the characteristics, buying process, and strengths and weaknesses of the primary print media—newspapers and magazines.

   Primary print media include newspapers and magazines. There are a number of characteristics unique to each. Newspapers are the number-one local medium, whereas magazines are highly segmented. Both are willing to carry a variety of sales promotion elements. Print has gone online during the last five years. There is a mixed review as to the role online technology will play in the future.

   Newspapers offer both classified ads and display ads. For the latter, ads are sold based on a rate per standardized column space. Magazines are sold based on a page or some increment of a page. Advertisers must also comply with three lead dates.

   The primary strength of the newspaper medium is its acceptance as a local news source. It also is quite flexible and carries sales promotions. Newspapers and magazines suffer from clutter. Magazines are highly targeted and possess excellent reproduction quality.

3. Describe the characteristics, buying process, and strengths and weaknesses of the primary broadcast media—TV and radio.

   Primary broadcast media include television and radio. Television includes a number of classifications, including network, local, cable, and satellite. Each offers certain advantages and disadvantages and is purchased in different ways. Mostly, television reaches a mass audience with a limited message at a low cost per contact. Specialty network television is much more targeted. Radio, like newspapers, is an important local medium. It is targeted and an excellent reminder medium, although it lacks a visual component, greatly limiting its use. TV media buyers have three options: prime-time network buys, national spot buys, or local buys. Radio offers local buy options.

4. Describe the characteristics, buying process, and strengths and weaknesses of the primary out-of-home media—outdoor and transit.

   Out-of-home media include outdoor and transit. It is an excellent reminder medium and is best used in close proximity to the product or service. However, there are many disadvantages, especially limited locations and poor image.

5. Explain the role that supplemental and new media play in the overall media strategy.

   Supplemental and new media are used with audiences and in places that are not fully reached by primary media. Examples include merchandising material, specialty advertising, in-store, direct mail, telemarketing, directories, videocassettes, infomercials, product placements in movies and TV shows, and so forth. The most important new media is interactive digital technology. This media will allow greater targeting and may dramatically change the nature of print and broadcast media.

points to ponder

Review the Facts

1. What is interactive digital technology?
2. List the strengths and weakness of radio as a media alternative.
3. What are the strengths and weaknesses of directories as a media alternative?

Master the Concepts

4. Why would a manufacturer of high-quality running shoes probably select magazines as its primary medium?
5. What techniques are used by rating services to gather and provide data concerning television viewership?
6. Under what circumstances would spot television advertising be more appealing than national television advertising? Network versus cable?

Apply Your Knowledge

7. Prepare an argument in favour of the use of radio instead of television as the primary medium for an integrated marketing communication strategy.
8. "Any ad agency that hasn't wholeheartedly accepted the interactive revolution is going nowhere." React to this statement.
9. Think of the university you attend as a product. Considering the characteristics of the product, develop an evaluation process that would allow you to assess media alternatives.

suggested projects 

1. (Writing and Oral Communication Project) Contact an ad agency that has an interactive media department. Interview the director and determine the role this media will play. Write a three-page report on your findings.
2. (Writing and Oral Communication Project) Interview a media buyer for a local independent retailer. Assess what he or she views as the pros and cons of the various media. Write a two-page report that summarizes your findings.
3. (Internet Project) Visit three Web sites for magazines or newspapers that also have print versions. Compare the print version with the online version of each magazine or newspaper. If you were the marketing communication media specialist for a kitchen appliance manufacturer, would you prefer to buy ad space in the print or online version of each magazine or newspaper you examined? Explain your answer. What if you were the media specialist for a software developer? Do your conclusions change? Why?

case 14 MAGAZINE PUBLISHERS LAUNCH THEIR OWN TV SHOWS

Shift is a monthly magazine on digital culture and, like several other magazines, ***Shift*** is attempting to extend its brand through such tactics as extensive Web sites, corporate trade shows, and TV spinoff series. ***Shift***'s television spinoff debuted in January 2000. Why a TV spinoff series? The theory is that such a move will increase magazine readership and attract more advertisers.

Perhaps a big step, but it is a move that seems logical for a publication like ***Shift***—which strives to be on the cutting edge of digital culture—to extend literally into the digital world. This marketing communication strategy—brand extension into the digital world—is catching on. For example, Rogers Media of Toronto recently launched ***MoneySense***, a monthly business magazine aimed at providing Canadians with practical, hands-on financial advice. Less than one year since its inception, the publication has expanded into MoneySense television, which—like its counterpart—aims to help people invest more wisely.

"We wanted to develop a brand extension for the magazine, and television was certainly there," says publisher Deborah Rosser, adding that the show's actual content is different from the magazine's, though the tone and topics covered remain the same.

Both MoneySense television and Shift TV air on Life Network, which handles all advertising for the shows. MoneySense's Rosser, however, says it's something she's hoping to control in the future so she can offer advertisers some sort of package deal. In the meantime, she has already referred many marketers to Life Network, especially those in the financial, automotive, and telecom sectors.

"I think it would be great if we could expand each other's markets," explains Rosser. "That would be the ideal scenario, where some marketers who might be focused on TV as a medium and be buying on Life Network suddenly turn around and say, 'Wow, there's a magazine connected with this show, isn't that great, we'll buy that!' and vice versa."

In a similar, yet different approach to both *MoneySense* and ***Shift***, Ruth Kelly has extended her role as publisher of Alberta Venture magazine by serving as host of a four-part series called Alberta Venture TV - We Mean Business. Unlike Shift TV and MoneySense television, however, Kelly will have full control of the show's advertising, which means she can grow her pool of advertisers by offering them corporate sponsorship. "We can now bundle together the powers of the magazine, the Web site, and television, and create a bigger, more horizontal campaign," Kelly says, adding that TV appeals to a slightly different group of advertisers, such as regional companies, than does print.

All of this sounds great but some publishers have discovered that a TV spinoff is not always an easy strategic move. For example, when Avid Media launched Canadian Garden Television in 1997, a spinoff of its popular ***Canadian Gardening*** magazine, the venture was quite a challenge. "It was a pioneering effort," recalls Tom Hopkins, senior vice-president, editorial at Avid Media. "The whole project was much more uncertain back then."

So just what has changed in a few short years? According to Hopkins, the popularity of specialty television has inspired more publishers to spin off their own series, a trend that has sparked advertisers to become more aggressive in reaching for a well-defined target audience. "The credibility of specialty TV has improved dramatically," Hopkins explains. "It has matured to the point where advertisers are far more accepting of its marketing power than they were even three years ago."

It seems TV spinoffs will remain a trend for the foreseeable future.

Case Questions

1. What are some of the marketing communication strategy implications of the multimedia approach discussed?
2. What are the potential problems with this approach?

Source: Shawna Cohen, "TV Spinoffs," ***Marketing,*** February 28, 2000, 22-23.

CBC VIDEO VIGNETTES

CBC

Turn Down the Volume

Have you ever noticed that television ads often seem louder than television programming? If you haven't, tune into your favourite television show and see if you can detect a difference between the sound level of the show and its ads.

Industry Canada's broadcast legislation prevents loud television stations but does not target individual advertisers. As a result, television stations must monitor the volume of submitted ads and adjust them accordingly. According to sound technicians, it's not uncommon for some advertisement developers to submit ads that exceed the legislated standard governed by Industry Canada.

Although advertisers run the risk of annoying their targeted audience, most advertising experts would agree that loud ads are attention getters. Given the level of competition for consumers' attention, it's little wonder some television advertisers exceed the limits of the broadcast standard by creating high-volume ads. For advertisers determined to have their ads heard even if the television station turns down the volume button before broadcast, a sound technology technique called compression enables them to apply a little magic. The compression technique provides a means of increasing the perceived volume level without actually exceeding volume standards. This is done by altering the recorded work so as to elevate the low level sounds. This makes the entire recorded work seem a little loader than it actually is. As a result, the ad is deemed to be within the volume standard but the audience perceives the volume level to be higher than the television programming.

QUESTIONS

1. Should broadcast legislation be changed in order to eliminate loud television ads? If so, specify the change(s) you would recommend.
2. Can you cite examples of advertisements in other media that attempt to gain attention by increasing the intensity of the message? Provide examples.

Video Resource: Based on "Turn Down the Volume," ***Undercurrents*** #104 (November 29, 1998).

Developing the Media Plan

chapter objectives

After completing your work on this chapter, you should be able to

- Explain how marketing communication and media interface.
- Describe the procedure for producing a media strategy.
- Discuss the tactics that are part of a media strategy.
- Explain how computer technology affects media planning.

The Changing Face of Media Buying and Planning

It has become hard to follow which global holding company controls which Canadian media buying company and what they're calling themselves. Companies are continuing to consolidate into fewer and larger entities. In addition to consolidation, the larger full-service agencies have completed a shift away from media departments towards separate media companies. For example, MacManus Group of New York recently bundled its media shops into a single entity called MediaVest Worldwide. In Canada, this name replaced TeleVest Canada.

Although even the largest of the consolidated media buying companies have not yet cornered the market, billings figures indicate a boom trend in media buys. The figures tracked by ***Marketing***'s sixth annual measure of media buying clout show that 1999 was a third straight boom year, though not quite as red-hot as the previous two years. The 12 top ranked firms (ranked by billings dollars), billed a total of $3.975 billion in 1999 (estimated). Billings were 8.6 percent higher than in 1998. This compares to increases of 5.7 percent in 1996, 11.1 percent in 1997, and 10.4 percent in 1998.

While the size and billings of media buying companies have grown by leaps and bounds, a new breed of media planner has also emerged. Known at Ammerati & Puris/Lintas as "marketing planners specializing in media," the new breed of media buyers are much more than media specialists—they're expected to have extensive product marketing knowledge. The forte of this new type of planner is creating low-cost, high-reach media plans and investigating and using the proper media (traditional or unconventional) needed to reach a marketing objective. "Because of the multiple media options available today we needed people who were much more marketing-oriented," explains David Martin, president and CEO of PentaCom. "The creative people and the media people must intertwine their work as much as possible. They have to understand that the overall project is part of a targeting process."

This marketing orientation is a decided trend at the small agencies that must compete with the much larger consolidated media buying giants. "Every account is run differently . . . and it's going to be a long time before the big ones cross over to integrated media-client relationships," say Erica Joseph, a senior media planner at Culver Moriarty and Glavin (CMG) in New York. The days of thinking of media planning and buying as a isolated function are quickly passing. In part because of the expectation of accountability, agencies now view media planning and buying as part of the creative and marketing mix.

Sources: Jim McElgunn, "Canada's Top Media Buying Companies," *Marketing*, November 29, 1999, 22, 24; "UPS Delivers at the Speed of Business With New Campaign," UPS home page (February 1, 1995): Internet (www.ups.com/news); Jane Hodges, "Say Hello to a New Breed of Planner," *Advertising Age*, July 24, 1995, S12.

Chapter Overview

Aperture
The point in place and time when the audience is most likely to use the marketing message.

To be effective, a marketing message must reach a particular audience in an optimal manner. It must attain **aperture**—that point in place and time when the audience is most likely to use the message.

Finding aperture is becoming more difficult for the marketing communication manager. The average consumer has more than 30 television channels from which to choose. Thousands of magazines are in print. Most Canadian cities have multiple AM and FM radio stations. Catalogues, direct-mail advertising, and out-of-home media bombard consumers at their homes, offices, and all points in between. Although the number of media choices is expanding, the time consumers have to spend with media is not.

DDB Needham Worldwide
www.mindadvertising.com

Keith Reinhard, chairperson and CEO of DDB Needham Worldwide, describes the task facing the media strategist: "In the future, the most important part of the promotion strategy will be to identify which media vehicles attract which consumers, and what media patterns those consumers follow through a day or week or month, and then to intelligently program messages on the consumers' own personal 'media networks'."[1]

Media strategists have a tremendous amount of factual information about media, including information about circulation, audience characteristics, buying patterns, rates, and competition. But because of the great difficulty in comparing media and the virtually unlimited number of media combinations possible, selecting the appropriate media plan is still quite arbitrary and somewhat subjective. In addition, as noted in the chapter opener, the modern media planner must also have a thorough understanding of marketing. Moreover, the planner must be capable of integrating the two.

This chapter discusses the process of developing a media plan. We explore the relationship between marketing and media planning first. Next we will examine the two stages in the media planning process: creating a strategy and implementing the media plan. We then look at the use of computer technology as a tool for media planners and close with an investigation of IMC's role in media planning.

Marketing and Media Planning

Media plan
A blueprint that maps out the best ways to send the marketing communication message to the target audience.

The **media plan** is a blueprint that maps out the best ways to send the marketing communication message to the target audience. To create the plan, media planners must evaluate and choose the channels of communication that will deliver the marketing communication message to the target audience at the right time, in the right place, and for the right cost.

Recall from Chapter 4 that marketing plays a critical role supporting a company's marketing program. Media planning, in turn, plays a key role in the marketing communication program. Just as the marketing communication plan and objectives are based on the firm's marketing plan, the media plan depends on the marketing communication plan and objectives. A simplified version of this relationship is shown in Figure 15.1.

Who is responsible for media planning depends on the size of the business and the size of the agency. For example, in a small manufacturing business with a marketing communication budget of $100 000, the vice president of marketing is likely to plan the entire marketing communication effort, including the

Figure 15.1 THE PLACE OF MEDIA PLANNING

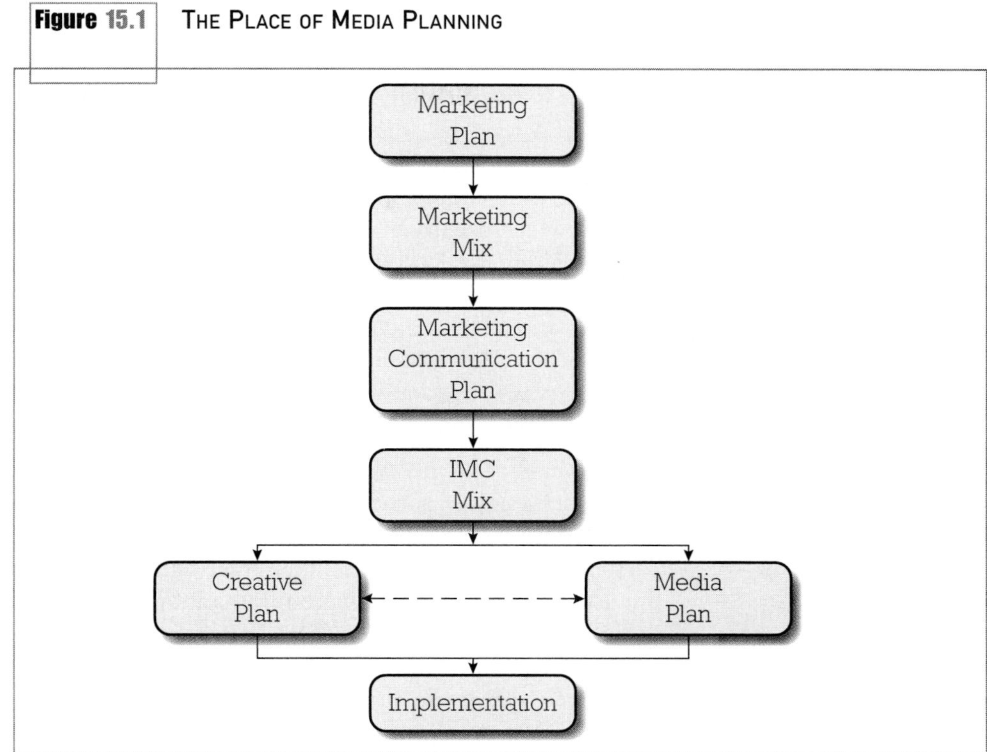

media plan. For Intel Corp., a director of marketing communication (under the vice president of marketing) is responsible for all the facets of communication, including the media plan. However, Intel has the media plan designed by the media planning department at J. Walter Thompson, an outside agency. We see, then, that people with very different titles may be engaged in media planning. Likewise, media buying may be the job of the marketing vice president or the media buyer working under the agency's media planner. A media buyer is typically the entry-level job in media planning.

We first look at seven marketing factors that affect media decisions: the firm's marketing objectives, the product, its profitability, its channels of distribution, the IMC strategy, marketing resources, and the target audience.

1. *Marketing objectives*: The media plan should support the firm's overall marketing objectives. Because the objectives should drive media decisions, the media plan must wait until those objectives are outlined in enough detail to support media direction. Most marketing objectives relate directly to market share; others relate to communication objectives.

2. *The product*: The product also influences the media effort. The price of the product, its newness, stage in the life cycle, and means of distribution suggest the type of consumer who purchases the product. This information also suggests what media mix will present the product to the right audience. A product such as an expensive fishing boat implies a unique group of media and a particular schedule. For instance, this product probably appeals to a prestige-conscious market segment, so it would not be promoted in the *National Enquirer*. It is also a seasonal product, so it would be best to promote it in the spring issues of *Sports Afield*, *Field & Stream*, and *Bass*.

3. *Product profitability*: Closely related to the influence of the product in media is the product profitability. It is difficult to justify expensive network television

for a product that has a small profit margin. A small margin may also affect the amount of retailer support for a marketing communication program.

4. *Channels of distribution*: The channels of distribution influence the media plan in several ways. First, it is wasteful to buy media in markets where the product is not available. Second, certain kinds of resellers are better able to use particular media. For example, wholesalers tend to be good at using direct mail and catalogues, which usually include a great deal of detailed information and require a good mailing list. Retailers are best at using local newspapers and radio. Third, particular resellers may be impressed by manufacturers who use certain media, such as national television. Fourth, consumers who buy the product at particular kinds of outlets may expect to locate product information in certain media. Consumers who purchase groceries at supermarkets, for instance, expect to find product information and coupons in both print media and direct mail.
5. *IMC strategy*: The media plan should take into account the other elements of the IMC strategy. In particular, the amount of effort devoted to advertising, personal selling, and sales promotion helps form the media plan. For instance, if personal selling is emphasized, then trade publications might be the only medium used. But if the marketing communication strategy relies on mass advertising, then planners should create a comprehensive media mix. If the strategy calls for coupon promotions, then media planners must include a print medium, such as newspapers, to distribute the coupons.
6. *Resources*: Obviously no business has all the resources it needs. This is particularly true in media planning where the cost of a comprehensive media plan is beyond the reach of most companies. In addition to a limited budget, another marketing constraint is lack of human resources. Some companies do not have a sales force or the media talent to discern a good media choice from a bad one.
7. *Target audience*: Though the factors discussed so far strongly influence the media plan, in an integrated marketing communication program the most critical factor is the target audience. Traditionally, media planners' knowledge of the target audience is limited to secondary research (discussed later in this chapter). Although this type of information is useful, it does not ensure that the media planner has in-depth knowledge of that audience. In integrated marketing communication programs, media planners must assess exactly how the target audience wants to receive information and how media are best combined to reach the target audience, including nontraditional media. This assessment may require a company to conduct media-related research on its target audience. As noted in the IMC Concept in Focus feature, understanding the customer is a prerequisite for integrated media planning.

concept review

Marketing and Media Planning

A media plan must consider the following marketing factors:

- Marketing objectives
- Product
- Profitability
- Channels of distribution
- IMC strategy
- Marketing resource constraints
- The target audience

Concept in Focus

It Begins with the Consumer

Media planners face a serious problem: how to integrate media. IMC expert Don Schultz contends that the real question is how to integrate from the view of the consumer. Why is an integrated media plan a problem? Most media planners think about media from the marketer's viewpoint, not the buyer's. They talk about target markets and media weights, effective reach, and cost per thousand. These concepts have little meaning for the prospective purchase or the loyal buyer of a brand.

Taking the marketer's view of media planning creates another terminology problem. Just what is "media"? Only those delivery vehicles that can be measured, such as radio, TV, newspaper, magazine, and outdoor? Or are "media" all systems that can deliver a message or an incentive to a consumer? For example, is packaging a medium? Is a T-shirt or key chain? That's a problem for many media planners who do not consider the buyer's perspective. From the buyer's point of view, anything that delivers the message is the medium.

Can planners integrate media without shifting their view from the marketer to the buyer? Probably not. What to do? Here's a modest proposal: Let's start over. Let's start with the understanding that integration needs to be done from the consumer's or customer's view. That means planners should no longer talk about media. Instead, they should talk about delivery channels or delivery systems. Delivery channels are any method marketers can use to deliver either a message or an incentive to a customer, prospect, gatekeeper—anyone the marketing communication program tries to influence. Second, planners should recognize that most consumers don't know the difference between advertising and sales promotion, direct marketing and public relations, and all those other functional activities. Consumers don't talk in terms of receiving a direct-mail promotion or seeing a brand-image advertising campaign. They talk about seeing or hearing or learning something about a brand, product, or company. And in most cases they think in terms of only two things: They receive a message, or they receive an incentive.

The message is something they put away in their heads, generally for later use. The incentive is something they have in their hands and can use right now: a coupon or discount or a key chain—yes, even a T-shirt.

Finally, media planners should forget all those nifty media terms such as "reach" and "frequency" and "gross rating points." Those are marketers' concepts. Instead, they should look at message delivery from the view of the consumer. When is the message or incentive most relevant to the consumer? Delivering a coupon to me on the reverse side of a magazine article I want to save is not relevant. If marketers want to talk to loyal coffee buyers, probably the best time is when they are making coffee in the morning. That suggests packaging and in-pack premiums and maybe some radio commercials. That's when the consumer is receptive.

How would this kind of message delivery approach work? Quite simple. Start with the consumer, then determine whether to deliver a message or an incentive to get a response. Then decide when and where and under what conditions the message or incentive would be most relevant and when the consumer would be most receptive.

Food for Thought

1. What problems could emerge if a company adopted this approach to media planning?
2. Is the consumer a reliable source for such information?
3. What would be the benefits of such an approach? Explain.

Source: Don E. Schultz, "Integration and the Media: Maybe Your Approach is Wrong," *Marketing News*, June 21, 1993, 15.

Creating a Strategy

The two stages of media planning are (1) creating the media strategy and (2) developing tactics to implement that strategy. The first includes a series of basic discussions about the situation, objectives, and the media strategy. The tactical part of media planning involves detailed directions for implementing the media strategy. The primary components of the entire process are shown in Figure 15.2. We describe the two stages in detail in the sections that follow.

The first stage of media planning, creating the media strategy, begins with a situation analysis and then moves to setting media objectives. Once the objectives are set, planners can outline a strategy that suggests specific activities to achieve objectives. In this section we examine these first steps.

Assess the Situation

Marketing exists in a very dynamic world that requires constant reassessment. Therefore, at the beginning of any planning process, planners need to take a measure of the situation in which the product will be marketed. The situation analysis includes an identification of factors relevant to the media plan, followed by a determination of the relative importance of each. A natural starting point is to address the seven marketing factors discussed in the previous section. Planners also need to assess environmental factors outside the business. Examples include the economic situation, the regulatory situation, and cultural and social factors. For instance, regulations virtually eliminate television advertising in Middle Eastern countries. Finally, the situation analysis should consider the activities of your competition. Virtually all the major computer software manufacturers advertise in the same set of media. Although it may not be strategically sound to copy the media strategy of a competitor, it may be necessary to be located in the same medium so that customers can make comparisons.

A great deal of this situational information may be available through the manufacturing department. In other cases research must be conducted. Once the media planner gathers the pertinent information, the next step is to identify which situational factors will have the greatest bearing on the media plan. Some companies, for instance, follow the lead of their competitors. In such a case a great deal of effort will be devoted to gathering additional information about their competitors' media plans, including a spending analysis across media categories. Planning for media in foreign countries presents other problems. A media strategist entering the Chinese market quickly realizes that cultural mores and regulations prohibit a host of media alternatives. Billboards cannot be used, for instance, and radio will not carry contest or sweepstakes messages.

Figure 15.2 The Two Stages of the Media Planning Process

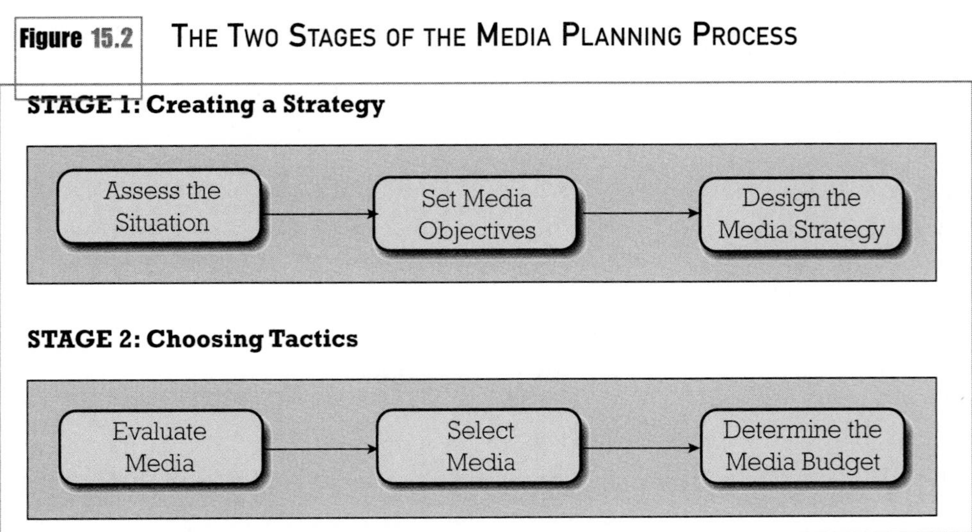

Horror stories abound of media planners who did not do their homework. For example, when Honda introduced the Acura Legend, the company assumed the car would appeal to white male executives earning over $105 000. The initial media plan emphasized business magazines, direct mail, and early morning television. In fact, the product appealed to a much broader target audience, and Honda had to expand its media plan accordingly. This cost Honda millions of dollars in wasted media placement and wasted time.

Conversely, some agencies have become so paranoid about collecting all relevant information that they risk crossing the line into potentially unethical behaviour (see the You Decide feature).

Set Media Objectives

Media objectives
Quantitative statements of what the plan intends to accomplish. They must be specific enough to provide guidance, realistic, measurable, and sufficiently achievable within the available budget.

As in any aspect of business, a media plan must begin with specific objectives, given the conclusions drawn from the situation analysis. **Media objectives** are quantifiable statements of what the plan intends to accomplish. Objectives must be specific enough to provide guidance, realistic, measurable, and sufficiently achievable to be practical within the available budget.

Media objectives are determined by the marketing communication objectives, which in turn are dictated by the marketing objectives. Media

The Spy Agency Is Alive and Well

I help conduct competitive media warfare. My tools aren't firearms or explosives but strategic media ideas. I don't arrange clandestine meetings with operatives, but we conduct our business with the secrecy of a spy agency. Our mission: to respond to competing brands' media strategy manoeuvres and to maintain and improve our clients' market share.

It's not easy being part of a competitive media "SWAT team." You can't tell anyone about that part of your job, let alone admit that this function exists. But it's a task that is becoming increasingly important in this era of strategic media planning.

In the old days the lowest person on the media department totem pole was assigned the competitive responsibility: How much did our competitor spend? What [TV time slots] and publications did they use? That's nice. Come back again next year and tell us the same thing. The inherent problem with this was that these analyses were not action plans. Brand managers would listen to your findings, smile, say "Thank you," and that's it—nothing more than an information presentation. But today more clients need to know the [strategy underlying the competition's media mix,] as well as the . . . execution. The emphasis a competitor puts on a certain execution tells lots about its marketing strategy. Any drastic or quick changes in a mix can say a lot about what they have in mind.

We have a dedicated group of strategists called the "Chess Team," whose job it is to act as the competitor and "live" two to three moves out in the future. The media department advises the "Chess Team" on media intelligence, weight levels, messaging mix and trends, as well as their strategic implications. . . . We can predict their moves and identify our client's opportunities and vulnerabilities.

Thanks to technology we seem to be moving to a world of real-time competitive monitoring. We spend quite a bit of time analysing competitive data. As technological advances are made, we can only be placed in a stronger position to outmanoeuvre our competitors.

You Decide

1. Do you feel this type of work is ethical? Is it useful? Explain.
2. What risks do businesses face if they rely on media warfare tactics? What risks do they face if they don't?

Source: Excerpted from Julie Chan, "A View From The Media War Trenches," *Advertising Age*, July 24, 1995, S2.

objectives may be stated implicitly in terms of reach, frequency, continuity, and cost. They may be explicitly stated in terms of geographic distribution and target audience. Implicit objectives suggest that these goals are not directly tied to a particular target audience. Explicit objectives indicate a direct connection with the audience.

For example, the marketing objective for American Greeting Cards is as follows: Introduce a new brand to an existing category and establish it as the dominant brand in the category with a 30 percent market share. The resulting media objective might read as follows: Allocate a disproportionate percent of reach and frequency weight in the first 13 weeks of the introductory period to achieve rapid awareness and induce early trial. This assumes that the target audience and geographic dispersion remain the same.

Having introduced the terms "reach," "frequency," "continuity," and "cost" as media objectives, let's turn now to a more thorough discussion of these concepts. Reach and frequency are often discussed together—that is, an objective might set a goal of desired monthly reach and frequency.

Reach and Frequency

Reach
The number of people or households exposed to a particular media vehicle (such as a specific magazine or TV program) or media schedule (the total number of vehicles across a period of time) at least once during a specific time period (usually weekly or monthly).

Reach is the number of people or households exposed to a particular media vehicle (such as a specific magazine or TV program) or media schedule (the total number of vehicles across a period of time) at least once during a specific time period (usually weekly or monthly). If CBC's *Market Place* is seen at least once in a four-week period by six out of ten homes, the reach is 60 percent (6 ÷ 10 = 0.6 or 60%). Although determining reach is complicated when dealing with several media vehicles, a variety of manuals and mathematical techniques exist to make the necessary calculations.

High reach goals are appropriate when the communication goals are very broad or cognitive—for example, if the goal is to achieve consumer attention, awareness, or knowledge. When reach goals are high, media planners need to choose a wide range of media vehicles that minimize the duplication between vehicles and media categories. That is, they should avoid media, such as women's magazines, where the same consumer may read several publications in the same category.

Frequency
The number of times within a given period that a consumer is exposed to a message (usually figured on a weekly and/or monthly basis).

Frequency is the number of times within a given period that a consumer is exposed to a message (usually figured on a weekly and/or monthly basis). If a Reebok ad is given a total of 21 exposures during a one-week period, the total frequency is 21 and the average frequency is 3 (21 ÷ 7 days = 3 exposures per day).

Chatelaine
www.chatelaine.com

High frequency goals make sense when the marketing communicator aims to change attitudes and behaviour. When frequency goals are high, the media plan should provide a great deal of duplication within and between media vehicles and categories. The media strategy then should focus on the continuous use of a group of media categories, subcategories, and vehicles. For example, Kraft salad dressings are advertised in all the traditional women's magazines, such as *Canadian Living* and *Chatelaine*, on daytime television, and advertised cooperatively with local supermarkets.

Gross rating point (GRP)
The combined measure of reach and frequency that reflects the total weight of a media effort. It is derived by multiplying reach times frequency.

Calculating GRPs. The two measures, reach and frequency, can be combined to reflect the total weight of a media effort. This combined measure is called **gross rating point** (GRP) and is derived by multiplying reach times frequency.

Gross impressions
The impressions of all viewers taken together.

All the viewers together are also called **gross impressions**. Say, for instance, that *The Simpsons* has an audience of 250 000 U.S. viewers, then each time the marketer uses that program, the value in impressions is 250 000. If Nestlé showed a Nestlé's Crunch chocolate bar ad four times during a program, the number of gross impressions would be 1 000 000 (250 000 × 4). The term **gross** is used because the planner has made no attempt to calculate how many different people view the show. Because rating points are equal to gross impressions, it is easier to use GRPs. To illustrate, assume three 30-second IBM spots were shown each day on *Wheel of Fortune* and the weekly rating was 29.3, the GRP would be as follows:

$$\text{GRP} = 29.3 \times (3 \times 7) = 615.3$$

This number is not necessarily good or bad. The experience and judgment of the IBM media planner play a big part in assessing whether 615 GRPs is adequate. Of course, GRPs would be calculated for the total media schedule, not just three 30-second spots. Table 15.1 gives an example of GRP calculations for a total media schedule. Note that without more information we cannot assess whether the total GRP figure of 883 in Table 15.1 is satisfactory.

The media planner must compare this figure with the media plan objectives to judge whether the number exceeds or falls short of the stated media objectives. This may be the least scientific aspect of media planning. In fact, based primarily on experience, media planners often rely on rules-of-thumb to determine minimum GRPs to make an impact in a particular market.

GRPs include the total audience and do not account for the wasted reach (that is, people seeing the message who are not in the target audience). A better

Table 15.1 CALCULATING GRPs

	Ratings (Reach)	×	Number of Messages (frequency)	=	GRPs
Television					
E.R.	21		4		84
North of 60	12		2		24
The City	2		1		2
Everybody Loves Raymond	18		5		90
Friends	19		4		76
Today Show	10		8		80
The National	14		12		168
Magazines					
Field and Stream	11		4		44
Maclean's	19		10		190
Playboy	23		3		69
Canadian Business	28		2		56
Total GRPs					883

Target rating points (TRPs)
An accurate reflection of the desired media schedule, this estimate includes only the numbers of people in the primary target audience who are reached by the message, as well as the number of times.

estimate is **target rating points** (TRPs) because it includes only the numbers of people in the primary target audience who are reached by the message, as well as the number of times. This adjustment is a much more accurate reflection of the desired media schedule. Suppose the TRPs that Lennox China & Crystal desires is 1250 (50 percent of the target audience, 25 times). However, to produce a TRP of 1250, a much higher GRP number might be required because several of the media choices would contain waste circulation (people not in the target audience).

Effective frequency
The number of times the prospect should receive the message to ensure the most effective communication.

Linear approach
This approach suggests that each exposure adds as much purchase probability as the one preceding it and supports the notion that greater frequency is better.

Decreasing return approach
The assumption that the first exposure is the most powerful, and each ensuing exposure is less effective.

Learning curve approach
This approach suggests that the effectiveness of each exposure increases up to a certain point and that subsequent exposures add little.

EFFECTIVE REACH AND FREQUENCY. Suppose a total media buy or schedule has a GRP of 1100. Does this media buy have more total weight than the example given in Table 15.1 of a GRP of 883? Yes is the tentative answer, but the specific reach and frequency levels must be appraised relative to one another. Gross rating points do not account for the varying impact of certain exposure levels (reach) combined with certain frequencies. Two measures, effective frequency and effective reach, try to adjust for these calculations.

Effective frequency is the number of marketing messages needed to affect individuals in the way the marketer desires. That is, what is the number of times the prospect should receive the message to ensure the most effective communication? The answer is often a judgment call. Although no one knows exactly what the optimum number of exposures is, three general approaches help solve the problem: linear, decreasing return, and learning curve. We summarize these approaches in Table 15.2.

The **linear approach** suggests that each exposure adds as much purchase probability as the one preceding it. If each exposure produces a purchase probability of two percent, then four exposures produce an eight percent probability and 10 exposures produce a 20 percent probability. The linear approach supports greater frequency as being better.

The **decreasing return approach** assumes that the first exposure is the most powerful, and each ensuing exposure is less effective. Advocates of this approach opt for low frequency. The **learning curve approach** suggests that the effectiveness

Table 15.2 APPROACHES FOR DETERMINING THE OPTIMUM NUMBER OF EXPOSURES

Approach	Description	What the Associates Say
Linear	Each exposure is as powerful as the previous one	The more frequency the better
Decreasing returns	First exposure is most powerful; all others are less and less effective	Low frequency is better
Learning curve	Up to a certain point, successive exposures are increasingly more powerful; after that point, the exposures have little power	Search for the optimum frequency

of each exposure increases more than an equal amount up to a certain point and that subsequent exposures add little. Exposure 1 produces a 2 percent probability, exposure 2 increases the probability to 5 percent, exposure 3 produces 9 percent, and so forth, up to 7 exposures. This approach searches for the optimum number of exposures and does not advocate frequency for its own sake.

Impact
The measure of whether the audience actually perceived the message.

When measuring effective frequency, impact should also be analysed. **Impact** is the intrusiveness of the message. That is, was the message actually perceived by the audience? Being in the room with the television on does not mean that the viewer actually sees every ad on the screen. Media planners use several research techniques to determine whether impact has actually taken place.

Effective reach
A measure of the number of prospects who are aware of the message.

Effective reach builds on the concept of effective frequency. However, in contrast to effective frequency, which measures the average number of times a person must be exposed to a message before communication occurs, **effective reach** measures the number of prospects who are aware of the message.

Recall that reach counts the percentage of people who are exposed to the message at least once, and perhaps only once. However, it is not enough to expose an audience to a message once; to ensure success, people must be aware of the message. For each marketing communication message, then, there are two reach components: empty reach (those in the audience exposed to a message who still have no awareness of it) and effective reach (those exposed enough times to be aware of the message).

Continuity

One key media plan objective concerns the timing of media messages. Media planners must determine how and when media dollars should be allocated throughout the campaign and plan the timing of the message. Should the message be delivered continuously and uniformly? Or should there be times when no media are purchased and other periods when a large part of the media budget is allocated? Product characteristics, market size, budget, and a number of other considerations determine the answers to these questions. For example, Mattel Inc. might allocate 10 percent of its budget in September, 20 percent in October, 20 percent in November, 40 percent in December, and 10 percent during the rest of the year. These allocations correspond to products that are seasonal, with the peak purchasing time preceding the winter holiday season.

Typically media planners consider three continuity options: continuous, pulsing, and flighting. The continuous pattern is one in which the planner schedules media at the same level throughout the year. Pulsing is media on an erratic schedule, timed to coincide with some factor (for example, a seasonal product). Flighting is a media schedule within a "flight," such as a 13-week period of time. These terms will be discussed in more detail when we consider scheduling later in the chapter.

Cost

Cost per thousand (CPM)
The cost of reaching 1000 people in the medium's audience.

Cost considerations represent a final media objective. Media planners usually receive a specific budget and must plan accordingly. They must be aware of factors such as unit costs (for example, the cost of a 30-second television ad on a national network), production costs, available discounts, and the various trade-offs between cost, production quality, size, and location. As a bottom-line cost figure, media planners normally use the **cost per thousand** (CPM) computation, the cost of reaching 1000 people in the medium's audience. The CPM figure allows the planner to compare vehicles within a medium (for example, one magazine with another or one program with another) or to compare vehicles across media (for instance, the CPM of radio compared with that of newspapers). Although the analyses can be done for the total audience, it is more valuable to base it only on the audience segment that has the target characteristics.

Unit
A measure used in calculating the cost per thousand (for example, per page or per 30-second spot).

To calculate the CPM, two figures are needed: the cost of the **unit** (for example, per page or per 30-second spot) divided by the unduplicated reach:

$$\text{CPM} = \frac{\text{Cost of unit} \times 100}{\text{Reach}}$$

Some media planners prefer to make cost comparisons on the basis of rating points instead of reach. This is called *cost per rating point* (CPRP), and the calculation is parallel to CPM:

$$\text{CPRP} = \frac{\text{Cost of unit}}{\text{Rating point}}$$

CPMs vary tremendously across countries and across mediums. These cost considerations will be discussed further in the section on the media mix.

In conclusion, the media planner can use reach, frequency, continuity, and cost as a basis for expressing goals. In addition, summary measures such as GRP, TRP, and CPM can be produced through these goals in order to make comparisons. For example, a local Ford dealership wants to develop a media plan to support an end-of-the-model-year short-term campaign to rid itself of inventory. The media objectives are to reach a relatively small number of prime prospects as many times as possible, on a daily basis, with a low CPM. Local television and radio would probably achieve these objectives. However, if a manufacturer were introducing a new, nondurable consumer product, and the marketing communication objective was to create a 75 percent level of brand awareness in the target market, the related media goal might be to achieve a high level of reach with moderate frequency levels.

Design the Media Strategy

Once the determination of the media objectives has been completed, the media planner must next develop a comprehensive strategy that specifies how these objectives will be reached. This detailed document addresses several questions. To whom should the message be targeted? Are there multiple targets? When should the targets receive the message? Does the selected media meet the unique requirements of the strategy? Next we discuss four elements that are part of a comprehensive media strategy: the target audience, dispersion and concentration requirements, qualities the media must have, and the media implications of the message content.

Describe the Target Audience

Although the overall marketing plan describes the target market, this information must be translated into a format for the media plan. Media strategists need information that will allow them to pinpoint the most effective means for delivering the message to the appropriate audience. Whereas creative strategists attempt to understand those for whom they will create marketing communication messages, media strategists ensure that a particular media audience matches the intended target audience. Media strategists want to select media that are most efficient in delivering messages to people who are in the target market and to avoid media that deliver a high proportion of messages to those outside that market.

Media strategists, then, are interested in information that helps them relate certain consumer characteristics to particular media. They are most concerned about media audience characteristics—especially product buying and usage. To make valid comparisons among media, media planners must have information about the audience characteristics.

Why is it important that media strategists have useful and comparable data? Suppose a media planner promotes a hot cereal that has two primary target markets—children and senior citizens. The manufacturer decides to deliver the advertising message to senior citizens. The media planner would want to know the characteristics of senior citizens. People in this age category tend to have lower incomes, have no children at home, live a more sedentary lifestyle, and have poorer health. Thus the media planner might identify lifestyle, health, and age characteristics.

Clairol
www.clairol.com

This task completed, the media planner must consider which of the many ways of describing consumers is most appropriate to the particular product. A general guideline will help: Limit the number or criteria to no more than three or four. For example, media planners for Clairol hair products might be most interested in demographics such as gender, occupation, income, and age. If more criteria are considered, comparing media across these characteristics becomes almost impossible. The more criteria included in the definition of a consuming group, the fewer the people who will meet all the criteria.

Note that the media planner can set audience objectives only in terms of those audience characteristics that have been measured. Although it would be desirable to collect demographic, psychographic, and product usage data from media sources, typically only demographics are available.

Determine Dispersion Requirements

Dispersion
A media policy that places the message in as many different programs and spots as possible to avoid duplicating the audience.

Maximum dispersion
Reach has priority over frequency: the media buyer should avoid duplicating programs as much as possible.

Many people believe that the primary objective of a media plan is to deliver a message to as many consumers as possible. **Dispersion** refers to a media policy that places the message in as many different programs and spots as possible to avoid duplicating the audience. The request for **maximum dispersion** means that reach has priority over frequency. In this case the media buyer should avoid duplicating programs as much as possible. Using different shows increases the opportunity for different or unduplicated audiences. For instance, a media planner might describe comparable strategies as follows:

- Plan I: Ten nighttime television appearances in a three-month period. This plan guarantees that 60 percent of the national television audience will see the message at least once during the three-month period.
- Plan II: Eight daytime television announcements during a three-month period. This plan guarantees that 50 percent of the television market will see the message at least once.

Because both plans cost the same amount, it appears that Plan I is superior to Plan II, but several other considerations should be examined before making this decision.

First, the coverage should be compared not only in gross impressions but also in terms of the specific target audience. For example, although Plan II appears inferior, if the target audience is women between the ages of 25 and 44, they are the main recipients of the daytime message in Plan II. Dispersion of messages means dispersion among the target audience, as defined by the marketer.

A second consideration is to specify more clearly what the phrase "at least once" really means in a given situation. Although a certain percentage of the audience will see the message at least once, a percentage of that group will also see it more than once. For example, an advertiser might follow Plan I and purchase a nighttime television scatter plan, which means that 24 messages appear in a variety of programs to achieve maximum dispersion.

Gross impressions
The term used to describe the total number of viewers taken as a whole. The planner has made no attempt to calculate how many different people view the show.

Net coverage
The number of people exposed to the message.

Average frequency of contact
This is determined by dividing the total number of homes reached by a media plan by the net coverage of the plan; it provides media planners with another basis for comparing plans.

The marketing communication message appears in six television programs (PGM) during the three-month period, and the total audience for these six programs is 51.5 million (PGM 1 = 6.3 million, PGM 2 = 9 million, PGM 3 = 4.7 million, PGM 4 = 11.2 million, PGM 5 = 9.4 million, and PGM 6 = 10.9 million). This total figure of 51.5 million is often referred to as **gross impressions**. However, because some of these audience members receive the message more than once, an adjustment must be made to determine how many new viewers are actually added by each additional program. That is, even though the first program delivers 6.3 million and the second 9 million, 3.1 million are the same people. After removing this redundancy from all six programs, the actual number of people exposed to the message is 12.8 million. This number is referred to as the **net coverage**. Dividing the total number of homes reached by a media plan by the net coverage of that plan produces the **average frequency of contact**. Average frequency of contact provides media planners with another basis for comparing plans:

Plan I: Average frequency of contact = 51 500 000 ÷ 12 800 000 = 4.02

Plan II: Average frequency of contact = 43 600 000 ÷ 16 500 000 = 2.6

The smaller the number, the better the coverage of the plan. Based on average frequency of contact, Plan II is the better plan.

A third consideration is the distribution of frequency of exposures. Research results indicate that the most effective media plan tends to concentrate message delivery at the middle of the frequency range rather than at the extremes (see Figure 15.3). Rather than achieving one exposure to many people and many exposures to a few people, it would be best for the majority of households to receive two or three advertising exposures, with the balance receiving only one or two. Media planners may wish to make such frequency distribution goals explicit in their media strategy statements so that these goals are included in the criteria established to evaluate alternative plans.

Determine Concentration Requirements

Marketers of products such as toys, turkeys, snow skis, and cold remedies face some special problems related to the continuity objective. Marketers must concentrate their message at a particular time of the year or in a particular part of the country. Under these conditions, the media planner must deal with a series of decisions. When should the campaign start? When should it peak? How should the budget be distributed? Can the same campaign be run in various geographic areas? The answers reflect not only traditional spending patterns but also pressures from retailers and the direct sales organization.

Figure 15.3 DISTRIBUTION OF FREQUENCY OF EXPOSURES

Ideally the majority of households should be subjected to three or more exposures.

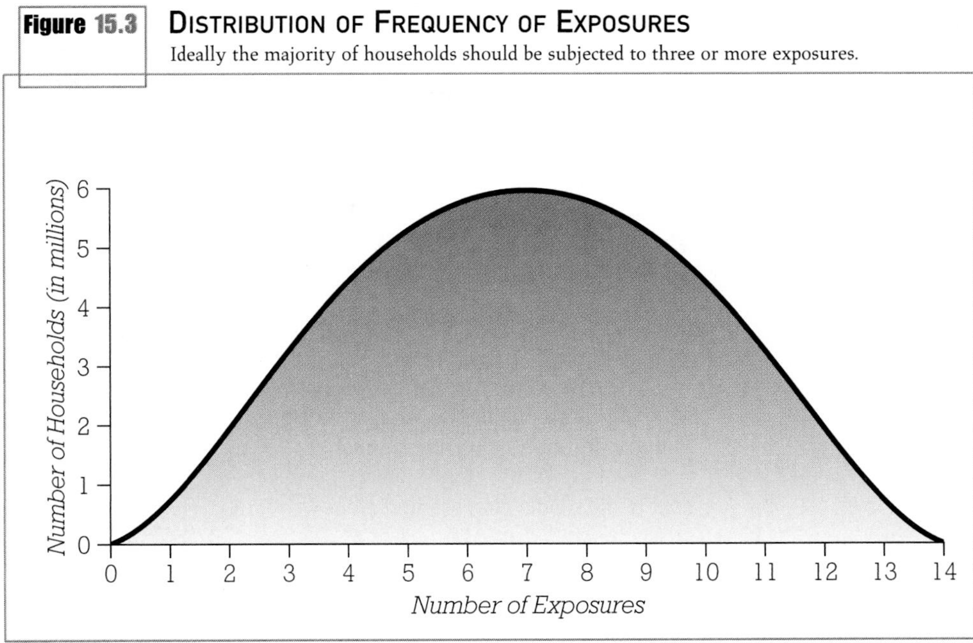

IDENTIFY INHERENT QUALITIES REQUIRED OF MEDIA

Qualitative media effect
What the media does to enhance or depreciate a message after the medium has delivered the message.

Many media exert qualitative effects on the messages they carry. The **qualitative media effect** is what the medium does to enhance or depreciate a message after the medium has delivered the message. As an example of this effect, the *National Post* might enhance the quality of a message because of the high-quality reputation of its editorials.

A media planner may want to place a message anywhere on this qualitative continuum. For example, a media planner might not be concerned with minimizing cost and may have little concern with the quality of the medium. Consider the products advertised in supermarket tabloids. These are often questionable, low-quality products. Consequently, the media planner could place a message about such a product on the sides of abandoned buildings, taxicabs, and matchbook covers. At the other extreme, promoters of high-fashion women's clothing may feel it is critical that their messages appear in fashion magazines such as *Glamour* and *Flare*. The perceived quality of these publications by the large target audience should enhance the message.

The important factor is that the interaction between the medium and the message should be complementary. If media planners cannot derive significant qualitative value by placing a message in a particular medium, they probably should not do so. Perhaps the qualitative goal can be met through some other means than the media strategy.

ANALYSE IMPLICATIONS OF MESSAGE CONTENT

A final consideration for the media planner is to match the medium with the message. Creative directors produce specific messages with a variety of factors in mind. We have previously discussed the influence of the product on message content. In turn, the resulting message content has a bearing on the medium selected to deliver it. Messages that carry a great deal of detailed information suggest print over broadcast. Messages with a strong emotional appeal suggest broadcast over print.

The possibility also exists that the medium will be selected first, and the message will be created with television or magazines in mind. Media strategists plan knowing the essence of the message that their media plan will deliver and adjust the plan accordingly.

concept review

Creating a Media Strategy

1. The process of media planning begins with a situation analysis. Gathering primary and secondary information and determining which information is pertinent to the media plan are first steps.
2. Media objectives determine direction and control for the media plan and are stated in four ways:
   - Reach: number of people or households exposed to a media vehicle at least once during a specified time period
   - Frequency: number of times within a given period that a consumer is exposed to a message
   - Continuity: the timing of media insertions
   - Cost considerations: several cost factors must be considered
3. The design of the actual media strategy includes the following factors:
   - Describe the target audience
   - Determine dispersion requirements
   - Determine concentration requirements
   - Identify inherent qualities required of media
   - Analyse *implications* of message content

Choosing Tactics

Once a media strategy is in place, what does a media planner do to implement it? Most of the tactics are carried out by the time and space buyers in the media department of advertising agencies. The process of selecting tactics usually consists of three stages:[2]

1. Evaluate media.
2. Select media.
3. Determine the media budget.

Evaluate Media

A thorough evaluation of all the media relevant to a particular strategy is an important aspect of any media plan. Chapter 14 described the strengths and weaknesses of the various media. And we have already discussed the objective and subjective factors to consider. Collecting the necessary information to appraise these factors may require extensive primary research by the sponsoring firm or its agency. This research is both expensive and time-consuming. As a result, many media planners rely heavily on research findings provided by the medium, on experience, and on subjective appraisal.

Every media planner should follow two guiding principles when evaluating media. The first is to realize that the medium simply carries the message; it is not the instrument that accomplishes the final effect. The medium should be evaluated not in terms of whether it will sell the product but in terms of how effectively it will deliver the message.

The second principle is to recognize that the total audience attracted to a particular medium may be much larger than the target audience actually reached. That is, fewer people see a particular marketing message within the newspaper than see the newspaper. Media planners must do the best they can to develop information or estimates of the relation between exposure opportunity and actual exposure. Effective reach is one measure of this process.[3]

Sometimes, as noted in the IMC Concept in Focus feature, technology has made the separation of media types even more complex.

SELECT MEDIA

Once media planners have considered the media objectives and the qualitative and quantitative characteristics of various media, they must make several important decisions. These decisions can be divided into two general categories: mix decisions and timing decisions.

Before beginning this discussion, it is important to note that these decisions are always restricted by the size of the budget. Budgets are never large enough to accomplish all that the media planner has in mind. The media planner must work within the budget provided, even though the media plan may turn out to be a compromise that may not totally satisfy the established objectives.

IMC Concept in Focus

Multimedia Clouds the Water

Depending on whom you ask, the term "multimedia" can mean almost anything. Multimedia is fairly new to the marketing world, which explains why there is so much confusion surrounding its definition and capabilities. This new technology can combine nearly all the elements of other media and use sophisticated software to display this information on a computer screen. More than that, the program can be made interactive. The user can touch a button and jump to other sections of the program, rewind, fast forward, or pause. With multimedia, you can integrate graphics, photography, animation, type, sound effects, voice, music, video, slides, special effects—almost anything—and weave it into a single interactive program.

The uses of this new technology seem endless. For example, Marketing Etcetera recently crafted a multimedia CD-ROM presentation touting the merits of Hewlett-Packard's OpenView Express product. The CD-ROM presentation program is intended for prospective buyers, resellers, and trade shows. The user simply loads the program onto their computers and lets the customized screen saver run to attract consumer attention. By touching any button, the core of the multimedia program would be activated, leading the viewer through the OpenView Express's benefits. At certain points, the viewer could choose to skip ahead to other points of interest. The entire program is a slick, entertaining presentation incorporating 18 minutes of animation, audio, and video.

Much of the animation was created in flash to enable the viewer to not only see the presentation on CD, but also on-line. The interactivity of multimedia makes it ideal for trade shows, sales seminars, point-of-sale solutions, electronic catalogues, product updates—anywhere where computers can tell the sales story. And because a live body doesn't have to be present to walk the viewer through the program, it can expand a firm's sales capability relatively inexpensively.

Food for Thought

1. Can you think of other communication applications for this technology?
2. Are there any risks?

Source: Elizabeth Weisiger, Marketing Etcetera, Personal Correspondence (March 6, 2000); Press Release from Marketing Etcetera (March, 2000).

Media mix
The combination of media.

THE MEDIA MIX

The media planner faces a series of decisions when selecting a medium or combination of media—the **media mix**. Media-mix decisions are usually made in conjunction with timing decisions. That is, the scheduling possibilities of a medium such as national network television may dictate the need for an additional medium to meet reach and frequency objectives. In this section we examine some of the key questions a media strategist should consider when drawing up the media mix.

NUMBER OF INSERTIONS. One key question for media strategists is determining the ideal number of insertions they should use in a particular medium in a given period of time. Armed with this information, media planners should be able to set up usage guidelines for different media and build an estimate of the cost of implementing various media mix plans. Say that the U.S. market media planner for Subaru determines that the ideal number of insertions during a year for magazines is 550 and the ideal number of TV insertions is 315. Given the rates for each medium, the planner knows the company must spend at least $7 million on print and $17 million on TV to launch a successful campaign.

As noted earlier, there is little agreement and no well-developed general knowledge about how many insertions in a particular medium are ideal. That number is likely to depend on the media objectives, the marketing communication program, and the ability of the message to connect with the audience. For example, if the objective is to reach a large number of people and have them recall the message in the short run, then it would probably be best to concentrate the messages during a 13- to 15-week period, to spread these exposures across a large group of consumers, and to reduce the exposure frequency as time progresses. Experience and research often guide planners' decisions about the number of insertions given the particular situation. Many sophisticated practitioners have developed their own rules for particular situations through continuous testing in the marketplace, through continuous analysis of sales patterns, or both. Of course, it doesn't matter how many insertions you buy if the message is not on strategy.

RELATIVE EFFICIENCY. Even if media planners have some research knowledge or arbitrary rules for determining patterns of media usage, they still need to know about the relative efficiency of each media type. Is television more efficient for my product or is radio? They will also want to know the efficiency of one media vehicle compared with another. Will an ad in *Chatelaine* reach the same objective for a lower cost than an ad placed in *Flare*?

The standard measure of relative efficiency within media is the cost per thousand (CPM) computation explained earlier. Suppose that a media planner wished to reach U.S. bank executives 24 to 34 years old and is considering three magazines: *Bankers Magazine, Bank News,* and *Bank Systems & Technology.* The media planner would start by learning the one-page cost (black-and-white or four-colour) and enter it into the numerator of the equation. For the sake of illustration, let us assume that the insertion costs for a black-and-white, full-page ad in the three publications are as follows:

Bankers Magazine	$1420
Bank News	930
Bank Systems & Technology	3670

Calculating the denominator of the equation is more difficult. One approach is to use the circulation of each magazine. This information is available and reliable. However, this figure does not reflect actual people, because it includes businesses, libraries, and other institutional subscribers. So the media planner may use some measure of the people reached by the particular vehicle as the denominator. The audience measure employed is contingent on the target audience characteristics specified in the media objectives. This type of information may be available through the medium itself or through private research companies. In our example the relevant audience is males, 24 to 34 years of age. Suppose the total audience fitting this description for each magazine is as follows:

Bankers Magazine	9511
Bank News	9279
Bank Systems & Technology	5692

The cost-per-thousand computations for a black-and-white, full-page ad for each magazine are as follows:

$$\textit{Bankers Magazine} = \frac{\$1420 \times 1000}{9511} = \$149.30$$

$$\textit{Bank News} = \frac{\$930 \times \$1000}{9279} = \$100.23$$

$$\textit{Bank Systems \& Technology} = \frac{\$3670 \times 1000}{5692} = \$644.76$$

Cost-per-thousand-target market (CPM-TM)
Cost computations that include an audience adjustment.

These values are referred to as the **cost-per-thousand–target market** (CPM-TM) because it includes an audience adjustment. The cost per rating point (CPRP), as described earlier, is another indicator used to evaluate media alternatives.

Comparing the efficiency of different types of media is quite different. The key question is whether the audience data are truly comparable from medium to medium. The answer is usually no, for three reasons. First, the audiences of different media are measured in different ways. For example, A.C. Nielsen measures audiences based on television viewer reports of the programs watched; outdoor audience exposure estimates are based on counts of the number of automotive vehicles that pass particular poster locations. Second, each of these measurements deals with different aspects of consumer involvement. The measurements for an outdoor poster audience assume that every passing automobile contains an attentive passenger. Electronic measurements of national television audiences assume that the set is on and the person is probably in the room, but the measurements do not assume that the viewer is watching the program. Third, comparisons based on audience exposure do not reflect the potential value of the medium, which depends on how well the promoter exploits the medium's ability to attract consumers. The ability to attract cannot be reflected in cost-per-thousand computations.

Despite these limitations, many media planners still resort to the cost-per-thousand computation. Table 15.3 displays other criteria a media planner can employ in comparing media categories.

EFFECTS OF MULTIPLE MEDIA. Finally, to select the appropriate media mix, media planners should gauge the pros and cons of using multiple media. Above

Table 15.3 SOME CRITERIA FOR COMPARING MEDIA

	Television			Radio			Newspapers			Magazines		
Audience Factors/Data	Network	Spot	Cable	Spot	National	Local	Supplemental	Consumer	Business	Farm (Specialty)	Out-of-home	Direct Mail
Typical adult rating (%)	16	16	2	2	14	40	25	20	20	20	60	21
Reach*	H	M	L	L	L	H	H	H	L	L	H	M
Frequency*	M	H	H	H	M	M	L	L	L	L	H	L
Selectivity		X	X	X		X		X	X	X		X
Seasonal usage				X						X		
Controlled circulation									X	X		X
Geographic flexibility		X	X	X		X		X	X	X	X	X
Local coverage		X	X	X		X		X			X	X
Ethnic appeal			X	X		X		X			X	X

*H = high, M = medium, and L = low.

Message Factors/Data	Network	Spot	Cable	Spot	National	Local	Supplemental	Consumer	Business	Farm Specialty	Out-of-home	Direct Mail
Typical adult rating (%)	80.0	72.5	62.5	37.5	35.0	35.0	35.0	52.5	52.5	52.5	47.5	65.0
Vehicle audience weight									X	X	X	
Long message life						X	X	X			X	
Simple message	X	X		X								
Emotional appeal	X	X	X	X			X	X				X
Immediacy				X	X	X						
Control ad placement	X	X	X	X							X	X
Editorial association	X		X		X	X	X	X	X	X		
Supporting medium		X	X	X	X	X	X		X	X	X	X
Good response measures					X	X	X	X	X	X		X
Good ad reproduction							X	X	X	X	X	X

all, they should consider the possible benefit of placing a message once in two media versus twice in the same medium. Some people see no media at all, and others concentrate on one medium to the exclusion of others. Both of these factors suggest greater coverage if media planners use a media mix instead of one medium.

A second benefit of a media mix program is its tendency to even out the frequency of exposure within the total audience. When 12 messages are played on two different media (for example, radio and television), the heavy users of each medium receive a lower, more even dose of the message than they receive when all 12 are played on radio. Finally, a mix of media allows media planners to send slightly different messages to those audience segments that are exposed to several media. An individual listening to the radio version of a message, for example, will pick up on different cues than those in the television version of the message. The person perceives two unique messages even though a large percentage of both messages are identical. Some media companies have tried to make all of this a little easier by selling media packages.

THE TIMING OF MEDIA

The timing of media refers to the actual placement of marketing messages. Timing includes not only the scheduling of promotions but also their size and positions. Timing decisions are dictated by the media objectives. For instance, the media objectives state that the target audience must receive the message at a particular time or with a certain level of impact.

SCHEDULING. The effectiveness of a media schedule depends in large part on four considerations.[4]

1. *Exposure*: How many exposures are created by the media schedule? As discussed earlier, evaluating this aspect of a media schedule entails counting the number of exposures that can be obtained. In the case of magazines, the number of exposures is the circulation figure converted into a CPM number; for television, the basic unit of counting is the GRP. In addition, this figure should reflect exposure to the advertising rather than to the media vehicle. If there is any reason to believe that readership for some vehicles is higher than for others, the basic CPM figures should be adjusted accordingly.

2. *Segmentation:* Who is exposed and what percentage represents members of the target audience? Delivering a message to people who are not in a target segment has little value. Data to consider in evaluating this aspect of a schedule might include demographics, lifestyle profiles, and product usage. Describing segments in terms of factors such as these allows further adjustment in the CPM and GRP figures.

3. *Media-option source effect*: Does exposure in one vehicle have more impact than exposure in another? The media-option source effect provides three qualitative measures of media alternatives. The first is the **media-class source effect**, which compares different types of media (for example, television ads versus magazine ads). The second qualitative measure, **media-option characteristics**, examines the effect of variations in size (full page or half page), length (30 seconds or 60 seconds), colour (black and white or colour), and location. Finally, the **vehicle source effect** compares the impact of a single exposure in one vehicle with a single exposure in another vehicle. A Pioneer Stereo ad in *Rolling Stone* might make a greater impact than the same ad in *Time*, even if the audience were the same.

4. *Repetition effect*: What is the relative impact of successive exposures to the same person? Although it may take a minimum number of successive exposures to penetrate the consumer's mind, beyond this point the value of successive exposures is uncertain. The key is to make the correct assumptions about the value of successive exposures. Such assumptions must consider the timing of the exposures (that is, people forget between exposures), differences in appeals, interest level, month, product characteristics, and so on. Some campaigns make a strong impact quickly; others take a long time to create awareness.

Media-class source effect
A qualitative measure that compares different types of media.

Media-option characteristics
A qualitative measure that examines the effect of variations in size, length, colour, and location.

Vehicle source effect
A qualitative measure that compares the impact of a single exposure in one vehicle with a single exposure in another vehicle.

Time
www.time.com

Rolling Stone
www.rollingstone.com

Some people conclude that three exposures within a purchase cycle are all that are needed to induce attitudinal or behavioural change.[5] Advertising theorist Herbert Krugman suggests that each of the first three exposures has a different purpose. The first exposure elicits a "what is it?" response. The second exposure continues the evaluation and information-gathering process. The third exposure provides a reminder that the audience member has not acted on the message. Exposures beyond the third simply repeat the process and serve no real benefits.[6] Of course, this rather simplistic explanation does not account for many other considerations.

Continuous
A continuity pattern called for if the audience constantly needs to be exposed to the message because of the nature of the product and excessive competition.

Flighting
A continuity pattern that calls for heavy scheduling during shorter time periods in order to increase reach and frequency with the hope that these effects will carry over into longer time periods.

The media planner sets the schedule after assessing the four considerations of exposure, segmentation, source effect, and repetitious effect. The schedule should specify the time and date of messages in each media vehicle. It should be based on the continuity objectives discussed earlier.

Recall that one of three continuity patterns may be followed, as Figure 15.4 illustrates. The first is **continuous**. This pattern is called for if the audience needs to be exposed to the message constantly because of the nature of the product (that is, it is purchased frequently and regularly) and excessive competition. A continuous pattern also assumes that the media budget is very large.

A second pattern, **flighting**, calls for heavy scheduling during shorter time periods in order to increase reach and frequency in the hopes that these effects

Figure 15.4 THE THREE SCHEDULING ALTERNATIVES

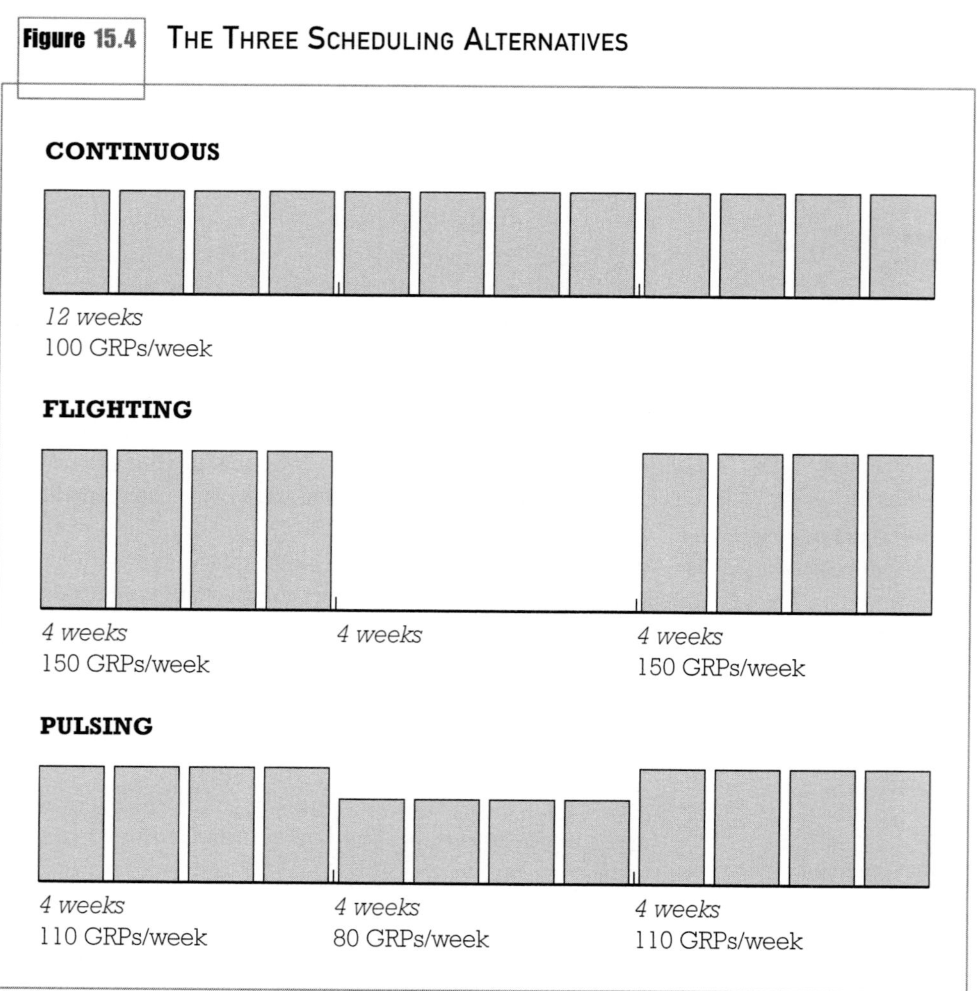

will carry over into longer time periods. A media planner may therefore concentrate media buys in a 13-week period rather than over 52 weeks. This strategy allows the media planner to buy media at better rates. Compared with a more diluted schedule, flighting also may create a much better impact on the consumer. This advantage is still debatable because a short-run impact may not carry over through the rest of the year. If impact does not carry over, the entire effort could be wasted. On the other hand, if the company has limited promotional funds, this strategy could be the most effective. Flighting might also prove appropriate for seasonal products whose season fits the 13-week time frame.

Pulsing

A combination of continuous advertising and flighting, with continuous advertising emphasized during the best sale months. This continuity pattern tends to minimize waste and thus represents the best of both techniques.

A variation of flighting is **pulsing,** which is a combination of continuous advertising and flighting, with continuous advertising "emphasized" during the best sale months. Because this approach tends to minimize waste (that is, delivering messages when the consumer is not in the market), it represents the best of both of these techniques. Not all marketers should use pulsing, however. It best fits products that are sold year-round but that have heavy sales at intermittent periods such as stationery products, hot dogs, beer, and linens and towels (often featured as white sales).

SIZE AND POSITION. Timing of the media effort also involves determining the size and position of a particular message within a medium. Although a great deal of research has been conducted in this area, the results are not conclusive.

We do know that simply doubling the size of an ad does not double its effectiveness. Although a larger promotion creates a higher level of attraction and greater opportunity for creative impact, the extent is still undetermined. Equivocal results have been reported for print media of various sizes and for television and radio commercials of various lengths. Depending on what advertisers have to say and how well they can say it, a 30-second commercial may do the job much better than a 60-second commercial. Bigger or longer may not always be better. Still, the media planner must consider the possible positive effects. The size or length chosen should also be related to the objectives.

Guidelines regarding positioning are only slightly more enlightening. In general, there is some evidence to suggest that within a print medium (1) the inside cover and first few pages get a slightly better readership, (2) placement of compatible stories adjacent to an ad may enhance its effect, and (3) having many competing ads on the same page detracts from effectiveness. Findings related to broadcast media are almost nonexistent.

DETERMINE THE MEDIA BUDGET

How much to spend on media is a strategic decision. It depends on sales potential, objectives, and affordability. The IMC budget must be viewed as a function of the marketing of the brand or company. It is not possible to reconcile ambitious marketing goals with a modest budget. Conversely, it makes no financial sense to have an ambitious budget if the marketing goals are modest. A comprehensive discussion of budgeting is given in Chapter 16. In most instances, because media represent 80 percent of that budget, they are carefully considered.

The media planner's role in this decision making can vary greatly. When top management gives the total dollar amount to the media planner, the media planner's control tends to be limited, especially when management gives the media planner a dollar figure that is insufficient to implement the media strategy.

Ideally the media planner is allowed to gather and present media cost information to management, which is considered part of the budget determination process. This information includes marketing communication expenditures by the competition, the cost of media, and the audience delivery affordable at given budget levels.

Media planners must cope with several timing problems related to the budget. They cannot always abide by the budgetary schedule used by the rest of the business, which often begins on January 1 or July 1. Due to product seasonality, media availability, and several other factors, media budgets can start or end on any date.

Another timing issue has to do with lead time. Media planners often have to move quickly to make media buys. Corporate executives may take weeks or months to evaluate and approve budgets, so it's best if the company gives the media planner some flexibility to make quick budget decisions.

A final issue related to timing is rooted in the dynamic nature of media planning. Media buying has often been compared with buying and selling stocks. Every day media buyers negotiate with hundreds of media about such factors as rates and special discounts. Media representatives are constantly putting together media packages and desperately trying to sell unsold space or time in minute-by-minute contact with media planners. Media buyers without adequate budgets or contingency funds are unable to engage in this negotiation process and may wind up spending millions of extra dollars on media. Again, flexibility is a crucial tool for managing the media budget.

Computer Technology and Media Planning

Undoubtedly, computer technology has simplified media planners' jobs in some ways. However, several issues limit practitioners' use of technology. First, there is no satisfactory way to compare several media simultaneously because each medium differs in its costs, ratings, size, and so forth.

For instance, media space and time offer quantity discounts, but these discounts may not be comparable. Similarly, the value a particular medium can deliver varies with the time and place. For example, the value of national network television is much greater when programs are being shown for the first time (as compared with the rerun period of the summer, when television

concept review

Choosing Tactics

Three tactical decision areas are associated with the media plan:

1. Evaluation of how media will facilitate the delivery of the message and what the actual exposure of a particular medium will be.
2. Media selection, which is based on the following:
   - The media mix—determining which media work best together
   - The timing of media—entailing scheduling and selecting size and position
3. The media budget

Canadian Business
www.canadianbusiness.com

viewing decreases significantly). Finally, the value delivered by a particular medium also depends on the media objectives. A software manufacturer specializing in banking might have a high-reach objective and value a magazine such as *Canadian Banker* over *Canadian Business.*

Another issue is that creating the best media schedule requires some judgment about how to combine all the elements—including message form, placement in time, and media vehicles—to produce the greatest effect. Ultimately, designing a media schedule is more art than science.

Because of these issues and others, practitioners have limited their acceptance of computer technology. Steve Farella, executive vice president and director of corporate media services at Wells Rich Greene advertising, explains: "There are some departments that see [the computer] as a very integral part of the media planning process. We don't do that. . . . We still think that media thinking can be done independent of the machine."[7] In fact, many practitioners have developed a good deal of specific knowledge about how media work for their products, services, or institutions on the basis of market testing. Other practitioners have reached conclusions about how best to use media based on their own extensive experience. Many practitioners readily accept the results of their own experience over the results produced by management scientists.

Still, there is a definite trend toward technology. Computerization has brought about many improvements and made things available that were not even possible before in media buying. For example, in the 1980s it was not unusual for a buyer to spend a day or more manually rating the programs that the television stations offered. Today these estimates can be made in seconds.

There have been four main lines of development: retrieval and estimation models, optimization models, simulation models, and media buying models. All four suggest that students interested in media as a career must be proficient in a broad range of computer software.

Retrieval and Estimation Models

The computer allows vast amounts of data to be stored and retrieved in a meaningful format. Companies collect a great deal of information about their customers. They can also purchase data about consumer characteristics, behaviours, and lifestyles. Some computer programs can combine this data, along with media usage data, to create alternative media schedules or campaigns and compute the relevant cost per thousands. These computer models can also estimate the potential reach for individual media or for various media combinations. Virtually all the syndicated research firms make data available in computerized forms, which can then be combined with other software to create a media schedule.

Optimization Models

Optimization models attempt to modify data on audience characteristics, measures of reach and frequency (in order to eliminate problems or irrelevant relationships), and so forth. The modified data can then be compared and the best plan selected. It is impossible for research to produce "perfect" information; its purpose is to produce better information than was previously available.

Simulation Models

These models compare media plans by simulating their effects on typical consumer behaviour such as purchase, store visits, coupon redemption, and

Craig Dawson

VP Director of Communications
Thompson Enterprise Media

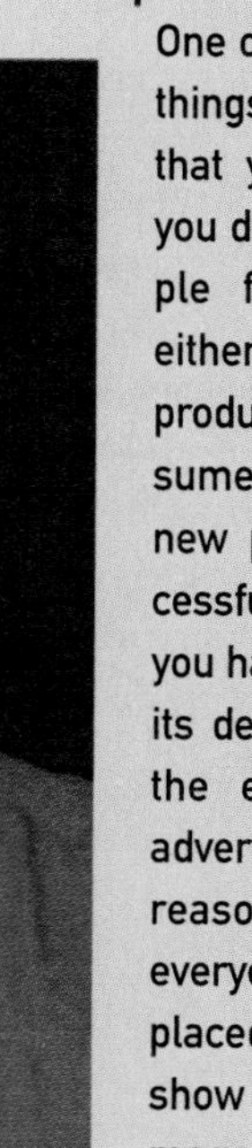

One of the most intriguing things about advertising is that you can tell if what you do is right by the simple fact that you have either changed sales of a product or changed a consumer's opinion. Seeing a new product launch successfully and knowing that you have had some part in its development is one of the exciting aspects of advertising. Knowing the reason a great ad that everyone talked about was placed on a specific TV show or radio station or magazine provides a strange little thrill. After all, if the creative is great, but it's in the wrong place or is targeting the wrong people, the product won't sell. And in the end, that is advertising's main objective—to sell.

As VP Director of Communications of one of Canada's largest media companies, my job requires me to oversee the planning and buying of media totalling over $50 million annually. With a staff of 15 to 20 people, we take the creative product and make sure that the right people see it at the right time at the best possible cost.

In terms of what I specifically do, I oversee (and in some cases do myself) the development of media/communications plans for all of the clients assigned to my group. We determine, with the help of an account and creative team, the best way to reach the target of each particular client for each particular campaign. Utilizing budgets that are usually set by the client, these plans can be written on a yearly basis with lots of preplanning or weeks before something needs to go to air. As such, there is no typical week and that is one of the challenging, yet exciting, things about media as you progress upwards in the media department—each day can be dramatically different.

As with the best plans, our media company works as a team with the account group and creative group from an agency to develop ideas and plans that suit each objective. Working with the other departments can help media by getting new ideas and we can assist in the strategy and creative by giving them ideas.

Once the plans are written, presented to the clients, and approved, our media buying team calls up the various media sales representatives and negotiates for placement of ads. This is done with all media, from TV and radio stations to newspapers, magazines, outdoor, transit, Internet, and even bathroom stalls. The buyers' job is to negotiate the best prices and I am charged with making sure they can rationalize any and all choices to both myself and the client. As the VP, I am ultimately in charge of anything that goes out of my department, so I have the right to refuse or ask for adjustments where I see fit, if any are needed.

Also, I am responsible for new business acquisitions, staff training, promotions, and morale. Given the speed of

information requests. The models allow media planners to compare many plans without committing to an actual plan. The models can even specify particular market segments and make comparisons for each.

Simulation models cannot eliminate the difficulty of comparing media. Selecting the appropriate consumer characteristics is not easy. Nor does this technique account for the impact of multiple combinations of media or the deterioration of media effect.

work and the constantly changing advertising environment (new media opportunities seem to crop up every week), maintaining an enjoyable working environment is one of the most important things I strive for. That and ensuring that my staff receive the accolades they deserve for outstanding work. This provides for an exciting, enjoyable, and ever-changing job day-by-day.

Academic Background and Career History

After deciding that I wanted to be like Darren Stephens on "Bewitched" (a 1960s sitcom), I studied Creative Advertising in Toronto at Centennial College of Applied Arts and Technologies, graduating from their three-year program in 1982. My first position was as a media assistant at J. Walter Thompson working on accounts such as Labatt's, RJR MacDonald, and Pepsi. After two years, the Labatt account moved agencies to Scali, McAbe, Sloves, and I was recruited to move with it. While at Scali, as a media planner, I also worked on Apple Canada and MGM/UA movies. In 1986, I was recruited to Saffer Advertising to head up their U.S. planning and buying division for a number of high-profile retail accounts. This job required travel to the U.S. and an entire new learning curve to understand the differences between Canadian and U.S. media planning and buying.

After nearly two years I left Saffer and became associate media director at Bozell Jacobs Kenyon and Eckhardt (which then became Bozell Inc. and eventually Bozell Palmer Bonner). At Bozell I worked on a number of high-profile accounts from American Airlines and Samsung to smaller-budget names such as Petersen Tools and the Greek National Tourist Board. After nearly four years, I left to become media director at Nathan Fraser Ross Roy, working on accounts including Kmart and Arby's. At age 28, I was one of the youngest media directors in Canada.

After just over one year, I decided to go out on my own and become a media consultant. In this position I was able to fulfill the dream of being in charge of my own destiny and worked for seven years in varying positions. As a "free-lancer" or "consultant," I had clients of my own who had no advertising agency support (so I was able to do more than just media), and I also had a number of creative agencies who required media/communications expertise and used me as their media department. As a result, I worked inside full-service advertising agencies for short periods of time when they required help. One of these agencies was Enterprise Creative Selling, and after freelancing in and out for over five years, I was offered a position as media director for enterprise under the JWT group banner.

Since that time, in 1998, Enterprise Media has merged with J. Walter Thompson media to form Thompson Enterprise Media, a division of WPP Inc. Within TEMedia I am one of two heads of "supergroups" working on clients including Tim Hortons, Merrill Lynch, McCormick Canada, Discovery Channel, and a growing number of dot.com businesses. At present, TEMedia is about to merge with Ogilvy and Mather media, another WPP company, to form Mindshare Canada. Mindshare Worldwide is currently the largest media buying/planning company in the world.

Advice

When you begin in media, you will be focusing most of your efforts in the beginning to a great deal of detail work. Although some people may think that this type of work can be monotonous, it helps to build the foundation of the library of knowledge necessary to progress in the media/communications field. You must learn to walk before you can run. No one person will "give" you the challenges to succeed and rise in media; you must continually ask for more and strive to grow in any organization. Find what you like and run with it.

Media Buying Models

The actual processing of media buys, along with invoicing, remains one of the most archaic dimensions of media planning. However, the barriers to efficient media buying are not technological. They are human. Media sales reps want to keep their jobs, users are reluctant to give up a paper trail of transactions, and companies do not want to foot the bill for developing the standards necessary for interchanging data electronically. There are a few breakthroughs, however.

With Media Management Plus, for example, agencies can explore "what if" scenarios with narrow audience segments, giving them as much if not more information than their reps have. Agencies can also do post-buy analyses and line-by-line comparisons of orders. With this system, Pizza Hut monitors its 26 U.S. regional agencies buying in 160 television markets.

Few people would disagree that computers are playing an increasingly important role in the media planning process. The use of computers saves time and frees the planner from a great deal of lengthy computations and routine paperwork that were formerly required. Some experts, however, are concerned about the possibility that planners could develop a blind acceptance of computerized data to such an extent that it could lessen the amount of judgment that goes into planning. These experts point out that no matter how valid formula models are, they do not justify uncritical acceptance of the data without being modified by experience and judgment.

A Closing Thought:

Keeping Media Under One Roof

Media is a different coloured "horse" than it was a few years ago. Once only accountable for a "low cost per thousand," media buyers are now required to run faster, jump higher, and get more "bang for the buck." Moreover, media planners must cope with new media forms that spring up almost daily and contribute to growing clutter. Some sources estimate that a person may now see as many as 2000 advertising impressions per day.

How can a media planner become an expert on all these choices? In fact, the solution appears to be absorbing special media areas (such as direct mail, telemarketing, and online) under one roof. The full-service agency now includes a full range of media specialists as well. This phenomenon is referred to as "splintering." Perhaps as a result of splintering, the most important question media buyers will address in the future will be "What percentage of the marketing communication dollar should be allocated to mass versus target marketing (and how should this ratio change as a product matures)?"

concept review

Computer Technology and Media Planning

Several types of computer technology can aid media planners.

1. Retrieval and estimation models collect vast amounts of audience and media data, combine them into alternative media schedules, and estimate the effectiveness and cost of each.
2. Optimization models provide a systematic way of selecting and modifying media-related information.
3. Simulation models allow the testing of various media strategies without committing actual resources.

Media buying models can help agencies explore "what if" buy scenarios, do post-buy analysis, and assess line-by-line comparisons of orders.

Rogers Group of Companies
www.rogers.com

At the same time that media is splintering, there is also a trend toward media moguls. The strong Canadian presence of the Rogers Group of Companies on the national information, communications, and entertainment services stage is a prime example. Rogers Cantel Inc. is Canada's largest wireless provider; Rogers Cable is Canada's largest cable television company serving more than two million customers in Ontario and British Columbia; while Rogers Media Inc., which includes Rogers Broadcasting Limited and Maclean Hunter Publishing, is Canada's integrated media company with such assets as radio stations across Canada, a home shopping network, and over 50 leading consumer, business, and specialty magazines.[8] With such a strong market presence the Rogers Group of Companies (like other media giants) can offer a powerful media package mix package to prospective clients. Although this may make media planning and buying more efficient, there is also a risk that such strong competitors will eliminate legitimate media choices.

At risk, as a result of these mergers, may be the independent media buying services. Rather than allowing the advertising agency to handle the media buying, independents offer advertisers significant cost benefits if they provide that service rather than the agency. However, agencies have fought back, and independents are looking for ways to compete other than price. Many are moving into strategic planning. Media giants may negate the limited advantages offered through independents.

This leads to another important media question. Is a global media buy possible? In addition to the differences in culture, laws, and availability that make global media planning very difficult, the prospect of a global media buy appears unlikely. The biggest impediment to global media buying deals is the lack of centralized client control. Most clients are decentralized by continent or by country. As a result, no one person has the authority to combine budgets across countries.

Finally, the most important question many media planners will address is how, given the tremendous growth in media choices, an integrated media plan will be possible. Rather than coordinating five or six major media alternatives, today's media planner is faced with hundreds of choices. Undoubtedly this task represents one of the more serious roadblocks to accepting IMC. It will mean that biases are eliminated and media planners will have to start with the target audience—their communication needs and wants.

summary

1. Explain how marketing communication and media interface.

   Finding aperture, the optimum point in time and place to reach the target audience, is the primary purpose of media planning and buying. If this is not done correctly, all the other marketing communication tasks performed will be diminished or doomed to failure.

2. Describe the procedure for producing a media strategy.

   The media plan is a blueprint that maps out the best way to send the marketing communication message to the target audience. It is dependent on the marketing communication plan and the creative plan. There are several issues that influence the media plan: marketing objectives, the product, product profitability, the channels of distribution, the integrated marketing communication mix, resource limitations, and the target audience. The media planning process includes a set of strategic considerations—situation assessment, media objectives, and strategy.

3. Discuss the tactics that are part of a media strategy.

   The media planning process includes several tactical considerations—how to evaluate, select, and budget for media. Each one of these tasks has many subactivities that are crucial to implementation.

4. Explain how computer technology affects media planning.

   Computer technology has evolved to assist in all facets of media planning and buying. Despite the technological advances, experience and judgment are still the most important factors in the media planning process.

points to ponder

Review the Facts

1. Describe the two levels of a media plan.
2. Define reach, frequency, continuity, and waste circulation.
3. Define what is meant by effective reach and effective frequency.

Master the Concepts

4. What are some problems that a media planner may encounter when executing the media strategy?
5. Explain the concept of gross rating points and demonstrate how it is derived.
6. How many repetitions are enough? Explain.

Apply Your Knowledge

7. Assume that you are on a committee to choose the best media plan from several alternatives. The other members favour Plan A because it reaches more people at least once at approximately the same cost as the other plan. What might you say to convince them that a judgment based on that criterion alone is erroneous?
8. How would you evaluate whether reach, frequency, or continuity is the appropriate media strategy?
9. Many practitioners rely on media-supplied information, experience, and their own subjective appraisal to evaluate media. Can you explain why more objective considerations are not used?
10. Perform the following calculations:

    Calculate the GRPs for a daily soap opera with a weekly rating of 3.8 for three 30-second spots that are run during the program five days a week. How would you evaluate this number?

suggested projects

1. (Oral Communication) Contact a local business, interview the people involved in media planning, and devise a one-year media schedule for the business.
2. (Writing Project) Survey at least two marketing communications firms. Ask them about their use of computers in media planning. Write a report on your findings.
3. (Internet Project) Suppose you were the media planner for a compact disc producer that markets alternative rock bands from Central Europe. Market research indicates that your target audience (men and women aged 18–27) spends approximately five to seven hours per week on the Internet.

   Visit three sites at which you think your company might want to advertise. Find out the advertising rates and other information that your marketing communication director might wish to know before authorizing the media buy. For instance, at Netscape, advertising space costs vary (as do CPMs) depending on where a company's ad appears. Some suggested sites include:

CANOE	www.canoe.com
Yahoo	www.yahoo.ca
AOL	www.aol.com

   Compile your findings in a memo to your marketing communication director. Be sure to make recommendations about where you think the company should advertise and why.

Crayola on the Comeback Trail

Background

What do you do when your chief product seems to be at the end of its product life cycle, when your customers have turned to newer, more modern substitutes, and when your brand name seems destined to evoke feelings of nostalgia rather than excitement? Some companies let the product die and try to succeed with new and different ones. Others rethink their approach and try to broaden their appeal.

That's what Binney & Smith, makers of Crayola crayons, decided to do in 1990. The company had done well for years by selling its products to parents. Parents bought crayons because they viewed them (and the company promoted them) as an educational tool and because the parents remembered what fun crayons were when they were kids. But our culture changes so fast that today's kids often have no use for toys that delighted their parents. And though parents still make most of the buying decisions for their kids' toys, children today have both more spending power and more influence over their parents' spending than did previous generations.

Targeting Different Markets

So now Crayola is marketing its product to both children and parents. Its first ad aimed directly at kids was called "Crayola Rock 'n Rolls." The commercial used rock music, eye-catching colours, and hip kids, and was aired at times when young kids were most likely to be watching TV.

At the same time, the company began a new campaign aimed at parents. The slogan emphasized nostalgia, trying to elicit fond memories of the parents' own early years: "Crayola. Childhood isn't childhood without it." But the copy, running in parents' and women's magazines, stressed how little effort crayons require from parents, allowing children to play independently.

With the two ends of the age spectrum covered, Crayola also reached for the middle. It now makes ColourWorks—coloured pens, pencils, and erasable crayon sticks, all aimed at a teenage audience. Traditionally, kids gave up crayons at about the age of seven, but Crayola is hoping that teens will decide that colouring can be cool and will make posters with their ColourWorks pens.

Colour Change Controversy

The company's most controversial move was to change colours for the first time in 32 years. A survey showed that kids, no doubt influenced by the popularity of loud, artificial colours in the culture at large, wanted brighter colours. So Crayola replaced eight of the older, subtler colours with more brilliant, eye-opening shades. The response was similar to that which greeted the production of New Coke. Many parents were outraged at the loss of their favourite colours, even though their kids preferred the new ones. So attached were parents to their favourite colours that protest groups were formed, including the RUMPS (Raw Umber and Maize Preservation Society) and the national campaign to save Lemon Yellow. So Crayola, taking its cue from Coca-Cola, reintroduced its classic colours, pleasing everyone and basking in the free publicity.

It's too soon to tell how well crayons can survive in a world of Nintendo and Sony Play Station, but by rethinking its audience and developing a varied media campaign, Binney & Smith has given its most important product a fighting chance.

Case Questions

1. Given the information provided in this case, outline the strategic and tactical considerations to evaluate in developing Crayola's media plan.
2. What other media alternatives might have worked for Crayola?

Sources: Crayola Web site (May 6, 1996): Internet (Crayola.com.80/trivia/triviasheet); Cara Applebaum, "Bright Ideas for Crayola Ads," *Adweek,* September 10, 1990, 64.

PART FIVE IMC Appropriation, Evaluation, and Campaign Planning

16

Developing the IMC Appropriation

chapter objectives

After completing your work on this chapter, you should be able to

- Explain how a strategic budgeting planning process works.
- Describe the budgeting techniques used in advertising, sales promotion, public relations, direct marketing, and personal selling.

FedEx Canada Invests: Using the Net and Getting Integrated

Hoping to cash in on an industry that is estimated to reach $1 trillion by 2003, businesses have been jetting their way to the Net. Although some call it the new-media industry equivalent to a gold rush, most businesses are "panning out"—just not getting the return on investment they anticipated. The interactivity and content are there. The navigation is sound and the products are great. Everything is by the book. Surely there is "gold in them thar hills." So what's missing? An IMC strategic plan and properly funded implementation. That's what's missing. E-business demands a unique strategy and a long-term investment perspective. The marketing communications must entertain and engage potential consumers. It must converge multiple marketing disciplines—incorporating both traditional and high-tech tactics. Otherwise, it will not successfully gain mind share in today's digital market space. Development and implementation of such marketing communications requires an investment that pays off over many years.

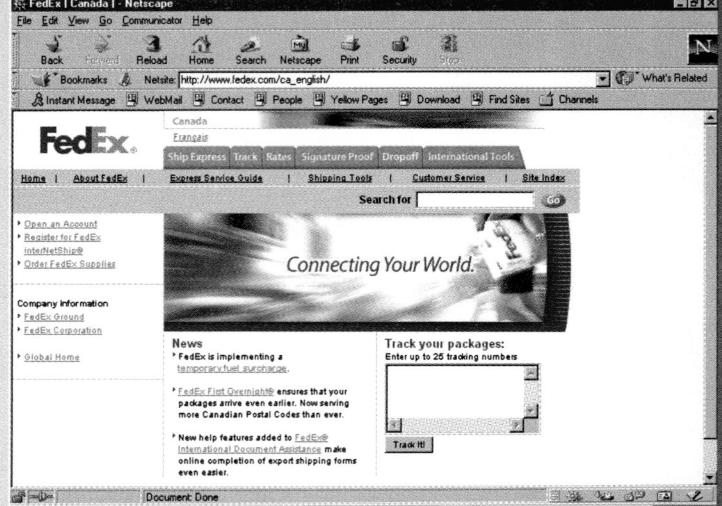

With the expertise of the ICE Group of Companies, Federal Express Canada Ltd. has invested in a unique integrated marketing communications strategy that has helped increase awareness and usage of FedEx interNetShip—the first bilingual browser-based shipping product on the Canadian market.

"Communicating the benefits of using FedEx interNetShip to customers is only part of the challenge. We also need to better educate our own employees," explains Vinoo Vijayaraghavan of electronic commerce at Mississauga, Ontario-based FedEx Canada.

Internal audience. External audience. Online media. Traditional media. So many choices—so many decisions. So many opportunities. ICE's solution was a "Think Fast" integrated marketing communications initiative that spans online, broadcast, and print media, and targets both external and internal audiences. This initiative was a textbook case of an integrated marketing communications campaign because all communications tools, from advertising to sponsorship, were used to send a defined target audience a consistent and persuasive message.

To grab attention, ICE developed a series of ads that bluntly address people without a second to spare. "Hey, business!" begins one radio spot. The ad is quick and to the point: "You're Ben Hur steerin' that chariot into the pack" and FedEx interNetShip provides the fuel to move faster.

"The tagline 'Think Fast! Think FedEx interNetShip' is full of positive associations," says creative director Steve Beinicke. "It totally captures the essence of the brand." Besides radio, the theme was carried into direct mail, online banners ads, and print. ICE also produced internal communications for FedEx in the form of posters to help drive home the benefits. "The clock's ticking and you've already got a million things to do," starts the copy—alluding to the massive number of FedEx shipments that must be picked up and delivered on a daily basis.

Federal Express
www.fedex.com

All of the creative was geared toward taking action, in this case, to visit www.fedex.com/ca. When potential customers arrive, an online, "flash-based" demonstration invites customers to test-drive FedEx interNetShip—effectively enabling them to engage with the brand—a key component in any e-business strategy.

Since the initial "Think Fast" integrative campaign launched, usage of FedEx interNetShip has spiked and shipments have increased dramatically. Using ICE's integrated marketing communications approach, FedEx interNetShip has been able to capture an ever-elusive target audience and reap the rewards of the Web's return on investment.

Source: Gayle Duncan, "High-Octane and Integrated," *Marketing* (July 19/26, 1999), 13.

Chapter Overview

The FedEx Canada situation suggests that allocating dollars to any business strategy, especially marketing communication, is a combination of careful analysis, experience, and luck. FedEx will never know whether the dollar amount it selected was just enough, too much, or too little. FedEx does know, however, that IMC and E-Commerce solutions require an investment that pays off over many years.

Many company executives still want assurance that marketing communication expenditures will improve the firm's bottom line. Even with these assurances, the most experienced and sophisticated executives are never sure whether they have allocated the right amount to marketing communication. Some marketing communication managers' solution? Ask for twice as much as your budget requires and hope that you will get half. Although all the major players may play this budgeting game, such an approach is certainly not strategically sound.

Appropriation
The maximum amount of dollars that management allocates to a specific purpose.

Budget
The details of how an allocated sum of money will be used.

In this chapter we investigate the planning process for marketing communication appropriation and budgeting. An **appropriation** is the maximum amount of dollars that management allocates to a specific purpose. In contrast, a **budget** is the nuts-and-bolts details of how this sum of money will be used. Usually the marketing communication manager asks for an appropriation and creates a related budget that reflects the marketing communication strategy.

Often the marketing director gives the marketing communication manager an appropriation amount and then the manager allocates these monies. Ideally the manager's allocation takes an integrated approach. That way, opportunities for saving money or producing more from the same amount would be more likely to occur. Unfortunately this integration rarely happens and budgeting tends to be done for each communication tool independent of the others. Thus the advertising manager fights for his or her share of the pie, as does the director of sales promotion, the PR manager, the national sales manager, and the vice president of direct marketing. Throughout this chapter we present separate budgeting criteria for each marketing tool, but keep in mind that the integrated approach taken by FedEx Canada and the ICE Group of Companies is the ideal, as shown in the opening vignette.

Planning for Marketing Communication and Budgeting

Figure 16.1 shows the planning framework used for marketing communication appropriation and budgeting using a strategic orientation. As noted, we present this as an ideal, recognizing that few companies approach budgeting this way. Note also that a prerequisite of determining an appropriation is forecasting both sales and cost. As we see later, decision makers must make appropriations based on accurate sales and cost estimates, so this element is integral to the appropriation decision.

Also, both cost forecasts and objectives are made at the marketing communication tool level. This suggests an objective-task approach (a technique discussed later), which means that the appropriation should be made by looking at the objectives of each marketing communication tool, and budgets built from the bottom up.

Figure 16.1 The Planning Process for Marketing Communication Appropriation and Budgeting

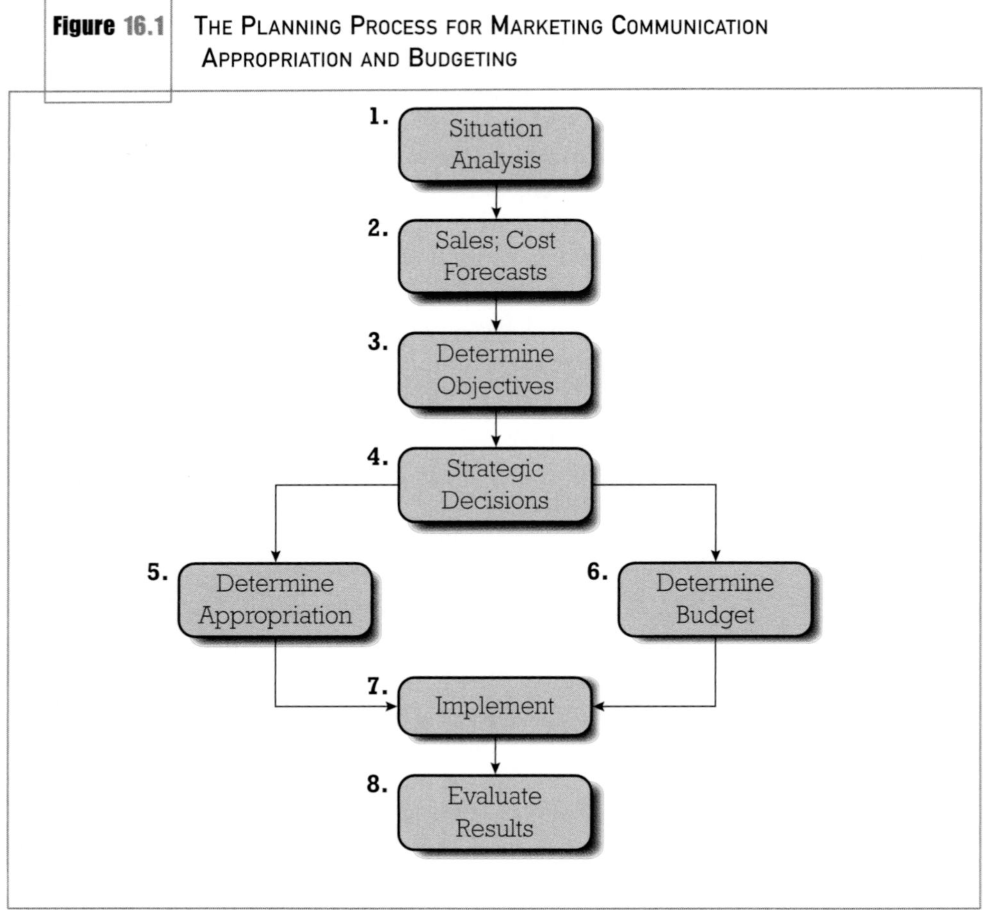

Preliminary Considerations

Though the appropriation and budgeting process relies on numerical information, the process is more art than science. It is usually based on educated guesses, tradition, or the financial condition of the company. One industry expert observed: "Of all the decisions marketing managers must make, questions concerning marketing communication allocations are thought to be most difficult."[1] To understand how appropriation and budgeting decisions are made, then, marketing communication should identify how the organization approaches the appropriation process, who the primary decision makers are, and how the marketing manager allocates marketing communication costs.

Most businesspeople recognize that marketing communication is important to corporate growth and health. Still, many businesspeople act as if marketing communication were an expense of selling rather than an investment in strong consumer relationships that generate higher sales. They often estimate sales for some ensuing period, establish the manufacturing, administration, direct-selling costs, and acceptable profit levels, and then determine the marketing communication budget with whatever money remains.

A company's marketing communication appropriation is often based on what is traditional for a company of its size in its industry. The general level of marketing communication expenditures within an industry tends to settle into a competitive equilibrium. That level remains more or less undisturbed until one firm finds a more successful or efficient manner of spending marketing communication dollars or settles on a marketing mix that is distinctly different from the industry pattern. Why? Many managers are afraid to depart from the normal range of marketing communication spending for similar products. They fear that if they reduce the percentage of dollars spent on communication, they will lose market share; if they increase it, they invite an equal and damaging response from competitors.

Instead of thinking about how marketing communication works to achieve objectives, then, marketing communication managers often set marketing communication appropriations by routinely applying a set of decision rules year after year. For example, in the cosmetics industry, five percent of forecasted sales often go to marketing communication. Chrysler Motors allocates $100 toward advertising for each unit forecasted. Like any business decision, the marketing communication appropriation is shaped by some established decision-making process. Whether the appropriation is wise and effective depends in part on who decides the amount of the appropriation and how the appropriation is defined and applied.

The Appropriation Decision Makers

A wide range of individuals can help determine the marketing communication appropriation. In a small mom-and-pop hardware store, virtually everyone working in that business might express an opinion about how much to spend on communication. As that store grows and becomes a member of the Home Hardware retailer-sponsored cooperative, the folks at Home Hardware may offer several guidelines and even mandate expenditure through the lure of cooperative dollars. There are also differences between companies that sell consumer products versus those that sell to other businesses. For instance, in a large consumer goods company such as Kraft Canada, the product manager has a strong impact, as does the advertising manager, promotion manager, and director of field sales, and its primary advertising agency.

In a business-to-business company such as Prestige Electronics, the decision is made by the director of marketing in conjunction with general advice from the CEO. In general, the greater the number of decision makers and the more removed those decision makers are from the marketing communication strategy, the more likely they will be to make conservative appropriations. Likewise, one shouldn't assume that larger companies are better able to make effective marketing communication appropriation decisions.

THE MARKETING COMMUNICATION APPROPRIATION: EXPENSE OR INVESTMENT?

Companies vary in their view of the marketing communication appropriation. For instance, many businesses charge any expense item relating to the consumer to 1) the cost of producing sales (such as personal selling), 2) the cost of creating the product (including research), or 3) the cost of communicating with the consumer. This last category would include all facets of communication, including letters to irate consumers, but most facets would have a strategic basis.

For companies that view marketing communication appropriations as a short-term expense, the strategic approach tends to be shortsighted as well. Communication efforts are viewed as 12 months long, with a tendency to start from scratch each year. For companies that adopt an integrated perspective, marketing communication appropriations are considered an investment, equivalent to machinery or a building, that pays off for many years. This perspective supports the notion of a campaign, which requires a much longer time frame than an individual ad or coupon drop. Rather, the integrated approach acknowledges that it may take time to achieve communication objectives, and that the payoff may be later than sooner. It represents a change in attitude and suggests that you don't give up on a brilliant communication idea simply because the results aren't immediately evident.

The budget planning process normally requires formal meetings in order to attain adequate consultation with interested parties.

Appropriation Issues

Although the marketing communication appropriation includes several communication areas, such as advertising, public relations, direct marketing, personal selling, and sales promotion, the majority of appropriation research comes from the advertising area. For example, researcher Gary Lilien suggests three important issues confront the executive who makes national advertising appropriation decisions:[2]

1. *Economies of scale*: Is there some relevant range in which increments of advertising yield increasing returns?
2. *Threshold effects*: Is there some minimum level of exposure that must be exceeded for advertising to have a discernible effect?
3. *Interaction effects*: Does advertising interact with each element of the marketing mix (especially personal selling) to produce effects that are greater than the sum of their separate effects?

Concept in Focus

An IMC Approach Toward Budgeting

Managers from restructured and downsized companies often have scarce resources—and little energy—to develop, implement, and evaluate corporate initiatives. This has been particularly true for marketing communication managers. Too often, top management equates IMC with lower cost. Instead, corporate management should re-evaluate how and why they allocate money to marketing communication.

Many organizations rely on microeconomic analysis as the basis for managing their operations, taking a stated corporate goal and using it as a basis for planning. Using this approach, the firm allocates a percentage of expected sales revenues for marketing communication. If the sales goal for the coming year is $1 million, the costs and desired profit are deducted from that amount, then the leftover funds are earmarked for various functional activities such as marketing communication. If sales revenues drop or management believes they soon will, management trims the budget for the functional areas.

Some firms, however, use an ROI (return-on-investment) approach to marketing communication spending. With this approach, the business focuses on the return it will reap from marketing communication spending. If the marketing communication manager can prove that the IMC meets the organization's ROI financial goals, then as long as cash flow is adequate, the organization should make the investment. Under an ROI approach, IMC dollars would no longer be treated as a fixed cost, that is, taken in the current accounting period. Instead, they would be treated as a variable cost that will provide returns in the future. Just like any other sound investment, the more you spend on IMC, the more you get back.

Don Schultz explains that he once calculated a projected ROI of about 200 percent for a proposed IMC in a service company. If the company invested $10 000 in the program, then it would have to generate $40 000 in additional sales. Could the IMC program do that? Historically, marketing communication programs generated incremental sales of 23 percent—much lower than the projected 200 percent. In that case the general manager's decision was easy: Don't invest.

If marketing communication expenditures are a variable, not a fixed cost, the marketing communication manager must track and evaluate marketing communication returns to see if they comply with the firm's required ROI. The problem with this approach is that such returns have been hard to measure. Today, however, technology and continuous improvement processes make measuring communication programs not only possible but practical.

Sources: Don E. Schultz, "How to Generate an Unlimited IMC Budget," ***Marketing News***, June 5, 1995, 7; Don E. Schultz, "Trying to Determine ROI for IMC," ***Marketing News***, January 3, 1994, 18; Don E. Schultz, "Spread Sheet Approach for Measurable ROI for IMC," ***Marketing News***, February 28, 1994, 12.

Unfortunately, executives tend to respond to these issues in a manner that is not strategic. Instead they often use mechanical decision rules that are routinely applied to make appropriations year after year. This mechanical process both excuses executives from careful thought about the task of determining just how marketing communication affects sales and ensures that the appropriation will fall neatly into the financial structure that exists within the company.

Of course, some businesses strive to apply an IMC approach to make strategic appropriation decisions. As indicated in the IMC Concept in Focus feature, this approach can be difficult to implement.

Assessing the Situation

In deciding the amount of money to allocate to marketing communication, the astute decision maker should evaluate the key situation factors. Which factors are influential depends on whether the marketing communicator is a manufacturer, a retailer, or a direct marketer.

Situational Factors Influencing the Manufacturer

Manufacturers consider the following six factors when determining the marketing communication appropriation:[3]

- The product, including its type, stage in the life cycle, and strategic components
- The market
- The competition
- The financial condition of the company
- Research guidelines
- The distribution system

The Product. Certain product elements have a tremendous impact on the marketing communication appropriation. We examined these elements in Chapter 2 when we discussed how the type of product, the stage in its life cycle, and its strategic components affect both the need for marketing communication and the effectiveness of particular types of marketing communication. For instance, it takes a larger amount of marketing communication dollars to launch a new product than to keep an old one selling. The same is true for convenience products compared with durable products. Marketing communication for consumable products such as milk, potato chips, and soft drinks use mass selling techniques to presell the product. Consumer durables, such as furniture and appliances, require an emphasis on personal selling because sales representatives can differentiate the products for consumers, tailor the presentation to meet prospects' needs, and use persuasive tactics to convince buyers to make such a high-cost purchase. Also, emotion-based products such as cosmetics, perfumes, and cars profit more from advertising than do products bought for primarily rational reasons, such as industrial machinery.

The Market. Both the size and nature of the market influence the marketing communication appropriation. Manufacturers who expect to cover a national market rather than a regional one will obviously spend more money.

Characteristics of the market, including demographics and psychographics, the attitudes and perceptions of the consumer toward the manufacturer, the amount of brand loyalty toward the firm and its competitors, and the amount of product use should also be considered in the appropriation process.

THE COMPETITION. Many companies monitor the expenditure of their competition and match these amounts either directly or proportionately. Expenditure information is available through observation or industry statistics. As we discuss later in this chapter, matching is usually an ineffective strategy. There are instances, however, when a major competitor dramatically increases the budget for a particular brand, and the only recourse is to match this increase.

THE COMPANY'S FINANCIAL CONDITION. When a company faces falling profits or during a general economic downturn, marketing communication budgets, especially advertising and public relations, are often cut first in firms that view marketing communication as a cost, not an investment. Then, when business booms, marketing communication is usually reinstated. This strategy can backfire. Firms that continue their marketing communication spending during poor economic conditions do better in the long run than firms that decrease or eliminate such spending.

Realistically, however, the marketing communication allocation is limited by what a company can afford. As a practical matter, a ceiling on the allocation always exists. The marketing communication manager should be aware of this approximate dollar limit before beginning the planning process.

RESEARCH GUIDELINES. Some companies, such as small companies in furniture manufacturing fields, use little research to guide their decisions; they rely instead on experience and tradition. For the more sophisticated organization, marketing surveys, media data, census material, forecasts, and many other types of research are available.

THE DISTRIBUTION SYSTEM. A channel of distribution can be quite long and include many intermediaries (that is, wholesalers and retailers). Or it can be quite short and direct, as it is for a manufacturer who uses a catalogue and the mail to distribute products. A long, complex channel may require a large marketing communication appropriation to support the product because of the divided efforts of the intermediaries. For example, Coca-Cola Enterprises Inc. follows an intensive distribution policy because its products must be available in every possible outlet. Because these outlets usually carry competing brands of soft drinks as well, Coca-Cola cannot expect the intermediaries to carry much of the marketing communication effort. A retailer may engage in some cooperative advertising, but little more. Consequently, Coca-Cola must make use of extensive mass-marketing communication, especially advertising and couponing, that will pull the product through the channel.

Tommy Hilfiger
www.tommy.com

In contrast, clothing designer Tommy Hilfiger distributes its products through an exclusive dealership arrangement. Because the retailers are guaranteed the sole right to sell the brand, they in turn provide certain efforts for the manufacturer. The retailer will engage in extensive personal selling as well as local advertising. Much of the marketing communication effort and cost, then, is taken off the shoulders of the manufacturer.

Although these factors are all important in determining the marketing communication budget, the manager must never lose sight of the fact that all communication tactics must be considered for possible funding. Take, for example, Lange Watches, a famous German luxury watch manufacturer whose factory was destroyed by Russian bombs at the end of World War II. Relaunched in October 1994 after the destruction of the Berlin Wall, great-grandson Adolph Lange plays the heritage benefit in his marketing. It began with a reception at a castle in Dresden and a print ad campaign. The print ads featured old and new Lange timepieces with the copy, "The economy in East Germany starts to tick differently. A Lange & Sohne has returned. A legend has become a watch again." Large watches sell for $14 800 to $148 900. Swiss agency GGK Basil, which handles Lange's $980 000 account, has also produced a 60-page catalogue titled, "When Time Came Home," detailing the history of the Lange family and their watches. The company prints 10 000 copies of the catalogue in German and recently added English and Italian versions. By the end of 1995, the company had sales of $20 million, and 700 watches were snapped up.[4]

Situational Factors Influencing the Retailer

Many of the factors just discussed have a direct bearing on the marketing communication budget for retailers as well as for manufacturers. However, retailers who engage in budgeting must also consider a variety of factors unique to retailing. Seven key factors follow:

- Age of store: New stores require more advertising.
- Location of store: Bad locations may require more promotion.
- Merchandising policies: Discount stores usually need a greater amount of mass selling to turn over product.
- Competition: The greater the level of competition, the more promotion is needed.
- Media availability: The size of the community often dictates the type and extent of the media that can be employed.
- Size of the trading area: Marketing communication tends to increase with market size.
- Support from the manufacturer: Manufacturers may provide retailers with advertising support, point-of-purchase displays, sales training, and other promotion support that will reduce the expenditures required of the retailers.

Situational Factors Influencing the Direct Marketer

A number of situational factors affect the direct marketer's budget allocation.

- The database: The more specific and the more frequent the update of the database, the more it will cost.
- The role of technology: Using new technology, such as interactive and artificial intelligence, will add risk and expense.
- Legal and regulatory implications: Several direct-mail techniques, especially telemarketing and direct mail, are heavily regulated. Compliance with these regulations can add greatly to the expected expense.

- Location of the target audience: Delivering a direct-marketing message usually is more costly the farther it must travel or the more isolated the recipient.
- Direct marketing via retailing: Factory outlets are like direct marketing and must consider the same factors found with retailing.

SALES AND COST FORECASTS

Executive judgment
The intuition of one or more executives.

Time-series analysis
The use of a company's historical data to discover a pattern or pattern's of the firm's sales over time.

Market tests
Making a product available to buyers in one or more test areas and then measuring purchases and consumer responses to marketing tactics.

A sales and cost forecast is a necessary part of the budgeting and appropriation process. Sales for the coming year can never be known exactly and therefore require a managerial estimate or "forecast." This estimate may be based solely on judgment (for a completely new product) or may be supplemented by previous experience with similar situations. A variety of techniques are used to produce this forecast. **Executive judgment** bases the sales estimate on the intuition of one or more executives. It is also possible to survey customers, the sales force, or experts in the field. Two techniques that are far more complicated are time-series analysis and market tests. **Time-series analysis** uses the company's historical data and tries to discover a pattern or patterns in the firm's sales over time. The method assumes that past sales patterns will continue. **Market tests** involve making a product available to buyers in one or more test areas and then measuring purchases and consumer responses to marketing tactics. These results lead to projections for the product in the total marketplace.

Sales forecasts are used to determine the appropriation in at least two ways. First, the general trend in sales (that is, up, stable, down) provides a general guideline for the direction the appropriation should take. Second, many companies set their appropriation as a percentage of projected sales. (This method will be discussed in more detail later.)

Cost forecasting also affects budget decisions. Costs must be forecasted to justify a budget request. Agency-related costs, media costs, production costs, special events costs, entertainment costs, and coupon distribution costs all must be estimated and totalled. Most of this information about costs is available either through secondary sources or through the provider of the service or product. References such as the *Canadian Advertising Rates and Data,* a Rogers Media monthly publication, report media costs for a specified period of time. Production houses readily provide cost estimates. Several calls may be necessary before all the cost information is gathered, but it can be done. There are also computer databases that provide a great deal of cost information. The databases usually guarantee information for a given period of time, note rate increases or decreases, and provide dates for revised cost information.

Canadian Advertising Rates and Data
www.cardmedia.com

SETTING OBJECTIVES

A strong relationship exists among the marketing communication objectives, the appropriation/budget objectives, and the expenditure of funds required to meet the marketing communication objectives. Assuming that an organization has specific marketing communication objectives, it should be a fairly straightforward matter to estimate the marketing communication expenditure necessary to reach these objectives. However, the appropriation and budgeting objectives also affect the appropriation process. These objectives provide an important link between the marketing communication objectives and the resulting appropriation. Essentially, appropriation/budgeting objectives tend to be either *quantitative* or *qualitative* (see Figure 16.2).

Figure 16.2 How Marketing Communication Objectives Lead to Appropriations

Quantitative objectives
An organization's objectives that concern an appropriation's ability to maximize profit, sales, or market share.

Quantitative objectives are concerned with the appropriation's ability to maximize profit, sales, or market share. (The theoretical foundation for these quantitative objectives is marginal analysis, discussed later in the chapter.) Maximization of profits suggests that the goal of marketing communications would be to contribute to profitability. The amount of profit depends on the costs associated with each marketing communication element. Complying with the profit maximization objective would emphasize keeping costs low or ensuring that high-cost items have very high payoffs. For example, media would be chosen that had a low CPM, or markets would be targeted that produced high profit margins.

Overspending
A saturation point at which continued spending would produce sales at a decreasing rate.

Underspending
Low marketing communication spending resulting in sales below their expected minimum.

Sales-based objectives attempt to maximize expected sales. A special concern is to avoid overspending. **Overspending** means that continued spending would produce sales at a decreasing rate. The saturation point has been reached and further spending is wasteful. **Underspending** is also a concern. If sales are below their expected minimum, marketing communication spending is too low. Forecasting and tracking sales are mandatory to achieve sales-based objectives.[5] Because constant monitoring of the market is part of this process, budget flexibility is important. That is, money should be available at a moment's notice to take advantage of sales trends.

Reaching market-share objectives is similar to maximizing sales in that the company must estimate competitors' sales curves which, together with the firm's, comprise the market. Estimating a competitor's sales curve is difficult because it also requires estimating how the competitor's sales will respond to a particular level of spending. This difficulty in making estimates is possibly why so many false budgets are leaked to marketing communication trade publications; either a high appropriation intimidates competitors altogether or a low appropriation induces competitors to underspend. Maintaining market share means matching competitors' spending, and gaining market share means outspending the leading competitors.[6]

Qualitative objectives
An organization's objectives that address the subjective issues achieved through the appropriation rather than the quantitative issues of profit, sales, and marketing.

Qualitative objectives address the subjective issues achieved through the appropriation rather than the quantitative issues of profit, sales, and market share. In this context the goal is to assess the extent to which the dollars spent achieve the qualitative objectives associated with the marketing communication plan discussed in earlier chapters. In the case of media selection, for instance, qualitative objectives focus on whether the medium selected matched the image of the company, whether the tone of the medium was appropriate, or whether the right people understood the message in the manner intended. Qualitative appropriation and budget objectives indicate the extent to which the dollars allocated will achieve these marketing communication objectives at the most effective level.

Strategic Decisions

Despite the fact that billions of dollars are spent on marketing communication every year, the majority of the companies spending these dollars use decision processes that are based on little if any strategic thinking.[7] Although this pattern has not proven detrimental to many of these companies, there is growing evidence that marketing managers are using more sophisticated techniques in setting marketing communication appropriations and budgets. Traditional subjective methods are gradually being replaced by data-driven approaches. These approaches may provide an additional competitive advantage to those willing to commit to them. First, however, we will discuss the subjective methods of appropriation for the main marketing communication areas.

Determining Appropriations for Advertising

The budgetary approach used by a particular advertiser typically varies with the product, the size of the appropriation, and tradition. In the following sections we describe the advantages and disadvantages of some of these methods.

Predetermined Budgetary Methods

Earlier, we suggested that marketing communication budgets are often handed down to the marketing communication manager by management fiat, with little or no input from the marketing communication manager. Next we examine four common budgetary techniques used under these conditions: the percentage-of-sales, unit-of-sales, competitive parity, and all-you-can-afford methods.

concept review

Planning for Marketing Communication and Budgeting

1. Distinction should be made between appropriation and budgeting.
2. The planning framework for marketing communication appropriation and budgeting determination includes the following:
   - Preliminary considerations
   - Assessing the situation
   - Sales and cost forecasts
   - Setting objectives
   - Strategic decisions

Percentage of Sales

The percentage-of-sales technique is probably the most popular of the marketing communication budgetary methods. Management bases the marketing communication appropriation on a fixed percentage of sales of the previous year, of an anticipated year, or of an average of several years. To illustrate, if sales were $3 million on average for the last three years, management using this technique might choose five percent of that average and allocate $150 000 to marketing communication. One advantage of this method is that expenditures are directly related to funds available—the more the company sold last year, the more it presumably has available for marketing communication this year. Another advantage is its simplicity. If businesspeople know last year's sales and have decided what percentage they wish to spend on advertising, the calculation is easy.

The percentage-of-sales method suffers from several serious limitations, however. Most notably, it assumes that marketing communication is a result of sales rather than a cause of sales. It does not take into account the possibility that sales may decline because of underspending on marketing communication. Also, this method does not include the possibility of diminishing returns—meaning that after a certain point additional dollars may generate fewer and fewer sales. In short, using the percentage of sales may mean underspending when the sales opportunities are high and overspending when the potential is low.

Perhaps the most effective manner in which to use the percentage-of-sales technique is to examine both past sales and forecasted sales. This examination also assures that market potential is accounted for when the forecast is considered. Regardless of its limitations, the percentage-of-sales method will no doubt remain popular.

Unit of Sales

The unit-of-sales method is very much like the percentage-of-sales technique. Instead of dollar sales, though, the base is the physical volume of either past or future sales. Toyota, for example, would base their appropriation for Camry on the number of units they expect to sell next year rather than the value of those units. This unit value is then multiplied by a fixed amount of money to derive a total marketing communication appropriation. This method exhibits the same strengths and weaknesses as the percentage-of-sales method, and the same solutions apply. It is commonly used for high-ticket items such as automobiles and appliances.

Competitive Parity

Many marketing communicators base their allocations on competitors' expenditures. Information on expenditures is available readily through sources such as *Marketing* magazine, *Advertising Age*, A.C. Nielsen, and government reports. This technique is rarely the sole determinant of the appropriation but normally complements other marketing communication methods.

The competitive parity technique has three advantages. First, it recognizes the importance of competition in marketing communication. Second, it often helps minimize marketing communication battles between competitors. Because competitors are all spending about the same on marketing communication, they tend not to try to outspend one another. Finally, this approach is simple to use because the only information required is the dollar amount expended by competitors.

The fact that this technique is based on a simple dollar amount also suggests a limitation. Important competitors may vary widely in the size and direction for their budgets, so comparisons may be hard to make. Another drawback is that competitive parity assumes that a company's marketing communication objectives are the same as its competitors, and this can be a treacherous assumption. It also assumes that competitors' allocations are correct. Finally, information on competitive advertising expenditures is available only after the money has been spent, so it may not indicate future selling.

All You Can Afford

With the all-you-can-afford method, the amount left over after all the other relevant company expenditures are made is allocated to marketing communication. Companies of all types and sizes use this method. It is particularly popular when introducing a new product. As unsophisticated as the approach appears, it often produces effective results. If a company is doing a good job allocating to the other elements of its business, it may not be surprising that the amount left over for marketing communication fits the needs of the company.

Strategy-Based Budgeting Approaches

In contrast to the predetermined budgeting methods that are based on simple rules of thumb and industry traditions, several budgeting techniques are based on the marketing communication strategy itself. These bottom-up approaches begin with the input of people implementing the marketing communication strategy, continue on to the marketing communication manager, and ultimately reach top management, accompanied with documentation supporting the budget amount requested. Admittedly, these techniques are more difficult to use but ensure that the marketing communication plan will be implemented effectively. We explore four strategy-based budgetary methods: the objective-task, mathematical model, experimental, and payout planning methods.

Objective-Task

The most popular strategic technique is the objective-task method. With this method, the marketing communication manager first studies the market and product thoroughly to set logical marketing communication objectives. Then the marketing communicator defines specific objectives (such as creating consumer awareness and increasing coupon redemption) for a particular time period. After setting the objectives, the marketing communicator determines how much money will be necessary to achieve them. If the associated costs are greater than the money available, then either the objectives are adjusted or more funds are found. This method is equivalent to the zero-based budgeting method discussed in Chapter 4.

The main advantage of this method is that it develops the budget from the ground up, so that objectives are implemented strategically. It does not rely on factors outside the control of the decision maker, such as past sales or competitors' spending. The second advantage is that the task method works well for new product launches, when advertising must be developed more or less from scratch or when the firm makes major changes in the marketing communication program for established products. In these "change" situations, historical and competitive information do not provide useful budgeting guidelines.

The objective-task method has one key drawback: Its results are only as good as the stated objectives and the accuracy of the dollar amounts assigned to each objective. Setting objectives and assigning accurate dollar amounts are difficult tasks. If done poorly, the budget and the marketing communication fare poorly.

Mathematical Models

During the last several decades, the use of quantitative techniques in marketing communication budgeting has grown but has not found wide acceptance in the industry. These quantitative methods may apply mathematical models from other fields, such as physics or psychology, or may use models developed specifically for marketing.

Mathematical models have not been widely accepted for a variety of reasons. First, they require experimental and formal analysis techniques beyond the capabilities of many companies. Second, the process is time-consuming and expensive. Third, models from other fields have not been successfully modified to apply to marketing, and little agreement exists as to the reliability of the marketing communication budgeting models. Although new quantitative budgeting models are being proposed, their extensive use in actual practice will probably be slow in coming.

The Experimental Approach

The experimental approach is an alternative to modelling. The marketing communication manager uses tests and experiments for different marketing communication budget options in one or more market areas and uses the results to guide budget decisions. For instance, a product might be tested simultaneously in several markets with a similar population, brand usage level, and brand share. Varying advertising and budget levels would be determined for each market. Before, during, and after the expenditure, sales and awareness would be measured in each market. By comparing the results, marketing communicators can estimate how the varying budget levels might perform nationwide. The budget that produced the best results would then be used.

To a great extent, this technique eliminates the problems associated with the other budgetary approaches. The major drawbacks of this approach are the time and expense involved in getting the data and the difficulty of controlling the environment. Dow Chemical Co. has used the experimentation approach for many years. The company has increased total sales and profits while decreasing advertising costs.

Payout Planning

The payout plan is often used with other budget-setting methods to assess the investment value of the marketing communication. It projects future revenues generated and costs incurred, usually for a two- or three-year period. Its purpose is to show what level of expenditures needs to be made, what level of return might be expected, and what time period is necessary before the return will occur. Payout planning is a useful budgetary technique when a new product is introduced with a commitment to invest heavily in marketing communication to stimulate awareness and product acceptance. It acknowledges the likelihood that this situation will diminish company profits for the first year or two.

Management naturally wants estimates of both the length of time that marketing communication dollars must be invested before sales occur and the expected profit flow once the brand has become established.

Table 16.1 illustrates a payout plan for a chain of bagel shops. In its first year the bagel shop chain spent $2 million of its $2.18 million in gross profit on marketing communication, plus $4 million on corporate investment, producing an operating loss. The second year the company invested $3 million on marketing communication and $1 million on corporate investment, producing a cumulative loss of $3.6 million. The third year showed a net profit of $1.28 million and a cumulative debt of $2.3 million. The fourth year of operation the organization profited after investing $4.1 million in marketing communication; the gain was $3.3 million, with a payout of $990 293.

The key to the payout plan is the accuracy of the forecasting. Forecasts must be made of sales over time, factors affecting the market, and costs. A successful brand typically grows in its early years and then levels off at a stable market share. Investment in marketing communication is high in the beginning and low later on.

The payout plan is a useful planning tool, but it has limitations. Most notably, it cannot account for all the uncontrollable factors that may affect the plan. New competitors, legislation, natural disasters, and new technologies are just a few of the contingencies influencing the plan. Also, the assumptions underlying the plan tend to be optimistic. What happens if the product has no competitive advantage or the marketing communication is ineffective? Clearly, top management would react badly to a payout plan that is two or three years behind the projected break-even point.

Table 16.1 EXAMPLE OF A PAYOUT PLAN FOR A BAGEL SHOP CHAIN

		Year 1	Year 2	Year 3	Year 4
Sales		$ 9 461 053	$16 588 017	$21 650 000	$37 200000
Ingredient cost	29%	2 743 705	4 810 524	6 278 500	10 788 000
Labour cost	21%	1 986 821	3 483 483	4 546 500	7 812 000
Materials cost	7%	662 273	1 161 164	1 515 500	2 604 000
Overhead	20%	1 892 270	3 317 634	4 330 000	7 440 000
Total operational costs	77%	7 285 070	12 772 733	16 670 500	28 644 000
Gross profit	23%	2 176 042	3 815 243	4 979 500	7 440 000
Marketing communication costs		2 000 000	3 000 000	3 700 000	4 100 000
Organization profit		176 042	815 243	1 279 500	3 340 000
Corporate investment		4 000 000	1 000 000	0	0
Corporate profit/loss		(3 823 958)	(194 757)	1 279 500	3 340 000
Cumulative profit/loss		(3 823 958)	(3 629 207)	(2 349 707)	990 293

concept review

Determining Appropriations for Advertising

The following methods are used for determining appropriations for advertising:

1. Predetermined budgetary methods
   - Percentage of sales: fixed percentage of last year's or forecasted sales
   - Unit of sales: fixed dollar amount of each unit sold
   - Competitive parity: proportionate match of the amount spent by competitors
   - All you can afford: amount left over after all other relevant expenditures are made
2. Strategy-based budgetary methods
   - Objective-task: costs budgeted to achieve objectives
   - Mathematical models: application of mathematical models to budgetary decisions
   - Experimental approach: tests of various budget allocations in various markets
   - Payout planning: projects future revenues generated and costs incurred

Determining Appropriations for Other Forms of Marketing Communication

The methods we have described for determining the appropriations for advertising are also used to set appropriations for other elements of the marketing communication mix. Most companies use more than one of these methods. In fact, the method used may vary from division to division or even between functional areas. For example, a company might use competitive parity to set its personal selling budget, percentage of sales to establish the advertising budget, and all-you-can-afford for the other marketing communication activities. In the following sections we examine appropriation techniques used with the other marketing communication elements: sales promotion, public relations, direct marketing, and personal selling.

Sales Promotion Budgeting

One serious difficulty associated with sales promotion is the vast number of activities that fall under this marketing communication tool. As a result, there is ongoing uncertainty about which activities should be the financial responsibility of sales promotion. The *Dartnell Sales Promotion Handbook* offers the following list of activities that should be covered by the sales promotion budget:[8]

1. Research
2. Travel
3. Sales education
   a. Training literature
   b. Films and visuals
   c. Housing and administration
4. Promotional literature
5. Dealer services
6. Sales tools and equipment
7. Fairs and exhibits
8. Educational material for schools
9. Sales contests and campaigns

10. Dealer and other meetings
11. Community relations
12. Speakers' bureau
13. Publicity
14. Trade associations

When these activities overlap with the other marketing communication elements, the costs should be shared. For the most part, the extent to which sales promotion is allowed to share its financial burden depends on who is in charge of sales promotion. Most large companies use a brand management system, and the brand manager is responsible for determining the total amount to be invested in sales promotion.

When the brand management system is not used, the marketing communication manager usually develops a total sales promotion budget for the department that includes all expected expenses. Salaries, sales promotion activities, department expenses, ongoing costs, and similar charges are individually budgeted. Either approach benefits from an internal accounting system capable of providing budgetary control.

Most of the budgetary methods discussed in determining advertising appropriations are also used with sales promotion. Five primary techniques are used to allocate funds to sales promotion:[9]

1. *Predetermined ratios*: These ratios involve rules of thumb based on company policy or historical precedent, possibly modified by the strategic position of the brand.
2. *Objective-task method*: Objectives for sales promotion are stated and plans are developed to accomplish these objectives at minimum cost.
3. *The build-up approach*: The budget begins with the necessary marketing communication expenses and successively adds the less important ones.
4. *Competitive parity*: The budget mirrors that of a close competitor, scaled up or down as needed.
5. *Optimal modelling*: A sales response model is used to find the budget that will maximize profits. The model is either solved analytically or by using a simulation approach. The "optimal" budget becomes a guideline or starting point for other budgets.

Although senior managers often specify predetermined ratio guidelines, historical precedent (that is, last year's allocation) is the most commonly used method of allocation in sales promotion.[10] This use of historical precedent is discouraging because the objective-task and theoretically optimal expenditure methods have much more intuitive appeal.

As indicated in earlier chapters, an ongoing concern of marketing communication managers is how to allocate dollars between advertising and sales promotion. The following factors influence this allocation decision:[11]

- Characteristics of the decision maker (preferences and experience)
- Power and politics in the organization
- The organization's structure (centralized or decentralized, formal or complex)
- Use of expert opinions
- Approval and negotiation channels
- Pressure on senior managers to produce an optimal budget

Public Relations Budgeting

Compared with the other areas of marketing communication, public relations uses the least sophisticated budgeting techniques. Essentially, public relations managers follow one of four strategies in setting budgets. The first is equivalent to the all-you-can-afford technique. Because public relations is often at the end of the line when funds are allocated, the amount given to public relations is typically much lower than that given to advertising, sales promotion, or other types of marketing communication.

Competitive parity is the second technique. However, because the amount that competitors spend on public relations is very difficult to gauge, the amount chosen is often based on an approximation of what competitors are spending on public relations. Because many public relations costs are hidden, however, budgeters often make serious miscalculations in their estimates.

A version of the objective-task method is a third budgeting technique used in public relations. This budgeting technique usually depends on the objectives established for the other marketing communication elements. For example, a sales promotion program such as a special event is also the responsibility of public relations. The objective established for the special event by sales promotion dictates the public relations objective, which in turn can be assigned a cost figure.

The final budgeting technique follows a cost accounting approach. Simply stated, the public relations manager develops a list of activities and events that he or she would like to implement in the upcoming year. The manager then creates an itemized list of costs that is compared with a budget ceiling or submitted to top management for approval. Adjustments then follow.

Direct-Marketing Budgeting

For the most part, direct-marketing budgets employ a cost-based approach tied to the techniques discussed in advertising. Direct-mail marketers, for instance, can estimate to the partial penny the cost of mailing out a direct-mail piece to a given number of people. The cost of the database, printing, sorting, bundling, postage, and so forth are well-known numbers. The same is true for a telemarketing campaign, a catalogue, or designing a Web site. Although there is no available information to support a particular budgeting approach, one might safely conclude that an all-you-can-afford strategy is predominant. Alternately, because a primary benefit of direct marketing is accountability, an objective-task approach makes the most sense, with a typical objective being response rate.

Personal Selling Budgeting

Direct selling expenses, or field selling expenses
These expenses arise from activities directly connected to personal selling.

Indirect selling expenses
Those expenses associated with personal selling but not directly associated with the product (such as moving expenses, special entertainment expenses, and special marketing expenses).

In most businesses the dollar figure allocated to personal selling is calculated independently from that of the other marketing communication functions. That is, the sales manager and marketing director determine the personal selling budget with little concern for what the other mix elements are spending. This tendency toward having a separate selling budget is a major reason why coordinated personal selling with advertising, sales promotion, direct marketing, and public relations has been so difficult.

The two cost categories associated with personal selling are (1) **direct selling expenses**, or field selling expenses; and (2) **indirect selling expenses**. This latter category includes moving expenses, special entertainment expenses, and special marketing communication expenses. Many companies have drastically reduced this cost area in recent years. Moving expenses have become prohibitive; tax law changes, costs, and attitude changes have also decreased the popularity of the seven-course expense account lunch and other entertainment expenses. This discussion will concentrate on direct-selling expenses.

Figure 16.3 shows a suggested process for developing a personal selling budget. The 15-step process begins with a list of the location of each sales territory, followed by a sales forecast for each metro area. Steps 3 through 9 indicate all the direct-cost items associated with each metro area. These cost items are totalled under step 10. Step 11 totals the specific cost items for all metro areas. Step 12 projects sales of the territory. Step 13 calculates the percent of the territory's sales that will be accounted for by total sales of the metro area listed. Step 14 enters the budgeted salaries. Step 15 enters total forecasted expenses for the metro areas from column 10. Step 16 adds steps 14 and 15 for a total budget figure. The derivation of the dollar amounts placed in each of the cost categories can be percentage of sales, objective-task, all-you-can-afford, or some combination of these methods. Here again, the simpler methods prevail.

Marginal Analysis: The Budgetary Ideal

Marginal analysis
The theoretical basis for determining the size of a marketing communication budget.

Hundreds of approaches are used to determine how much to spend on marketing communication. However, the theoretical basis for determining the size of the marketing communication budget is **marginal analysis.** In theory it means that a business adds to the budget as long as the marginal revenues from the expenditures exceed the amount of the expenditures. The point at which the marginal revenue and marginal costs are equal shows the optimal budget level.

Figure 16.3 Preparing a Sales-Costs Budget

Preparing a Sales-Costs Budget

1. Metro areas	2. Projected sales	3. Lodging costs	4. Meal costs	5. Auto rental	6. Misc. expenses	7. Entertainment	8. Transportation	9. Promotional	10. Total metro expenses
11. Metro totals									
12. Projected total territory									
13. Percent of total	%	%	%	%	%	%	%	%	%
14. Budgeted salaries									
15. All-metro total									
16. Actual expenses									

concept review

Determining Appropriations for Other Forms of Marketing Communication

1. Sales promotion, public relations, and direct marketing use many of the same budgeting techniques as advertisers.
2. Budgeting for personal selling considers two categories:
   - Direct selling expenses
   - Indirect selling expenses

This model is illustrated in Figure 16.4. The optimal level of marketing communication expenditure is that level that will maximize profits. To find that level, we must start by assuming that the only determinant of dollar sales (S) was the amount spent on marketing communication (MC). So, sales is a sole function (F) of marketing communication.

$$S = F(MC)$$

Also, assume that the general shape of the sales curve is represented by the top line in Figure 16.4. In addition, the expenditure on marketing communication is represented by the upward sloping linear line labelled *(MC)*. The line designated as *MF(MC)* represents the relative difference between the projected sales and marketing communication expenditures, that is, gross margin. Gross margin is also reflected as a profit curve in the lowest line. Accordingly, the most profitable point of expenditure is P*. Any expenditures beyond this point would provide a lower and lower level of profitability. As long as sales exceeded costs, it would be wise to continue a budget increase. However, a dollar invested in marketing communication above the level P* would yield less than $1 profit.

Figure 16.4 Illustration of Marginal Analysis

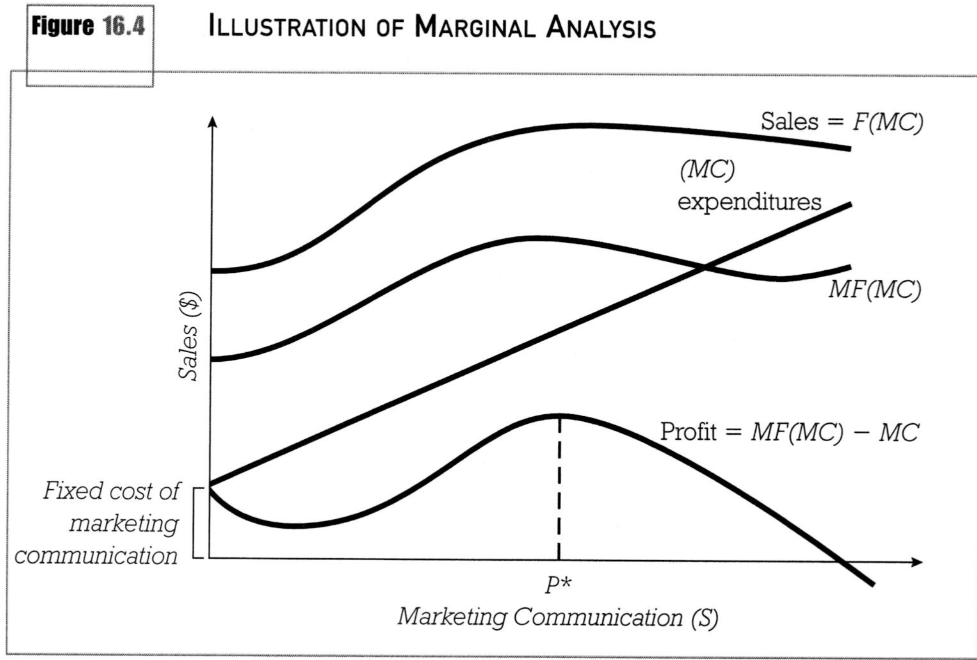

Although the *F(MC)* is portrayed as being S-shaped (see Figure 16.4), the shape and parameters determining the curve can vary tremendously. However, at least in the case of advertising, there are several reasons why an S-shaped curve seems justified: (1) there is always some sales return for additional advertising investment, but the rate of return declines as more money is spent, (2) no amount of advertising investment can push sales above some limit imposed by the culture and the competitive environment, (3) there are threshold levels of advertising such that expenditures below the threshold have no effect on sales, and (4) some sales will be made even with no advertising investment. These conclusions are depicted in Figure 16.5.

Marginal analysis has also been applied to budgets for personal selling. Although the primary benefit of marginal analysis in this context is to determine the optimum size of the total sales organization, it has a secondary advantage of providing a basis for making adjustments in the sales force throughout the year. Both decisions have a direct impact on the personal selling budget. The application of marginal analysis is straightforward. If an additional salesperson is hired, total sales should increase as should total selling costs. If a person is let go, sales will decline and so will expenses. In general, the manager will hire another person if the gross margin on the additional sales raises more than the selling cost increases—that is, if the extra salesperson will contribute more in gross margin than in cost. When replacing salespeople, the opposite reasoning applies. That is, salespeople will be replaced if they don't contribute marginally.

This decision-making process is illustrated in the following example. Suppose that a company currently has 50 salespeople at a total cost of $800 000 and a total profit of $1 060 000 (see Table 16.2). One of the salespeople has announced the intention to quit and the human resources manager has reported that three qualified people are available as replacements. The information found in Table 16.2 can be used to evaluate the following alternatives:

Figure 16.5 ADVERTISING EXPENDITURE

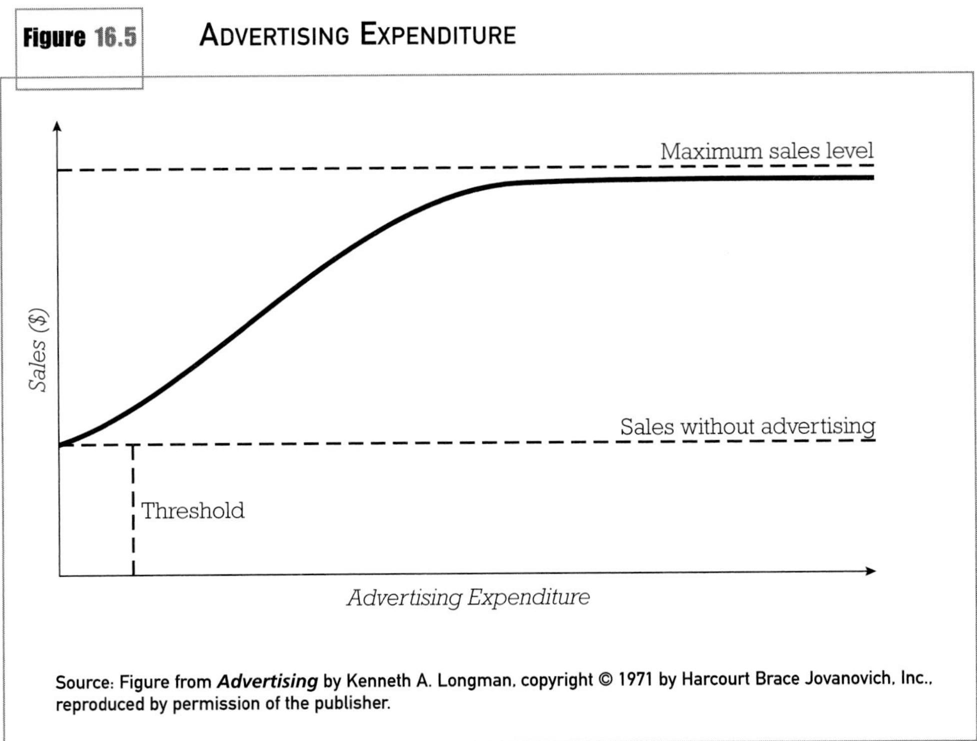

Source: Figure from ***Advertising*** by Kenneth A. Longman, copyright © 1971 by Harcourt Brace Jovanovich, Inc., reproduced by permission of the publisher.

Table 16.2 MARGINAL ANALYSIS OF SALES FORCE

	Profit Contribution		Selling Cost	
Number of Salespeople	Total	Marginal	Total	Marginal
49	$ 900 000		$780 000	
50	1 060 000	70 000	800 000	20 000
51	1 120 000	60 000	820 000	20 000
52	1 170 000	50 000	840 000	20 000
53	1 210 000	40 000	860 000	20 000

1. Do not replace the salesperson.
2. Replace the salesperson.
3. Expand the force by one or more.

If the salesperson is not replaced, the gross margin will drop by $70 000 and $20 000 will be saved. Hiring one person to replace the departing salesperson will generate a $40 000 differential, hiring two people will increase net profits by $30 000, and hiring three people will generate another $20 000 and a larger market share. Thus, 52 salespeople represent the optimum sales-force size because the marginal profit is still greater than the marginal cost.

Although there are no examples of marginal analysis applied to sales promotion or public relations, there is no reason why this rationale would not work. In sales promotion the applicable units relate to levels of couponing, sampling, or price discounting. For public relations, the units of input are information releases, special events, or participation in open houses. The marginal unit sales from any given increase in these inputs can be calculated, producing a similar curve to that in Figure 16.4. With the exception of the threshold level, most of these propositions have been widely accepted in the advertising industry.[12]

Although marginal analysis reflects an important ideal, applying it in practice has been difficult, if not impossible. The first problem relates to the assumption that sales are a direct result of marketing communication expenditures. This assumption may be valid in the case of direct-mail promotion, but it is questionable in most other types of marketing communication. The assumption that sales are determined solely by marketing communication expenditures is obviously faulty in practically all situations. Even if a researcher could isolate and control all the relevant variables for one time, there is no guarantee that the derived response curve would be valid in the future.

Second, marginal analysis ignores how the sales-response relationships change if copy strategy, media strategy, or other elements of the marketing mix are changed. Some changes can cause the response relationship to become more or less efficient by making dollars work harder or easier.

Third, marginal analysis does not account for the cumulative effect of past marketing communication effort on future sales. A consumer who buys a microwave oven in February could be affected by marketing communication seen in December and an encounter with a salesperson six months earlier. There is also the possibility that marketing communication might attract buyers who become loyal customers for many years. To date, marginal analysis is unable to accommodate this **lag effect** of marketing communication.

Lag effect
The cumulative effect of past marketing communication effort on future sales.

There are continuing efforts to adjust the marginal analysis technique to reduce these limitations. Some researchers have developed sophisticated experiments in which the various budget variables affecting sales are manipulated and the results are compared. Elaborate statistical regression models are added to these experiments to provide even greater predictability. However, the high level of expertise required to implement these techniques has discouraged their use. Instead, marketing communication managers opt for simpler budgetary methods.

concept review

MARGINAL ANALYSIS: THE BUDGETARY IDEAL

1. Marginal analysis is a theoretical basis for setting a marketing communication budget.
   - A business continues to supplement the marketing communication budget as long as the incremental expenditures are exceeded by the marginal revenue that they generate.
   - The optimal level of marketing communication expenditure is the level that will maximize profit.
2. Marginal analysis is difficult to implement because of the following reasons:
   - It is impossible to judge whether sales are the direct result of marketing communication.
   - It does not consider changes in different elements of marketing communication strategy.
   - It does not account for the cumulative effect of past promotions.

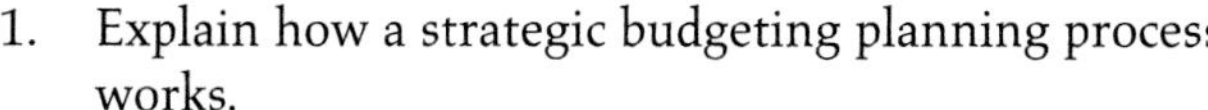

summary

1. Explain how a strategic budgeting planning process works.

   An appropriation is the maximum amount of dollars that management allocates to a specific purpose, such as marketing communication. A budget is the nuts-and-bolts details of how this sum of money will be used. The budgetary planning process includes the following steps: situation analysis, sales and cost forecasts, communication objectives, determining the appropriation, determining the budgets, implementing, and evaluating results. Key preliminary issues to consider are (1) who are the appropriate decision makers, (2) whether the appropriation is viewed as a cost or investment, and (3) theoretical considerations.

   In assessing the situation the budget planner should consider aspects of the product, the market, the competition, the financial condition of the company, research, and distribution. A number of techniques are used to forecast sales and costs, such as executive judgment, market tests, and secondary information sources. Relevant objectives to consider can be quantitative or qualitative.

2. Describe the budgeting techniques used in advertising, sales promotion, public relations, direct marketing, and personal selling.

   Using advertising as a reference model, appropriation approaches can be considered as predetermined (percentage of sales and units, competitive parity, all-you-can-afford) or strategy-based (objective-task, mathematical models, experiments, payout planning). Sales promotion, public relations, personal selling, and direct marketing all use one or more of these appropriation approaches. Marginal analysis represents the budgetary ideal in that your budget should maximize profits.

points to ponder

Review the Facts

1. Differentiate between the terms "appropriation" and "budget." What is the role of each?
2. Discuss the factors that influence the absolute size of the appropriation.
3. What factors influence the promotion allocation of the retailer?

Master the Concepts

4. Describe both the marginal analysis and the objective-task methods of determining the appropriation. How are the two methods comparable?
5. What is the problem with using the competitive parity approach when developing the appropriation for a new product? Suggest an alternative approach.
6. In addition to selecting the method of budgeting and subsequently determining the size and allocation of the budget, what other factors should the manager consider?
7. Describe the experimental approach to budgeting. What are the drawbacks associated with this method?
8. There are several difficulties in appropriating a budget for sales promotion. Discuss them.

Apply Your Knowledge

9. What are the first two budget decisions that a marketing communication manager must make? How is the manager influenced by competition when making these decisions?
10. What procedure would you use to develop a payout plan for a new product?

suggested projects 

1. (Oral Communication) Interview two local businesspeople (one retailer and one manufacturer), and ask them to discuss the method they use to establish their marketing communication budget. Compare your findings from the two interviews.
2. (Writing Project) Write a two-page memo defending the use of predetermined budgeting methods.

case 16 United Way Changes Its Ways

Few business organizations have gone through more changes than the United Way. The organization began in Denver in 1887 when the first United Community Campaign was organized. It was known as the Community Chest from the 1920s through the 1940s. Then the organization became known as the United Fund or the United Givers. It was not until the 1970s that United Way took its current name.

The intent of the United Way remains consistent—to raise money simultaneously for several worthwhile causes, thus cutting down on duplication of fundraising drives and saving time and frustration for donors. Individual charities within local United Ways receive on the average one-fourth of their funding from the annual United Way campaigns. The remainder of funding comes from grants and bequests, from government agencies in fees for contracted services, and from supplemental fundraising drives.

As one would expect, the marketing program for United Way to date has been very simple. The national office was responsible for coordination, long-range planning, and providing some services to the approximately 2100 local United Ways in the United States and Canada. Headquarters furnished the local organizations with technical support for local campaigns and tried to build and maintain good relations with large corporations. More specific activities had to do with the development and production of films and other materials for use by voluntary solicitors and the media, development and production of planning and budgeting manuals, review of national agency programs, publication of various newsletter series, training of locals in management techniques and fundraising, maintenance of a lending library of pertinent reports, and the execution of public opinion and market research. For example, one research effort found a direct correlation between contributor knowledge of United Way and support.

All the advertising for the United Way has been through the support of the Advertising Council, a social marketing organization formed for the purpose of supporting selected nonprofit causes with the creation and placement of donated professional advertising. Advertising agency Bozell & Jacobs, International, volunteered to create the advertising, and the National Football League agreed to support the United Way on its televised games. Later, the National Hockey League and National Basketball Association agreed to similar arrangements. The entire cost to United Way for the NFL series was $200 000, the cost of production.

Marketing communication efforts at the United Way have changed, however. The United Way is planning to develop a series of print, television, and radio ads that will be targeted at the general public. These ads will run the entire year, not just during campaigns. United Way faces one other unusual problem. Because the money spent on marketing communication has been donated and should go to the various charities, the public is very critical about spending on other programs.

Top management at United Way has never had to develop a marketing communication budget before, so there is a great deal of confusion as to where to begin and what the process should look like. There appear to be two camps thus far. One group simply wants to come up with a total appropriation based on the experiences of for-profit businesses with comparable revenue and cost figures. This group has identified six such businesses and has estimated that $11 million would be necessary to support a one-year advertising program. The allocation of money to the various components of the advertising strategy would be based on cost figures submitted by the people responsible for each component.

The second group, headed by staff economist John Blair, wishes to employ a marginal analysis approach in deriving the appropriation. The group argues that having detailed support for such a large financial decision is particularly important when an organization is spending donated money. Admittedly, there will be some problems making all the necessary forecasts that are part of the marginal analysis approach. In the worst-case scenario, intelligent assumptions can substitute for hard data.

Case Questions

1. Given the situation faced by United Way, assess the appropriateness of the two appropriation techniques suggested.
2. Are there other techniques United Way should consider? Which ones? What advantages are offered by these alternative techniques?

17

Measuring IMC Performance

chapter objectives

After completing your work on this chapter, you should be able to

- Address the main issues in measuring the performance of marketing communication.
- Explain the specific testing methods used with advertising, sales promotion, public relations, direct marketing, personal selling, and other IMC tools.

What's in Store for Canadian Coffee Chains

When the last decade began, Tim Hortons had just hired the agency it still uses, Enterprise Creative Selling of Toronto, and had been spending about $3 million a year on advertising. For much of the decade, the chain's ads attempted to get consumers to see Tim Hortons as more than a doughnut shop by focusing on products such as bagels, sandwiches, and soup. According to Doug Fisher, restaurant consultant and author of ***Successful Restaurant Strategies***, broadening the menu allowed Tim Hortons to "get more out of the market in terms of sales, but also improved the franchisees' ability to sustain themselves in the market and make money."

But even as the ads were featuring different products and deals, they were driving a consistent brand message, says Doug Poad, vice-president of strategic planning at Enterprise. The brand identity was one of "relaxed, caring, friendly, and honest." The "True Stories" campaign, launched in 1997, capitalized on this feel-good theme: it put the focus on Tim's coffee and the emotional connection Canadians have to coffee. Even a 1999 Roll Up the Rim to Win spot in which a customs agent allows people who can name the contest to cross the border plays on the chain's place in Canadians' hearts. That loyalty has enabled Tim Hortons to grow to almost 1600 locations across the country, sell brand coffee for home use, and even offer branded coffee makers.

By all accounts, Tim Hortons is a Canadian success story due in no small measure to its marketing communication strategy. Today, Tim Hortons accounts for 13.1 percent of Canada's quick-service restaurant sales, according to numbers provided by the Canadian Restaurant and Foodservice Association. To aid in this success the chain spent $21 million on advertising in 1998, according to A.C. Nielsen of Markham, Ontario. But what does the future hold for Tim Hortons?

"Coffee wars" may be brewing as three Toronto-based coffee chains continue to introduce changes to their outlets. Although it can be argued that these chains do not compete head-to-head with Tim Hortons, a new wave of intense competition has opened up. Second Cup is moving ahead with its first TV campaign, a six-month effort through Toronto-based Ammirati Puris Lintas. This ad campaign comes as Second Cup undergoes strategic changes, such as increasing its number of cafés. Other changes include introducing new products such as branded mints and chocolates and its Energy Latte coffee drink. The chain is also rolling out a lunch program of salads and sandwiches. Meanwhile, Starbucks Coffee Co. introduced lunches in a number of its Toronto-area stores. And mmmuffins Canada Corp., the parent company of mmmuffins and Michel's Baguette chains, is repositioning its Michel's locations to keep up with changing consumer tastes. Michel's is dropping its French motif for a more multicultural position, adding gourmet sandwiches and expanding its salad offerings.

Enterprise Creative Selling
www.enterprises.com

No one really knows what the future holds for Tim Hortons. Certainty, Tim's competition is "heating up" in the Canadian coffee-brewing business. With this competition, success will be difficult to assess accurately because Tim Horton's marketing effort has become much more complex.

Sources: Lesley Daw, "More Than Just a Doughnut Shop," *Marketing*, December 20/27, 1999, 17. Astrid Van Den Broek, "Changes Brewing at Coffee Chains," *Marketing*, November 15, 1999, 2.

Chapter Overview

One of the most difficult problems marketing communication managers face is determining whether they have met their objectives. For marketing managers and product managers, the measures of success are often quantifiable, such as sales, market share, or profits. The marketing communication manager, however, must assess qualitative results that are difficult to gauge and are less concrete. Is communication performance best measured through awareness, recall, attitude change, coupon redemption, sales, or some other indicator? Tim Hortons could measure the success of its communication strategy by the percentage of market sales. Should it also assess the cost of creating awareness of its extended product lines? Or the cost of differentiating itself from new competitors?

Simply stated, marketing communication managers want to be guaranteed that the measurement of marketing communication performance is done accurately and responds directly to the marketing communication objective. This mandate is constant regardless of the type, size, or location of the business.

Complying with this request has been neither easy nor universal. There are serious and unresolved questions regarding what to measure, how to measure, and what the measurements mean. In this chapter we address the philosophical issues related to the evaluation of marketing communication performance. We also examine specific evaluation techniques for advertising, sales promotion, public relations, direct marketing, personal selling, and other IMC tools.

Marketing Communication in Perspective

Recall from Chapter 1 that all marketing communication is driven by one or more objectives, such as creating brand awareness or increasing market share. The objectives, however, are meaningless unless some mechanism can measure the extent to which they have been reached. Marketers' objectives range from the very subtle to the definite (for example, market share). Generally, the task of marketing communication is to dispose people to change their attitudes, their behaviour, or both as requested by the marketer.

In this chapter we examine evaluative research, which measures the effectiveness of the marketing communication planning process. It differs from the research conducted to analyse target markets or to select media, which we discussed in earlier chapters. Though evaluative research may take place at various times throughout the marketing communication process, it is carried out with the specific purpose of assessing the effects of various strategies. Thus, evaluative research allows the marketing communication manager to evaluate the performance of specific program elements and provides input into subsequent situation analyses. It is a necessary ingredient of a continuing planning process.

To conduct evaluative research the marketing communication manager should ask four related questions: What should be tested? Should we test? If so, when? And how? We investigate the answers to these questions next.

WHAT SHOULD BE TESTED?

The basic problem in assessing marketing communication is to show that a specific effort produced specific results. Did the new Tylenol ad increase the viewers' understanding of the drug's benefits? Did the 25-cent coupon for a President's Choice product increase its sales? Whether the effort caused the results is difficult to discern.

Several other factors may have contributed to increased understanding or a change in behaviour. An increase in product quality or the deletion of a competitor may offer a better explanation. In addition, controversy surrounds the question of which results to measure to assess marketing communication—short-term or long-term effects, the change in sales level, or some other benchmark. Top management often argues, for instance, that unless dollars spent on marketing communication generate sales, then they have been wasted. Still others argue that too many uncontrollable factors affect sales and market share for marketing communication to be held accountable for them.

The hierarchy of effects model, discussed in Chapter 4, provides one way of resolving this debate. The model assumes that consumers move through seven steps to the point of purchase: unawareness, awareness, knowledge, liking, preference, conviction, and purchase. Because marketing communication helps move consumers through these steps, each step, then, suggests a legitimate objective for a marketing communication strategy. Figure 17.1 lists some appropriate marketing communication activity for each step, and corresponding ways to measure effectiveness.

In this text we categorize all results and efforts into just two components: communication and behaviour. That is, we assume that the effectiveness of marketing communication equals the extent to which the communication worked and, if appropriate, changed behaviour.[1]

To see whether the communication worked, managers should consider the marketing communication objectives. For example, assume that a manager wanted to evaluate the effectiveness of a 20 percent discount in a line of children's play clothes. Say that discount was offered to move 70 percent of the company's out-of-season merchandise. In measuring the effects of the discount, counting inventory before and after the discount would provide reliable sales results. Although sales-related objectives are appropriate for sales promotion and personal selling, they are not usually appropriate for advertising and public relations.[2] These marketing communication tools are more closely linked to other marketing communication objectives, such as building product awareness and knowledge and changing attitudes and preferences. Sales promotion and

Figure 17.1 A Matrix of Evaluation Measures Used in Marketing Communication

	COMMUNICATION Source, Message Media	BEHAVIOUR Pseudo-purchase, Purchase
PRETESTS	• *Focus groups* • *Checklists* • *Split-run* • *Readability* • *Physiological* • *Direct mail* • *Theatre* • *On-the-air*	• *Test marketing* • *Single-source*
CONCURRENT	• *Recall* • *Attitude* • *Tracking* • *Coincidental*	• *Single-source* • *Diaries* • *Pantry checks*
POSTTESTS	• *Readership* • *Recall* • *Awareness* • *Attitude* • *Association* • *Audience assessment*	• *Single-source* • *Split-cable* • *Inquiry* • *Sales counts*

personal selling provide the impetus to take action. The impetus provides the necessary motivation (conviction) to get up and dial a toll-free number, visit a store, sign on the dotted line, pay cash, or hand over a Visa card (purchase).

Communication Factors

Recall from Chapter 8 that persuasive communication depends on the proper manipulation of the message, the source, the means of delivery, and the control of noise. Given the importance of these communication factors in effective marketing communication, we must determine the measurable elements of each factor and choose the best way to make these measurements. Next we explore how to find the measurable elements of each factor. Later we discuss the measurement techniques.

Message Variables. There are numerous elements in a typical marketing communication message. Words, music, colour, visuals, layout, headlines, and the logo can all affect the outcome of a marketing communication message. All these message elements are more or less important to the various individuals involved in the message creation. For example, the marketing manager or product manager who initiates the communication and provides the primary direction for its design is most concerned that the focal concept is delivered clearly through the message. A **focal concept** is the key idea that the message contains. Sometimes the focal concept is very specific, such as product safety in the case of Volvo. In other cases the focal concept is a general mood or attitude that the message is supposed to deliver. Coke ads suggest that drinking Coke and having fun go together.

Focal concept
The element in a marketing communication message that becomes the key idea that is delivered.

The copywriter or commercial director may have an entirely different set of message variables to test. The copywriter is concerned with whether the headline attracts attention. Is it understood as intended? Are funny words perceived as funny? Is the long technical copy interesting to the reader? Is "25%

off" easier to understand than "now $1.99"? The art director wants to know if the photograph works better than the line drawing. Is the red background more soothing than the yellow? There are literally hundreds of questions such as these that are asked during and after the creative process.

Source Variables. The source could be a celebrity, an animated character, a background voice, an actor, or someone singing a jingle. Key questions include whether the source that delivers the message creates the desired result. Factors to evaluate might include the following: the attitude change produced through the source, the trust or credibility associated with the source, the likeability of the source, and the possibility that the source will dominate the message (that is, the consumer will not remember the name of the sponsor). Once these source-related variables have been identified, there are a number of techniques available to measure attitude, likeability, credibility, wearout, and so forth.

Delivery Variables. Marketing communication messages can be delivered in a variety of ways. Advertising messages are normally delivered through the mass media. A tremendous amount of research is available to support mass media decisions. This research not only aids in placement decisions but also provides measures of effectiveness. The marketing communication manager can compare the effectiveness of one medium class with another (for example, newspaper versus television), size or length of the ad, and position in the vehicle. The marketing communication manager can specify very precise media objectives and be fairly sure that the measures are available to assess these goals.

Sales promotion messages can be delivered through conventional mass media as well as nonconventional media. For example, Campbell Soup Co. can deliver a coupon for its new soup through print advertising, a freestanding insert, or a direct-mail coupon drop. The company can also offer samples of the product at the point of sale by setting up a soup kettle at the end of a supermarket aisle and having a person pass out cups of soup. How is this variable evaluated? Campbell's marketing communication objective is to get the new product into 50 percent of Canadian kitchens within 30 days of market entry. Speed of coupon delivery, coupon redemption, and product trial are the responsibility of sales promotion. Measuring these factors is quite complicated, and sales figures are often considered a result of the strength of sales promotion.

The process becomes even more confusing when we consider public relations. In the case of publicity, counting the number of lines and/or stories appearing in the popular media is often considered an indicator of success or failure. But how does one compare the relative goodwill produced through a story in *Maclean's* to a plant tour with elementary students to the sponsorship of a 10K run? Goodwill is a vague phenomenon: Public relations still finds it difficult to develop objectives and measures that help select the best delivery mechanisms. More will be said about measuring public relations later in the chapter.

Even personal selling has the capability to compare delivery mechanisms. Issues such as the timing of message delivery, who should deliver the message, and the size of the message are all considerations. Typically, the measure of performance is sales. However, other intermediary measures might also be considered. Examples include the number of sales calls made, the percentage sold, the type of products sold, the cost per sale, and the profit per sale. A good sales manager is constantly taking measures such as these and making adjustments as needed.

Behavioural Factors

The behavioural factors associated with marketing communication include intent to buy, purchase, and brand loyalty. In the hierarchy model, these factors lead to conviction and purchase. We have already alluded to the difficulties in integrating advertising with sales. Nevertheless, advertisers are faced with increasing pressure to produce sales. In some cases advertisers are willing to opt for action measures that suggest an intent to buy but fall short of actual purchase. Among these action measures are brand choice, store visits, and contact (such as calls or written responses). These action measures are appropriate early in the product life cycle, when creating awareness or educating the consumer is a prerequisite to commitment.

Where these action measures prove unsatisfactory, advertisers have turned to sales tracking companies such as Nielsen Marketing Research. Sales tracking can involve three primary methods of obtaining sales data: monitoring warehouse shipments to resellers, cash register scanning at the stores, and conducting household diary panels. The ultimate sales test is to set up specific controls so that the advertiser can manipulate the ad, control who receives it, and then determine the results. Experiments can be done by the advertiser: Test cities with comparable characteristics are found, and one city receives the ad and the other one does not, then sales are measured.

Incremental sales
The additional sales that are produced by a specific sales promotion.

Sales promotion and personal selling consider all the behavioural variables just discussed, including sophisticated sales tracking. For example, sales promotion often considers incremental sales rather than sales. **Incremental sales** are the additional sales produced by the sales promotion. The calculation of these sales eliminates people who would have purchased the product anyhow, regardless of the availability of a coupon, rebate, or price reduction. Personal selling often considers sales figures relative to profitability. In other words, the costs associated with producing one dollar in sales are just as important as the sales themselves. Likewise, the cost of gaining one percent of market share may be greater than the benefits. As indicated in the You Decide feature, sometimes test results can be misleading.

Should We Test?

Several benefits come from testing communication efforts. First, testing increases the efficiency of marketing communication by helping managers eliminate unproductive alternatives. Nissan found this to be the case when it introduced the Infiniti through a series of ads entitled "the rocks and trees approach" by critics. Initial tests showed that an automobile ad that does not show the car raises curiosity but does not give reasons to buy. The campaign was changed. Second, information from testing can help managers avoid disasters that can destroy the campaign or even the organization. Finally, tests provide feedback to those who create and implement the marketing communication campaign.

There are also problems that may preclude testing. First, testing costs a great deal of money. A complete testing program for one year ranges from $140 000 to $700 000. Second, windows of opportunity for marketing communication can be very short and may not allow enough time for testing. Third, the adequacy of the testing instruments and the meaning of the results are often questionable. High recall scores may be more a reflection of an unusual appeal than effective communication. Fourth, testing can create internal tensions and squabbles.

The Mystery of Online Ads

When people buy magazines, they leaf through the pages, getting impressions of ads. When people watch TV, they see ads on the screen. If they take car trips, they see billboards along the road. Thanks to researchers in each medium, marketers can more or less tell how many and what kinds of people will see the message, based on circulation, viewership, or traffic-flow data analysis.

The Internet, however, combines elements of all of the above media: As nothing less than integration of print and broadcast—an interactive text-and-picture magazine, catalogue, or billboard delivered on-screen at the consumer's request—it's no wonder the advertising community has had trouble pinning it down. Without a standardized method of tabulating audience exposure and impact, much less a way for marketers to know who's on the other end of the mouse, companies that advertise on the Internet have been doing so largely on the basis of trust.

Internet content providers already set rates according to the available figures. But the science of quantifying the Web is only in its infancy. Disadvantaged against competitors in traditional media who have well-established methods of auditing circulation and measuring audiences, Canadian Internet advertising professionals have measurement services that are just now being introduced. Media Metrix Inc. in association with ComQuest Research Inc., a unit of BBM Broadcast Bureau of Measurement has introduced its independent, objective audience measurement services in Canada. These services offer Internet statistics such as size, reach, frequency, time spent on the Internet as a whole, by category, and for specific Web sites. These audience data are linked to demographic profiles, collected from panellists. Other service providers such as Markham, Ontario-based Nielsen Media Research Ltd. are following suit with similar measurement services.

This type of site measurement data is welcomed by Internet advertisers. Advertisers feel much better with independently collected site data. According to Ted Boyd, president of the Internet Advertising Bureau (IAB) of Canada, this is "... good news for the industry all around." Measurement tools like the ones now being developed could solve the problem of building demographic information about Internet users. Why? Because these tools go beyond the software tools used by Internet providers themselves that do little more than track "hits" and "click-throughs."

Perhaps the arrival of Internet measurement data services will take the mystery out of this anonymous medium and encourage continued growth in Internet advertising. The latest numbers from IAB and Ernst & Young, partners in producing bi-annual Internet advertising surveys, indicate Internet advertising continues to grow rapidly. In 1998 Internet advertising in Canada was a $24.5-million business. At the current rate of growth, Internet advertising could be a $900-million business by 2004.

You Decide

1. Will the new measurement services provide the credibility that Internet advertisers need?
2. What could be done to make advertising on the Internet more reliable?

Sources: Kevin Marron, "TV-Style Ratings Track Net Surfers," (Report on E-Commerce), ***The Globe and Mail***, January 28, 2000, E2; Information extracted from www.iabcanada.com, February 27, 2000; Information extracted from www.bbm.ca/Press_Releases/body_press_releases.html, February 27, 2000; Laura Rich, "Measure For Measure: What Is The Web Worth? ***Adweek***, November 11, 1996, 32-3; Ian P. Murphy, "On-Line Ads Effective? Who Knows For Sure?" ***The Marketing News***, September 23, 1996, 1, 38; Michael Schrage, "The Internet's Promise," ***Adweek,*** June 3, 1996, 36.

Internet Advertising Bureau of Canada
www.iabcanada.com

Ernst and Young
www.ey.com

People may disagree about what to test, especially because management is reluctant to support tests that are not related to sales. Creative people, especially copywriters, resent having research dictate the words they must use. Finally, testing encourages people to engage in activities that increase ratings but have little to do with objectives. For instance, a designer knows he or she can improve recall scores by simply including a cute baby or puppy in the ad.

To decide whether to test, managers should weigh the costs and benefits of testing. Unfortunately, most marketers tend either to ignore this step or to concentrate on just one or two key factors. The decision to test is often based on the testing capabilities offered by the marketer's agency.

When Should We Test?

If testing is worthwhile, the next question concerns the timing of the testing process. The possible answers may be classified as pretesting, concurrent testing, and posttesting. Ideally, all three would be employed.

Pretesting, or evaluative research
Research that is conducted before the audience is exposed to the marketing communication.

Pretesting (also known as evaluative research) is research conducted before the audience is exposed to the marketing communication. Pretests are useful when managers need to examine possible problems before resources are spent on the actual message. For example, a manager may want to know whether a potential spokesperson is credible. A survey might satisfactorily answer the question before the commercial is actually produced and distributed.

Concurrent testing
Evaluation of a marketing communication effort while it is running in the marketplace.

Concurrent testing evaluates the marketing communication effort while it is running in the marketplace. This form of testing may be the most difficult to implement and maintain, but it has several advantages. It allows the researcher to quickly determine to what extent the message is reaching the desired target market. Concurrent testing may also indicate whether the message is being interpreted properly and may measure the effects of the message. Most important, this technique allows adjustments to be made immediately.

Posttesting
Research that is conducted after the audience has been exposed to the message, medium, or spokesperson.

Posttesting is research conducted after the audience has been exposed to the message, medium, or spokesperson. It is designed to determine to what extent the marketing communication objectives have been attained. It allows researchers to evaluate how well they did and then to make appropriate changes.

How Should We Test?

Hundreds of specific tests can be used to evaluate marketing communication. However, all these measurement devices can be placed into three categories: experiments, surveys, and mechanical measurement techniques.

Experiments
Giving individuals a controlled exposure to a message to change their opinion, attitude, or cause some other action.

Experiments give individuals a controlled exposure to the message and change their opinion, attitude, or cause some other action. Experiments may take place in the laboratory or in the field. For example, an advertising agency designs three print ads in which the copy, illustrations, size, and other factors are all kept the same. The only difference among the three ads is the spokesperson; one is Cree, one is Caucasian, and one is Asian. The experiment's objective is to measure the effect of these manipulations on attitude toward the product. A thousand names are randomly selected from a master list. (In randomization, everyone has an equal chance of being selected or assigned.) Then these people are randomly assigned to view only one of the ads. All the people complete an attitude questionnaire. Finally, the evaluator conducts statistical tests to assess the difference in attitude among the three groups.

Validity
When a concept is confirmed through testing to be what it claims to be.

Reliability
When the same test results are repeated time after time.

An experimental design is valuable because it provides results that can be evaluated through the most advanced statistical tests. Such tests determine the validity and reliability of the results. **Validity** means the concept is confirmed to be what it claims to be. **Reliability** means that the same results are repeated time after time. Companies balk at using experimental designs because of their high costs.

Survey
Interviews or questionnaires that are used to obtain information about people's exposure to a particular message, medium, or person, and the resulting changes in their attitude or actions.

In a **survey** interviews or questionnaires are used to obtain information about people's exposure to a particular message, medium, or person, and the resulting changes in their attitudes or actions. People are simply asked what they think, feel, remember, or do. Statistical analysis of the responses yields a measure of correlation between the reports of exposure and the changes in attitude or action.

Like the experimental approach, the survey method requires that the researcher deal with conceptual and technical matters. If a survey is to have any use at all, the researcher must take care that the design of the sample, the questionnaire construction, and the interviewing methods do not bias the results. Surveys are much easier and faster to conduct than experiments. However, the fact that surveys do not control for unknown variables means that alternative factors could be producing the measured results.[3]

Mechanical measurement
Information collected through a device that measures involuntary responses of the automatic nervous system.

Mechanical measurement techniques collect information through a device. Physiological devices, the most common type of mechanical techniques, will be discussed later. These devices usually measure involuntary responses of the automatic nervous system; thus these techniques offer objectivity.

MEASURING ADVERTISING PERFORMANCE

Until the 1920s, copy and media testing were practically unknown in advertising. Today they are a common part of the research efforts of most medium- and large-sized agencies. In addition, syndicated researchers conduct independent research. Because most of the performance research techniques were developed in the advertising industry, it is not surprising that most of the discussion will be in an advertising context. Essentially, managers in sales promotion, direct marketing, and public relations have adapted these techniques for their respective fields.

Syndicated media research may be purchased directly by the advertiser, or it may be sold to agencies and provided to the clients. Usually done on a regular basis, media research is designed to meet the needs of current as well as potential clients. The television rating services of A.C. Nielsen and the radio rating services of the Bureau of Measurement (BBM) are well-known examples. Media trade associations such as Audit Bureau of Circulations (ABC) conduct syndicated research as well.

Tables 17.1 and 17.2 summarize studies of practices in advertising research. Table 17.1 reports on a survey of 94 of the top U.S. ad agencies. The respondents were asked to indicate their usage patterns in areas of advertising research:

concept review

MARKETING COMMUNICATION IN PERSPECTIVE

1. Evaluative research helps determine whether marketing communication has reached its objectives and suggests ways to improve communication efforts.
2. The evaluative process requires answers to four questions:
   a. What should be measured?
      - Communication factors, which include message variables, source variables, and delivery variables
      - Behavioural factors, which include intention to buy, purchase, and brand loyalty

   b. Should we test?

   c. When should we test?
      - Pretesting
      - Concurrent testing
      - Posttesting

   d. How should we test?
      - Experimental approach
      - Survey design
      - Mechanical measurement

Table 17.1 REPORT ON MEDIA, AUDIENCE, AND COMMUNICATION MEASURES USED IN ADVERTISING RESEARCH

Factors Evaluated in Media	Percentage
Reach	90.4%
Gross rating points	89.4
CPM to target	88.3
Average frequency	87.2
Effective reach	86.2
Frequency distribution	75.5
Quintile distribution	43.6
Others	30.8
Communication Effects Evaluated	
Recall	58.5
Advertising exposure	52.1
Awareness	47.9
Attentiveness	43.6
Purchase	31.9
Recognition	24.5
Preference	18.1
Attitude toward brand	18.1
Prepurchase behaviour	17.0
Comprehension	16.0
Interest	16.0
Knowledge	14.9
Intentions	12.8
Attitude toward ad	11.7
Conviction	8.5
Others	9.6

Source: P.J. Kreshel, K.M. Lancaster, and M.A. Toomey, "How Leading Advertising Agencies Perceive Effective Reach and Frequency," *Journal of Advertising* 14, no. 3 (1985): 32–8. Used with permission.

(1) media factors, (2) methods for evaluating communication effects. The percentage reported reflects the number of people using each technique or measure. The results indicate that these top agencies measure media performance in terms of reach, gross rating points, CPM to target, average frequency, effective reach, and frequency distribution. Finally, communication effectiveness is measured primarily through recall, advertising exposure, awareness, and attentiveness.

In contrast to the general research-related findings shown in Table 17.1, the information in Table 17.2 reports on the specific type of television copy research used by a survey sample of 112 advertising agencies. The second column shows the percentage of those surveyed that use a particular method. The top three reported tests were evaluating finished ads (93.8 percent), undertaking preliminary background or strategic research in preparation for advertising commercials (92.9 percent), and evaluating rough commercial execution of other

Table 17.2 GENERAL FINDINGS REGARDING COPY RESEARCH

Type of Copy Research	Percentage
Evaluate finished commercials.	93.8%
Undertake preliminary, background, or strategic research in preparation for advertising campaigns.	92.9
Evaluate rough commercial execution of other formats prior to finished commercial.	91.1
Evaluate television campaigns.	90.4
Evaluate copy ideas, storyboards, and other formats prior to rough commercial.	88.7
Test competitive commercials.	56.1
Test commercials for wearout.	42.9

Source: B. Lipstein et al., "Television Advertising Copy Research: A Critical View of the State of the Art," *Journal of Advertising Research* 24, no. 2 (April/May 1984): 21–5. Used with permission.

formats prior to finished commercial (91.1 percent). It is interesting to note that two of the three techniques were pretests, and the top-rated test was a posttest. This fact suggests a strategic orientation in at least this facet of advertising. Correctly, advertising copy should be evaluated before being implemented.

PRETESTING: COMMUNICATION AND BEHAVIOUR

The appeal of testing an ad before running it in the media is obvious. The test gives some assurance of success before money is spent. Although there is no surefire way of predicting success, certain methods of pretesting can give helpful information if used intelligently.[4] These methods include tests of consumer opinion or awareness, physiological measurements, readability tests, and test marketing. These methods and their descriptions are summarized in Table 17.3.

TESTS OF OPINION OR AWARENESS

Opinion method
A simple method of evaluating an advertisement by showing members of the general public a proposed advertisement and asking their opinion of it.

Opinion methods is a catchall classification for the simplest method of evaluating ads. People readily give their opinions. When shown a proposed ad, they will state whether they think it would get their attention, how interesting they think it is, which advertising claims they believe, and how likely they believe it would cause them to buy the product or service. They will also compare ads on the basis of all of these functions and give opinions at any stage of an ad's development. Most opinion methods are simple, fast, and inexpensive.

Opinions may be solicited from any member of the general public—from the prospective consumer to the creative person to the advertising expert. However, researchers must watch out for pitfalls associated with each of these sources. People associated with the advertising business are usually prejudiced. This prejudice may be unconscious, based on allegiance to client brands or on conviction regarding the superiority of particular techniques. Conversely, when consumers give their reactions to ads, rather than explain how the ad influenced them, they frequently try to give "expert" opinions on ads. It is common for individuals to want to report what they think other people like or dislike rather than to speak directly for themselves.

Table 17.3 PRETESTING METHODS FOR ASSESSING ADVERTISING EFFECTIVENESS

Method	Description
Tests of opinion or awareness	People express their opinions about different characteristics of an ad or their awareness of its existence.
Focus groups	A focus group, consisting of eight to ten potential buyers, evaluates the ad's copy, creative concept, product name, or campaign.
Program analyser/ mechanical voting	Designed for broadcast media, it allows audience members to continuously record their likes and dislikes of a program and the associated commercials.
On-the-air tests	Viewers see a test commercial in selected markets and are asked to express their attitudes toward the brand, their ability to play back the commercial, and their brand knowledge.
Anteroom trailer method	A trailer is parked near a mall, and volunteers are asked to view test commercials and are then interviewed as to their effectiveness.
Physiological measures	This series of techniques is designed to assess physiological responses to an ad.
Readability tests	A variety of tests assess the general readability and understandability of the ad.
Test marketing	Different versions of an ad are placed in different markets, and the results are compared.

Opinions about behaviour entail a special problem: They are likely to be speculative. When respondents are shown ads and asked such behavioural questions as whether the ads would catch their attention or motivate them to send in the coupon, the respondents can only guess.

Consumer jury
The collective sampling of opinion ratings obtained by interviewing respondents individually.

Opinion ratings are usually made by interviewing respondents individually. When a sufficient sample has been obtained, the total is called a **consumer jury**. In a variation respondents are brought together to get the benefits of group discussions and judgments. Specific procedures used to obtain ratings include focus groups, program analysis, and on-the-air testing.

FOCUS GROUPS

A typical focus group consists of eight to ten people who are potential users of the product. A moderator usually supervises the group, providing direction and control. The format depends on what is being evaluated. For example, when Kellogg Co. wanted to test the concept "Corn Flakes are a high-fibre alternative," it conducted nearly 100 focus groups of people aged 40 to 55. Some groups were all male, some all female, and some mixed. Groups were videotaped, and management evaluated the tapes.

Usually focus groups serve as a pretest device, but they are also useful for concurrent and posttesting. They may be used to evaluate copy, a concept, a product name, or a campaign. To compare ads for the same product, two or more ads are presented, and members of the group are asked, "Which of these ads do you like least?"

The rating given by focus groups appears to have a high positive correlation with the success of the ad. Therefore, there is general agreement that focus groups do reflect the consumer's point of view. Focus groups are also relatively inexpensive, and they can be organized and completed quickly.

Still, research reveals problems with some focus groups. Foremost is the inability to draw concrete conclusions from focus groups. These groups often view only parts of a marketing communication. Some are asked to make value judgments that are beyond their capabilities. For example, it would be impossible for members of a focus group to determine whether a particular ad would prompt them to buy the product without a great deal of additional information. It is therefore important not to have expectations of a focus group that are beyond its capabilities. Also, focus groups are small and may not be representative of the target market. Careful selection and evaluation of focus group participants can lessen this problem. Finally, because members are being paid, they tend to say what they think the researcher wants to hear.[5] The group moderator must always be sensitive to this problem.

Program Analysis

Program analyser
A technique designed specifically for broadcast media that allows members of an audience to indicate likes and dislikes continuously throughout a program, including the commercials.

A technique specifically for broadcast media is called the **program analyser**. It allows members of an audience to indicate likes and dislikes continuously throughout a program, including the commercials. Each seat in a room or auditorium is equipped with right-hand and left-hand switches for signalling likes and dislikes as the presentation proceeds. When neither control is operated, the evaluators assume the person is indifferent.

Other types of mechanical voting equipment have been developed, but some investigators find paper ballots satisfactory. Schwerin Research Corporation, for example, uses a procedure in which people mark their reactions on a ballot when numbers are flashed on a screen. Each critical point in the script has a number assigned to it, and the ballot has corresponding places in which to indicate favourable or unfavourable reactions.

Like many other procedures, program analysis permits researchers to apply a variety of approaches. Investigators usually go beyond collecting ballots. In order to test a group's memory of commercials, they may ask the members to write down all the sales points they can remember. Then the group is likely to be invited to discuss its reactions to the program and commercials at any selected point.

On-the-Air Testing

On-the-air testing
A method of pretesting opinions that analyzes a new commercial by comparing it with an existing commercial.

Another method of pretesting opinions, called **on-the-air testing**, analyses a new commercial by comparing it with an existing commercial. The test commercial is aired in one or more cities, either in place of the regular commercial or in a new time period. Viewers who saw the new commercial are interviewed by telephone to determine their brand attitudes, their ability to recall the commercial message, and their brand knowledge. This information is compared with the responses of people who saw only the existing commercial.

Anteroom trailer
A pretesting opinion method in which people are invited into a comfortable room, in a mobile home or recreational vehicle usually parked in a busy shopping area, and are shown test commercials interspersed with a prerecorded show. These people are then interviewed and the effectiveness of each commercial is ascertained.

Other Methods

Another popular way of pretesting opinions is the **anteroom trailer** method. A mobile home or recreational vehicle is parked near a shopping centre. People are invited into the trailer and may be offered some incentive for participating. They enter a comfortable room that contains easy chairs, magazines, and a television set showing a prerecorded program. Test commercials are interspersed throughout the program. After the commercials have been shown, the subjects are interviewed and the effectiveness of each commercial is ascertained.

Opinion tests with standardized formats are readily available to any advertiser who has the necessary resources. However, agencies and advertisers have designed many opinion pretests to meet special needs.

Physiological Measures

Over the years, advertisers have experimented with assessing people's physical reactions to ads to measure effectiveness. Of the many techniques tried, five are worthy of special note:

1. *Eye movement tracking*: Participants are asked to look at a print ad or television commercial while a sensor aims a beam of infrared light at their eyes. A portion of the light reflected by the cornea is detected by the same sensor, which electronically measures the angle between the beam reflected by the cornea and the centre of the eye's pupil. This information can be processed to show the exact spot in the ad or on the television screen where the eye is focused.

2. *The pupillometer*: This device measures pupil size when a person is exposed to a visual stimulus such as an ad or a package. The assumption is that pupil size increases with interest.

3. *The psychogalvanometer*: This device is part of the lie-detector apparatus. Two zinc electrodes are attached to the subject, one on the palm of the hand and the other on the forearm. When the subject is exposed to an ad, emitted perspiration on the palm results in lower electrical resistance, which is recorded on a revolving drum.

4. *The tachistoscope*: This device controls exposure to a print message so that different parts of the ad can be shown without revealing the other parts. That way, the tester can tell at what point each part is perceived. Advertisers can thus find out how long it takes respondents to get the intended point of an illustration or headline.

5. Brain waves: Through the use of the electroencephalograph (EEG), data can be collected from several locations on the skull. Several electrical frequencies at each location are checked up to 1000 times per second. By measuring the electrical activity in various parts of the brain, this technique can tell the researcher when the subject is resting or when there is attention to a stimulus.[6]

These physiological tests suffer from several limitations. First, because respondents may feel threatened by these devices, the validity of the results is questionable. Second, there is a great deal of uncertainty as to what this machinery actually measures. Increased perspiration may provide a measure of emotional arousal, but is it a meaningful reflection of advertising effectiveness?

Readability Tests

An ad must be readable before it is set in final form. The length of the words and sentences and the impersonality of the writing are some of the elements that influence readability. Short words and short sentences make for easier reading.

The Flesch formula, developed by Dr. Rudolph Flesch, is a widely accepted technique for measuring readability. The formula uses four elements as they appear in 100-word writing samples:

Average sentence length

Average number of syllables

Percentage of personal words

Percentage of personal sentences

For example, Flesch contends that "fairly easy" sentences average 14 words in length and have 139 syllables per 100 words. The Flesch formula cannot be used for radio and television writing because a good announcer can make difficult copy sound very simple.[7] The ad for Wrigley's Freedent is considered very readable.

Test market
One or more cities that serve as a test area for an ad or media mix.

The copy for this ad is clear, simple, and easy to read.

Test Marketing

A **test market** might be used to test some elements of an ad or a media mix in two or more potential markets. The test markets should be representative of the target market. In a typical test market, one or more of the test cities serve as controls while the others are the test. In the control markets the researcher can either (a) run no advertising or (b) continue to run the old ad. The new ad is used in the test cities. Before, during, and after the advertising is run, sales results in the test cities are compared by checking inventories in selected stores.

In addition, test markets can measure communication variables such as recall, awareness, and correct message interpretation. Kraft Foods conducted a rather sophisticated market test. Two versions of a cross-promotion print ad were tested. One version contained the headline, "Super Choices Sweepstake" and the other, "The More Super Choices Coupons You Redeem, the More Chances You Have of Winning." Coupon redemption was used as the performance measure.[8] The second headline won.

Materials for Pretesting

Even if an ad has been completed, it may still be pretested before being distributed in case some elements have the potential for causing problems. To preview print ads, advertisers use several types of special material. In folio (short for portfolio) testing a cross-section of consumers examines a portfolio of ads, usually at home. A dummy publication is specially prepared by a magazine or newspaper for testing purposes. It includes editorial material and 15 to 20 ads. Copies of the dummy publication are distributed to a sample of consumers who are asked to read the publication in a normal fashion. A tip-in is a page that is glued to the binding of a real magazine in such a way that a reader cannot tell it from the regular pages. Some copies will have the tip-in ad, some will have the regular ad. Later, people who have read the publication with the tip-in page are questioned.

For broadcast commercials it is often too expensive to produce several completed commercials for testing. In such cases animated or live-action roughs fill in. An artist draws key frames of the commercial in sequence, then the drawings are photographed and a sound track recorded. Finally, a film is made of the drawings. Admittedly, a live-action rough does not contain all the elements of the finished commercial, but the essence is there. This technique is best suited for researching brand awareness and recall.

Concurrent Testing: Communication and Behaviour

As mentioned earlier, concurrent testing takes place while the advertising is actually being run. There are three primary techniques: coincidental surveys, attitude tests, and tracking studies. The first two techniques assess communication effects. Tracking studies evaluate behavioural results.

Coincidental Surveys

This technique is most often used with broadcast media. Random calls are made to individuals in the target market. By discovering what stations or shows are being seen or heard, the advertiser can determine whether the target audience is hearing the message and, if so, what information or meaning the audience members receive. This technique can be useful in identifying basic problems.

Attitude Tests

In Chapter 6 we discussed the relationship between an attitude—an enduring favourable or unfavourable disposition toward a person, thing, idea, or situation—and consumer behaviour. Researchers measure consumers' attitudes toward elements of an ad or toward a brand being advertised either concurrently or as a posttest. The measurement techniques for print and broadcast are virtually identical. Researchers survey individuals who were exposed to the ad, asking questions about the spokesperson, the tone of the ad, its wording, and so forth. Results that show strong negative attitude scores may prompt the advertiser to pull an ad immediately.

There are five techniques to measure attitudes in this context:[9]

1. *Direct questions*: Respondents express how they feel toward a particular brand, ad, or element of the ad through an open-ended format.
2. *Rating scales*: Respondents indicate their feelings on a progressive scale (for example, from "strongly agree" to "strongly disagree" or from "easy" to "very hard to use").
3. *Checklists*: Respondents check characteristics or feelings considered appropriate. For example, in response to the question "Which is the primary benefit of Gold Medal Flour?", participants might list price, quality, or convenience.
4. *Semantic differential*: Characteristics of concern are displayed as bipolar opposites on a seven-point scale. For example, "Would you say the Jeep Cherokee is economical to drive? Expensive to drive?" "How does it compare with the following competitors?"

5. *Partially structured interviews*: Rather than getting feedback on ads, the interviewer asks broad questions that allow respondents to discuss the product in general and reveal attitudes.

Attitudinal tests are considered more valuable than survey opinion evaluation because they tend to reflect a direct emotional reaction. Recall that people have opinions about a great many things but hold strong attitudes about relatively few. There is also the assumption, right or wrong, that a favourable attitude indicates that the person is more likely to purchase a brand than if he or she has an unfavourable attitude. There is little solid evidence that this correlation is always accurate.

Tracking Studies

Market tracking study
Research that follows the purchase activity of a specific consumer or group of consumers over a specified period of time.

Studies that follow the purchase activity of a specific consumer or group of consumers over a specified period of time are **market tracking studies**. These studies combine conventional marketing research data with information on marketing communication spending. Compared with other tests, tracking studies provide fuller integration of data and a more complete view of the market.

Researchers use market tracking for both concurrent testing and posttesting. It may serve two basic objectives: (1) to show how the marketer's product sales or market share compares with the competition, at a point in time after implementing some marketing communication, and (2) for reassessment, that is, to help understand how the market responds to changes made in the marketing communication strategy.

Tracking studies evaluate copy media and changes in sales. Higher sales for one strategy, compared with those produced by an alternative strategy, implies that the former strategy is better. Tracking studies have had an impact on many decisions, ranging from pulling advertising to changing copy to altering a campaign strategy.

Marketing communicators use several methods to collect tracking data: wave analysis, consumer diaries, pantry checks, and single-source tracking.[10]

Wave Analysis. Wave analysis involves a series of interviews during a campaign. The tracking begins with a set of questions asked of a random sample of consumers on a predetermined date. The first questions usually qualify the person as someone who remembers hearing or seeing the ad. Once the person is qualified, a series of follow-up questions is asked. The answers serve as a benchmark and allow adjustments in the message content, media choice, and timing. Perhaps two months later, another series of calls is made and the same questions are asked. The second wave is compared with the first. The periodic questioning may continue until management is satisfied with the ad's market penetration.

Consumer Diaries. Sometimes advertisers, such as Frito-Lay, ask a group of representative consumers to keep a diary while a campaign is being run. The consumers may be asked to record activities such as brands purchased, brands used for various activities, brand switches, media usage, exposure to competitive promotions, and use of coupons. The advertiser can then review these diaries and determine factors such as whether the message is reaching the right target audience and if the audience is responding to the message as intended.

PANTRY CHECKS. The pantry check provides much of the same information as the diary method but requires little from the consumer. A researcher goes to homes in the target market and asks what brands or products have been purchased or used recently. In one variation of this procedure, the researcher counts the products or brands currently stocked by the consumer. The consumer may also be asked to keep empty packages, which the researcher then collects and tallies. The purpose is to correlate product use with the introduction and completion of the campaign.

Single-source tracking system
The use of computers and scanners to monitor participants in a study that evaluates the relationship between advertising and sales.

SINGLE-SOURCE TRACKING. Thanks to scanners, combined with computer technology and data and the use of electronic media, researchers are very close to showing a causal relationship between advertising and sales. To set up a **single-source tracking system**, researchers first recruit people living in a particular market to join a consumer panel. The system has four elements:

1. Participants receive a card (with an identification number) that they give to the checkout clerk each time they make a purchase in a supermarket. Scanners identify the person and record their purchases so researchers know who they are and what they buy.
2. The panel members (who are all cable subscribers) are split into matched groups, with each group receiving a different version of a television ad. Electronic test market services transmit the appropriate commercial to the appropriate home so the advertiser knows which household sees which commercial.
3. Meters record the television viewing by panel members. Thus researchers know whether members saw the commercial, when they saw it, and how many times they saw it.
4. Print advertising, coupon distribution, and other marketing communication activities are all controlled. Researchers therefore know what else influences a household's decision to buy or not to buy.

The possibilities for isolating single variables in electronic test markets are almost limitless. Researchers can increase the frequency of advertising or try a different media schedule. They can see whether an ad emphasizing product convenience will stimulate sales to two-career families. They can try an ad that plays up the product's fibre or vitamin content or compare the effectiveness of a two-for-one promotion and a cents-off coupon.

Critics contend that current single-source data systems are just fancy versions of the old paper-and-pencil diary and provide little insight into which elements in the marketing communication mix are making a difference and why the consumer reacts in a particular manner to particular cues. In fact, current single-source methods provide a great deal more information than traditional methods.

Table 17.4 summarizes these concurrent testing measurement techniques.

POSTTESTING: COMMUNICATION

More testing occurs after the advertising has run than before, even though resources have already been spent on the ad. The popularity of posttests is explained in part by the limitations of pretesting. In addition, posttests indicate who listened to the message and can thereby provide a basis for planning future messages. The most widely used methods of posttesting fall into three categories: readership, recall, and attitude change.

Table 17.4 CONCURRENT TESTING METHODS FOR ASSESSING ADVERTISING EFFECTIVENESS

Method	Description
Coincidental surveys	Random calls are made to assess whether people are watching a commercial while it is actually running and what they understand.
Attitude tests	Researchers survey individuals who were exposed to the ad, asking questions about the spokesperson, the tone of the ad, its wording, and so forth.
Tracking studies	These studies follow the purchase activity of a specific consumer or consumer group and correlate this with spending on marketing communication. Techniques include wave analysis, consumer diaries, pantry checks, and single-source tracking.

READERSHIP (RECOGNITION)

Daniel Starch is credited with being the primary developer of readership (recognition) tests. Readership tests provide a mechanism for breaking a print ad into its more important components (that is, headline, visuals, body copy, logo) and then measuring how these elements are remembered by a sample of readers. The intent of the test is to show advertisers that the mere presence of an ad does not mean that readers notice it. The primary Canadian supplier of this testing service is Daniel Starch (Canada) Ltd. The test procedures follow:

1. The Starch organization sends copies of a recent issue of a magazine or newspaper to a certain number of interviewers.
2. The interviewers find a certain number of people who saw the publication (within 10 days after the date of publication for weeklies).
3. The interviewer goes through an unmarked copy of the publication with respondents and asks them to indicate the ads they read. When the ads are a half page or larger, the interviewer asks respondents which components they saw.

Starch regularly covers most of the major magazines. The expense of the readership tests is borne partly by the publishers, which use the results to bolster advertising sales, and partly by ad agencies, which use the results to indicate the impact of an ad. The agencies receive copies of the magazine with a set of stickers on each ad showing what percentage of men and women observed each part; the Timberland ad shows an example. Each ad is evaluated in terms of several criteria: (1) noted includes the percentage of people who remembered seeing the ad, (2) associated includes those who not only noted the ad but also saw or read some part of it that clearly indicated the brand or advertiser, and (3) read most includes the percentage who read half or more of the written material.

Readership tests allow the advertiser to compare ads across several dimensions, such as colour, size, and copy. This technique also suggests which elements are most successful in gaining attention. Against these strengths, three weaknesses should be weighed. First and foremost, the Starch test measures

The Starch scores are shown on the labels for this Timberland ad.

Courtesy: Timberland and Roper Starch.

readership, but readership does not necessarily translate into sales or penetration of an idea. Second, readership scores may lead advertisers to use trick means of getting high readership. Finally, results can be misleading because readers are frequently confused. They are often unsure whether they saw a particular ad in one magazine or another, or if they really saw it at all.

Recall Tests

Recall test
A test that measures the depth of impression an advertisement leaves on the reader's mind.

Like the readership test, the recall test depends on the memory of the respondent. In readership tests researchers show specific ads to respondents. In contrast, **recall tests** give little or no aid to respondents because the object is to measure the penetration or impact of the ad.

Perhaps the most famous recall test is the Magazine Impact Research Service offered by Gallup and Robinson, a prominent research firm. Before respondents are interviewed, they must answer questions to prove that they have read the magazine. After being accepted, they receive cards showing the names of all the products advertised in full or double pages in the issue. After respondents have listed each ad they think they have seen, they are asked to tell what the ad looks like. They are next asked to tell all they can about what the advertiser said—what the sales points were, what message the advertiser tried to get across, and the like. Respondents are also asked to tell the interviewer what they got out of the ad. Next they are asked whether the ad made them want to buy the product or find out more about it. And finally the interviewer asks questions to determine whether the respondent is a prospect for the product advertised.

Gallup and Robinson
www.gallup-robinson.com

The Impact method is designed to measure the depth of impression an ad leaves on the reader's mind. Three dimensions of an ad's impression are reported: proven name registration (the percentage of qualified readers who can recall the ad and describe it with the magazine closed), idea penetration (the respondent can describe the contents of the ad), and conviction (the respondent wants to see, try, or buy the product).

Check out Gallup and Robinson's Web site at for the Ad Games that illustrate the results of their Impact research.

Day-after recall

A test in which people conduct telephone interviews with a sample of television viewers the day after the commercial is aired to determine the extent of brand-name recognition as well as recall of various selling points communicated by the commercial.

To evaluate television commercials, Burke Research Corporation has developed a **day-after recall** test. The day after a commercial is aired, interviewers conduct telephone interviews with a sample of television viewers to determine the extent of brand-name recognition as well as recall of various selling points communicated by the commercial. Typical scores range from 15 to 30 percent recall.

Recall tests do a good job of providing information on the penetration of copy. They also help gauge the extent to which a message provides the correct impression. On the negative side, there is not necessarily a relationship with sales. Recall tests are also quite expensive, and not all companies can afford them. There is also the problem that some people have better memories than others. Recall tests cannot account for these differences.

Attitude Change Measures

When used for posttesting, attitude measurement tests generally try to assess the effectiveness of advertising or other marketing communication in changing the consumer's evaluation of the company and/or its brands. As noted earlier, it is assumed that a favourable change in attitude predisposes people to buy a product. Recall and attitude tests are often combined to determine if there are major differences between consumers who remember the advertising messages and those who do not. Attitude tests at this stage in the process are also used to measure changes in consumer perceptions of a brand or measure degrees of acceptance of various claims made in the advertising.

Because attitude change is perceived to have more bearing on purchase than recall, attitude measures are highly regarded and heavily used by many marketing communication managers. In addition, testing attitudes can be done with ease and minimum expense.

Posttesting: Behaviour

Although most marketers feel the ultimate payoff from advertising should be a change in behaviour—phone response, store visit, or direct sales—measuring advertising's contribution to sales has proven extremely difficult and expensive. Researchers have two key testing methods that try to measure advertising's effect on sales: inquiry tests and sales tests.

Inquiry Tests

Inquiry test

A test designed to check the effectiveness of ads by asking those who have seen them to respond to questions.

Inquiry tests check the effectiveness of ads by asking those who have seen them to respond to questions. The advertiser runs a certain number of ads and offers some inducement to reply to them. The offer may be a booklet, a sample of the product, a toll-free number, or something else of value. The marketing communicator finds the cost per inquiry by dividing the cost of the ad by the number of inquiries.

Inquiry testing may be used to check media, individual ads, or campaigns. To check the effectiveness of two ads, a promoter might run ad A one day and ad B the next in the local paper. The ad that produces the most inquiries per dollar is deemed more effective.[11]

Another version of the inquiry test is the split-run test. Split-run refers to the practice of testing ads by running two or more versions of the same ad on the same issue date but in different editions of a newspaper or magazine. The different ads appear on the same day in identical positions. Each version of the ad may change only one element—copy, illustration, headline, coupon redemption, or readership. Or the advertiser might run four entirely different ads.

Split-run is also available on cable television. The cable system is able to show different commercials for the same product in different households simultaneously. Later, viewers' opinions are surveyed by phone, mail, or personal interview.

Split-run testing can be used as a pretest or posttest. Sometimes a split-run test is conducted on alternative versions of an ad for different market segments and wants to find out whether a standardized ad would suffice; posttesting with a split-run may provide the answer.

There are several advantages of inquiry testing. The results indicate that the person not only read or saw the ad but also took some action (that is, responded to the inquiry). Action is a much stronger indicator than recall or awareness. Moreover, there is fairly good control of the variables that influence action, especially if split-run is used; the only variable that changes is the ad itself. However, one can question the sincerity of a person who expresses an interest in the product or service being offered. Also, unless one element is being modified, one is never sure why one ad is better than another. Finally, inquiry tests are time-consuming. It may take three or four months before replies are measured.

Sales Tests

Several posttests presumably reflect a relationship between a particular ad and a particular sale. Comparing past sales with current sales is a common approach, particularly with the big catalogue houses like Sears. These businesses assume that a particular ad placed in a catalogue is responsible for the sales generated. If sales increase from year to year, the ad is given credit.

Field tests are also used to examine the impact of ads on sales. For example, various ads may be run in several comparable markets, targeted to different market segments. Then evaluators compare the sales in each test market or segment.

Although these various measures of advertising effectiveness provide important insights, the ultimate question is, "Does advertising work?" If we go back to the assumption that every ad has a different objective, ranging from

concept review

Measuring Advertising Performance

Three types of effectiveness measures are used in advertising:

1. Pretesting includes opinion/awareness, mechanical, readability, and test marketing.
2. Concurrent testing includes coincidental surveys, attitude tests, and tracking.
3. Posttesting includes readership, recall, attitude change, inquiry, and sales.

Can Marketing Communication Create Sales?

There remains a great deal of controversy about the ability of marketing communication to cause sales. Take a look at the following sample of studies. All suggest that a causal relationship exists.

- To find out just how effective business-to-business advertising is, the Association of Business Publishers and Advertising Research Federation designed a study in which two products (a $14 portable safety product and a $14 000 commercial transportation component package) were advertised for a year in similar business publications. The study proves through the tracking of actual product sales that business publication advertising produces more sales than would occur without advertising. It also proves that increased advertising frequency can increase product sales. Results also suggest that a single advertising campaign may be effective for a full year or longer.

- Gerald Tellis conducted a study in which 250 volunteers were each given an identification card that notified a grocer's computerized checkout counters to track all the items they bought. The subjects' TV sets were outfitted with a device that continuously monitored which channels were being watched and hence which commercials the family was viewing. Daily newspapers were monitored for coupons and store specials. Tellis found that in the case of laundry detergent, television advertising's effect on sales was minimal; lowering prices through coupons and store specials, however, resulted in a large boost in sales.

- According to a 10-year study of data from Information Resources' BehaviourScan, TV advertising produces long-term sales growth even two years after a campaign ends. Also, a shift from a daytime media schedule to prime-time produced better sales results; a bigger ad schedule worked better during a new-product introduction; and better results were produced by concentrating increased advertising into fewer weeks than by a sustained but lower-level effort.

- *Family Circle* tracked the supermarket purchases of its readers before and after an issue of the magazine was released. Scanner-derived data from Citicorp POS Information Services made it possible to track the sales of 22 products advertised in that issue. Sales differences between *Family Circle* households and control households increased for 15 of the products advertised, with an average increase of 20 percent.

- According to John Philip Jones, who researched and authored the book *When Ads Work: New Proof that Advertising Triggers Sales*, advertising has a real but temporary short-term effect in 70 percent of the products he studied. Further, the average market share of all advertised brands is higher than that of unadvertised brands. Prices of advertised brands are also higher, and sales growth of advertised brands is three percent above unadvertised ones.

Food for Thought

1. Armed with this information, do you think it would be tough to convince a CEO to spend money on marketing communication if the business was suffering from financial trouble? Why?
2. If you were attempting to prove that marketing communication caused sales (and money for research was plentiful), what methods would you use? What if your funds were limited?

Sources: John P. Jones, ***When Ads Work: New Proof that Advertising Triggers Sales*** (New York: Lexington Books, 1995); "Print Advertising Proves Itself," ***American Demographics*** (January 1992): 16; Howard E. Potter, "IRI Study Confirms Some Conventional Wisdom," ***Marketing News***, January 6, 1992, 22; Gary Levin, "Ads Outperform Promotions in Profits Study," ***Advertising Age***, April 17, 1989, 4; "Science 1, Advertisers 0," U.S. News & World Report, May 1, 1989, 60–1; Jerome W. Vozoff, "Ad Effectiveness: A New Study," ***Adweek***, May 16, 1988, 56; "On the Effectiveness of Advertising," ***Adweek***, May 26, 1987, 19.

creating awareness to purchase, then the answer is yes—advertising works. The IMC in Action feature offers support for this position. The same conclusion can be drawn for the other communication mix tools.

Table 17.5 provides an overview of the posttesting measurement techniques just discussed.

Table 17.5 POSTTESTING METHODS FOR ASSESSING ADVERTISING EFFECTIVENESS

Method	Explanation
Readership (recognition)	An ad is broken into its more important components, and researchers determine how these elements are remembered by a sample of consumers.
Recall tests	Recall tests give little or no aid to respondents because the object is to measure the penetration of the ad.
Attitude change	This measurement assesses the effectiveness of measures advertising or other marketing communication tools in changing the consumer's evaluation of the company and/or its brands.
Inquiry tests	An advertiser runs a certain number of ads and offers some inducement to reply to them in order to check media, individual ads, or campaigns.
Sales tests	Sales are compared before and after an ad is run.

MEASURING THE PERFORMANCE OF SALES PROMOTION

Measuring the effectiveness of sales promotion can be just as complicated as measuring the effectiveness of advertising. Part of this complexity is a result of the nature and diversity of sales promotion objectives. Recall from Chapter 10 that these objectives can range from stimulating immediate action to enhancing product value and brand equity to match the competition. Several sales promotion objectives are directly related to sales, and many of the same sales-based measurement techniques discussed in earlier sections are also used with sales promotion. Intermediate objectives, such as trial purchase, trading up, and multiple purchases, are more difficult to measure and require customized methods developed by sales promotion managers. Sales promotion also attempts to accomplish communication objectives. Coming up with valid ways to measure these responses while separating the effect of the media has proven very difficult.

A second reason for the complexity in measuring sales promotion performance revolves around the organizational structure supporting sales promotion. Two dimensions of the structure are particularly relevant. First, sales promotions are often delivered to the end user through one or more resellers. The effectiveness of a sales promotion, then, depends on the abilities of the reseller as well as on the marketing communication strategy. Wholesalers and retailers who actively support a marketer's sales promotion can greatly enhance its performance. The opposite is also true.

Another organizational problem is the diversity of sales promotion service agencies. Some service companies build trade-show booths or supply audiovisual equipment for sales promotion events. Others plan or implement marketing communication strategies. No matter how broad or narrow their scope of operations, all these suppliers are known as sales promotion agencies. This generic title often confuses potential or current clients because they are unaware that an agency may have expertise in only one facet of sales promotion and is incapable of measuring effectiveness of the other areas.

Despite these limitations, a great deal of effort has been devoted to improving the quality of sales promotion performance measures. Simple measures, such as counting the number of coupons redeemed, are still used and provide valuable information. Advanced mathematical models have recently found their way into sales promotion testing. For example, elaborate regression models are able to determine the contribution of various sales promotion tactics on sales. Sales promotion has borrowed heavily from advertising measurement techniques as well. For instance, the pretest, concurrent test, and posttest framework is also used in sales promotion. There is one major difference, however, between the evaluation of advertising and the evaluation of sales promotion. Evaluations of advertising tend to emphasize communication measures. For sales promotion, evaluation tends to focus on behavioural measures. As the field of sales promotion grows in sophistication, the evaluation of communication variables will increase.[12]

Pretesting Sales Promotion

In general, sales promotion managers are reluctant to pretest. Short lead time and concern for alerting competitors are two reasons for this hesitation. Instead, managers tend to rely heavily on experience ("What worked before will work again") and determine that sales promotion is best evaluated through sales, its ultimate goal. Although experience and sales are important, there are benefits in pretesting before spending the money or committing unresolvable strategic mistakes. Pretests consider communication and behavioural variables. Because many of these measurement techniques were discussed earlier, only brief mention will be made in the discussion that follows.

Pretesting Communication

Perceived value
The calculations that consumers make in their minds of the extra value contained in a sales promotion compared with the risks in accepting the offer.

There is a wide variety of measures used to pretest the communication elements of sales promotions. In addition to the typical communication elements found in advertising (that is, headline, copy, and visuals), an overriding communication element contained in most sales promotions is perceived value. **Perceived value** is the calculation the consumer makes in his or her mind of the extra value contained in the sales promotion compared with the risks in accepting the offer. For example, a consumer may weigh the benefit of 40 percent off on an unknown brand of shoes compared with the risk of buying an unfamiliar product. Measuring perceived value is complicated because consumers are unsure what these promotions are worth. Some promotions—price-offs, bonus packs, rebates and refunds, and trade coupons—provide an immediate value. Others, such as premiums and continuity programs, give gifts to enhance value. A third group—samples, demonstrations, warranties, contests, and sweepstakes—provides a promised or implied value. Consumers might be asked to evaluate the trade-off through a survey questionnaire. Or the researchers can vary the type of value offered and assess how consumers respond to each.

Ballot method
A pretesting process that consists of mailing out sales promotions to be evaluated. Consumers are asked to vote for the promotion they like and return the ballot to the research firm.

Portfolio test
A pretesting method that is conducted in person and consists of showing consumers sales promotions to be evaluated. They are then asked to vote for the one they like the best.

Jury method
A combination of the ballot and portfolio methods of pretesting, except the jurors are paid for their evaluation and may be knowledgeable about sales promotions.

Mall intercept
A pretesting method that involves stopping people at random in a mall and showing them the various promotions for evaluation.

This assessment can be done through several different devices. Focus groups and consumer panels are common. Other techniques include the ballot method, portfolio tests, the jury method, and mall intercepts. The **ballot method** consists of mailing a printed ballot to a list of consumers. The sales promotions to be evaluated and some additional information are given about each one. Consumers are asked to vote for the one they like best and return the ballot to the research firm. **Portfolio tests** are similar to the ballot method except a portfolio of sales promotions is developed and shown to consumers in person. Although portfolio tests are more expensive than the ballot method, the information obtained is considered more accurate. The **jury method** is a combination of the previous two techniques except the jurors are paid for their evaluation and may be knowledgeable about sales promotions. The **mall intercept** technique involves stopping people at random in a mall and showing them the various promotions for evaluation. Although print and television can be tested, it is the most expensive device.

Pretesting Behaviour

The most common device used to pretest the behavioural response to sales promotion is the market test. Depending on the specific sales promotion technique, the behavioural response considered could be trial purchase, purchase, repeat purchase, incremental purchase, and so forth. We have already discussed the process of market testing. In sales promotion pretesting, market tests usually consist either of testing two separate markets against each other or matching several stores in the same market against one another. In either case the sales promotion device or program being tested is the only variable manipulated. All else is kept constant.

Pretesting Sales Promotion with Resellers

If resellers are unhappy with the sales promotion effort, they will either reject it outright or give it only partial support. It is therefore important to get the evaluation of resellers before implementation. It is possible to pretest some aspects of sales promotion programs with resellers—particularly materials that are used in-store or that rely on the reseller's cooperation to make them work. The easiest way to pretest a sales promotion program is simply to go to several key retailers or wholesalers and discuss the plan with them.

Concurrent Testing of Sales Promotion

Concurrent testing is evaluating the performance of sales promotion while it is still running. As noted in the advertising section, this testing allows the marketing communication strategists to modify the sales promotion to increase performance or eliminate it to reduce negative consequences. For sales promotion, essentially all concurrent tests measure changes in sales or some variation of sales in response to the promotion. Thanks to advances in scanner research capability, sales information can be combined with consumer information to provide a very elaborate analysis of a specific sales promotion device or program. For marketers who do not have access to such technology, traditional sales comparisons (actual and forecasted sales figures or sales among competing stores, for instance) are still employed.

Posttesting Sales Promotion

Because the main objective of sales promotion is to stimulate immediate action, it is not surprising that the most valid and reliable measures of performance are posttests. Although sales and market share remain the predominant areas of interest, researchers also measure communication and behavioural factors.

Communication Posttest Measures

Usually the information sought to measure the effectiveness of communication elements relates to consumer awareness and attitudes. The information-gathering devices, however, are much simpler than the techniques used in advertising research. For example, the most common methods for measuring consumer awareness and attitudes are telephone calls, mailed questionnaires, and personal interviews. Direct mail is the least expensive method, and personal interviews are by far the most expensive. The information sought is usually related to changes in consumer awareness, attitude, or actions in reference to a specific sales promotion event.

Posttesting is also done through in-store observations and interviews and in follow-up survey interviews with responders and nonresponders to a promotion. In-store observations and intercept interviews with shoppers at the point of purchase are particularly relevant for store-distributed promotions such as samples and premiums.

Behavioural Posttest Measures

Techniques are available that assess the extent to which sales promotion affects the behaviour of resellers and consumers. Monitoring sales is the most common technique. Data-gathering techniques include market testing and tracking studies. The interpretation of these figures varies. For example, traditional break-even analysis can be employed. First, fixed costs and variable costs of the promotion are determined; second, the variable contribution margin of the brand is determined; and finally, break-even sales volume for the promotion is calculated. Multiple regression analysis is a statistical technique that estimates the contribution of several variables acting jointly on a single dependent variable—sales. By its basic nature, the analysis of sales promotions tends to fit this technique well. Finally, there are statistical models built into the scanner systems that can provide a very detailed analysis.

Measuring the Performance of Public Relations

Ascertaining the results of a public relations effort is, for several reasons, the most neglected branch of the art. Such evaluation deals with the most difficult thing to measure—changes in human opinion. Public relations' contribution is difficult to measure because it is used along with other marketing communication tools. If PR is used before the other tools come into action, its contribution is easier to evaluate.[13]

This evaluation process may be informal or scientific. It may involve a few people seated around a table or a massive survey. It can take a few hours or a few weeks. Basically the process seeks to answer the question, "How did we do?" As is the case with all marketing communication elements, public relations needs to understand to what extent its programs achieved the objectives.

In Chapter 11 we described some of the primary methods used to evaluate a public relations effort: focus groups, content analysis, monitoring, and informal observations. These methods can be used to measure exposure, psychological change, or behavioural change.

Exposures

The easiest measure of PR effectiveness is the number of exposures created in the media. Publicists supply the client with a clipping book showing all the media that carried news about the product and a summary statement such as the following:

> Media coverage included 3500 column inches of news and photographs in 350 publications with a combined circulation of 79.4 million; 2500 minutes of airtime on 290 radio stations and an estimated audience of 65 million; and 660 minutes of airtime on 160 television stations with an estimated audience of 91 million. If this time and space had been purchased at advertising rates, the cost would have amounted to $1 047 000.

This exposure measure is not very satisfying. There is no indication of how many people actually read, heard, or recalled the message, nor what they thought afterward. There is no information on the net audience reached since publications overlap in readership. Because publicity's goal is reach, not frequency, it would be useful to know the number of unduplicated exposues. Nor does this exposure measure indicate whether these figures reflect positive or negative coverage.

Change in Awareness, Comprehension, or Attitude

A better measure is the change in product awareness, comprehension, or attitude resulting from the PR campaign (after allowing for the impact of other marketing communication tools). For example, how many people recall hearing the news item? How many told others about it (a measure of word-of-mouth)? How many changed their minds after hearing the news item?

Sales and Profit Contributions

Sales and profit impact, if obtainable, are often the most satisfactory measure of the results of public relations. For example, sales of 9-Lives increased 43 percent at the end of the "Morris the Cat" PR campaign. However, advertising and sales promotion had also been stepped up, and their contribution was considered too. Suppose total sales increased $1 500 000; based on experience, management estimates that PR contributed 15 percent of the total sales increase. Then the return on PR investment is calculated as follows:

Total sales increase	$1 500 000
Estimated sales increase due to PR (15%)	225 000
Contribution margin on product sales (10%)	22 500
Total direct cost of PR program	– 10 000
Contribution margin added by PR investment	$12 500
Return on PR investment ($12 500 ÷ $10 000)	125%

Measuring the Performance of Direct Marketing

Direct marketing has been around for a long time and has developed evaluation techniques unique to that industry. For example, an outgoing telemarketer keeps careful records of calls made, characteristics of people called (those that reject/accept the marketing pitch), and the general conversion rate. Telemarketers know that a conversion rate of two to four percent is average and can actually test various scripts to determine which message is producing the best results. Likewise, a direct-mail company now has the capability of carefully controlling its database, so that it can customize direct-mail pieces to reach specific audiences. Analysis of response rates is then fairly easy. In addition, direct-mail experts know that previous buyers are far more likely to buy again and require different messages. Earlier we discussed the current difficulty of assessing the performance of online direct marketing. New technologies will have to be developed to bring this area into the realm of valid and reliable testing.

Measuring the Performance of Personal Selling

Because of the typical organizational separation, the performance measures developed in personal selling are quite different from those found in other areas of marketing communication. To begin with, the personal selling function is evaluated by the sales manager and the marketing manager. Their task is twofold: (1) to evaluate the sales production of various sales territories and (2) to evaluate the performance of the salespeople responsible for that territory. Performance standards are compared with actual performance and adjustments are made. Marketing communication managers need to evaluate the relative performance of personal selling in the marketing communication mix, as opposed to sales performance. Each level of evaluation will be discussed.

Evaluating the Salesperson

The goal of this evaluation is to determine appropriate corrective action. To do that managers must assess the factors that affected performance and determine which ones the salesperson could or could not control. The three most important controllable factors are volume, activities, and quality.[14]

Volume Analysis

Sales volume is the simplest type of sales performance measurement and the most often used. Volume analysis can be appraised in terms of both effectiveness and efficiency. In terms of effectiveness, actual sales performance of a particular salesperson can be compared with the previous year's sales, the present year's budget, the sales performance of other salespeople, the number of sales closed, the number of accounts in the territory that are inactive, and the concentration on sales of special merchandise.

As with effectiveness, sales efficiency can be measured in many ways. Experience suggests four measures: gross margin on sales, contribution to profit, expense-to-sales ratio, and market share. The employment of basic accounting procedures quickly provides the appropriate data to run these tests for an individual salesperson, across salespeople, or across territories.

Activity Analysis

A manager's understanding of salespeople's performance has often been increased by examining their activities as well as their sales volume. Again, the possibilities are numerous.

The effectiveness of the sales force can be evaluated with respect to the number of sales calls, new accounts opened, and complaints received. The precision of these analyses might be improved by looking at both efficiency and effectiveness. For example, calls per day and costs per call might provide more useful information than just the raw number of calls. It might also be interesting to look not just at the number of new accounts opened but at the size of each account. Perhaps the number of complaints should be balanced by the number of sales. Finally, sales representatives may be putting in long hours, but they may not be selling hours. A look at the ratio of selling time to total time can also provide useful insights.

Evaluating Personal Selling as a Part of Marketing Communication

Poor cooperation between sales management and marketing communication management has meant that this type of evaluation is rarely performed. Personal selling is often reluctant to provide the information requested by the marketing communication manager because of distrust and a sense of separateness.

However, a more inherent problem is that there is little evidence that companies actually have objectives that specify how personal selling should contribute to the overall marketing communication effort. The nature of the evaluation therefore relies heavily on subjective criteria developed by the marketing communication manager. For example, a marketing communication manager may be very concerned with whether the salesperson uses the sales promotion materials provided, including point-of-purchase displays, catalogues, brochures, pamphlets, and cooperative advertising programs. It might also be important to know whether these materials were used correctly. How is this information gathered? Surveys of the sales reps is one possibility, although the reps are reluctant to answer such surveys. Another possibility is to monitor the sales force—but that is costly and creates more distrust. Consequently, the validity and reliability of this information are suspect.

The other area in which salespeople might be evaluated is communication. Do salespeople provide feedback from customers about programs, competition, market information, or program effectiveness? This information is difficult to quantify, and the results may produce simple yes-or-no categories. This facet of evaluation remains the weakest in promotion. It is unlikely that the situation will improve until the organizational and perceptual boundaries separating personal selling from the other marketing communication elements are removed.

Evaluating Other Types of Marketing Communication

As indicated throughout this text, there are many elements or techniques that fall under integrated marketing communication. Trade shows, point-of-purchase, packaging, sports marketing, and licensing are just a few of these communication techniques. Many cross over into the more traditional communication areas and rely on the same evaluation tools. For example, marketers often view event marketing and sports marketing as part of public relations and evaluate them accordingly.

However, the demand by marketers to hold events more accountable has prompted the development of new measures to evaluate sponsorships.[15] The beauty of event promotions is that results easily can be measured against sales by counting retail displays and impressions via pre- and post-event attitude surveys.

Also, there are a number of research companies that specialize in measuring employee satisfaction and customer satisfaction. This can be done through focus groups, personal in-depth interviews, or the survey technique. These measures assume that satisfaction is a result of good customer service, so strong satisfaction implies good service.

As the number of communication techniques grow, it will be even more important to develop evaluation tools that are appropriate for each technique. More important, it would be best to have evaluation tools that work across all these communication techniques simultaneously.

concept review

Measuring the Performance of Sales Promotion, PR, Direct Marketing, Personal Selling, and Other Types

1. Sales promotion uses pretest methods, concurrent testing methods, and posttesting methods, similar to those used in advertising, to measure performance.
2. Techniques used to measure the performance of public relations include focus groups, content analysis, monitoring, and informal observation.
3. Direct-marketing techniques to assess performance are unique for each direct-marketing tool.
4. Personal selling performance is measured through volume analysis and activity analysis.
5. A number of other communication techniques, such as trade shows, point-of-purchase, packaging, and so forth, are beginning to develop their own performance measures.

A Closing Thought:

The Search for a Universal Measure

One of the key issues in successfully integrating marketing communication is to be able to measure the effectiveness of a communication strategy simultaneously. That is, how do the individual components blend together to achieve objectives? Although we have techniques and technologies that have been applied to each of the mix components separately, a universal measure that applies across all communication tools does not yet exist.

Scanner and single-source techniques are capable of assessing advertising and sales promotion simultaneously but have not incorporated public relations and personal selling as well. Until this challenge of a cross-functional measurement system is met, total integration remains quite difficult.

summary

1. Address the main issues in measuring the performance of marketing communications.

   In conducting evaluative research, four preliminary questions should be answered: What should be tested? Should we test? If so, when? And how?

2. Explain the specific testing methods used with advertising, sales promotion, public relations, direct marketing, personal selling, and other IMC tools.

   Measuring advertising performance can be done as a pretest, concurrent test, or posttest. Common pretest methods include tests of opinion/awareness, focus groups, program analysis, on-the-air tests, physiological methods, readability tests, and test markets. Concurrent testing methods include coincidental surveys, attitude tests, and tracking studies. Posttest methods include readership (recognition), recall tests, attitude change measures, inquiry tests, and sales tests. Techniques used to assess the effectiveness of sales promotion include measuring perceived value, market testing, sales, tracking studies, and in-store observations. Techniques used to assess the effectiveness of public relations include focus groups, content analysis, monitoring, and informal observations. Analysts use specialized techniques for each area of direct marketing to assess direct marketing's effectiveness. To measure the effectiveness of personal selling, researchers use volume analysis and activity analysis.

points to ponder

Review the Facts

1. What prominent decisions should the marketing communication manager consider when measuring promotional performance? Elaborate.
2. What are the most common measures of advertising effectiveness?
3. What information would you require to assess public relations performance?

Master the Concepts

4. What are the major limitations in measuring the effectiveness of the sales promotion program?
5. Explain the utility of the model for measuring advertising effectiveness. What are the stages involved in the model?
6. Why were inquiry tests developed? In what ways can they be utilized?
7. What mistakes are made by sales managers who use sales volume alone to measure sales performance?

Apply Your Knowledge

8. The marketing manager for a large cereal manufacturer wishes to increase sales by 10 percent through a massive communication effort including television, print, coupons, a sweepstakes, and event sponsorship. Evaluate whether the sales objective is an appropriate way to evaluate performance of this promotional strategy.
9. Select an advertising objective and create several rough ideas for ads that relate to the objective. Finally, devise an experiment that can measure the relative effectiveness of those ads.

10. Assume that a severely limited budget motivated your firm's marketing communication manager to re-evaluate the methods used to test advertising. Pretests, concurrent tests, and posttests were used in the past. In light of the budget constraints, your associates feel that only posttesting should be considered. Do you agree? Explain.

suggested projects 

1. Outline a performance evaluation program for a fast-food retailer such as McDonald's, Burger King, or Kentucky Fried Chicken.
2. (Oral Communication) Visit a marketing communication firm and discuss its techniques for measuring effectiveness with an account executive or top-level manager. How does the firm's approach compare with the techniques discussed in this chapter?
3. (Writing Project) Visit your campus library and identify three or four secondary research sources that provide companies with assistance in measuring performance. In a brief one- to two-page memo, describe the type of information they provide.
4. (Internet Project) Conduct some research on the Web to find at least two sources that provide companies with assistance in measuring Internet advertising performance. In a brief one- to two-page memo, describe the information the sources provide. Be sure to note how each source measures performance.

Advertisements That Are Good for Your Health

People who work for advertising agencies have to get used to negative public perceptions about the work they do. Consumer advocates charge agencies with subliminally coaxing people to buy products they can't afford or don't want or need. Public-service ads have a reputation for being unrealistic and preachy, and even the anti-drug ad campaigns are criticized for using inaccurate information and ignoring deadly but legal drugs.

A Healthy Victory for Ads

But ad agencies have been feeling a little better about public acceptance of their work as a result of the state of California's anti-smoking campaign. The campaign's ads have won the respect of viewers and media critics and have apparently done their job—getting smokers to quit.

The anti-smoking campaign is the result of a taxpayer referendum in 1988. California voters approved a 25-cents-per-pack tax on cigarettes, with the money to be used to warn citizens, particularly those in high-risk groups, of the perils of smoking. The state wanted at least half of its 30.5 million residents to be aware of the ads, a goal that was quickly reached. Ten years later, the campaign is still a success story.

Targeting Minority Groups

Part of the success of the ads is attributed to their specific targeting of young people, pregnant women, Spanish speakers, Asians, and African-Americans. A Los Angeles advertising agency, Keye/Donna/Perlstein, was the lead agency, but Muse Cordero/L.A. and The Hispanic Group/Santa Monica, two minority-owned shops, get credit for the effectiveness of ads directed at ethnic markets. Early studies showed that 78 percent of California's African-Americans, 85 percent of its Spanish-speaking population, and 65 percent of its Asian population had seen or heard at least one of the campaign's television or radio spots.

The Results

Within six months of the start of the campaign, three out of four California residents indicated that they were aware of the ads. Almost half of the adult smokers who had seen the ads said they intended to quit, as compared with 39 percent of those who hadn't seen the ads. The ads have led to more positive attitudes toward good health among both adults and students, and early surveys showed a slight drop in smoking by students.

The ads break the stereotype of bland, unrealistic public-service messages. Rosemary Romano, director of public information for the Federal Office on Smoking and Health, says they "are hard-hitting, the quality is excellent, and they cover a range of issues."

Although the tobacco industry fought hard against the original referendum, it had no plans to organize a counterattack. The industry trade group, the Tobacco Institute, disputes claims of success by the anti-smoking campaign, pointing out that tobacco sales had fallen 14 percent statewide in 1989, before the campaign began. Some people may, in fact, be quitting more because of the extra cost of smoking than because the ads are having the desired effect. But judging from the requests from around the nation and around the world to borrow or buy the ads, the particular agencies involved, and the entire industry, should view the California anti-smoking campaign as a major sign that ad agencies can do effective work for the public good.

Case Questions

1. What are the problems associated with the effectiveness measures mentioned in this case?
2. Suggest a measurement process that would better meet the assessment objectives cited.

Sources: California Cancer Institute home page (September 4, 1996): Internet (www.CA.cancer.org:80/Prop 99/wewon); California State Government Health Statistics (February 3, 1996): Internet (www.ao.ca.Gov1CgHlth3); Pat Hinsberg, "Anti-Smoking Ads Capture An Audience," *Adweek*, November 5, 1990, 18.

CBC VIDEO VIGNETTES

CBC

Overbranding

Branding was the marketing tool of choice in the late 1990s but some marketing experts now believe that overbranding can be a very real problem. What is overbranding? Overbranding is the term used to describe the negative impact of having either too many brands in the marketplace or having too many products associated with the same brand name. For marketing communicators charged with the task of creating brand recognition, one such negative impact of overbranding is that it becomes very difficult to build recognition for new brands. For established brands, a possible impact of overbranding is that your targeted consumers may reach a saturation point where they just can't stand you anymore.

According to Professor Alan Middleton of the Schulich School of Business at York University, overbranding has become an issue because of the amount of clutter in the marketplace—so much clutter that Middleton says there is "frustration out there." Also of concern is a young and hip Gen-Xer segment that is known to marketers as the "anti-brand kids." Middleton explains that this segment exhibits a lack of trust when branded products are promoted as being too hip. Middleton believes this anti-branding sentiment could grow beyond this segment into the general population.

Sound plausible? Don Green, co-founder of Roots Canada Ltd. seems to at least agree with the general notion that overbranding is a very real phenomenon and a potential problem for a company like Roots. Roots is a Canadian branding success story. Having succeeded in a carefully crafted brand extension strategy, Roots has increased the number of Roots-branded products. From sweaters to a line of pet products, Roots offers high-quality Canadian-made products that its customers are willing to pay a premium price for. According to Green, one way to avoid overbranding is to be selective: "Don't slap your name on any product just to get your name out there."

QUESTIONS

1. Do you agree that overbranding is a real phenomenon? Explain.
2. If you were a marketing communications adviser to Roots, how would you suggest the success of its brand extension strategy be measured? Would it be possible for you to determine if overbranding has become a problem?

Video Resource: Based on "Over Branding," Venture #705 (November 24, 1998)

18 Campaign Planning

chapter objectives

After completing your work on this chapter, you should be able to

- Distinguish between a campaign and a one-shot marketing communication effort.
- Outline the steps in the campaign planning process and explain the campaign planning document.

Chapters Online Inc.: A Different Kind of Book Retailer

Chapters Online believes that its close relationship with Chapters superstores and its many strategic alliances, portal, and affiliate relationships are important elements in attracting customers to its Web site. Moreover, Chapters Online knows that everything it does sends a message.

Since its inception in 1995, Chapters has developed and established a nationally recognized brand in Canada, operating more than 70 book superstores under the Chapters name and more than 230 traditional bookstores. In October 1998, Chapters' launched its e-comm initiative, Chapters Online. Chapters Online's close relationship with Chapters provides it with a number of competitive advantages: established brand recognition in Canada; strategic portal partners and affiliates; access to Chapters' sophisticated distribution and fulfilment capability at the same volume discounts enjoyed by Chapters; access to Chapters' experienced management team; an extensive customer database; a successful Chapters 1 Club loyalty program; and the added benefit of Chapters' ability to effectively communicate the online business through its store network.

Chapters Online is a good example of relationship marketing based on an understanding of the importance of all stakeholders, company actions, and delivery of value to the consumer. The integrated approach to marketing communication started at the same time the online concept was being developed. The case study used throughout this chapter illustrates how communication can remain consistent and true to a company vision across all types of communication.

Chapters Online's marketing communications began with an aggressive national print, billboard, and radio advertising campaign to enhance its brand awareness. Chapters Online also sponsors various high-profile community events to increase its visibility and profile. It also utilizes online advertising on portals' and affiliates' Web sites. Chapters Online believes that its marketing and communication efforts were recently validated by a Kubas Consultants survey, commissioned by Chapters Online, which ranked Chapters Online's Web site and Amazon.com as approximately equal. What's important, however, is that the initial strategic vision that guided the development and launch of Chapters Online continues to provide marketing communication direction.

Source: Adapted from "About chapters.ca," http://www.chapters.ca/AboutUs/Background, extracted March 31, 2000.

Chapter Overview

This chapter introduces the campaign planning process. It shows how everything we have discussed thus far can be used to produce a consistent, creative set of messages that accomplishes various objectives. More important, the campaign process provides a framework for integrating all the marketing communication elements into one coordinated whole. Even though the concept of a campaign is most commonly used in the context of advertising, the marketing communication manager must view the entire communication effort as a campaign that extends across time, across different message delivery systems and functional areas, and across different target audiences.

The Chapters Online story is one of a complex integrated campaign whose strategy has been maintained with consistency throughout the retailer's history. We use this campaign case study throughout this chapter to illustrate how an IMC campaign is planned and managed.

Planning a Campaign

A campaign is not created in a vacuum; it is guided explicitly by the realities of the situation and implicitly by the marketing and corporate business plans. Campaign planners create a blueprint for all messages delivered over time, across various media, and to various audiences. A **campaign** is a series of marketing communication messages designed to meet a set of objectives based on a situation analysis and delivered over time (at least one year), through several marketing communication activities, and through various media. By taking a campaign approach, marketing communication planners increase the likelihood that the communication efforts will create synergy.

Campaign
A series of marketing communication messages designed to meet a set of objectives based on a situation analysis and delivered over time (at least one year), through several marketing communication activities, and through various media.

In contrast, companies that create one marketing communication message at a time (such as one TV or print ad, one direct-mail piece, or one billboard) are not involved in a campaign planning process. This one-message-at-a-time strategy is called the one-shot approach and can lead to problems with inconsistent messages.

In Chapter 4 we discussed general approaches to planning. In this chapter we consider the specific process used to develop a comprehensive campaign, from the situation analysis to creating the message to the media plan to the final evaluation. Table 18.1 describes eight steps that are important in campaign planning.

The end result of the campaign planning process is a document—called a campaign plan—that summarizes all the campaign planner's recommendations. The main sections of the campaign plan are similar to the steps in the campaign planning process. In other words, the outline in Table 18.1 can also be used as an outline for the **campaign plan** document. This document is reviewed by everyone who will execute the campaign. The review usually generates feedback, the document is revised, and ultimately it must be approved by the external agency's top management (if developed out of house) and the client.

Campaign plan
A document that summarizes all the campaign planner's recommendations and is the end result of the campaign-planning process.

When the campaign plan is developed by an external agency, it is presented to the client in a formal business presentation that may last several hours. The presenters usually provide listeners with a campaign book that details the recommendations and "leave behinds"—handouts used during the presentation that call attention to key proposals. Presentation skills are extremely important

Table 18.1 PLANNING AN INTEGRATED CAMPAIGN

1. Situation analysis
   - Conduct appropriate research
   - Identify stakeholders
   - Analyse the strengths, weaknesses, opportunities, and threats (SWOTs)
2. Strategic decisions
   - Set message objectives
   - Define target audiences
   - Target the competition
   - Develop a positioning strategy
3. Marketing mix decisions
4. Marketing communication tool selection
   - Match strengths and weaknesses of marketing communication tools to the objectives
   - Identify which tool(s) should lead the effort; and which will be used to support it
5. Budget planning
   - Determine the appropriation
   - Decide how it is to be split among the various marketing communication activities
6. Message design
   - Develop a "big idea" or campaign theme
   - Develop the creative strategy for the various targeted stakeholders
   - Write and design the messages (for each marketing communication area)
   - Pretest the messages
7. Media/message delivery system
   - Identify the contact points and message sources
   - Select vehicles that deliver to those points
   - Schedule the media activities
   - Estimate the costs; compare against the budget
8. Evaluation
   - Develop a research proposal to evaluate whether the campaign met its objectives
   - Evaluate retention

for people who plan and manage campaign efforts because the agency's recommendations must be "sold" to the client.

Marketing communication programs don't run by themselves. And integrated marketing communication programs are even more complicated to steer because, instead of one leader from the client and the agency, the operation is usually managed by a team of people from different functional areas—advertising, public relations, and so on—who plan, implement, and monitor the work. Managing and working with this team often require tremendous effort, but, the payoff can be great—a creative, cohesive campaign that can last for years.

concept review

PLANNING A CAMPAIGN

1. A campaign is a series of messages that are disseminated in a variety of different ways, that are designed to meet a set of objectives, and that are based on an analysis of the marketing communication situation.
2. There are eight steps in the campaign planning process:
   - Analyse the situation.
   - Make strategic decisions: objectives, targeting, competitive positioning.
   - Analyse the communication dimensions of the marketing mix.
   - Select the best marketing communication tools.
   - Establish and allocate the budget.
   - Design the message: big idea, creative strategy, executions.
   - Design the media or message delivery system.
   - Evaluate the success of the campaign effort.

SITUATION ANALYSIS

The situation analysis summarizes everything that's known about the marketing situation—the economy, trends in the industry, the competition, the company's strengths, and the buyer's decision making, among other information. These facts are gathered through formal primary and secondary research and informal marketplace assessment. Once all the information is gathered, planners look for windows of opportunity in their analysis.

RESEARCH

Although research cannot substitute for careful analysis or creative solutions, sound research can provide insight into difficult marketing communication problems. A framework for determining the types of research needed is illustrated in Table 18.2. The table suggests, for example, that concept testing research would be useful in selecting an appropriate campaign theme. A concept test employs a focus group format: Eight to ten people are gathered in a room and asked to assess whether they understand and like various message approaches such as "saving money," "personal safety," and so forth.

Five general types of research are particularly important in campaign planning:

1. *Corporate/brand*: Analyse the strengths and weaknesses of the organization for whom the campaign planning is being developed. Which strengths can be leveraged?
2. *Industry/competition*: Analyse the industry's growth and downturns to determine its economic health. Within the industry, who are the leaders and who are the followers? What are the market shares? What marketing communication programs are being used by the competition, and how much are they spending? Where are the threats and opportunities?
3. *Product*: Review the product (goods, service, idea) in terms of its uses, packaging, quality, price, unit of sale, brand image, distribution, competitive positioning, and product life cycle.

Table 18.2 CAMPAIGN PLANNING RESEARCH

To make this decision	One must choose/identify	Using
Key SWOTs	Internal/external factors; competitive situation; sociocultural factors	Industry studies; economic studies; primary and secondary consumer research
To whom	Stakeholder groups; prioritize to target	Stakeholder analysis; segmentation studies; attitude, opinion, and behaviour studies; ethnographic analysis
What to say	Theme; copy platform; appeals; selling points; position	Concept tests; perceptual mapping and positioning studies; likeability studies
How to say it	Marketing communication activity	Zero-base analysis of strengths and weaknesses; effectiveness analysis
How often	Frequency of exposure	Repetition studies; memorability and irritation analysis
Where	Media/delivery systems	Media models; syndicated data; readership/viewership studies
How much to spend	Budget level	Sales analysis; payback/break-even analysis
And afterwards		
Did it work	Objectives to be measured	Copytesting (awareness, attitude, behaviour, comprehension, likeability)

4. *Consumer behaviour*: Describe the consumer demographically and psychographically so that campaign planners can answer the following kinds of questions: Who buys—or doesn't buy—the product? In particular, who isn't buying the product and why? If one in ten people buy the product or brand, what is going on in the minds of the other 90 percent? (This tells what product or service features should be improved, changed, or deleted.) What other related products do they buy? What other activities or lifestyle associations relate to this product? When do they buy? How frequently do they buy? How do they use the product? Who else is involved in the purchase decision? What factors are most important in the purchase decision? Why do they repurchase or not repurchase the product?
5. *Target markets*: Analyse the stakeholder groups that affect and are affected by this situation and what kind of influence they have on the success of this program. How do you define the various stakeholder groups and estimate their size? How do you prioritize them in terms of their importance? Where are the best prospects in terms of demographic/psychographic characteristics, geographic location, and degree of product usage? How accessible are the target markets? If the company thinks it might use direct-mail advertising, for example, the availability of an accurate database is critical.

Communication audit
A formal or informal process that collects all communication materials, sorts them, compares them, and finally determines if they are working to support a set of integrated objectives.

COMMUNICATION AUDIT

One key factor that affects the success of an IMC program is whether the messages being sent are consistent, focused, and on strategy. This information is best gained by doing either a formal or informal **communication audit** that collects all communication materials, sorts them, compares them, and finally determines if they are working to support a set of integrated objectives.[1] Content analysis of the messages is a useful tool for this exercise.[2] A formal IMC audit also looks at the processes and organizational structure used to create marketing communication and the materials produced.[3]

ANALYSIS

The objective of the research is to identify key problems and opportunities, or if you are using a S.W.O.T. analysis—to identify those strengths, weaknesses, opportunities, and threats that should be either leveraged or minimized. Not every problem uncovered in a situation analysis can be solved with a communication campaign; nor are all of them equally important. So a key aspect of a situation analysis is the analysis—the assessment of which factors are important enough to affect the success of the marketing program and which of those factors can be addressed by marketing communication.

CHAPTERS ONLINE'S SITUATION

In Chapters Online's case, Chapters wanted to capture the new dimensions to book and book-related product-buying provided by the Internet: at-home shopping, leisurely browsing, and an unimaginably broad selection of titles. Chapters Online was Chapters' means of responding to the market opportunity to provide consumer value by means of extensive selection and convenience. It seems many consumers have responded. As noted by Rick Segal, president of Chapters Online, "We often have 1000 Canadians visiting our site at 2:00 a.m. when all of our stores are closed."[4]

Organized as a separate corporation, Chapters Online was given independence from Chapters. The intention was to build on the advantages of its

concept review

SITUATION ANALYSIS

1. The situation analysis is based on both primary and secondary research.
2. It gathers information from five key areas:
   - Corporate/brand
   - Industry/competition
   - Product
   - Consumer behaviour
   - Target market
3. Conclusions are drawn in terms of problems and opportunities or SWOTs—strengths and opportunities that can be leveraged and weaknesses and threats that need to be addressed.
4. The key to a situation analysis is the analysis—determining which factors are important enough to affect the success of the marketing effort and which of those factors can be addressed by marketing communication.

affiliation with Chapters' mall and superstore formats while differentiating itself as a leading online retail destination for Canadians.

Chapters Online gained early entry into the online marketplace and the absence of a dominant online retailer in Canada provided the company with an opportunity to position itself as a leader in Canadian electronic retailing. International Data Corporation, an information technology market research firm, has reported that 23 percent of Canadians (or approximately 6.9 million people) used the Internet in 1998 and that this figure is expected to increase at a compound annual growth rate of 26 percent calculated from 1997 to 2003, such that 64 percent of Canadians (or approximately 19.2 million people) are expected to be using the Internet by 2003. One of Chapters Online's objectives from the start was to make inroads into this growing Canadian market.[5]

International Data Corporation
www.idc.com

Strategic Decisions

The strategic direction of an integrated campaign depends on decisions about objectives, positioning, and targeting. Strategic marketing communication planning can be handled in a number of different ways. First, the client can do all the planning and let the agency implement these decisions. In this kind of an approach, the agency is more of a service provider than a partner. A second approach is to allow the agency to do more of the strategic planning for the communication activities. If strategic planning is the agency's responsibility, an account planner or an account executive and the account management team handle the planning.

Account planning is a British marketing communication concept that has found some acceptance in North America. An account planner is a person skilled in both research and account management who has the insights to speak with authority about the customer's needs and wants. In most marketing communication efforts, the traditional partners are the agency, represented by an account executive, and a client, represented by a marketing or advertising manager. Account planning adds a third viewpoint to the strategy development—that of the customer.[6]

What the account planner brings to the table is a wider range of research tools, including an emphasis on more qualitative research methodologies used to develop deeper consumer insights. As Lisa Fortini-Campbell explains in her book, *The Consumer Insight Workbook*, today's marketing communication demands that brands connect with consumers. To create that connection, planners must go beyond just knowing and describing the consumer and develop deeper insights that lead to understanding, respect, and empathy.[7] The account planner takes on that responsibility by proactively recommending strategies that are thought to be more customer-focused and by reacting to creative ideas from the customer's viewpoint—will that message speak to customers in a meaningful way?

Objectives

Every campaign should be guided by a clear, precise, and measurable statement of objectives. Objectives serve three functions.[8] First, they are a communication device. That is, campaign objectives are a practical method of informing all levels of management about goals and tasks. Second, objectives act as a decision-making guide for management. Objectives indicate the anticipated results of the campaign. Planners can evaluate the objectives to identify feasible approaches to tackle weaknesses and take advantage of opportunities. Finally, and most important, campaign objectives can be used to measure the specific results of the program so the company can learn from the experience.

Ultimately, the measure of success for any marketing communication campaign is its ability to increase sales and market share for the company. Sponsors naturally want every dollar they spend to trigger increased sales, but, as discussed in previous chapters, some areas of marketing communication (sales promotion, direct marketing) are better at that than others (advertising, public relations).

Planners should set objectives for a campaign as well as for each marketing communication tool used. In designing the campaign objectives, the components of a campaign should build on each other and create a positive synergy, thereby improving the chances that the consumer will select the company's brand. Planners refer to this sequence as movement from awareness to direct action—in other words, from communication objectives to sales objectives.

The plan's objectives also move from general to specific. The marketing plan objectives are the most general; the marketing communication plan objectives are more specific, especially in each subsection that focuses on a communication activity such as advertising or sales promotion. When the objectives are aligned like this, they "cascade" from one level to another, as shown in Figure 18.1.

Many types of stakeholders—customers, creditors, employees, suppliers, the media, community members, shareholders, and governmental agencies—are concerned with the operation of the firm. The process of objective setting must recognize the relative importance of these groups, and plans must incorporate and integrate their interests. Determining the relative weight given to any particular interest group is usually the campaign planner's responsibility, with the approval of management.

Stating Objectives

Objectives must be stated in terms that are understood and acceptable to those who will work to achieve them. Unrealistic goals, for instance, would not be acceptable to all involved. Therefore, planners should develop objectives with the input of all those expected to implement them. The campaign planner should set up a system to provide feedback during the planning process from all relevant people—both inside and outside the organization.

Furthermore, the objectives should be clear and specific. Precise wording enhances clarity. A campaign objective should specify who is to be affected, by what, how, when, and exactly what the result should be. In the following example, objectives for an ad campaign for Campbell's Chunky Soup are put in the context of the campaign's overall strategic directions:

- Who? Caucasian men, ages 35 to 55, blue-collar occupations, with incomes under $50 000; Campbell's Soup wants to reach 40 percent of this target audience with this message
- By what? An appeal to the virtue of obtaining the hearty taste of homemade soup by buying a premium-price canned soup
- How? Through a greater understanding of the product's benefits

Figure 18.1 SAMPLE CAMPAIGN OBJECTIVES

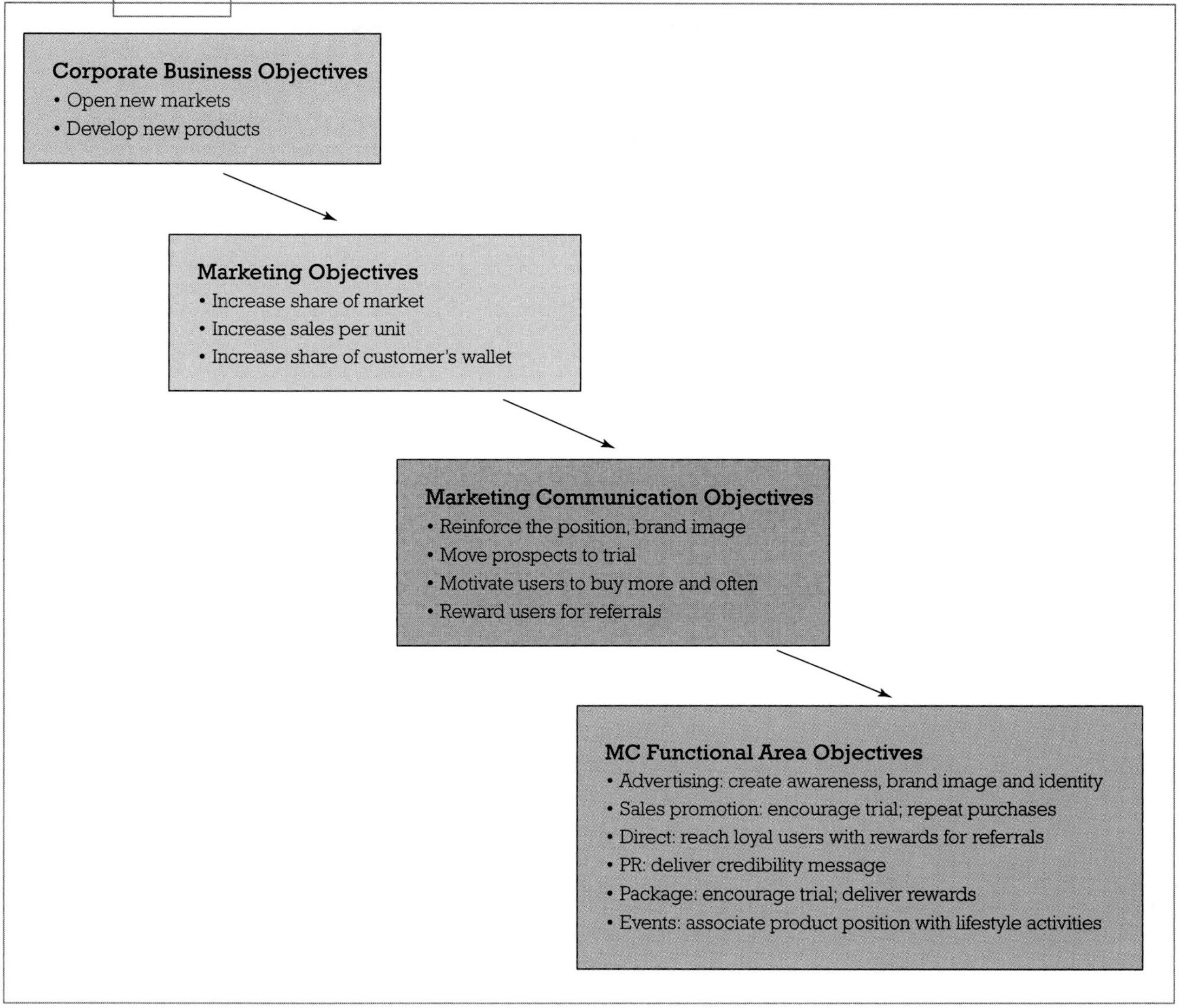

- When? During the next six months
- Objectives/results? Awareness of the product benefits increases by 20 percent from 40 percent to 48 percent; and an increase of 12 percent in sales
- Supporting communication objectives? The attitude score of the benefits of Chunky Soup versus homemade soup should reach 3.5 on a 6-point attitude scale after the individual has seen the ads

Planners assign numerical values to as many components as possible so they are measurable. Furthermore, the starting point and anticipated results are necessary for measuring change or impact. For example, the awareness result for Campbell's Chunky Soup listed the current awareness level of 40 percent as a point of comparison for the anticipated result of 48 percent. Then the percentage difference was calculated (an 8-point change equals 20 percent) to give a sense of the magnitude of the change.

concept review

Strategic Decisions (Objectives)

1. Campaign objectives may be classified as either sales objectives or communication objectives.
2. Planners should set both marketing communication objectives for each marketing communication activity and campaign objectives that link the campaign to the ultimate goal of increasing sales or market share.
3. Objectives must be stated in terms that are understandable and acceptable to all those who must meet them. They must be specific and state who is to be affected and by what; they must be measurable; and they must be assigned a time duration.

Chapters Online's Objectives

Chapters Online's overriding objective is to remain a leading Canadian electronic-commerce company. Another Chapters Online objective is to position itself to take advantage of Canada's expanding market for books and book-related products such as audio books, CDs, DVDs, magazines, and educational- and entertainment-oriented software on CD-ROM. Estimated to be approximately $2 billion per year, the Canadian book market is highly fragmented and regionalized. The largest number of per-capita book purchases are made by 35- to 54-year-olds and this population segment is expected to grow by approximately 20 percent in the next decade.[9] Of course, Chapters Online's marketing communication is expected to contribute every year to meeting Chapters' sales and marketing share objectives.

Competitive Positioning

Campaign planners usually target competitors to see how their brand compares with the competition. To target the competition, planners identify all the other options a consumer considers when making a product decision. A position statement identifies the core characteristics of the brand that differentiate it from the competition and summarize its appeal to consumers. IMC expert Tom Brannan states that "without a clear positioning, there can be no true integration." He believes that positioning "is an essential prerequisite to integrated communication since it provides the single focus around which every aspect of our communication will be constructed."[10] Positioning strategies are developed when a brand is new, but they are also reinforced in every campaign. Strategic planning means using your messages and vehicles to outflank the competition by creating a more attractive position or making your position more appealing. One strategic purpose for a campaign, as is illustrated in Figure 18.2, is to create, reinforce, or reposition a brand.

The strategy for Chapters Online is to position itself as the book and book-related product provider that goes beyond mere satisfaction. The idea is to complement and build upon Chapters' other retail formats to outperform competitors in the delivery of customer value. To accomplish this leadership position, Chapters Online knows it must continue to execute its strategy better than competitors on the dimensions of people, costs, and technology.[11] As stated by Rick

Figure 18.2 POSITIONING STRATEGIES

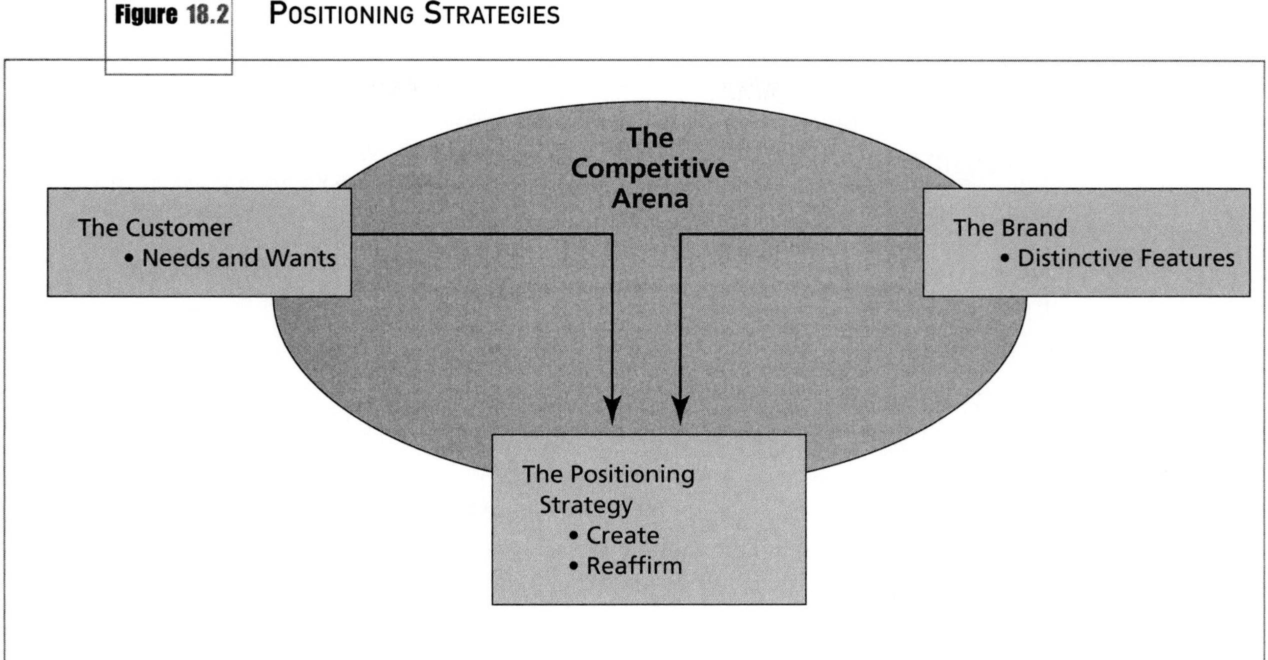

Segal, president of Chapters Online, "At Chapters Online, we understand the value of our people. Brain power is the prime factor driving this country's smartest companies. More than ever before, huge value is being leveraged from smart ideas, and the winning technology and business models they create. As a company leading the way in Canadian e-commerce, our team is the best and brightest in the business. Our success relies on it."[12]

TARGETING STAKEHOLDERS

Once the objectives have been identified, every campaign should have a clear sense of who the important stakeholders and the targeted audiences are for the various messages. It is necessary to decide the relative importance of each stakeholder group, of segments within each group, and how these groups can best be reached by various types of marketing communication activities.

Figure 18.3 illustrates a stakeholder targeting worksheet that could be used in an IMC campaign. In a planning document like this, you would identify the key stakeholder groups and diagnose what they think about the brand and what motivates them. It's also useful to note the ways they can be reached through their contact points. Finally, you would decide how important the various stakeholders are for this campaign and prioritize them.

CHAPTERS ONLINE'S TARGETED STAKEHOLDERS

The Chapters Online approach represents a well-rounded program of integrated marketing communication. One of the most important aspects of an IMC program is the recognition that all stakeholders are important, and they should be considered in planning the company's total communication program. Furthermore, stakeholders often overlap, so the messages must have a consistent theme, style, look, and feel—even if the messages themselves vary according to the needs of different stakeholders.

concept review

STRATEGIC DECISIONS (COMPETITIVE POSITIONING)

1. Targeting the competition is done by identifying all the other options a consumer considers when making a product decision.
2. Positioning strategies are built on an understanding of the competitive situation; a position is the location the product holds in the mind of the consumer relative to the competition.

Chapters Online's approach is to build partnerships with important stakeholders. Two of the most important Chapters Online stakeholders are the Chapters retail stores and *The Globe and Mail*. Chapters Online has achieved early recognition and credibility due to its association with the Chapters brand. Chapters Online has utilized, and will continue to utilize, Chapters' national network of superstores for highly targeted in-store marketing activities promoting the use of its online operations. Computer kiosks located in Chapters superstores permit Chapters customers to access Chapters Online's Web site to locate and purchase out-of-stock books, thereby increasing its marketing penetration.[13]

Chapters' partnership with *The Globe and Mail* is an agreement to form ChaptersGlobe.com, a strategic alliance that focuses on promoting the Canadian book community and the online sale of books. The ChaptersGlobe agreement provides for advertising and other promotional support of the ChaptersGlobe.com Web site, marketing alliances, and the linking of the ChaptersGlobe.com Web site to Chapters.ca and other Web sites. Chapters Online believes that forming long-term strategic alliances is a key component in achieving its strategic objectives of expanding the breadth of its product offerings and increasing online traffic to its Web site.[14]

The following is a discussion of other important stakeholder targets in Chapters Online's IMC program.

THE CUSTOMER TARGET

Chapters Online's primary target market includes the growing book and book-related product buyers aged 35 to 54 years who enjoy using the Internet to browse an unimaginably broad selection of titles while they're at home or at work. Chapters Online's target market shares a primary characteristic with Chapters' superstores customer target—shoppers who enjoy a broad selection. This factor highlights the importance of the previously discussed partnership with Chapters' retail stores.

Toronto Dominion Bank
www.tdbank.ca

Infospace Canada
www.infospace.com

PORTAL AND WEB-CONTENT SITES

Chapters Online has entered into marketing agreements with leading Canadian portal and Web-content sites including Alta Vista Canada, AOL Canada, Bid.Com International, Canoe, CHUM Limited, ClickThrough Interactive, Infospace Canada, Microsoft Network Canada, Toronto-Dominion Bank, TSN.ca, and Yahoo!Canada. Portal agreements allow Chapters Online to

Figure 18.3 STAKEHOLDER WORKSHEET: EVALUATION TOOL

Stakeholder	*Perceptions of Brand*	*Wants and Needs*	*Contact Point*	*Priority*

advertise by way of an advertising banner and a click-through button on the portal. Users of the portal then access Chapters Online's Web site directly. The use of portal agreements has become significant in e-commerce as popular portals have the ability to direct substantial online traffic to a particular site and are an important marketing and promotional tool. The typical portal agreement includes some form of exclusivity and may include payment by Chapters Online of fees based on traffic and purchases generated by the portal.[15]

AFFILIATE PROGRAM

Chapters Online's affiliate program, which was launched in October 1998, currently includes over 2000 affiliates and is growing rapidly. The affiliate program allows other Web-site owners to link to Chapters Online's Web site and direct their visitors to purchase products from Chapters Online.

Each time a purchase is made by a visitor who has followed an affiliate's link, such affiliate receives a referral fee. Chapters Online's affiliate program is an important component of its overall marketing and promotion strategy.

Chapters Online's affiliate program is superior to that of many of its Canadian-based competitors as it remunerates affiliates with relatively high referral fees. Affiliates also benefit from online sales reporting and an automated link generator that makes it easy for affiliates to create links to any Web page within Chapters Online's Web site.[16]

Employees

Employees are another important stakeholder group. Chapters Online has one overriding focus, one mission, and one goal—to be the best at whatever it does. This is accomplished through teamwork. To execute this approach, Chapters Online's continuously works at building the best team in e-commerce. By combining leading-edge technology and cyber-savvy cohorts with a loft-style workspace that inspires creativity and facilitates interaction, Chapters Online leads the way in Canadian e-commerce.[17]

Community

As suggested by the listing of events on the cover of the accompanying calendar of events document for one of Chapters' superstore locations, Chapters and Chapters Online are committed to support literacy, Canadian culture, and education. In keeping with these commitments, Chapters and Chapters Online have committed to purchase for inventory every new Canadian book presented to its buyers by a member publisher of the Association of Canadian Publishers' Council. Also, ongoing support is offered to endeavours such as the following:

- Frontier College, a volunteer-based organization that teaches people across Canada to read and write;
- Sponsorship of multiple awards and events that promote Canadian authors; and
- Sponsorship of the annual Chapters/Books in Canada First Novel Award, which is considered Canada's most important honour for first-time novelists.

This ad features Chapters Online's Strategic partners Compaq and Microsoft®.

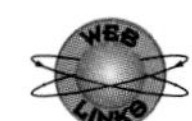

PEN Canada
www.pencanada.ca

Also, every year, Chapters donates hundreds of books and gift certificates to schools, daycare centres, women's shelters, senior's residences, health-care institutions, and many other community organizations such as the Writers' Trust, Canadian Children's Book Centre, and PEN Canada.[18]

This cover of calendar of events planned for a Chapters superstore location communicates Chapters commitment to the communities in which it operates. Note also that this document provides Chapters Online's Web sites address.

concept review

Strategic Decisions (Targeting)

1. Targeting involves identifying and prioritizing the key stakeholder groups, then targeting specific audience segments within these stakeholder groups.
2. How the target audiences are defined has a substantial impact on other campaign decisions such as the message and media strategies.
3. The various audiences are addressed with a central theme, but separate messages address each target group's particular concerns.

THE MARKETING MIX

In Chapter 3 we described how the marketing mix can communicate messages and dictate message strategies. How the product is designed, priced, distributed, and serviced are some of the most important factors in developing a message strategy. In the case of Chapters Online, a number of marketing mix factors communicated messages about the retailer and its personality.

SELECTION AND CONVENIENCE

Chapters Online offers a broad selection of about three million book titles, as well as over 240 000 music CD titles, and over 70 000 videotape and DVD titles that customers can conveniently browse from the comfort of their home. What more could a book, CD, video, or DVD buyer want? Finding that special title you're looking for with a minimal expenditure of time and effort. No time and effort spent finding the store, a parking space, and the title you're looking for on the shelf. True hassle-free shopping. That is the Chapters Online experience. Moreover, unlike the Web sites of other retailers, the site is easy to access and navigate as suggested by the user-friendly layout of the accompany Chapters Online Web site home page.

If the traditional shopping experience is what the buyer enjoys, Chapters Online benefits from its relationship with Chapters' national network of superstores, which offer e-commerce kiosks to enable shoppers to conveniently access the millions of titles offered by Chapters Online.

The offer of an unimaginably broad selection of titles via its connection with Chapters Online has paid off for Chapters' large-format superstores. Industry market research indicated selection as the primary criterion for customers choosing a large-format bookstore, over other factors such as location, ambience, price, and service. This finding has been validated for Chapters. The primary competitive advantage of Chapters' superstores—selection—has in great part contributed to Chapters being listed first in this area in the 1997, 1998, and 1999 Kubas survey. This annual Canadian retail sector survey found that Chapters outpaced every other retail chain in Canada, in all product categories, including those retailers with decades of experience.[19]

The home page for Chapters.ca is designed to be user friendly so that visitors can navigate the site with ease.

Customer Service, Security, and Loyalty

To assist all Web-site visitors, Chapters Online offers assistance in the form of answers to frequently asked questions. If customers can't find answers in the Web site's Help section or in its Frequently Asked Questions section, a Contact Us section provides customers multiple ways in which to contact Chapters Online's customer service department. The customer service department can be contacted via e-mail or by 1-800 phone contact, seven days a week.

Security remains one of the primary concerns that inhibits Internet shopping for many consumers. Chapters Online has used technology to ensure that personal and payment information remains confidential and secure. One of today's most advanced security systems—Secure Socket Layers (SSL)—encrypts all customer-provided information before sending it to Chapters Online's server. Only when this information reaches the Chapters.ca servers is it decrypted.[20] To ensure that potential buyers learn of Chapters Online's safe shopping environment, the accompanying Securities & Guarantees statement is communicated to shoppers. Like all other aspects of Chapters Online Web site, navigation to the Securities & Guarantees Web page is easy to find and access.

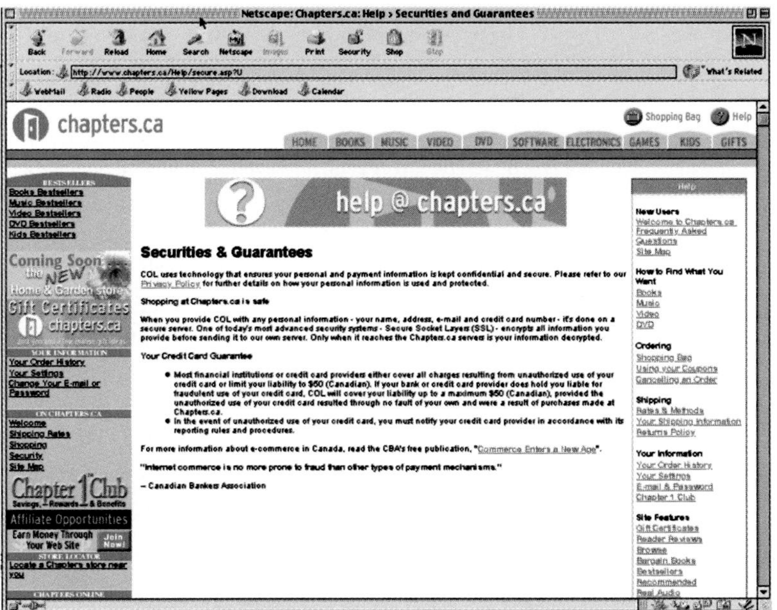

"Internet commerce is no more prone to fraud than other types of payment mechanisms." This message from the Canadian Bankers Association and Chapters Online's use of cutting-edge security technology are communicated by this Web page.

Marketing Communication Tools

The next step in campaign planning is to decide which marketing communication tools to use to develop the campaign and which one should lead the effort. In Chapter 4 we presented general strengths and weaknesses for the key marketing communication areas. The decision about which area to use depends on the problems to be solved and the stated objectives. The planning process involves analysing the objectives, strengths, and weaknesses of the various marketing communication tools and then matching objectives to the tools that can best deliver success.

Advertising, for example, is particularly effective for reminding people of established brands and their positive past experiences. If you have an announcement to make, then public relations and advertising can work hand in hand as shown in the many case examples highlighted in this text. Public relations is also useful for building or rebuilding credibility, particularly when there is a believability problem. If you want to build excitement and enthusiasm, then an event may target your market and involve the right audience in your message. Many times, a number of different areas can be used, so the lead area becomes the one that generates the best "big idea."

For example, to reposition Black Gold, a Scandinavian beer, from an older market to a younger, yuppie market, the local DDB Needham agency used an event—a film noir festival—as the centrepiece of the campaign. The event may not seem to be the strongest marketing communication activity to lead a repositioning, but the strength of the creative idea—film noir and its association with the product name—made the event a winner. The festival was supported with advertising to announce the event, publicity, collectors' posters, postcards, and tabletop cards in bars.

Some marketing communication activities work together naturally. For a new product launch, for example, public relations will often lead to take advantage of the news angle, and then the advertising kicks in to build high levels of awareness and motivate people to look for the product. In most cases advertising and sales promotion also interact closely; advertising is used to build excitement for sales promotion, and sales promotion is used to reinforce an action message carried in the advertising. Other than the obvious differences in technique, the major differences between advertising and sales promotion are expectation and accountability. Recall from Chapter 10 that the intent of sales promotion is to provide an incentive to action through the addition of some kind of extra value. Thus, sales promotion is tied to immediate sales or response. In contrast, advertising tends to have several intermediate objectives leading to sales, such as creating awareness and building brand equity, and accomplishing these objectives takes time. Advertising relies heavily on the other mix elements, especially personal selling and sales promotion, to close the sale. The proper blending of advertising with sales promotion has proven to be very effective. A print ad containing a coupon, for example, has been shown to increase recall scores eightfold as compared with the same ad without a coupon.

Chapters Online's Marketing Communication Mix

Chapters Online's marketing communication is dominated by online advertising, a natural medium for attracting Internet shoppers. But online advertising is only one of the marketing communication tools used to build the program.

The other marketing communication tools used, such as traditional print ads, frequently acknowledge one or more of Chapters Online's partnerships or promote a relationship-building activity. Chapters Online's philosophy is that building and maintaining long-term relationships of various forms optimizes its ability to effectively interact with its target market. The objective is to present the company in such a way that customers and other stakeholders feel strongly about being identified with Chapters Online.

Many people think we're American, but the truth is, Chapters was founded and built right here in Canada. And since opening our first store in 1995, we've grown to become the country's premiere retail success story. In fact, we've been ranked Canada's favourite retailer for three years in a row.* We take great pride in our heritage and so we support Canadian authors through store programs and awards. We also encourage reading beyond our stores, through contributions to literacy programs across the country. So, to separate fact from fiction once and for all, Chapters is Canadian. End of story.

* Of the top 130 retailers in Canada, Chapters was voted #1. Kubas & Consultants, Major Market Retail Report, 97, 98, 99.

This print content on the backside of a book marker communicates Chapters' pride in being Canadian and its support of Canadian authors.

As discussed earlier in this chapter, Chapters Online has entered into many marketing agreements with leading portal and Web-content sites, and has launched an affiliate program. By establishing these types of relationships, Chapters online benefits from increased market exposure and penetration while relationship partners also receive benefits such as referral fees.

Consistent with the relationship approach, Chapters Online has teamed up with acclaimed broadcast journalist Pamela Wallin to launch a virtual book club. Check it out at www.chapters.ca/wallin. This partnership provides Chapters Online visitors with access to Chapters and Verse, a regular column that deals with current affairs. Visitors also enjoy a link to Pamela's weekly column and Pamela's Picks. Instead of being a review of recent releases, Pamela's Picks represents recommended reading and notable titles and authors from all aspects of Pamela's professional and personal experiences.[21]

Chapters Online's loyalty program, Chapters 1 Club, not only works to cement customer relationships by entitling members to discounts on future purchases at Chapters' stores or at Chapters.ca, but it also provides Chapters Online with a database of frequent shoppers. This enables Chapters to apply direct marketing tools using the Customer Lifetime Value approach as discussed in Chapter 12. It also provides insightful customer information that can be used to enhance the efficiency and potential effectiveness of all marketing mix tools.

The Budget

As discussed in Chapter 16, the appropriation governs all proposed activities by placing upper limits on what can be spent. Often the overall marketing communication appropriation is set as part of a marketing plan, so the problem becomes fitting the campaign into this framework. One of the truisms of the business is that there is never enough money to do it right, so the planner is always endeavouring to make the greatest impact with less money than he or she believes is needed. Once the appropriation level is determined, then the budget is developed, which determines how the money will be allocated.

Most important, campaign planners have to decide how to allocate the money among different marketing communication activities and different types of message delivery systems. Television commercials, for example, are expensive to produce and run. However, they reach large audiences and their per-impression cost is quite low. Personal sales is extremely expensive on a per-impression basis, and yet in some industries—particularly business-to-business marketing—a personal sales call on a limited number of key buyers may be the only way to do business. Campaign planners constantly juggle costs and reach as they try to decide where to best put the money.

The campaign budget is developed by estimating the costs for all the various elements in the plan. Once those estimates are totaled, then the planner compares that amount with the appropriation. Inevitably the campaign plan will then have to be adjusted to keep the activities on budget and the expenses aligned with the available money.

concept review

Marketing Mix, Marketing Communication Tools, and Budget

1. The marketing mix decisions communicate important information and contribute to the message strategy.
2. The decision about which marketing communication activities to use is based on the problems to be solved and the objectives to be achieved.
3. The lead marketing communication activity is often the one that can contribute the most to support the big idea. Many, if not all, of the other marketing communication tools can be used in support of the big idea once the lead activity has been chosen.
4. The budget level must be established if it is not a given, and then the total budget must be allocated among the various marketing communication activities.

Message Design

Message design is the creative side of marketing communication planning. You are trying to determine what to say and how to say it. Every campaign is focused on a central big idea that holds the communication efforts together. Without a coherent concept, there is no way to make a complex set of messages mesh together.

In the case of much of Chapters Online's advertising, the central big idea that holds the communication efforts together is the no-hassle selection provided by a company that takes pride in its Canadian heritage and support of Canadian content. Is the message delivered in the accompanying advertisement that appeared in *Canadian Business* consistent with this central big idea?

Creative strategy
An outline of what to say to the various target audiences who may have different message needs.

Once the big idea has been decided, then the creative strategy can be designed. The **creative strategy** outlines what to say to the various target audiences who may have different message needs. Trade members, for example, will want to know how they can make money by supporting this promotion. Employees need to be informed about the campaign so they can reinforce its messages. Sales representatives will need a variety of sales support materials to use in their sales calls to buyers. They will also need motivational programs to encourage them to work hard in support of the campaign. Finally, the targeted consumer audience will need a different set of messages that get attention, build awareness, and lock the information in memory. All of these messages are different in terms of what they say. However, their overall theme and tone should reflect and reinforce the general campaign theme.

Copy platform (workplan)
In advertising, the translation of the creative strategy into a document that specifies what will be said to whom and with what effect and that gives directions about the executions.

In advertising the creative strategy is translated into a **copy platform**, a document that specifies what will be said to whom and with what effect. It often gives direction about the executions. For instance, the copy platform might describe the tone of voice and product personality for the ad. Other elements might include a statement of the product position, the psychological appeal, and the selling premise.

There are many different approaches to creative strategy, as discussed in Chapters 3, 4, and 9. Generally, the approaches focus on information, argument, image, emotion, or entertainment. In a marketing communication campaign plan, these various strategies may relate to the different audiences. For example, employees may respond most effectively to information, the trade to reason or argument, sales personnel to an emotional appeal, and consumers to entertainment.

Creative tactics
The details in the execution of the creative strategy.

Creative tactics provide the details of the executions in all the various areas. What will the ads say and look like? What will the press releases focus on? How will the events be organized? What sales support materials are needed, and what will they say and look like? The campaign plan will spell out as many of these details as possible, so the managers who are approving the plan will have some idea of the scope and scale of the effort. Budgets will also be estimated for all of the individual execution activities.

Evaluation

With rapidly rising costs, overwhelming numbers of advertising messages, and more and more advertising voices seeking to be heard, most authorities agree that advertising should be pretested. Pretesting is done to avoid costly mistakes; to predict the relative strength of alternative concepts, strategies, and tactics; and to increase the efficiency of the campaign effort. Posttesting is done to determine if the campaign met its objectives.

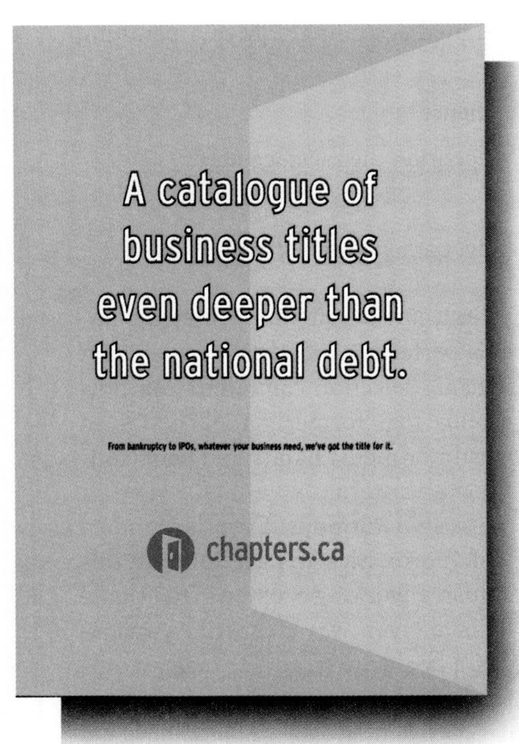

What is Chapters Online attempting to say with this advertisement?

Companies concerned with whether their campaign messages will be heard and understood will do concept testing to check the power of the big idea as it is being developed. They will also test various message strategies to compare their impact on the target audiences and do execution testing to evaluate various approaches to the actual construction of the messages. In the final analysis pretesting is done to select the best appeals and provide benchmarks against which the communications can be measured. The basic advantage of campaign pretesting is to gain some measure of assurance in the creative product for a rather modest investment. In the end, however, the campaign planner must appreciate that good pretest results simply mean that the likelihood of success is good, not guaranteed.

Posttesting involves developing research methods to test whether or not the campaign reached its objectives. Copytesting services can provide information about levels of awareness, comprehension, attitude, and likeability. Sales tracking can provide sales data, and other behavioural responses can be measured by tracking inquiries, coupons returned, phone calls, and Web page hits. The methods used in pretesting and posttesting were described in detail in Chapter 17.

concept review

Message Design

1. Every campaign is held together by a central big idea.
2. Creative strategies describe the general message approaches to be used with the various stakeholder audiences, including the targeted consumer audience.
3. Executions are the actual ads and other materials produced by the various functional areas involved in the campaign.
4. Pretesting is used to determine if campaign messages will be heard and understood. Concept testing checks the power of the big idea. Pretesting is also used to test various message strategies and executions to evaluate alternative approaches.
5. Posttesting is used to determine if the campaign met its objectives.

Media/Message Delivery System

The media—or message delivery—plan is just as important as the creative plan. The two plans are usually developed simultaneously. Sometimes the campaign planner may have already decided that a certain medium—such as direct mail—must be used, and the creative effort is designed accordingly. Media planning involves the following steps:

1. Selecting the best vehicles to reach the audience
2. Deciding on the frequency—the level of repetition the message needs
3. Scheduling the media efforts across time
4. Estimating the costs and allocating the budget among the various vehicles

Because the world of media planning is extremely complex, a media planner's ability to select a media mix that blends perfectly with the creative effort is both an art and a science. In advertising media selection computers can now perform media-related data analysis in seconds that formerly took hours. In addition, the information available about consumer media habits and behaviour has made media selection far more exact and less wasteful.

Clorox Company
www.clorox.com

Still, the choices appear endless and the costs enormous. Even large marketers such as the Clorox Company, maker of Clorox Bleach, have found it difficult to find the right media to reach the elusive working woman. Traditional daytime television and women's magazines have given way to specialty magazines and direct mail. And university students, a favourite target for many clothing and sports manufacturers, are even more difficult to reach with conventional media. That's why special programs such as on-campus events are used so extensively. As discussed in Chapters 14 and 15, choosing the media plan has become a major undertaking.

In Chapters Online's case, its heavy usage of online advertising and a Web site destination to interact with customers requires innovative use of Internet technology. Those who frequently visit Chapters Online's Web site are accustomed to the creative use of cutting-edge technology to provide safe and hassle-free brows-

This virtual scratch-and-win card is an example of Chapters Online's effort to be creative in its application of technology.

ing of the listings of new books, CDs, DVDs, and gift suggestions. However, visitors beware, you just might be in for a treat. Take, for example, the opportunity to scratch a virtual scratch-and-win card on your computer. Visitors to Chapters.ca recently had this opportunity as part of a limited-time offer promotional contest. The interactive appeal of this contest was reinforced by the fact that the customer's drawing of a mouse over the virtual card made a scratching sound.

To execute this contest, Chapters Online partnered with Ford Motor Co. of Canada Ltd., to offer, as its largest prize, a 2000 Ford Focus ZTS. It also gave away three Com Palm Connect Organizers, five $200 Web site shopping sprees, and coupons worth $5 and $10 for use at Chapters. The smaller prizes were instant wins and all entrants were offered an opportunity to enter into a draw for the car. Contest rules restricted card scratching to once daily, but clearly many participants made subsequent scratches thus indicating a high degree of involvement in this contest. Participants averaged four to five scratches in total.

David Hainline, executive vice president for merchandising and marketing at Chapters Online, says the goal was to build traffic on our site," adding: "It allowed us to present to a lot of people who haven't been to our site for awhile. When they come for multiple visits, we can show them more. We're adding product lines and enriching the lines we have all the time."[22]

Evaluation

Evaluation is the final and, in some respects, most important step in developing a campaign because it is the point where a company learns from its experiences. Many companies overlook this step, which is unfortunate because that makes it difficult to develop progressively more effective communication plans. Campaign evaluation is concerned with questions of effectiveness: Does the campaign work? Does it do what needs to be done? What were the results? It is also concerned with questions of taste and judgment: Is the campaign fair and accurate? Does it mislead?

Two problems make evaluation particularly difficult. First, there is little agreement on how to measure the success of a campaign—how much emphasis should be placed on communication effects and how much on sales? Though it is true that most managers understand, for example, that advertising does not necessarily lead directly to sales, the expectation is still there. A second problem is that it is sometimes difficult to diagnose the nature of the problem. Sometimes it takes a sophisticated research effort to deconstruct a campaign to find out what went wrong.

Nevertheless, evaluation must take place. Essentially, two types of evaluations may be made: ongoing evaluation—tracking studies—while the campaign is running, and post-evaluation at the end of the campaign. The former allows the advertiser to make adjustments before the problems become too severe. Maxwell House Coffee discovered that consumers were afraid that its new coffee was a potential health risk, so it opted for an ongoing evaluation. Using the information collected, Maxwell House was able to quickly develop print and broadcast ads that carefully explained the controversial issues. Had Maxwell House been concerned only with evaluating sales rather than communication effectiveness during the campaign, it would have been too late to solve the problems as they were uncovered.

Cadillac Motors
www.cadillac.com

Post-evaluation allows marketing communicators to make major adjustments so that mistakes will not be repeated. Cadillac Motors, for example, went through a period where its campaigns were changed every six months because post-evaluation indicated that the target audience was having a difficult time determining the primary idea in Cadillac ads.

Chapters Online's Success

Chapters Online has been successful in many ways. Its Web-site visitors consistently receive a no-hassle opportunity to browse its huge selection of books and book-related products. Also, Chapters Online has a loyal base of customers as indicated by its successful Chapters 1 Club loyalty program.

Chapters Online continues to meet and exceed performance expectations, thereby generating marketplace recognition and impressive performance statistics:

- Chapters Online received the Canadian Web site of the year award in 1999 by *Internet World*, an industry publication that focuses on the Internet.[23]
- Chapters Online completed a successful initial public offering (IPO) in September 1999, issuing 3.4 million shares at the IPO price of $13.50 a share.
- Revenues at Chapters Online continue to increase substantially. For example, in the second quarter of 1999, revenues reached $6.4 million, an increase of 74.4 percent from the first quarter.
- Customer site visits continue to increase. Customers on the site in the second quarter of 1999 totalled more than 262 000, an increase of 88 percent over the first quarter.[24]

Despite its success, Chapter Online is not without its critics. Since 1995, Chapters and its CEO Larry Stevenson have come under fire from publishers, authors, politicians, and independent bookstores. The primary complaint has been that Chapters is trying to monopolize the Canadian book industry—not an unexpected criticism given the size and success of Chapters and Chapters Online. However, the existence of this criticism serves to illustrate that Chapters must remain consistent in its efforts to demonstrate commitment to support literacy, Canadian culture, and education.

It seems that a consistent commitment to Canadian authors is paying off. According to Stevenson, "In 1995, 35 percent of the books that Canadians were reading were Canadian. Now it's 46 percent. We haven't done it all but we've been a part of it. As a result, there are more Canadian authors selling more Canadian books."[25]

No matter how experts and critics view the impact of the company, there's no doubt that Chapters Online is a successful marketing communication case study on how to build a brand by focusing on how customers and other stakeholders relate to its product offerings and the company itself.

concept review

Media/Message Delivery System and Evaluation

1. Media planning involves:
   - Selecting the best vehicles to reach the audience
   - Deciding on the frequency of the message
   - Scheduling the media efforts across time
   - Allocating the budget among the various vehicles
2. Campaign evaluation is concerned with questions of effectiveness.
3. Evaluation is the point where a company learns from its experiences, either through ongoing evaluation or post-evaluation.

A Closing Thought:

A Success Story

The Chapters Online story is about how a company, through planning and action, can create positive relationships with its key stakeholders. Chapters Online understood the total range of communication contact points that deliver a company's message and worked hard to send a consistent message from all those points. Finally, the Chapters Online experience shows the organization necessary to manage communication messages delivered in a variety of ways by multiple partner and affiliate organizations. The Chapters Online integrated marketing communication program helped develop a strong brand image, one of hassle-free, convenient shopping for books and book-related products, from a quality Canadian company that cares about its customers and is committed to support literacy, Canadian culture, and education.

Chapters Online has been able to create a successful marketing communication program. It remains to be seen whether the program will continue. What would you recommend for the future if you were the new marketing communication director for Chapters Online?

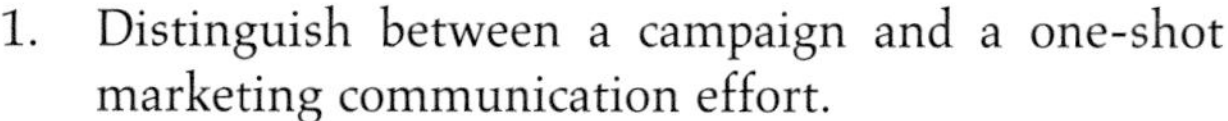

summary

1. Distinguish between a campaign and a one-shot marketing communication effort.

   A campaign is a series of marketing communication messages designed to meet a set of objectives based on a situation analysis and guided by the marketing and corporate business plans. Campaign messages are delivered over time, through different media and message delivery systems, and to various audiences. Campaigns normally mean a commitment to a message strategy that will last at least one year. In contrast, companies that create one marketing communication message at a time—such as an advertisement, a public relations press release, or a direct-marketing piece—are not involved in a campaign planning process. This one-message-at-a-time method is called the one-shot approach.

2. Outline the steps in the campaign planning process and explain the campaign planning document.

   Planning a campaign involves eight steps: analysing the situation, deciding on a set of key strategic decisions (objectives, targeting, and competitive positioning), analysing the communication dimensions of the marketing mix, identifying the best functions to lead and support the effort, determining and allocating the budget, designing the creative strategy, designing the media or message delivery system, and evaluating the success of the campaign. These are also the major sections in the campaign plan document.

points to ponder

Review the Facts

1. What is a one-shot approach, and how does it differ from a campaign?
2. What is a campaign plan?
3. What is a marketing communication audit, and how can it be used in campaign planning?
4. What is account planning, and what does it add to the campaign planning effort?

Master the Concepts

5. Why do you think many marketing communication professionals regard campaign planning as a complicated task?
6. Discuss how campaign objectives are set. How would campaign objectives differ from objectives for an individual ad?
7. Explain the difference between creative strategies, message strategies, and creative tactics.
8. Explain how a planner should select the marketing communication activities used in a campaign. What is one way to determine the marketing communication activity that will lead the effort?
9. Explain what is meant by the notion that the marketing mix (other than marketing communication) can deliver messages.
10. "A company should evaluate a campaign to learn from its experiences." Explain what might be learned from such an exercise.

Apply Your Knowledge

11. Assume that you are working on the campaign to launch a new Wish-Bone Cheddar and Bacon dressing. What research would have to be done to support this campaign?
12. In planning the media or message delivery systems to be used in a campaign, what are the four decisions a planner must make? Suppose you are the media planner for the launch of a new Wish-Bone Cheddar and Bacon dressing. Develop a set of recommendations demonstrating that you understand how these four decisions are applied to a campaign.
13. Adopt a non-profit association in your community and develop a marketing communication budget for it. Identify its most important activities, the expenses associated with them, and its income sources. How much money needs to be raised through donations to make the income cover the expenses?

suggested projects

1. (Writing Project) Find an example of at least one print and one broadcast ad that belong to the same campaign. Compare and contrast the ads. Do they seem to follow the same campaign strategy in a consistent theme? How are they similar and how are they different? Write a brief report that explains what you think the reasons are for the differences.
2. (Team Project) Break into small groups of four to six students. Each member should find one article about a current campaign in any of the trade magazines—*Marketing Magazine, Advertising Age,* or *Adweek,* for example. As a group, discuss each campaign article and select the one the group would like to evaluate. Using the information available in the article, outline the campaign using the eight sections in a campaign plan. Then critique the campaign and assess ways to improve it, if any. Select a group spokesperson to present your findings to the class.
3. (Writing Project) Based on the Chapters Online case discussed in this chapter, outline the different types of marketing communication activities used in this retailers marketing program. Explain how they are integrated. Is there any marketing communication area that wasn't discussed? In that area, or any other area that you feel was underutilized, what might you recommend that Chapters Online marketing communication planners include in next year's campaign plan? Write your proposal.
4. (Internet Project) Assume that you are the new media communication specialist for Chapters Online. Visit the Chapters Online page (http://www.chapters.ca) and investigate the site. Assess whether the current site sends the same message as other Chapters Online advertising in print, TV, or through other methods. What stakeholders does the site target? Is the site easy to navigate? Is it engaging? Does it provide enough information? Write a brief memo analysing the current site and making recommendations for next year.

case questions

1. Watch for some current Chapters Online advertising on television and in magazines. Explain the strategy behind these new ads and how they link (or don't link) with the previous campaign efforts discussed in this chapter.
2. How many different ways are being used to communicate the Chapters Online message? Develop an analysis of the Chapters Online message delivery system.
3. If you were in charge of Chapters Online's current campaign, how would you evaluate its success? Develop an evaluation plan that will help you determine whether the Chapters Online marketing communication program is effective.

NOTES

CHAPTER 1

1. Don E. Schultz, Stanley I. Tannenbaum, and Robert F. Lauterborn, *Integrated Marketing Communications* (Chicago: NTC Business Books, 1993), xvii.
2. NPO Group. Reprinted with permission from *Advertising Age*, 22 March 1993: 3. Copyright, Crain Communications, Inc. 1993.
3. Tom Duncan, "A Macro Model of Integrated Marketing Communication," American Academy of Advertising Annual Conference, Norfolk, Va., 1995.
4. Jeffrey E. Barnhart, "Small Firms Look to Integrated Marketing," *Sales and Marketing Strategies & News* (July/August 1994): 13, 15.
5. William Weilbacher, *Brand Marketing* (Lincolnwood, Ill.: NTC Business Books, 1993).
6. Regis McKenna, *Relationship Marketing* (Reading, Mass.: Addison-Wesley, 1991), 4.
7. Terry G. Varva, *Aftermarketing* (Homewood, Ill.: Irwin, 1992), xiii.
8. Frank K. Sonnenberg, "If I Had Only One Client," *Sales & Marketing Management* (November 1993): 4–107.
9. Frederick E. Webster, Jr., "The Changing Role of Marketing in the Corporation," *Journal of Marketing*, 56 (October 1992): 1–17.

CHAPTER 2

1. Quoted in Frederick Webster, Jr., *Market Driven Management* (New York: John Wiley & Sons, 1994), 7.
2. "AMA Board Approves New Marketing Definition," *Marketing News*, March 1, 1985, 1.
3. Tom Duncan and Sandra Moriarty, *Driving Brand Equity* (New York: McGraw Hill, 1997); Don Schultz, Stanley I. Tannenbaum, and Robert F. Lauterborn, *Integrated Marketing Communication*, (Lincolnwood IL: NTC Business Books, 1993), 45.
4. Theodore Levitt, "Exploit the Product Life Cycle," *Harvard Business Review* (November/December 1965): 81–94.
5. Dan Scherk and Andrea Southcott, "Fun in a Bottle," *Marketing*, 1 February 1999, 15.
6. John Markoff, "Microprocessor Boom Dooms Cray," *The Sunday Camera*, 26 March, 1995, 15.
7. David W. Stewart, Gary Frazier, and Ingrid Martin, "Integrated Channel Management: Merging the Communications and Distributions Functions of the Firm," in *Integrated Marketing and Consumer Psychology*, Esther Thorson and Jerri Moore ed. (Hillsdale, N.J.: Lawrence Erlbaum Associates, 1996).

CHAPTER 3

1. Michael Hammer and James Champy, *Reengineering the Corporation* (New York: HarperCollins, 1993), 28.
2. Tom Duncan and Steve Everett, "Client Perceptions of Integrated Marketing Communications," *Journal of Advertising Research* 33 (May/June 1993): 30–5.
3. Polly Labarre, "This Organization is Dis-Organization," *Fast Company* (July/August 1996): Internet (www.fastcompany.com).

4. Tom Duncan, "The Concept and Process of Integrated Marketing Communication," *IMC Research Journal* 1, no. 1 (spring 1995): 3–10.

5. William C. Taylor, "At Verifone It's a Dog's Life (And They Love It!)" *Fast Company* (November 1995): Internet (www.fastcompany.com).

6. Tom Duncan, "The Concept and Process of Integrated Marketing Communication," *IMC Research Journal,* 1:1 (Spring 1995): 3–10.

7. Glen M. Broom, Martha M. Lauzen, and K. Tucker, "Dividing the Public Relations and Marketing Conceptual Domain and Operations Turf," *Public Relations Review* 17, no. 3 (1991): 219–26.

8. Extracted from http://www.ddbm.com/goodnews/, October 23, 1999, and http://www.strategymng.com/articles/, October 23, 1999.

9. Dan Logan, "Integrated Communication Offers Competitive Edge," *Bank Marketing* 26 (May 1994): 63–6.

10. Stephen J. Gould, Dawn B. Lerman, and Andreas F. Grein, "Agency Perceptions and Practices on Flobal IMC," *Journal of Advertising Research* (January/February 1999): 9-20.

11. Anders Gronstedt, "Integrating Up, Down and Horizontally: Lessons from America's Leading Total Quality Corporations," *Integrated Marketing Communications Research Journal* 1, no. 1 (Spring 1995): 11–5.

12. Michael McCarthy, "GM to Redefine Agency Roles, Fees," *Brandweek* (October 17, 1994): 3.

Chapter 4

1. John D. Leckenby, "Conceptual Foundations for Copytesting Research," University of Illinois Advertising Working Papers, No. 2 (February 1976).

2. Russell Colley, *Defining Advertising Goals for Measured Advertising Results* (New York: Association of National Advertisers, 1961).

3. Michael L. Ray, "Communication and the Hierarchy of Effects," in *New Models for Mass Communication Research,* P. Clarke, ed. (Beverly Hills, CA: Sage Publications, 1973): 147–75.

4. Robert C. Lavidge and Gary A. Steiner, "A Model for Predictive Measurements of Advertising Effectiveness," *Journal of Marketing* (October 1961): 59–62.

5. Sandra E. Moriarty, "Beyond the Hierarchy of Effects: A Conceptual Model," in *Current Issues and Research in Advertising,* 1 (1983): 45–56.

6. David W. Stewart, "The Market-Back Approach to the Design of Integrated Communication Programs: A Change in Paradigm and a Focus on Determinants of Success," AAA Special Conference on Integrated Marketing Communication, Norfolk, WV (March 1995).

Chapter 5

1. Milton Rokeach, *The Nature of Human Values* (New York, 1973), 5.

2. J. Michael Munson and Edward F. McQuarrie, "Shortening the Rokeach Value Survey for Use in Consumer Research," in *Advances in Consumer Research,* vol. 15 (Cambridge, Mass.: Association for Consumer Research, 1988), 381–6.

3. Leon G. Schiffman and Leslie Lazar Kanuk, *Consumer Behavior,* 3rd ed. (Englewood Cliffs, N.J.: Prentice-Hall, Inc., 1987), 506.

4. Henry Assael, *Consumer Behaviour and Marketing Action*, 3rd ed. (Boston: Kent Publishing, 1990), p. 275.

5. Martha Farnsworth Riche, "Psychographics for the 1990s," *American Demographics* (July 1989): 25–6, 30–2.

6. Information referenced extracted from http://www.goldfarbconsultants.com/gc_report.html, February 10, 2000.

7. Philip Cateora and John M. Hess, *International Marketing*, 4th ed. (Homewood, Ill.: Irwin, 1979), 90.

8. Hazel Kaban and David Mulryan, "Out of the Closet," *American Demographics* (May 1995): 40–7.

9. Nancy Coultun Webster, "Playing to Gay Segments Opens Doors to Marketers," *Advertising Age* (May 30, 1994): 5–6.

10. Theodore Levitt, "The Globalization of Markets," *Harvard Business Review* (May-June 1983): 92.

11. Philip Kotler and Gary Armstrong, *Marketing: An Introduction* (Englewood Cliffs, N.J.: Prentice-Hall, Inc., 1990), 477.

12. Rupa Chatterjee, "A McDonald's Outlet Opens in New Delhi," *India Abroad* (October 18, 1996): Internet (indiaworld.com/openbin/show/ia/sub scribe/961018/economy-index).

13. Jim McElgunn, "Foot Puts the Boot to Current 'Life-Cycle' Trends," *Marketing*, June 15, 1992, p. 1; Daniel Stoofman, "Completely Predictable People," *Report on Business*, November 1990, pp. 78-84; and "Boomers Slowing Pace of Leisure," *Toronto Star*, June 20, 1993, G3; as cited by Philip Kotler, Cary Armstrong, and Peggy H. Cunningham, *Principles of Marketing* 4th ed. (Prentice Hall Canada Inc., Scarborough, ON., 1999), p. 81.

14. Adapted from: http://www.statcan.ca/englsih/Pgdb/People/Population/demo23a - demo23c.htm. Extracted July 21, 1999.

15. http://www.statcan.ca/english/Pgdb/People/Population/demo23c.htm. Extracted July 21, 1999.

16. Adapted from: http://www.statcan.ca/english/Pgdb/People/Population/demo25b.htm Extracted July 21, 1999.

17. Philip Kotler, Cary Armstrong, and Peggy H. Cunningham, *Principles of Marketing*, 4th ed., (Prentice Hall Canada Inc., Scarborough, ON.), 1999, p. 81

18. Robert B. Settle and Pamela L. Alreck, *Why They Buy: American Consumers Inside and Out* (New York: John Wiley & Sons, 1986), 129.

19. Schiffman and Kanuk, *Consumer Behavior*, 318.

20. Settle and Alreck, *Why They Buy*, 171.

21. Alvin Toffler, *The Third Wave* (New York: William Morrow, 1980), 248.

Chapter 6

1. C. N. Coffer and M. H. Appley, *Motivation: Theory Research* (New York: John Wiley & Sons, 1964).

2. K. Levien, *A Dynamic Theory of Personality* (New York: McGraw-Hill, 1935), 88–91.

3. Barnaby J. Feder, "At Motorola, Quality is a Team Sport," *New York Times*, 21 January 1993, 15.

4. Meryl Gardner, Andrew Mitchell, and J. Edward Russo, "Strategy-Induced Low Involvement with Advertising," paper presented at the first Consumer Involvement Conference, New York University, June 1982.

5. Richard Petty and John T. Cacioppo, "Issue Involvement as a Moderator of the Effects on Attitude Advertising Content and Context," in *Advances in Consumer Research*, ed. K. B. Monroe, vol. 8 (Ann Arbor, Mich.: Association for Consumer Research, 1981): 20–4; Richard E. Petty and John T. Cacioppo, *Attitudes and Persuasion: Classic and Contemporary Approaches* (Dubuque, Ia.: William Brown Co., 1983).

6. L. Festinger, *A Theory of Cognitive Dissonance* (Stanford, Calif.: Stanford University Press, 1957).

7. Feder, "At Motorola, Quality is a Team Sport," 15.

8. Susannah Baker, "College Cuisine Makes Mother Cringe," *American Demographics* (September 1991): 10–11.

9. Henry Assael, *Consumer Behavior and Marketing Action*, 3rd ed. (Boston: Kent Publishing, 1987), 84.

10. R. Kelly, "The Search Component of the Consumer Decision Process—Theoretic Examination," in *Marketing and the New Science of Planning*, ed. C. King (Chicago: American Marketing Association, 1968), 273.

11. James Bettman, *An Information Processing Theory of Consumer Choice* (Reading, Mass.: Addison-Wesley, 1979).

12. Richard E. Petty, John T. Cacioppo, and David Schumann, "Central and Peripheral Routes to Advertising Effectiveness: The Moderating Role of Involvement," *Journal of Consumer Research* 10 (September 1983): 135–46.

13. F. H. Nothman, "The Influence of Response Conditions on Recognition Thresholds for Taboo Words," *Journal of Abnormal and Social Psychology* 65 (1962): 154–61.

14. Peter H. Webb and Michael L. Ray, "Effects of TV Clutter," *Journal of Advertising Research* 19 (June 1979): 7–12; Thomas J. Madden and Marc G. Weinberger, "The Effects of Humor on Attention in Magazine Advertising," *Journal of Advertising* 11, no. 3 (1982): 8–14; Michael A. Belch, Barbara E. Holgerson, George E. Belch, and Jerry Koppman, "Psychophysiological and Cognitive Responses to Sex in Advertising," in *Advances in Consumer Research*, vol. 9, ed. Andrew Mitchell (Pittsburgh: Association for Consumer Research, 1982), 424–7.

15. Junu Bryan Kim, "Generation X Gets Comfortable with Furnishings, Housewares," *Advertising Age*, January 10, 1994, S-2.

16. Bruce G. Posner, "The Future of Marketing Is Looking at You," *Fast Company* (October-November 1996): 108–9.

17. William Keenan, Jr., "Surveys as a Sales Tool," *Sales & Marketing Management* (January 1996): 65.

18. Michael D. Hutt and Thomas W. Speh, *Industrial Marketing Management* (Chicago: Dryden Press, 1981), 15–6.

19. William A. Dempsey, "Vendor Selection and the Buying Process," *Industrial Marketing Management* 7 (1978): 257–67.

CHAPTER 7

1. Extracted from www.info.ic.gc.ca December 15, 1999.

2. Adapted from material extracted from www.crtc.gc.ca December 15, 1999.

3. C.J. Michael Flavell and Christopher J. Kent, *The Canadian Competition Law Handbook* (Carswell Thomson Professional Publishing, Scarborough, ON, 1997.)
4. Adapted from "About Dairy Farmers of Canada," www.myrecipes.org/engl/policy/home.html., December 17, 1999.
5. C.J. Michael Flavell and Christopher J. Kent, *The Canadian Competition Law Handbook*, (Carswell Thomson Professional Publishing, Scarborough, ON), 1997, 164-165.
6. Ibid., 165.
7. Ibid., 165-166.
8. Ray O. Werner, "Legal Developments in Marketing," *Journal of Marketing* (July 1991): 66.
9. C.J. Michael Flavell and Christopher J. Kent, *The Canadian Competition Law Handbook* (Carswell Thomson Professional Publishing, Scarborough, ON), 1997, 169.
10. Michael Durham and Jan Rocha, "Amazon Chief Sues Body Shop," *The Observer*, March 3, 1996, 5.
11. Ronald E. Dimock, *Canadian Marketing Law Handbook* (Thomson Professional Publishing Canada, Scarborough, ON, 1991), 259.
12. Ibid., 259.
13. Extracted from an Industry Canada press release, "New Electronic Principles to Protect Consumers," November 9, 1999.
14. Internet expert example (from US).
15. C.J. Michael Flavell and Christopher J. Kent, *The Canadian Competition Law Handbook*, Carswell Thomson Professional Publishing, Scarborough, ON, 1997, 169.
16. Ibid., 73.
17. Scott Donation, "Publishers Bracing for Smoke-Free Pages," *Advertising Age*, March 12, 1990, 3.
18. William H. Bolan, *Advertising* (New York: John Wiley & Sons, 1984), 59.
19. Nancy A. Reese, Thomas W. Whipple, and Alice E. Courtney, "Is Industrial Advertising Sexist?" *Industrial Marketing Management* (1987): 231-9.
20. National Science Foundation, *Research on the Effects of Television on Children* (1977): 45.
21. Michael J. Miller, "The Web Wore Black," *PC Magazine*, March 26, 1996; Fritz Messere, "Analysis of the Telecommunications Act of 1996," (September 11, 1996): Internet (www.oswejo.edu/~messere.telcom2).
22. The Broadcast Code for Advertising to Children, The Canadian Association of Broadcasters. Reprinted October 1998.
23. Extracted from the May 1999 revision of the Canadian Code of Advertising Standards, www.adstandards.com/asc/ccas.html.
24. John B. Broder, "The Chairman of the FCC. Starts a Crusade Against Hard Liquor Ads on Television," *New York Times*, 9 April 1997, C7; Sally Goll Beatty, "Seagram Again Challenges Ban on TV Advertising," *Wall Street Journal*, 24 September 1996, B16; Chuck Ross, "FCC Taking Look at Seagram Ads," *Advertising Age*, September 30, 1996, 2, 63.
25. John Heinzl, "Ad Watchdog Barks Back," *The Globe and Mail*, 1 March 1999, B13.
26. Extracted November 5, 1999 from Advertising Standards Canada's Web site, www.adstandards.com/asc/overview.
27. For updated statistics on the WTO, refer to www.wto.org.

28. Marcus W. Brauchli, "A Change of Face: China Has Surly Image, But Part of the Reason is Bad Public Relations," *Wall Street Journal,* 16 June 1996, A1.

29. Barbara Crossette, "Globally, Majority Rules," *New York Times,* 8 August 1996, S4,P1.

30. Ray E. Hiebert, "Advertising and Public Relations in Transition from Communism: The Case of Hungary, 1989-1994, *Public Relations Review* (Winter 1994): 364.

31. David Lieberman, "Wired Up or Beamed In, It's Coming Cheaper, Faster," *USA Today,* 11 June 1996, 2B.

32. Darren McDermott, "Singapore Unveils Sweeping Measures to Control Words, Images on Internet," *Wall Street Journal,* 6 March 1996, B8.

Chapter 8

1. "Communicating Differential Advantage is Essential," *Marketing News* 25 (October 1985): 26.

2. Frank X. Dance and Carl E. Larson, *The Functions of Human Communications: A Theoretical Approach* (New York: Holt, Rinehart and Winston, 1976).

3. Werner J. Severin and James W. Tankard, Sr., *Communication Theories: Origins, Methods, Uses* (New York: Hastings House, 1979).

4. Frank Rose, "The End of TV as We Know It," *Fortune,* December 23, 1996, 66.

5. C. David Mortensen, *Communications: The Study of Human Interaction* (New York: McGraw-Hill, 1972).

6. B.S. Greenberg and G.R. Miller, "The Effects of Low-Credible Sources on Message Acceptance," *Speech Monographs* 33 (1966): 127–36.

7. Jon B. Freiden, "Advertising Spokesperson Effects: An Examination of Endorser Type and Gender in Two Audiences," *Journal of Advertising Research* 24 (1984): 33–41; Denis McQuail, *Mass Communication Theory* (Beverly Hills, Calif.: Sage, 1984).

8. Barry L. Bayers, "Word-of-Mouth: The Indirect Effects of Marketing Efforts," *Journal of Advertising Research* 25, no. 3 (June/July 1985): 31–9; Blaine Goss, *The Psychology of Human Communication* (Prospect Heights, Ill.: Waveland Press, 1989).

9. Albert Hirschman, *Exit, Voice, and Loyalty: Response to Decline in Firms, Organizations and States* (Cambridge, Mass.: Harvard University Press, 1970); Roobina Ohanian, "The Impact of Celebrity Spokespersons' Perceived Image on Consumers' Intent to Purchase," *Journal of Advertising Research* (February/March 1991): 46–54.

10. Jagdip Singh, "Voice, Exit, and Negative Word-of-Mouth Behaviors: An Investigation Across Three Service Categories," *Journal of the Academy of Marketing Science* (Winter 1990): 46–54.

11. Stephen Weitz, *Nonverbal Communication,* 2nd ed. (New York: Oxford University Press, 1979).

12. R. Buck, "Nonverbal Behavior and the Theory of Emotion: The Facial Feedback Hypothesis," *Journal of Personality and Social Psychology* 38 (1980): 811–24; Christy Fisher, "Wal-Mart's Way: No. 1 Retailer Relies on Word-of-Mouth, Not Ads," *Advertising Age,* February 16, 1991, 3, 48.

13. Elizabeth C. Hirschman, "The Effect of Verbal and Pictorial Advertising Stimuli on Aesthetic, Utilitarian, and Familiarity Perceptions," *Journal of Advertising Research* 15, no. 2 (1986): 27–34.

14. James MacLachlan, "Making a Message Memorable and Persuasive," *Journal of Advertising Research* 23, no. 6 (December 1983/January 1984): 58–9; Paul M. Herr, Frank

R. Kardes, and John Kim, "Effects of Word-of-Mouth and Product-Attribute Information on Persuasion: An Accessibility-Diagnosticity Perspective," *Journal of Consumer Research* 17 (March 1991): 454–62.

15. Larry Percy, "A Review of the Effect of Specific Advertising Elements Upon Overall Communication Response," in *Current Issues and Research in Advertising*, vol. 2., ed. James H. Leigh and Claude R. Martin, Jr. (Ann Arbor, Mich.: University of Michigan, 1983), 77–118.

16. C. Hovland, *The Order of Presentation in Persuasion* (New Haven, Conn.: Yale University Press, 1957).

17. Michael Ray and Alan Sawyer, "Repetition in Media Models: A Laboratory Technique," *Journal of Marketing Research* 8 (1971): 20–9.

18. Betsy D. Gelb, Joe W. Hong, and George M. Zinkhan, "Communications Effects of Specific Advertising Elements: An Update," in *Current Issues and Research in Advertising*, vol. 11, ed. James H. Leigh and Claude R. Martin, Jr. (Ann Arbor, Mich.: University of Michigan, 1985), 75–98.

19. George W. Booker, "A Comparison of the Persuasive Effects of Mild Humor and Mild Fear Appeals," *Journal of Advertising* 10 (1981): 29–40.

20. I.L. Janis and S. Feshback, "Effects of Fear-Arousing Communications," *Journal of Abnormal and Social Psychology* 48 (1953): 1, 78–92; B. Sternthal and C.S. Craig, "Fear Appeals: Revisited and Revised," *Journal of Consumer Research* 1 (9174): 22–34; J.J. Burnett and R.E. Wilkes, "Fear Appeals to Segments Only," *Journal of Advertising Research* 20 (1980): 21–4.

21. B. Sternthal and C.S. Craig, "Humor in Advertising," *Journal of Marketing* 37 (1973): 12–8.

22. Donald L. Duncan and James Nelson, "Humorous Advertising in Radio," *Journal of Advertising Research* 25, no. 4 (October/November 1985): 84–7.

23. William B. Beggs, Jr., "Humor in Advertising," *Link* (November/December 1989): 12–5.

24. Gelb, Hong, and Zinkhan, "Communications Effects," 75–98; Herbert Fried, "Humor Is Our Best Fool," *Advertising Age*, April 8, 1991, 26.

25. Judith A. Wiles and T. Bettina Cronwell, "A Review of Methods Used in Measuring Affect, Feelings, and Emotion in Advertising," in *Current Issues and Research in Advertising*, vol. 13, ed. James H. Leigh and Claude R. Martin, Jr. (Ann Arbor, Mich.: University of Michigan, 1990), 261.

26. J. Nunally and H. Bolerex, "Variables Concerning the Willingness to Receive Communications on Mental Health," *Journal of Personality* 27 (1959): 38–46.

27. W.J. McGuire, "Resistance to Persuasion Confirmed by Active and Passive Prior to Refutation of the Same and Alternative Counter Arguments," *Journal of Abnormal and Social Psychology* 63 (1961): 326–32.

28. Joan Meyers-Levy and Brian Sternthal, "Gender Differences in the Use of Message Cues and Judgments," *Journal of Marketing Research* 28 (February 1991): 84–96.

29. Diane McGuinness and Karl H. Pribram, "The Origins of Sensory Bias in the Development of Gender Differences in Perception and Cognition," *Cognitive Growth and Development*, ed. Morton Bortner (New York: Bruner/Mazel Publishers), 3–56.

30. P.S. Raju and Subhash C. Lonial, "Advertising to Children: Findings and Implications," *Current Issues and Research in Advertising*, vol. 12, ed. James H. Leigh and Claude R. Martin, Jr. (Ann Arbor, Mich.: University of Michigan, 1990), 231–74.

31. Mary Ann Strutts and Garland G. Hunnicutt, "Can Young Children Understand Disclaimers in Television Commercials?" *Journal of Advertising* 16, no. 1 (1987): 41–6.

32. Leslie Isler, Edward T. Popper, and Scott Ward, "Children's Purchase Requests and Parental Responses: Results from a Diary Study," *Journal of Advertising Research* 4 (October/November 1987): 28–39.

33. Ibid.

34. Jessica M. Bailey, "The Persuadability of Elderly Consumers: A Study of Focus on Control and Responsiveness to Fear Appeals," in *Current Issues and Research in Advertising*, vol. 10, ed. James H. Leigh and Claude R. Martin, Jr. (Ann Arbor, Mich.: University of Michigan, 1987), 213–47.

CHAPTER 9

1. Peter D. Bennett, *Dictionary of Marketing Terms* (Chicago: American Marketing Association, 1988), 4.

2. "Does Advertising Pay? The Impact of Advertising Expenditures on Profits for Consumer Business" (San Francisco: The Strategic Planning Institute and the Ogilvy Center for Research and Development, 1986).

3. "How Advertising in Recession Periods Affects Sales" (New York: American Business Press, Inc., 1979); McGraw-Hill Research Report No. 5262.1, Laboratory of Advertising Performance (New York: McGraw-Hill, 1985).

4. "Remington Finds the Numbers Don't Lie," *Focus* (NDL magazine) (Winter 1992): 10–11.

5. Kathy Haley, "In the Changing '90s Market, the Infomercial 'Here to Stay'," *Advertising Age*, March 11, 1996, 2A.

6. Jane Hodges, "CMR Takes Ad Tracking Service to the Internet," *Advertising Age*, March 4, 1996, 24.

7. Tom Duncan and Sandra Moriarty, "Global Advertising: Issues and Practices," *Current Issues and Research in Advertising* 13, nos. 1 and 2 (1990): 313–42.

8. Tara Parker-Pope, "Ford Puts Blacks in Whiteface, Turns Red," *Wall Street Journal*, 22 February 1996, B5.

9. Stan Sutter, "The Cannes Experience," *Marketing* (July 5, 1999), 4-8.

10. Marilyn Much, "New Research Quantifies the Effect of Ads," *Investor's Business Daily*, 24 April 1995, A4.

11. "Frederick G. Crane, E. Stephen Grant, and Steven W. Hartley, *Marketing: Canadian Insights and Applications*, (Toronto, ON: Irwin/McGraw-Hull Companies Inc., 1997), 87.

12. Raymond Serafin, "GM Will Standardize Assessment of Ad Work," *Advertising Age*, December 18–25, 1995, 1, 30.

CHAPTER 10

1. John F. Luick and William L. Ziegler, *Sales Promotion and Modern Merchandising* (New York: McGraw-Hill, 1968), 11.

2. "Shaping the Future of Sales Promotion," Council of Sales Promotion Agencies (1990): 3.

3. J. Brian Robinson, "Promotion is a New Way to Make Brand Contact With Buyers," *The Marketing News*, April 12, 1994, 2, 16.

4. Scott Hume, "Rallying to Brands' Rescue," *Advertising Age*, August 13, 1990, 3.

5. Scott Hume, "Brand Loyalty Steady," *Advertising Age*, March 2, 1992, 19.

6. Michael Schrage, "Reinventing the Wheel," *Adweek*, April 6, 1993, 23.

7. Sally Goll Beatty, "IBM Combines In-Store Promos Seemingly Out of the Big Blue," *Wall Street Journal*, 23 February 1996, B4.
8. "Carol Wright Survey: 'Trade Promotion Still Dominates'," *Promo* (June 1996): 107.
9. Betsy Spethmann, "Crowning the New Brand Kings," *Brandweek's Superbrands '96*, special edition, October 19, 1995, 25–8.
10. R. Craig MacClaren, "Creativity Can Burst the Trade Spending Balloon," *Promo* (October 1995): 54.
11. "Our Favorite Incentives," *Adweek*, October 19, 1992, 20.
12. Jack Neff, "This Space for Rent," *P-o-P Times* (September 1993): 36–42.
13. Keith, J. Tuckwell, *Canadian Advertising in Action*, 4th ed., (Scarborough, ON: Prentice-Hall Canada Inc., 1998), 534.
14. Betsy Spethmann, "Coupons Shed Low-Tech Image," *Brandweek*, October 24, 1994, 30–1.
15. Scott Hume, "Coupon Use Jumps as Distribution Soars," *Advertising Age*, October 5, 1992, 3.
16. Glenn Heitsmith, "Rebates are Getting a Bad Rap," *Promo* (March 1993): 10, 42.
17. Glenn Heitsmith, "Prosecutors Eye 'No Purchase' Claims," *Promo* (March 1993): 1.
18. Pam Weisz, "Body Shop, in Lieu of Ads, Hits the Road," *Brandweek*, April 24, 1995, 42.

Chapter 11

1. Walter W. Seifert, "The Outlook for Public Relations: Brighter Than Ever," *Public Relations Quarterly* (summer 1973): 18–30.
2. Adapted from www.cprs.ca/accredit.htm, p. 2, extracted August 23, 1999.
3. Ibid., p. 1.
4. "Applying PEW Typologies to an Issue: Big Business," *PR Reporter*, April 8, 1996, 2.
5. "Kekst, Fleshman, Burson Tops in Harris Survey of PR Firm Clients," *Inside PR*, September 9, 1996, 1, 3.
6. Mark Landler, "Corporate Insurer to Cover Cost of Spin Doctors," *New York Times*, 10 September 1996, C1.
7. "Case: When You're Wrong, the Best Course is To Say So," *PR Reporter*, January 15, 1996, 1.
8. "Management Wants Integrated Communication and Impact Measurement," IABC Communication World (November 1994): 32.
9. William D. Novelli, "Stir Some PR into Your Communications Mix," *Marketing News*, December 5, 1988, 40.
10. Yustin Wallrapp, "How Advertising-PR Partnership Can Succeed," *Advertising Age*, September 18, 1989, 40.
11. Mark Maremont, "Ben & Jerry Tell on Themselves," *Business Week*, June 26, 1995, 8.
12. Mark Lewyn, "See a Game, Shop for a Car, Surf the Net," *Business Week*, January 29, 1996, 53; John Riley, "Fields of Green," *Newsday*, 18 August 1996, A4; "NBC's 'Seinfeld,' 'ER' Bags $1 Mil per Ad Minute," *Advertising Age* (April 18, 1997): Internet (www.adage.com/bin/viewdataitem.cgi.articles&articles418); Wendy Tanka, "High-Tech Firms Lift Their Profiles at Sports Venues," *Rocky Mountain News*, 15 August 1996, 16B.

13. John McManus, "Despite Its Huge Economy and Growth, Event Marketing is Still Evolving," *Brandweek*, April 17, 1995, 16.

14. McManus, "The Ring Cycle."

10. McManus, "Despite Its Huge Economy."

15. Thomas L. Harris, *The Marketer's Guide to Public Relations* (New York: John Wiley & Sons, 1993), 199.

16. John Bennett, "Shopping for Sponsorships? Integration is Paramount," *Brandweek*, February 14, 1994, 18.

17. Brian Metzler, "Swoosh! CU Deal Boon for Nike," *Daily Camera*, 24 December 1995, 1E, 4E.

18. Kristen Traeger, "Mission Marketing: The Next Strategic Step on the Philanthropy Continuum," *IMC Research Journal* 1, no. 1 (spring 1995): 35–8.

19. Paul Carringer, "Not Just a Worthy Cause," *American Advertiser* (spring 1994): 17.

20. Goeffery Smith and Ron Stodghill, "Are Good Causes Good Marketing?" *Business Week*, March 21, 1994, 64.

21. Tom Duncan, "Why Mission Marketing is More Strategic and Long-Term than Cause Marketing," in 1995 Winter Educator's Conference, vol. 6, ed. David W. Stewart and Naufel J. Vilcassin (Chicago: AMA), 469–75.

22. Craig Smith, "The New Corporate Philanthropy," *Harvard Business Review* (May–June 1994): 107.

23. Alex Nieroth, "Success Takes Strategic, Olympic Effort," *Brandweek*, August 21, 1995, 22.

24. Bennett, "Shopping for Sponsorships?"

CHAPTER 12

1. *Direct Marketing* (July 1995): 4.

2. Cited in David Chilton, "New Tools Promise No End in Sight for the DM Boom," *Marketing*, 2 February 1998, 8-9.

3. Ibid.

4. Extracted from www.cdma.org/membership/more/html, November 13, 1999.

5. "DM Marketplace," *Direct Marketing* (August 1986): 8.

6. Robert Kestanbaum, "Growth Strategies for Direct Marketers," Direct Marketing Association, Release 110.2 (January 1984).

7. Robert Stone, *Successful Direct Marketing Methods* (Lincolnwood, IL: National Text Book Co., 1986), 2.

8. Ibid.

9. Alan Sharpe, "Eight Consumer Direct Mail Mistakes," *Marketing*, 2 February 1998, MD6.

10. Adapted from "Web Workings," *Atlantic Process*, June 1999, vol. 6(5), 22.

11. Anita Brown, "Pay to Play," *Marketing and Media Decisions* (September 1990): 16–17.

12. "Behavior and Attitudes of Telephone Shoppers," *Direct Marketing* (September 1987): 50–1.

Chapter 13

1. Ben M. Enis, *Personal Selling: Foundations, Process and Management* (Santa Monica, Calif.: Goodyear, 1979), 1.
2. G.D. Bruce and B.M. Bonjean, "Self-Actualization Among Retail Sales Personnel," *Journal of Retailing* 44 (Summer 1969): 73–83.
3. J. W. Thompson and W. W. Evans, "Behavioral Approach to Industrial Selling," *Harvard Business Review* 47 (March–April 1969): 69–83.
4. Marvin A. Jolson, "Should the Sales Presentation be 'Fresh or Canned'?" *Business Horizons* 16 (October 1973): 83–5.
5. John I. Coppett and William A. Staples, "A Sales Mix Model for Industrial Selling," *Industrial Marketing Management* (1980): 32.
6. Ibid.
7. Stan Kossen, *Creative Selling Today*, 2nd ed. (New York: Harper & Row, 1982), 423–24.
8. "Sales Incentives," *Incentives* (September 1990): 55–8.
9. Barry Norton, "Growth Spurts," *Contact*, vol. 2(2) March 1999, 9.

Chapter 14

1. Kevin Goldman, "Consumers Like Print Ads Better Than Those on TV, Study Says," *Wall Street Journal*, 6 June 1995, B9.
2. Canadian Media Directors Council Media Digest, 1996-97, p. 35 as cited by Keith J. Tuckwell, *Canadian Advertising in Action*, 4th Edition, Prentice Hall Canada Inc., Scarborough, ON, 361.
3. WWW.southam.com/About/Index.html, extracted November 13, 1999.
4. David Chilton, "In the Right Neighbourhood," *Marketing*, November 15, 1999, 28.
5. Chris Cobb, "Ottawa Plans $90m Subsidy for Magazines to Protect Canadian Periodicals After Settlement with U.S., "National Post Online, August 16, 1999, extracted from www.nationalpost.com, December 6, 1999.
6. "Study of Media Involvement," *Audits and Surveys* (March 1996): 14.
7. Michael Schrage, "Newspapers are Jointly Venturing On-Line, But The Flaw Is In Themselves," *Adweek*, May 22, 1995, 14.
8. Lisa Hrabluk, "iMagicAct," *New Brunswick Business*, November 1999, 9-11.
9. JBBM Bureau of Measurement, www.bbm.ca, extracted November 22, 1999.
10. Cyndee Miller, "P.O.P. Gains Followers as 'Era of Retailing' Dawns," *Marketing News*, May 14, 1999, 2.
11. Jack Neff, "This Space for Rent," *P-o-P Times*, September 30, 1993, 36-42.
12. "Consumers Notice Specialty Items," *Promo* (June 1992): 74.
13. Scott Donaton, "The Next 50 Years," *Advertising Age* (Spring 1995): 54.

Chapter 15

1. Bickley Townsend, "The Media Jungle," *American Demographics* (December 1988): 8.

2. Anthony F. McGann and J. Thomas Russell, *Advertising Media*, 2nd ed. (Homewood, Ill.: Irwin, 1988).

3. J.M. Agostine, "How to Estimate Unduplicated Audiences," *Journal of Advertising Research* (March 1961): 11–14.

4. David A. Aaker and John G. Myers, *Advertising Management*, 4th ed. (Englewood Cliffs, N.J.: Prentice-Hall, Inc., 1990).

5. Michael J. Naples, *Effective Frequency: The Relationship Between Frequency and Advertising Effectiveness* (New York: Association of National Advertisers, 1979), 79.

6. Herbert E. Krugman, "What Makes Advertising Effective?" *Harvard Business Review* (March/April 1975): 96–103.

7. Dennis H. Gensch, "Computer Models in Advertising Media Selection," *Journal of Marketing Research* 5 (November 1968): 423–4.

8. Information extracted from www.rogers.com/rogers/employ/profiles.html, December 12, 1999.

Chapter 16

1. Donald C. Marschner, "Theory Versus Practice in Allocating Advertising Money," *Journal of Business* 40 (July 1967): 286–302.

2. Gary L. Lilien et al., "Industrial Advertising Effects and Budgeting Practices," *Journal of Marketing* 40 (January 1976): 16–24.

3. Leonard M. Lodish, *The Advertising and Promotion Challenge* (New York: Oxford University Press, 1986), 92–4.

4. Dagmar Mussey, "Selling Esteemed Watch With Limited Ad Budget," *Advertising Age*, February 12, 1996, 18.

5. John Philip Jones, "Ad Spending: Maintaining Market Share," *Harvard Business Review* (January–February 1990): 38–42.

6. Nigel F. Piercy, "The Marketing Budgeting Process: Marketing Management Implications," *Journal of Marketing* 51 (October 1987): 45–59.

7. James E. Lynch and Graham J. Hooley, "Increasing Sophistication in Advertising Budget Setting," *Journal of Advertising Research* 30 (February/March 1990): 67–75.

8. Ovid Rio, *The Dartnell Sales Promotion Handbook*, 7th ed. (Chicago: The Dartnell Corp., 1987), 91–2.

9. Paul W. Farris and John A. Quelch, *Advertising and Promotion Management: A Manager's Guide to Theory and Practice* (Radner, Penn.: Chilton, 1983).

10. Roger A. Strang, *The Promotional Planning Process* (New York: Praeger, 1980).

11. George S. Low and Jakki J. Mohr, "The Budget Allocation Between Advertising and Sales Promotion: Understanding the Decision Process," AMA Educators' Proceedings, Chicago, Ill. (Summer 1991): 448–57.

12. Julian L. Simon, "Are There Economies of Scale in Advertising?" *Journal of Advertising Research* (June 1965): 15–20.

Chapter 17

1. Charles Ramond, *Advertising Research: The State of the Art* (New York: Association of National Advertisers, 1976).
2. Robert J. Lavidge and Gary A. Steiner, "A Model for Predictive Measurements of Advertising Effectiveness," *Journal of Marketing* 25 (October 1961): 59–62.
3. Johan Arndt, "What's Wrong With Advertising Research?" *Journal of Marketing Research* 16 (June 1976): 9.
4. H. D. Wolfe, J. K. Brown, S. H. Greenberg, and G. C. Thompson, *Pretesting Advertising Studies in Business Policy*, no. 109 (New York: National Industrial Conference Board, 1963).
5. David W. Stewart, "Measures, Methods, and Models in Advertising Research," *Journal of Advertising Research* (June/July 1989): 54–60.
6. Michael L. Rothschild, Ester Thorson, Judith E. Hirsch, Robert Goldstein, and Byron B. Reeves, "EEG Activity and the Processing of Television Commercials," *Communication Research* (April 1986).
7. Rudolph Flesch, *The Art of Readable Writing* (New York: Harper & Row, 1974).
8. Julie Liessee, "KGF Taps Data to Target Consumers," *Advertising Age*, October 8, 1990, 3, 88.
9. Don E. Schultz, *Strategic Advertising Campaigns*, 3rd ed. (Lincoln, Ill.: NTC Business Books, 1990), 550.
10. James F. Donius, "Market Tracking: A Strategic Reassessment and Planning Tool," *Journal of Advertising Research* (February/March 1985): 15–19.11
11. Simon Broadbent, *Spending Advertising Money* (London: Business Books, 1975).
12. Robert C. Blattberg and Scott A. Neslin, *Sales Promotion: Concepts, Methods, and Strategies* (Englewood Cliffs, N.J.: Prentice-Hall, Inc., 1976), 377.
13. Robert L. Dilenschneider and Dan J. Forrestal, *The Dartnell Public Relations Handbook* (Chicago: The Dartnell Corporation, 1987), Chapter 6.
14. Richard B. Still, Edward W. Cundiff, and Norman A.P. Govoni, *Sales Management*, 3rd ed. (Englewood Cliffs, N.J.: Prentice-Hall, Inc., 1976), 377.
15. David Barboza, "Research Firms Say They Can Tell Companies if Sponsoring an Event Is Worth the Money," *New York Times*, 18 November 1996, C11.

Chapter 18

1. Ian Linton and Kevin Morley, *Integrated Marketing Communications* (Oxford, U.K.: Butterworth Heinemann, 1995), 43; Chris Fill, *Marketing Communications* (London: Prentice-Hall, Inc., 1995), 172-3.
2. Audrey Ward and Jeremy Herbert, "The IMC Audit Content Analysis," *IMC Research Journal*, 2, No. 1(Spring 1996), 28-31.
3. Tom Duncan, "Is Your Marketing Communication Integrated? *Advertising Age*, January 24, 1994, 24.
4. Lawrence N. Stevenson, Joseph C. Shlesinger, and Michael R. Pearce, *Power Retail: Winning Strategies from Chapters and Other Leading Retailers in Canada*, McGraw-Hill Ryerson, 1999, 84.
5. "About chapters.ca," http://www.chapters.ca/AboutUs/Backgrou. . ., Extracted March 31, 2000, [1].

6. Shelly Garcia, "The Knights of New Business," *Adweek*, July, 1992, 21-2, 24, 26-7; Warren Berger, "The British Reinvasion," *Creativity* (June 1993), 36-7.
7. Lisa Fortini-Campbell, *The Consumer Insight Workbook* (Chicago: The Copy Workshop, 1992), ii.
8. David A. Aaker and John G. Myers, *Advertising Management: Practical Perspectives*, 3rd ed. (Englewood Cliffs, N.J.: Prentice-Hall, Inc., 1987), 85.
9. "Welcome to Chapters Corporate Website!," http://chaptersinc.com/welc.htm, Extracted March 31, 2000, 2-3.
10. Tom Brannan, *A Practical Guide to Integrated Marketing Communications* (London: Kogan Page, 1995), 23.
11. Lawrence N. Stevenson, Joseph C. Shlesinger, and Michael R. Pearce, *Power Retail: Winning Strategies from Chapters and Other Leading Retailers in Canada*, McGraw-Hill Ryerson, 1999, 242-247.
12. "Careers@chapters.ca," http://www.chapters.ca/Help/Careers.asp? . . . p. 1, Extracted March 30, 2000.
13. "About chapters.ca," http://www.chapters.ca/AboutUs/Backgrou. . ., Extracted March 31, 2000, 2.
14. Ibid., 3.
15. Ibid., 3.
16. Ibid., 3-4.
17. Adapted from: "Careers@chapters.ca," http://www.chapters.ca/Help/Careers.asp? . . . p. 1, Extracted March 30, 2000.
18. Adapted from "Chapters in the community," http://www.chaptersinc.com/mednews.htm, Extracted March 31, 2000, 1-3.
19. Lawrence N. Stevenson, Joseph C. Shlesinger, and Michael R. Pearce, *Power Retail: Winning Strategies from Chapters and other Leading Retailers in Canada*, McGraw-Hill Ryerson, 1999, 85.
20. Adapted from: "Securities & Guarantees," http://www.chapters.ca/Help/secure.asp?U . . . , Extracted March 6, 2000., 1.
21. "Pamela Wallin," Extracted from www.chapters.ca/wallin/, March 8, 2000. 1-2.
22. Contest details and quotation from "Scratch and Save at Chapters," *Marketing*, January 24, 2000, 9.
23. "About chapters.ca," http://www.chapters.ca/AboutUs/Backgrou. . ., Extracted March 31, 2000. 1.
24. Statistics cited from "CHAPTERS INC. 2nd Quarter Report," October 2, 1999," http://www.chaptersinc.com/invrel.htm, 3.
25. As quoted by Mark Vaughan-Jackson, "All the World's a Page," The Telegram, St. John's Newfoundland. Extracted from Canada.com, www.canada.com/cgi-b...stories/, March 5, 2000.

Photo Credits

Chapter 1

p. 2 Dick Hemingway; **p. 4** reproduced with permission of PepsiCo, Inc., 1997, Purchase, New York; **p. 8** Courtesy of Kenex LTD.; **p. 14** Courtesy of Nancy Dennis and Ch!ckaboom; **p. 16** Wolf Kutnahorsky Photo

Chapter 2

p. 26 Courtesy of Cows Inc.; **p. 28** UPS and UPS Shield Design are registered trademarks of United Parcel Service of America, Inc. Used by permission; **p. 32** Courtesy of Boehringer Ingelheim Pharmaceuticals; **p. 36** Courtesy of The Marketing Store Worldwide; **p. 40** "2000 Microsoft Corporation. All rights reserved. Microsoft and Encarta are registered trademarks of Microsoft Corporation in the United States and/or other countries; **p. 42** Courtesy of Bill Flora; **p. 44** Courtesy of the Coca-Cola Company; **p. 45** Pierre Tremblay/Masterfile. Ad courtesy of Quicken.ca. "F-WORD" campaign by Virginia Nells and Katya Gitlin; **p. 46** Courtesy of Ch!ckaboom

Chapter 3

p. 55 Courtesy of Kraft Foods, Inc.; **p. 60** Courtesy of Xerox Corporation; **p. 61** "1994 Lotus Development Corporation. All rights reserved. Used with permission of Lotus Development Corporation; **p. 68** Courtesy of Mediacom Inc.; **p. 72** Courtesy of ACCPAC International

Chapter 4

p. 80 Courtesy of Healthy Choice; **p. 84** Courtesy of Silver Fox Developments Inc.; **p. 90** Courtesy of Waterman Pens; **p. 91** Courtesy of The Gillette Company

Chapter 5

p. 102 David Bray, Senior Vice President/Creative Director, EthnoWorks Inc., a division of Hennessy/Bray Communications; **p. 108** Greater Montreal Convention and Tourism Bureau; **p. 109** Courtesy of *Out*; **p. 112** of Bijan Designer for Men Beverly Hills; **p. 116** Courtesy of MasterCard International; **p. 118** Advertisement provided courtesy of AOL Canada Inc.; **p. 119** Scotia McLeod Inc.; **p. 120** Fairchild Television—the only national Chinese TV network in Canada. ACNielson•DJC Research; **p. 124** Reprinted with the permission of Ford of Canada; **p. 127** Courtesy of London Life

Chapter 6

p. 132 Courtesy of Frank Herholdt/Tony Stone Images; **p. 136** Rogers AT&T Wireless Advertisements; **p. 137** Courtesy of Boxell Worldwide, Inc. as agent for National Fluid Milk Processor Promotion Board; **p. 141** Qantas Public Affairs; **p. 143** Courtesy of South Shore Industries Ltd.; **p. 146** Courtesy of Kim Race; **p. 151** Courtesy of Tele-Pages Inc.; **p. 154** Reprinted with permission from Melitta Canada Inc.; **p. 157** Courtesy of ENN–The Elevator News Network and Fauveshaus Advertising Inc.

Chapter 7

p. 164 Copyright ©1996 by The New York Times Co. Reprinted by permission; **p. 168** Courtesy of Dairy Farmers of Canada; **p. 170** Courtesy of Eric Swetsky; **p. 171** Rogers AT&T Wireless Advertisements; **p. 179** Courtesy of Advertising Standards of Canada; **p. 181** Copyright American Association of Advertising Agencies. Reprinted with permission; **p. 182** Courtesy of the Campbell Soup Company; **p. 188** Courtesy of Toyota Canada Inc.; **p. 190** Courtesy of Black Star and Dennis Chamberlain

Chapter 8

p. 198 Courtesy of iCraveTV.com; **p. 208** Reproduced courtesy of Chesebrough-Pond's, Inc.; **p. 209** Courtesy of MetLife and United Features Syndicate, Inc.; **p. 213** Courtesy of CBC

NEWSWORLD; **p. 215** Business Development Bank of Canada; **p. 219** Courtesy of North Bound Leather; **p. 220** Courtesy of Jennifer Nagle

CHAPTER 9

p. 230 Courtesy of Unilever Canada; **p. 236** Courtesy of United Colors of Benetton; **p. 237** Ad provided by Foote, Cone & Belding/New York. Reprinted by permission of British Virgin Islands; **p. 238** Courtesy of PETA; **p. 239** Stewart, McKelvey, Stirling, Scales and The CCL Group; **p. 247** Reproduced with permission of PepsiCo, Inc., 1997, Purchase, New York; **p. 248** Fauveshaus Advertising Inc.; **p. 250** Courtesy of The Net Idea Telecommunications Inc.; **p. 252** Reprinted by permission of CMA Canada

CHAPTER 10

p. 262 Crayola, the serpentine and chevron designs are registered trademarks of Binney & Smith. Used with permission; **p. 281** Courtesy of Fleishman Hillard, Inc.; **p. 285** The trademarks of Canadian Tire Corporation, Limited and its copyrighted work have been reproduced with permission; **p. 286** Courtesy of CIBC and Air Canada

CHAPTER 11

p. 291 Courtesy of The Gillette Company; **p. 300** All rights reserved. Used with permission of Kellogg Canada Inc. © 1999 and The Centre for Research in Women's Health, a joint initiative.; **p. 302** Courtesy of The Gillette Company; **p. 307** Courtesy of The Gillette Company; **p. 309** Courtesy of the University of New Brunswick; **p. 310** Courtesy of Royal Bank of Canada; **p. 312** Courtesy of University of Victoria Communications; **p. 315** Courtesy of Bank of Montreal; **p. 317** The Canadian Press/Paul Chiasson; **p. 318** Courtesy of Enterprise Creative Selling

CHPATER 12

p. 326 Courtesy of American Express Canada; **p. 330** Used with permission from *TIME for Kids* magazine, copyright 1996; **p. 330** Courtesy of Commport Communications International, Inc. and EDI OutSourcing Inc.; **p. 332** Advertisement reproduced with the kind permission of Canada Post Corporation; **p. 341** ©2000 Dun & Bradstreet Canada; **p. 345** Courtesy of Black Star and David Graham; **p. 346** Reprinted with permission from nGage Electronic Commerce; **p. 347** Courtesy of NorstarMall.ca Inc.; **p. 349** Courtesy of Janice MacPherson, The Net Idea Telecommunications Inc.

CHAPTER 13

p. 355 Photo courtesy of Andy Freeburg Photography. © Andy Freeburg; **p. 361** Courtesy of H&R Block Tax Services, Inc.; **p. 366** Courtesy of Results International

CHAPTER 14

p. 382 Courtesy of WebTV Networks, Inc.; **p. 394** Courtesy of Treehouse TV; **p.398** Courtesy of McCain Foods (Canada); **p. 406** Steve McCurry/National Geographic Society; **p. 408** Toronto Transit Commission; **p. 409** Courtesy of Point-of-Purchase Advertising Institute; **p. 410** Courtesy of Enterprise Creative Selling

CHAPTER 15

p. 417 Courtesy of Doug Goodman Photography; **p. 442** Courtesy of Mr. Craig Dawson

CHAPTER 16

p. 450 Courtesy of Federal Express Corporation; **p. 454** PhotoDisc

CHAPTER 17

p. 477 Courtesy of Enterprise Creative Selling and Tim Hortons; **p. 491** Wrigley Canada; **p. 496** Courtesy of Timberland and Roper Starch

CHAPTER 18

pp. 513, 528, 529, 533, 535 Courtesy of Chapters Online Inc.; **p. 526** Courtesy of Compaq Canada Inc., photography by Curtis Lantinga; **pp. 527, 531** Courtesy of Chapters Inc.

Company/Name Index 

***Note: Boldface pages indicate weblinks**

Subject Index

***Note: Boldface pages indicate definitions**